Painting Shakespeare

Painting Shakespeare explores the tradition of critical and interpretive painting and engraving that developed when eighteenth-century artists rejected the depiction of Shakespeare's plays in performance to produce images based on the new scholarly editions. The opening chapter locates Shakespeare painting alongside contemporary performance, editing and criticism, and discusses its relation to art history and practice. The book proceeds to examine Hogarth's use of ironic allusion, and the development of this and other techniques of critical visualisation by artists of the succeeding decades. Later chapters discuss the arcane allusions and supernatural visions of Fuseli; the gestural immediacy of Romney; the fluid, critical mythologising of Blake; and the compound subtleties of Reynolds. The book concludes with a study of the Boydell Shakespeare Gallery and the radically new reading practices it constituted. Richly illustrated with over a hundred pictures including a colour plate section, this study provides a complete critical history of Shakespeare painting and engraving in this period.

Currently Professor of English at the University of Bergen, STUART SILLARS was previously a member of the Faculty of English at the University of Cambridge, and has been a visiting professor at universities in Texas, Washington and Croatia. He has written extensively on the relationship between literature and the visual arts, with books including *Art and Survival in First World War Britain* (1987) and *British Romantic Art and the Second World War* (1991), and has had many articles and reviews published in major journals in the UK, Europe and the USA.

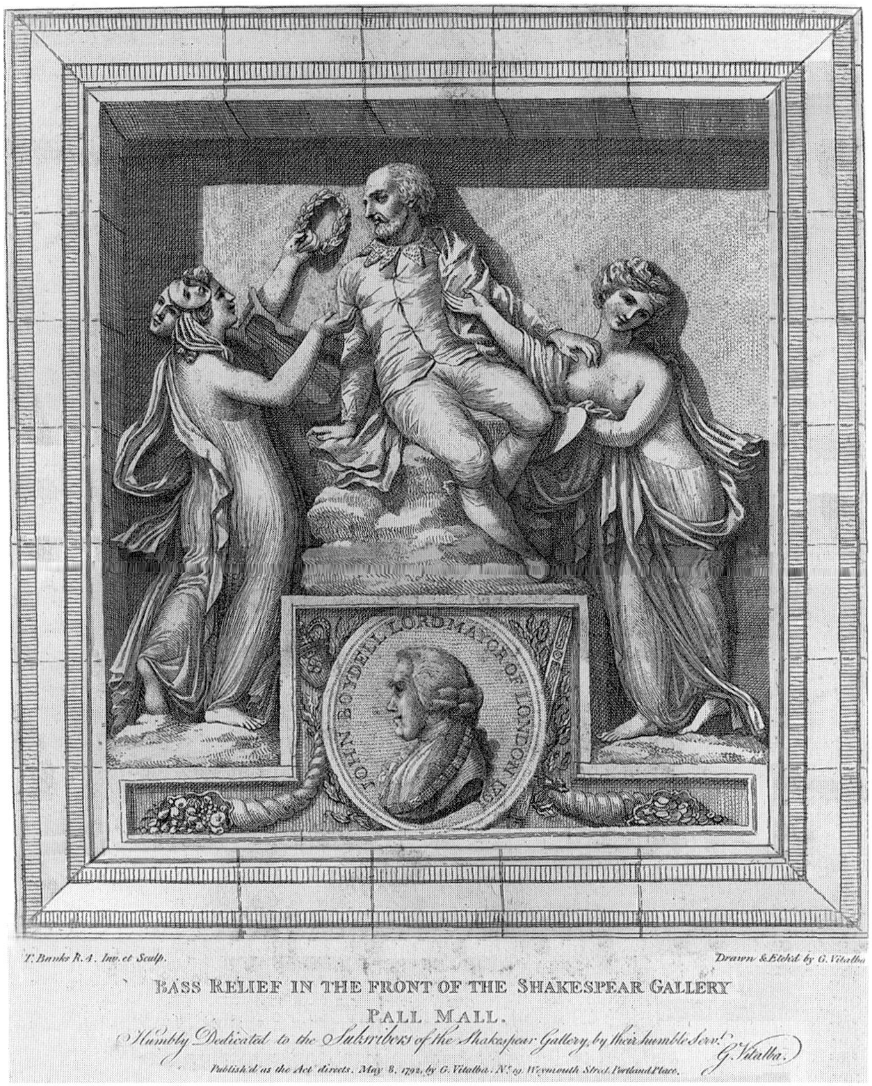

Frontispiece: Bas-relief in the front of the Shakespeare Gallery, drawn and etched by G. Vitalba, published 8 May 1792. From an extra-illustrated copy of *Illustrations of Shakespeare, and of Ancient Manners* by Francis Douce, reproduced by permission of the Folger Shakespeare Library, Washington D.C. The etching shows a version of the sculpture by Thomas Banks for the façade of John Boydell's Shakespeare Gallery in Pall Mall, together with the commemorative medallion struck for subscribers to the *Collection of Prints* and the edition of the plays. Banks' sculpture, *Shakespeare between the Dramatic Muse and the Genius of Painting*, presents a visual allegory of the mediating function of the gallery: see Fig. 2 and Chapter 9.

PAINTING SHAKESPEARE

THE ARTIST AS CRITIC
1720–1820

STUART SILLARS

CAMBRIDGE
UNIVERSITY PRESS

CAMBRIDGE UNIVERSITY PRESS
Cambridge, New York, Melbourne, Madrid, Cape Town, Singapore, São Paulo

Cambridge University Press
The Edinburgh Building, Cambridge CB2 2RU, UK

Published in the United States of America by Cambridge University Press, New York

www.cambridge.org
Information on this title: www.cambridge.org/9780521853088

First published 2006

Printed in the United Kingdom at the University Press, Cambridge

A catalogue record for this book is available from the British Library

Library of Congress Cataloguing in Publication data
Sillars, Stuart, 1951–
Painting Shakespeare : the artist as critic, 1720–1820 / Stuart Sillars.
p. cm.
Includes bibliographical references (p.) and index.
ISBN-13: 978-0-521-85308-8
ISBN-10: 0-521-85308-7
1. Shakespeare, William, 1564–1616 – Illustrations. 2. Art and literature – England – History – 18th century. 3. Art and literature – England – History – 19th century. 4. Painting, English – 18th century. 5. Painting, English – 19th century. 6. English drama – Illustrations. I. Title.
PR2883.S45 2006
822.3′3–dc22

ISBN-13 978-0-521-85308-8 hardback
ISBN-10 0-521-85308-7 hardback

For my graduate students in
Texas, Cambridge, and Norway
with affection and gratitude

CONTENTS

COLOUR PLATES

12 George Romney, *The Tempest*. Colour stencil engraving by Benjamin Smith, 1797. Fine Arts Museums of San Francisco, Achenbach Foundation for Graphic Arts, 1963.30.10223

13 Henry Fuseli, *The Tempest*. Line and stipple engraving by Jean Pierre Simon, with hand colouring, 1797. Fine Arts Museums of San Francisco, Achenbach Foundation for Graphic Arts, 1963.30.20006

14 Robert Smirke and Joseph Farington, *1 Henry IV*. Colour stipple engraving by Samuel Middiman, 1797. Fine Arts Museums of San Francisco, Achenbach Foundation for Graphic Arts, 1963.30.11891.

15 W. Jeayes after William Hodges, *The Merchant of Venice*, after 1807. Watercolour in grangerised Heath's Shakespeare. By permission of the Folger Shakespeare Library.

16 Francis Wheatley, *The Opening of the Shakespeare Gallery*, 1790. Victoria and Albert Museum, London.

ILLUSTRATIONS

ACKNOWLEDGMENTS

This book has benefited greatly from the advice, expertise and kindness of many people. The following have contributed in diverse ways to the book's content, clarified its expression or aided in other ways: Julie Ainsworth, Catherine Alexander, Charles Armstrong, Erin Blake, Kent Cartwright, Johanna Drucker, Charles Edelman, Antonia Forster, Nicholas Friend, Claire Haynes, Ludmilla Jordanova, Sandra Kroupa, Laurence Lerner, Raimonda Modiano, Ruben Moi, Jane Monro, Charles Moseley, William L. Pressly, Ren Renfro, William Sherman, Bettina Smith, Valerie Wayne, Gary Jay Williams, William Williams, Mary Williams, Claire Wills, Clive Wilmer, David Worrall, Georgianna Ziegler, Orm Øverland.

I am grateful to the Bergen-Seattle Exchange Committee of the University of Bergen for making possible an extended research trip to the University of Washington, the Historisk-Filosofisk Fakultet of the University of Bergen for granting a sabbatical semester, and the Bergen University Fund for a generous grant towards the book's production.

The staffs of the following libraries were unfailingly helpful: the University Library, Cambridge; Selwyn College Library, Cambridge; the University of Bergen; the Library of Congress; and the Library of the University of Washington. The bulk of the research was carried out in the Folger Shakespeare Library, and I owe a special debt to the Reading Room staff whose professionalism, skill and patience were a continuing source of encouragement: Harold Batie, LuEllen DeHaven, Leigh Anne Palmer, Camille Seerattan, and Betsy Walsh. The dedication reflects a debt perhaps too often overlooked within the academic community.

At Cambridge, Sarah Stanton gave generous support to the project from the outset, and Rebecca Jones and Alison Powell oversaw the production process with great efficiency. Laurence Marsh edited the text with tact, precision and patience. I am deeply grateful to them all for their help and kindness.

It should not be necessary to add that those errors and inadequacies that remain are the product of my own unaided perversity.

SJS
Bergen, January 2005

CHAPTER 1

PLACING SHAKESPEARE PAINTING

I

In 1750 John Wootton, an artist with a small but honourable reputation for sporting paintings and landscapes in the style of Gaspard Dughet, painted *Macbeth and Banquo meeting the Weird Sisters* (Plate 1).[1] The circumstances under which it was produced are unclear, but its size (152.5 × 146 cm, or 60 × 57 in) and what little is known of its provenance[2] suggest a commission from a relatively wealthy individual, probably not from the highest financial or social rank, who wished to display it as part of his private collection. That Wootton was a friend of Pope, Gay and Prior, all of whom owned examples of his work, might explain the literary nature of the painting, although this needs to be seen within the larger context of the burgeoning interest in Shakespeare through performance and textual editing, and as representative of the instinctive, untutored power that was the essence of the national imagination. The painting's date places it at a time when these movements had begun to gain significant momentum. Theobald's *Shakespeare Restored* of 1726[3] and his edition of the plays in 1733[4] had begun the attempt to recover an original, authentic text that was to drive Shakespeare editing for the rest of the century, and marked the beginning of a split between a reading and a performance practice. When Garrick revived *Macbeth* in 1744 after its absence from the stage since 1671, he claimed to present it 'as written by Shakespeare',[5] but nonetheless retained some of the songs added by Davenant and omitted the porter scene and various other passages deemed unsuited to contemporary tastes. There was as yet very little that could be termed critical writing. John Dennis, following Dryden, had continued the process of freeing the 'naturally learn'd'[6] Shakespeare from unfavourable comparison with the Ancients, with assertions resting on general principles; Johnson had published a pamphlet on *Macbeth* in 1745 which discussed individual passages.[7] The work of Murphy, Farmer and Montagu was still some years off, and the establishment of an *apparatus criticus* of the sort assumed by present-day readers would take several generations.

In Wootton's painting the figures of Macbeth, Banquo and the witches are placed within a naturalistic scene that owes much to the conventions of European landscape painting. The windswept trees and extreme chiaroscuro, light almost overcome by darkness spreading from the left of the canvas, draw on Gaspard Dughet; the rocks framing the witches' cave to the right echo the stone formations of Salvator Rosa. The relation between the figures and the landscape resembles that found in Poussin, not only as Michael Bellamy has remarked[8] in terms of their scale but also because of the way they are arranged to suggest a narrative progress that recedes into the space of the painting. The reader's eye is led across from the two central figures to the horse that turns its head towards them from the left, and then by the curve of its body to the second horse, which in turn leads the eye back to the line of figures in the middle distance. From this movement the reader identifies the horses of Macbeth and Banquo being held by their grooms and the line of troops returning from battle, to locate the events within the play's third scene.

This narrative presentation suggests that the image grows out of an art historical rather than a theatric frame of reference. For reasons that will shortly become clear, Wootton's setting departs from both Shakespeare's 'heath' (1.1.7)[9] and the 'open Place' and '*1st Grove*' of Garrick's prompt book,[10] but imports the witches' cave from Act IV. The thunder and lightning that Garrick stipulates are absent. Wootton's Macbeth and Banquo combine the dress of classical soldier and Scots warrior, whereas Garrick's costume for the role was his customary eighteenth-century court dress, Macklin being the first to attempt something closer to authentic Scottish costume. The witches' high-crowned hats could draw on Garrick's production, as could the headgear of the central figure, which suggests the 'torn mobs' worn in his production, but the absence of 'blue-checked aprons' and broomsticks suggests a freer interpretation of the roles.[11] Perhaps the gesture of Macbeth recalls Garrick's pose of recoil familiar from other images, such as Benjamin Wilson's painting from 1754 recording the encounter with the ghost in *Hamlet*;[12] but the presence of the staff instead of the open palm with spread fingers argues against this. That the open hand was also described as showing horror and dismay in the *Conférence de M. Le Brun sur l'expression générale et particulière*, the handbook of ready-made gestures and expressions that was influential in the earlier eighteenth-century theatre,[13] suggests that it, too, was a source avoided by

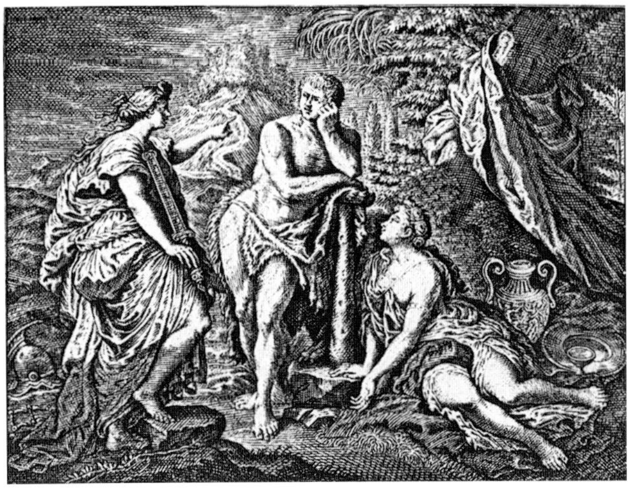

1 Paolo de Matteis, *The Choice of Hercules*. Engraved by Simon Gribelin, 1714.

Wootton. All this points away from the theatre and towards an imaginative reading of the text – and Shakespeare's text, perhaps as available in Theobald's edition, rather than the adaptations of Davenant or Garrick – as the basis of the painting's invention, in dialogue with conventions taken from the practices of landscape and narrative painting. Little is known about Wootton, so that it is impossible to determine a factor that will be important for later Shakespeare painters: the way in which the artist's knowledge was acquired, most particularly which edition was used as the basis for visual presentation. It is quite clear, however, that the painting rests on detailed study of the printed text rather than an acquaintance gained from the theatre.

In translating the temporal unfolding of the play to the spatial presentation of the painting, Wootton employs not only the recessional forms borrowed from Nicolas Poussin, but also a compositional element that had recently become fashionable in English history painting. The principal characters of the image are presented within a trope known as the Choice of Hercules, used in many Renaissance paintings and made popular by the Earl of Shaftesbury in an influential essay on the production of narrative in painting published in 1713,[14] supported by a painting that Shaftesbury commissioned from Paolo de Matteis (Fig. 1.)[15] The essay argues that the moment of selecting virtue over pleasure contains all the greatness of the hero's future life; in adopting and adapting the same figure, Wootton follows the essay's advice in narrative terms but neatly inverts the moral implication by showing the moment when Macbeth turns away from the honest, doubting Banquo towards the witches. Not only is there a physical reversal of the Hercules trope, Macbeth turning in the opposite direction to reject virtue; the allusion is deeply ironic in positing an equivalence with this earlier moment of moral crisis that is far more benevolent in outcome.

Wootton supplements the presentation of the moment of choice by implying its results through another technique suggested by Shaftesbury: the use of emblematic detail to suggest future events. These are set within a larger telescoping of events, in the inclusion of the witches' cavern from Act 4. Inside it may be seen the shape of the 'brindled cat' referred to by the First Witch (4.1.1); perched above is a magpie, recalling the 'maggot-pies' that Macbeth mentions as ill omens (3.4.125). Next to it sits an owl, 'the fatal bellman' (2.2.3) that shrieks before the death of Duncan, the 'mousing owl' (2.4.13) whose unnatural killing of a falcon is recorded by the Old Man, and itself the predator against which 'the poor wren/ The most diminutive of birds, will fight' (4.2.9–10). The inclusion of these figures, quite naturalistic within the darkening landscape, extends the breadth of the image and reveals the scope of evil that Macbeth embraces as he turns towards the witches.

Another detail is used to broaden the painting's reference through an allusion to a later passage of the play that brings with it associations of darkness and the rebellion of nature against Macbeth's crimes. Almost at the centre of the painting, silhouetted against the cloud, two dark birds are shown flying towards the trees. They recall words from Macbeth's pivotal speech in Act 3:

Light thickens,
And the crow makes wing to th' rooky wood;
Good things of day begin to droop and drowse,
While night's black agents to their preys do rouse.
(3.2.50–53)

In presenting the crows flying towards the wood, paralleling Macbeth's movement towards the witches, the painting shows the play's descent into evil signalled in this speech just before the murder of Banquo. The birds also reveal themselves as part of another essential aspect of the image's visual reading of the play: its emphasis on landscape. The shift into darkness, so common a feature in the baroque landscapes of Rosa, is here instilled with a more immediate critical purpose, revealing itself as a reading of the function of the dark landscape as a moral dimension of the play's movement. The tree blown back on itself at the right is a statement of the many references to the storm on the night of the murder which, like all the images of revolted nature, are the result of the murder and are 'unnatural,/ Even like the deed that's done' (2.4.10–11). The broken tree in the left foreground provides a focus for the insinuations of destruction and reversal of nature that climax in Macbeth's plea to the witches to answer his questions regardless of the consequence: 'Though you untie the winds . . . Though bladed corn be lodged and trees blown down' (4.1.51, 54). Seen thus, it anticipates the climax of the same speech that reveals the collapse of natural order when 'the treasure/ Of nature's germen tumble altogether/ Even till destruction sicken' (4.1.57–9). The landscape, the essential feature of the collapse of the play's moral world into what Lady Macbeth calls 'the blanket of the dark' (1.5.51), is powerfully visualised in Wootton's painting. This is far more than a representation of any stage setting. Just as the Choice of Hercules trope is appropriated from Old Master tradition and more recent theoretical debate, so the atmospheric landscape of Rosa and Gaspard Dughet is turned into a major critical reading of the play's direction. Added to the specific details of the birds and the inclusion of the witches' cave to convey future events, it confirms the function of the painting: far more than a simple representation, this is an image that narrates the play's pivotal moment of action and mediates its larger movement of language and morality to offer a consistent and suggestive critical reading.

Wootton's painting is an early example of a discursive medium increasingly significant during the eighteenth century: the visual image that offers a critical reading of one of the plays of Shakespeare. This it does in three linked ways. It stresses the collapse of Macbeth's moral universe as implicit within the first meeting with the witches; it suggests later events by the use of emblematic detail in the presence of the owl, magpie and crows; and it visualises the language of the disturbance of the natural world and its order. Today familiar from critical scrutiny over many generations, these textual operations were not discussed in explicit terms until much later: it was probably Bradley, for example, who first drew attention to the function of landscape in the text's moral trajectory, in a critical text founded on structural analyses in which the influence of painting, and perhaps even performance, was minimal.[16] Wootton's painting makes these critical points with striking visual immediacy a hundred and forty years before Bradley lectured on *Macbeth*, and in this it is representative of the special power of eighteenth-century Shakespeare painting. It is the recovery of this tradition that is the purpose of this book.

II

That Wootton's painting was capable of sustaining a reading of such depth for its contemporary viewers is explained by the tradition of narrative in the theory of painting on which it rests. If the critical analysis of Shakespeare's language was at best embryonic in the mid-eighteenth century, the practice of analysing the composition of paintings and the way that it influenced meaning, especially in the presentation of narrative, was increasingly the subject of theoretical discussions that determined both how paintings were produced and how they were read. Early in the century the discussion of the theory of painting in terms of its aesthetic identity, procedures and meanings began to establish itself as a significant discourse within the larger debate around the nature of taste. Historical painting, based on the sculptural practice of the ancient Greeks and Romans, often as transmitted by Renaissance Old Masters, was regarded as the highest form of art. From it developed both the Grand Style and the related vogue for paintings of events in British history. Images of literary narratives, from Greek, Roman and English texts, were given similar weight; and, with the canonisation of Shakespeare as the national genius, the visual treatment of the plays became a major concern. The development of a precise theoretical basis by the preceding generation meant that when Wootton painted Macbeth there was both a clear set of procedures for the artist to follow and a body of educated readers to decode and interpret the image.

Wootton's painting has already disclosed the effects of the seminal work in the theoretical tradition, the Earl of Shaftesbury's *A Notion of the Historical Draught or Tablature of the Judgement of Hercules* (1713), which should be read in conjunction with the painting commissioned by its author and which, in an engraving by Simon Gribelin (see Fig. 1), was included in the second edition of 1714. Shaftesbury begins by stressing the importance of presenting 'one single Intelligence, or Design' (p. 4), an approach fundamental to the visual treatment of the plays in asserting the dominance of a concept uniting composition, narrative and theme. Shaftesbury is, however, most concerned with the moment of the narrative sequence that is selected for depiction. Arguing closely from the Choice trope, he defines three possibilities: the initial meeting between Hercules, Pleasure and Virtue; the moment 'when they are enter'd on their Disputes' (p. 6); and the moment 'when *Virtue* seems to gain her Cause' (p. 6). Of these he finds the last the most effective because it contains the fullest implications of event and character, expressing as it does 'the *Grand Event*, or consequent Resolution of HERCULES' (p. 6) and thus encompassing the moral significance and implicit consequences of the choice. Depiction of earlier events is rejected as productive of 'a mere confus'd heap', but the suggestion of later happenings in the use of emblems, as in Wootton's painting, is treated more sympathetically:

> It may however be allowable, on some occasions, to make use of certain *Enigmatical* or Emblematical Devices, to represent future Time. (p. 9)

This would have had clear resonance for educated readers. 'Emblematical devices' are the visual embodiment of virtues or attributes that depend on traditions of presentation that in some instances date back to Judaeo-Christian images, formalised in medieval and Renaissance painting and catalogued in the emblem books fashionable in the 1590s. The most widely read, Cesare Ripa's *Iconologia*, remained in print in new editions throughout the eighteenth century, with new illustrations, giving practical enactment to Shaftesbury's concept.[17]

What Shaftesbury establishes in specific terms, Jonathan Richardson makes both more general and more widely accessible in his *Essay on the Theory of Painting* (1715),[18] *Essay on the Whole Art of Criticism as it Relates to Painting* and the *Science of the Connoisseur* (1719).[19] These explain both the qualities of paintings themselves and the attributes needed in those wishing fully to interpret and evaluate them. Significantly, Richardson's discussion of painting makes no distinction between the presentation of historical events and that of literary texts, exploring them interchangeably as examples of the visual mediation of sequential events. Arguing in the *Theory of Painting* that the immediacy of the art remedies the defects of language, Richardson allows the painter the 'liberty of heightening' (p. 13) in adding or deleting details or circumstances, and the freedom '*sometimes to depart even from Natural, and Historical truth*' (p. 49) to clarify a larger principle – thus implicitly allowing the possibility of critical interpretation. Shaftesbury's detailed discussion of the selection of a moment is simplified into the advice that it should contain '*That in the Story which is the most Advantageous*' (p. 53), supported by an Aristotelian assertion of the centrality of a 'Unity of Time' (p. 56) stated visually by the 'Principal Action in a Picture' (p. 56). Richardson is less cautious than Shaftesbury in accepting emblems, which he refers to as 'Insignia' (p. 74) and supports by direct reference to Ripa's *Iconologia*. Pragmatically, he allows the development of new emblems by the artist, with a significant proviso: 'if any be necessarily of his Own Insertion, his meaning should be apparent' (p. 74). The owl and crows in Wootton's painting precisely embody this principle.

The approaches of Shaftesbury and Richardson have substantial implications for Shakespeare painting. The selection of a single moment, its interpretation with what Richardson in the *Theory* calls 'latitude' (p. 47) through the use of a principal action, with some liberty to select, clarify or elaborate, and the use of emblems either already in existence or specially devised, the whole being capable of ready understanding by the educated reader who will in consequence receive moral instruction and improvement, constitute a clear set of ground rules. They facilitate the treatment of a text in both immediate generalities and encrypted detail, making possible the interpretation of language, character and action central to the provision of an interpretive or critical reading in visual terms. That Richardson's essays were republished in 1725, 1773 and 1792 reveals their continuing influence throughout the century.

Later theorists and commentators, Reynolds by implication in the *Discourses*[20] and Fuseli much more directly in the *Instructions for the Connoisseur*,[21] will modify and clarify these concerns, but not seriously undermine them; Lessing's *Laocoön*, published in 1765, was not translated into English until 1836, when it became influential on narrative painting and book-illustration in England. While some artists, notably Fuseli, were aware of it, it was Shaftesbury and Richardson – in addition, of course, to Fuseli and Reynolds – who were still the main foci of theoretical debate. In consequence time, action, emblem and morality remain principles that will guide the work of an increasing number of Shakespeare painters to generate a range of supple and complex insights. They should be seen in counterpoint with a range of larger concerns that assume various degrees of prominence through the century. The debate about the origin of beauty, held between the poles of the classical ideal presented by Reynolds and the forms of nature advanced by Hogarth, remains an important dynamic; in turn, it forms part of the discussion of taste that flourished in the writings of Steele, Fielding and many others. Another part of the debate was the distinction raised by John Locke[22] between simple and complex ideas which, while relating to mental processes, uses terms that might almost be applied to paintings and prints, a duality explored and developed by Joseph Addison's claims for the simple immediacy of visual perception as one of the 'Pleasures of the Imagination' in the *Spectator* (1712).[23] It received practical form in the range of meaning attributable to the moral subjects of Hogarth in the 1730s and 40s, and might also be seen as hypostatising a division between painting that merely presents and that which critically interprets.

In various ways all of these concerns relate to the increasing importance of the onlooker and the reading function. Only if narrative devices are understood and allusions recognised may the moral and critical principles that underlie them be assimilated. This process depends on a grasp of the fact that, while its spatial structure would suggest the instantaneous identity of painting in opposition to the temporal nature of literary forms, narrative is implicit within visual structures in their construction and, correspondingly, in how they are read; the opening pages of this chapter implicitly reveal Martin Baxandall's lucid comment, 'if a picture is simultaneously available in its entirety, *looking* at a picture is as temporally linear as language'.[24] The balance between these two frames of temporal construction is one that will be exploited and developed in different ways throughout the century, but it rests on statements made in the early years, most particularly by

Richardson in his *Theory*, which asserts directly: 'Painting is a sort of Writing, it ought to be easily legible' (p. 74). Through the processes this implies, that aspect of connoisseurship concerned with understanding structure and meaning assumes central importance: it generates a discourse of critical discussion and analysis of painting which is actively engaged in by educated onlookers as a demonstration of their taste and understanding. This takes place within the growth of gallery visiting as both a social event and a critical activity, and the process of reading engravings as an intimate discursive exchange. The latter in particular had become an established formal discipline by the century's end. Lamb asserts of Hogarth, 'Other pictures we look at – his prints we read;'[25] discussing what to do on a winter evening, Leigh Hunt asks 'shall we read an engraving from Poussin or Raphael?'[26] and Keats recalls 'all the pleasant flow/ Of words at opening a portfolio'.[27] These discussions are stimulated and in part recorded in the reviews of paintings and galleries found increasingly from the 1780s in periodicals such as the *Analytical Review* and the *Morning Post*, and publications dedicated to individual exhibitions, such as Humphry Repton's discussion of the paintings in the Boydell Shakespeare Gallery, *The Bee*.[28] Those who could not afford to buy prints were not excluded: the number of images that show crowds examining the contents of print-sellers' windows suggests that this was a popular substitute for gallery-going.[29]

The nature of the reading practice, and the codes in which critical statements are encrypted, depend throughout the century on the concepts established by Richardson and Shaftesbury. At the level of instantaneous event, a strong impetus is provided by Richardson's sharpening of Shaftesbury's reference to the use of traditional or innovative emblems. More significant in terms of larger critical statement is the allusion to earlier conventions of meaning in Shaftesbury's use of the Choice motif. The simplest dimension of this lay in the prominence it gave to classical myth, a ready way to establish *gravitas* in both style and subject. In the succeeding years, the former would accord well with the idea of a national school of Neo-classical Painting; the latter might be seen as a visual parallel to the nascent discipline of Shakespeare criticism, often concerned with morality within character analysis. Such values were often embedded in the Choice motif itself. Hogarth was the earliest eighteenth-century English artist to use it as an instrument of critical commentary. It appears, for example, in *The March to Finchley* (1746)[30] and the first plate of *The Harlot's Progress*[31] in contexts quite distant from its original placing, to generate satire both comic and biting. Later, it is important in Shakespeare images, becoming, for example, the basis of Reynolds' 1762 portrait of Garrick, and the *alto relievo* of Shakespeare by Thomas Banks for the façade of Boydell's Shakespeare Gallery (Fig. 2), both discussed in later chapters.

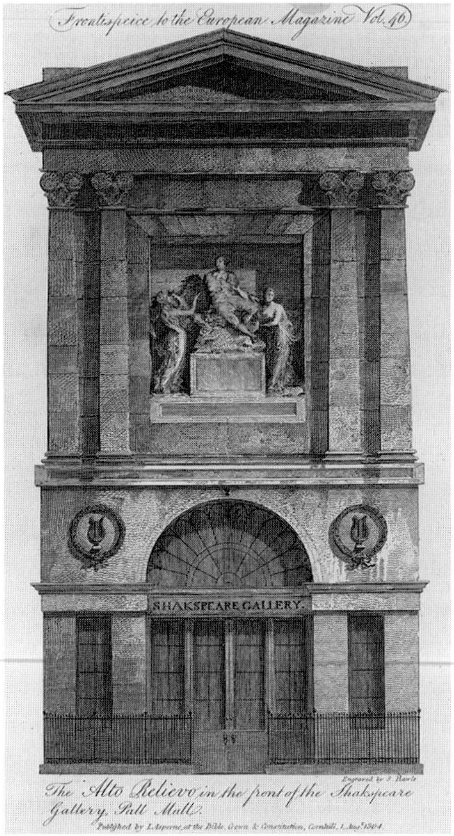

2 S. Rawle, *The alto relievo in the front of the Shakspeare Gallery*, Pall Mall.

That the initial encounter between Macbeth and the witches was one of the most frequently painted scenes from Shakespeare owes much to contemporary interest in the supernatural, but it may also reflect the popularity of the Choice motif. Once established as a model of the temporal and moral visualisation of narrative, it is used by artists in a variety of situations – historical, satirical, literary, Shakespearean. Its importance lay in far more than the presentation of a sequence: the most effective instances, like those of Hogarth, used the figure to create meaning or critical comment through the dialogue established between its original meaning – a moment of high moral election that would decide the future life of a hero in classical epic – and that which it carried in its new setting, comically or satirically inappropriate to this ethical elevation. In this it is representative of a larger practice that is central to Shakespeare painting as visual criticism.

The ironic potential of such dialogue is clear in Wootton's use of the trope for Macbeth's choice between the good Banquo and the evil witches, but this is only one of the levels of meaning that may arise. The dialogue generated by allusion may ennoble or debase the new circumstances, revealing a serious or satiric thrust; alternatively, it may illumine the new events conceptually by placing them in the wholly new light of the original figure to suggest a range of critical readings through comparison. Such exchanges are, of course, familiar from two main directions. In art historical criticism they constitute the process of iconographical reference, which draws attention to the development of conventions of representation where particular compositions are used in, for example, a painting of the annunciation, deposition or other Biblical narrative. In such conventions meaning is generated by tradition, supplemented by symbols or attributes – the dove of the Holy Spirit, say, or the keys that designate St Peter. That such tropes are found most often in Biblical painting reveals their didactic purpose: in pre-literate cultures, such images immediately convey both narrative and moral impulse.

The other practice is ultimately more influential as a drive towards the production of paintings as critical statements on Shakespeare's texts. Shaftesbury's *Historical Draught* appeared in 1713, the year between the publication of the two canto and the four canto versions of a much more familiar text, Pope's *Rape of the Lock*. The effect of this poem relies largely on the convention of the mock-heroic – the application of tropes familiar from classical epic to events of a commonplace and domestic nature. The discrepancy generates satiric comedy, but depends on the reader's recognition of the original figure and the absurdity of its use in the new situation. A little later, a similar technique is used by Fielding in *Tom Jones*. The battle in the churchyard (Book Four, Chapter 8) is mock-heroic in a manner directly reminiscent of *The Rape of the Lock*, as is the scene (Book Nine, Chapter 2) in which Tom leads Mrs Waters to safety without looking back, 'her cloaths being torn from all the upper part of her body',[32] in comic parody of the progress of Orpheus and Eurydice. In 1728, John Gay adopted a similar approach in music, using traditional airs as the basis of the songs in *The Beggar's Opera*: the words originally sung to the tune form an inaudible but insistent presence beneath those of the opera, allowing a similar act of criticism through comparison. The song 'Through all the employments of life/ Each neighbour abuses his brother',[33] for example, is enriched by being set to a melody traditionally having the words 'Down, down with political fools'. That this appears just after the overture in which the song 'Walpole' appears, embeds the politician's corruption within a context of much deeper inevitability;[34] the song is traditional, and so is political corruption, suggesting satire within a tone of boisterous acceptance. By contrast, many visual artists who followed Hogarth's use of iconographical allusion frequently appropriated classical or Biblical elements for more serious purposes. Benjamin

West's *Death of General Wolfe* (1771)[35] elevates the scene by using the trope of a deposition, to intensify the seriousness of both event and painting, as the death may be equated with the death of Christ on the cross, placing the image within the convention of Old Master religious painting. This dual aim is, of course, quite appropriate to the new seriousness with which contemporary British history and the creation of a national school of history painting were being viewed in the third quarter of the century. The proper understanding of the series of referential frames governing his complex allegorical paintings for the Society of Arts, still visible in the Great Room of the RSA in London, so concerned James Barry that he published an analysis of them that ran to 249 pages and was sold alongside prints reproducing the images themselves.[36]

Satiric or ennobling, serious or comic, musical, literary or visual, all of these uses of allusion have the same function: the comparison they generate acts more powerfully upon the current than the original meaning of the figure. A fundamentally similar conceptual stance underlies the use of the technique in paintings of Shakespeare's plays. The difference lies in the fact that a greater critical depth is often provided by the parallels that the allusion sets up so that the reader or connoisseur, trained by the advice of Richardson and versed in the developing practices of both the analysis of paintings and the discussion of Shakespeare's plays, may explore intellectual and moral debates of the sort declared as the object of painting by Richardson and Shaftesbury. If, after all, Shakespeare is being advanced as the national genius, quite equal to the ancients, then his work is both worthy of the close attention they have received and capable of producing moral insights and examples equal to theirs. The general principle has a direct practical result: the use of the Choice trope forces moral comparison with Hercules, and from this flows a critical discussion of, for example, character and action in *Macbeth*.

This raises a question insistent in any discussion of interpretive practice and authorial direction: how far is the critical use of iconographic allusion the result of an identifiable purpose on the part of the artist? The answer will depend on the stance of the onlooker, which will fall between two extremes. Confronted with such images we may dismiss doubts as a version of the intentional fallacy and, with Derrida, give the images our own 'countersignature'[37] and assign to them any number of associative meanings. At the other extreme, we may restrict interpretation to concepts and practices firmly demonstrable from the artist's other work, written intention or similar direct evidence. Both positions are untenable, the first because it renders impossible the recovery of insights genuinely part of an eighteenth-century critical conspectus, the second because it denies the imaginative life of the painting itself, through litigious insistence on verbal proof. Finding an acceptable position between them depends upon a rigorous analysis of general and specific critical and creative standpoints contemporary with the work, to remain inside what Umberto Eco calls 'the rights of the text'.[38] This process is itself revitalised by subsequent theory and practice, so that the two constitute a dialogue reflecting that between the two voices of the iconographic allusion itself. In this way, legitimising the images as aspects of contemporary critical intelligence is facilitated through the use of methods and concepts disclosed by later stances. The resultant reading will itself become the subject of debate, since the answer to such questions can never be absolute or static; but a deeper exploration of individual images and artists may act as a safeguard and go some way towards allaying fears of ahistoricism and over-ingenuity.

With Hogarth the production of meaning through dialogue with earlier texts and their conceptual and critical frames is beyond question. His employment of the Choice trope stands as a fine example of the way in which allusion becomes not only an assertion of satiric meaning but a forceful rejection of the neo-classical pantheism associated with that kind of Whiggism that Shaftesbury represents.[39] With Reynolds, the use of allusion is equally clear but causes problems that can never be fully resolved because of his own statements about borrowing compositional elements from Old Master paintings simply as the basis of visual structures, apparently devoid of meaning generated in reference to their original significances. Yet his own use of reference for comic effect, through the practice that has come to be called 'borrowed attitudes'[40] – the use of comically inapposite references, most commonly in portraits – reveals a shrewd critical intelligence and an awareness of production and reading practices that carefully manipulate inferences generated through dialogue with tradition. A similar tension can be seen in the theory and practice of Fuseli: advocating in his third Royal Academy lecture[41] an apparently neutral 'Judicious Adoption of Figures' from Old Master paintings, he manipulates complex networks of reference to produce sharp critical insights in his paintings.

Despite problems and uncertainties that, as the following pages will show, arise with individual images, the evidence all points in one direction. The production of meaning by iconographic allusion in music, poetry, the novel and history painting is without doubt a major component of the aesthetic ideology and practice of the period. Its use in Shakespeare painting as an instrument of interpretation constitutes a lateral extension of a well-established technique, that cannot be dismissed as an invention of the later analyst. To this should be added a further argument. That the interpretations offered in these chapters were not made explicit in critical writings contemporary with the paintings does not mean that original readers were not aware of their implications at some deeper, unexpressed level. Similarly, that the terms of critical discussion of the plays evolved only in twentieth-century academic writing, and the techniques of iconographical analysis were formalised by Erwin Panofsky as recently as the 1930s,[42] suggests not that the complex structures the approaches reveal were not present, but rather that the vocabularies for disclosing them were established much later.

The notion of painting as critical interpretation of Shakespeare of course depends on the painter's familiarity with the plays. In part, this was achieved through familiarity with production, and here another tradition of representation assumes importance alongside that of iconographical reference: the idea of the schematic representation of the passions. First established by Descartes, the idea gained ground most completely in the lectures and writings of Charles Le Brun. Translated into English at least twice during the early eighteenth century these theoretical works, with the copious illustrations that accompanied them, were very influential in the theatre, Garrick himself following many of the suggested postures and expressions. They were supplemented by British writings such as the explorations of the language of the hand made by John Bulwer,[43] and other treatises published up to the end of the century, retaining some influence on the style of both performance and painting.[44] But in general their significance as a method of textual interpretation in painting was limited, and they never became a universal language of the kind their advocates intended. After the middle years of the century, in which paintings often combined a reflection of performance with a setting not possible on stage, a more immediate imaginative recreation of the texts displaced the stereotyped emotions that Le Brun's idea of the passions became when applied to static visual representation.

Leaving aside the tradition of portraits of actors in character – an important tradition, but one marginal to the discussion of paintings as textual criticism – it is clear from both general and specific evidence that paintings were based on reading the plays. This reflects an intellectual climate where a knowledge of Shakespeare and an interest in the aesthetics of visual representation were closely connected; a telling detail here is that Richardson's theoretical writings and Theobald's edition of Shakespeare shared the same London publisher. In practical terms, knowledge of the published texts is most obvious in paintings of plays that had received no recent productions. Elsewhere, the painter's use of editions that pursue the chimerical grail of Shakespeare's authentic text rather than contemporary adaptations is evidenced by the inclusion of characters omitted from performance, most frequently the Fool in paintings of *King Lear*. The extent of individual artists' knowledge of the plays may sometimes be deduced from other sources. Reynolds produced a number of detailed notes to the texts, some of which were included in Johnson's edition of 1765 (see Chapter 7); Fuseli's writings make clear that he, too, knew this edition, and later also that of Steevens (see Chapter 4). In this way, the theory of painting, the practice of textual editing and the process of critical interpretation find an overlapping focus in the tradition of visual criticism. Here it is worth recalling that, to Johnson, 'illustration' meant textual elucidation and comment;[45] only in 1816 is the first use of the word in the meaning now commonly accepted, 'an illustrative picture,' recorded in the OED (4b). In the second half of the eighteenth century, the two significances were given tangible form in paintings that constituted rich and subtle Shakespeare illustrations: the texts of the plays are given powerful critical readings, often with the aid of iconographic allusions, in a manner that followed the published theory of painting, to be decoded and discussed by an increasingly educated body of readers.

III

How did the visual treatment of Shakespeare's plays develop through the eighteenth century, alongside the growth of editing, criticism and performance? What were the effects of the theories and practices developed by Shaftesbury, Richardson and their followers, and how did Shakespeare imaging relate to the larger currents of painting, print-production and the growth of the public gallery? Within the tradition of Shakespeare visualisation, driven by the interpenetration of social, economic and aesthetic forces, certain themes and transformations are apparent. The images are prolix and contradictory in their mediation of the plays: themes coalesce, and differences in treatment follow no linear sequence. Yet it is possible to trace recurrent concerns and map changes that govern, influence or redefine Shakespeare painting during the years with which this study is concerned.

Increasingly, the painting of the plays became part of several networks of aesthetic and social exchange. The practice of reading the plays, already growing with the work of Theobald and Warburton, developed into the major initial experience of the plays after Johnson's edition of 1765. As well as furthering the concept of establishing an authentic text, this did much to stimulate critical discussion. At one level, this consisted of the examination of textual detail: at another, it involved the exploration of character, morality and action within the possibilities and constraints of Shakespeare's dramatic structures. William Hawkins had given the first lectures on the dramatist, in Latin, at Oxford in the early 1750s; Arthur

Murphy, Charlotte Lennox, the Earl of Orrery, Lord Kames and others all extended the discussion in different directions. As the century continued the beginnings of a critical practice began to emerge, albeit one far removed from the practices of textual and critical study that evolved in the twentieth century, even allowing for the beginnings of the analysis of verbal imagery evident in the work of Walter Whiter.[46]

Similarly, in the middle years of the century the relation between painting and the theatre changed, at first revealing a play of relationships between stage and landscape or interior. Wootton's treatment of Macbeth's encounter with the witches is representative of many other paintings that, in different ways and with variable effectiveness, explore the balance between classical figure tropes, stage practice carefully selected and re-ordered, and settings depicted with different degrees of naturalism. An opposite impulse is seen in images including Johann Zoffany's *Garrick and Mrs Pritchard as Macbeth and Lady Macbeth* (c. 1768) which, while modifying the setting a little from what would be possible in the theatre, records the actors with an accuracy confirmed by contemporary written accounts. Theatrical conversation pieces of this kind, and portraits of the actor in character, began to form categories distinct from painting based on critical reading. The shift from these theatre-pieces to the purely imaginative images of Fuseli, Blake and others is the most extreme transformation and, while in one sense it parallels the move from seeing to reading Shakespeare, in another it reveals a difference of objective between the two genres. The combination of theatre record and larger interpretive initiative on the part of the artist can sometimes be revealing, however, and such overlaps constitute a thread that surfaces intermittently through the period.

Fundamental to the move out of the theatre is the use of landscape, which becomes important in terms of composition, symbolism, sentiment and ideology. Early images use the manner of Rosa or Poussin, supported by emblems from the natural world to underline morality, or follow Watteau in offering airy Rococo settings. Later paintings use indigenous settings to reveal the innate Englishness of character and event. Increasingly, too, landscape becomes the vehicle of multiple and various ideological inflections, offering a range of possible construals in terms of national, familial and gender politics. The one strand that runs through almost all later landscapes is a stress on apparently uncultivated natural forms as a reflection of the instinctive, untamed freedom of the English spirit: it is the most complete visualisation of Shakespeare as the instinctive genius whose identity with the English countryside had been established in the 1740s by Akenside, Warton, Gray and Collins. The idea of 'Shakespear's warblings wild'[47] as the antithesis of classical restraint, embodying the national identity in its full untutored splendour, is explicitly linked with the hope that the plays will find visual form in Collins' verse epistle to Hanmer, which begins with a reference to 'th'unlettered Bard' (l. 16) and closes with the invocation 'O might the Muse with equal Ease persuade/ Expressive Picture to adopt thine Aid!' (ll.119–20).[48]

Shakespeare's place as the national bard was confirmed by Garrick's Shakespeare Jubilee of 1769, an event that widened the schism between the plays themselves and the writer as cultural determinant first apparent in the 1740s. This is particularly important in another dimension of the creation of nationhood, the idea of history, which assumes various forms as the century passes. Once Shakespeare is established as the essence of national identity, what is perceived as his version of history takes on a special kind of cultural truth, and this in turn is reflected in visual treatments. Changing notions of authenticity, seen in costume and setting, generate the most insistent form of exchange between past and present. Many earlier images, for example Benjamin Wilson's paintings of Lear and Hamlet, apparently ignore the idea of the past by locating the events, and dressing the characters, in strictly contemporary forms. This apparent ahistoricity betrays its own use of history, representing one extreme of the debate between past and present apparent with great diversity elsewhere. A highly idiosyncratic view of British history merges in William Blake's Shakespeare images with Christian myth and the supernatural to produce close and many-faceted readings of the play's metaphoric language that, in his later work, are absorbed into his own private mythology. The images of the Boydell Gallery are generally more providentialist: the elaborate imaging of the christening of Elizabeth in *Henry VIII* by Matthew Peters, and the preponderance in the same collection of treatments of *The Merry Wives of Windsor*, replete with depictions of the newly restored Windsor Castle, suggest a newly self-aware nation creating its past within its present.

Within the dual senses of history and political identity the idea of religion forms an important subsidiary thrust. First apparent in the painting of Hogarth, whose treatment of *The Tempest* uses the questioning of iconographic elements to reject Catholicism, the approach is later developed obliquely by Fuseli and more directly in some of the Boydell prints. In a broader sense, too, the displacement of an elaborate iconographic reference of the sort employed in the Old Master tradition, itself largely founded on a Catholic tradition of Biblical exegesis, by an allusive vocabulary referring to pragmatic concerns such as the indigenous landscape discussed above, may be read – within the larger growth of Romantic experiential nature – as another dimension of the move towards a Shakespeare embodying ideal Englishness.

History, nationhood and iconography had by the mid-1760s come together in the adoption of the Grand Style, one manifestation of the period's larger concern to define itself through reference to the past that became known in stylistic terms as Neo-Classicism. In terms of subject matter, this began with treatments of classical myth and legend by West, Barry and Angelica Kauffman,[49] but then moved to embrace Biblical subjects and treatments of English history and contemporary events in the nation's political and military life, according them a status equal to those from the history of Greece and Rome. Between 1759 and 1778 the Society of Arts stipulated that its Premiums would be awarded only to paintings of English or British historical subjects;[50] that such images – and the literary topics that were largely identified with them – were at least equal to their classical antecedents as late as 1795 is suggested by a review of the enlarged Boydell Shakespeare Gallery that begins with the line 'On Greece and Rome why lavish all your praise – Shakespeare'.[51] Richard Samuel's painting of a celebrated group, *The Nine Living Muses of Great Britain*,[52] painted in 1778 and exhibited at the Royal Academy in the following year, includes as proof of the nation's aesthetic stature Charlotte Lennox, Angelica Kauffman, Elizabeth Montagu and Catherine Macaulay, all figures of importance in different ways in the discussion and visualisation of Shakespeare's plays. Lennox suggested the plays' failure in comparison to the novel, causing readers and painters increasingly to re-create the texts as seamless narratives told from a single omniscient viewpoint; Kauffman contributed to Boydell's Shakespeare Gallery, having already had many paintings reproduced and published by him. Elizabeth Montagu was one of the earliest to establish criticism as a serious intellectual discipline; and Catherine Macaulay produced a version of English history that, continuing the approach of the earlier historian Paul Rapin – a very early, and very successful, proponent of serial publication in 1732 – openly declared its Whiggism in opposition to Hume's Tory narrative, extending a debate that insinuated itself at a deep ideological level into Shakespeare painting.

Alongside the classical restraint and intellection that images such as Samuel's painting embody, another convention was increasingly evident from the 1760s that instead celebrated an immediate emotionalism. The primacy of feeling gained currency after the publication of Rousseau's works in English translation, and the appearance of Sterne's *Tristram Shandy* in 1759, and was made respectable – and also ironised – in Henry Mackenzie's *The Man of Feeling* in 1774. The move towards the novel as the primary literary form, and the emotional and imaginative engagement it engenders, reveals itself in many images from the century's last quarter, by involving their readers with greater emotional directness through gesture, action or landscape. James Northcote, William Hamilton, Francis Wheatley and

John Opie established themselves within this new tradition, offering images that reveal the new *sensiblité* by dwelling on moments of emotional intensity without relating them critically to the plays' larger ideas. Feeling was not only aesthetic in its manifestations; its impact on education, social reform and the growing movement against slavery was forceful, and itself contributed to the circles of discourse in which the reading, production and painting of Shakespeare participate. It also mediated the perception of landscape, running alongside and in some cases merging with other cultural currents. Of these the most important was the cult of the Gothic, which not only influenced architectural forms both in actual buildings and in their painterly representation but also brought new concerns to present historical scenes within a heavily stylised notion of accuracy, and valorised landscapes of a wild barrenness. In this it overlapped with the particular definition of the Sublime advanced by Edmund Burke in his *Philosophical Enquiry* of 1757.[53] The dominant effect of the Sublime lay in its power to inflict terror on the beholder, with a consequence that was both aesthetic and cathartic. Like the Gothic and the cult of *sensibilité*, the Sublime made its impact upon Shakespeare painting, as indeed on most other aspects of Shakespeare activity.

Shifts in emotional temper were matched by developments easier to quantify, by which painting, engraving and the place of the visual image in British society were transformed. Changes in approaches to the plays in which they were seen as a national possession are manifested in the greater importance of Shakespeare painting as both a site and a focus of social interaction. At the beginning of the period it is probably still true to say that the individual painting, often a portrait or a view of a country house, commissioned by a patron, was viewed as the most important species of artistic production; it was accessible only to its owner and his – or, rarely, her – household, or to the increasing number of connoisseurs to whom private collections were made available upon request. As early as the 1740s this began to change, when Francis Hayman produced images for the pavilions in Jonathan Tyers' Vauxhall Gardens (see Fig. 3), at the heart of the recreational activity of the rapidly growing merchant citizenry. The exclusivity as an individual painting was also progressively diluted by the move towards public exhibition. The Foundling Hospital had begun the practice in the same decade, to be followed by the Society of Artists in 1760, the Free Society in 1765 and the Royal Academy in 1768. Between these displays, allowing public discussions of paintings, and the large engravings produced by Boydell and other print-publishers, facilitating the discussion of images in private, stand the many varieties of social awareness of images in the collections of connoisseurs, at galleries of many kinds, in shops selling books and prints (see Fig. 4) and even in the street outside them. All

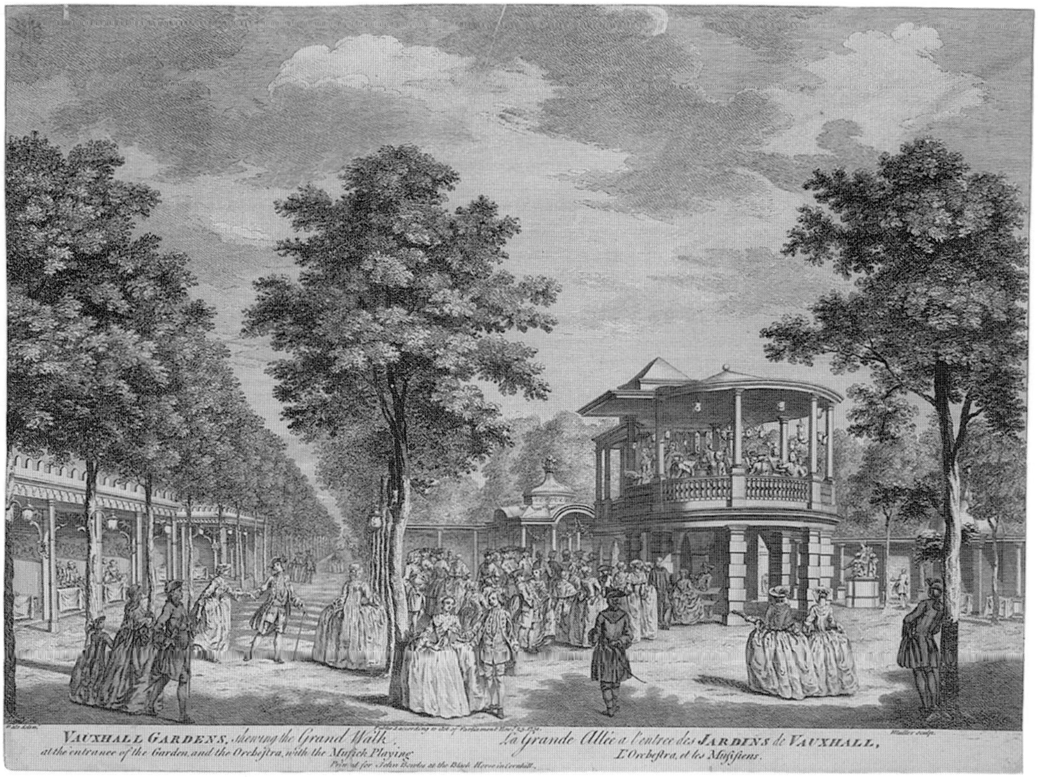

3 Samuel Wale, *Vauxhall Gardens shewing the Grand Walk*. Engraved by J. S. Muller, after 1751.

these are a function of the greater involvement of Shakespeare and Shakespeare discussion in the new social grace of conversation, and of the new social spaces in which it occurred. The conversations themselves ranged in focus from the amused contemplation of Reynolds' 'borrowed attitudes' – perhaps the most sociable form of iconographic allusion, concerned as it is with decoding comic visual allusions and the insights they show into the sitter's character – to the scholarly discussion of the play texts themselves, with political satire, relations to the theatre, the idea of history and the concept of Shakespeare as national genius as overlapping discourses in between.

For the artists, exhibition had a more commercial end. Many, including Turner and Blake, had their own galleries, and Blake's *Descriptive Catalogue*[54] makes clear the strong financial drive behind them. This was, of course, essential for the professional artist. Joseph Wright followed the convention of pricing portraits according to size and, as the artist became better known, the fees rose accordingly. A portrait measuring 30 × 25 in (76.2 × 63.5 cm) was six guineas in the 1760s but rose to fifteen in the 80s and 90s; group portraits and larger genre paintings could

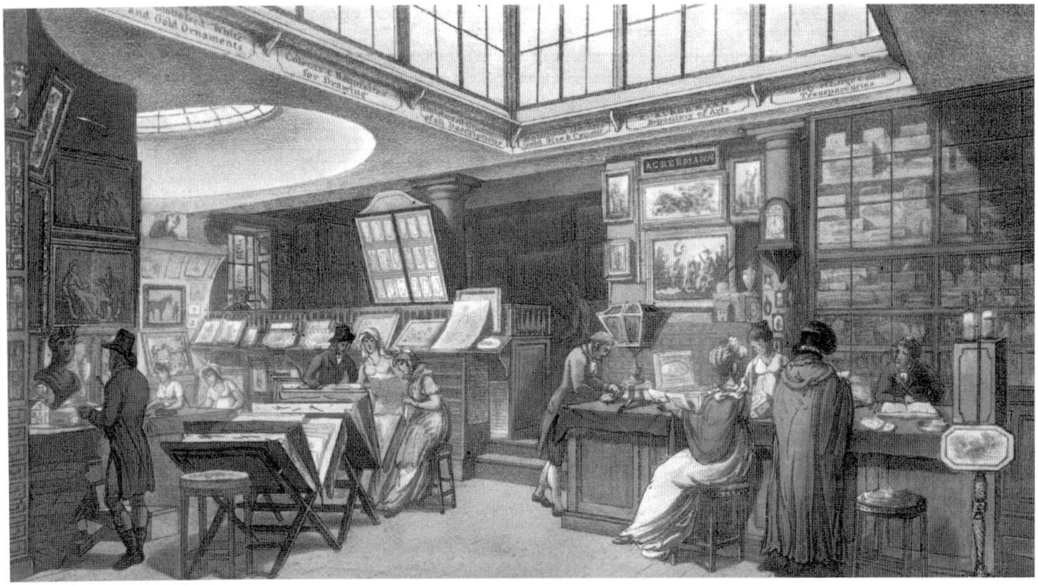

4 Charles Augustus Pugin, *Ackermann's Room in the Strand*, 1809.

cost over £100.[55] Price was also dictated by fashion and individual taste. Wright's restrained yet intense *Juliet in the Tomb* (1790)[56] failed to sell at auction at Christie's and was bought in by the artist for £47 5s; his *Ferdinand and Miranda in Prospero's Cell* (1789),[57] full of incident and of much rhetorical power, was purchased by Boydell for the Shakespeare Gallery for £315.[58] The inference that it had a more immediate and far wider appeal when reproduced is hard to avoid.

The strong commercial thrust of the later years was also evidenced in the public display of individual images. In May 1784, for example, two paintings by John Singleton Copley, *The Death of Major Peirson*[59] and *The Death of Lord Chatham*[60] – an image that, like West's *Death of Wolfe*, elevates its subject by the use of the deposition motif – were shown in the Haymarket. The Great Room was open every day from 8.00 a.m. to midnight and one shilling was charged for admission. In August the exhibition transferred to the upper gallery in Boydell's house in Cheapside. This event is in a sense exceptional, exploiting the national events the two paintings chronicle; but the display shows the degree of interest in painting, especially that with a topical subject, that was now manifesting itself as a form of social activity. By the end of the century some understanding of painting, in terms of both subject and style, was no longer the preserve of the wealthy patron; connoisseurship, as defined and popularised by Richardson in his 1719 treatise, and refined by Fuseli's of 1765, had been made available to a wider audience by publications such as Dodsley's *Preceptor* of 1748,[61] and the later editions of

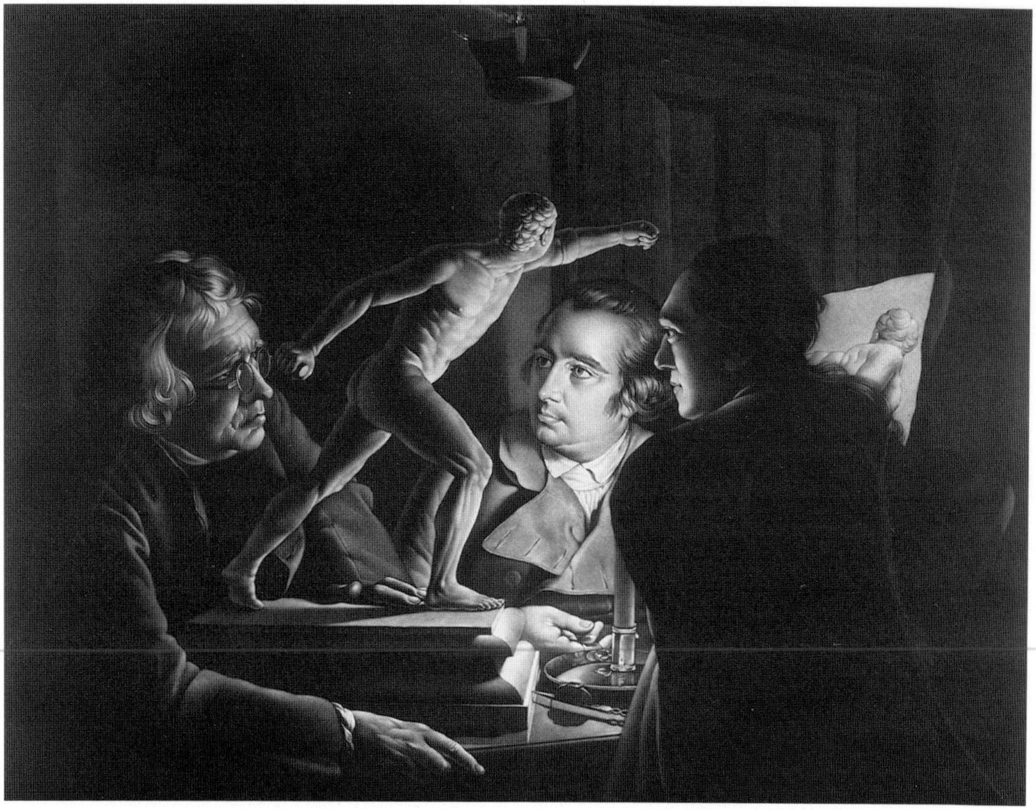

5 Joseph Wright, *Three Persons Viewing the Gladiator by Candle-light*. Mezzotint by William Pether, 1769.

Chambers' *Cyclopædia*.[62] It had become as much a part of the rounded education of anyone with social, aesthetic and intellectual interests as an awareness of the theatre, or a knowledge, actual or pretended, of the plays of Shakespeare.

A major impetus behind the public display of many paintings was the wish to publicise and sell prints reproducing them. The rapid expansion of print publishing in the second half of the century was the result of technical advances, growing national expertise and a carefully nurtured market. At the start of the period, one of the most popular techniques in England was the mezzotint. In this process a copper plate is prepared by being worked over completely with a fine-toothed roller so that its surface consists of fine indentations and burrs. The burrs are then pressed down with a scraping tool, to create a surface of different degrees of density that reflects the design to be printed.[63] Because the burrs and indentations are very efficient in holding ink, the finished plate produces a wide range of tonal gradations, which include velvety black textures (see Fig. 5) and deep tones in the rare instances where mezzotints are produced in colour (see Plate 3). The most accomplished engravers, such as Valentine Green, James McArdell and William Pether, were known for the subtlety of their mezzotints in the 1740s, and contributed significantly to images of Shakespeare's plays.

The very subtlety of the mezzotint plate also made it very fragile, however, and prints were produced in very small editions; a run of twenty-five or thirty impressions was not uncommon, making them expensive and exclusive. Engraving allowed a much larger edition. Again using a copper plate, the process involves gouging out lines with a V-shaped chisel known as a burin. The plate is covered with ink and the surplus removed so that the ink fills the incised lines; dampened paper is then pressed on to the plate and forced into the incisions, giving a very clear, sharp image which can be reproduced between one and two thousand times.[64] A little later, in the 1750s, stipple engraving was developed, in which a series of dots, circles or other geometric figures was stamped into the plate using hardened steel punches. As well as producing subtle effects of texture and gradation the technique made engraving much quicker, an important advance when prints made from commissioned paintings were needed rapidly to recoup the initial outlay. For a similar reason, engraving was often supplemented by etching. In this process the copper plate is covered with a layer of varnish, which is then scraped away by an etching needle and the plate immersed in acid which bites away the metal. The plate is then cleaned and impressions are taken from it as from an engraving.[65] All three techniques are often used in the same plate, to save time and give variety, from the sharp lines of engraving through the softer gradations of etching to larger background textures made by stippling. Etching offered another advantage. If the first proof print was found lacking, areas could be 'stopped out' by the addition of more varnish and the plate bitten again in the acid, to make the printed area denser or in some cases to change the image. In this way, Caroline Watson removed the devil behind the head of Cardinal Beaufort in her print of Reynolds' painting from 2 *Henry VI* (see Chapter 7).

When Shaftesbury wished to include an engraving of *The Choice of Hercules* in the 1714 edition of his *Historical Draught* he turned to the Frenchman Simon Gribelin, then living in London; similarly, Hogarth used Ravenet and Scotin to engrave his *Progress* series in the 1730s. Twenty years later, following the pioneering work of William Woollett, British engraving was second to none: James Heath, Thomas Burke and Francesco Bartolozzi were among the best-known names.[66] In 1780, the publisher William Wynne Ryland organised an exhibition of paintings by Angelica Kauffman *On Purpose for Engravings in various Manners*[67] at which both paintings and engravings were displayed, in what is probably the earliest overt reference to such a hierarchy. Engraving a large painting was lengthy and complex: in December 1795 Boydell wrote 'After Six Years absence, I have got the Picture of Major Pierson home,'[68] referring to the Copley image mentioned above, that had been borrowed for copying and engraving by James Heath. He continued 'it will take at least three Months to Print it'; it actually took nine, to produce an edition of 1,500.

These movements, social and technical, all reach their climax in the most significant public event of eighteenth-century Shakespeare imaging, the Boydell Shakespeare Gallery. The initial 34 paintings grew to an eventual total of 167. It was not the paintings themselves but the engravings that reproduced them that were Boydell's major concern: in 1805 two imperial folio volumes were published, reproducing one hundred of the finest paintings, with further images commissioned to illustrate an edition of the plays. It is tempting to see this as the climax of a process of continuous enfranchisement, in which engravings become increasingly available to those of lower social rank, but this would be a misreading, as the size and cost of the Boydell prints restricted them to those of higher income. Not until the next century, with the growth of lithography and wood-pulp paper that allowed images to be reissued in smaller format and larger print runs, were they freely available at significantly lower cost.

Producing a hundred large engravings was a long and expensive undertaking, and the delay contributed to the financial collapse of the Boydell Gallery in 1805. The best engravers could command fees superior to those of the painters whose work they were reproducing. For his Boydell painting of *King Lear* (see Chapter 4), Henry Fuseli received £262 10s; for engraving it, Richard Earlom was paid £420.[69] Sold at auction, the collection was dispersed and many of the paintings are now known only as engravings. Some were coloured by hand; while they lack the subtlety of the paintings, it is possible to infer from those reproducing surviving paintings that their colours were reasonably faithful, offering some idea of the coloration of the lost paintings.

One of a number of ventures that sought to present literary works in visual form, of which James Woodmason's *Irish Shakespeare Gallery* and Thomas Macklin's *British Poets* were other important representatives, the Boydell Gallery is significant in revealing the variety of style, approach and critical direction of Shakespeare painting at the end of the century. But the venture effectively closes the great period of Shakespeare visualisation: thereafter, treatment of Shakespearean themes becomes concerned once more with theatre, character and sentiment and the major critical thrust moves into other fields of endeavour.

IV

These themes – theatre, landscape, history, and the production techniques and social exchanges which governed the images – are essential strands throughout this book, but its larger purpose is rather different. It is concerned with individual images as interpretive statements, of a variety of kinds, to reveal the importance of visual criticism as an endeavour parallel in importance to performance, production and editing. While it does chart major movements and transformations in visual practice, it does not attempt to present an encyclopaedic coverage of the period; more specifically, except within its larger exploration of stances and techniques, it is not concerned with relations between paintings and theatre practice, a topic already explored in great depth by theatre historians. Certainly, there are links between stage and easel, which are discussed where appropriate; but the book rests on the premise that images from the period increasingly spring from the plays as they are printed rather than as they are performed. In consequence it is a range of readings, of a range of kinds, that are here considered.

With such an extensive body of material, severe limitations are necessary, and significant omissions have been made, the broadest being the discussion of illustrated editions, except where related to individual paintings and engravings. The earliest visual treatments of Shakespeare in the eighteenth century were the frontispiece engravings for Rowe's editions of 1709 and 1714 (see Fig. 6): important documents in the history of the book, they offer in some instances suggestive interpretations of the plays. Thomas Hanmer's edition, which appeared in the 1740s, had frontispieces by Francis Hayman, and is uniquely significant as presenting the only series of images based on written instructions specifying scenes and treatment. Many other artists and engravers produced thoughtful images offering insights of many kinds that do much to enrich and redefine the experience offered to eighteenth-century readers of the plays. Yet the pulse of an illustrated edition is inherently different from that of a self-defining easel-painting, concerned as it is with *mise-en-page* and the location within the individual reader's progression through a printed text. For this reason these dual texts stand to one side of the tradition of visual criticism, and will be touched on only when they have a direct bearing to the establishment of a tradition of representation or, as is the case with Hayman, reveal a change in composition or altered emphasis in a related painting.

Another tradition of painting that has been largely excluded is that which focuses on the experiential immediacy of a single moment of the text, and becomes increasingly important in the work of Wheatley, Opie, Smirke and others in the

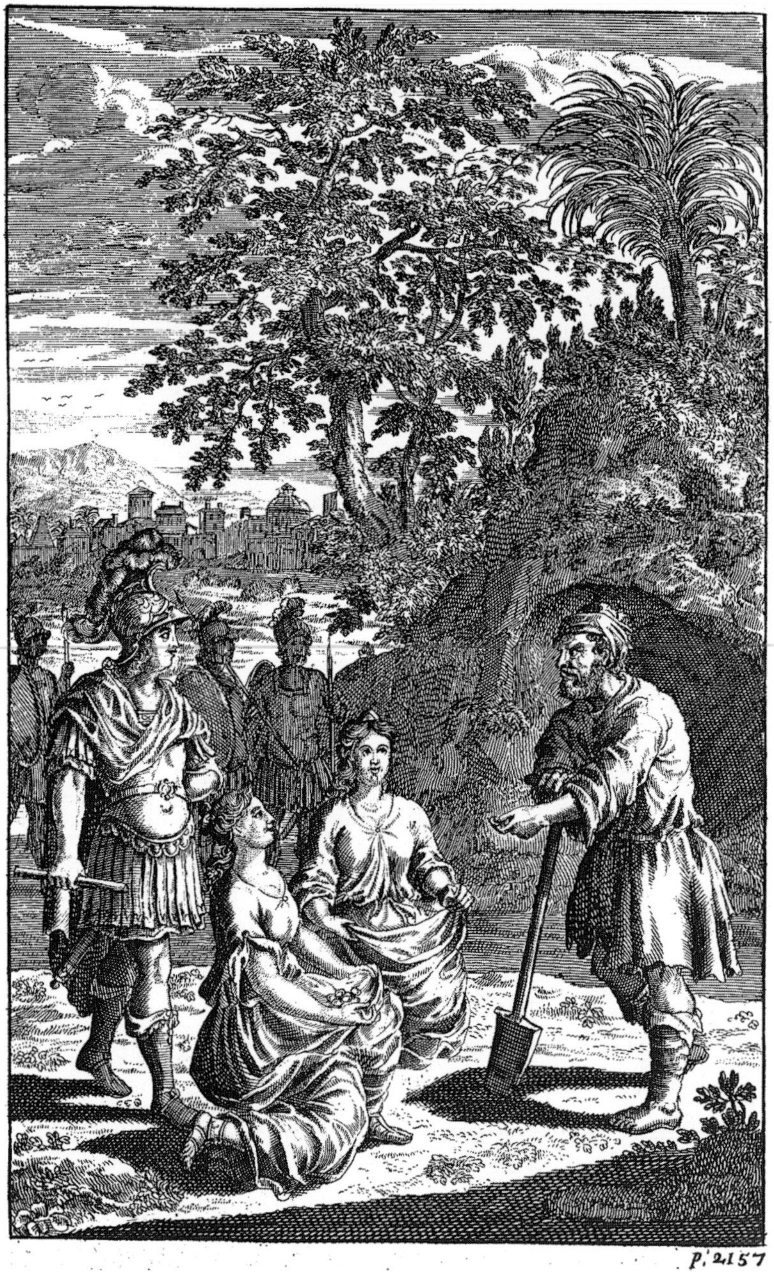

6 Elisha Kirkall, after François Boitard, Frontispiece to Rowe's *Timon of Athens*, 1709.

larger cultural shift towards the privileging of feeling. Work of this kind, however 'charmingly drawn', whatever its 'sweetness of pencil',[70] inevitably becomes peripheral to images of conceptual concentration. The comic paintings of William Bunbury, revealing though they are, have similarly been excluded. All these have much to say about the commodification of the plays within a range of social settings, and an exploration of this would further extend our knowledge of the century's varieties of Shakespeare assimilation, but such works are not the concern of this book since they do not primarily contribute to the critical or interpretive exploration of the plays.

As eighteenth-century performance and editing encompassed a range of different and sometimes contradictory practices, so the visualisation of the plays takes a variety of forms. The drawing together of a pivotal moment with emblematic indications of succeeding events, often through visual translation of the play's linguistic patterning in a manner that seems to anticipate twentieth-century close reading, has already been explored in Wootton's *Macbeth*. Other approaches include the rapid mediation of scene or subject through bravura wash-drawings; the implication of wider structures of meaning through patterns of iconographical reference; and dialogue between the play texts and ideas of history current in the artist's temporal and social frame. Yet to approach the visual tradition by following each of these, like a series of thematic corridors, would be to falsify; the workings and values of the images from which tradition is constructed emerge with greater clarity when they are approached, like most critical and theoretical positions, as a series of statements by significant individuals or groups, who inflect the developing language of visual criticism with their own usages to make personal contributions to the growing interpretive debate. The distinct stances adopted by single painters become increasingly evident from Hogarth onwards, albeit that the period between his work and the early images of Henry Fuseli is defined rather by significant works than by important individuals. Within the frame of the foregoing general account, the chapters that follow look in detail at important individual images or groups of images produced by the most significant figures. Comparisons between them and performance practice, and accounts of the critical reception they received when first exhibited, have been included only where they clarify the images by offering other voices in the critical and cultural debate to which they contribute.

Like most accounts of recent English art, the study begins with the work of Hogarth: the four images he produced that deal directly with Shakespearean themes lay the foundations of many of the techniques of visual criticism on which the individuals that followed erected their own structures. His sketch of Falstaff reviewing his troops reveals insights into character and action, as well as making visible right at the start of the period the compound reflexivity between performance and painting that will trouble and enthrall many subsequent painters. His *Scene from Shakespeare's 'The Tempest'* (1736?) postulates, with several kinds of wit, an alternative to the narrative hypotheses of Shaftesbury and Richardson that translates the diachronic text into a spatial composition, itself an arena for critical debate. Reflexivity and interpretive probing are again insistent in Hogarth's *Mr Garrick in the Character of Richard III*, which brings together theatrical portraiture, the presentation of stage action and the use of emblematic detail to offer a critical reading of great force and widespread influence. All his works raise insistent issues concerning the social and political functions of Shakespeare imaging and its role within an historiography that sees the past as a forum for debating the present, with a lancing insight into both. In their use of iconographic reference, and their confrontation with contemporary ideological issues, they instigate processes and address problems that recur throughout the subsequent decades, as well as revealing issues peculiar to their own time in the idea of Shakespeare and the plays they present.

In the years immediately following Hogarth, no single figure emerges as a major force, but the movements that occur all to some extent turn away from the theatre towards the imagination as the basis of painting the plays. Hayman's work for Vauxhall Gardens becomes part of a new social exchange in which Shakespeare has become implicit, and provokes in the early guide books the beginning of a published discussion of Shakespeare painting: the developing function of landscape within such hybrid forms is apparent also in the work of Benjamin Wilson. The need to locate Shakespeare painting within stylistic traditions that is demonstrated by these paintings is continued, and perhaps more completely fulfilled, in works by Francesco Zuccarelli and Nathaniel Dance. They suggest that Shakespeare painting has by now acquired a dual identity, being both a self-defining genre and a contribution to the mid-century debate on the establishment of a native style in English painting. At the same time a convention of representing Lear in the storm is evolving, doing much to establish a common ground between image and reader while allowing for brilliant departures in the work of John and Alexander Runciman.

Henry Fuseli began to produce serious visual treatments of the plays in the 1770s with a series of wash-drawings based on the tragedies, most particularly *Hamlet* and *Macbeth*, that mediate text and character through an eclectic range of iconographic reference to generate insights of great breadth and intensity into the plays' narrative and psychological processes. These and his fresco designs for *The Tempest* and *Twelfth Night* already raise an issue that will be troublesome in the images he produces on returning to London: the very depth of their readings, generated by arcane allusions, makes them inaccessible to almost all their potential readers. The struggle to resolve this dilemma is evident in many of his images, including the arabesque *Queen Katherine's Dream* and several of his Boydell paintings.

The predominantly iconographic mode of visual criticism developed by Fuseli is almost completely opposite to the approach taken by his contemporary George Romney. While he produced four paintings for the Boydell venture, only two were treatments of the plays: one, a version of the first act of *The Tempest*, offers a visual synchronisation of temporally discrete moments, striking in its difference from Hogarth's; the other addresses Shakespeare painting through a totally different perspective and equates character with society portraiture to locate the plays within one kind of national identity. Romney's genuine contribution to Shakespeare painting lies in his wash-drawings, multiple bravura sweeps that hover around a single moment, never reaching finality but of immense power in their suggestiveness. At times, too, such an immediacy is apparent in the Shakespeare paintings of Romney's friend William Blake: the early watercolour *Oberon, Titania with Puck and Fairies Dancing* voices its critical understanding through a tough rhythmic grace. Elsewhere, Blake demonstrates acute complexes of the visual and the verbal: the monoprint *Pity* and the watercolour *Fiery Pegasus* provide precise visual equivalents for Shakespeare's tropes but paradoxically reveal their purely verbal identity in the provision of further, and wholly visual, metaphoric regenerations. This inventiveness based on Shakespearean responses goes further with Blake than with any contemporary painter, as images resting on *A Midsummer Night's Dream* and one of the Sonnets are developed into emblems fundamental to the personal mythology manifested in the widening circles of the Prophetic Books.

The *Discourses* of Sir Joshua Reynolds, that Blake had annotated with such passionate disdain, become a principal theoretical source of a major stream of English painting, the Grand Style, and in this some individual paintings represent the most complete Neo-Classical readings of the plays. Benjamin West and James Barry are key figures, but so in a different way are Thomas Lawrence and the sculptor Anne Damer, who produced bas reliefs of *Coriolanus* and *Antony and Cleopatra* exhibited in the Boydell Gallery and reproduced on the title pages of its *Collection of Prints*. In the light of the rest of his work, rich in visual comedy, 'borrowed attitudes' and multiple resonances, it is perhaps unsurprising that Reynolds himself produced, in his three Boydell paintings, images full of subtle and arcane allusion within a style generally remote from idealised Neo-Classicism. His own deep knowledge of the plays, evident also in his writings, is apparent in images teasingly suggestive in the visual criticism they offer.

Fuseli's later work, still concerned with uniting his own iconographic methods with a style that would gain popular acceptance, frequently focused on the supernatural, reflecting an area in which Shakespeare had been regarded as supreme at least from critics such as Addison,[71] and which was of compelling interest for Shakespeare painters through most of the century. Treatments of *A Midsummer Night's Dream* address the text's ambivalences with Renaissance *sprezzatura*, while paintings of *The Tempest* concern themselves more with the different dimensions of magic in Prospero, Caliban and Ariel. A group of tondi or small circular paintings explore the identities of *The Winter's Tale*, meditating on the character of Perdita and reflecting the narrative deferral of the tale Mamillius never completes, and together transform the tradition of sentimental paintings of individual characters in a thoughtful fusion of criticism and invention.

Many of the images discussed in these chapters are part of the Boydell Shakespeare Gallery, but the organisation and assumptions of the venture and the works of many less well-known painters and engravers are also important, most particularly in showing how critical mediation shades off into ideological appropriation in dialogue with contemporary concerns. The variety of ideological valencies given to the landscape, the debate about history, and the idea of nationhood are among the directions that this takes. Within and around them, however, is the new reading experience and reading structure offered by the two volumes of the *Collection of Prints*. A sequence purely visual, almost always presenting the plays in three, four or five images by different hands, it constitutes a focus for varieties of critical reading, and returns the debate about interpretation and criticism to the readers, reinforcing the social, as well as the critical, function that Shakespeare painting has had since Hogarth and Hayman, now within a setting redefined and sharpened by intervening years of war, industrialisation and social change.

Any study of the present kind will be indebted to the work of its predecessors, and the visual history of the years under consideration has been explored in several directions by earlier scholars. The work of T. S. R. Boase[72] recognised the importance of many overlooked images, to build an armature for later studies. Of these, W. Moelwyn Merchant's *Shakespeare and the Artist* remains the most important, its ambitious narrative scope enfolding stage design, the illustrated edition and some dimensions of operatic adaptation as well as offering detailed readings of individual paintings. The term 'visual criticism' is only one of the many things within it for which the critic working in this field should still be grateful. The study of the Boydell Shakespeare Gallery edited by Walter Pape and

Frederick Burwick contains a number of essays on the paintings, their markets and their relation to history painting, as well as essays on individual artists and the contemporary reception of their work.[73] It also reproduces all the prints from the two volumes published by Boydell. The earlier edition by A. E. Santaniello has all the prints, but on a rather larger scale, and also usefully reproduces the original prefatory material. Hildegard Hammerschmidt-Hummel's recent work provides an encyclopaedic survey of Shakespeare visualisation, and is especially helpful in providing a scene-by-scene listing of images for each of the plays.

A number of shorter studies have appeared that both seek to redefine the identity of visual mediations and to locate them within the larger encounter from which, as readers, playgoers and critics, we construct our essential ideas of the plays. Jonathan Bate's essay 'Pictorial Shakespeare: Text, Stage, Illustration'[74] makes powerfully clear the ways in which an image in an illustrated edition offers its meanings through procedures of structure and reference quite different from those of a production, regardless of how directly it may appear to record stage practice. Stephen Orgel explores the image – both engraved frontispiece and easel-painting – in the larger cultural history of the plays in *Imagining Shakespeare*, and in 'The Authentic Shakespeare'[75] reflects on the value and limitations of paintings as documents in theatre history. John Harvey's 'Shakespeare and the Ends of Time: The Illustrations'[76] focuses more directly on the tradition of visual mediation, offering both a survey and astute analyses of individual works.

Exhibition catalogues provide a further essential source. Geoffrey Ashton's *Shakespeare and British Art* is one of the most wide-ranging, with invaluable material on paintings, drawings and engravings from all periods, as well as entries on Shakespeare memorials. The catalogue to the Heim Gallery's exhibition *The Painted Word* has important discussions of the larger course of literary painting during the period, and contains essays useful in locating Shakespeare painting within it. *Shakespeare in Art*,[77] published alongside the Dulwich Picture Gallery exhibition of 2003, offers an impressive collection of illustrations and incisive discussions of the visual tradition within the history of Shakespeare assimilation. Jonathan Bate's opening essay on 'The Shakespeare Phenomenon' sets larger cultural markers for the study of the plays' visualisation, and is followed by a discussion of Shakespeare painting and the print market by David Alexander. Shorter essays explore other visual territories, and the volume's entries on individual paintings are invaluable. Yet its main purpose is to offer an introductory survey and place key images within this larger movement through accounts of their provenance and subjects: it does not often explore the paintings as readings of the plays, although when it does, as later references will show, its insights are revealing. The work of art historians in preparing *catalogues raisonnés* and monographs on individual artists and movements provides an essential factual basis for an interpretive study of the present kind, and the work of Gert Schiff, Martin Postle and many others underpins the specific analyses and larger ideas of the present volume.

During the period of roughly a century that probably constitutes its richest phase, the visualisation of the plays moves through concepts, stances and techniques that repeatedly overlap and separate, like a series of *coulisses* that provide a formalised yet apparently naturalistic recession in a stage set or a Claudean landscape. As the century passes, the tradition is transformed and reinvented in response to, and sometimes in confrontation with, the social, political and aesthetic forces that move around it. In translating dramatic narrative across to the seemingly instantaneous time of the canvas or print, the work of visualising Shakespeare presents a complex of interlaced opportunities and perils. Seen as an entity in its own right, without overt comparisons with the theatre, theatrical portraiture or the illustrated edition, it combines the immediacy of performance with the intellectual insight of critical writing and locates them both within a new order of aesthetic imagining that becomes a major vehicle for the mediation of the plays.

NOTES

Sizes of paintings are given first in centimetres and then in inches, with height preceding width. Except where otherwise stated the medium is oil on canvas.

1. Rafael Valls Gallery, London.
2. It is recorded as being in the ownership of the Rev. E. Thistlethwaite of Anfield Plain, Co. Durham, in 1904, suggesting a family descent. For this information I am indebted to Lucy Bestwick of the Rafael Valls Gallery.
3. *Shakespeare Restored: or, A Specimen of the Many Errors, as well Committed, as Unamended, by Mr Pope in his Late Edition of this Poet* (London: Franklin, Woodman, Lyon and Davis, 1726).
4. *The Works of Shakespeare*, ed. Lewis Theobald, 7 vols. (London: Bettesworth, 1733).
5. Announcement in January 1744, quoted by Kalman A. Burnim in *David Garrick: Director* (first publ. 1961) (Carbondale Ill.: Southern Illinois University Press, 1973), p. 103.
6. John Dryden, *Of Dramatick Poesie, An Essay* (1668) *The Works of John Dryden. XII. Prose 1668–1691*, ed. Samuel Holt Monk (Berkeley and Los Angeles CA and London: University of California Press, 1971), p. 55.
7. *Miscellaneous Observations on 'Macbeth'* (London: E. Cave, 1745).
8. *The Painted Word: British History Painting: 1750–1830*, ed. Peter Cannon-Brookes (London: Heim Gallery, 1991), p. 46.
9. All quotations from Shakespeare's plays, except where otherwise identified, are from the most recent New Cambridge Shakespeare edition.

10. Burnim, *David Garrick*, p. 109.
11. Ibid., p. 109.
12. *David Garrick as Hamlet*, untraced; mezzotint by James McArdell, 41.9×33 ($16\,{}^{1}/_{2} \times 13$), published 1 November 1754.
13. The volume was first published by E. Picard, Paris, 1698. A French edition was published in London by David Mortier in 1701; the most influential English edition was *A Method to learn to Design the Passions*, trans. John Williams (London: J. Huggonson, 1734).
14. Anthony Ashley Cooper (3rd Earl of Shaftesbury), *A Notion of the Historical Draught or Tablature of the Judgement of Hercules, according to Prodicus, lib II Xen[ophon] de Mem[orabilia] Soc[ratis]* (London: A. Baldwin, 1713).
15. Also known as *Hercules at the Crossroads between Virtue and Vice*, 64.1×76.8 ($25\,{}^{1}/_{4} \times 30\,{}^{1}/_{4}$), Temple Newsom House, Leeds.
16. *Shakespearean Tragedy: Lectures on 'Hamlet', 'Othello', 'King Lear', 'Macbeth'* (London: Macmillan, 1904), Lecture IX, pp. 333–4.
17. One of the earliest was *Iconologia: or, moral emblems*, ed. Pierce Tempest and Isaac Fuller (London: B. Motte, 1709). This was presumably known to Shaftesbury and may have been the edition used as the basis of Richardson's reference. More significant was a much later version, with a text rewritten from Ripa's original by George Richardson: *Iconology; or, A collection of emblematical figures: containing four hundred and twenty-four remarkable subjects, moral and instructive; in which are displayed the beauty of virtue and the deformity of vice: the figures are engraved by the most capital artists from original designs; with explanations from classical authorities.* (London: G. Scott, 1779). Conveniently available with introductory notes by Stephen Orgel (New York and London: Garland Publishing, 1979).
18. London: Bettesworth, 1715. Reprinted Menston, Yorkshire: Scolar Press, 1971. Page numbers refer to this edition.
19. *An Essay on the Whole Art of Criticism as it Relates to Painting* (London: Bettesworth, 1719). Reprinted, with *An Argument in Behalf of the Science of the Connoisseur*, as *Two Discourses* (London: Bettesworth, 1719). Reprinted as *Aesthetics: Sources in the Eighteenth Century*, 4. (Bristol: Thoemmes Press, 1998).
20. These were published shortly after being delivered as addresses at the prizegiving ceremonies of the Royal Academy. The standard modern edition is *Discourses on Art*, ed. Robert R. Wark (New Haven and London: Yale University Press, 3rd edn, 1997).
21. First published with his translation of Winckelmann, *Reflections on the Painting and Sculpture of the Greeks: with Instructions for the Connoisseur, and an Essay on Grace in Works of Art* (London: Printed for the Translator, and sold by A. Millar, 1765).
22. *An Essay Concerning Human* Understanding, ed. John W. Yolton (London: Dent), II. XXXI.12–14, pp. 190–1. The idea is also developed in II.XXXII.10, p. 194, III.X.1, p. 252 and IV.III, pp. 278–97.
23. Nos. 411–421, June 21–July 3 1712.
24. *Patterns of Intention: On the Historical Explanation of Pictures* (New Haven and London: Yale University Press, 1985), p. 3.
25. 'On the Genius and Characters of Hogarth', *The Reflector*, II, 1811, p. 61.
26. *Indicator*, I.10 (No. 2, 20 October 1819).

27. 'Sleep and Poetry', ll.337–8. *John Keats: The Complete Poems*, ed. John Barnard (Harmondsworth: Penguin, 1988).
28. Humphry Repton, *The Bee; or, a Companion to the Shakespeare Gallery; containing a catalogue-raisonné of all the pictures; with comments, illustrations and remarks* (London: T. Cadell, 1789).
29. For example, *A Real Scene in St. Pauls Church Yard, on a Windy Day*. After Robert Dighton, 1783, which shows Bowles' Map and Print Warehouse, and *A crowd outside a print shop*, by J. Elwood, 1798.
30. *March of the Guards towards Scotland in the year 1745*, 101.6 × 133.3 (40 × 52 $^1/_2$), Thomas Coram Foundation, London.
31. Engraving, 30.48 × 38.1 (12 × 15), British Museum, London.
32. *Tom Jones*, ed. R. P. C. Mutter (Harmondsworth: Penguin, 1966 repr. 1985), p. 401.
33. Daniel O'Connor, ed. *The Beggar's Opera* (London: Gowans and Gray, 1922) 1.
34. The point is also made by Ronald Paulson in *Emblem and Expression: Meaning in English Art of the Eighteenth Century* (London: Thames and Hudson, 1975), p. 85. For a fuller discussion of the device see Stuart Sillars, 'Musical Iconography in *The Beggar's Opera*'. *British Journal for Eighteenth-century Studies*, 1.3 Autumn (1978), pp. 182–5.
35. 152.6 × 214.5 (60 × 84 $^1/_2$), National Gallery of Canada, Ottawa.
36. *An Account of a Series of Pictures, in the Great Room of the Society of Arts . . . with Addenda* (London: Printed for the Author by William Adlard, sold by T. Cadell and J. Walter, 1783).
37. *Acts in Literature*, ed. Derek Attridge (London and New York: Routledge, 1992), p. 18 and *passim*.
38. *The Limits of Interpretation* (Bloomington, Ind.: Indiana University Press, 1990), p .7.
39. For a full exploration of this, see Ronald Paulson's introduction to his edition of Hogarth's *Analysis of Beauty* (New Haven and London: Yale University Press, 1997), pp. xx–xxiii.
40. The term was coined by Horace Walpole. *Anecdotes of Painting in England*, Advertisement to Vol. IV, 1771 ed. Ralph N. Warnum (London: Swan Sonnenschein, Lowrey, 1881), I, p. xvii, n. 2. It has been fully explored by Edgar Wind in '"Borrowed Attitudes" in Reynolds and Hogarth', *Journal of the Warburg and Courtauld Institutes*, II, (1938–9), pp. 182–5.
41. *The Life and Writings of Henry Fuseli*, ed. John Knowles, 3 vols. (London: Colburn and Bentley, 1831), II, p. 180.
42. Most influentially in the chapter headed 'Introductory' in *Studies in Iconology: Humanistic Themes in the Art of the Renaissance* (New York: Oxford University Press, 1939), pp. 3–31. Reprinted as 'Iconography and Iconology: An Introduction to the Study of Renaissance Art' in *Meaning in the Visual Arts* (New York: Doubleday 1955 and Harmondsworth: Penguin, 1970).
43. *Chirologia: Or, the Naturall Language of the Hand, Composed of the Speaking Motions and Discoursing Gestures thereof, whereunto is added Chironomia: Or, the Art of Manuall Rhetoricke.* (London: Tho. Harper, 1644).
44. As late as 1807 a volume of schematic gestures was published as an aid to stage performance, a translation of J. J. Engel's *Ideen zu einer Mimik*, 1785: Henry Siddons, *Practical Illustrations of Rhetorical Gesture and Action* (London: Richard Phillips, 1807). For surveys of the influence of such writings, see Alan T. McKenzie, '"The Countenance You Show Me": Reading the Passions in the Eighteenth Century', *The Georgia Review* 32 (1978), pp. 758–83; and Alastair

Smart, 'Dramatic Gesture and Expression in the Age of Hogarth and Reynolds', *Apollo* 82 (1965), pp. 90–97.

45. The full title of his edition is *The Plays of William Shakespeare, in eight volumes, with the corrections and illustrations of various commentators, to which are added notes by Sam. Johnson.* (London: J. and R. Tonson, 1765).
46. *A Specimen of a Commentary on Shakespeare* (London: T. Cadell, 1794). Available with the author's own revisions in an edition by Alan Over completed by Mary Bell (London: Methuen, 1967).
47. Joseph Warton, 'The Enthusiast, or the Lover of Nature', 1744, l. 131.
48. *Verses humbly address'd to Sir Thomas Hanmer on his Edition of Shakespear's Works. By a Gentleman of Oxford* (London: M. Cooper, 1743). The verses appeared in slightly altered form in a second edition of 1744 and reprinted by Dodsley and elsewhere. *The Poems of Gray and Collins*, ed. Austin Lane Poole (London: Oxford University Press, 1919), p. 238.
49. This is the spelling used in contemporary references and in the Boydell collection.
50. For a full exploration of this see John Sunderland, 'Mortimer, Pine and some Political Aspects of English History Painting', *Burlington Magazine*, CXVI (1974), pp. 317–26, especially p. 325.
51. *Morning Chronicle*, 21 April 1795, p. 4. That the quotation is spurious – perhaps a half-remembered allusion to Jonson's memorial verses – rather accentuates than denies the point.
52. 52 × 61 (132 1/8 × 154 7/8), National Portrait Gallery, London.
53. *A Philosophical Enquiry into the Origin of our Ideas of the Sublime and Beautiful* (London: R. and J. Dodsley, 1757).
54. *A Descriptive Catalogue of Pictures, Poetical and Historical Inventions...* (London: D. N. Shury, 1809). Conveniently available, along with the texts of advertisements for both the exhibition and the catalogue, in *The Complete Poetry and Prose of William Blake*, ed. David V. Erdman (New York: Doubleday, 1988), pp. 526–51. The first section of the catalogue is headed 'CONDITIONS OF SALE'.
55. The figures are taken from Benedict Nicolson, *Joseph Wright of Derby: Painter of Light*. 2 vols. (London: Routledge and New Haven: Yale University Press, 1968), I, p. 17.
56. Romeo and Juliet. *The Tomb Scene. 'Noise again! Then I'll be brief'*. 177.8 × 241.3 (70 × 95), Derby Art Gallery.
57. 259 × 365.8 (102 × 144), untraced.
58. Nicolson, *Joseph Wright of Derby*, I, 245.
59. *The Death of Major Peirson and the Defeat of the French Troops in the Market Place of Saint Helier, in the Island of Jersey, Jan. 6 1781*, 1784; 238.9 × 363.2 (94 × 143), Tate Britain.
60. *The Collapse of the Earl of Chatham in the House of Lords, 7 July 1778*, 1779–80; 228.6 × 307.3 (90 × 121), Tate Britain.
61. *The Preceptor: Containing A General Course of EDUCATION. Wherein the first principles of polite learning are laid down in a way most suitable for trying the Genius, and advancing the Instruction of YOUTH* (London: R. Dodsley, 1748).
62. *Cyclopaedia; or, an universal dictionary of arts and sciences, with the supplement, and modern improvements*, 6 vols. (London: Strahan (vol. 1) and J. F. C. Rivington (vols. 2–5), 1786).
63. The process is explained and illustrated in detail in Carol Wax, *The Mezzotint: History and Technique* (London: Thames and Hudson, 1990).

64. In the 1830s this was extended to much larger runs by the technique of facing the copper with steel. This was eventually to displace both copper engraving and the technique of engraving on the end-grain of boxwood blocks popular in Victorian illustration. See Stuart Sillars, *Visualisation in Popular Fiction, 1860–1960* (London and New York: Routledge, 1995), pp. 16, 31–3.
65. The processes and their different uses are discussed in Timothy Clayton, *The English Print 1688–1802*, Paul Mellon Centre for Studies in British Art (New Haven and London: Yale University Press, 1997).
66. This topic is covered in more detail in David Alexander, 'Print Makers and Print Sellers in England, 1770–1830', in Peter Cannon-Brookes, ed. *The Painted Word: British History Painting: 1750–1830* (London: Heim, 1991), pp. 23–38. The following paragraphs rely heavily on his account.
67. *Original Pictures, Historical and Emblematical, Painted by Angelica Kauffman On Purpose for Engravings in various Manners exhibiting with the above, coloured and plain.*
68. Letter to Geo. Hollington Barker, 20 December 1795. Folger Shakespeare Library Y.c.255.3.
69. Winifred H. Friedman, *Boydell's Shakespeare Gallery*, PhD thesis, Harvard University, 1974 (London and New York: Garland, 1976), p. 222.
70. Review of Wheatley's *The Winter's Tale Act IV Sc 3* in the Boydell Gallery, *St James's Chronicle*, 16–19 May 1789.
71. *Spectator*, No. 419, 1 July 1709.
72. 'Illustrations of Shakespeare's Plays in the Seventeenth and Eighteenth Centuries', *Journal of the Warburg and Courtauld Institutes*, X (1947), 83–108.
73. *The Boydell Shakespeare Gallery*, ed. Walter Pape and Frederick Burwick, in collaboration with the German Shakespeare Society (Bottrop: Peter Pomp, 1996).
74. *Book Illustrated: Text, Image and Culture, 1770–1930*, ed. Catherine J. Golden (New Castle, Delaware: Oak Knoll Press, 2000), pp. 31–59.
75. The title essay in *The Authentic Shakespeare and Other Problems of the Early Modern Stage* (London and New York: Routledge, 2002), pp. 231–56.
76. *The Cambridge Review*, May 1996, pp. 25–48.
77. Ed. Jane Martineau et al. (London and New York: Merrell, 2003).

CHAPTER 2

PLAY, ICONOGRAPHY AND SOCIAL DISCOURSE IN HOGARTH'S SHAKESPEARE

I

When Hogarth painted Garrick as Richard III in the mid 1740s, his reputation was already firmly established. His painting of *The Beggar's Opera*,[1] first produced between 1729 and 1731, proved so popular that he was commissioned to paint five further versions, and in the engraving by Blake would remain one of his most widely distributed images. If this suggests that both his close relationship with the theatre, which included a friendship with Garrick, and his willingness to satisfy the demands of the print market are important in his Shakespeare images, it should not distract attention from other key elements of these and other works. The *Progress* engravings of the 1730s reveal Hogarth's grasp of narrative as the most innovative as well as the most secure of any painter of his generation. Rather than simply following Richardson's advice he developed a reading structure to lead the eye through a series of signs assimilated not only for their direct mimesis but also through their reference – often in a satiric manner – to classical, Renaissance and more recent iconography, often including and extending tropes such as the Choice of Hercules. This merging of innate and referential, clear and obscure, not only makes the images accessible to all kinds of readers; the combination of direct statement and reflective critical insight both defines and deepens Hogarth's visual mediations of Shakespeare's plays.

These images are revealing in a larger sense, suggesting a number of wider, and more fluid, relationships and outlooks. At the time of Hogarth's images the verbal identity of the texts, and the very idea of what constitutes a Shakespeare play, are both in flux, with stage adaptation and editing producing versions that, simply because they have gone through a social processing to make them fit for contemporary aesthetics and morality, are intricately imbricated in larger patterns of exchange. Yet although the plays have not at this time acquired anything like the independent nature or assumed authenticity that they would have in the 1770s, they are still presented under the name Shakespeare. To declare Hogarth's images non-Shakespearean because they do not record performances, or because they present a version of the text remote from any notions of accuracy, is to overlook their importance in revealing the centrality of Shakespeare activity of various kinds to a whole series of other discourses, and thus to deny them a very important role in Shakespearean assimilation. Two of his images, in different ways and to different degrees, demonstrate these qualities very clearly: two others address the texts in forms now more recognisable as kinds of visual criticism. Studying them today reveals not only many of the social and textual relations and reflections of the 1730s, but also discloses their fusion of textual commentary, contemporary satire, and a forcefully original approach to translating temporal structures into spatial ones. It also reveals how they establish iconographical reference as a major determinant for critical commentary, anticipating the compound reflexive forms of Fuseli, Reynolds and others from much later in the century.

Just as the larger body of Hogarth's work initiates a tradition of narrative social commentary in English art, his contribution to the visual criticism of Shakespeare's plays can be seen as exploring a set of techniques that both suggest a practice of visual criticism and facilitate immediate, transhistorical engagement with the texts' issues. The Shakespeare images open out varieties of critical analysis, and raise questions about interpretive practices, that will remain insistent until the end of the century. Except for the widely-reproduced *Richard III* painting, to say that they were influential upon subsequent Shakespeare painting is to overstate their importance and their circulation; but since the narrative and allusive practices they display were a part of Hogarth's art in general, they clearly share in furthering the intellectual and moral impulse in English painting, of which Shakespeare images are a major component.

That Hogarth produced so few Shakespeare images certainly shows that his major concerns lay elsewhere, but does not lessen their force. That they use many of the approaches, and indeed many of the iconographic elements, of the artist's better-known satiric paintings and prints locates them at the centre of his output, and also gives those who came after a vocabulary of supple and suggestive critical practices to emulate and extend. In the debate they enable between theatrical text and visual satire, past and present, morality and aesthetics, they establish modes of utterance and exchange that have much to suggest about the plays' intellectual and aesthetic currencies.

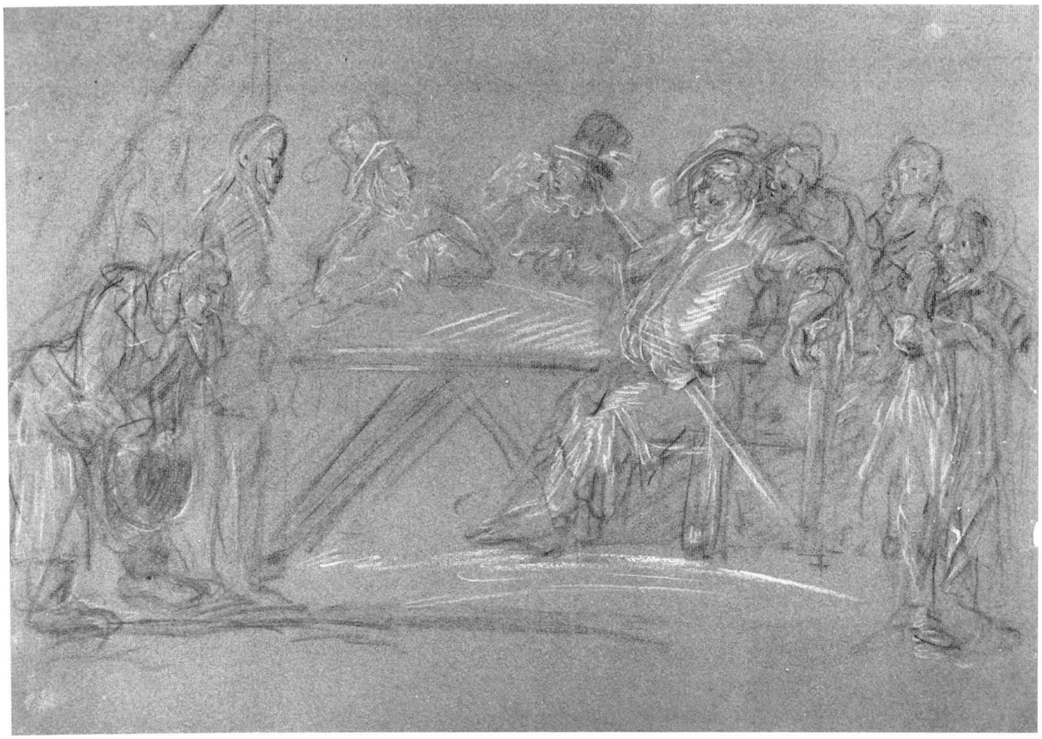

7 William Hogarth, *Falstaff Reviewing his Troops*, c. 1728.

II

The charcoal sketch known as *Falstaff reviewing his Troops* (c.1728: Fig. 7)[2] has been described as 'a swift and vivid presentation of a dramatic moment',[3] an assessment hard to contest. In origin it refers to a performance of 2 *Henry IV*, in Betterton's adaptation, in which John Harper played the role of Falstaff at Drury Lane in 1723, with a revival in 1728, and may well offer something of a theatrical record. The vestigial background, lacking the heavily naturalistic setting of later, more historicised images, argues for this, and within the loose drawing the characters are incisively individual; but the depiction relies on painterly, not theatrical, techniques to make its impact. Falstaff himself is fully realised. His posture, emphasised by the parallel diagonals of the table legs, the beam in the top left and the poses of figures before him and to the left, combines relaxation with the self-conscious authority that he attempts to exert over his companions in the Eastcheap scenes, and this is echoed in the formality of sword, boots and hat. Yet the very sketchiness of the image has implications that take it beyond the theatre, which become clearer in comparison with the oil painting developed from it, with the same title, in 1730.[4] There, tension dissolves into comic exaggeration and the explicit detail of the setting dilutes the concentration of gesture and mood so that, unusually for Hogarth, it becomes simply another painting that relocates familiar stage personages within a naturalistic setting, a practice common in the 1740s and 50s. A version of the same moment produced nearly seventy years later reveals a similar approach. James Durno's painting of the scene for the Boydell Gallery[5] comes from a tradition in which Falstaff's girth is metonymic of a character now become merely comic, in a reading of the scene underlined by the ironic use of a classical frieze for the recruits and Bardolph's hand extended to receive a bribe.

What is lacking here but abundantly present in Hogarth's sketch is a sense of energy: this earlier Falstaff is corpulent but not absurdly obese, and the taut compositional line that extends across the table to the figure bowing before him suggests a distance of power that reveals the catechising as something that, while comic to the audience, is tense with anxiety for those at whom it is directed. This is enhanced by the individuation of the characters: the cipher in profile is presumably Shadow, so that the man bowing under Falstaff's interrogatory gaze is identifiable as Wart, a reading supported by his elaborate, though ill-fitting, clothes. Both are depicted with an economy that suggests astringency, rather than caricature, and this limitation of the comic, a spicing of the absurd with the fearful, shows an insight into the play's interactions that goes against the later habit of stressing laughter above all else. It serves, also, as a reminder that both Shakespeare's audience and Hogarth's viewers included displaced soldiers for whom the comic overtones of such a recruitment would have been securely muffled by their own subsequent experience. Falstaff's mingled antecedents in the *miles gloriosus* and the morality Vice produce, as David Bevington puts it, 'an inextricable mixture of farce and high moral seriousness';[6] the character of the old soldier has about it elements of Hašek's *Good Soldier Švejk*, and this quality of the survivor depends upon the ability to capitalise on a situation and exploit it for his own benefit. It is this mingled quality that is captured in Hogarth's sketch. Dating from nearly fifty years before Maurice Morgann's study of Falstaff as a dramatic character,[7] which looks beneath the assumption that Falstaff is merely a coward, it forms a valuable corrective to a single, comic reading.

Important in the drawing's taut network of relationships are its medium and execution, and the equation they generate between the two kinds of performance that together they enact: that of the image, and that of the play-text. In essence a series of bravura strokes, the drawing's energy is forceful and abrupt, stressing process rather than product. In this it suggests a parallel with the process on stage – another skilful, bravura improvisation by Falstaff, as he interrogates the recruits with insults and puns at their expense. Hogarth's sketch, in short, presents another sketch: the medium discloses Falstaff as an actor in an improvised, darkly comic performance. Rather than merely recording something that happens in the theatre, the drawing offers the onlooker a way of reading the scene and its characters as performance of quite another kind, presenting a visual embodiment of one of Falstaff's brilliant inventions. Perhaps most fully developed in his extemporisation on the battlefield – 'Honour is a mere scutcheon' (*I Henry IV* 5.1.140–1) – these are at their most subversive in his silence in playing dead – ''Sblood, 'twas time to counterfeit' (*1 Henry IV* 5.4.112) – and climax with the self-preserving brutality of stabbing the dead Hotspur. A later chapter will explore the balance of theatrical and visual imagination in one of these scenes as developed in the wash-drawings of George Romney, but Hogarth's much earlier sketch reveals a very specific astuteness simply in its choice of medium. In appearing to show a fragment of action, the sketch penetrates beneath comic character-drawing to release the play's darker energies and operations. In so doing it reveals one major function of critical interpretation through visual criticism, stressing another kind of performance through a parallel between orders of performance that forces us to address the nature of play and playing, sketch and sketching, in both media.

Hogarth's treatment of Falstaff is Hogarth's most direct address to the plays, effecting through its selection of moment both a record and a metaphor of performance: but it may also contain an implicit political statement. Frederick Antal (*Hogarth*, p. 61) points out that it is drawn on paper from the same pad as a preparatory drawing for the *Beggar's Opera* painting, and Elizabeth Einberg (*Shakespeare in Art*, p. 52) sees this as evidence of its sharing with that work a concern with bribery and the perversion of justice, adding a political thrust that is most likely directed at Robert Walpole. Such a thrust is made much more openly in the engraving *Henry VIII and Anne Boleyn* (1728–9: Fig. 8),[8] an image that raises a different series of issues about Shakespeare visualisation by enfolding a celebrated production of the play within the discourse of national politics and history. At this time, Shakespeare's plays are defined very largely through their fitness for performance, a criterion resting on canons of contemporary taste and stage practicality. Pope's edition of 1725 had moved material thought corrupt or inauthentic to the foot of the pages, and acting versions cut or replaced matter likely to offend, or sometimes wholly recast character and action to accord with the current temper. Over the next two decades the practice would be displaced by the attempt to recover an authentic text; but in the 1720s the idea of a Shakespeare play is still fluid, without losing the notional identity conferred through

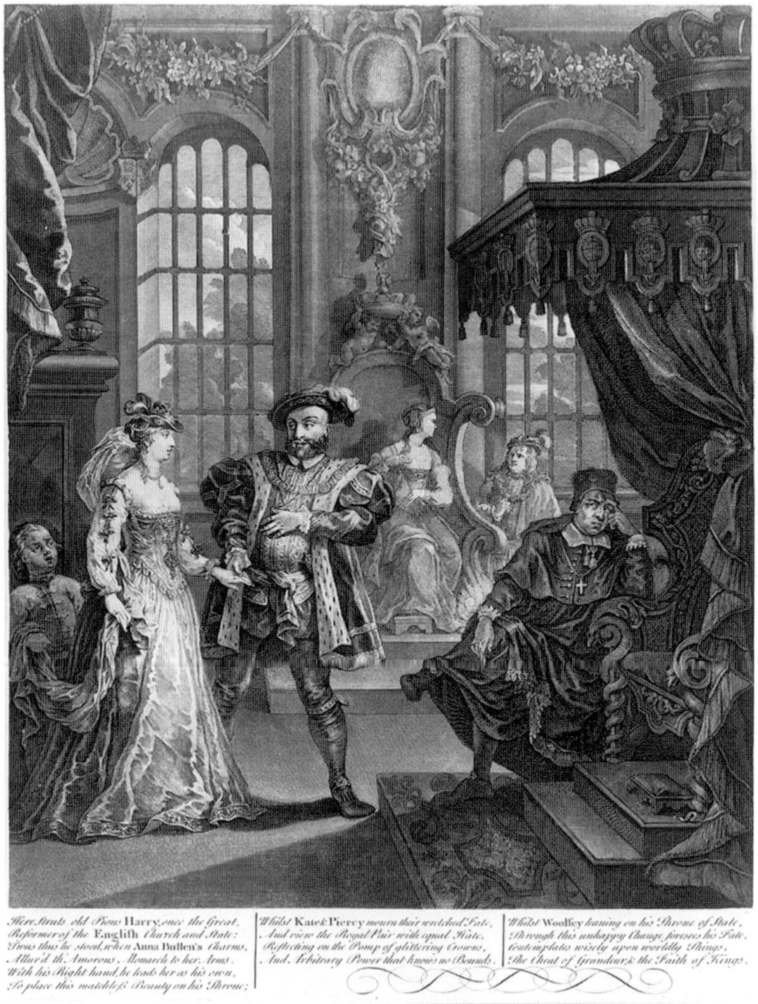

8 William Hogarth, *Henry VIII and Anne Boleyn*, 1728–9.

its authorship. Hogarth's *Henry VIII* is important because of the light it throws on this practice, and on the place of Shakespeare visualisation within it, negotiating as it does between text, performance and a series of larger discourses to reflect one very particular contemporary ideology. It demonstrates the cultural assimilation of a Shakespeare play just as insistently as many images from the century's close, but in a markedly different way. This is reason enough for giving it serious consideration, but two other aspects, one technical and one conceptual, make it even more significant: its use of iconographical reference to convey a critical and moral purpose, and its approach to the larger identities of history and historiography.

The image has no immediate reference to Shakespeare's *Henry VIII*, and nor do the verses beneath it, attributed to Allan Ramsay, yet the date of its production makes clear that the play is fundamental to the political debate to which it contributes. On 11 June 1727 George II was crowned in Westminster Abbey; on 26 October, Colley Cibber mounted a revival of *Henry VIII* that became the success of the season. Its popularity was due largely to an interpolated pageant in which the Queen's Champion issues a challenge to all comers in Westminster Hall. Although advertised as including 'The Military ceremony in Westminster Hall, with proper Decorations never seen before', the play was nevertheless billed as 'Written by Shakespear',[9] revealing well the prevailing attitude towards the plays that simultaneously claimed them for the national dramatist and facilitated their adjustment to contemporary popular tastes. The scene became so popular that it was performed as an afterpiece on seventy-five occasions[10] and became the subject of a burlesque afterpiece *Harlequin Anna Bullen* at Lincoln's Inn Fields.[11] The production of a Shakespeare play has thus become a way of both celebrating and ridiculing contemporary royalist fervour, establishing the centrality of the text and its adaptation within the construction and satiric debate of contemporary history. Hogarth's engraving builds upon this to voice a political statement so that, while it records neither text nor performance, the image rests irrefutably on a Shakespearean frame.

The basis of the engraving's satiric thrust is the depiction, in the role of Cardinal Wolsey, of the Prime Minister, Sir Robert Walpole, then an intensely distrusted figure. His Whig libertarianism, his personal arrogance and the widespread rumours of his abuse of power, bolstered by his imprisonment in the Tower in 1712 on charges of peculation – never proved – ensured that, to many observers, he was both the pinnacle of corruption and a threat to the new king. The parallels with Wolsey, eager to assume King Henry's authority, are thus immediately presented in Hogarth's engraving. Two lines in particular from the supporting text verbalise the image's presentation of the cardinal:

Whilst Woolsey *leaning on his Throne of State*
Through this unhappy Change foresees his Fate.

As Wolsey was removed by Henry VIII, so, the image implies, should Walpole be discharged by George II. This use of immediate and insistent reference to contemporary affairs within a Shakespeare image may not be the first of its kind, but it is certainly one of the most direct: and, despite the apparently restricted code of its style, with its formal elegance, Hogarth's engraving uses historical allusion as a medium of contemporary satire that operates at all levels of aesthetic

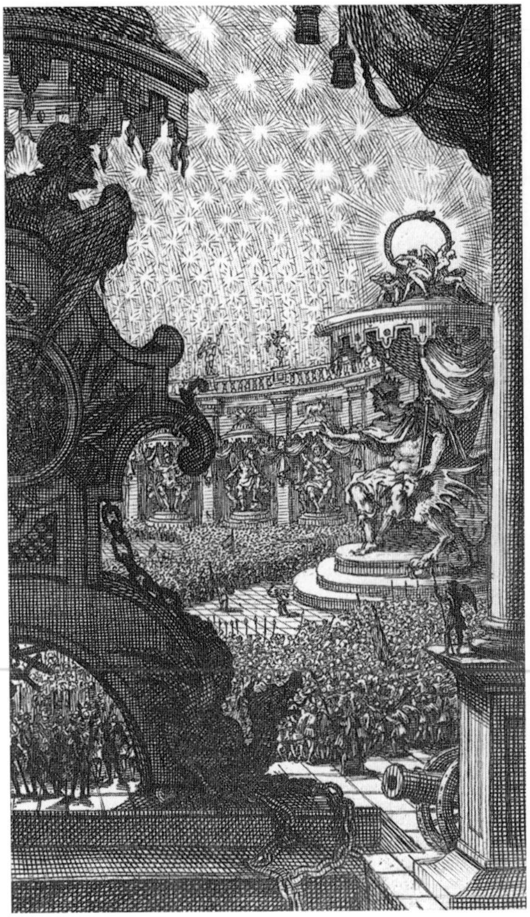

9 William Hogarth, Illustration to *Paradise Lost*, Book II, 1725?

production, and needs to be seen alongside both the musical allusiveness in *The Beggar's Opera* (see Chapter 1) and the many broadsheet caricatures in which Walpole features. Shakespeare's play is involved within a contemporary satiric spiral, but the very insistence of this reveals its theme as timeless: corruption in Wolsey, equated with corruption in Walpole, reveals the innate and recurrent presence of political self-serving.

The satiric thrust is enhanced in the image by iconographic reference – indeed, it is probably the earliest Shakespeare image to employ the device to make a critical or interpretive point. The throne of state beneath which Wolsey sits is a frequent element in Hogarth's satiric images, as a later section of this chapter will further explore: the most pertinent earlier use occurs in the artist's illustration to *Paradise Lost* II, 1–6, (1725?: Fig. 9) depicting Satan addressing the rebel angels in

Pandaemonium.[12] For those who had seen that image, the allusion had a simple meaning; Walpole's presiding over parliament is an exact parallel to Satan's hold over the rebel angels, and both are figured metaphorically in Wolsey's doomed over-reaching. The reference thus exerts critical pressure both on Wolsey, familiar to the engraving's readers through the recent production of Shakespeare's play, and on Walpole, the immediate perceived threat.

This dialogue between present and past, theatrical chronicle and political actuality, is continued in other ways. The baroque elegance of the setting locates the events not so much within a specific past as within a contemporary idea of that past: the setting suggests more Caroline indulgence than Henrician reform. The inclusion in the background of Northumberland (Lord Percy, the former lover of Anne Boleyn) with the rejected Queen Catherine places them both within a more local temporal scheme, reminiscent of displaced former lovers elsewhere in Hogarth, commenting on the human cost of the abandonment of Henry's wife and perhaps hinting metaphorically at the transitory nature of political allegiances. The propriety of the setting, reinforced by the cultural respectability of the reference to Shakespeare, constitutes an ideal medium for sophisticated satire, the popularity of the recent production ensuring that the allusions are readily understood. In using this cluster of reference, Hogarth initiates another impulse of critical reading in eighteenth-century Shakespeare painting: the voicing of recurrent patterns of corruption by showing them in their strictly contemporary iteration. This sharpening of the original onlooker's perception of the plays also makes audible to later viewers the dialogue between past and present in earlier Shakespeare production; in echoing the use of contemporary references in *Henry VIII* and the history plays in general, the image reveals a conceptual circularity between stage and studio that facilitates an intellectual engagement in visual form that will support textual criticisms and appropriations of many kinds in the decades to come.

This confirms the engraving's place in the development of Shakespeare imaging: for the first time, an historical play has been used as the basis of a directly contemporary political satire, introducing a dialogue between past and present to contribute to the debate on the latter, rather than to present a supposedly accurate history. The anachronistic adaptation of Shakespeare's play is in one sense responsible for this, but the result is wholly positive: instead of the narrowing mathesis of the much-vaunted historical authenticity pursued by later painters, Hogarth freely adapts the play, as did Cibber, to engage with contemporary preoccupations. The direct result is that Shakespeare's play moves to the centre of national debate: in the process a narrow, mimetic historicism has been rejected and a critical interpretation made by iconographic allusion.

III

One way of looking at Shakespeare iconography in the eighteenth century is as an opposition between those images that use reference as a critical medium to universalise, locating the plays within the Neo-Classical tradition of Platonic forms, and those that use it to draw local or individual readings of character and incident, revealing specific insight or critical commentary. This polarity is suggested in Hogarth's paintings of *The Tempest* and *Richard III*. One visualises the tensions the play generates within a composition based on no single scene: the other explores a significant moment redolent of all that has been and pregnant with all to follow. In the complex presentation of the plays' temporality the images employ iconographic reference in different modes, one substantive, the other ironic, one suggesting wholly new readings, the other exposing discrepancies against an earlier ideal.

At some time in the early 1740s Hogarth painted David Garrick in the first of his most celebrated roles.[13] The painting's title, *Mr Garrick in the Character of Richard III*, asserts its content and context as the presentation of an actor playing a role, and from this it is reasonable to suppose that, as it shows a scene from the play instead of an isolated figure, it represents stage action. There is much to support this and, given the degree of Garrick's fame, the same is true of Shearer West's assertion, made of theatrical portraits from the 1780s, that many who bought the original print cared little for 'the exact meaning of the image', wishing only 'to find a successful likeness' of the actor as hero.[14] Yet the painting offers far more than this. Its mediation of narrative and idea reveal it as a sophisticated intellectual and moral consideration of the play, achieving this status through a technique of embedding iconographic reference within a fabric of temporal re-ordering that offers a wholly visual translation of the play's unfolding. Its status as one of the most frequently reproduced images of any of the plays further testifies to its power: the version reproduced in Fig. 10[15] accords it central significance within a series of visual elements that incorporates Tudor roses, Richard's emblem of the Boar and simplified versions of James Northcote's Boydell paintings of the play (see Chapter 9).

Hogarth's image presents the moment of Richard's awakening in Act 5 of Cibber's text, the adaptation used by Garrick. In many of the engraved versions, the

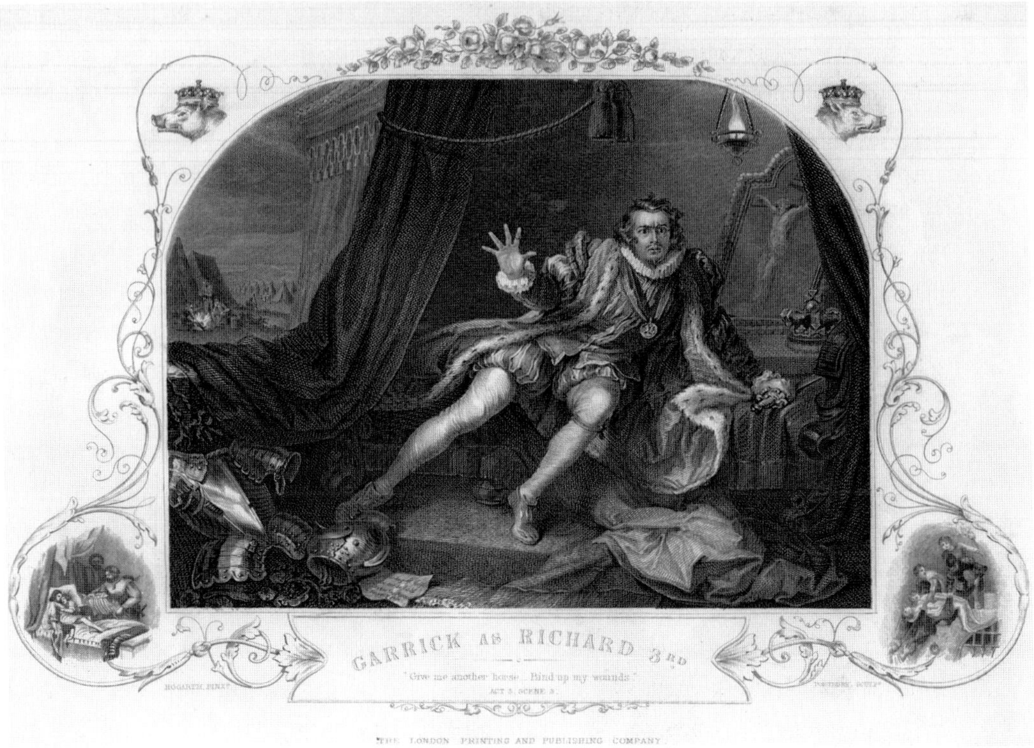

10 William Hogarth, *Mr Garrick in the Character of Richard III*. Tallis Shakespeare, *c*. 1850.

line 'Give me another horse, bind up my wounds' appears as caption.[16] This fixes the moment very precisely: it comes immediately after Cibber's stage direction 'Richard starts out of his sleep', and shows him still confusing his dream with the reality of the night before battle. The posture shows very precisely Richard's disorientation on awaking and thinking he is on the battlefield. The staring eyes and deep frown recall the expression worn by Garrick in Zoffany's portrait of him as Macbeth,[17] and are clearly related to the facial archetype of horror mentioned in Le Brun's *Conférence*.[18] Le Brun's advice about gesture seems also to be a source, speaking as it does of 'the Hands quite open, and the Fingers separated wide from each other'; but the difference is made clear as the passage continues to prescribe 'the Arms close pressed to the Body; and the Legs in the Action of Flight' (p. 48). The raised right hand, palm open towards the audience, is an expansive gesture of exactly the kind for which Garrick was famed, perhaps based on Le Brun. Hogarth was well acquainted with Le Brun's physiognomic studies, but used them rather as starting points than final statements: in the *Analysis of*

Beauty he refers to the *Conférence* as 'for the use of learners', and something offering 'but imperfect copies' (p. 97) of the emotions. The expression and posture are those of Garrick himself, but within a self-defining and continuous dramatic actuality, not as an isolated declamatory presence, a moment within an intense psychological continuum, not an acting 'point' or an element in a rhetorical trope. It seems that both actor and artist agree in using Le Brun's postures, if at all, only as a basis on which to build a complete expression. Partly as a result of this, Hogarth's image is direct and spontaneous: it involves the whole body to show the king struggling to evade his dream as he awakes. This does more than evidence the circulation of imagery between stage and easel: it reveals a difference between those depictions that simply follow Le Brun's codes and those presenting scenes within a longer continuum that may or may not make reference to theatrical practice. The difference recurs throughout the century, and often becomes a principal determinant of an image's critical weight.

Dialogue between theatrical and painterly continues in the costume and attributes of the figure of Richard, to merge with Hogarth's habitual iconographic detail and, in one precise element, to establish a tradition in the presentation of Richard. The costume is that developed for the character by Garrick himself, supplementing the ermine-lined cape, Elizabethan tunic and trunk hose with the star of the order of the garter and the garter itself bearing the royal motto 'Honi soit qui mal y pense'. While the order was instituted by Edward III about 1344, and the garter worn by its members from that date, the star was added by Charles I, so that its presence on stage and in the canvas is anachronistic to both the period in which the play was written and that in which it is set. Despite this, the addition is theatrically powerful: it is a strikingly visible emblem of Richard's status, and it also reveals Garrick's awareness of the telling power of the detail of costume, constantly reminding the audience of the disparity between the nobility of the order and the ignominy of its wearer. Characterisation by attribute is familiar from other paintings by Hogarth, which adopt the technique from earlier European imagery and turn it to satiric use, so that once again the methods of studio and stage overlap, and the exchange between past and present continues.

One aspect of the costume has been developed in a peculiarly painterly way by Hogarth. The garter is worn on Richard's leg so that only one word is legible: 'mal'. While it is feasible that this was the case in performance, logic would suggest otherwise: only those at the very front of the stalls would have been able to read the inscription and, even for them, and even considering the static nature of Garrick's acting style, more than one word of the inscription would have been visible as the actor subsequently moved around the stage. Appropriated from the theatre, the detail becomes a visual speech-act stating Richard's character that is taken up in numerous subsequent images including Nathaniel Dance's painting of Garrick (1771),[19] William Hamilton's *John Philip Kemble as Richard III* (1787),[20] ceramic figures of Garrick from later in the century,[21] and even a book of cut-out dolls of famous Shakespearean characters (1811).[22]

A more direct tradition of characterisation by attribute, activated by Shaftesbury and Richardson but learned ultimately from medieval and Renaissance painting, is also used in the image. The framed painting of the crucifixion, and the crown and sword beneath it, together constitute a meditation on the divinity of kingship, the right to reign coming directly from Christ, and the power of the sword issuing from the crown, as revealed, for example, in the 'Ermine' portrait of Elizabeth I.[23] Their presence here serves to undermine Richard by the contrast they reveal. Richard has no divine right: his crown has been achieved by the abuse of the sword which should properly be wielded only to preserve the state. The irony is enhanced by the recent presence in the play of the ghosts of Richard's victims, even in Cibber's much shorter text that includes only the ghosts of Henry VI, the young princes and Queen Anne. Sword and crown are present throughout the play, assuming symbolic and associative functions as its action changes: placed in the static space of the painting, their force is magnified, inviting reflection upon the general situation of Richard as false monarch. To this is added the significance of the picture of the crucifixion, on which Richard has literally as well as morally turned his back in rejection of Christian values. Hogarth here uses a picture-within-a-picture in a form of commentary found frequently elsewhere in his work.

Cibber's Act V dispenses with Richmond's tent and the ghosts appearing to him, the loss of the ritual antiphony this causes presumably being less important than the greater practicality on the Restoration stage and the concentration it thrusts on to the evil Richard. The tent in which he sits is a classical structure complete with elaborate hanging tassel, and is rich in referential meaning that undermines deeply Richard's character. In its design and detail, and in its location to the right of a composition that also includes a hint of a battlefield and some small figures at the left, it is clearly based on Le Brun's *The Family of Darius before Alexander* (1660–1: Fig. 11).[24] In *The Analysis of Beauty*, Hogarth refers to 'one of Alexander's battles painted by Le Brun' (p. 7) which could refer to any of the series the painter produced for Louis XIV; but it is more likely that Hogarth knew this painting, since it was widely reproduced in England. The most likely source is an engraving by Simon Gribelin, published and sold in London in 1693 (Fig. 11),[25] which has a dual text in French and Latin with the title 'Il est d'un Roy

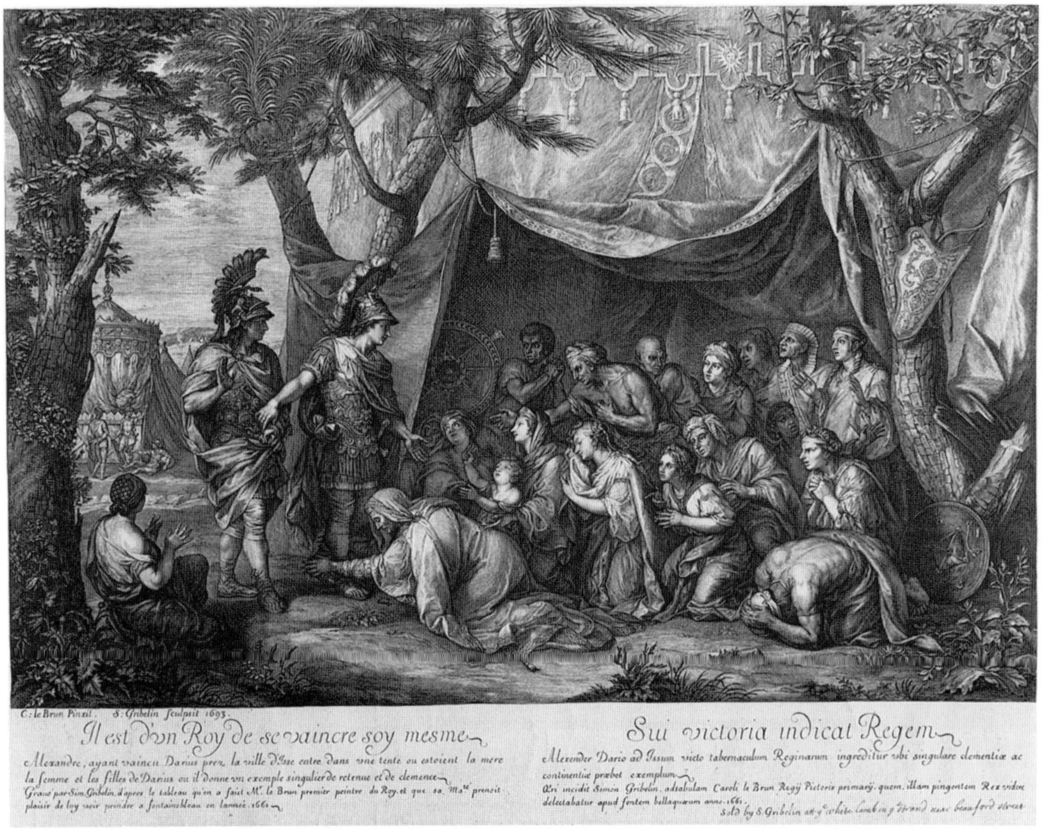

11 Charles Le Brun, *The Family of Darius before Alexander*. Engraved by Simon Gribelin, 1693.

de se vaincre soy mesme' and 'Sui Victoria indicat Regem'. The motto adds further critical force to Hogarth's image suggesting a characteristic exactly opposite to Richard's behaviour.

The tent motif is a frequent device in Hogarth, as is apparent from the earlier discussion of his treatment of Satan and Cardinal Wolsey: later, Hayman and Reynolds would use it for similarly satiric purposes. Here its force is considerable, both in itself and in revealing the nature and depth of the iconographic imagination that Hogarth brings to Shakespeare. Its main effect is to place the image within the tradition of European historical painting. In so doing it suggests a link between Shakespeare and the stress on the validity of English painting in comparison with Old Master designs that typifies the desire to see English art as their equal in intellectual achievement and aesthetic commodity, since it shows the use of a style elevated to match the richness of Shakespeare's language, anticipating a similar approach in some later paintings.[26] But the main function of the reference is to stress the darkness implicit in Richard's character by implicitly contrasting it with Alexander's magnanimity. Le Brun shows the family of Darius addressing Alexander with gestures of gratitude and supplication, depicting the moment when the classical hero arranged for them to have safe harbour while he continued his pursuit of Darius himself, a key moment within the hagiographic life of Alexander presented by, among others, Plutarch, whose text Hogarth might well have known in Dryden's translation. It embodies the twin virtues of the soldier: ruthless pursuit of the enemy and compassion for the defeated innocent. The allusion to such moral strength – coupled, of course, with the mere reference to Alexander in a painting of Shakespeare's Richard – reveals the gulf between Richard and the ideal classical hero.

The tent draws further accretions of meaning from its use elsewhere in Hogarth's work. As well as in the *Paradise Lost* illustration discussed above, it features in the first *Marriage à-la-mode* image as the canopy beneath which Lord Squanderfield sits as he receives the mortgage for his property in return for the marriage of his son. The resonances are clear: Richard is both a Satanic usurper and an aristocrat who has laid waste his birthright, in addition to the moral opposite of the noble Alexander. Another aspect of Le Brun's painting is a concern with mistaken identity, in which Darius' elaborately dressed subordinate is mistaken for him by the imploring figures. Richard, too, is misplaced, playing a role for which he is morally ill-fitted, and this suggests another layer of performance: while not portraying a theatrical event, the painting both shows Garrick performing as Shakespeare's character and constitutes a level of social performance in the act of sitting for a portrait.

The static commentary provided by this iconographic allusion is balanced by the painting's enactment of the play's dynamic currency through careful elision of elements temporally separate in the action. This it does in a number of ways. The soldiers standing before a brazier in the right middle ground visualise Cibber's interpolation of lines from *Henry V* (4.0.6–7,12,14) where the Chorus describes the stillness of the two armies encamped before battle recalling events from before Richard's awakening from his dream. A combination of sequential abridgement with moral comment is evident in the scrap of paper at the left of the canvas, which reads:

Jockey of Norfolk
be not so bold
For Dickon thy master
is bought and sold

The lines, read by Richard from a paper found by Norfolk in his tent a little later in the same scene, prophesy Richard's fall, and foreshadow the equestrian imagery of Richard's final cry 'My kingdom for a horse!' (5.4.13).

Hogarth's achievement in this image goes beyond the delineation of an actor in his most famous role, and beyond the searching analysis of the character of Richard that it offers. It reveals the emotional and moral intensity of the action, not only of the individual moment of supernatural horror but through its consequences for Richard himself and for the soldiers in the battle to come, and also explores the responsibilities of kingship through its inclusion of elements that visualise the Tudor emblematology of divine rule. These comments show its stature as a critical interpretation of the play: but the exchange that it presents between the diachronic unfolding and the intensity of the moment reveals its larger awareness of the relation between visual and theatrical forms. The selection of Richard's moment of waking does more than stress a turning point of great power in the action: this is the one point in the play where time is suspended, since just for an instant Richard thinks he is in one place but in reality is in another. Playfully, the image paradoxically exchanges the temporal natures of theatre and painting: the play's only moment of inactivity is selected for visual treatment, and the apparently static nature of an easel painting is used to foretell the future, so that the usual functions of drama and painting as respectively dynamic and static are reversed. The self-reflexive examination of theatre and image seen in the Falstaff sketch is repeated: here, enclosing as it does the iconographic and other meanings in which the painting abounds, the reversal gives the image an unusual concentration.

A Scene from Shakespeare's 'The Tempest' (Fig. 12)[27] was painted at some time between 1736 and 1738. Despite its title, the image does not represent a single moment of the action: although many have suggested that it presents Act 1 scene 2, this cannot be the case since it shows both Ferdinand and Caliban, whereas the two are not on stage together. Instead of offering a frozen moment of theatrical time in the manner of the *2 Henry IV* sketch, the painting's composition reveals in a single, instantaneous statement the forces that drive the play. Lacking the left-to-right reading structure of the *Progress* engravings, in which the eye is led across the image to uncoil the narrative from a sequence of details, the painting must be seen as a visual equation to which each element contributes simultaneously at both a conceptual and sensory level. The result constitutes a reading of the play that discloses within it an alternative structure of belief and ideology, offering a visual and theological parallel to the other world structured within the island and its inhabitants.

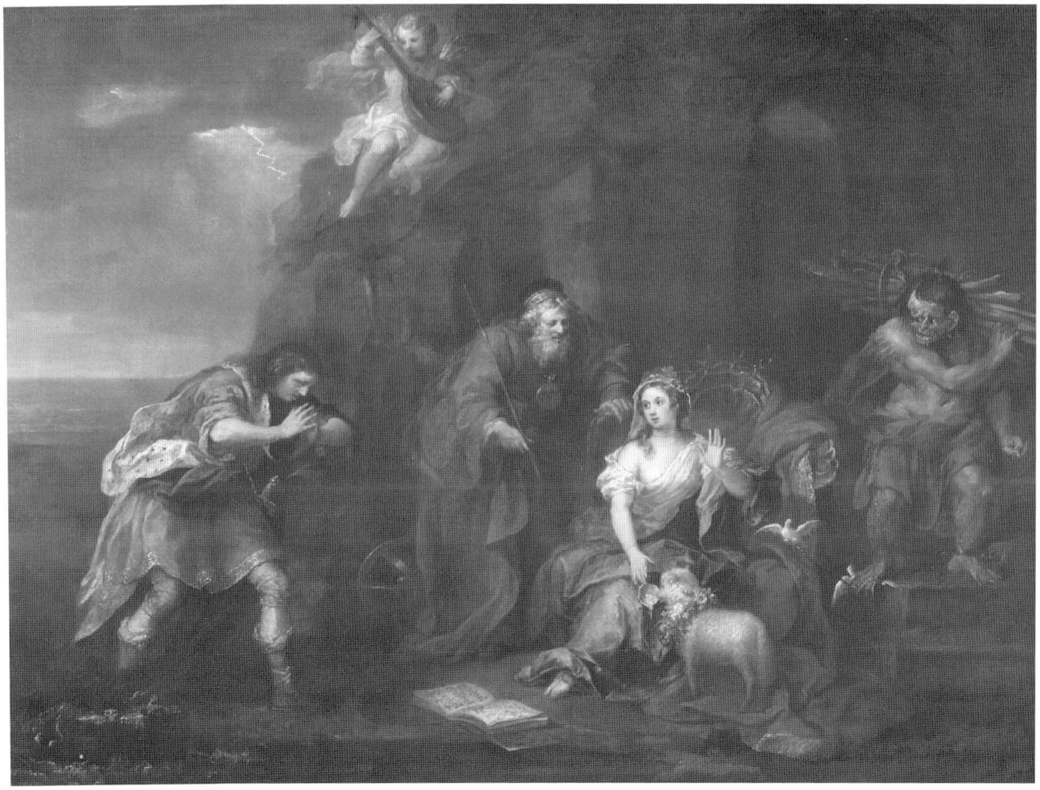

12 William Hogarth, *A Scene from Shakespeare's 'The Tempest'*, 1736–8.

The key to this is the reinvention of Renaissance and Baroque Biblical painting in a manner that, rather than ironising through iconographic reference, makes its points by the complete displacement of earlier, sacred meanings by the play's new order. The similarity between Miranda and the Virgin Mary in a Renaissance nativity is instantly apparent; the displacement of the infant Christ by the lamb suggests the native innocence and purity of the island by appropriating a much older Christian symbol for a use both literal and metonymic. The Marian blue of Miranda and the red drapery of her throne both reinforce this, and the figure of Caliban, bearing logs and not myrrh, becomes a parody Magus, a thought that inevitably destabilises the role of Prospero, who instead stands in the posture traditionally associated with Joseph. The presence of Ariel as a lute-playing *putto* above recalls the angel-musician, symbolising celestial harmony, from early Netherlandish nativities and Italian frescoes.

The parody nativity might be completed by the presence of Ferdinand as another Magus, yet his posture is that of the Archangel Gabriel in an annunciation – a link that, once established, reveals a meaning in Miranda's uplifted hand that differs from the shock at beholding the wondrous being that is understood from the play. The allusion is completed by the presence of the open book, often used in annunciations to represent the fulfilment of Old Testament prophecy, and the two birds which, as well as being naturalistic, refer to the dove of the Holy Spirit. Still another Renaissance genre is represented by the coronet that Miranda wears, suggesting a coronation of the virgin. In this trope, Prospero becomes one of the Old Testament prophets officiating in the crowning.

These levels of allusion are offset by naturalistic elements that reflect the characters as they appear in the play. Prospero's wand and the astrolabe at his feet suggest his magic; his brown robe suggests this is natural or earth magic, confirmed by the animals' bones and body parts that writhe in the container at the left foreground. Ferdinand's robes are contrastingly baroque, recalling the civilisation of Naples he has recently left. The sea to the left and the rocks to the rear suggest the difference of the play's two worlds. Caliban bears logs, and treads on the doves, suggesting an animal crushing of the idea of human love: yet curiously he stands on steps that are geometrically perfect, and the arch behind him is similarly formal, embellished with an ambiguous bird that, in combining elements of a bat and an eagle, balances the natural world of the island and the imperial orders that it displaces.

Despite their lack of circumstantial synchronicity, these fragments of Catholic iconography work together, hovering around each other to convey the central conceit of the image. What is being suggested through an assemblage of elements is that the world of the island offers a parallel and an alternative to the western Christian ideal, whose images it does not parody but appropriates and redefines, just as it does the forms of Renaissance architecture. In place of a crowned virgin is Miranda, the thing of wonder; in place of wise men, a 'poisonous slave got by the devil himself' (1.2.321); in place of the infant Christ, an actual rather than a symbolic lamb; in place of Old Testament prophecy, the magical book of Prospero. That all these forces are held in balance against each other, their hierarchy destabilised by the absence of sequence, gives the painting another dimension of freedom: lacking narrative, it also lacks explicit parody and instead postulates direct equivalence between the two worlds. It is this that gives the painting its originality and force. Within it may also be contained a more direct political comment. In rejecting religious iconography the painting is also rejecting Catholicism, and the image thus becomes one of many in which Hogarth privileges English empiricism over European dogma. Although Ferdinand advances making an elegant baroque *congé*, Miranda's upraised hand may be read as a gesture of rejection of this richly robed foreigner, while the figure behind her, Caliban, is a part of the island in a manner that Ferdinand is not because of the likeness of colour and texture that he bears to the rocks behind him. That Caliban treads on the doves reveals his innate absence of human amorousness, and perhaps also hints at rejection of Catholic ritual: it is a rejection paralleled in a later and better-known image of Hogarth's, the use of the dove as an inn sign just above the procession bearing the sacraments in the background of *O the Roast Beef of Old England* (1748).[28] The suggestion that Prospero's island is Protestant England is insidious, but hard to ignore.

While the image has no single narrative location within the play's sequence, it does perhaps have one that is generated by this system of antitheses, that is as much an emblematic opposition as a situation: the first encounter between the two worlds that is the foundation of Prospero's plotting. The painting embodies the order of reversal apparent within Miranda's 'O brave new world, / That has such people in't!' (5.1.183–4): that which comes to the island may well be brave, but this splendour is also threatening. Hogarth's painting makes this clear through the unity of colour and form in the island, and the offsetting of alien sophistication of dress and gesture against the subtlety of its natural magic and architectural precision. What results is a critical study of a play not performed in Shakespeare's text during Hogarth's lifetime that draws together political and social commentary within an appropriation of religious elements and symbols that now float free of their conventional meanings. As social and political criticism it is remarkable, offering what seems a complete equality between the two worlds of the play in which Caliban is by no means the weaker rival to Ferdinand, and in which the discussion of Gonzalo's idea of a Utopia (2.1.144–65) is perhaps also implicit.

Two details of the composition complete the rejection of emblematic language, both Catholic and classical, which unite to reject the whole tradition of western civilisation against which the island is posited. The crushing of the doves under Caliban's webbed foot refers to more than his rejection of human love, spiritual in the emblems of annunciation painting and physical in the attribute of Venus. Caliban's attempted rape of Miranda is not immoral but amoral, driven by the need to people the isle with Calibans (1.2.350–1): consequently, he treads on the dove not as an act of conscious brutality but because he is driven by quite different imperatives. Similarly, the milk spilling from the cup that Miranda holds out to the lamb is both a rejection of the sacrament and an index of the disturbance wrought on the island by Ferdinand's intrusion, which brings with it the ponderous threat of Catholic symbolism. Symbol and actuality in both these elements combine to place the main moral valency of the play with the island, not the visitor. These insights make it a truly outstanding image, unique in its total displacement of iconography and narrative while forceful and provocative in its reading of the play. Despite this uniqueness, the painting has in common with a tradition of later paintings a stance in which time is collapsed and iconography revivified by context. The resultant breadth is one of the major sanctions used in the visual treatment of the plays over the next eighty years, though rarely with such force. The complete absence of reference to stage action or precedent is again significant: Hogarth the theatre-goer and friend of Garrick moves away from theatrical mimesis to present instead a philosophical meditation in which events and drives are wound into a single magnetic field acting to unsettle assumptions about Shakespeare's text.

IV

Within the tough, reasoned satire evident in all his work, Hogarth's Shakespeare images convey multiple, acutely individual insights into the plays. Iconographic reference, the telescoping of dramatic sequence and the dialogue between past and present are key devices; but their conceptual essence is a grasp of the multiple dialectics between text, stage and easel that formed one constituent of the fluid state of contemporary Shakespeare activity. In the treatments of *1 Henry IV*, *The Tempest* and *Richard III* this is enriched by a supple play between the different modes of utterance of drama and visual image, and the varieties of social relationships involved in the varieties of portraiture and the processes they enact.

Two further points remain. Hogarth's images depend on an awareness of the plays of Shakespeare that derives from the theatre not because they mimic scenes from the stage but in their reference to the texts as used by the major theatrical figures of the day, notably Betterton, Settle, Cibber and Garrick. Yet this awareness is balanced by a knowledge of published editions aiming at the elusive target of restoring Shakespeare's own text. The most direct instance of this is the painting of *The Tempest*, which rejects Dryden and Davenant in favour of the text in the First Folio followed by Rowe – a decision facilitated by the relatively straightforward nature of the text. It is also apparent in the *Richard II* image, where the 'Jockey of Norfolk' passage differs from that used by Cibber, preferring the 'so bold' of both Folio and all the Quartos. Similarly, the line from the stage direction used as a title in some versions of the print uses 'another horse', again the reading of Quartos and Folio, instead of Cibber's 'a horse'.[29]

Small details, admittedly; but they may be revealing. There is no record of which text of Shakespeare Hogarth possessed, if any; but it may be suggestive that in the *Self-portrait with a Pug*[30] there is a single folio volume titled *Shakespeare*, and that in the *Masquerades and Operas* (1724),[31] the first print that Hogarth published independently, a woman is carting away, in a wheelbarrow, two volumes headed 'Shakespere'. Both the images show volumes that physically resemble the Folio rather than any more recent edition, certainly not Rowe's small octavos. The slight textual disparities prefigure an important shift in which painters moved to the use of the more trustworthy editions of Theobald, Johnson and Steevens instead of the adapted and abbreviated texts used for performance, to produce readings that rest on a more secure footing when seen from anything approaching modern critical stances.

The second circumstance has to do with the images' destinations rather than their textual origins. In existing in both painted and engraved forms, two of Hogarth's Shakespeare visualisations respond to the social and commercial imperatives that come increasingly to dominate Shakespeare painting in the later years of the century. The need to address issues of text and visual convention in a way that could be understood by the variety of audiences that together constituted the print-buying public was a generative tension that instigated and determined many of the most important paintings and engravings of the period. In his Shakespeare images as in his other work, Hogarth successfully combined literary and moral insights in a manner accessible to a range of readerships. The works discussed here demonstrate the full complexity of the techniques, and treat many of the themes, that increasingly become evident in the most sophisticated Shakespeare paintings. That they do so within a complex of relationships to do with adaptation, readership and social consumption, to explore issues of contemporary political and religious debate, reveals that the immanence of Shakespeare activity within these frames is strengthened rather than limited by the changing forms that text and performance assumed at this time.

This is most particularly true of Hogarth's *Henry VIII and Anne Boleyn*. Horace Walpole records seeing a painting of Henry VIII in a setting that is of major significance in the early assimilation of Shakespeare images into social and political discourses: 'It was at Vauxhall in the portico of the old great room on the right hand as you enter the garden.'[32] Vauxhall Gardens had been opened in June 1732. Hogarth was certainly involved in their planning, advising the developer Jonathan Tyers on the design and being rewarded by him with a gold medallion for the ways in which he assisted 'more essentially than by a few pieces he painted for the decorations'.[33] The painting that Walpole saw was most likely a copy of the engraving, by Hogarth himself or by some other hand. That it should be displayed there suggests that its satiric import was not only still recognised but still strong; to the satiric use of an allusion to a Shakespeare play in the print must therefore be added its contribution to the varieties of conversational exchange undertaken by the merchants, soldiers and court functionaries who visited the Gardens, many of whom would also have seen Cibber's version of the play on which it rested.

This placing of Shakespeare within a number of contemporary ideological frames stands as a mirror of the functions that Shakespeare visualisation would adopt much later in the century, within the different borders of a more firmly established, notionally authentic text, and a stronger sense of Shakespeare as the lodestone of national values. Before either these, or the tradition of iconographic visual criticism in which Hogarth again occupies a foundational place, would come to dominance, a generation of painters would explore the relationship between scenes from the theatre, portraits of actors in character and several orders of landscape naturalism to develop practices and conventions in the critical visualisation of the plays. These images also contributed to a series of social, intellectual and political discourses, that ranged from the connoisseur's exploration of a scene within European traditions of allegory to the compound social and political debates at Vauxhall. It is to these images, and these frames, that the next chapter turns.

NOTES

1. 57.15 × 75.88 (22 $^{1}/_{2}$ × 29 $^{7}/_{8}$), Tate Britain.
2. Charcoal heightened with white chalk on toned paper, 38.9 × 54 (15 $^{5}/_{16}$ × 21 $^{1}/_{4}$), Royal Library, Windsor Castle.
3. Merchant, *Shakespeare and the Artist*, p. 35.
4. 49.5 × 58.3 (19 $^{1}/_{2}$ × 23), Private collection.
5. Untraced; smaller version, oil on canvas, 71.2 × 104 (28 $^{1}/_{4}$ × 42), Heim Gallery, London. Engraved by Thomas Ryder, published 1 December 1798, 49 × 63 (19 $^{1}/_{4}$ × 24 $^{3}/_{4}$).
6. *Henry IV, Part I*, The Oxford Shakespeare (Oxford: Oxford University Press, 1987), Introduction, p. 25.
7. *An Essay on the Dramatic Character of Sir John Falstaff* (London: T. Davies, 1777). Conveniently available in *Shakespeare Criticism*, ed. Daniel A. Fineman (Oxford: Clarendon, 1972).
8. First State, 43.97 × 36.35 (17 $^{5}/_{16}$ × 14 $^{5}/_{16}$). British Museum, London.
9. *The London Stage 1660–1800: Part 2: 1700–1729*, 2 vols. ed. Emmett L. Avery (Carbondale, Ill.: Southern Illinois University Press, 1960), II, p. 946. For Cibber's description of the adaptation, see John Genest, *Some Account of the English Stage*, 10 vols. (Bath: H. E. Carrington, 1832), III, pp. 200–2.
10. The figure is given in an account by W. R. Chetwood quoted in George C. D. Odell, *Shakespeare from Betterton to Irving*, 2 vols. (New York, Scribner's, 1920), p. 307.

11. *The London Stage*, I, p. cxix.
12. Engraving, 13 × 7.46 ($5\frac{1}{8} \times 2\frac{15}{16}$). This was possibly produced for Tonson's edition of 1725 but never used. See Ronald Paulson, *Hogarth's Graphic Works*. 2 vols. (London and New Haven: Yale University Press, 1965), I, pp. 112–3.
13. *Mr Garrick in the Character of Richard III*, c.1741–6? Oil on canvas, 190.5 × 250.2 ($75 \times 98\frac{1}{2}$). Walker Art Gallery, Liverpool.
14. *The Image of the Actor* (London: Pinter, 1991), p. 38.
15. *The Complete Works of Shakespeare Revised from the Original Editions*, edited by J. O. Halliwell (London: London Printing and Publishing Company, 1850).
16. *The Tragical History of King Richard III*, V.iii.60, in *Shakespeare Made Fit: Restoration adaptations of Shakespeare*, ed. Sandra Clark (London: Dent, 1997). The line is the same in both Quartos and Folio: see *William Shakespeare: the Tragedy of King Richard the Third. Parallel Texts of the First Quarto and the First Folio with Variants of the Early Quartos*, ed. Kristian Smidt (Oslo: Universitetsforlaget and New York: Humanities Press, 1969), pp. 208–9.
17. *Garrick and Mrs Pritchard in Macbeth*, 1768; mezzotint by Valentine Green, 1776, 41.9 × 55.2 ($16\frac{1}{2} \times 21\frac{3}{4}$), National Portrait Gallery, London.
18. *Conférence de M. Le Brun sur l'expression générale et particulière* (Paris: E. Picard), 1698. Translated by John Williams in 1734 as *A Method to Learn to Design the Passions*. The Augustan Reprint Society Publication Numbers 200–201 (Los Angeles: University of California Press, 1980). Subsequent page numbers refer to this edition.
19. Exhibited 1771; 236.2 × 150 (93 × 59), Shakespeare Memorial Theatre Gallery, Stratford-upon-Avon.
20. c.1787; Oil on panel, 55.6 × 46.3 ($21\frac{7}{8} \times 18\frac{1}{4}$), Folger Shakespeare Library, Washington D.C.
21. Folger Shakespeare Library, Washington D.C.
22. William Henry West Betty, *Young Albert, the Roscius, exhibited in a series of characters from Shakespeare and other authors* (London: S & J Fuller, 1811), Folger Shakespeare Library, Washington D.C.
23. Attrib. William Segar, 1585; oil on panel, 94.7 × 50 ($37\frac{5}{16} \times 19\frac{11}{16}$), Hatfield House, Hertfordshire.
24. 297.8 × 419.1 ($117\frac{1}{4} \times 165$), Musée du Louvre, Paris. The allusion was first noted by Antal (*Hogarth*, p. 69). Paulson (*Hogarth's Graphic Works*, I, p. 191) suggests that the composition also owes something to the frontispiece to *Coriolanus* in Rowe's 1714 edition; but the tent here is a far smaller structure than that in Le Brun's picture, which Hogarth's image far more closely resembles. That Hogarth mentions the painting in passing in *The Analysis of Beauty* (xi) suggests the degree of his familiarity with it: like the illustrator and readers of Rowe's edition, he would have known the image from its reproduction in a 1703 translation of André Felibien's *The Tent of Darius explain'd; or the Queens of Persia at the feet of Alexander*. Translated from the French of Mr F., by Collonel [sic] Parsons. London, 1703.
25. Engraving, 28.4 × 36.4 ($11\frac{3}{8} \times 14\frac{3}{8}$), Worcester College, Oxford.
26. See the discussion of James Barry's Boydell painting of *King Lear* in Chapter 3.
27. 80 × 101.6 ($31\frac{1}{2} \times 40$), St Oswald Collection, Nostell Priory, Wakefield.
28. 78.8 × 94.5 ($31 \times 37\frac{3}{8}$), Tate Britain.
29. Smidt, *Parallel Texts*, 216 and 217, 208 and 209.

30. 78.7 × 94.6 (31 × 37 $^{1}/_{4}$), Tate Britain.
31. Engraving, 12.7 × 17 (5 × 6 $^{11}/_{16}$), Royal Academy of Arts, London.
32. Letter to John Nichols, 31 October 1781. *Horace Walpole's Miscellaneous Correspondence*, II, ed. W. S. Lewis and John Riely with the assistance of Edwine M. Martz and Ruth K. McClure (New Haven: Yale University Press and Oxford: Oxford University Press, 1980), p. 451.
33. Account by John Phillips quoted in *The Genuine Works of William Hogarth illustrated with biographical anecdotes, a chronological catalogue, and commentary*, by John Nichols and George Steevens, 3 vols. (London: Longman, Hurst, Rees, and Orme, 1808–1817), I, p. 47.

CHAPTER 3

LANDSCAPE, READERSHIP AND CONVENTION, 1740–90

I

Although Hogarth convincingly initiated the practice of critical interpretation through visual mediation of the plays, his work had little immediate influence in establishing a tradition: only in the 1770s did other figures emerge who would continue and develop the process at the same level of intellectual complexity. This is not to deny that visual treatment of the plays grew in popularity and extent in the intervening years; rather, it is to suggest that paintings and drawings adopted different stances, concerned mainly with the problem of transforming the expressive and technical aspects of stage performance into the idiom of static presentation. This exploration took place within the limitations and demands of the growing interest in and market for images related to the theatre that Hogarth himself had helped to fuel. The strongest demand was for portraits of actors in character, with Quin, Garrick, Henderson and Siddons dominating, with images following the lead established by Hogarth in *Garrick as Richard III* yet never attempting its conceptual depth. Through the work of artists like Wilson and Zoffany, from the 1760s onwards, this tradition begins to develop into the genre of theatrical conversation pieces, group portraits that purported to show, with different degrees of mimetic intention or achievement, scenes as acted on stage. Related to them are portraits of aristocratic patrons as Shakespearean characters, forming a sub-set of the genre that might be termed 'personation', often exploiting references of special significance to the sitter and her or his family in a manner that, as Chapter 7 will clarify, was later used to much deeper critical and referential import by Reynolds. The three groups are clearly related, and while mainly concerned with presenting individual likenesses they allow the possibility of larger critical interpretation through revelation of character or delineation of event.

As readership of the plays independent of performance became more widespread, another kind of picture became popular, the study of an individual character as opposed to an image of an actor or an aristocratic subject presenting the role. While this suggests that visual mediation of the texts was reflecting the growing interest in the discussion of character, the images rarely approached analytical objectivity. One of the latest and most popular series of these images, begun in 1782, was known as *Picturesque Beauties of Shakespeare*,[1] a title that reveals much about their nature. As the genre of picturesque landscape strove to fix the emotional imprint of the scene on the perceiver, so these portraits offer an immediate response of sentiment to the characters they depict. Ultimately this tradition grows into the convention of portraits of characters as idealised types that is popular in the next century, culminating in works such as Charles Heath's *Heroines of Shakespeare* (1883).[2] Some studies of individual characters, however, show a broader awareness of the intellectual, emotional and aesthetic current of the unified work of which they are only one constituent. The twelve *Shakespeare Heads* by John Hamilton Mortimer (1775) are of a completely different order, and influential in a later move to greater depth. As a later part of this chapter will show, Mortimer's head of Lear, building on close textual reading, the physiognomic theory of Le Brun and the tradition of depicting prophets taken from the Sistine Chapel, becomes an essential component in images reflecting the dramatic interactions and intellectual drives of the play from the later years of the century.

Two or three decades before this, a development occurred that was of greater significance in Shakespeare imaging. In response to the growing interest in the plays as experienced both when performed and when read, painters began to offer images that relocated scenes within landscape or architectural settings. They addressed the problems of moving out of the theatre, while remaining accessible in showing famous actors, and of presenting scenes that would both recall the impact of the theatric moment and offer some kind of transformation of the play's larger movement into the spatial structure constituted by painting. The site of this more complex exploration of the plays lies at the confluence of diverse existing conventions. At first, it is formed of the negotiations between the representation of theatric action, the expressive vocabularies of the portrait and conversation piece, and the adoption of more thoroughly painterly approaches to composition and chiaroscuro. Added to these, in different proportions and degrees according to artist and subject, are conventions of landscape that range from the Rococo to the Gothic, embracing indigenous mimesis and European allegory along the way. Later, the taste for the Sublime, the fashion for 'moonlight' painting, and a concern for the historical Grand Style were subsumed into Shakespeare paintings. All transplant the plays from the theatre into a landscape of the imagination, a shift aided by the canonisation effected by Garrick's Jubilee of 1769 which confirmed the status of Shakespeare as the embodiment of the English genius, a spirit most often expressed through an ideal of the countryside. Alongside these imperatives was the search for a style that concentrated national identity in similar measure: seen in this light, the conception of the Boydell Shakespeare Gallery is revealed as an event based on logical inevitability.

That no single figure emerges as dominant in these years is a reflection of the developing state of Shakespeare painting through complex exchanges with genres that were themselves adopting multiple, and fluid, identities; but it is also a function of the market. Individual images emerge not only through their use of a wider range of methods of presentation, that allow broader critical insights, but also in their negotiations between theatre, text and specific audiences. From images of this sort emerge conventions of representation, both general and specific, that come to be defining elements of Shakespeare imaging for both viewers and subsequent generations of artists. The intellectual interrogation of the idea of theatre and the visual mediation of the text that drives the change from a depiction of a single scene to the visual gathering of the play's temporal progress, and the growth of a sophisticated readership aware of the subtleties that both these shifts imply, come together to supply the foundation for the greater complexities of visual criticism produced in the maturity of both traditions later in the century. This chapter explores first the presentations of scenes, and increasingly of larger movements in the plays, within particular production contexts for particular viewers, and then the development of an iconographical tradition in the representation of *King Lear*, again revealing a growth of sophistication in both image and readership.

II

While many paintings that address the plays critically were produced for individual patrons, one series of images from the earlier years stands out because of its production for one particular, and very public, site; the paintings commissioned by Jonathan Tyers from Francis Hayman for display in Vauxhall Gardens. By the 1740s, when the works were completed, Hayman had begun to move out of his employment as a scene-painter at Drury Lane to produce portraits and conversation pieces, and from early in this decade date both the Vauxhall paintings and the commission from Hanmer for the frontispieces for his edition of the plays.[3] The result is that the Vauxhall images combine a knowledge of the theatre with an awareness of the plays in a reliable, recent textual form; at the same time, because of their setting, they are part of a series of discourses, social, political and literary.

Jonathan Tyers took over the lease of what were then known as Spring Gardens in 1728 with the intention of raising it above its earlier status as 'a much-frequented rural Brothel'.[4] The Shakespeare paintings contribute to this elevation, but are given a sombre tinge by the intimations of mortality by which they are surrounded, in even the most ebullient of the large number of other images painted early in the 1740s by Hayman and his circle for permanent display at Vauxhall. Concerned largely with games and recreations, they make iconographic references to English and Dutch emblem books stressing transience and vulnerability, often include sexual advances and bawdy insinuations, and repeatedly reveal the dangers implicit within apparently innocent plays and pastimes.[5] At some time in the later 1740s Hayman contributed two paintings to Tyers' private garden at Denbies, near Dorking, which reflected the theme of mortality in having a Temple of Death before a Valley of the Shadow of Death and a gateway formed of coffins topped by a male and female skull, with monitory verses close by.[6] These circumstances suggest a subtlety and ambivalence of meaning within the Shakespeare images: they contribute to what David Solkin, in his survey largely concerned with the images' social functions, calls 'a site devoted solely to the cultivation of refined pleasure',[7] but suggest that this pleasure was at the very least enhanced by a fashionable awareness of mortality. This duality is of particular resonance in the Shakespeare paintings.

Exactly how many images Hayman produced is unclear; certainly his Shakespeare images numbered at least seven, defining their major contribution to a visual scheme as much literary and moral as it was decorative, and that at one level was doubtless planned to stimulate the new art of refined conversation among the diners. The images fall into two groups. First are those that decorate the 'Pavilions' or supper-boxes. *The Wrestling Scene in 'As You Like It'* (c. 1740–2: Fig. 13),[8] probably painted as a sample of Hayman's work of this kind, immediately declares its convergence of theatrical and painterly practice. It takes as its central characters the cast of the Drury Lane *As You Like It*, revived on 20 December 1740 with Hannah Pritchard as Rosalind and Kitty Clive as Celia. They are, however, relocated within a Rococo landscape of the kind made popular in England through the influence of Watteau. Light, airy and made loosely classical by the colonnade at the left, it conveys a mood that, apart from the shadows over the Duke, is lucent and ebullient. The action rests on a taut compositional armature that conveys the narrative

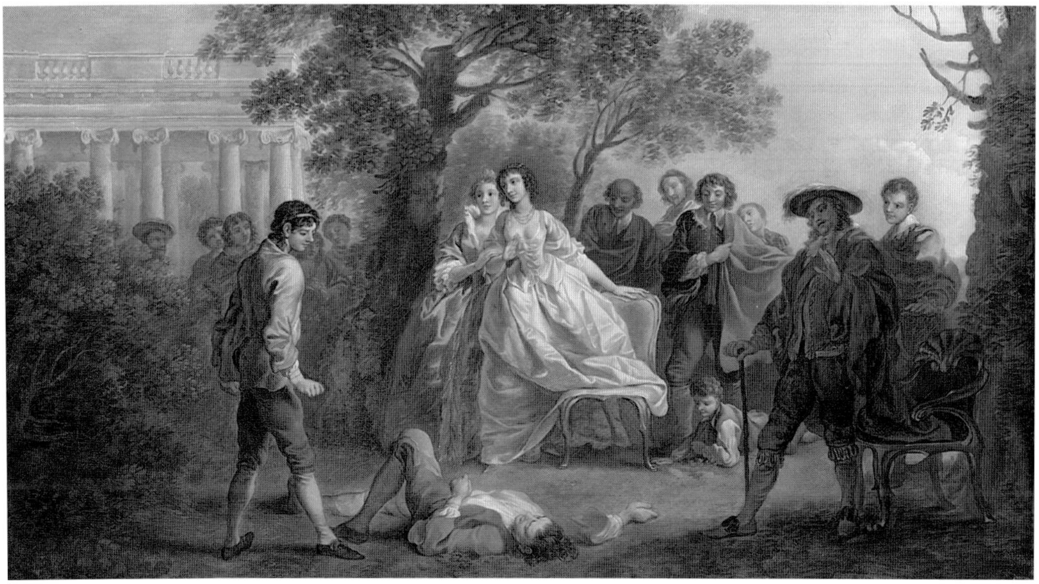

13 Francis Hayman, *The Wrestling Scene in 'As You Like It'*, c. 1740–2.

forces in a wholly painterly manner that offsets and redefines the direct theatrical references. Rosalind and Celia look towards the left, drawing the onlooker's eyes to Orlando, who in turn looks down at Charles. His extended right hand, and the fall of light across the painting, point towards the figure of Duke Frederick in the right foreground, from whom an irregular horizontal extends across the line of courtiers behind him and ultimately back to Rosalind and Celia. In contrast to the brightly lit Rosalind and Orlando, the Duke appears in shadow, and through this painterly means a basic critical reading of the play is disclosed: the scene is revealed as a generative turning point from which will follow Orlando's retreat from the Duke's anger and the subsequent banishment of Rosalind. The combination of theatrical recollection with painterly light and composition functions to convey the pivotal moment, bringing together a grasp of the play's workings and the pavilions' larger theme of the pleasure and perils of games. Yet the implications of the scene, and its larger place in the play's unfolding, are less apparent than the immediate sensory pleasure offered by colour, texture and movement – and, for the original audience, by the recognition of the actors and the performance on stage.

Similar is the painting listed as *The Fairies Dancing on the Green by Moonlight*[9] in the anonymous *Description of Vauxhall Gardens* of 1762. While suggesting Titania's reference to 'our moonlight revels' (2.1.141), the image also includes recognisably human figures, so that the overall effect is to imply the complex choreography of amorous reversals in the mortal and fairy lovers. But the links are remote, and the uncertain history of the image makes it an unlikely source of direct Shakespearean visualisation, perhaps relating instead to Settle's adaptation of the play as *The Fairy Queen*.[10] Much more resonant are the group described by an early guide as 'four large beautiful *Pictures*, the Subjects of which are from our divine *Shakespeare*' (*A Sketch*, p. 4) displayed in a large chamber known as the Prince of Wales' Pavilion. The only one of these to survive is a depiction of the play scene in *Hamlet*, which shows Claudius rising during the dumb-show and is unusual in omitting Hamlet himself.[11] The result is to place the viewer in this role, a strikingly innovative act of complicity that becomes uncomfortable when the image and the play, are read in the light of contemporary politics. The implication is that the viewers are visually enfolded within a desire to see the present king deposed – a stance much more forthright in its support of the Prince than those of the Pavilion's other images, if surviving records have any validity. This is an appropriation of the play similar in effect to Hogarth's *Henry VIII*, though radically different in style and rhetoric. A closer reading of the play's theatrical identity is provided in the small oil-sketch, *The Play Scene from 'Hamlet'* (c. 1745; Plate 4),[12] which dates from the same period and which in its composition mediates between the Vauxhall canvas and the Hanmer design. The onlooker's attention is directed to Claudius, rising in the middle ground, by the strong horizontal tension between the eyes of Polonius and Gertrude beside him and Horatio at the extreme right, and this is matched in the gaze of Hamlet that extends from low down at the very front of the image's recessive space. Only Ophelia looks not at the king but instead at Hamlet. These compositional lines go beyond the presentation of a key moment to visualise one of the essential modes of the play, the tense observation with which the characters constantly regard each other. At the same time, the painting conveys Ophelia's confusion over Hamlet's behaviour, suggesting the later course of their relationship as implicit within this pivotal event. Seen in the Vauxhall context of darkened play, the scene has another resonance: a doomed innocence particularly relevant to Ophelia, suggested by the similarity of costume between Hamlet and Ophelia and the young men and women in Hayman's Vauxhall images of games, in particular the couple at the extreme left of *The Play of See-Saw* (c. 1741–2).[13] The resonances are suggestive: in this painting, the young woman is falling backwards into the arms of the man, with an obvious sexual innuendo that parallels Ophelia's songs. The see-saw, a frequent metaphor of political advancement and failure, offers itself as an ironic parallel to the relationship between Old Hamlet and Claudius; the dark humour that it provides is exactly of the kind found in *The Beggar's Opera* or *Tom Jones*, and is totally fitting as a contemporary comment on Shakespeare's play in its mock-heroic mixture of genres.

The other paintings in the Pavilion showed scenes from *King Lear*, *The Tempest* and *Henry V*, and are now known only through written accounts of the Gardens. Of these, the most valuable is that in the *Description* of 1762, which supports its account of each painting with up to a page of carefully selected quotation from Hanmer or Pope, comments on the disposition and depiction of character, and in some cases raises other points that offer a simple engagement with the images as critical visualisations of the plays. From the accounts it is clear that the images in part resemble the frontispiece wash-drawings for Hanmer's edition on which Hayman was working at about the same time.[14] The link seems closest in the image of Lear, shown on the heath in the convention established by Rowe: the inclusion of the Fool, mentioned in the *Description*, makes clear that the image follows Shakespeare's text and not Tate's, or any compromise version from the contemporary theatre. That from *The Tempest* shows the first encounter between Miranda and Ferdinand, making clear Prospero's wish to control and restrain their love. Like Hogarth's earlier painting, which Hayman may well have seen, it includes both Caliban and Ariel, presenting all the play's forces in diagrammatic opposition, although it seems to have differed in composition and detail from the Hanmer engraving.

The compound dialogue involved between the lost painting, the written account in the *Description* and the various discourses of the social conversation that resulted at the site of the painting's original display is most directly suggested in the treatment of *Henry V*. Surviving accounts reveal that it closely resembled the drawing for Hanmer's edition (Fig. 14) in presenting the visit of the French envoy Mountjoy before the Battle of Agincourt. The *Description* contrasts the 'vanity and pride' (16) of Mountjoy with Henry's 'dignity suitable to a sovereign' (17), but goes on to claim that 'the brave old standard bearer' is the 'finest human figure' (17). This figure is an addition to the play's text, and in commenting on it the author of the *Description* reveals the sensitivity involved in the addition, as well as implying an awareness of the fact that a high proportion of visitors to the Vauxhall pavilion were soldiers, linking a vestigial critical comment with a sound ideological appropriative gesture: that England was once more at war with France when the pamphlet appeared makes of this image, and of the play itself, a reflection of immediate contemporary concerns.

The account continues: 'Henry seizes the bridle of his white horse in order to mount him for the battle' (16). This action, absent from the frontispiece, is another significant addition, not simply in reinforcing the contrast between English vigour

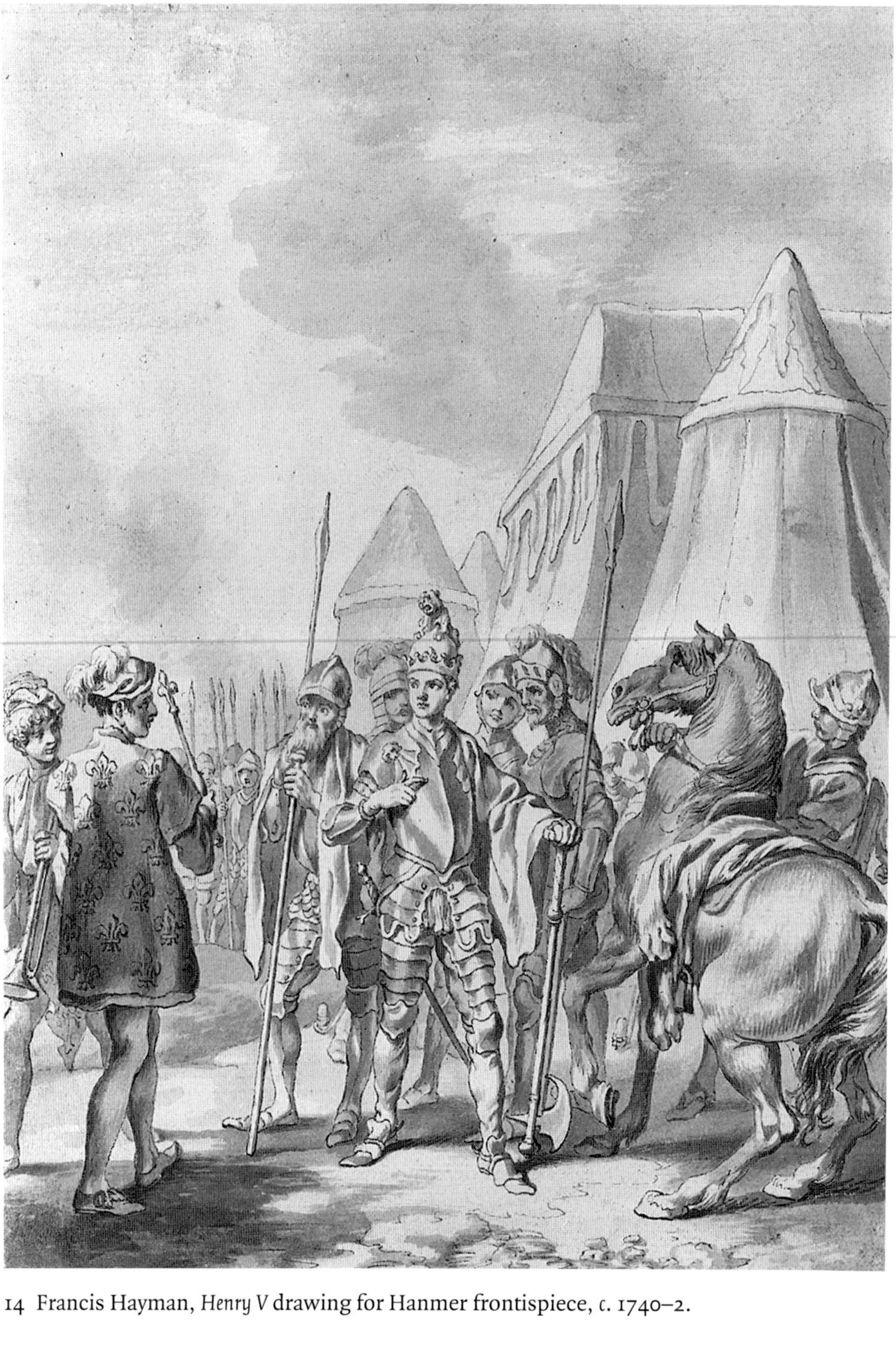

14 Francis Hayman, *Henry V* drawing for Hanmer frontispiece, *c.* 1740–2.

and French vanity but by compressing the play's action and recalling the words in which Vernon describes Henry's energy in 1 *Henry IV* where he leaps into the saddle 'All furnished, all in arms' (4.1.97). This visual insight is complemented in the *Description* by six lines praising the horse:

How firm the manag'd war-horse keeps his ground,
Nor breake his order though the trumpet sound!
With fearless eye the glitt'ring host surveys,
And gaze directly at the helmet's blaze:
The master's word, the law of war he knows,
And when to stop and when to charge the foes.[15]

Unidentified in the text, these come from the *Cynergetica* by Oppian of Apamea, a paean in praise of hunting translated at least twice in the first half of the eighteenth century,[16] and stress the perfect understanding between a fine rider and his mount. The metaphoric equation between statecraft and horsemanship is a common trope in the Renaissance and beyond, evidenced in 1 *Henry IV* in Vernon's claim that Hal will 'witch the world with noble horsemanship' (4.1.110): that Hayman's image refers implicitly to it, and that the *Description* makes the link more directly, shows both an understanding of the visual operation of the trope and a wish to state it in classical terms. In turn, this suggests that the readers of the account and the painting will understand such a reference at some level, and absorb it into their own discussions, the soldiers among them enriching it through their own experience and the others seeing it as another demonstration of English superiority. Not only is Shakespeare wound into a spiral of patriotism, classical education and noble governance, but this is achieved through a visual mediation of the plays resting not on recollections of performance or adaptation but on a careful reading of the text. From this, some idea of the kind of discussions that took place before the paintings may be derived: these images are far more than self-conscious discussions of the pleasures and perils of amorous games, and instead represent the extension of serious discourse about the plays and their nationalist significance into a new social space.

The image of young Prince Hal grown to manhood as the ideal monarch is given further power, as are the other three paintings, by the circumstance that the patron and landlord of Vauxhall Gardens was Frederick, Prince of Wales. As Edelstein makes clear, Frederick was in the mid-1740s 'the symbolic head of the Opposition and, as such, the embodiment of the Opposition's ideal of a patriot king' (p. 31): the *Sketch*, written just after his death, refers to him as 'The Prince, who, lately formed the Nation's delight, and is now the just Subject of their unfeigned Sorrow' (p. 6).

This infuses the four paintings with an immediate political and even emotional resonance at the time of their painting, paralleling the adulation in which the young Henry Frederick was held in the early seventeenth century. Seen through this perspective, Hayman's paintings take on another ideological configuration: the *Hamlet* image becomes a coded reference to the succession, Prospero becomes the old king holding back the youthful heir, Lear embodies the inadequacies of governance, and Henry is revealed as the ideal young monarch into whom – the suggestion can hardly be far away – the young prince will grow.

The impact of these four paintings, estimated to have measured three metres (10 feet) in width, presented within a pavilion already potent with political and social charges, must have been striking. Even though they no longer exist, the verbal discourse in which they are inscribed in the *Description* suggests that they do far more than simply move Shakespeare painting out of the theatre. Hayman's images, seemingly more subtle in detail and suggestion than the smaller versions produced for Hanmer, as well as gaining far more rhetorical power by their sheer size, present the action and language of the plays, most particularly *Henry V*, in an idiom much amplified by their place of display. The verbal discussion they receive in the *Description*, as well as making quite clear that they are textual, not theatric, visualisations, is valuable evidence of the levels of discourse into which Shakespeare imaging could be drawn, both in terms of its analytical approach and as a bridge towards the ideological involvement within contemporary political and social debates. For these reasons, the pamphlet remains an essential document in revealing the place of Shakespeare imaging at the beginning of the period, forming an incisive and original balance to the commentaries offered alongside the Boydell Shakespeare. In practical terms, it goes further than they do; although the images have already been seen as visualising the work of 'our divine *Shakespeare*' (the possessive adjective indicates already a national ownership), they offer a directness that many later images, with their concern for chronological, providentialist history, cannot quite match.

III

At the same time as the Vauxhall paintings were presenting a focus for the social discussion of Shakespeare, other images were addressing the shift from theatrical record to visual textual criticism in more private settings. The complexity of the process and its multiple roots are exemplified in two images by Benjamin Wilson, an artist whose career charts the negotiation of conflicting forces that, in different proportions, acted upon most early Shakespeare images. Of the five paintings exhibited in his lifetime, four were portraits and one a history painting. In 1766 he took on the role of supervising scene painting at the private theatre of the Duke of York, where he recruited Johan Zoffany as his assistant. Three years later he was the main painter for Garrick's Jubilee at Stratford. Portraiture, history and scene-painting provide the major generic impulses for his painting; to these forces should be added a fashionable interest in the Gothic, the supernatural and the nascent form of moonlight painting.

Wilson's *William Powell as Hamlet encountering the Ghost* (1768–9: Plate 2),[17] like Hayman's *Wrestling Scene*, combines the depiction of popular actors with a larger landscape setting based on painterly principles that facilitate critical commentary in visual form. That the painting was long thought to depict Garrick reveals its reliance on what by then had become a conventional acting style, and the grouping again reflects stage practice. Yet while the setting may owe its origin to scenography in its general arrangement and in the fashionable Gothic castle, it moves away from stage illusion by using barely relieved darkness to intensify the emotional temper. Scale is important here: the setting dominates the characters, providing an overwhelming mood to which they supply textual focus. The painting lacks the tight links to the play's imagery provided in Wootton's *Macbeth*, but in its use of landscape a similar manipulation of feeling is apparent. This double approach, of recording a performance within a larger emotional suggestion, is employed in a different way in Wilson's earlier *David Garrick and George Anne Bellamy as Romeo and Juliet* (1753: Fig. 15).[18] It uses the simple expedient of taking the tomb scene and depicting the two actors within it, Garrick in one of his most familiar poses, Bellamy with arm raised, fingers outspread in an exaggerated theatric posture of surprise. The dominant element is a depiction of the tomb, lit from above by a chandelier much of the sort providing lighting in Drury Lane for the performance that opened in September 1750. The scene is enclosed within a dark landscape composed largely of trees seen in silhouette, relieved on the right by the moon shining through clouds and distant trees.

As a comment on the text it is much limited by the fact that it shows Garrick's adaptation. In the scene depicted, Juliet awakens and Romeo 'Brings her from the tomb';[19] after a brief exchange, Romeo dies from the poison he has taken earlier, and Juliet then stabs herself. The image contributes to the shift from theatrical depiction to more directly painterly visualisation. Earlier commentators[20] have seen it as a representation of the stage set in Covent Garden, in which two doors open in a pair of shutters to reveal the interior of the tomb. Kalman Burnim goes so far as to claim that the image is 'a highly valid theatrical rendition, as valid perhaps as a photograph'[21] in the evidence it provides of the performance. Clearly,

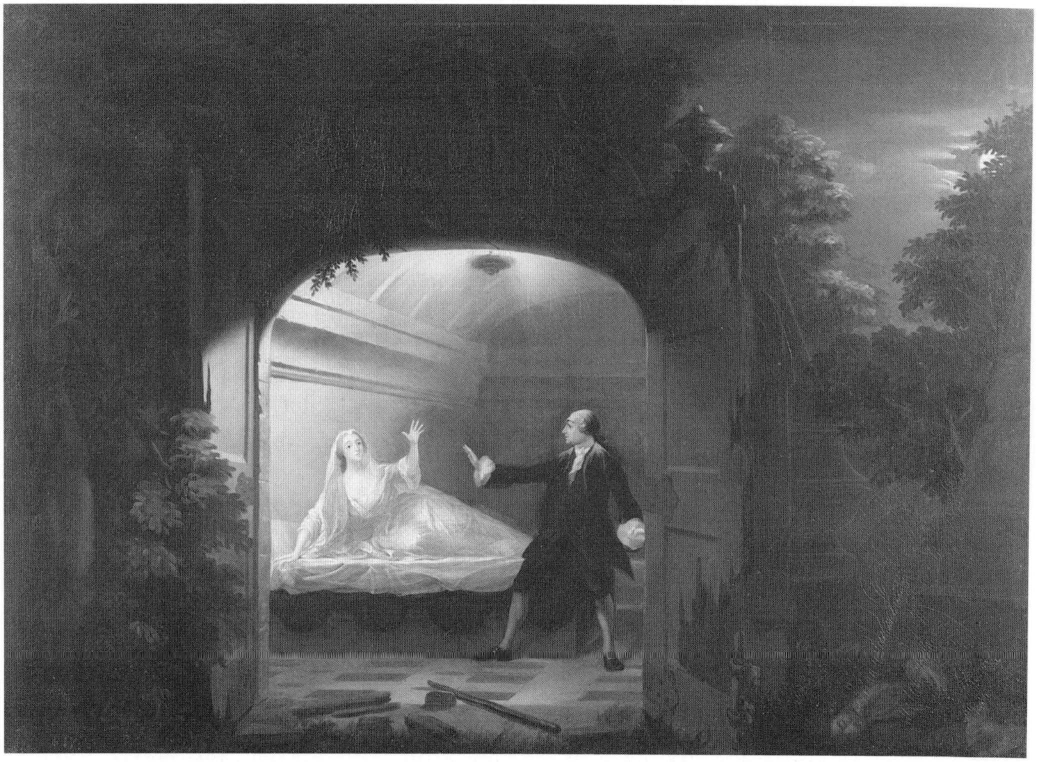

15 Benjamin Wilson, *David Garrick and George Anne Bellamy in Romeo and Juliet, Act V, Scene iii*. 1753.

the figures are modelled on Garrick and Bellamy in their famous roles, but the rest of the painting betrays no sign that a stage set rather than a painted landscape is being presented. Burnim's claim that the moon to the upper right depicts an elaborate stage lighting device is belied by its appearance, which, like the rest of the landscape, is very much that of the ruggedly picturesque nocturnal scenes then becoming fashionable. If this is an accurate representation of a stage set, then the set must indeed have been very fine; and this is contradicted by the record of Christlob Mylius, who declared 'The costumes are mediocre and the decorations positively bad.'[22] Mylius had collaborated with Lessing in founding a periodical on the theatre, and written plays based on the work of Molière and Holberg, so it may be assumed that he looked with a professional eye on the performance; his account hardly tallies with the fine draughtsmanship and painterly style of Wilson's depiction. It may well be that Wilson drew on the physical structure and mechanical arrangements of the performance, but they are certainly translated into the idiom of contemporary landscape. This enfolding of theatre within recorded nature is a combination that can perhaps only be achieved once, but it demonstrates well the difficulties encountered by those wishing to create a convincing single image from the dual sources of stage and study. It also shares with Hayman's Vauxhall paintings a key attribute in the growth of Shakespeare painting. In placing the stage action within a setting resting on forms and styles borrowed from fashionable landscape, it is locating Shakespeare painting within the mainstream of contemporary artistic practice, facilitating if not fulfilling the use of its techniques of intellection and moral commentary.

Despite their increasing value in moving the Shakespearean text to the centre of various kinds of larger discourse, these images should not be seen as part of a continuous historical growth. Some years after Wilson's paintings, for example, Francis Wheatley's *The Duel Scene from Twelfth Night* (1772)[23] presents the cast of the 1771 Drury Lane production against an ideal landscape, in a light, undemanding pastoralism that does nothing to visualise the action's sombre potential beneath its apparently comic surface. Zoffany offers a tragedic equivalent, with a fashionable interior setting, in *David Garrick and Hannah Pritchard as Macbeth and Lady Macbeth* (*c.* 1768).[24] The representation of the central figures accords with contemporary accounts of the two players, and it is primarily as a record of the performance that it has interested earlier commentators. In its Strawberry Hill Gothic, the setting may present something of the original design, matching the use of contemporary dress in relocating the scene to the mid-century present. Yet once more the lighting, carefully constructed to show diagonal shafts of light from offstage and a moon shining from behind clouds through a window upstage, reflects a fashionable concern for mood-setting that develops and extends the very limited possibilities of stage lighting into the more emotionally suggestive potential of painterly chiaroscuro. In an exploration of the two versions of this painting as theatrical documents, Stephen Orgel stresses their use of the conventions of contemporary portraiture, and concludes that the images show 'not the play but the world of real action the play represents',[25] suggesting the movement towards visual criticism to which the paintings contribute. The images may reflect the contemporary theatre's concern for emotionally powerful 'points' of action; but they do so in a wholly painterly fashion.

Although the works of Wilson, Wheatley and Zoffany move away from stage record in their lighting and locations, they remain essentially depictions of a single scene. Hayman's images demonstrate most fully what is hardly suggested in the others: an implicit awareness of the play's progression, although even they lack the syncretic visual invention shown by Wootton or Hogarth in implicating language or action from elsewhere in the text. In the 1760s, however, other paintings began to appear that moved towards this more extensive textual explication.

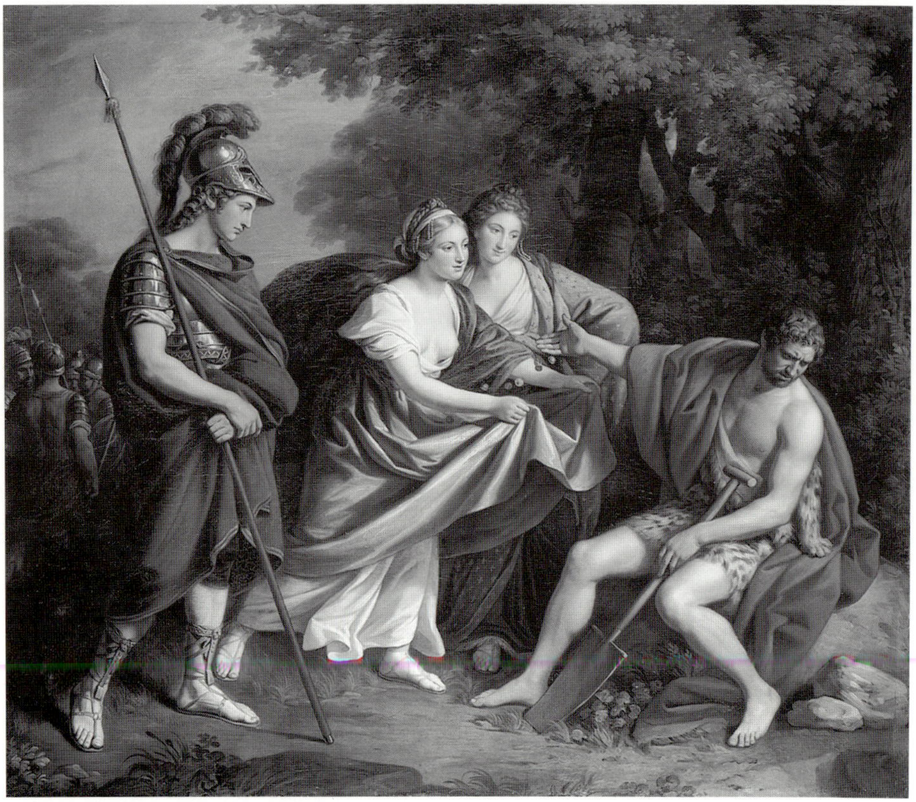

16 Nathaniel Dance, *Timon of Athens*, 1767.

Nathaniel Dance's *Timon of Athens*, exhibited at the Society of Artists in 1767 (Fig. 16),[26] completely displaces the stage relocation model and, in the process of appropriating another convention, makes a critical comment on the play as a whole. There can be no reference to performance here, since the play's only recent productions, in 1736 with revivals in the 1740s, had been in Shadwell's 1678 adaptation that completely omitted Phrynia and Timandra, who are shown by Dance. The frontispieces in the editions of Rowe and Hanmer also show this episode from 4.3, but Dance follows them only in selecting the moment. That the image rests wholly on painterly formulations is apparent in the use it makes, probably for the first time in Shakespeare painting, of the historical Grand Style, with its single light source, characters arranged largely in the same plane, and concentration on effects of drapery. Lighting and composition are fundamental to the painting's meaning. The alienation of Timon is shown by his averted, darkened face and location at the extreme right, while a group of soldiers, the companions of Alcibiades and representatives of Athens, are at the far left, symbolising the play's moral extremes. These features broaden the painting's immediate narrative situation, the final act of rejection where Timon flings money towards Phrynia and Timandra:

> Hold up, you sluts,
> Your aprons mountant; you are not oathable,
> Although I know you'll swear, terribly swear
> Into strong shudders and to heavenly agues
> Th' immortal gods that hear you.
> (4.3.136–40)

In their use of the bawdy gesture of the raised apron, the lines concretise the equation between money and sexuality that underscores the whole play. The passage also stresses the consequences of this link that Timon obsessively explores throughout the scene, the corruption of humankind both moral and physical that he metaphorically expresses through the syphilitic plague spread by the two women. It is here that Dance's use of the Grand Style makes its full impact: the depiction of such imagery in a visual vocabulary of classical restraint and poise imbues the painting with great satirical force. The image gained wider currency in an engraving by John Hall published in 1771,[27] and so powerful was it that a quarter of a century later John Opie, painting the play for Boydell, produced an almost identical composition,[28] the only differences being a change in the position of one of the women and the replacement of Alcibiades' soldiers by a dog, a visualisation of Timon's words on his appearance, 'For thy part, I do wish thou wert a dog,/ That I might love thee something' (4.3.55–6) to show his rejection of human company in favour of the animal world.

The effect of Dance's image essentially rests on the viewer's ability to understand the discrepancy between its style and subject, and this perhaps reveals the growing sophistication of both painting and audience. It also suggests that – unlike the work of Hayman and Wilson, that functions within a more popular cultural echelon – the painting operates within the highest levels of connoisseurship. The difference is reflected in the ownership and subsequent engraving of Dance's *Timon* and Wilson's *Romeo and Juliet*. The Dance painting was purchased for the royal collection, where it remains; the Wilson entered the collection of the banker Henry Hoare, then building a collection of English and European paintings to furnish his recently completed house at Stourhead. Both were the subject of engravings published by Boydell, but were marketed very differently. In 1779 Boydell issued a 130-page catalogue in French, offering prints of *les plus beaux tableaux qui soient en Angleterre*.[29] Hall's engraving after Dance is described (p. 30) as *d'après le Tableau du Cabinet du Roi*, and offered for '15 chelins' (15 shillings). It is advertised as appearing in the second volume of a collection of the 'plus célèbres tableaux de l'Angleterre,' along with engravings of works by Claude, Poussin, Rubens, and the great champion of English historical painting, Benjamin West. It is accompanied by a paragraph that places the event shown within the narrative of Timon, and ends with a majestic claim:

Nous ne pouvons pas entrer d'une manière convenable dans le detail de ce tableau, non plus que de quelques autres peints par des modernes. Les rapides progrès de l'art en si peu d'années doivent faire sentir qu'il ne dépend nullement du terroir, mais uniquement de la culture.

Nowhere in the account is any reference made to Shakespeare; significantly, it is as a statement of classical culture that the engraving is presented. That it is being offered for sale in France both shows the major advances in the production and marketing of engravings in England – as indeed the whole catalogue, remarkable for its extent, declares – and suggests that the use of Shakespeare as an emblem of English cultural hegemony, that will be exploited very soon afterwards by Boydell, has not yet established itself as a commercial lever.

By contrast, the Wilson image, engraved by Ravenet, is described only as 'd'après un Tableau du Cabinet de M. Hoare' (p. 43) and is included in the Tome Troisième, in a section headed 'Portraits' (p. 38), with a brief secondary reference in a section of 'Acteurs Anglois dans les principaux roles des tragédies & comédies Angloises' (p. 119). The difference is revealing. While neither is being regarded primarily as a work providing a commentary on Shakespeare, the hierarchical relationship is clear, with a portrait of two actors by implication less prestigious than an historical painting of a classical subject in Neo-Classical style. The difference is reflected in the price: the Wilson is priced at five shillings, exactly a third of the Dance, despite their being roughly the same size. The comparison reveals the compound intersections and partings of the various orders of Shakespeare painting at this time. Not yet regarded as embodying national character through its literary origin, it can nonetheless represent English painting as equalling that of the Old Masters and form part of a socio-commercial milieu that embraces continental marketing; at the same time, the distance between a classical history and a theatrical portrait is established in clear hierarchical terms.

A similar complex of critical reading, stylistic allusion and engagement with a range of social and mercantile exchanges is apparent in Francesco Zuccarelli's *Macbeth Meeting the Witches*, (1760: Fig. 17).[30] That it alludes to a convention employed by no other Shakespeare painting of its time reveals much about the aesthetic,

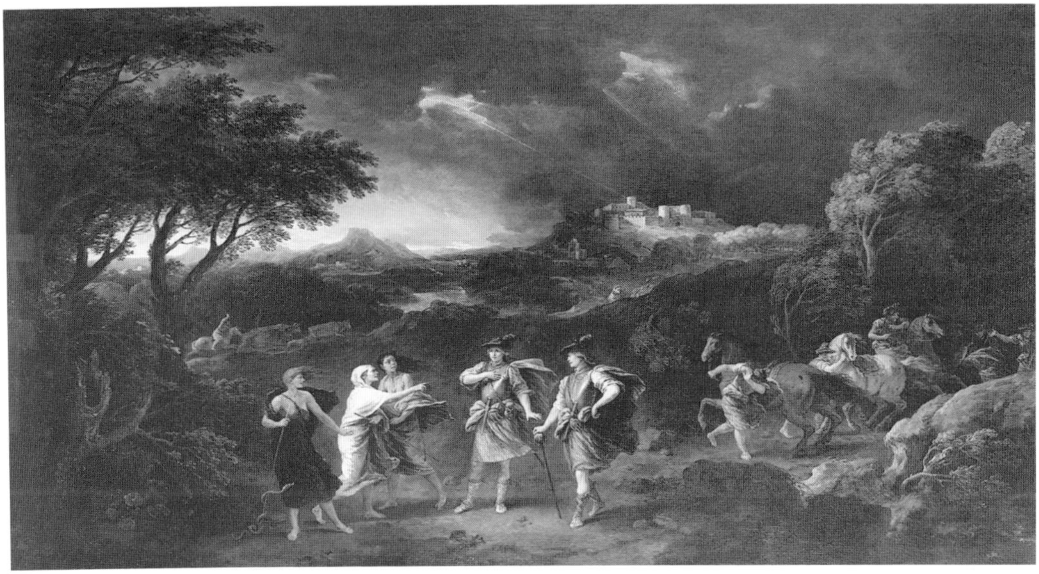

17 Francesco Zuccarelli, *Macbeth Meeting the Witches*, 1760.

intellectual and social frames within which it was produced and seen: that, like Dance's painting, it moves towards a higher rhetorical level in its idiom suggests once more the increased status of Shakespeare painting in the decade of Johnson's edition and Garrick's Jubilee. Like Hamlet's initial encounter with his father's ghost, Macbeth's meeting chimes fortuitously with a series of movements in English taste of its time: the developing concern for landscape as an emotional code; an interest in the Gothic; a fascination with the supernatural; and an interest in the nature of the heroic, negotiated between a variety of European styles and ideas of classicism and a more indigenous concern for folk-heroes. John Wootton's painting of 1750 is the first to employ some of these elements but bases them, as Chapter 1 has shown, on a combination of elements temporally separated in the play. Zuccarelli's treatment extends some but not all of these features, principally the trees blown back on themselves at the right and the birds flying towards them, to visualise later elements of the play's verbal imagery; although it does not, like the Wootton, assimilate the cauldron scene, it uses painterly devices of composition, lighting and convention to convey an awareness of the larger structure and growth of the play. While this may suggest some influence, or the beginning of a tradition of depicting the scene, the later painting establishes its difference immediately in its style, resting expansively on European models and elevating the scene by the imposing rhetoric thus employed.

Again, biography is relevant. Born near Orvieto in 1702, Zuccarelli established himself in Venice as a painter of religious landscapes in the pastoral tradition before travelling to London in 1752. He became a fashionable landscape painter, exhibited at the Society of Artists, gained the support of George III and became a founder member of the Royal Academy. The *Macbeth* painting was first owned by Sir William Hamilton, but sold very soon afterwards to Richard, first Earl of Grosvenor, at an auction forced on Hamilton by mounting debts.[31] The artist also painted at least one other version,[32] owned and probably commissioned by Hamilton's friend William Lock, a connoisseur and amateur artist whose drawings, especially those of Emma Hamilton, were much admired by Henry Fuseli, a circle that gives some indication of the currency of one level of artistic endeavour at this time. Yet already, the circle was being extended: exhibited at the Society of Artists in 1767 and engraved by William Woollett in 1770,[33] the image became available to a much wider constituency. It is significant that a fashionable Italian painter living in England should paint a landscape on a Shakespearean theme, and then receive a commission for another version. Before this, the only paintings on remotely related subjects that had been produced in multiple copies had been images of the theatre, most notably Hogarth's several variants of *The Beggar's Opera*. The original painting is in an unusual format, much longer than customary for landscapes, which may suggest that it was commissioned by Hamilton for a specific place in his gallery. Such an action by a notable collector who owned work by Rosa, Gaspard Dughet, Veronese and Titian,[34] suggests that Shakespearean subjects were becoming more prominent. Its subsequent purchase by the Earl of Grosvenor, another major private patron, further demonstrates the absorption of Shakespeare painting into the very centre of the age's cultural commerce: its engraving by the most celebrated print-maker of the period shows this interest spreading outwards from the individual connoisseur into the gallery-going public and the rapidly growing ranks of the upper-middle class city dwellers.

What did the painting convey to the aristocratic patron and to the wider audience who saw it in Woollett's engraving? William Pressly argues[35] that both rest heavily on a painting well known in England, Gaspard Dughet's *Landscape with Storm* (1653–4: Fig. 18),[36] and the image seems certain to be one of its sources: Shakespeare's play has been transplanted into the Roman *campagna*, representing a taste in English connoisseurship exploited in landscapes by artists from Richard Wilson onwards. It also resembles very closely another *Landscape with Storm* (1651: Fig. 19),[37] by Dughet's more celebrated brother-in-law, Nicolas Poussin, which may divulge more about its critical insight into the play. Even without this detailed meaning, the allusiveness is revealing about the cultural politics of the

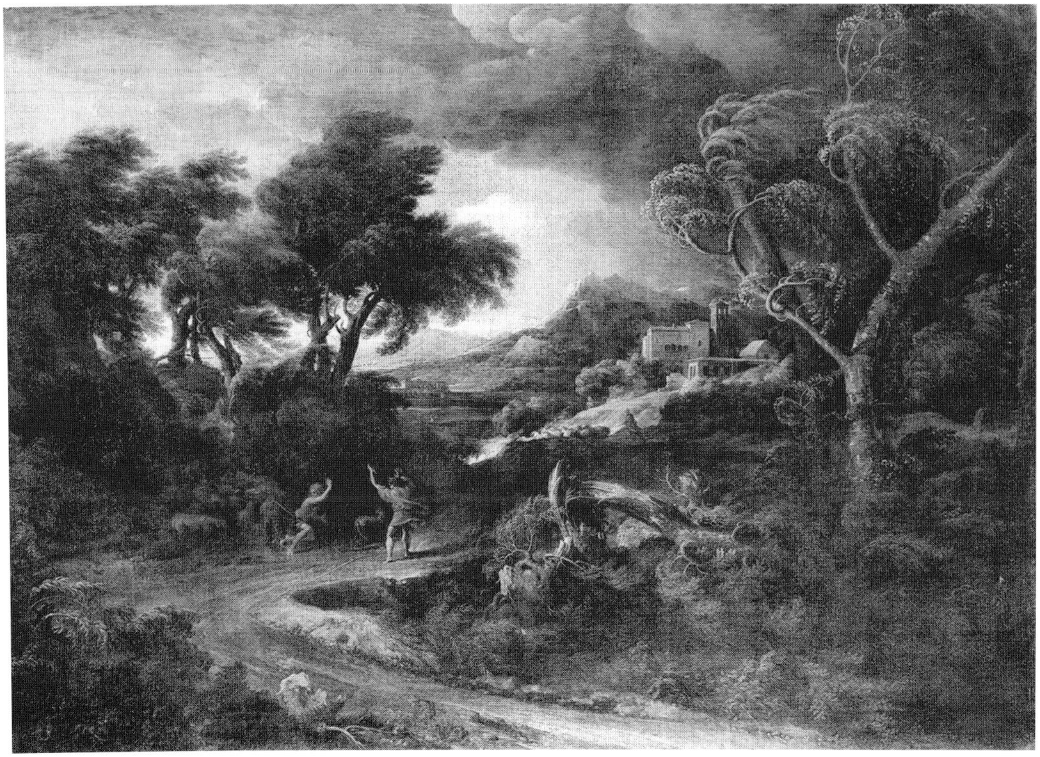

18 Gaspard Dughet, *Landscape with Storm*, 1653–4.

image: in the distance between Wootton's and Zuccarelli's versions of the scene, Shakespeare imaging has travelled from something merely indigenous to a form that asserts nationhood by appropriating styles from international elite culture.

The most far-reaching consequence of this change in rhetorical register is the rejection of all links with the theatre and the placing of the events at the centre of a European pastoral landscape tradition, complete with sheep in the version now in the Folger, and this has implications in the reading of the play it offers. The move away from the stage is also shown in the use of Scottish dress, not present in London until Macklin's 1773 production. The Choice trope used by Wootton is softened, although Macbeth still stands between the witches and Banquo; in the Lock version he holds both hands outstretched at his sides as if physically weighing the decision. The castle in the middle ground is familiar from European landscapes in general and Dughet's *Storm* in particular, but it has another purpose, suggesting the moral storm that will descend on the castle when Duncan visits: in the Lock version this is made explicit by the bolt of lightning, itself a natural concomitant to the thunder associated with the witches, that strikes the building and causes its upper masonry to fall. The Poussin is a more concentrated image,

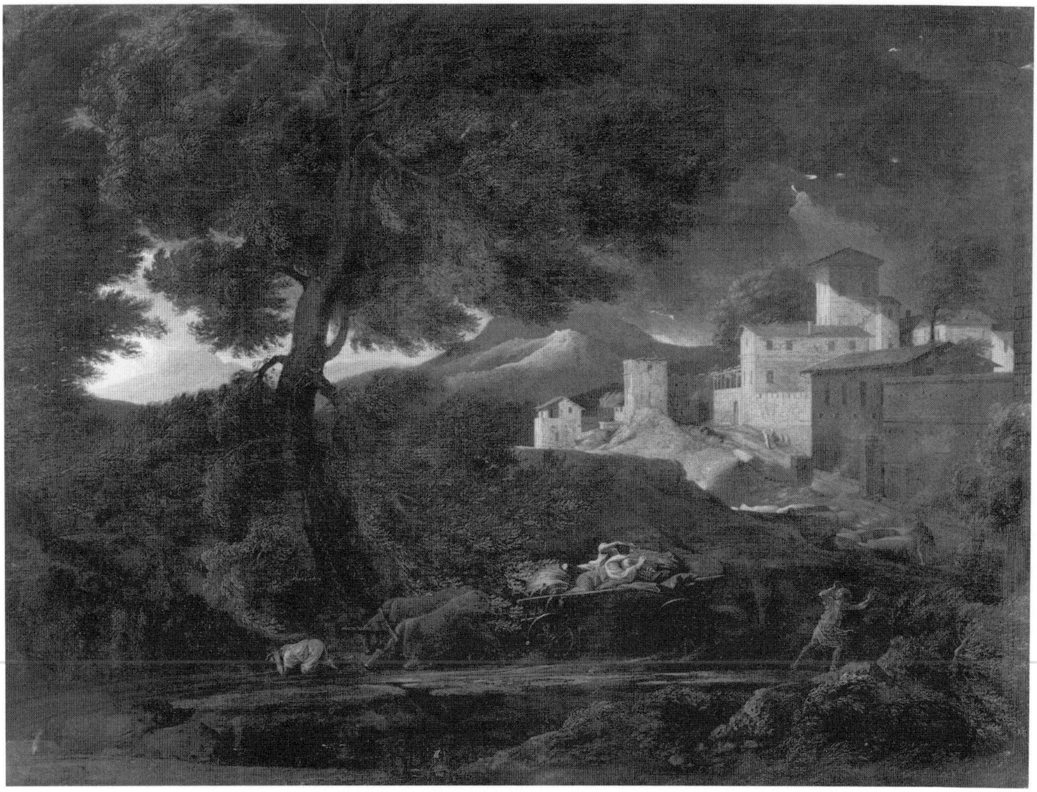

19 Nicolas Poussin, *Landscape with Storm*, 1651.

and its influence as a source for the Zuccarelli is apparent in the mountains, the castle and the light that shines through and beneath the trees.

A landscape that has extremes of light and dark, in which the trees are bent back by the powerful wind and a stroke of lightning flashes against the distant castle, provides a vigorous emotional equivalent of the scene's intensity, conveying fashionably Gothic extremes. It also has a more specific function within the play, revealing a larger structural awareness. The storm discussed much later by Ross and the Old Man in 2.4 is made forcefully literal here, and the reference to Duncan's horses 'Turned wild in nature' (2.4.16) is hinted at in the two horses in the Lock version. This shows the tradition of exploring the play's imagery established by Wootton being powerfully extended; yet, when the painting is seen in the context of its resemblance to Poussin, it may be taken a stage further still.

Poussin's landscapes exist within the tradition of European allegorical painting, to the extent that their structures convey a narrative sequence that must be properly read to achieve full understanding. As Sheila McTighe[38] and others have made clear, the storm for Poussin is a powerful allegory of the workings of fate, very often shown in conjunction with images of blindness to show humankind's inability to see its operations. When read in this way, Zuccarelli's painting reveals a much more extensive level of critical interpretation. Macbeth's failure to understand the nature of the witches leads on to the death of Duncan, symbolised in the lightning striking the castle, and the unnatural events that follow from it, revealed in the storm coiling around Macbeth. The light shining through the trees may be seen in narrative terms as the resolution offered by Macduff; within an allegorical frame, it suggests the alternative that Macbeth himself considers in his soliloquy at the start of 1.7. In the painting, the path of light offers a moral judgment on Macbeth's actions, in McTighe's terms, 'to make the viewer aware of the virtue of firmness and immobility in the face of Fortune's storms'.[39] The effect of the storm is thus threefold: it shows, in the bolt of lightning, the actual moment of evil in the murder of Duncan; it prefigures the cosmic echoing of the murder, 'unnatural,/ Even like the deed that's done' (2.4.10–11); and it presents a balancing force of good that Macbeth has rejected.

Just how far the image was read in this way by its first onlookers is, of course, an unanswerable if insistent question: McTighe's suggestions about the power of fate in Poussin's image are themselves qualified by questions of this sort.[40] But one essential point argues in favour, if not of readings as explicit as this, then of others that are closely bound to them. In choosing to paint in this manner, Zuccarelli has allied himself to the tradition of European allegorical painting, represented most completely by Poussin. We may choose to read the presence of the light not as an emblem of choice but as a prefiguration of the redemptive return of Macduff; yet even this reading moves the painting out of the arena of simple narrative representation and into a subtler conjunction of critical and moral purposes.

Zuccarelli's painting represents a radically new dimension in the visual mediation of the play, and suggests a possible new direction for Shakespeare imaging, in opening the path towards European allegorical painting. That it exists in two versions, and was reproduced just at the time when English engraving was becoming a major cultural force, suggests that it achieved widespread exposure. Yet the fact that it produced no imitators, even within the very specific constituency defined by aristocratic patronage and the subject area of the supernatural sublime, implies that its rhetoric was not sufficiently accessible, possibly because of the competing interest in history painting that was given a major spur by the foundation of the Royal Academy and the first of Reynolds' *Discourses* in 1768. Perhaps the rhetoric of European allegorical painting was judged unsuitable to the innately English qualities of Shakespeare; perhaps the cultivation of Neo-Classical painting concerned with the actualities of national history supervened, to generate the literary and Shakespearean sub-genres that later become popular. Whatever the reason, Zuccarelli's image remains unique in stance and style, notable both in itself and as an index of the change in cultural status that Shakespeare painting has undergone since Wootton: the distance between it and the paintings of Hayman and Wilson is of major importance in the growth of visual criticism.

A curious equivalent to the elevated rhetoric of Zuccarelli is found in another treatment of the same scene that exists almost at the opposite polarity of style, Francis Towne's watercolour of the same scene, produced at some time in the last quarter of the century. Undated, and currently unknown apart from its discussion and reproduction by Moelwyn Merchant,[41] it is close stylistically to the topographical watercolours the artist produced in the 1780s. As a reading of the play it offers little, save to place the events within a landscape of rocky outcrops and wind-bent trees constructed in the large planes of colour familiar from Towne's work. Its significance lies in something rather different. Hayman's images speak to a city audience familiar with images of irony, some of whom would have seen the references to play and playing in both *Hamlet* and *As You Like It* as resonant with political overtones. By contrast, Wilson's are directed more towards a readership concerned both with the theatre and with emerging forms of landscape painting. Dance and Zuccarelli, in accommodating Shakespeare painting within different forms of elite visual culture, make subtle readings of the plays' moral progressions. These, too, in the forms of popular engravings, become available to another kind of audience, the new print-buying public, located both within and between the various cultural strata so far encountered – somewhere between Vauxhall and Grafton Street, in short. The Towne watercolour addresses yet another constituency, in placing Macbeth in the landscape of popular topographic painting. Alongside the shift from the theatre into the arena of critical analysis, another movement is evident: the visual re-enactment of the plays has become part of cultural, social and political debate at a large number of levels, revealing much about the sophistication of both paintings and readers.

IV

The establishment of conventions of representation of particular events or themes is an essential stage in the maturation of any visual discourse. It institutes a dialogue between one generation of artists and the next that enables both continuity and change; and it also enables a parity of understanding between artist and viewer that provides common ground of idea and expectation. Significant as they are, none of the paintings discussed above facilitates the growth of such a convention, as they exist as single images, either in the depiction of the particular plays they explore, or in more general terms. While there are some links between the *Macbeth* images of Wootton and Zuccarelli, their stylistic differences are great, showing no developing sense of tradition. Something of a convention is seen in the relation between Dance's use of key elements from earlier treatments of *Timon of Athens* (see Fig. 6), and their replication by John Opie, but this is too limited to constitute a mature iconographic current. There is, however, one tradition of depiction that emerges during the middle years of the century to form an iconographic convention. King Lear in the storm is first depicted in the frontispieces to the play published in Rowe's editions of 1709 and 1714, and is then developed by Hayman in his Hanmer frontispiece. As John Harvey remarks in his astute discussion of the tradition, '*King Lear* has always been a sensitive subject, probably because of its dangerous politics',[42] and this dimension of the play has already been hinted at in the discussion of Hayman's Vauxhall paintings. This significance, along with the sheer scale and public exposure of the Vauxhall *Lear*, no doubt combined with the inherent emotional intensity of Lear on the heath to make it the most frequently depicted Shakespearean scene in the middle years of the century, and ultimately a key component of the grand historical paintings of the Boydell Gallery. The depictions go some way towards establishing the practice of Shakespeare painting as a continuing and developing strand within the larger cultural stream of English painting and aesthetic discourse; through this, shifts in the visualisation of one play may be charted and revealed as a significant strand in its critical reception.

An early form of this tradition is evident in Benjamin Wilson's *David Garrick as King Lear*, now known only through the mezzotint by James McArdell, dated 1 November 1754 (Plate 3).[43] The image combines something of Garrick's stage presence with the tradition established by the Rowe frontispieces. These show Lear before a thatched hovel, accompanied in the earlier version by Gloucester and Kent, with Edgar at a little distance away to the right, and in the later with the additional presence of the Fool. They refer to Rowe's stage directions which specify, at the start of Act III:

> SCENE *A Heath*
> *A Storm is heard with Thunder and Lightning*

and continue in scene three:

> *Part of the Heath with a Hovel.*[44]

Hayman followed this convention in his Hanmer frontispiece and the Vauxhall painting, and McArdell's image continues it in the use of a single stroke of jagged lightning; but the use of a horizontal rather than a vertical format allows Wilson to continue his practice of moving from the theatre into a fully-realised setting within the convention of Gothic landscape.[45] Behind the more naturalistic, wind-bent trees the landscape is far more barren, and without the hovel, and is realised largely through aerial perspective. The more open composition suggests far greater isolation, the distant mountains conveying a bleakness in place of the shelter offered by the trees and hovel of the engravings. In consequence, Lear's disturbed state is visualised in terms of a contemporary intellectual landscape of distress, and to the actual storm is added another level that draws Shakespeare's text into a way of seeing and feeling that is part of the mid-century's mindset. This repositioning of the play is also seen in two other aspects of the mezzotint. The use of present-day costume and the posture of Garrick himself both reflect his version of the text, constructed largely from Nahum Tate's adaptation, and this is confirmed by the absence of the Fool, not present on the London stage until Macready's revival of 1838.

Whereas Wilson's painting, so far as may be judged from the mezzotint, moves away from the theatre, Pieter van Bleeck's *Mrs Cibber in the role of Cordelia* (1755)[46] is much more concerned with the actors. This rather uneasily places Cordelia and her maid Arante before a stormy landscape and frames them between the ruffians sent by Edmund to abduct her in Tate's Act 3 Scene 4. Even here, though, the lightning and storm clouds remain, and a key element of the tradition is retained. The convention is continued in one of the earliest paintings of an artist later to emerge as a major figure in the imaging of Shakespeare. George Romney's *Lear in the Tempest tearing off his Robes* (Fig. 20) dates from 1762,[47] and employs many conventional elements. Lear is shown on the heath, in the company of the Fool as well as Edgar, Kent and Gloucester, and the lightning still strikes; but the painting breaks with convention in its very dark setting, relieved by Gloucester's torch. This follows the practice of Hayman and Wilson in uniting Shakespeare's text with contemporary taste: the extreme chiaroscuro, later developed by Joseph Wright, is itself perhaps a dimension of the taste for the Sublime following Burke's study that had appeared five years before. Both paintings show that, as the convention develops, it takes with it accretions of contemporary feeling that move it further away from performance practice and give it a double effect of familiarity for the reader, by recalling both the events and the painterly style of their presentation.

Romney's *Lear* is significant for reasons rather similar to Zoffany's *Macbeth*: its mere existence reveals that painting Shakespeare is now regarded as a valuable

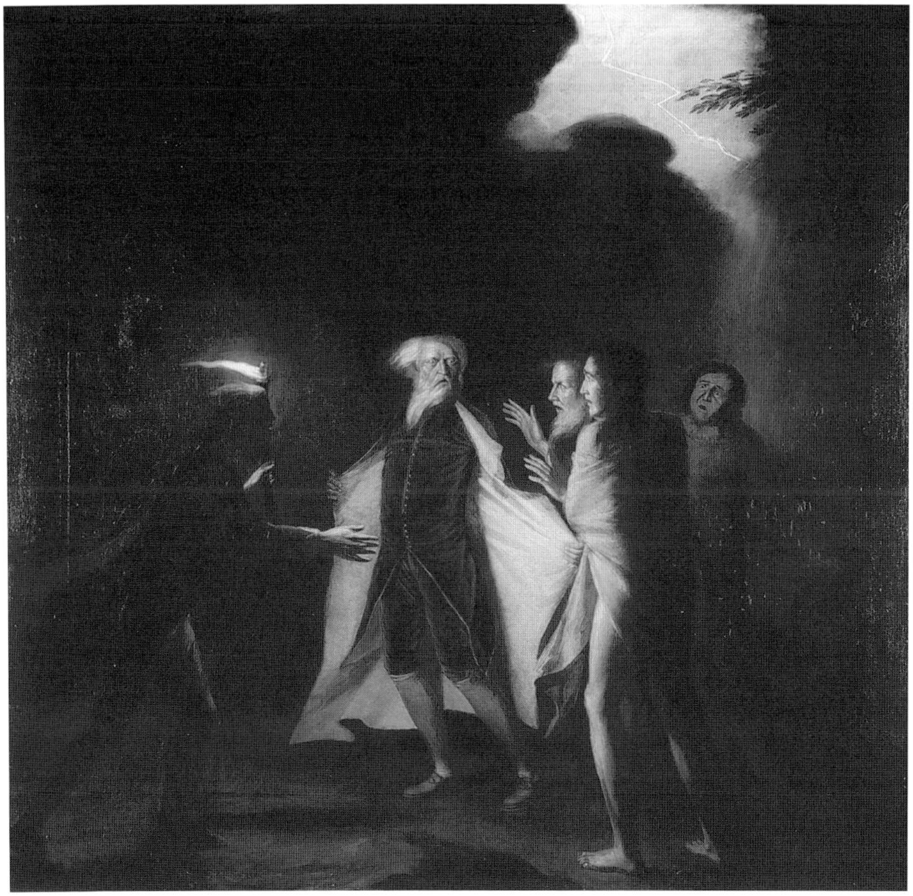

20 George Romney, *Lear in the Tempest tearing off his Robes*, 1762.

branch of history painting, and that an energetic and ambitious young painter should choose such a subject as one of his earliest essays reveals much about its growing prestige. Two other paintings continue the tradition. One is a *Lear* by Reynolds, dating from some time before 1762 (Fig. 21), that again makes use of the flowing hair motif;[48] the other, perhaps existing in two forms, is by William Hodges,[49] and reveals his interest in Shakespearean subjects – or perhaps a shrewd understanding of their fashionable status – before his two paintings for Boydell's Gallery.

Two paintings by the brothers John and Alexander Runciman gain added power through forcefully rejecting the conventional forms used by Romney and Reynolds. Each uses landscape differently, and both are among the earliest images to convey a serious critical reading of Shakespeare's *Lear*. John Runciman's *King Lear in the Storm* (1767: Fig. 22)[50] follows the same procedure as Wootton's *Macbeth*

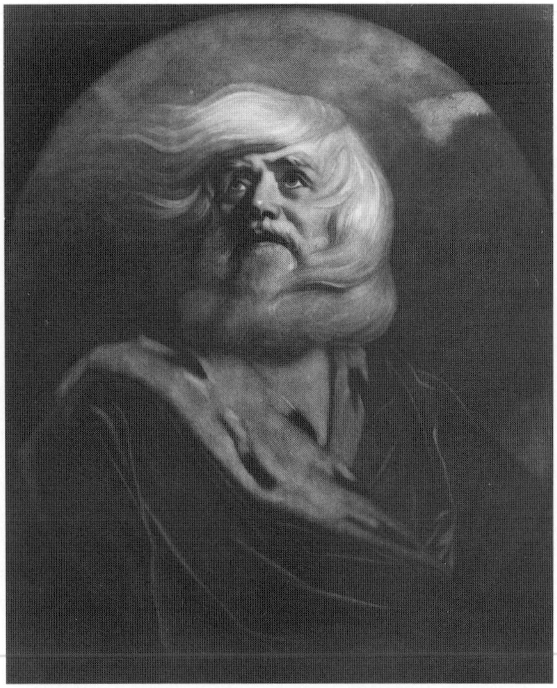

21 Joshua Reynolds, *Lear*, before 1762. Mezzotint by Giuseppe Marchi.

in taking an element of verbal imagery and giving it visual form. The painting places Lear on a heath that abuts a raging sea, a visualisation of the repeated references to the sea as a measure of the violence of the storm, as Moelwyn Merchant was the first to note.[51] Merchant does not add the reference that is probably the most striking: Cordelia's description of the king's being 'As mad as the vexed sea' (4.3.2). Landscape is used here as a way of revealing the linguistic workings of the play in drawing attention to Lear's psychological state, extending the function of the landscape far beyond the fashionable role it has had in conventional versions of the scene. The painting also includes the Fool, betraying its origin in reading, not performance. As Lear puts a protective arm around him, he reveals the compassion shown when he orders him into the hovel – 'In, boy, go first' (3.4.26). This suggests that Lear outfaces the destructive forces of the natural world through his new-found compassion: the effect is simultaneously to prove and disprove that his madness is as great as that of the sea, and a valuable interpretive statement results. As well as offering a powerful textual reading, the painting is unusual at this time in locating Shakespeare painting within an Old Master tradition, since it draws on Rubens for its composition and van Dyck and Rembrandt in the characters'

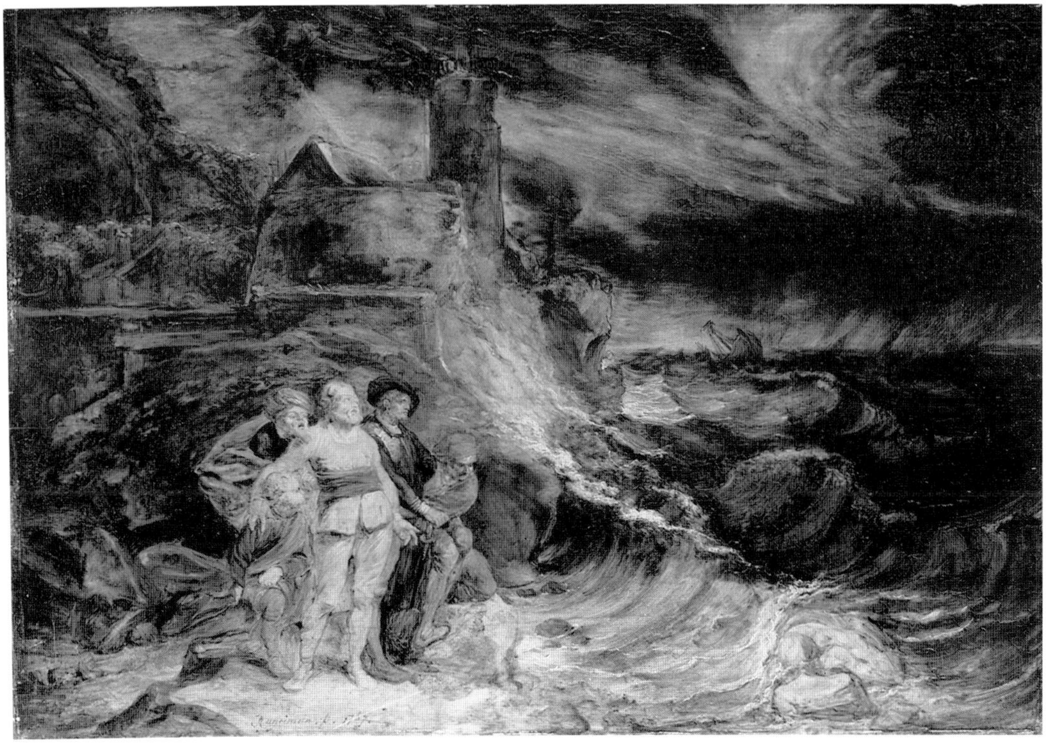

22 John Runciman, *King Lear in the Storm*, 1767.

costumes.[52] The result is to elevate both scene and dramatist to a higher rhetorical and cultural plane.

Alexander Runciman's *King Lear on the Heath* (*c.* 1767: Fig. 23)[53] conveys a quite different reading. Lear is shown in the act of tearing off his cloak, apparently in compassion for 'Poor Tom' and the 'poor naked wretches' (3.4.28) whom he addresses at the core of the scene. Once more, Lear towers before the storm, its turbulence revealing the new-found moral power that lies within his compassionate concern. This is countered by the figure of the Fool who stands, head bowed and arms crossed, a little apart from the central action. That the Fool is depicted semi-naked, with exposed genitals, adds another layer of meaning: this is a 'bare forked animal' (3.4.96) and a cynically distant Fool who sees through the power of Lear's fellow-feeling, unable to accept it as more than mere rhetoric. The lowered viewpoint, accentuating both Lear's size and the disparity between him and the Fool, further emphasises this uncertainty: has Lear genuinely learnt compassion, or is he just as inflated with rhetoric as at the start of the play? Runciman invites us to deliberate this question through an image powerfully ambiguous in its human relations, enhanced in its effect by its refusal

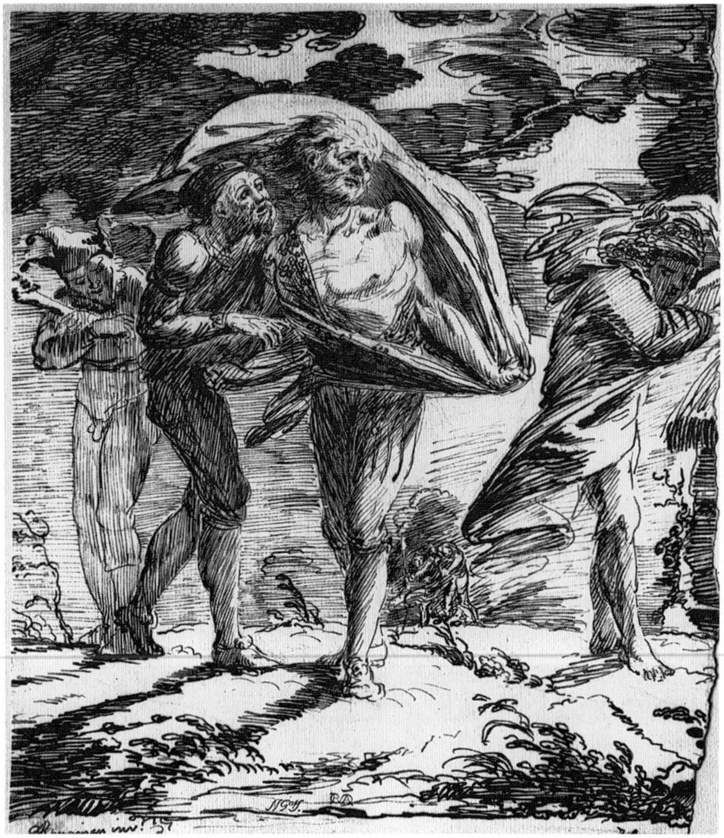

23 Alexander Runciman, *King Lear on the Heath*, c. 1767.

of convention. The two Runciman images make valuable critical interventions in the discussion of the play, and their pairing also foreshadows a major device of later Shakespeare painting: the manipulation of medium and scale for rhetorical effect.

The mid-1770s saw the development of a related convention of the depiction of Lear, both on the heath and in later scenes. It crosses freely over boundaries of medium and scale, being found in drawings, etchings and works on canvas, and culminates in some of the images produced for the Boydell Gallery. One of its earliest forms is found in one of a series of engravings depicting the heads of Shakespeare's characters. Eight years after Dance showed his *Timon* painting at the Society of Artists, John Hamilton Mortimer used the same forum to show his *Twelve Characters from Shakespeare*. That they go beyond the convention of character studies is suggested by the fact that they include a figure headed 'Poet' pausing, quill in hand, in the act of composition, over Theseus' lines on the poetic

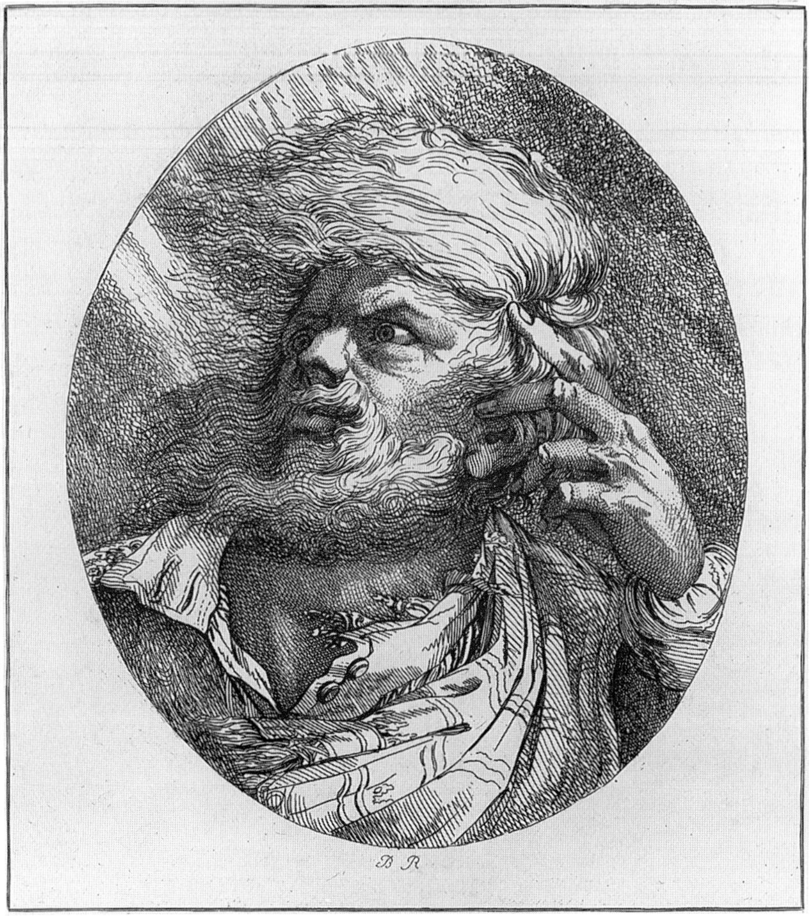

24 John Mortimer, Head of Lear, *Shakespeare Heads*, 1775. Engraving by 'B. R.', 1820.

process beginning 'The poet's eye, in a fine frenzy rolling' (5.1.12) in *A Midsummer Night's Dream*. Mortimer himself produced etchings of the series, published in two sets that year and the next. The head of Lear (1775: Fig. 24)[54] belongs to the second set – the original drawing is now lost – and was published above these lines:

Here I stand your Slave,
A poor infirm, weak and despis'd old man
But yet I call you servile ministers
That have with two pernicious daughters joind
Your high engender'd battles 'gainst a head
So old and white as this, oh! Oh! Tis foul-
King Lear Act III, scene 3^{d}.

The text allows a fairly precise identification of the edition used and hence of the artist's knowledge of the play. In this passage Rowe follows the Folio's 'That will with two pernicious daughters join,' Warburton emends 'Slave' to 'Brave', and Pope has 'O, ho, tis foul'. Apart from the misattribution to the third rather than the second scene, and some slight differences in spelling, Mortimer's text might be taken from either Theobald or Johnson. This preference for an edition aspiring to textual authority as much as validity in the theatre clearly reveals Mortimer's allegiance, and shows the distance travelled from the practices of Hayman and Wilson. That Garrick was involved in support of Mortimer's venture is well known; it is also recorded that George Steevens, whose edition would later form the basis of the Boydell Shakespeare, was one of the subscribers.[55] Indeed, since his edition does not alter the lines from Johnson's 1765 version, it is conceivable, although unsupported, that Steevens' 1773 revision of Johnson was the source of the quotation.

This does not mean that Mortimer's image relies solely on textual study. The dominant element of the image, Lear's wild hair, certainly has its origin in the text, where Lear refers to 'a head/ So old and white as this' (3.2.22–3), but this is made even more explicit in Tate's adaptation, where it becomes 'a head/ So old and white as mine' (III.i.19–20).[56] McArdell's engraving of Garrick in the role is much in accord with contemporary written accounts, which talk of his performance as presenting a 'little, old, white-haired man'[57] who stood on the heath 'with his old grey hair standing, as it were, erect on his head'.[58] There may also be other sources, including the depictions of the emotions by Le Brun, although the resemblance is perhaps more in the effort visually to depict a very specific moment of emotion and intellect: wild hair has no direct relation to any emotion in the schematic catalogues, although it does figure incidentally in Le Brun's depiction of Anger.[59] To these sources should be added the likeness between the head and those of the Old Testament prophets in the Sistine Chapel and Old Master paintings in general, giving Lear the more general resonance of an old man of immense dignity. In Old Master paintings the flowing white beard appears most often in images of prophets and apostles: Rubens alone, for example, uses the figuration in images of Abraham, Joseph, Simeon, Jeremiah, the apostle Paul and Saint Peter. From this it is apparent that the form denotes venerable status, probably as much from the matter of simple human ageing as from iconographic tradition. The same is perhaps true of the disorder of the hair, suggesting a breach of decorum in appearance to mirror psychological or physical disturbance, doubly appropriate in images of Lear suffering the effects of the storm and his mental anguish. The figuration reveals the innate dignity of the character, the extremity of distress, and the essential incongruity of circumstance in which a venerable figure is displaced both in mind and locale.

Probably in conjunction with other similar depictions – both the Runcimans use a similar form – the windswept head became an accepted and recurrent icon, Blake using it as the essential element in *Lear Grasping His Sword*,[60] one of seven Shakespeare miniatures dating from some time before 1785, and in his watercolour *Lear and Cordelia* of about 1780 (see Chapter 6). It also has one more source which, together with the images of John and Alexander Runciman, presented a different scene of the play in a manner that both developed and rejected existing conventions: James Barry's *King Lear Weeping over the Body of Cordelia*, shown at the Royal Academy in 1774.[61] This is the first of a series of images by Barry which are the culmination of the two traditions of visualising Lear, combining the icon of the head with more detailed readings of the play that incorporate and transcend the tradition of heath paintings. Barry's work is of consequence because of the diversity of its forms, itself an index of the stature that Shakespeare imaging has now assumed: all five images use the same basic compositional elements, to show Lear carrying the dead Cordelia. The etchings of 1776[62] and 1790[63] and the pen lithograph of *c.*1803,[64] which abstracts from the earlier compositions only the head of Lear, placing it against a setting of roughly sketched rocks, all share the central figure, with hair blown wildly astray by the wind, and one hand raised to his forehead. The element also forms the central trope of the vast painting completed for the Boydell Gallery in 1786–7 (Fig. 25)[65] and subsequently engraved by Francis Legat,[66] although here it is placed within the historicist incarnation of the Grand Style. Like Dance's *Timon* painting, Barry's composition follows many of Reynolds' practical rules but adds an imitation of Old Master tradition in using the trope of the deposition, taken directly from Annibale Carracci's *The Dead Christ Mourned*.[67] In this system of references the image generates a powerful critical statement about the play, elevating Lear's grief to that of the classical ideal of the suffering father and intensifying Cordelia's death by the parallel with the crucifixion while simultaneously denying the power of the resurrection, and forcing us to experience immediately the unnaturalness of the death of the child before the parent in a human, not a divine, frame. Here iconographic allusion makes an essential contribution to the operation of the image as critical reading, ennobling the events and increasing their emotional power rather than, as with Hogarth's use of the technique, ironically undermining them.

Much of the Boydell painting's force derives from its sheer scale. As has been noted,[68] it presents an epic parallel to the grandeur of Shakespeare's verse and the setting with its triliths suggests a massive inviolability in ancient Britain to

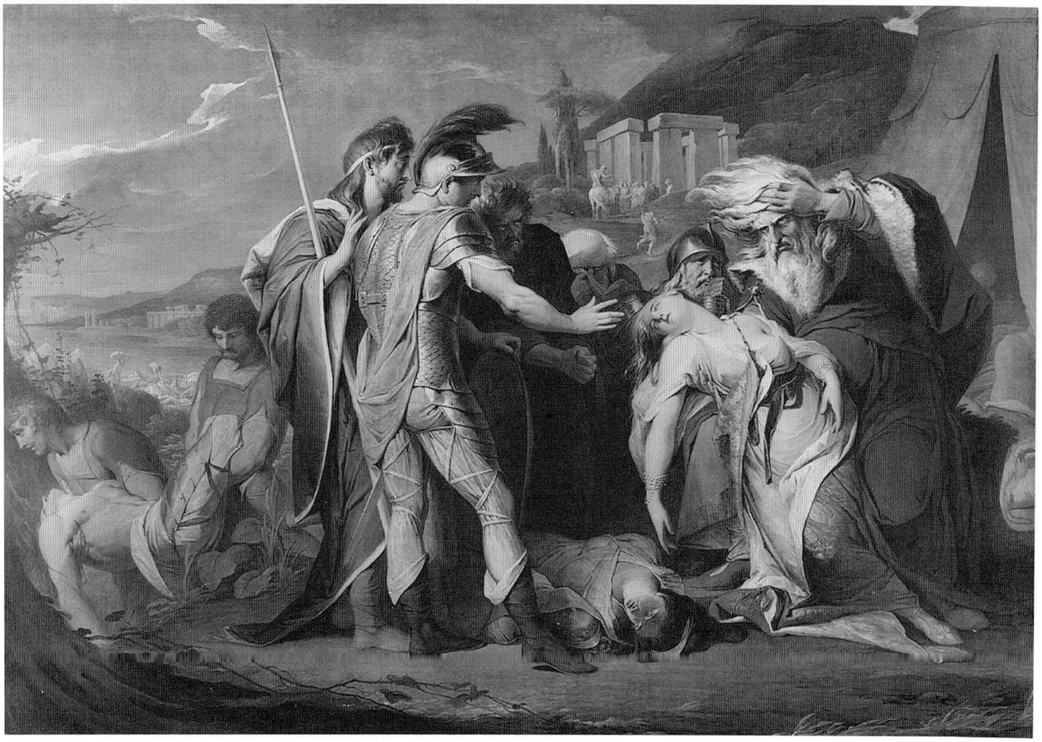

25 James Barry, *King Lear Weeping over the Body of Cordelia*, 1786–7.

parallel that of classical civilisation.[69] This anticipates Malone's addition of the stage direction 'The British Camp near Dover' at the beginning of 5.3, tightening the link between historical and literary painting and, in locating the scene within a specific temporal plane, simultaneously revealing a contemporary concern for national identity and asserting as a part of that identity the universal heroic values of Shakespeare. Local and ideal, human and universal combine to offer a reading quite in accord with aristocratic principles of taste and ideology; and, of course, it is Shakespeare's play that is being presented, not Tate's, and in this Barry reveals once more the disparity between theatre practice and reading practice at the end of the century.

The tradition of character depiction in the head of Lear during the 1770s evidences the growth of interest in character studies as an aspect of Shakespeare criticism in imaging, as much as in the growing production of critical writing of the time: as John Sunderland indicates,[70] Mortimer's *Heads* not only include carefully selected quotations in their engraved form, but they also present details of these speeches in visual terms, showing a textual focus absent from many character depictions, such as those of Robert Edge Pine. This will assume major proportions when the tradition is combined with historical painting at the close of the century, and the rhetorical paintings of Barry and West are issued as part of the Boydell collection. But by the end of the 1770s enough had been done to establish a tradition of visualising Lear on the heath to facilitate the recognition of the trope, and to establish the face and head as a recognisable, self-defining icon of the character and his sufferings. The images of the Runciman brothers skilfully deposed the first of these conventions to produce critical visualisations of the play; in the hands of Barry and West, the icon of the head of Lear would become a major component of some of the most forceful paintings of the last quarter of the century. The head of Lear is also significant in a larger dimension: it is the first and most insistent recurrent iconographic element in Shakespeare illustration, with all the critical and cultural resonances that this role brings with it in the coming of age of Shakespeare imaging.

V

The two currents of Shakespeare visualisation charted in this chapter show its growing strength as a cultural form through the middle years of the century in different, but related, directions. The first reveals its significance in contributing to a series of social dialogues, both national and international; the second, its growth in establishing an iconographical tradition that assigns common ground between artists and readers. The intensity of critical reading in individual images within these imperatives is variable; the greater concern is the search for idioms that itself reveals the depth and range of Shakespeare activity in the mid-century. At its most sophisticated this can itself be the source of critical comment, as the ironic use of a Neo-Classical history style in Dance's *Timon* painting well shows. The location of action, whether or not representing in some degree recognisable stage performances, within landscapes or interiors of various kinds, at first facilitates a dialogue between the period of the play and that of its later onlookers; but in its more complex manifestations it becomes a critical act in itself by suggesting directions of mood or idea, in a manner familiar to much later onlookers conditioned to the use of carefully considered anachronistic settings in the theatre. The growth of conventions both evidences and extends the influence of Shakespeare imaging, educating the paintings' readers and so building a common ground in representation that, in turn, facilitates incisive critical judgments when tradition is sharply displaced.

In terms of the adaptation of the plays from the temporal sequence of the stage and reading experience to the spatial order of painting, the selection of the moment for depiction remains the principle on which hangs not only an individual painting's structure, but also its critical intensity. Important though this is in the work of Hayman and others, the major development comes when paintings move beyond the visualisation of a single scene to adopt visual equivalences for themes or images throughout the play. It is in this development that John Wootton's painting of *Macbeth* is so outstanding: Hogarth apart, it is the first painting successfully to undertake this act of mediation, showing the moral darkening of the play and the ultimate collapse of Macbeth as contingent directly upon the initial meeting with the witches. That it presents this critical enactment in an idiom within the mainstream of contemporary landscape painting further reveals its power. Less well known than the treatment of the same events by Zuccarelli, it is ultimately more significant because it visualises the play more extensively, and in a style that is arguably more accessible to the majority of its contemporary readers than the allegorical form of the later painting.

At the same time, in its deliberative and ironic use of the Choice of Hercules trope, Wootton's canvas furthers the habit of constructing paintings and drawings through reference to conventions, facilitating the importing of images that are apparently of no immediate relevance for the purpose of critical commentary and textual reinvention. This is related to the quotation of elements from other conventions, in the use of iconographic allusion for critical purposes in the manner of the reference to the traditional trope of the deposition of Christ used by Barry to show Lear and Cordelia. As the activity of painting the plays becomes more firmly established, drawn into the accelerating currents of historical and literary painting and the idealisation of Shakespeare as the English spirit, the manipulation of conventional iconography reveals itself as one of the major methods by which interpretation and criticism is constructed. It is a practice not without uncertainty or controversy; but it is one on which many of the most resonant Shakespeare paintings erect complex and supple critical fabrics.

NOTES

1. *The picturesque beauties of Shakespeare, being a selection of scenes, from the works of that great author.* The series was issued by Isaac Taylor the younger.
2. *The heroines of Shakespeare; comprising the principal female characters in the plays of the great poet. Engraved in the highest style of art, from drawings by eminent artists* (London and New York: London Printing and Publishing Company, n.d. [1883]).
3. Sir Thomas Hanmer, ed. *The Works of Shakespear. In six volumes. Carefully revised and corrected by the former editors, and adorned with sculptures deigned and executed by the best hands* (Oxford: Printed at the Theatre, 1744). Hanmer's instructions as to scene and treatment are published by Marcia Allentuck in 'Sir Thomas Hanmer instructs Francis Hayman: an Editor's Notes to

his Illustrator (1744)', *Shakespeare Quarterly* 27 (1976), pp. 288–315. Reprinted in *Shakespeare and the Arts*, ed. Stephen Orgel and Sean Keilen (New York and London: Garland Publishing, 1999), pp. 290–318.

4. [John Lockman?]. *A Sketch of the Spring-Gardens Vauxhall. In a letter to a noble lord* (London: G. Woodfall, n.d. [1751?]), p. 27.
5. The images, their iconography and other levels of meaning are explored in T. J. Edelstein, *Vauxhall Gardens* (New Haven: Yale Center for British Art, 1983), pp. 25–35.
6. Brian Allen, 'Jonathan Tyers's Other Garden'. *Journal of Garden History*, 1.3 (1981), pp. 215–38.
7. *Painting for Money: The Visual Arts and the Public Sphere in Eighteenth-century England* (New Haven and London: Yale University Press, 1992), p. 120.
8. 52.7 × 92 (20 3/4 × 36 1/4), Tate Britain. For a full account of the place of the painting within the project see Brian Allen, *Francis Hayman* exh. cat. (London and New Haven: Yale University Press, 1987), pp. 15–17.
9. *A Description of Vauxhall Gardens. Being a proper companion and guide for all who visit that place* (London: S. Hooper, 1762), p. 37.
10. The complex history of attributions and analyses of this image may be traced in the following: Lawrence Gowing, 'Hogarth, Hayman and the Vauxhall Decorations', *Burlington Magazine*, XCV, (1953), pp. 4–19; W. Moelwyn Merchant, *Shakespeare and the Artist*, p. 45 and '"A Midsummer Night's Dream": A Visual Re-creation', *Early Shakespeare* ed. J. Russell Brown and B. Harris, Stratford-upon-Avon Studies 3 (London: Edward Arnold, 1961), pp. 165–86; Ronald Paulson, 'Hogarth the Painter', *Burlington Magazine*, CXIV (1972), pp. 71–9; Robin Simon, 'Hogarth's Shakespeare', *Apollo*, CIX (1979), pp. 213–20; Alastair Smart, 'Hogarth or Hayman', *Apollo*, CIX (1979), pp. 208–12.
11. Collection of the late Sir Ellis Waterhouse. The image is discussed by Karen Newman in 'Hayman's missing Hamlet', *Shakespeare Quarterly* 34.1 (Spring 1983), pp. 73–8.
12. 34.8 × 29.6 (13 3/4 × 11 5/8), Folger Shakespeare Library, Washington D.C.
13. 137 × 241 (54 × 95), Tate Britain.
14. The drawings themselves are bound in an edition of Hanmer's *Works of Shakespear* in the Folger Shakespeare Library, PR 2752 1744 copy 2 Sh Col.
15. The fourth line has 'glazes' instead of 'gaze', presumably an error of copying or memory.
16. One was a version by John Mawer in *Oppian's Cynergeticks. Translated into English Verse* (York: Thomas Gent, 1736). The other, that quoted in the description, is unidentified.
17. 126.4 × 116 (49 1/2 × 45 5/8), Folger Shakespeare Library, Washington D.C.
18. 138.75 × 184.15 (54 5/8 × 72 1/2), Yale Center for British Art, Paul Mellon Fund, New Haven, Conn.
19. David Garrick, *Romeo and Juliet by Shakespeare with Alterations and an additional scene* (London: J. and R. Tonson and S. Draper, 1750). Stage direction to V. v., p. 65.
20. For example, Kalman Burnim in *David Garrick: Director*, p. 137 and Desmond Shawe-Taylor, *Shakespeare in Art*, p. 124.
21. *David Garrick*, p. 137
22. Tagebuch, October 23 1753. Quoted in John Alexander Kelly, *German Visitors to English Theaters in the Eighteenth Century* (Princeton: Princeton University Press, 1936), p. 25.

23. 99.8 × 124.8 ($39\frac{1}{4}$ × $49\frac{1}{8}$), City Art Gallery, Manchester.
24. 102 × 127.5 ($40\frac{1}{8}$ × $50\frac{1}{4}$), Garrick Club, London; another version, Baroda Museum, India.
25. *The Authentic Shakespeare*, p. 249.
26. 123.2 × 137.2 ($48\frac{1}{2}$ × 54), Her Majesty the Queen.
27. 50.4 × 57.6 (21 × 24).
28. Untraced; engraved by Robert Thew, 29 September 1799, 49.5 × 63 ($19\frac{1}{2}$ × $24\frac{7}{8}$).
29. *Catalogue raisonné d'un receuil d'estampes d'apres [sic] les plus beaux tableaux qui soient en Angleterre. Les planches sont dans la possession de Jean Boydell, et ont été gravées par lui, & les meilleurs artistes de Londres* (A Londres: Chez le Proprietaire [sic], Graveur, & Marchand d'Estampes, Cheapside, 1779).
30. Oil on panel, 81.7 × 142.5 ($31\frac{9}{16}$ × $56\frac{1}{4}$), Folger Shakespeare Library, Washington D.C.
31. The auction records are reproduced in Ian Jenkins and Kim Sloan. *Vases and Volcanoes: Sir William Hamilton and his Collection* (London: British Museum, 1996), p. 79.
32. 68.6 × 91.4 (27 × 36), Royal Shakespeare Company Collection, Stratford-on-Avon.
33. Published 20 December 1770.
34. Works by all of these were included in the same auction, the catalogue of which describes them as coming from 'a Well-known and approved Collection'. See *Vases and Volcanoes*, p. 79.
35. *A Catalogue of Paintings in the Folger Shakespeare Library: 'As Imagination Bodies Forth'* (New Haven and London: Yale University Press, 1993), pp. 172–3.
36. 1653–4, 137 × 185.2 (54 × 73), National Gallery, London.
37. 1651, 99 × 32 (39 × $12\frac{5}{8}$), Musée des beaux-arts, Rouen.
38. *Nicholas Poussin's Landscape Allegories* (Cambridge: Cambridge University Press, 1996).
39. Ibid., p. 50.
40. Ibid., pp. 51–2.
41. *Shakespeare and the Artist*, pp. 86–7 and Plate 36a.
42. 'Shakespeare and the Ends of Time', p. 31.
43. 41.27 × 39 ($16\frac{1}{4}$ × $15\frac{3}{8}$), British Museum, London.
44. *Works*, V, pp. 2509 and 2513.
45. James Ogden, 'Lear's Blasted Heath', in *Lear from Study to Stage: Essays in Criticism*, ed. James Ogden and Arthur Scouten (London: Associated University Presses and Madison, Wis.: Fairleigh Dickinson University Press, 1997), pp. 135–145.
46. 210 × 205 ($82\frac{3}{4}$ × $80\frac{3}{4}$), Yale Center for British Art, Paul Mellon Fund, New Haven, Conn.
47. 106 × 104 ($41\frac{3}{4}$ × 41), Abbot Hall Art Gallery, Kendal Town Council.
48. 75 × 62.5 ($29\frac{1}{2}$ × 25), Private Collection. As well as being reproduced in mezzotint by Giuseppe Marchi, it was engraved by William Sharpe in 1780.
49. See Isabel C. Struebe, *The Life and Works of William Hodges*, PhD dissertation, New York University 1978 (New York: Garland, 1979), pp. 340–1.
50. Oil on panel, 44.4 × 61($17\frac{1}{2}$ × 24), National Galleries of Scotland, Edinburgh.
51. *Shakespeare and the Artist*, pp. 190–6.
52. Maria Grazia Messina stresses this debt in *Shakespeare in Art*, p. 66.
53. Pen and ink on paper, 11 × $19\frac{1}{4}$, National Galleries of Scotland, Edinburgh.
54. Etching, 1776, 40.4 × 32.6 (16 × $12\frac{13}{16}$).

55. Steevens wrote to Garrick in June 1775 asking if the prints were ready. See John Sunderland, *John Hamilton Mortimer: His Life and Works* (London: Walpole Society, 1988), pp. 76–9.
56. Nahum Tate, *The History of King Lear*, ed. James Black (London: Edward Arnold, 1975). Future references are to this edition.
57. John Hill, *The Actor: A Treatise on the Art of Playing*. 2nd edn, revised (London: R. Griffiths, 1755), p. 151.
58. Thomas Davies, *Dramatic Miscellanies* (London: T. Davies, 1784), II, p. 280.
59. *A Method to Learn to Design the Passions*, p. 45.
60. Water-colour, oval, 9 × 11.7 (3 × 3 1/4), Museum of Fine Arts, Boston.
61. 101.5 × 128 (40 × 50 1/2), Kathleen, Countess Plunkett.
62. *King Lear and Cordelia*, etching and aquatint in dark brown ink, 55.3 × 55.1 (21 3/4 × 21 11/16), Yale Center for British Art, Paul Mellon Fund, New Haven, Conn.
63. *King Lear and Cordelia*, c. 1790; etching with engraving in black ink, 51 × 55.4 (20 1/8 × 21 13/16), Museum of Art, Rhode Island School of Design (Mary B. Jackson Fund), Providence, R.I.
64. Pen lithograph, black ink, 23.5 × 32.2 (9 1/4 × 12 11/16).
65. 269 × 367 (106 × 144 1/2), Tate Britain, London.
66. Published 1 August, 1792, 49.5 × 62.5 (19 1/2 × 24 5/8).
67. Full title *The Dead Christ Mourned (The Three Maries)*, c. 1604; 92.8 × 103.2 (36 1/2 × 40 5/8), National Gallery, London.
68. Ronald Paulson, in *Book and Painting: Shakespeare, Milton and the Bible: Literary Texts and the Emergence of English Painting*, The Hodges Lectures (Knoxville: University of Tennessee Press, 1982), p. 26.
69. It is interesting that in this it shares the link that is often asserted between the classical acting style of John Philip Kemble and the Grand Style advocated by Reynolds. See West, *Image of the Actor*, p. 81.
70. John Sunderland, *John Hamilton Mortimer: His Life and Works* (London: Walpole Society, L II, 1988), pp. 79–80.

CHAPTER 4

FUSELI AND THE USES OF ICONOGRAPHY

I

Henry Fuseli is probably the most important Shakespeare painter of the last quarter of the century. To his nine canvases for Boydell must be added the wash-drawings of the 1770s; some designs for Shakespeare frescoes; paintings for Woodmason's Irish Shakespeare Gallery and Macklin's *British Poets*; a large number of individual canvases and watercolours; and innumerable sketches and designs, many of which were used in illustrated editions such as the Rivington Shakespeare edited by A. C. Chalmers. At its finest, his work combines a deep knowledge of Shakespeare's texts, a thorough understanding of the structures and devices of Renaissance art, and an imaginative and intellectual percipience that sprawls across almost every aspect of Neo-Classical and Romantic invention to produce innovative and forceful critical readings of the plays. The energy and visual immediacy of Fuseli's paintings, their depth of textual understanding and response, and their self-defined placement within the tradition of Renaissance iconography, coupled with a very specific stylistic redefinition of anatomy and the natural world, distinguish his output in approach and quality from that of almost all his contemporaries.

Studying theology with Johann Jakob Bodmer in Zurich, Fuseli was introduced to Homer, the *Nibelungenlied*, Dante and Milton, all of which he read in their original languages. In 1761 he was ordained into the Zwinglian ministry, but the following year had to leave Zurich after publishing a pamphlet criticising a corrupt local official. In Germany he collaborated with Johann Georg Sulzer on his *Allgemeine Theorie der Schönen Kunst*, writing among other articles an account of the Sublime, based on the work of Longinus and the ideas of Bodmer. Moving to London in the

1760s he began to visit the theatre and became friendly with Garrick: from this period date his first Shakespeare paintings, his English version of Winckelmann's *Reflections on the Paintings and Sculptures of the Greeks*, and his pamphlet on Rousseau. At Reynolds' urging he went to Italy in 1770 and developed a passionate respect for classical and Renaissance models. Returning to London in 1778 he began to make a name for himself with literary painting, especially after *The Nightmare* (1781). He became a friend of Blake, whom he asserted was 'd****d good to steal from';[1] he published his *Aphorisms on Man* (1788), was involved in the preparation of Lavater's *Physionomische Fragmente*, worked on an unfinished 'History of Art in the Schools of Italy',[2] and wrote for the *Analytical Review* and other periodicals. Fuseli was elected R.A. in 1790 and became Professor of Painting in 1801, giving some of the earliest and most influential lectures in English on Renaissance and more recent art, where his 'great learning' and 'vast mental resources' made him 'the idol of the students'.[3] Over the turn of the century he produced his Boydell paintings and many other images of Shakespeare's plays and other literary subjects. He died in 1825.

These biographical details reveal a combination of forces driving his work: a concern for classical values, an extensive knowledge of Renaissance paintings and their iconography, a close study of literary and linguistic forms and a deep and polemical concern for political issues. The artists of the Renaissance, especially Michelangelo, were for him unsurpassed, but he also found their heroic universality in the writings of Homer and Shakespeare. The exchange between the verbal and visual stands at the core of his work, whether in a serious play with macaronic visual puns or in a fascination with the statement of moral narratives in graphic form. Painting is matched by translation, his own writing, and an art historical awareness that informs all his work, most particularly in the construction of composition and meaning through iconographical allusion. This Renaissance temper is overlain by a Romantic sense of the Sublime, in which vastness of spirit is all. The combination makes him a unique figure in Shakespeare painting, producing images relating language, art history and art practice to a knowledge of the text informed by literary and philological awareness.

Fuseli's interest in literature was broad, resting on deep knowledge of Greek and Roman texts. His paintings and drawings include subjects from Virgil, Homer, Ovid, Plutarch, Aeschylus and scenes from Greek mythology; northern legends such as the *Edda* and the *Nibelungenlied*; and scenes from Dante and Milton, with some treatments of Chaucer and Spenser. His reading recent and contemporary writers produced images from *The Rape of the Lock*, *The Task* and the writings of Scott and Wieland. Within this complex of scholarship Shakespeare has a central place. Despite this, the artist shares the common contemporary view that the plays must be admired despite their irregularities. One of the *Aphorisms* reveals this, using an image from nature that immediately equates Shakespeare with the ancients while verbalising his taste for extreme chiaroscuro: 'Shakespeare is to Sophocles what the incessant flashes of a tempestuous night are to daylight.'[4] John Knowles records that even in his youth he was 'enamoured of the plays of Shakespeare, and attempted a translation of *Macbeth* into German' (I.13). No other record exists of this, and the text has not survived, perhaps being lost in the fire of 1769 which also destroyed his manuscript *History of German Poetry*. Knowles gives no date for the translation, but the implication is that it was begun while Fuseli was a student, probably placing it in the late 1750s. Wieland's translation of *Romeo and Juliet* dates from 1765, and Goethe's influential speech on Shakespeare was not given until 1771;[5] Schlegel began his project of translating all the plays in 1797, and Schiller's *Macbeth* appeared in 1800. Had Fuseli's work been published, it would have been the first German version of the play. The choice of play is revealing, reflecting again Fuseli's concern for historic and supernatural frames for the heroic, a placement that again demonstrates his relation of classical and Romantic concerns.

The artist's interest in the plays extended beyond reading into performance. From his first visit to London he was a frequent theatre-goer, seeing Garrick as Richard III and Macbeth and recording his performance in a handful of early paintings. Later, when London was his permanent home, his letters are peppered with references to the theatre. In 1814 he invites the merchant and print-collector Robert Balmanno to 'the Usual Box' to see *Othello* at 'Drury';[6] later, he asserts that 'Mrs Pritchard was the allowed Lady Macbeth of her day.'[7] Mary Balmanno records in her memoir that 'Fuseli was very fond of theatrical representations',[8] but apart from the references in the letters he wrote no extended critical statement on the theatre as an interpretive medium, confirming what is clear from the paintings: after an initial engagement with stage-painting, Fuseli's main visual source was the close imaginative reading of the texts themselves.

That he read Shakespeare in Johnson's edition is suggested by a footnote in his *Remarks on Rousseau* of 1767:

> When Shakespeare, to lesson mankind, afflicts innocence and virtue, nor, in the latitude of the ravings, crimes, follies he exposes, can find any reward this side the grave for them; when, to warn fathers against the dotage of predilection, the fury of prejudice and the destructive consequences of flattery, he destroys the family of Lear, and wraps Cordelia in the storm, one gentle feeler changes her dagger to a husband, and adulterates the simplicity of filial piety with love, and another could not for all the world read the play a second time, till he turned commentator.[9]

Fuseli's tone here suggests the intense immediacy of his experience of Shakespeare's text; his passion is consistent throughout, aroused as much by those who seek to adulterate the text as by the force of the play itself. The rejection of adaptations in favour of the restored versions is implicit in the final clause. This refers to Johnson's remark 'I know not whether I ever endured to read again the last scenes of the play till I undertook to revise them as an editor,'[10] that appeared only in his afterword to the play. Coupled with the detailed knowledge constantly apparent in his paintings, this suggests very strongly that at this time Fuseli used Johnson's edition. Later, in August 1794, under his usual pseudonym of 'Z.Z', Fuseli wrote a review of Steevens' edition for the *Analytical Review*,[11] concentrating on issues of textual editing that again reveal his close familiarity with the texts: this edition was presumably the basis of his subsequent readings. References in the letters are less certain. One of 27 September 1805[12] uses the phrase 'dusky death' in quoting from *Macbeth* (5.5.22), the reading Johnson preferred to the now more common 'dusty death'; but as Theobald, Hanmer and Warburton made the same choice this is not conclusive. It does, though, make clear that he did not remember the quotation from Rowe or Pope, who followed the First Folio and adopted the other usage. Tantalisingly, a letter of 25 December 1795[13] thanks George Steevens for 'His magnificent present, almost "privatis majore focis"': could this be Steevens' own edition?

Fuseli's knowledge of Shakespeare's texts was enriched by a reasoned, if conventional, awareness of the innate difference between verbal and visual structures. A discussion of the theories of Simonides and Plutarch concludes:

> *Successive action* communicated by sounds, and *time*, are the medium of poetry; *form* displayed in *space*, and momentaneous energy, are the elements of painting.[14]

From this he constructs a means of translating verbal continuum into visual immediacy:

> The middle moment, the moment of suspense, the crisis, is the moment of importance, big with the past and pregnant with the future.[15]

Both these concepts begin with the ideas of Shaftesbury, but Fuseli takes them much further. For him, the key term is 'invention', the subject of two of his twelve Academy lectures.[16] It denotes the unity of interpretive idea and painterly composition that results from the selection of a generative moment of the action, a central principle of the language, or a bringing together of aspects held temporally separate in the diachronic movement of the text. The 'invention' thus becomes a visual and conceptual armature that subsumes past and future events and motivations to present a central textual principle. The concentration with which Fuseli unites moment and totality in this single interpretive composite, and the way that it is enabled and informed by his acute literary sense, produces visual readings of great subtlety.

Fuseli's extensive study of Renaissance art brings another feature to his paintings: the use of iconographical reference not simply to follow a convention of depiction but to generate meaning through the equation between an element's signification in its original context and that which it conveys in its new setting. Paradoxically, in some of Fuseli's work the practice is developed so far that it endangers meaning: often, references to obscure sources, or to several distinct and disparate ones in the same image, make decoding arduous if not impossible for most onlookers. At its most inventively eclectic, Fuseli's allusive vocabulary can embrace classical sculpture and Renaissance painting, so-called Etruscan vase paintings, and the work of his contemporaries in Rome. It is used to locate the plays within a large cultural span, in Fuseli's personal version of the universalising impulse of Neo-Classicism, but also to produce innovative critical interpretations.

The radical exploration of textual ideas through an idiosyncratic use of iconographic reference is at its most extreme in Fuseli's earlier images. Later work, including many of the images for Boydell and the less successful Irish Shakespeare Gallery, shows a concern to make Shakespearean imagery accessible, although not always with success in popular or commercial terms. Fuseli's most successful solution to this dilemma occurs in paintings of the supernatural that employ complex and arcane references in a manner immediately compelling through their exoticism and emotional extremity. The critical effects of this approach will be the subject of Chapter 8: some of the more significant earlier images are explored in the pages that follow. They fall into three groups: the wash-drawings made during his Italian tour from 1771 to the mid-1780s; a series of designs for Shakespeare frescoes; and some paintings from the 1780s that, produced for public display and reproduction, move towards a more accessible style and referential vocabulary.

II

Although Fuseli had a strong interest in the theatre, paintings of performances do not feature prominently in his output. His earliest Shakespeare image, *Garrick as the Duke of Gloucester* (1766),[17] is crowded and confused, conveying neither performance nor intellectual commentary and instead, as Stephen Orgel memorably notes, presents Richard as 'the traditional snarling machiavel'.[18] Two later images of Garrick and Mrs Pritchard, discussed in Chapter 8, make their effect

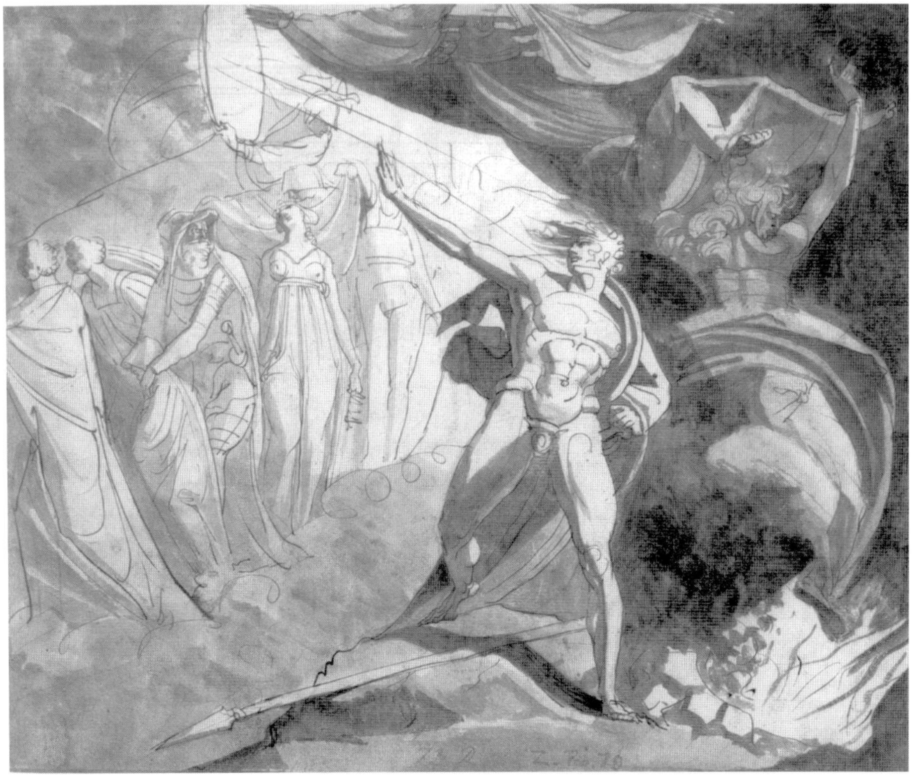

26 Henry Fuseli, *The Witches show Macbeth Banquo's Descendants*, 1773–9.

by straining against theatric mimesis to present a more purely imagined vision. By contrast, the watercolour wash-drawings that he produced at a far distance from the London theatre present several of the plays with a compositional concentration that offers original and provocative readings. Those treating *Macbeth* and *Hamlet* are the most striking.

The Witches show Macbeth Banquo's Descendants (1773–9: Fig. 26)[19] uses a figure that Fuseli employs repeatedly as an image of classical heroism, compounded of the *Dioscuros* Horse Tamer from the Monte Quirinale in Rome and the classical sculpture known as the Borghese Gladiator. Fuseli sketched the first of these several times in his stay in Italy (see Fig. 27), but the second is more revealing about his approach to classical antiquity and its relation to more recent themes. Cast in bronze for Charles I, the figure was much reproduced and used as a model for students, as shown in Joseph Wright's *Three Persons Viewing the Gladiator by Candle-light* (see Fig. 5). But whereas Wright uses the figure in an essentially static contemplation of the nature of antiquity that allows him to explore extreme effects of light, Fuseli uses it to invigorate moments of heroic struggle. In one of his

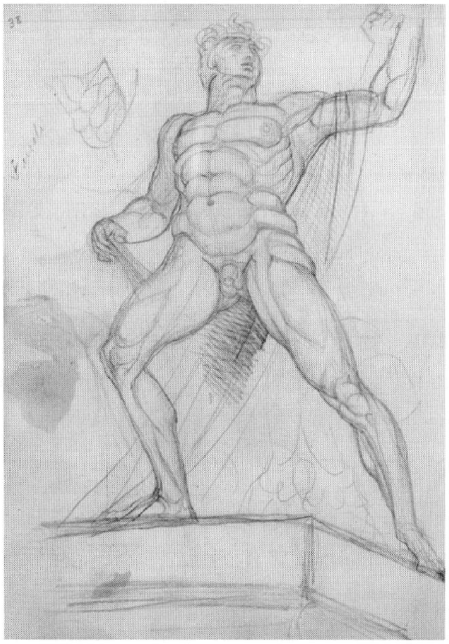

27 Henry Fuseli, Sketch after the Quirinale Horse Tamer, 1770–8.

Academy lectures he spoke of the figure in terms that rest on a full understanding of the mingled tone of the current idea of Aristotelian tragedy: it is 'a figure whose tremendous energy embodies every element of motion, whilst its pathetic dignity of character enforces sympathies'.[20] It is this quality that is embodied in Fuseli's first reference to the figure, in *Brutus throwing himself against his own sword held by Strato*[21] (1780–5). This shows Brutus running against the sword held by the seated Strato in simple visualisation of classical heroism in Mark Antony's line 'This was the noblest Roman of them all' (*Julius Caesar* 5.5.67).

In the *Macbeth* image, the gladiator figure is used to model an heroic protagonist who dominates the composition, cloak blown wildly around his nude body by the violent forces of nature that balance and re-present his own energy and power, the outstretched arm providing a link to the show of spirits. The strong light of the group is countered by the darkness of another gathering of witches behind him, the top one of which uses another form that will recur in the artist's work and is most fully developed in *Samuel appearing to Saul, before The Witch of Endor* (1777).[22] In the Book of Samuel, Saul consults the sorceress the night before the battle of Gilboa in which he is killed; the use of the figure in the *Macbeth* drawing adds a Biblical prophecy of death to those made by the witches, deepening the moral intensity of the scene. One of the figures in the show of descendants is female, clad in the fashionable *empire* style that presents the body almost naked.

This figure will reappear throughout Fuseli's work to suggest sexual predation in a variety of guises: here, it implies that Macbeth is drawn to the witches by their sexuality, in an early exploration of the relationship that would form part of the critical and performance tradition more than a century after Fuseli's image.

These three elements, all of which will appear frequently in Fuseli's later Shakespeare paintings, together convey a reading of the text striking in its breadth. The central witch reveals moral retribution at a Biblical level; the eroticised witch provides a metaphor of the power of the uncanny over Macbeth; and the gladiator, especially when read in conjunction with the artist's description, reveals the mingled heroism and frailty of the play's central character. Together with the extreme chiaroscuro, which places the events in the emotional frame of early Romantic *Sturm und Drang*, these elements offer a powerful visualisation of the play that goes beyond a moment of action to suggest its larger moral progress, and reveals not only the workings of Fuseli's iconographic method but some of the key elements that it repeatedly employs.

Stephen Orgel has discussed the use of classical formal allusions, and their interpretive effect, in another early wash-drawing, *Macbeth and Lady Macbeth* (1774),[23] and similar effects may be seen in other images from that play; but the eclectic referential vocabulary of these early sketches is shown with greatest effect in the treatments of *Hamlet*. *Hamlet, King of Denmark, poisoned by his brother Claudius while sleeping in the garden* (1771: Plate 5)[24] is one of the earliest examples of an approach later common in Shakespeare painting, the presentation of a passage reported rather than presented on stage – although, of course, the event is mimed by the players in Act 2. Apparently a literal reading of the king's death, the drawing is qualified and enlarged by its compositional basis in an Etruscan vase decoration generally known as *Pederastic scene with spectators* (see Fig. 28).[25] This shows an adolescent about to climb onto the lap of a tumescent male while the two are observed by a man standing before them and a woman half concealed within an architectural form. Fuseli's drawing transforms this: the adolescent becomes Claudius leaning up to pour poison into Old Hamlet's ear, the classical column is replaced by a tree, and instead of the two observers there is only Gertrude, who sits head in hand at a window at the extreme right. The uneasy sexual current, with Claudius seemingly about to climb on to Old Hamlet's lap, is implicit even without a knowledge of the source: once it becomes known, the scene becomes a darker and more extensive construal of the play. In a discussion of the images that focuses largely on early Romantic reinventions of antiquity, Jonah Siegel comments that Fuseli has 'allowed his model to bleed through the surface of his subject',[26] but the significance of the relationship is far greater when considered within the frame

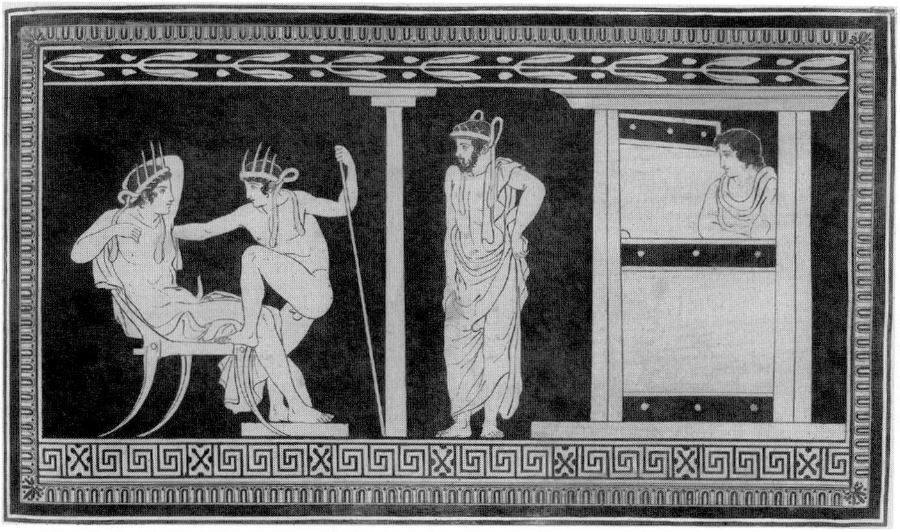

28 Etruscan vase painting, *Pederastic scene with spectators.*

of visual criticism of the text. One component of this is its detailed translations of the play's language, the most direct of which in making explicit the sexuality of the image is that noted by Schiff, the comparison between Old Hamlet and Claudius as 'Hyperion to a satyr' (1.2.140). A later account of the murdered king as having 'Hyperion's curls, the front of Jove himself' (3.4.56) is also made visible; so, too, is Hamlet's vision of the court as 'an unweeded garden/ That grows to seed' (1.2.135–6). These references serve to sharpen the presentation of the play's larger atmosphere. Equally striking is the depiction of Gertrude, watching yet unable to watch, in a way that reveals her shamed complicity and distils the tropes of obsessive, clandestine observation in which the play abounds into a single, powerful image of dark, claustrophobic scopophilia. Envy and murder reveal their roots in introverted, incestuous sexuality: the infusion of poison into the ear becomes an image of invasive sexuality fusing the details of the ghost's account of his death with the fear of sexual depravity and political decay that drives his injunction to revenge:

Let not the royal bed of Denmark be
A couch for luxury and damned incest.
(1.5.82–3)

An early instance of the imaginative concentration seen repeatedly in Fuseli's work, the *Hamlet* image concretises the driving mood of the whole play within a single visual moment, translating its temporal sequence into a compelling yet analytic

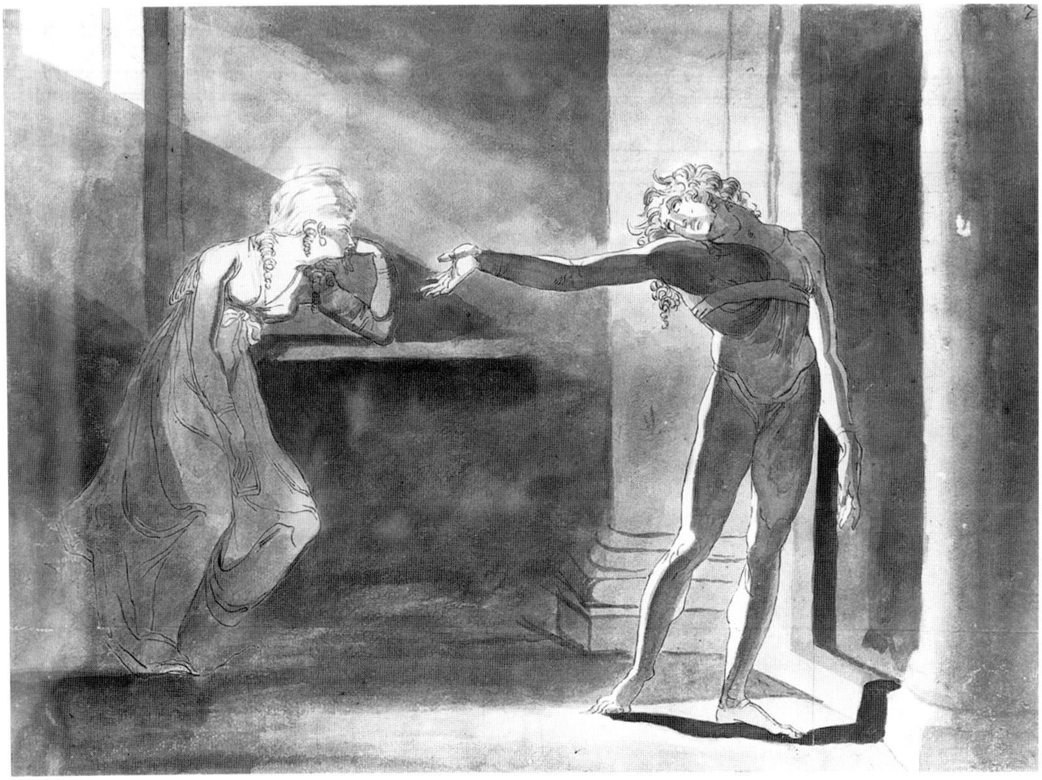

29 Henry Fuseli, *Hamlet and Ophelia*, 1775–6.

'invention' that works largely through the use of an iconographic reference as powerful as it is unexpected.

The second wash-drawing, known simply as *Hamlet and Ophelia* (1775–6: Fig. 29),[27] addresses a different area of the play's sexuality. While the postures do not correspond exactly to those described in 2.1, there is enough resemblance to them, and to the tone of the scene as a whole, to suggest that it is this part of the play and not the nunnery scene (3.1) that the watercolor relates. Here once again an episode that is reported, not enacted, becomes the basis of a visual treatment, suggesting that the play has been subtly redefined through the narrative perspective of the omniscient narrator in a novel. The composition alludes to another vase decoration (see Fig. 30),[28] this one showing a satyr entreating a dancing maenad who moves away from him with outstretched hand and gracefully arched body, recording part of a Grecian feast where 'lamentations made an essential part of devotion',[29] a mingled tone exactly suited to the complex relationship between Hamlet and Ophelia. Fuseli reverses the genders of the image, so that Hamlet stands with arm outstretched while moving away from Ophelia, and she leans

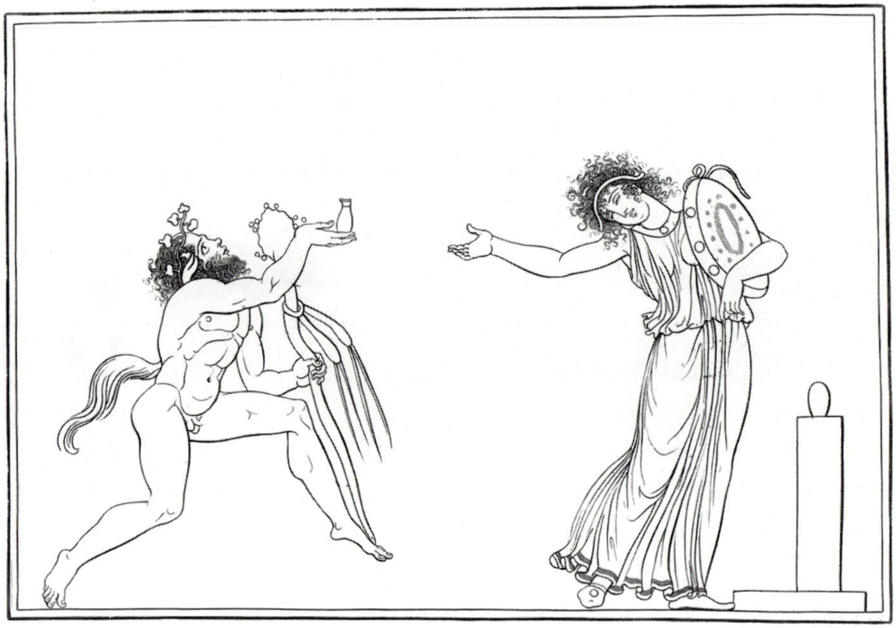

30 Etruscan vase painting, *Satyr and Maenad*.

rejected and dispirited against a shelf. The setting is bleakly classical, columns to the right illumined by light falling diagonally from the left, enhanced by weak washes of grey and pink. The relationship is one of exhausted erotic tension where, in apparent reversal of the situation in the vase painting, Ophelia's desires are being rejected by Hamlet. Hamlet becomes the neurotic, Wertheresque man of sorrows while Ophelia is the forceful yet thwarted woman who, like the earlier Lady Macbeth figure, suggests through her features and angular profile a version of the erotically powerful female. The effect is intense: not only is there a new reading of Ophelia as a woman cognisant of her sexuality, uttered long before the bawdy songs signal her mental distress, but the 'antic disposition' of Hamlet is rendered visually as an etiolated loss of libido, a sexual dysfunction today commonly associated with psychological disturbance. Perhaps there is another significance, which testifies to Fuseli's verbal wit: located firmly in the antique style of the vases, the painting offers a punning gloss on Hamlet's 'antic disposition', drained as he is of colour and sexual energy and locked in a balletic pattern of refusal, a negative equivalent of Keats's Grecian urn.

The depth of reading these images provide is not only rare in late eighteenth-century painting, but of a quality seldom approached elsewhere in Fuseli's own work as it moves towards greater public acceptance. They are perceptive critical statements, employing startlingly original iconographic reference systems to clarify in their inventions whole areas of dramatic mood and movement as well as close readings of individual moments. In them, Fuseli is using what he needs of the Neo-Classical tradition of allusion, but adapting it to suggestively complicate critical aporia with a sensitivity that far outmeasures other contemporary criticism.

III

In the mid 1770s Fuseli sketched a series of fresco designs based on four of the plays, *The Tempest*, *Twelfth Night*, *King Lear* and *Macbeth*. The scheme has obvious conceptual resonances of the Sistine Chapel, an allusion that immediately defines the cultural status of the project in establishing parity between Shakespeare and Michelangelo in the ability to convey universal humanity. Once again, the Renaissance impulse is filtered through Romantic concern for the individual, most clearly in the political and emotional inflections of the designs. Never advancing beyond preparatory sketches, the designs nevertheless reveal subtle critical readings through their use of iconographic allusion and the relationships of character and event they achieve through spatial disposition. The classical-Romantic dualism derives from the poised tension generated by the placing of loosely sketched figures within a tight architectural structure of separate fields. Gert Schiff points out[30] that these take a form that no actual building would permit; this suggests an analogy with the great Romantic verse dramas that remain on the page because of the impossibility of stage realisation. The designs also share with these works the thrusting of the burden of interpretation firmly onto the educated reader.

When approached with a sensitivity to its various meanings, the design for *The Tempest* (1777–8: Fig. 31)[31] reveals itself as a study of the play's exploration of domination in a range of political and personal frames, reading the play through a Romantic concern for the individual. The ambivalence of the colonising impulse even at its apparently most beneficent is suggested in the figure of Prospero that dominates the composition from its central position in the upper central field. The figure's head recalls that of God from the Sistine 'Creation of Adam', but just as significant is its likeness to the Bard Ossian[32] from the Penicuik House paintings that Alexander Runciman was developing when he knew Fuseli in Rome.[33] The dual allusion instils in the figure the values of the Romantic poet in a god-like act of creation. Seated and leaning forward, he holds a giant folio under his arm and points to it with his right forefinger, in a clear reproduction of the pose

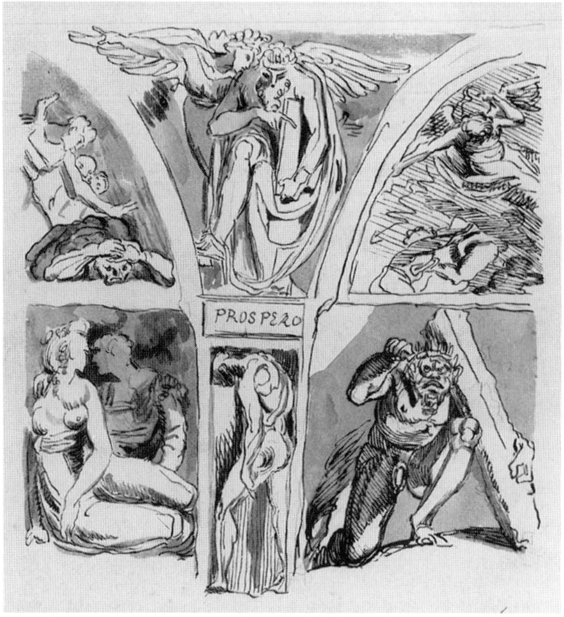

31 Henry Fuseli, Fresco design for *The Tempest*, 1777–8,

of Isaiah from the Sistine Chapel, adding prophecy and vengeance to Romantic creativity. The emphasis on the book reveals the source of Prospero's strength – 'Remember/ First to possess his books; for without them/ He's but a sot, as I am', says Caliban (3.2.83–5) – but the reference also undermines textual authority: the book enshrines language, the corrosive that gives Caliban only the knowledge 'how to curse' (1.2.364). Further, because Prospero is here presented in an image, not in language, the value of the verbal text is as much questioned as reinforced: Prospero's power, seemingly godlike and unchallenged, is deeply qualified. This is furthered by the ambiguity assigned to Ariel. Apparently angelic, the figure is compromised through its resemblance to the Witch of Endor figure already encountered in the *Macbeth* wash-drawing, that, in its suggestions of imminent death in battle, undermines the angelic function of Ariel, implying a vulnerability in Prospero that matches in physical terms the ambivalence of his textual authority.

Prospero is flanked by the forces he contains and controls. On the left Caliban is shown beneath the tarpaulin, as discovered by Stephano and Trinculo; on the right, the shipwrecked mariners are saved by Ariel. It is a precarious balance, for the opposition encloses conflicting views of the initial encounter between colonist and colonised, reflecting the importance of Montaigne's essay 'Of the Canniballes' as a major source within the ambivalence of Shakespeare's text. To the left, the colonists invent a monster; to the right, the island exerts its redemptive powers on the visitors. Together with the depiction of Prospero himself, the images of the upper level enact his mingled identity as prophet-magician and colonist, presenting it both as a power for good and a force of exploitation.

Below, in the centre, Ferdinand is presented as a desolate caryatid. The form transmits in bodily terms the containment visited on him by Prospero – 'My spirits, as in a dream, are all bound up' (1.2.485) – when, seeing him as a potential usurper who has come to the island 'to win it/ From me, the lord on't' (1.2.454–5), he rejects him as a suitor for Miranda. This conveys more than Prospero's wish to control, illuminating the links between political and marital colonisation that Ferdinand's arrival represents. To the left, the tensions of this metaphoric colonisation at first appear resolved as Ferdinand and Miranda sit in close embrace. The curves of Miranda's body and the dark tones and apparently classical apparel of Ferdinand show Fuseli's customary sensuality and gender polarity, linking a classical ideal in the suggestion of Greek sculpture with the immediacy of Romantic eroticism to unite universal and individual. Yet Ferdinand's darkness and Miranda's taut posture generate an unresolved tension that suggests another current of the play's movement. Ferdinand has travelled far from the desolation of the central figure, but he and Miranda are still subject to Prospero's control: their tension reflects the warning voiced in one of the latest, and consequently most troublesome, statements of the great chain of being:

If thou dost break her virgin-knot before
All sanctimonious ceremonies may
With full and holy rite be ministered,
No sweet aspersion shall the heavens let fall
To make this contract grow; but barren hate,
Sour-eyed disdain and discord shall bestrew
The union of your bed with weeds so loathly
That you shall hate it both. (4.1.15–22)

It is a second fall that Prospero here presents to Ferdinand; the close intertwining of Ferdinand and Miranda at the foot of the lunette, recalling the embraces of Adam and Eve in Fuseli's images of Milton's paradise, strengthens the allusion. Prospero's accusation that Ferdinand has come to 'usurp' him (1.2.452) inflect a human relationship with the dialect of colonialism, but in the design, as in the play, this has multiple dimensions. The dark shape of Ferdinand as colonist is offset by the suggestion in the figure of Miranda of the dominant females from the *Macbeth* wash-drawing and elsewhere, and the close opposition of their faces suggests conflict. This reminds the onlooker that Miranda herself turns colonist when finding her own 'brave new world' (5.1.183) inhabited by Ferdinand's people. The meanings of Fuseli's design follow the contours of colonial power, gender, willing surrender and annexation that circle each other in the verbal text of *The Tempest*.

A similar play of colonisation, fall, and redemption is explored in the image at the foot of the right hand field. This is Caliban, shown kneeling and bearing a baulk of timber, in extension of his frequent depiction as log-bearer from the references in 1.2. But the wood that he carries is far larger, and the resemblance is to quite another image, that of Christ falling under the weight of the cross in a Renaissance *via dolorosa*, the link strengthened by the horns on his head which suggest a crown of thorns. This is a parody Christ, but one close enough to rekindle ideas of the noble savage with which Fuseli was familiar from his study of Rousseau. In visual opposition to the lovers, it offers a version of compassion from the least expected quarter that sets the concepts of authority, colonisation, and redemptive love in a powerfully new frame.

Revealing as it does the implosion of textual power and the unresolved confrontations of colonisation and exploitation, the design finds amplification elsewhere in Fuseli's outspoken rejection of the slave trade. In *Remarks on Rousseau* he talks of 'the chains with which inequality and despotism have shackled the limbs of slavery':[34] invited in 1804 by his friend and patron William Roscoe to comment on the great improvements made to the port of Liverpool he responds 'methinks I every where smell the blood of slaves'.[35] Reviewing Morland's *Execrable human traffic, or the Affectionate Slaves* he is angrily dismissive: 'Some cannot feel for distant misery. The painter of this picture is of their number. The horrors of Sierra Leone, the Gambia and Niger, sound feebly in his ear.'[36] Perhaps most forceful is his painting *The Negro Revenged* (1806–7)[37] to illustrate Cowper's 'The Negro's Complaint'. Again, universal and individual combine. The central black figure is cast in the form of the Borghese Gladiator, used frequently by Fuseli to epitomise virtue; he watches the sinking of a slave ship in the storm that in the poem embodies divine justice redressing the evils of the slave trade, but which seems also to indicate a retrospective glance at the mechanism of retribution and reconciliation in *The Tempest*. These references make clear the larger political thrust of Fuseli's reading of *The Tempest* as a play about the moral processes of colonisation: the tensions implicit in Shakespeare's text in 1610, and reactivated by readings from the 1960s onwards, are made powerfully clear in this visual invention of 1777. At one level, it should be seen within the mounting surge of opinion against slavery,

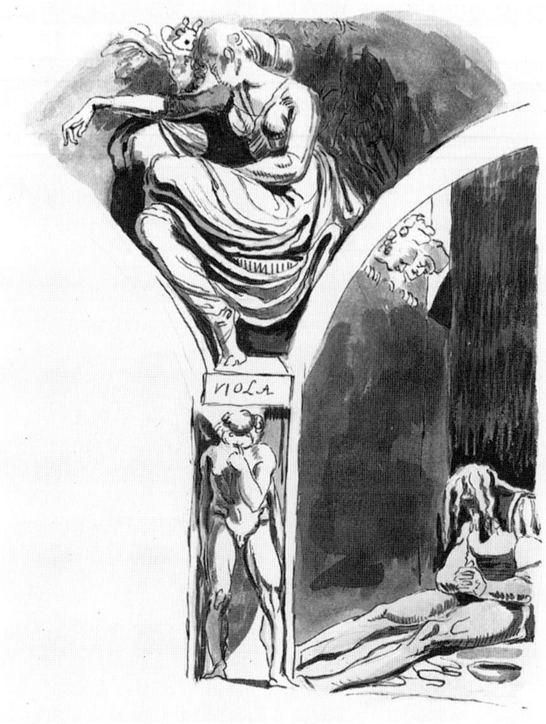

32 Henry Fuseli, Fresco design for *Twelfth Night*, 1777–8.

producing books, pamphlets and public debates urging in one case '*ABSTINENCE from SUGAR, RUM, &c.*' until 'measures are taken for the abolition of slavery'.[38] As an act of visual criticism, Fuseli's image is valuable today for its bringing together in a multiple, supple statement the complexities of the play's concern with the exploitations and enrichments of the colonial process, and placing them by implication in dialogue with an insistent humanitarian cause of its day.

The design for *Twelfth Night* (Fig. 32)[39] operates on a far smaller scale both physically and morally. Once more the play's forces are drawn together to work in generative opposition, although the fact that the design is unfinished and has only three images implies a pattern less clear than that of *The Tempest*. The largest element is the central upper field, containing a seated woman in profile above the caption 'Viola'. The figure presents difficulties of interpretation since, dressed as a woman, with long hair and presented in static, seated profile, it is clearly not the dynamic, cross-dressed Viola-Cesario. David Weinglass[40] reads the caption as a simple error, seeing the image as a representation of Olivia at the play's opening where, immobile in grief, she has 'abjured the sight/ And

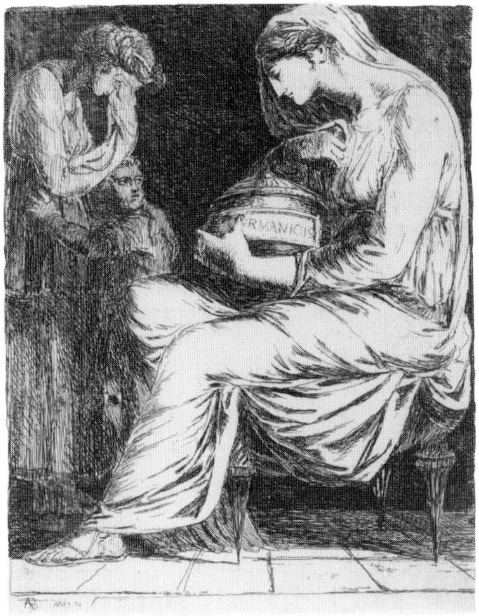

33 Alexander Runciman, *Agrippina weeping over the Ashes of Germanicus*, c. 1772.

company of men' (1.2.40–1). Peter Tomory[41] notes the resemblance between this and Alexander Runciman's *Agrippina weeping over the Ashes of Germanicus* (c. 1772: Fig. 33)[42] and this is clearly the element's source, bringing with it echoes of heroic grief from compositions in Caravaggio and an appropriate narrative context in mourning: Agrippina sat motionless with the ashes of her dead husband, eventually dying from starvation. This link suggests that the caption 'Viola' refers to neither Olivia nor Viola, but instead offers a realisation of Viola's words to Orsino in 2.4. Exploiting her adopted liminal identity, Viola speaks of herself as a separate person – 'My father had a daughter loved a man' (2.4.103) – and in so doing detaches for analysis the condition of emotional immobility, whether inflicted by mourning, gender uncertainty or personal insecurity, that broods over the play, afflicting Olivia and Orsino most palpably but also informing the varieties of inaction in Malvolio, Aguecheek and Sir Toby.

She never told her love,
But let concealment, like a worm i'th'bud,
Feed on her damask cheek. She pined in thought,
And with a green and yellow melancholy
She sat like Patience on a monument,
Smiling at grief. (2.4.106–111)

Fuseli's invention embodies these lines in several ways. The posture suggests immobile grief; the attitude implies pining in thought; and the classical costume seen in profile suggests an actual, sculpted monument to patient suffering. The image is a visual abstract not only of Viola's speech but of one of the essential states of the play, presenting it not as one of the emblems that Fuseli abhorred – as 'paltry subterfuges contrived by dullness to palliate the want of invention'[43] – but as a direct treatment of a linguistic figure. The result is to reveal not the nobility of mourning but its exaggeration and the resultant human cost, stressing an aspect of the play often overlooked.

To the right is a treatment of the brutally comic passage where Malvolio sits 'in hideous darkness' (4.2.25) while Feste, in the guise of Sir Topas, questions and maligns him. It is no surprise that Fuseli, alone among painters of a play rarely presented in visual terms, should focus on this scene and its disturbing dual tone, leaving the darker direction unresolved as it is in the play. Malvolio is a broken figure, head bowed and hands clasped as if in prayer, while Feste, joined by Maria, looks down with an air of detachment, suggesting the scene's location just before Sir Toby urges 'To him in thine own voice' (53). That Malvolio is seen from within the dark house adds to the intensity: seen from the standpoint of Feste and Maria, he is merely ridiculous. In this arrangement the image precisely catches the layers of observing and manipulation that are fundamental to the scene. Conjecture about the missing left-hand field is purposeless, but it is probable that it might have offered some image of the play's carnivalesque quality, or even its ending of qualified epiphany in the disclosures of identity and the marriages that follow, to reveal the play's full moral traverse.

In holding together the oppositional forces of *Twelfth Night*, such a scheme would follow the practice established in the design for *The Tempest*, and this is further suggested by the figure in the *trompe-l'oeil* niche in the lower centre. As the design for *The Tempest* has Prospero as a lowering directorial presence above the layers of action, so this design has the small, impish nude as its dominant force. Weinglass suggests that 'la figura e quella d'un amorino' (p. 120), but this is unlikely: Fuseli rarely uses unidentified *putti* or *amorini*. The clue to the *Twelfth Night* figure lies in another work by Runciman, *King Lear on the Heath* (see Fig. 23),[44] discussed in Chapter 3. Fuseli knew Runciman well in his Italian years, and called him 'the best *Painter* of *us* in Rome':[45] it is hard to believe that he had not seen this drawing. The Fool appears at the rear left of the composition and is clearly the source of the figure in the niche, revealing Feste as the guiding force of the play who shares the witty gravity of the Fool in *Lear* and recalling the fact that, on the heath, Lear's Fool sings what might well be a stanza from Feste's last song. In both images the figures are naked, giving them a suggestion of classical heroes while stressing their vulnerability. By the allusion Feste's constant awareness of the passage of time is transplanted to the world of Lear's 'bare forked animal' (3.4.96) and illuminated with the sombre shafts of his detached wit. The romance movement of 'O mistress mine' (2.3.33–8) is displaced by the darker tone of 'Come away death' (2.4.49–64), alone in Feste's songs in rhythmically resembling the melancholy songs and related viol fantasies of John Dowland. Nudity also reveals another dimension of *Twelfth Night*: beneath the elegant conversation, the verbal comedy of rhetorical dilation, the identity confusions, and the darkness of Malvolio's maligning lies the feral sexuality of the Fool's songs on the heath – a constant current in Fuseli's visions. Though unfinished, the design offers a disturbed *Twelfth Night* that accords with a reading of the play as one of the darkest of the comedies that never resolves the forces it releases: in disclosing the world of physical and moral exposure and stasis it reads the play as defined less by the joviality of Feste's *carpe diem* than by the darker motif of *tempus edax rerum*.

In their form, the Shakespeare fresco designs erect a parity between Shakespeare and Michelangelo that reveals Fuseli's placing of the dramatist within the highest category of Renaissance humanist aesthetics, seen through the storm clouds of a very idiosyncratic Romantic imagination. Allied with this is the implication, through the use of figures taken from the Sistine Chapel, that the creative power of the artist is parallel to the divine process of creation. Fuseli would later reject such an inflated view, and already here it is ironised in the many levels of meaning with which Prospero is endowed, far more serious and self-reflexive than the contemporary fashion of bardolatry. Instead of the vague claims of universal human understanding made, for example, in Garrick's preface to the Shakespeare Jubilee, the designs for *The Tempest* and *Twelfth Night*, perhaps because of their incompleteness of idiom, offer supple, multivalent interpretations of the plays to reveal their probing readings of human relationships, physical and psychological, intimate and political.

IV

While Fuseli's Italian images make incisive readings of the plays, they are representative of a cultural frame already quite anachronistic. Working through complexes of allusion to an eclectic montage of Renaissance texts they are accessible only to a small circle of readers educated to recognise the points of reference and skilled in reading the resultant meanings; executed in a size and medium never intended for public display, and nearly impossible to reproduce with contemporary techniques, their identity as objects of minority culture is abundantly clear. They constitute a form more appropriate to medieval illuminations produced for a single enlightened patron than to images painted for the public art market of which Shakespeare imaging increasingly formed part. That the sketches are contemporary with Mortimer's *Shakespeare Heads* and Dance's *Timon* painting, and come several years after the *Macbeth* images of Wootton and Zuccarelli, makes this very clear.

In Italy, isolated from the rapidly expanding art market, Fuseli relied on the patronage of the banker Thomas Coutts, the physician-poet John Armstrong, and Sir Robert and Lady Smyth, with whom he stayed in Bologna. Denied the ready income of the portraitist, he had difficulty in making a living, an early reference placing his likely income at '50L yearly'.[46] Hardship continued long after his return to London and election as an R.A. In 1790 he wrote to his friend William Roscoe 'my Situation continues to be extremely precarious'.[47] The return itself, in 1779, was in no small measure driven by economic necessity, coupled with a desire to establish himself in the first rank of literary and history painters. His timing was opportune. Somerset House opened the next year as the permanent home of the Royal Academy's exhibitions; the display of individual history and literary paintings was an established and highly lucrative practice; and the machinery developed by Boydell, Macklin and others was feeding the growing public demand for engravings, simultaneously creating a need for paintings as subject matter. Such works had to be accessible to as wide a readership as possible: aware of this, Fuseli sought ways to exploit it, in his involvement with not only the Boydell Shakespeare Gallery but with Macklin's *British Poets*, Woodmason's Irish Shakespeare Gallery, the foundation of his own Milton Gallery, and the supervision of large numbers of engravings from his own existing or specially executed works to illustrate editions of poems and plays that included the Rivington Shakespeare of 1805.[48] The search for an idiom that would both facilitate critical visualisation and be accessible to the wider public he had of necessity to court was to occupy him for the rest of his life, manifesting itself in frequent changes of style in his paintings.

Fuseli's efforts to combine sophisticated critical reading with a more accessible creation of meaning are well demonstrated in *Queen Katherine's Dream* (1781: Fig. 34),[49] a scene from *Henry VIII* that was very popular in the contemporary imagination. One of a series of paintings commissioned between 1781 and 1789 by Sir Robert Smyth, it moves some way towards wider acceptance in two ways: by selecting a single moment of emotional intensity rather than attempting to convey the narrative and thematic drive of the whole play, and by employing an idiom far closer to the conventions of English Neo-Classicism in place of the

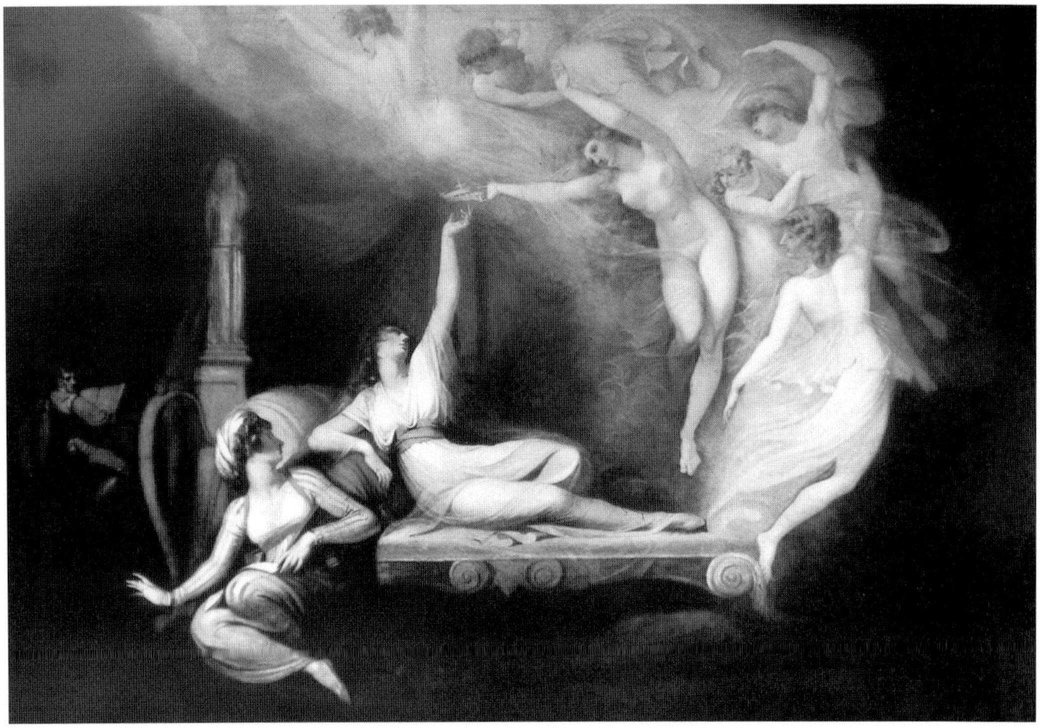

34 Henry Fuseli, *Queen Katherine's Dream*, 1781.

fusion of styles common in his earlier work. These changes do not result in a dilution of critical intensity: Fuseli knew Smyth well, and many of the references seem calculated to appeal to a sensitive and widely-read connoisseur. They also take up allusions more widely accessible than those of the Italian wash-drawings by moving towards the play as it was performed – not in any sense offering a production record, but instead acting upon the onlooker's imaginative receptiveness with a directness similar to that of a live performance. Yet although it uses a more accessible style and a deep palette of sumptuous richness, the painting still exists very much within a restricted circle of allusiveness, and the heavily compromised form of the engraving after it reveals just how far Fuseli's vocabulary still was from the wider tastes being satisfied by many of the artists discussed in Chapter 3.

While spectacle often ensured the popularity of *Henry VIII* throughout the century, the dignity of Katherine maintained its seriousness of tone and theme. This mood dominates Fuseli's painting. The upraised hand of Fuseli's habitual classical hero is apparent in Queen Katherine's gesture, but it is carefully modulated against the hand of the nearest visionary form to reveal the imaginative distance between her and the female nudes who present the 'spirits of peace' of the text

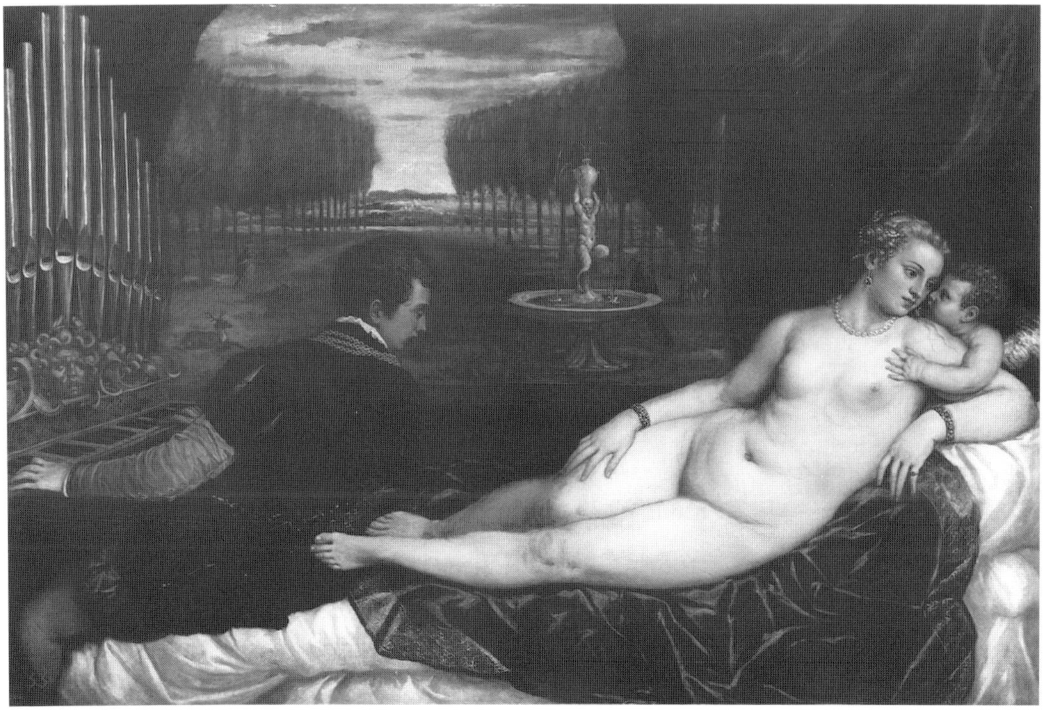

35 Titian, *Venus and Cupid with an Organist*, 1545–8.

(4.2.83) with a circling grace that approaches Hogarth's ideal line. It is clear that Griffith and Patience do not share Katherine's vision: Griffith looks diagonally across to Patience, directing attention to the fact that she sees only Katherine, not what she herself sees. As Fuseli himself said of Poussin's narrative constructions, which in this motif he clearly follows, the 'agents only appear, to tell the fact; they are subordinate to the story'.[50] In this way the image combines separate narrative viewpoints, enabling the reader to see simultaneously the whole scene, Griffith and Patience unable to see anything other than Katherine, and the vision that Katherine alone sees. Fuseli's presentation of the narrative skilfully exemplifies his own advice that the 'invention' of a painting must 'constitute one whole, that it fully pronounce its own meaning, and tell itself'.[51] In a larger sense, however, it hints at a willingness to make the narrative frame more easily read by those familiar with the techniques of Poussin.

With the addition of the line of spirits, the painting has a single iconographic source: Titian's *Venus and Cupid with an Organist* (1545–8: Fig. 35),[52] a painting that also forms the basis of the immediately contemporary *Nude Woman listening to a Girl playing upon a Spinet* (*c.* 1800).[53] The central element of the composition has been reversed to maintain narrative continuity, but the figure of Griffith to the left follows that of the organ player and the posture of the Queen, with the single alteration of the upraised hand, is that of Venus. The red drapes and complementary golden colorations also echo Titian's painting, and the statue that divides the two spaces at the left repeats the fountain. In taking a well-known image from classical mythology by a revered Old Master, Fuseli is following the dual codes of the value-system of the historical style. Additionally, the interpretive significance of the pairing accords with popular sentiment: Queen Katherine, divorced by Henry after years of devoted marriage, presents a version of the goddess of love in which Agape displaces Eros, and the heroic female virtues of tenderness and passivity are made explicit, in a reading of the play quite in accord with its construal in contemporary productions. The displacement of the open eroticism of Titian's painting[54] in this way seems unlikely to have escaped Fuseli's imaginative grasp: it is one of several aspects in which a self-conscious wit is apparent in the image.

One of these is the displacement of the earlier image's concern with the sense of hearing by a stress on sight. In turn this offers itself as a metaphor of the larger thrust of *Henry VIII* in which European Catholicism is displaced by an essentially English Protestantism, at the same time as promoting the new history painting in England as superior to its continental Old Master equivalents. For Fuseli to mediate such a shift through the mechanisms of iconographic reference, in one of the first major public paintings he produced on coming to England, suggests that he is approaching a concept of national identity – which, of course, takes Shakespeare the national genius for its site – with indirectness and subtlety.

All of this implies a successful uniting of Fuseli's former literary and art historical insights with a grasp of wider public interest, allowing the image to be reproduced directly with hope of commercial success. While it offers no extensive critical reading of the play, it certainly conveys the emotional power of the moment through the disposition of the figures and the narrative they contain, reinforcing this strongly by its sensuous tonalities and graceful patterning. In 1788, a version of the same scene was published in a stipple engraving by Francesco Bartolozzi in Thomas Macklin's *British Poets*, a serially-published collection of 'prints illustrative of the most celebrated British poets' (see Fig. 36).[55] The suggestion has been made that Fuseli produced a different painting of this subject as the basis of the engraving, and fragments of another version exist,[56] but the surviving oil and the engraving have many similarities, and from this and from Fuseli's own comments it seems likely that this painting was the basis of the reproduction. If this is the case, then the engraving considerably coarsens the rhythms and meanings of the

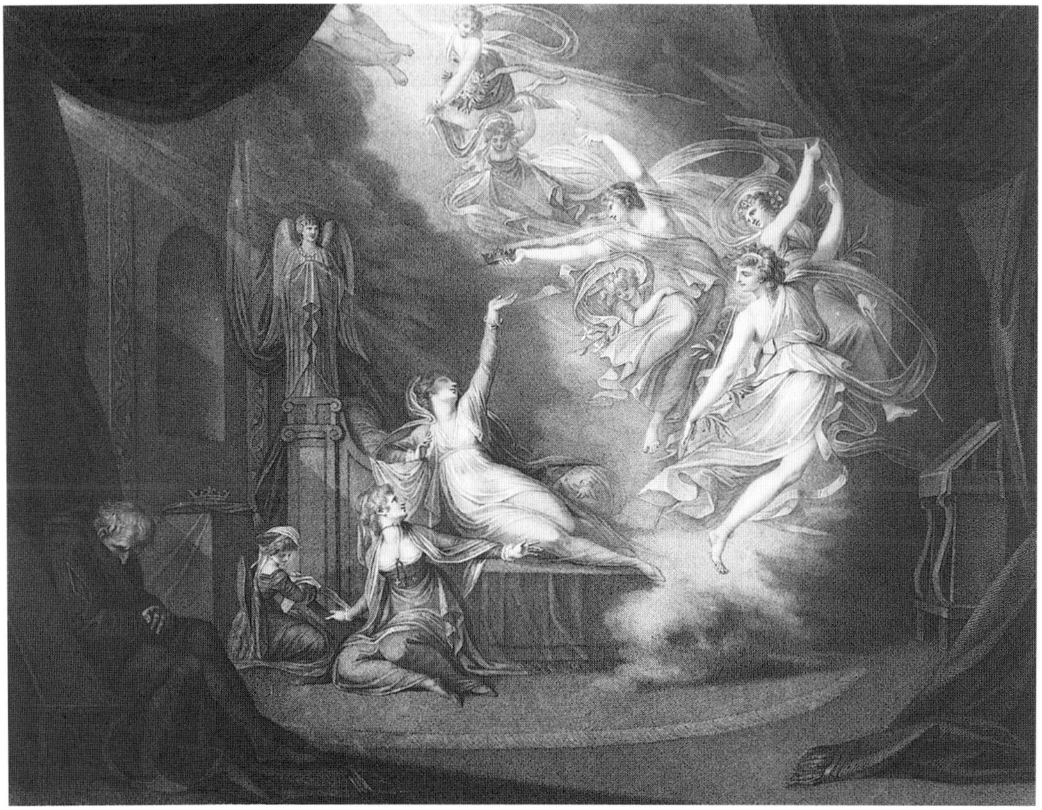

36 Henry Fuseli, *Queen Katherine's Dream*. Engraved by Francesco Bartolozzi, 1781.

painting. The whole composition is surrounded by a frame of swagged classical drapes to suggest a stage, and the figure of Griffith is moved in front of this as if onto an apron stage. The resultant absence at the rear is balanced by the addition of another waiting maid, the classical statue is replaced by a funerary angel, and a lectern is placed at the right – changes that add nothing to the interpretive value of the image. The gap between Katherine's hand and that of the lowest spirit is greatly enlarged, so that the painting's sense of tantalising closeness is lost. But the most significant change is that Patience now gazes at the dream-figures rather than the Queen, so that the separateness of the levels of vision is compromised. What in the painting is precisely narrated and carefully poised becomes in the engraving awkward and diffuse.

That the engraving does indeed attempt to reproduce the Smyth painting but loses much of its rhythm and meaning is suggested by Fuseli's own anonymous review of his work:

> Those who have not seen the painting will do great injustice to the painter, if they judge him from the print, though it is decorated with the name of Bartolozzi: *Katherine* and *Patience* have lost their character and individual expression, *Griffith* his limbs, the *Vision* its splendour.[57]

The painter's anger that the gentle narrative pointing had also been coarsened is perhaps suggested in another comment in the same review: 'The passage, which is inserted in the catalogue, makes Katherine repeat the vision, which the painter has represented.'

The perceived need to appeal to less sophisticated readers is surely a driving force behind Bartolozzi's work of adaptation: these are major compositional changes, not shifts caused by the move from mass to line. Though Macklin's publication was by no means cheap – three guineas to subscribers, four to others – it was still clearly designed to appeal to a far wider market, for whom a more direct style was apparently judged appropriate; the inclusion of references to the stage suggest a very basic clarification of the scene's origin. Fuseli's attempt to move towards greater accessibility in an image that combines sensual immediacy with intellectual implications of no little subtlety has been thwarted by the drive towards larger circulation.

Seven years after Fuseli's return from Italy, Boydell announced the formation of his Shakespeare Gallery. From the start Fuseli was enthusiastically involved, eventually having nine canvases on display. Eight were engraved for the folio collection; the remaining one, *Puck*,[58] was engraved by James Parker and included in the edition of the plays. Five of the nine address subjects concerned with the supernatural; the remaining four adopt approaches quite different both from these supernatural fantasies and from the earlier iconographic studies, and show how Fuseli sought to broaden the appeal of his work, in so doing exemplifying again the shift in the production and consumption of Shakespeare imagery that is a major dynamic in this period.

The most immediate is *Henry V Reveals the Conspiracy of Cambridge, Scrope and Grey* (1786–9).[59] Painted in the historical Grand Style, it employs a bold composition using forceful diagonals to convey the moment of Henry's giving the three traitors their death sentences. This departs from Fuseli's earlier practice in not moving beyond this single instant, however, and for this reason it lacks much of the painter's usual interpretive vigour. A parallel movement is made in the two best-known images, those that convey the initial encounters between Macbeth and the witches[60] and Hamlet and his father's ghost.[61] The former presents Macbeth again in the familiar Gladiator pose, while the latter shows Hamlet struggling to free himself from Horatio's grip to engage the ghost; in both, the result is an effect of vigorous yet contained energy. To this is added an effect of lighting that, even in the engraving, gives a spectral, unearthly feel to the spiritual forms. To judge from contemporary reviews, Fuseli was still struggling towards popular acceptance: while the *St James's Chronicle* found 'something uncommonly great' in the *Hamlet* image, of the *Macbeth* it concluded, 'We cannot be reconciled to its wildness and extravagance.'[62] Both demonstrate a radical simplification of approach to concentrate on a direct visualisation of the moment of initial encounter. In this they are striking paintings; but they do not approach the intellectual depth found in Fuseli's other contemporary images of the supernatural.

Quite a different approach is taken in *Falstaff and Doll Tearsheet* (1795: Fig. 37).[63] Just how far this has been modified to suit a wider audience can be seen by comparing it with an earlier treatment of the same scene. Known by the same title, this is another of the Italian wash-drawings, and dates from 1771 (see Fig. 38).[64] It depicts 2 *Henry IV* 2.4, with Poins and Prince Hal standing behind the two central characters. While they are disguised as drawers, continuing the satire at Falstaff's expense, the frozen time of the canvas adds to them an element of threat, a momentary pause in which Hal's disavowal of Falstaff is shown as if in abeyance behind him. A hint of the inevitability of this future rejection is perhaps also implicit in the disparity in age between Falstaff and Doll, achieved by a chiaroscuro which places Falstaff in dark shadow against Doll's brightly-lit face. This is countered by the eroticism of the image, shown directly in Doll's sitting almost astride Falstaff, and the latter's widely-splayed legs and the suggestion of genitals, a figuration that appears in some of his later erotic drawings. At the same time, in its low viewpoint and extreme foreshortening, as well as the exaggerated cod-piece, it suggests Hans Baldung Grien's *The Bewitched Groom*,[65] an image well known in England by an artist whose mingled concerns with eroticism and the supernatural would have appealed strongly to Fuseli. These elements come together to suggest a mixture of erotic drive, the future rejection in Hal's 'I know thee not, old man' (5.5.47), and the poignancy of the passing of time that is introduced at Falstaff's death, together with a comic note introduced by the discrepancy with the Old Master drawing.

The contrast with the Boydell image is profound. The loosely-sketched Renaissance setting has been replaced in the engraving by formal hangings and an elaborately sculpted boar's head on an ornate transom, suggesting something far more regal than the Eastcheap tavern. The large *stein* of the earlier version is replaced by a full goblet of wine. Hal and Poins stand decorously in the doorway, their elegant postures slackening the urgency of the earlier image where only

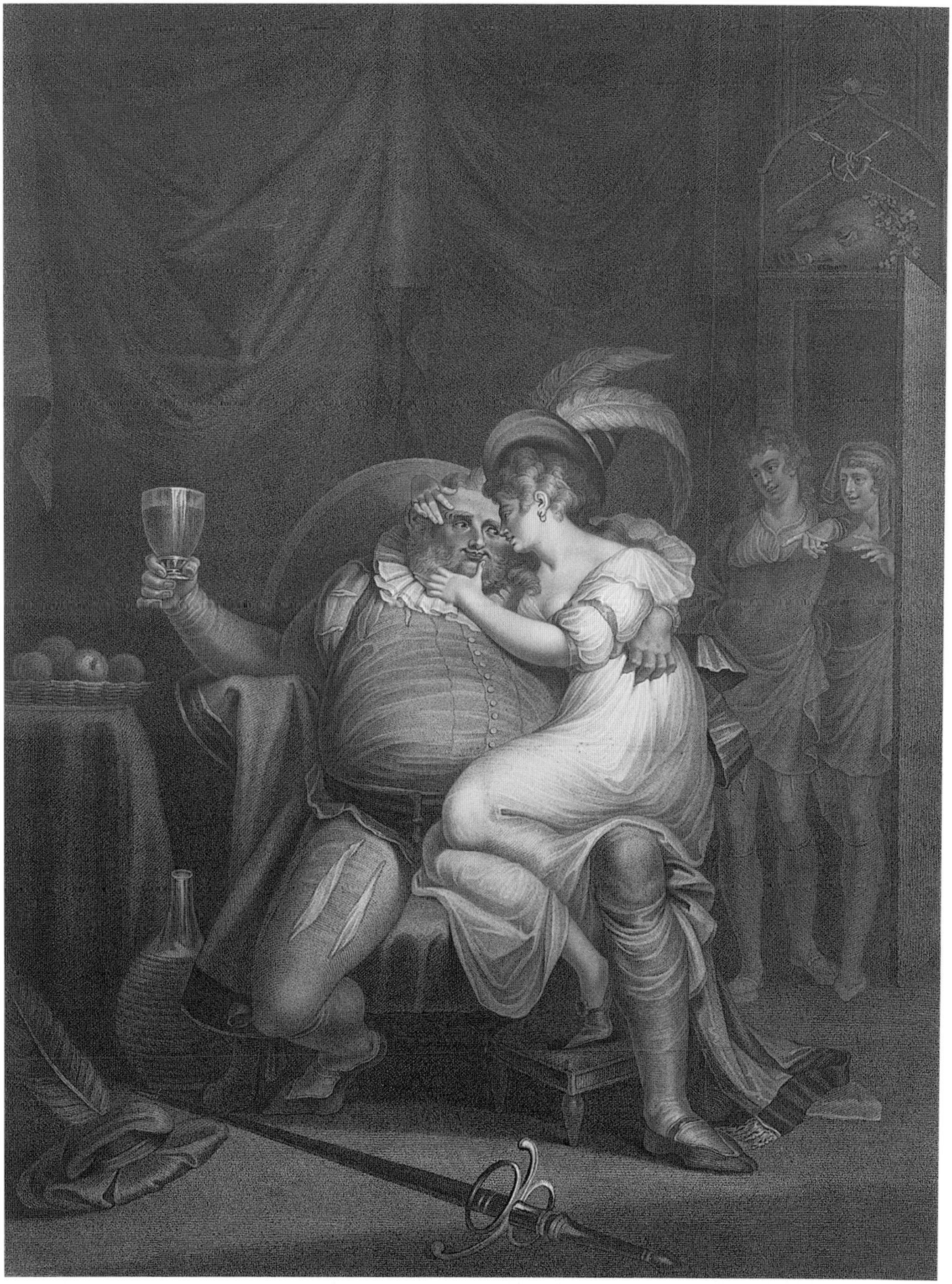

37 Henry Fuseli, *Falstaff and Doll Tearsheet*. Engraved by William Satchwell Leney, 1795.

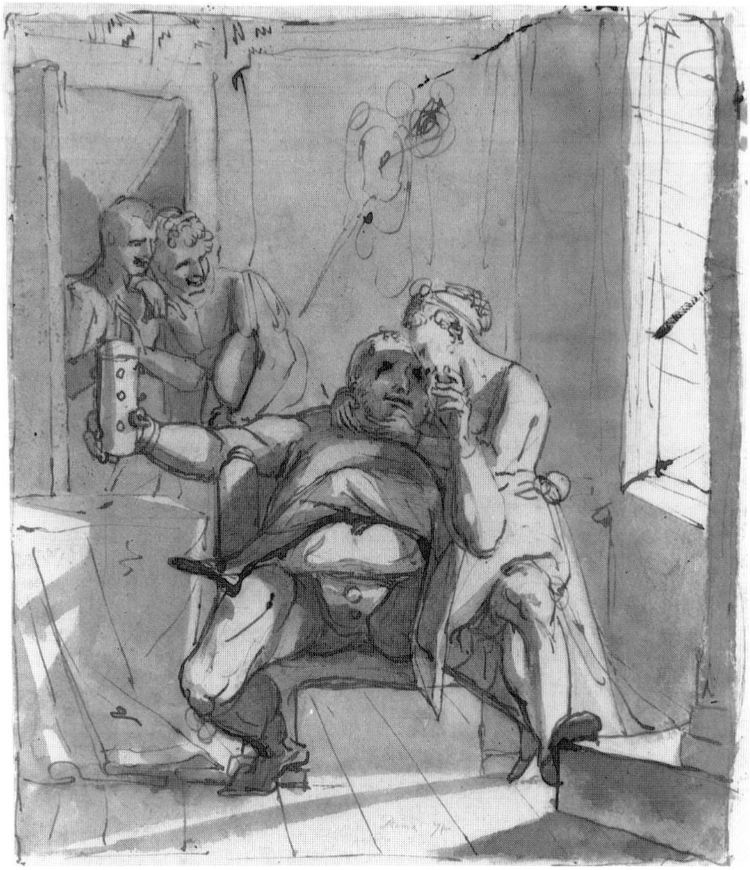

38 Henry Fuseli, *Falstaff and Doll Tearsheet*, 1771.

their torsos are shown, and where Hal's seriousness contrasts with Poins' laughter, hinting at the rejection to come. The largest change is in the central figures. Both are shown from a higher viewpoint, so that Falstaff appears more upright. Doll's posture is far more decorous; instead of having one leg extended across Falstaff she sits on his knee, and her legs conceal the genitals suggested in the earlier version. The scene has been moved towards a single reading: drained of its erotic power and implied decadence, it becomes a sentimental depiction of the two central characters, shown most directly in Doll's expression and the way she holds Falstaff's head. That it also depicts the actor John Henderson places it within a more popular genre: even in the engraved form, it is clear that Fuseli has moved a long way from his earlier studies of the relation between eroticism and power in the effort to appeal to a broader readership.

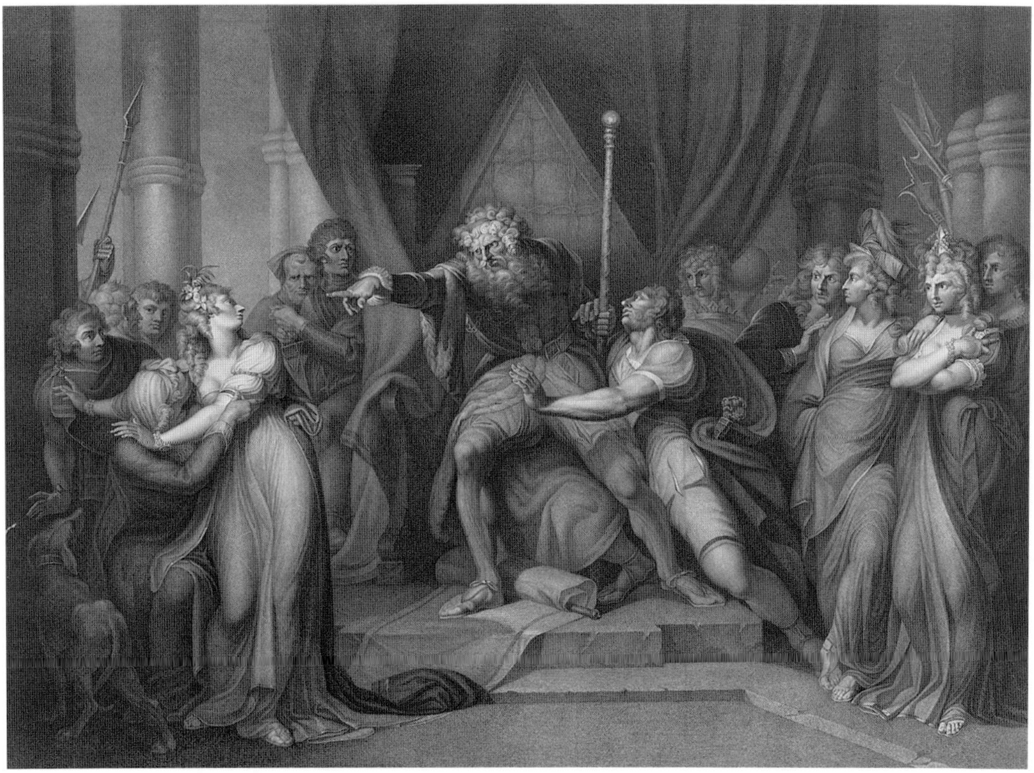

39 Henry Fuseli, *Lear Banishing Cordelia*. Engraved by Richard Earlom, 1792.

A rather different approach is seen in *Lear Banishing Cordelia* (*c*. 1786–9: Fig. 39).[66] In 1779 Fuseli had begun supervising the translation and illustration of the *Essay on Physiognomy* by his Zurich friend Johann Casper Lavater, himself producing some notable images. From this work he extended his practice of using bodily features to disclose character, instead of the more prescriptive depiction of the passing mood or 'passion' fashionable in some theatrical and painterly circles. In the Boydell *Lear* this is combined with a simple, forceful compositional structure of diagonals and exaggerated by the painting's size, which realises Fuseli's earlier theories about the importance of heroic scale. The composition focuses on a single moment in Act I but, unlike the *Henry V* image that its composition recalls, it suggests the action to follow by careful delineation of character. The scheming of Goneril and Regan is foreshadowed by their appearance in versions of the familiar sexual predators, and Kent's redemptive function is suggested by the way his cloak falls around him in echo of earlier embodiments of the heroic. But it is the figure and most especially the head of Lear that lift the image and its presentation of the play from the local to the universal, allowing Fuseli's ideas of the parallel grandeur of

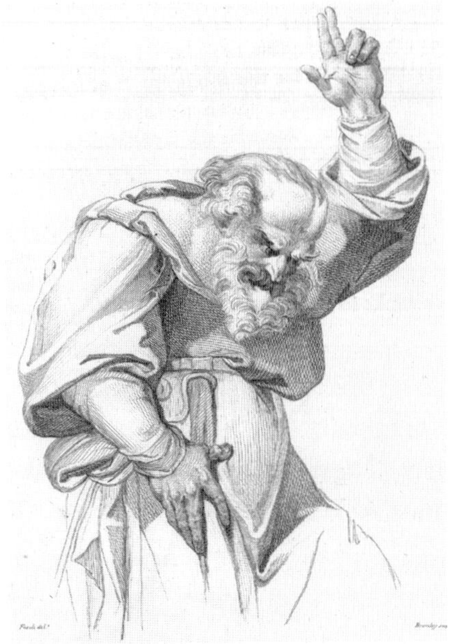

40 Henry Fuseli, Head of a Prophet. Engraved by William (?) Bromley from Lavater's *Essay on Physiognomy*, 1779.

Michelangelo and Shakespeare to be presented to an audience eager for versions of Shakespeare as the voice of timeless human feeling. With its glaring eyes and sharply pointed nose, coupled with the ferocity of the gesture, the head of Lear strongly recalls an engraving that Fuseli produced almost at the same time as the painting for 'Fragment Thirteenth' of Lavater's book (see Fig. 40), where it was accompanied by the following paragraph:

> Here is another figure full of fire, of dignity and energy, but defective in respect of truth and correctness. I imagine it represents a Patriarch or a Prophet bestowing his benediction. Nothing can be more solemn than this face. If that mouth had anathemas to pronounce, it would strike terror into the most obdurate hearts. Who could resist the adjuration of such a person?[67]

In stressing the power of the figure in pronouncing 'anathemas', the lines refer directly to the situation of Lear in Fuseli's painting while simultaneously containing the solemn dignity he displays much later in the play. It is revealing that Lavater offers no reason why this physiognomy suggests such a reading, simply asserting it from the engraving. This paragraph, the image beneath it and the likeness that both bear to Fuseli's Lear reveal one of the foundations of the artist's depiction of character and feeling: what would later be termed psychological characterisation is being accomplished at the end of the eighteenth century by distortion of external features, not by following any predetermined formulae but rather according to the instincts of the artist. This quality makes it accessible to those who have never encountered Lavater's writings, while a knowledge of them serves as a gloss to explain the full range of feeling it presents.

There are other recognisable sources in Fuseli's Lear, most notably a general reminiscence of heads of prophets and patriarchs from classical sculptures and from the Sistine Chapel, but these are given differentiation and astringency by the exaggerated anger of the expression. All these resonances imply a combination of terror and pity that parallels Fuseli's praise of the Borghese Gladiator as embodying the tragic hero's 'tremendous energy' while it simultaneously 'enforces sympathies'. The complex of responses locates itself directly within the idea of tragedy as instilling both pity and fear in the beholder, following the version of Aristotelian theory advanced by later eighteenth-century critics. In this figure Fuseli has attained a balance between an appeal to the contemporary readership and his own sense of the universal: with the liberating influence of Lavater, which allows him to present extremes of character by physiological directness, not iconographic encoding, the image unites Shakespeare, Michelangelo and the classics. While it lacks the intense originality of the earlier critical inventions, the painting shows Fuseli finding a way of combining his own approach to the play with that demanded by popular taste.

That it in part succeeded is suggested by early reviews. Humphry Repton called it 'one of the boldest effusions of a daring pencil' and commented on 'the wicked indifference of the two sisters, in one of which we read ambition, in the other lasciviousness'. While stressing that energy should be preferred to simple mimesis, he nevertheless enumerated some of the painting's 'enthusiastic failings', including the bending back of the fingers 'to a degree which few hands can ever reach'. The approval was not unqualified; Repton went on to criticise the presentation of Cordelia:

> Shakespeare makes her bear her fate in silence; therefore the violence here represented is not warranted by the text.[68]

The criticism was echoed in other reviews, but Fuseli himself patiently explained the figure's rationale:

> Goneril and Regan, with unblushing fronts, stand erect; but we own we expected to see the gentle Cordelia with down cast eyes, shrinking from the anger which terrified, even while it wounded, her ingenuous mind. The contempt which the hypocrisy of her sisters

inspired, might naturally dictate her answer; but, at the moment the painter has chosen, she may be supposed to be overwhelmed with fear and tender compassion, for her still dear but mistaken father.[69]

Again, the depth of Fuseli's textual reading is made clear. In the image of *King Lear*, Fuseli brings together his own system of unified invention with a direct representation of psychological states built on his work with Lavater, depending only in small measure on his earlier complex systems of iconographical reference. In using such a system he has moved a long way towards the demands of his new readers; in the process, much of the intellectual complexity and provocative depth of textual reading found in the earlier, intimate drawings has been lost, displaced by the sheer power of immediate effect. This mediation of sources so that the external form is to some degree distorted to offer a metaphor of the inner psychological state links Fuseli with Blake to hold them both apart from almost all other artists working at the time, lifting them above systems of representation borrowed from Le Brun or classical conventions of representation.

Intended to make the large public paintings more accessible, on occasion, as with the figure of Cordelia, it had an opposite effect. Yet there were other paintings in which Fuseli's concern for extreme detail, range of sources and complex imaginative imagery chimed more completely with the public taste of the time, and these paintings, concerned with the supernatural in Shakespeare, will be explored in Chapter 8.

NOTES

1. Alexander Gilchrist, *Life of William Blake*, 1863, 2 vols. (London: Macmillan, 1880), I. p. 52.
2. Published in *The Life and Writings of Henry Fuseli*, ed. John Knowles. 3 vols. (London: Colburn and Bentley, 1831).
3. 'Reminiscences of Henry Fuseli, Esq, RA', *Pen and Pencil* (New York: D. Appleton, 1858), pp. 193–209. Quotation from pp. 197–8. The account also gives rare insights into Fuseli's domestic life.
4. *Aphorisms on the Fine Arts* No. 214. Knowles, III, p. 140.
5. 'Zum Shakespeares-Tag', written and delivered 1771 but unpublished until 1854. Translated as 'On Shakespeare's Day' by Timothy J. Chamberlain in *Eighteenth-Century German Criticism* (*The German Library*: 11, New York: Continuum, 1992), pp. 171–4.
6. *The Collected English Letters of Henry Fuseli*, ed. David H. Weinglass (Millwood, New York: Kraus, 1982), 12 May 1814, p. 403.
7. Letter to unknown addressee, 1822. *Letters*, p. 474.
8. Mary Balmanno, 'Reminiscences of Henry Fuseli, Esq., R.A.', *Pen and Pencil* (New York: D. Appleton, 1858), p. 197.

9. *Remarks on the Writings and Conduct of John James Rousseau* (London: Printed for T. Cadell, (successor to Mr. Millar); J. Johnson and B. Davenport; and J. Payne, 1767), footnote to pp. 67–9.
10. 'General Observations' on *King Lear*. *Dr Johnson on Shakespeare*, ed. W. K. Wimsatt (Harmondsworth: Penguin, 1969), p. 126.
11. Vol. 19, August 1794, p. 350.
12. *Collected English Letters*, p. 325.
13. Ibid., p. 145.
14. Third Lecture: Invention. Knowles, II, p. 134.
15. Aphorism 96; Knowles, III, p. 94.
16. Lectures III and IV, reprinted in Knowles, II, pp. 131–186 and 187–235.
17. *Garrick as the Duke of Gloucester Waiting for Lady Anne at the Funeral procession of her Father-in-Law, King Henry VI*, pen and wash, 31.7 × 45.7 (12 ½ × 18), Kunsthaus Zurich.
18. *Imagining Shakespeare*, p. 34.
19. Pen and wash, 36 × 42 (14 ⅛ × 16 ½), Kunsthaus Zurich.
20. Third Lecture, Knowles, II, p. 147. For a discussion of the wider importance of the figure in early Romantic iconography see Peter Tomory, *The Life and Art of Henry Fuseli* (London: Thames and Hudson, 1972), pp. 78–9.
21. 1780–5; charcoal and chalk on paper, 55.3 × 66.9 (21 ¾ × 26 ⅜). British Museum, London.
22. Pencil and watercolour on paper, 30.2 × 40.2 (11 9/10 × 8 13/16), Kunsthaus Zurich. Reproduced in Lavater's *Essays on Physiognomy* in an engraving by T. Holloway, 1792, p. 289.
23. Pen and wash, 27.5 × 39.5 (10 13/16 × 15 ½). British Museum, London. Orgel's discussion occurs in *The Authentic Shakespeare*, pp. 252–6.
24. Pen and wash, 43.6 × 59.6 (17 ⅛ × 23 ½"). Graphische Sammlung der Eidgenössischen Technischen Hochschule. Line engraving by Johann Heinrich Lips, 20.6 × 30.5 (8 ⅛ × 12), *Fuessli's Sämmtliche Werke*, 1807.
25. The image is reproduced in *Collection of Etruscan, Greek and Roman Antiquities, from the Cabinet of the Honble Wm. Hamilton*, 2 vols. (Naples: F. Morelli, 1766–7), II, p. 32. The allusion was first noted by Gert Schiff in *Johann Heinrich Füssli, 1741–1825, Text und Oeuvrekataloge*, 2 vols. (Zurich: Schweizerisches Institut fur Kunstwissenschaft, 1973), I, p. 445.
26. *Desire and Excess: The Nineteenth-Century Culture of Art* (Princeton and Oxford: Princeton University Press, 2000), p. 52.
27. Pen, ink and wash on pink card, 36.0 × 47.8 (14 ⅛ × 18 ⅞), British Museum, London, Roman Album, Inv.no. 1885-3-14-204.
28. *Collection of Engravings from Ancient Vases, mostly of pure Greek workmanship discovered in sepulchres in the kingdom of the Two Sicilies but chiefly in the neighbourhood of Naples during the course of the years 1789 and 1790 now in the possession of Sir Wm. Hamilton*, 4 vols. (Naples: W. Tischbein, 1791–5), III, plate 20, facing p. 28.
29. Ibid., p. 28.
30. *Henry Fuseli 1741–1825*. Exh. cat. (London: Tate Gallery, 1975), pp. 72–3.
31. 1777–8; pen, ink and wash on card, 27.2 × 19.7 (10 ¾ × 7 ¾), British Museum, London, Roman Album, Inv.no. 1885-3-14-256.

32. *Ossian Singing*, 1772, pen and brown wash touched with oil, oval, 46.7 × 59.9 (18 $^{3}/_{8}$ × 23 $^{5}/_{8}$), National Galleries of Scotland, Edinburgh.
33. In 1767 Runciman was commissioned by Sir James Clerk to produce decorations including a painted ceiling for the new Penicuik House he was building in Edinburgh. The building was destroyed by fire in 1899. See Duncan Macmillan, *Painting in Scotland: The Golden Age* (Oxford: Phaidon, 1986), pp. 52–9.
34. *Remarks on the Writings and Conduct of J. J. Rousseau*, 1767, ed. Karl S. Guthrie, The Augustan Reprint Society (Los Angeles: Clark Memorial Library, University of California, 1960), pp. 5–6.
35. Recorded by Knowles, I, p. 377.
36. *Analytical Review*, I, June 1788, p. 221.
37. 91 × 71 (35 $^{7}/_{8}$ × 28), Zurich, Zollikon, Martin Hürliman.
38. *The Diary; or, Woodfall's Register*. No. 876. Thursday, January 12, 1792, p. 3.
39. 1777–8; pen, ink and wash on card, 35.5 × 20.8 (14 × 8 $^{1}/_{4}$), British Museum, London, Roman Album, Inv.no. 1885-3-14-259.
40. *Füssli pittore di Shakespeare: Pittura e teatro 1775–1825*, ed. Fred Licht, Simona Tosini Pizzetti and David H. Weinglass, exh. cat. (Milan: Electa, 1997), p. 120.
41. *The Life and Art of Henry Fuseli* (London: Thames and Hudson, 1972), pp. 82–3.
42. Etching, 13.5 × 10.3 (5 $^{5}/_{16}$ × 4), Mackelvie Trust Collection, Auckland City Art Gallery Toi o Tamaki.
43. Fourth Lecture: 'Invention Continued', Knowles, II, p. 201.
44. *c.* 1767; pen on paper, 27.9 × 48.9 (11 $^{1}/_{8}$ × 19 $^{1}/_{4}$), National Gallery of Scotland, Edinburgh.
45. Letter of 27 April 1771 to Miss Mary Moser, *Letters*, p. 13.
46. Letter from Patrick Murdoch to Sir Andrew Mitchell, 13 December 1768, *Letters*, p. 9.
47. 17 August 1790, *Letters*, p. 61.
48. *The Plays of William Shakespeare* (London: Rivington, 1805). This used the text of Steevens revised by A. Chalmers.
49. 151.1 × 212.1 (59 $^{1}/_{2}$ × 83 $^{1}/_{2}$), Town Hall, Lytham St. Anne's, Lancashire (Fylde Borough Council Collection).
50. Lecture II; Knowles, II, p. 101.
51. Lecture IV; Knowles, II, p. 190.
52. 148 × 217 (58 $^{3}/_{8}$ × 85 $^{7}/_{16}$), Museo Nacional del Prado, Madrid.
53. 71 × 91 (27 $^{7}/_{8}$ × 36 $^{7}/_{16}$), Kunstmuseum, Basle. See Antal, Frederick, *Fuseli Studies* (London: Routledge, 1956), p. 102.
54. This is explored in Rona Goffen, *Titian's Women* (New Haven and London: Yale University Press, 1997), pp. 159–69.
55. Title page to *A Series of Prints illustrative of the most celebrated British Poets*, No. 1 (London: Boydell, 1788–9).
56. See *Füssli pittore di Shakespeare*, p. 100.
57. Fuseli's own anonymous review of the print in the *Analytical Review*, IV, July 1789, p. 369.
58. 106 × 82.5 (41 $^{3}/_{4}$ × 32 $^{1}/_{2}$), Sciaffusa, Museum zu Allerheiligen. Engraved as plate no. 21, 16.5 × 26 (6 $^{1}/_{2}$ × 10 $^{1}/_{4}$).
59. 92.5 × 113 (36 $^{7}/_{16}$ × 44 $^{1}/_{2}$), Private collection, Switzerland.

60. Untraced; engraved by James Caldwell, 23 April 1798, 50 × 63 (19 11/16 × 24 3/4).
61. Untraced; engraved by Robert Thew, 29 September 1796, 50 × 63 (19 11/16 × 24 3/4).
62. 5–7 May 1789.
63. Untraced; engraved by William Satchwell Leney, 25 March 1795, 55.5 × 40.5 (21 7/8 × 15 7/8).
64. Pen and ink and wash on paper, 30.8 × 22 (12 1/4 × 8 5/8), Kunsthaus Zürich.
65. 1544; woodcut, 33.9 × 19.9 (13 5/16 × 7 13/16), National Gallery of Art, Washington D.C.
66. 259 × 363 (102 × 143), Art Gallery of Ontario, Toronto. Engraved by Richard Earlom, 1 August 1792.
67. John Caspar Lavater, *Essays on Physiognomy: designed to promote the knowledge and the love of mankind*, translated from the French by Henry Hunter, 3 vols. (London: printed for John Murray; H. Hunter; and T. Holloway, 1789–98), II, p. 292.
68. *The Bee; or, a Companion to the Shakespeare Gallery; containing a catalogue-raisonée of all the pictures; with comments, illustrations, and remarks* (London: T. Cadell, 1799), p. 48.
69. *Analytical Review*, 1788–9, p. 112. This article is not listed by Eudo C. Mason as one of Fuseli's contributions, but the style of writing and the fact that a second part of the same review in a subsequent volume is attributed to Fuseli make it clear that the artist is responsible. See *The Mind of Henry Fuseli: Selections from his Writings with an Introductory Study* (London: Routledge and Kegan Paul, 1951), p. 356.

CHAPTER 5

GEORGE ROMNEY: MEDITATIONS OF A VOLATILE FANCY

I

'Mr Romney (said Lord Thurlow one day to the artist) before you paint Shakespeare I advise you to read him.'[1] Too much weight should not be placed on this remark, qualified as it is by its uncertain context and its quotation by Romney's proprietorial friend William Hayley; but, as Alex Kidson points out,[2] Thurlow spoke from experience, having translated and glossed a passage from Virgil's *Georgics* so that Romney could paint it. The comment is useful in focusing doubts that have been raised about the extent of Romney's acquaintance with the plays, and his literary sensibility in general. Romney certainly lacked the close critical reading skills of Fuseli or Blake, and his knowledge of literature even at a surface level was limited, since his early education was far more extensive in visual and practical domains. Yet to dismiss his treatments of the plays would be to take a very narrow view of Shakespeare visualisation, privileging textual close reading above other interpretive techniques. Throughout his creative output the artist shows a compulsive interest in the plays, repeatedly presenting favoured episodes to which he responded with deep feeling in a series of ways which, as the following pages will make clear, offer an alternative to the readings of his contemporaries that is immediate and individual. Yet Thurlow's comment is helpful in directing attention to an area of uncertainty around Romney's working method, since little is known about the ways in which the artist experienced the plays. Isaac Reed gave him a copy of his edition of Shakespeare after having his portrait painted in 1796,[3] but this comes many years after most of Romney's serious Shakespeare work, and the evidence of his reading depends circumstantially on the presence of the editions of Johnson and others in the library of William

Hayley, in whose house at Eartham, near Chichester, he stayed every summer after their first meeting in 1776.[4] A more firmly documented source is provided by Romney's visits to the theatre, followed by discussions in the company of 'The Unincreasables', a group of eight including Reed and the actor John Henderson, formed in 1777.

In his biography of the artist, Hayley gives an account suggesting that Romney's knowledge of the plays rested on discussion and imaginative sympathy:

> He had a quick and keen relish for the beauties of that wonderful poet, altho' his own fancy was so volatile, and his mode of reading so desultory, that it may be questioned, if he ever read, without interruption, two acts of the dramas that he most cordially admired. (*Life*, pp. 113–14)

In his memoir of his father, John Romney makes clear that Shakespeare was a major force for the artist, pointing out that *King Lear* was the subject of the first and last painting that he produced (*Life*, p. 26), and claiming that his father proposed the scheme of a National Gallery of Shakespeare painting to Alderman Boydell (*Life*, p. 151). The actuality is far from clear, but it is certain that he responded to the scheme with great enthusiasm and had apparently long wished to spend more time in painting the plays.

Hayley also records that Romney used the 'riding-house' that he had built at Eartham 'to meditate on the various pictures from Shakespeare, that he hoped to produce' (*Life*, p. 127), and later relates this to a more directly Shakespearean frame, speaking of the 'meditation, in which Romney often loved to indulge with a degree of solemn humour, resembling the moody reflexions of Jaques, in As You Like It' (*Life*, pp. 265–6). A similar approach is hinted at by John Romney's assertion that *The Tempest*, *A Midsummer Night's Dream* and *Macbeth* were the artist's favourites, 'over which his imagination frequently brooded with congenial enthusiasm and delight' (*Memoirs*, p. 127).

This meditative process was probably marshalled in particular directions by Hayley. His claim to have assisted the artist by reading aloud to him while he painted (*Life*, p. 327) does not refer explicitly to Shakespeare, although the plays may well have been included. Hayley certainly suggested passages for the artist to paint. In a letter of 21 January 1787 – during the most productive period of Romney's Shakespeare output – Hayley assures his friend that he is reading the plays and 'perusing keenly for yr sake' (*Life*, p. 120). In reply, the artist voices gratitude 'for the subjects you have pointed out' (letter of 3 May 1791, *Life*, p. 157) and later writes 'I am delighted with the ideas you have suggested' (11 October 1793, *Life*, p. 207). That this relationship extends into composition and treatment is strongly hinted at elsewhere. The artist's son refers to 'some officious individual' (*Memoir*, 153) as having suggested the rearrangement of the painting of *The Tempest* for Boydell to exclude Caliban and incorporate the shipwreck: the reference is similar in tone to many other allusions to Hayley. If this is so, then Hayley assumes a directorial role rather similar to that of Hanmer, a circumstance that raises the teasing question of how far the sensibility that produced *The Triumphs of Temper* influenced the resultant images – although the probable answer is that both men shared a quality of sensibility in the fashion of the day, to which Hayley provided a degree of textual focus.

What emerges as a probable sequence is that Romney would read a passage at Hayley's suggestion, hear it read aloud, or see a performance, and discuss it with Henderson, Reed and others before, with suggestions and support from Hayley, entering a period of contemplation. His many notebooks suggest that initial, visceral responses to character, theme and setting were developed over long periods and in many images that present the same episode, or ones drawn from slightly different stages of the same scene. It is in these visual meditations around key moments that Romney makes one of his most individual contributions to Shakespeare visualisation.

One of the difficulties in reading and assessing Romney's work arises from its medium. The bulk of his output consists of images that are intimate in scale and rhetoric – drawings in watercolour wash, sometimes with outlines in pencil or pen and ink, occasionally heightened with chalk. That these are often described as sketches, with the implication that they are merely preparatory exercises for paintings never completed, both reveals and perpetuates an approach that seriously distorts their meaning and value: while some are executed in preparation for Romney's few large Shakespeare paintings, most are self-sufficient designs with an integrity of composition and meaning that demand consideration on their own terms. Those groups of images that treat closely related scenes should be read almost in the same manner as suites of engravings: only in this way does the full richness of Romney's mediation of the plays become clear.

Important though they are, Romney's wash-drawings constitute only one part of his output of Shakespeare images. There are also a handful of Shakespeare paintings of the kind that the age demanded – large, formal oils that imposed a high rhetorical stance towards the onlooker, and formed the basis of subsequent engravings. Others, in a range of media that include watercolour wash and formal oils, work in dialogue with significant contemporary conventions of representation. While perhaps lacking the immediacy of the wash-drawings, they nonetheless offer a new approach to the treatment of the plays. These images do much to reveal, by contrast, the originality of many of the more intimate works; yet they also have a value of their own, constituting a different kind of Shakespeare imaging that assimilates the plays into a variety of wider cultural domains. To categorise Romney's Shakespeare output into these three groups is, like any such division, a simplification; but as well as suggesting the range of his work it throws into sharper relief the particular identity of the wash-drawings. It is these that reveal the workings of his visual imagination at its most acute intersection with the plays of Shakespeare.

II

Writing to Hayley in February 1788 Romney complained 'This cursed portrait-painting! How I am shackled with it' (*Life*, p. 123). For most of his working life in London, Romney was an established and successful portraitist – so successful that his reputation at times exceeded that of Reynolds. His outburst reflects the frustrations of working with unsympathetic sitters, acute for someone of his hypersensitive nature, but it also rests on the contemporary belief that history painting was the highest form of art. The simple opposition that this suggests is misleading. Apart from his fine society portraits and conversation pieces, many of Romney's best-known paintings, and those with which he clearly sought to increase his reputation, are deliberative in their combination not only of these two apparently opposed genres but of other forms that occupy a middle ground between them. They include a small number of Shakespeare images that, in their considered use of a mingling of genres, need careful exploration to reveal their nature as mediations of the plays and their place within larger aesthetic currents of the day. Chief among them is the painting of *Troilus and Cressida* that Romney produced for the Boydell Gallery generally known as *Cassandra Raving* (1792–5? Fig. 41).[5]

As well as presenting an episode from the play, the painting exemplifies a particular kind of portraiture to which both Romney and Reynolds contributed, in which the subject is painted in the persona of an historical or literary character. Prominent among sitters so depicted was Emma Hart, later Lady Hamilton, whom Romney met in 1782 and painted with a frequency suggesting obsession. Famous for her 'attitudes', the adoption of poses and expressions imitative of other figures, she became an inevitable source of such images, and Romney painted her as Circe, Calypso, Magdalen, a Bacchante, and Saint Cecilia. Hayley makes the following comment, which perhaps suggests one reason for Romney's choice of her for this image:

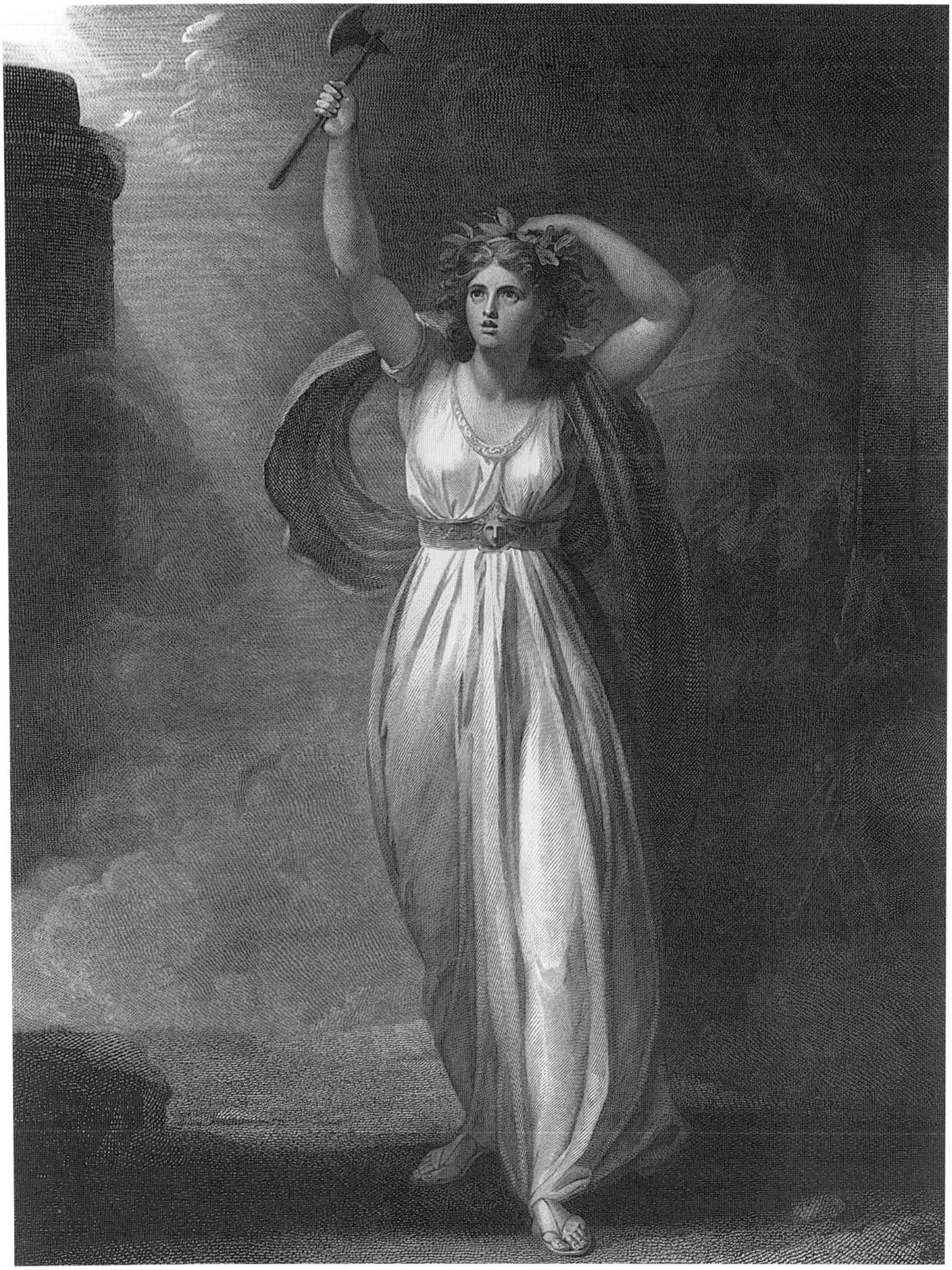

41 George Romney, *Cassandra Raving*. Engraved by Francis Legat, 1795.

> Her features, like the language of Shakespeare, could exhibit all the feelings of nature, and all the gradations of every passion, with a most fascinating truth, and felicity of expression. (*Life*, p. 119)

The painting shows Cassandra wearing a crown of laurel and wielding an axe. The engraving includes these lines:

> Cry, Troyans, cry! lend me ten thousand eyes,
> And I will fill them with prophetic tears
> (2.2.100–1)[6]

The reference provides a direct focus for the scene depicted behind Cassandra. To the left is one of the towers of Troy; on the right some soldiers descend on a ladder from the belly of the Trojan horse. Text and image work together here to reveal the main thrust of the image, which is to convey the accuracy of Cassandra's prophecy. Yet this is a general statement of the events of the siege of Troy, not a direct discussion of Shakespeare's play, which takes place before the events Romney shows and makes no mention of them. The painting's history implies its origins in classical myth rather than Shakespeare's play: although exhibited in the Boydell Shakespeare Gallery in 1792, with an engraving published three years later, it was begun in 1786, before the dinner at which the Gallery was proposed.[7]

This would seem to support Thurlow's comment about Romney's approach to his literary sources, and it certainly shows that the image lacks any immediate textual engagement beyond a limited extension of Cassandra's character by showing the truth of her prophecy. The value of the image as a Shakespearean document lies in other directions. In presenting Emma Hart as a Shakespearean figure Romney is propounding a new kind of relationship between Shakespeare and contemporary culture which, by implication, relocates the plays on the same level as the episodes from Greek mythology and classical tragedy which are the origins of other fashionable portraits of aristocrats adopting personae. A celebrated figure from high society and the nation's tutelary genius are thus brought together, so that what it lacks in textual reading the image makes up in its assimilation of Shakespeare into another level of social practice. This approach does not accord with the practice of painting as critical commentary, but through its style and socio-literary allusions it offers a valid alternative method of founding a national school of history painting as the equal of any in Europe. Ultimately, the combination of genres constitutes another major strand of Shakespeare activity, the inclusion of the Bard in aspects of national life and culture without detailed reference to the plays, that follows the enthronement of Shakespeare as national genius. In short, the crucial thing about what the Cassandra painting says about Shakespeare's text is that it says nothing at all, but a great deal about how Shakespeare was being processed as a cultural commodity.

Elsewhere, Romney's work continues this negotiation between genres to produce different kinds of Shakespearean commentary, most particularly in the two large allegorical images produced for Boydell, *The Infant Shakespeare Attended by Nature and the Passions* (c. 1791–2)[8] and *The Infant Shakespeare Nursed by Comedy and Tragedy* (1791).[9] In the former the infant playwright is placed between a series of passions drawn from Le Brun's personifications, the aim being to show the perfection with which Shakespeare's art can express each one – an assumption perhaps carried over into John Romney's comment about Lady Hamilton's powers of imitation. The second places the child between Tragedy and Comedy on the right and an undoubtedly English group of trees at the left, suggesting that the infant is a phenomenon not only of nature but of specifically English nature. Emma Hamilton again has a role here, appearing as the model for Comedy. As before, nationalism, portraiture and the Grand Style are united and Shakespeare conscripted into their service.

While these images move away from the plays to locate the dramatist within broader cultural domains, a pair of drawings of Henderson as Falstaff return to the theatre to present aspects of performance. This they do by appropriating the familiar genre of 'before and after' painting used to comic or satiric effect by Hogarth and others. In approach they are very different from Romney's two formal portraits of the actor, which do little to illuminate the scenes they show: *John Henderson as Macbeth* (c. 1787)[10] presents the initial encounter in the habitual windswept landscape, and *Macbeth and the Witches* (1785)[11] offers a ghostly outline of the show of kings and a Garrick-like gesture of recoil from Macbeth. These are clearly portraits in character, and have more to say about Henderson, and the idealisation – or idolisation – of the actor, than about the play.

The two drawings of Henderson as Falstaff show him just after his supposed killing of Hotspur. In the first he drags the body away to claim his reward; in the second, on the approach of Hal, he rapidly lets it fall.[12] The two function together as a static equivalent of stage humour through the skilful use of the 'before and after' trope. Many accounts record Henderson's pre-eminence as a comic Falstaff,[13] and these images, and the many related sketches of the actor's head, suggest that the resemblance is very close. Seen together, the two images suggest one of the sources of humour in Henderson's performance: the speed with which he releases the body, his furtive yet amused expression enhanced by small eyes twinkling above full cheeks. While no records survive, it is perhaps

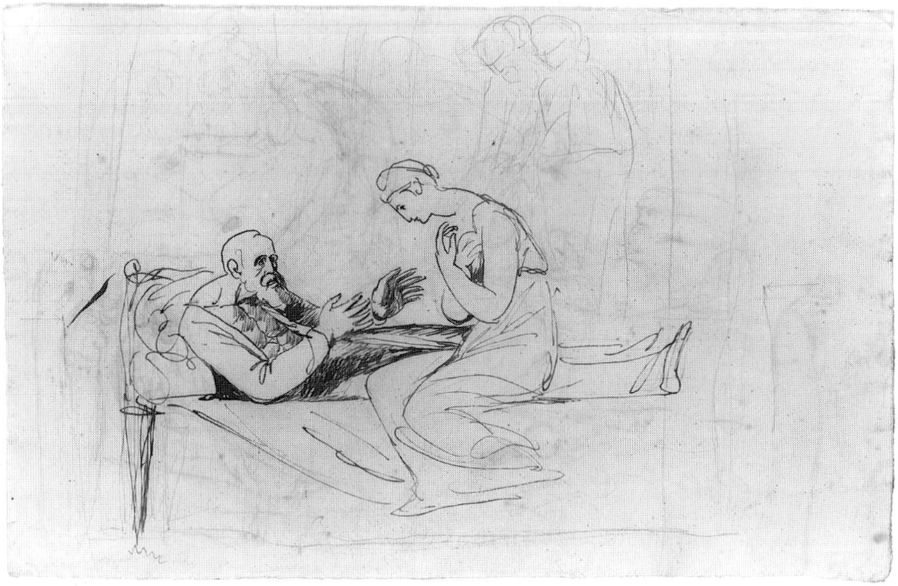

42 George Romney, *Lear Awakening from Madness*, c. 1777.

a not unreasonable conjecture that the sketches caused much amusement at a meeting of The Unincreasables. Offering little in terms of textual interpretation, they are significant in the performance history of Falstaff and perhaps unique in the immediate relation of the two moments they present, using the tradition of paired images to show the dynamism of theatrical action, in the process revealing the strength of Henderson as a comic actor and invigorating both the genres to which they contribute.

The tensions between styles and the contingent fusions they generate serve in the above instances to locate Romney's images within a range of arenas of Shakespeare activity, social, theatrical and patriotic; but they do not facilitate a close analysis of the plays. An instance of how the elision of styles may work to this end is provided in two very early images of King Lear. The first is *Lear Awakening from Madness* (c. 1777: Fig. 42),[14] the second *The Death of Cordelia* (c. 1775–7: Plate 6).[15] Both make their effect by using divergent stylistic vocabularies for each of their two central characters, resulting in an immediate utterance of the moral gulf between them at the key moment depicted. Much of the effect resides in the act of selection; whether by Hayley's recommendation or the artist's own choice, the two follow a common procedure by freezing the play's movement at an instant of particular emotional force, enhanced by the contemporary cult of feeling. Yet the composition and technique in both generate deeper reflections on character and action. The first drawing uses the differences in physical substance between the two figures to treat very short passages with great immediacy:

You do me wrong to take me out o' th' grave.
Thou art a soul in bliss (4.6.42–3)

and a little later;

You are a spirit, I know. Where did you die?
(4.6.46)

The two figures are quite different, the dark shading that defines Lear giving a heaviness that is the reverse of the delicate outline of Cordelia. To classify them as Romantic and Neo-Classical is to simplify and distort; the two styles present different orders of being, and the encounter is greatly enriched by its compound location within the range of late eighteenth-century visual diction. The image is also effective because of the two figures' separation, Lear's outstretched hands seemingly in a different plane, visually and existentially, from Cordelia's bowed body. A final element adds to the concentration. Rather than attempt a detailed visualisation of the imagery Lear uses in the intervening lines – to present visually the 'wheel of fire', or the tears that 'scald like molten lead' – Romney is content to offer a broad statement of human and spiritual separation through an opposition of styles.

The contrast works to even greater effect in the second image. Here the classical purity of line used for Cordelia is slightly softened by the introduction of a pale wash, but the emotion is focused and the classical atmosphere heightened by the addition of three female attendants. Lear is in contrast huge, almost ape-like, as he holds Cordelia's body, the form emphasised by the single, strong curve of arms, back and head, extended by the dark cloak falling from his shoulders and the very heavy shadow by which he is surrounded, and which occupies the right side of the image with almost geometric precision. Yet this clumsiness engenders a tenderness that is enhanced by the coloration of Lear's face, a soft brown-pink that gives a calm lightness to this focal point of the composition. The scene is precisely located in 5.3: one of the attendant women has brought the looking-glass Lear calls for (235) and he himself holds a feather to Cordelia's face, depicting the line 'This feather stirs! she lives' (239). Again the image discloses the immense disparity of character and moral imagination between Lear and Cordelia.

That both images achieve their mediations of the play almost entirely through the use of contrasting styles of drawing, yet maintain an integrity of composition, reflects powerfully upon their value in making critical readings possible only through their visual medium. In the formal painting of Cassandra, merged stylistic frames move the reference away from Shakespeare's text; in these wash-drawings, the poised balance of styles is fundamental to the insight with which they address it.

III

Romney's treatment of *The Tempest* for the Boydell Shakespeare Gallery has frequently been dismissed as a failure. Hayley asserted that even the artist himself was aware of its 'striking defects' (*Life*, p. 141) before going on to cite the compositional imbalance stressed by almost all subsequent critics; John Romney implicitly blamed Hayley for modifying the subject from Romney's original invention and so producing 'an anomaly in composition' (*Memoirs*, p. 153). The painting itself, of a size intended to match its heroic aspirations as a history painting, deteriorated badly through being kept rolled up in an iron foundry: it survives only in a series of fragments, so that the image must be judged from a surviving oil sketch (*c.* 1787–90: Fig. 43)[16] and the engraving by Benjamin Smith.[17] In all three of its incarnations the image attempts to draw together two spatially discrete compositions, with a difference in viewpoint that much disturbed its first viewers; yet seen in retrospect, through eyes accustomed to Modernist disjunctions of plane and perspective, it may not look quite so flawed. John Romney's judgment that it is 'rich in colouring, without being overcharged with gums and varnishes' (*Memoirs*, p. 153) is borne out by the oil sketch. The deep red of the clothes of Ferdinand and some of the sailors is echoed in the red-browns that dominate the canvas and intensify a mood more immediately suggestive of the Burkean Sublime. The image has an energy absent from the engraved version, caused partly by the precipitous slope of the ship towards the left, but mainly by the loose, full brushwork. Some idea of the qualities added in the final painting may be gained from a rare copy of the engraving that has been hand coloured (Plate 12).[18] In this the darkness produced by the density of the engraving is displaced by a greater sense of energy and movement in the sea and sky; the figures in the centre appear with more articulation, clarifying the composition through an enlarged sense of recession. The fault-line between the two passages of which the image is built is still apparent, but the greater vigour the composition acquires with the colouring defines

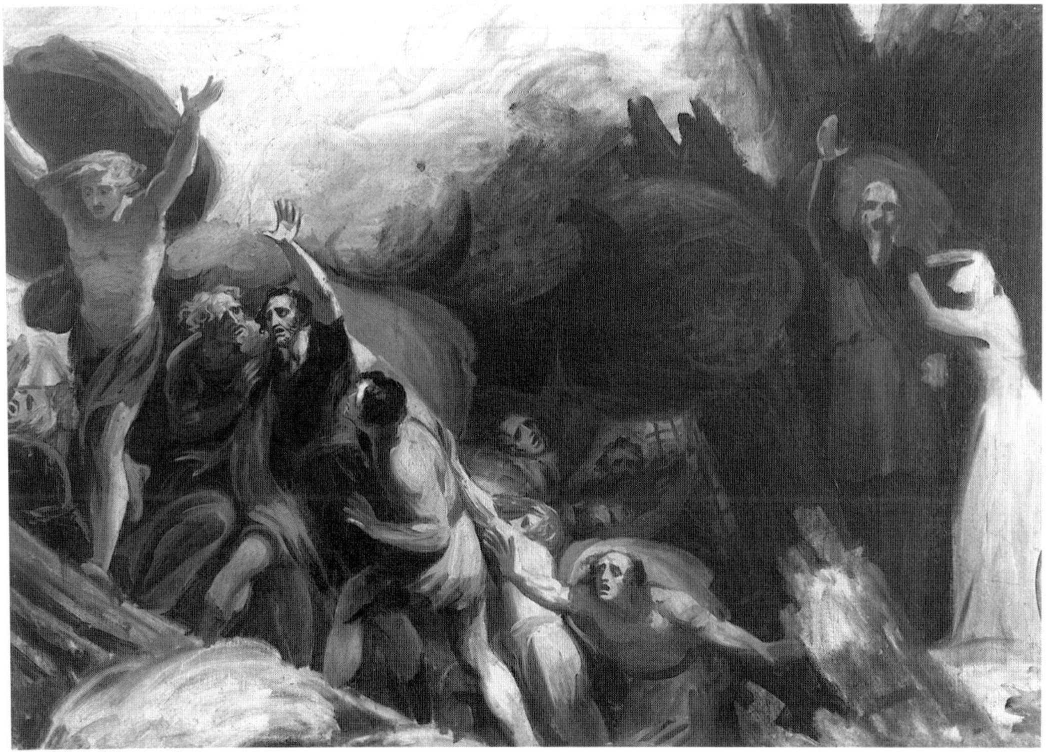

43 George Romney, Oil sketch for *The Tempest*, c. 1787–90.

this as a deliberate statement of synchronicity as much as an awkwardness of construction.

The major portion of the engraving shows the shipwreck, with Alonso apparently being restrained from jumping into the sea by his attendants and the Boatswain while, at the extreme left, Ferdinand, hands above his head and surrounded by a swirling cloak, leaps from the boat. Above him, three figures represent Ariel, the multiple presentation here embodying Ariel's lines 'Now on the beak, / Now in the waist, the deck, in every cabin, / I flamed amazement' (1.2.196–8), an arrangement far more vigorous than the single figure shown in the oil-sketch. The turbulent masses of cloud and spray reveal the force of the storm, though the presence of a patch of light perhaps hints at the redemptive uses to which it will be put by Prospero, its conjuror.

Beneath these figures, Ferdinand is seen leaping into the sea in a fairly direct presentation of Ariel's later report to Prospero that is printed below the engraving:

Not a soul
But felt a fever of the mad, and play'd
Some tricks of desperation. All but mariners
Plung'd in the foaming brine, and quit the vessel,
Then all afire with me: the King's son, Ferdinand,
With hair up-staring, – then like reeds, not hair, –
Was the first man that leap'd; cried, 'Hell is empty,
And all the devils are here.' (1.2.208–15)

As well as presenting a detail of the text, Ferdinand's windswept hair – absent from the oil-sketch – and upraised hands serve a compositional function in offering a link to the figure of Prospero at the extreme opposite end of the image, in a spatial dimension whose difference from the main focus so disturbed the original onlookers. In a classical grouping that contrasts forcefully with the Romantic sweep of the shipwreck, Prospero stands before his cell, robed as a magus and clearly modelled on a Renaissance Old Testament prophet. To his left stands Miranda, classically draped and in elegant *contrapposto*. These traditional figurations are matched by more recent techniques in Prospero's forthright gaze, Miranda's right hand raised in appeal and her left, fingers spread, moving towards her face in a statement of anxiety that combines the stereotypes of Le Brun with more immediate human observation. In these gestures, this passage of the painting condenses the essence of the scene's opening exchange. Miranda's first lines:

If by your art, my dearest father, you have
Put the wild waters in this roar, allay them.
(1.2.1–2)

are thus visually balanced by her father's answer:

Be collected:
No more amazement. Tell your piteous heart
There's no harm done. (1.2.13–15)

Whether the composition was devised by Hayley or by the artist himself, its effect is to offer a doubly telescoped statement of the play's action and driving forces. It combines Ferdinand's diving figure, an element later reported, not shown, with a depiction of the shipwreck of the first scene, and links it to the discussion of the storm and its moral purpose with which Prospero and Miranda begin scene two, a fusion of three moments that shows a fine sense of the adaptation of temporal sequence into spatial presentation. As well as compressing the action, the image encapsulates the main forces of the play. Prospero's magic is presented in its full ambivalence, the multiple figures of Ariel showing its dynamic power; the physical resemblance between Prospero and Antonio subtly introduces into the mind of the onlooker both the unnatural act of usurpation and the human-kindness of the forgiveness that Prospero will later advance towards his brother. Ferdinand and Miranda, polarised to the very edges of the composition, exhibit the romance drive that is the play's other major propellant. The engraving may be unsatisfactory in purely visual terms, but as a statement of the forces of the play it is powerfully suggestive, revealing in its multiple stagings another approach to the spatial presentation of the progressive time of the theatrical text and offering in its stylistic opposition of classical and expressive forms a metaphor of the play's own vital contrasts. In this it forms a strikingly appropriate image as the first visual presentation of the plays in the volume of large prints from the Boydell Gallery: it both elucidates character and action and presents itself as a comment on the essential difference between the forms of painting and drama, implicitly alerting the reader to the complexities of *ekphrasis* at the beginning of a collection that will explore and exploit the compound relationships it embraces.

In addition to its identities as a painting and an engraving within the Boydell collection, this image acquires further resonances when seen as part of the collection of treatments of the opening of the play produced by Romney in more intimate media. Together they represent not a narrative sequence but rather an exploration of the forces unleashed in the first act; but they may usefully be first approached in the order of the play's chronology. The earliest moment is presented in two wash-drawings in the Folger Shakespeare Library, *Miranda kneeling on the seashore alone watching the storm*[19] and *Miranda watching the storm* (Fig. 44).[20] In the first, Miranda is shown in profile, surrounded by billowing clouds generated by bravura wash strokes familiar in much of Romney's work; at the top left, a figure that replicates the outermost of the three Ariels from the Boydell painting appears as if on a wave-crest. The second is very similar but shows more clearly the foundering ship in the middle ground, with Ariel again in the upper left of a composition once more dominated by swirls of brown wash. In both, Miranda's distress is emphasised by her hands and arms, caught between reaching out to the suffering mariners and holding her body in anguish. The two drawings visualise the opening fears of Miranda, echoed in her first appeal to Prospero: they suggest the power not only of the storm but of the magician's conjurations, and reveal its ambivalence to Miranda at the outset of the action, reminding us that, to her at this moment, its purpose is for ill as much as for good. They also add to the depth of Miranda's character, extending her compassion at the shipwreck and establishing

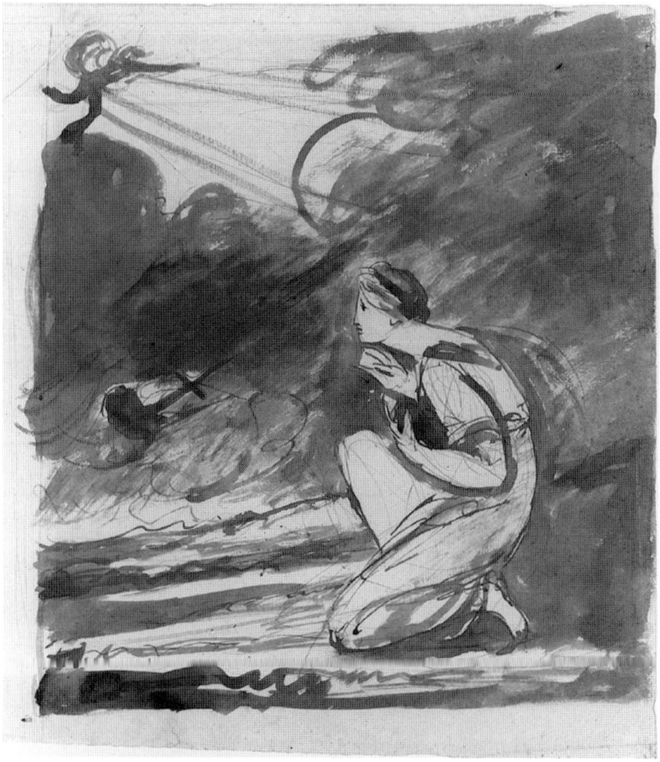

44 George Romney, *Miranda watching the storm*, c. 1786–90.

for her an identity independent of Prospero by showing her responses before he appears. This places her within the tradition of Shakespearean heroines defined through their compassion, then growing towards its climax in the next century; but it also reminds us that the outcome of the play is by no means certain at its beginning.

An untitled drawing in the Fitzwilliam Museum, Cambridge[21] continues the discussion of the ambivalence of Prospero's power by showing him in a significantly different posture. Instead of standing reassuringly before Miranda he sits some distance behind her in the drawing's recessive space, half concealed within a cave, and hunched downwards looking at a book at his feet, presented in frontal composition. This suggests a mood of conjuration at best ambivalent and at worst sinister; he is 'rapt in secret studies' (1.2.77) that might just as easily result in the destruction of Alonso, Gonzalo and Ferdinand as in their redemptive progress on the island. The uncertainty is echoed in Miranda's posture, one hand held to her forehead and the other outstretched towards the shipwreck in partial embodiment of Le Brun's picture of fear.

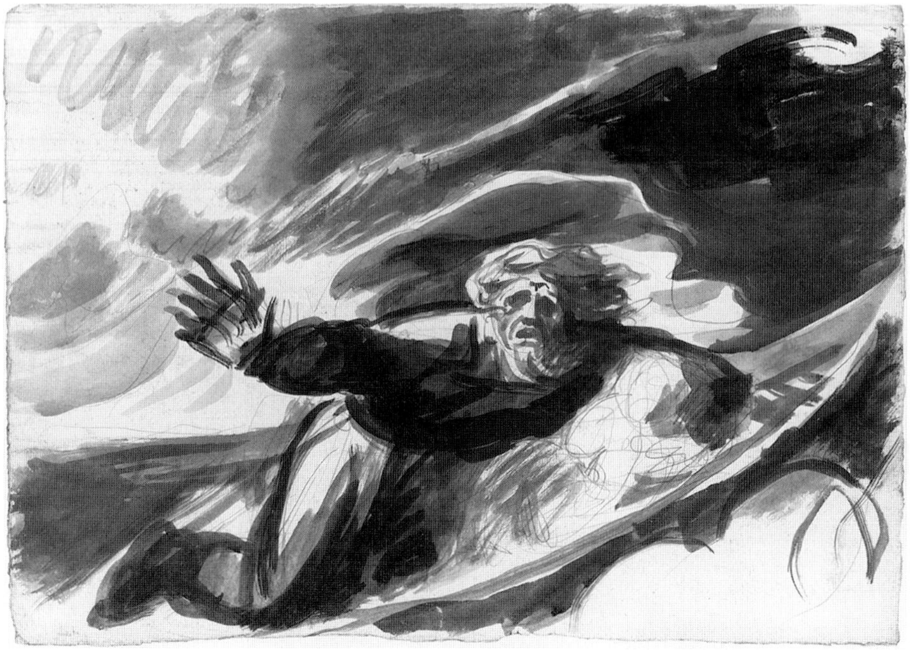

45 George Romney, *Man and Child in a Boat*, c. 1786–90.

This negative image is balanced by another wholly different reading of the opening of the play, that takes as its basis events subsequently narrated by Prospero. Catalogued in the Folger as *Man and Child in a Boat* (Fig. 45),[22] this presents Prospero and Miranda setting out to sea when exiled from Milan. The figure of the man has the flowing hair and beard familiar from the Prophet-Prospero, perhaps owing something to the figure of God in the Sistine Chapel ceiling, and the image as a whole has all the energy of the loosely sketched wash-drawings frequent in this period of Romney's work. The figure stares straight out of the composition, arms spread wide in a gesture of embrace which culminates in his left forearm folded protectively around Miranda, in visual recreation of the passage of Prospero's narrative in lines 144–151. The overall effect is to suggest a gentler aspect to his nature, a lyrical tenderness balancing the violence of the storm conjuration shown in his earlier lines: 'I have done nothing but in care of thee – / Of thee my dear one, thee my daughter' (1.2.16–17).

The next image in the play's sequence is a delicate Neo-Classical sketch, described in a pencilled inscription as 'an intended companion' to the Boydell storm image to show 'Ferdinand led by music in the air' (Fig. 46).[23] This may be a version of the projected 'large picture in the *Correggiesque* style' of which John Romney speaks (*Memoirs*, p. 128), but once again speculation about uncompleted

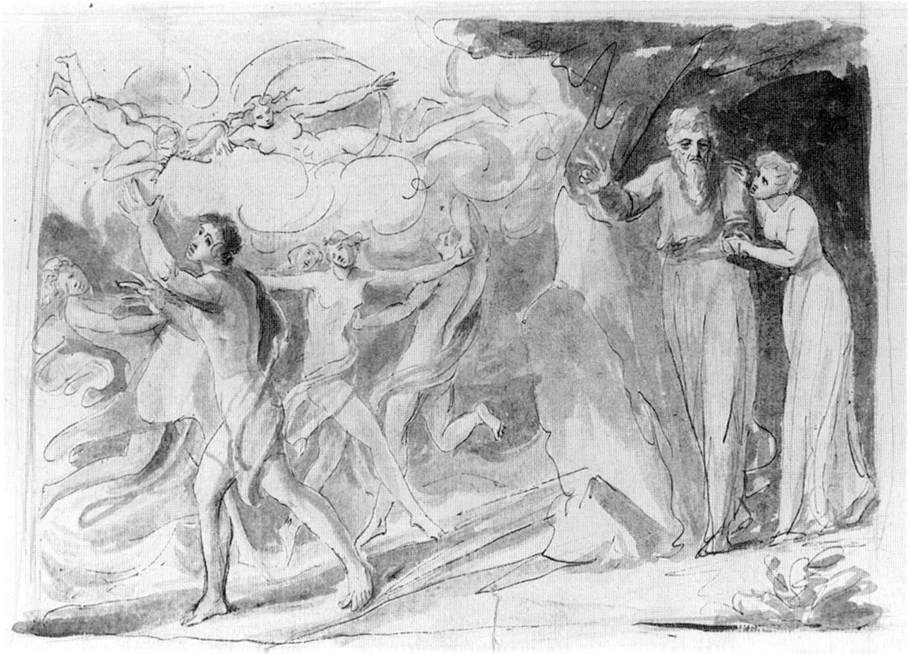

46 George Romney, *Ferdinand led by music in the air*, c. 1786–90.

oil paintings serves only to detract from the values of the surviving wash-drawings. Here, Prospero enacts his words (at 1.2.407–8) by pointing across from right to left, taking Miranda by the hand and showing her Ferdinand, who walks away from them at the left foreground. Above him fly two small female nudes; behind him four classically dressed figures dance in a circle. These are a conventional trope, recalling numerous versions of the seasons; but what makes them especially significant here is their resemblance to one of Blake's first watercolours, *Oberon, Titania and Puck with Fairies Dancing* (see Fig. 57), an image completed in 1785 and thus one with which Romney might well have been familiar. It carries with it the mood of magical reconciliation between the fairy king and queen, and the link to this pivotal moment adds to Miranda's first sight of Ferdinand a quality of intense richness, telescoping the play's movement to make clear its eventual outcome, and offering a metaphor of her 'What is't? A spirit?' (1.2.408) in terms both of another of the plays and of one of its most sensual visual embodiments. An alternative, and perhaps more likely, source is Poussin's *A Dance to the Music of Time* (c. 1639)[24], which Romney had seen in Rome and probably alluded to in *The Leveson-Gower Children* of 1777.[25] Here the association would suggest a grace transcending the temporal limitations of the island, adding another dimension of richness to the relationship between Ferdinand and Miranda. Regardless of reference, the image is particularly striking because of its idiom: rather than the bold, free washes of the earlier, threatening images that reveal the ambivalence of Prospero's power and the forces of the natural world, it uses the taut lines and poised grace of his earlier classical drawings to imply calm and resolution. The subtlety of the image is reinforced by comparison with two roughly contemporary versions of the same scene. Robert Edge Pine's *Miranda* (1782)[26] sets the events within a lush landscape, but fails to transmit the encounter's tensions or implications; the anonymous *Prospero, Miranda and Ariel* (*c.* 1770–90)[27] visualises the three figures in poses borrowed from classical sculptures without deploying the allusions to convey any larger critical meanings. In the Romney, by contrast, medium, reference and invention work together to offer a sensitive and suggestive reading of this essential turn in the play's movement.

Romney's vision of the play does not cease here; this would too easily complete the progress and ignore Prospero's intervention 'lest too light winning/ Make the prize light' (1.2.450–1). Another Folger image (see Fig. 47)[28] shows Prospero with arm upraised holding a wand, left arm outstretched with open palm to restrain Ferdinand, while Miranda stands before him open-mouthed, head tilted back in mute appeal. Her left hand, fingers open, is held out to the viewer, her right placed flat on Prospero's chest, and the whole combines elements of Le Brun's vocabulary with an observation of instinctive bodily movements to suggest a shocked appeal for restraint. The image presents the moment after Prospero has threatened Ferdinand and rendered him motionless, where Miranda pleads

O dear father
Make not too rash a trial of him, for
He's gentle, and not fearful.
(1.2.465–7)

This image, and a related one showing Miranda alone in similar posture,[29] reveal the destructive current still potent in Prospero's magic, balancing the apparent resolution hinted at elsewhere.

Romney's *Tempest* images circle around the forces of power and nurture displayed in the play's first act, laying bare its key determinants while giving due weight to the ambivalence of Prospero's magic, revealed both at its most threatening and through an intense protectiveness towards Miranda. They also endow Miranda's misgivings with more than usual force, and imply the resolution of the play's ending. As a group, they provide a visual mediation of the opening act's

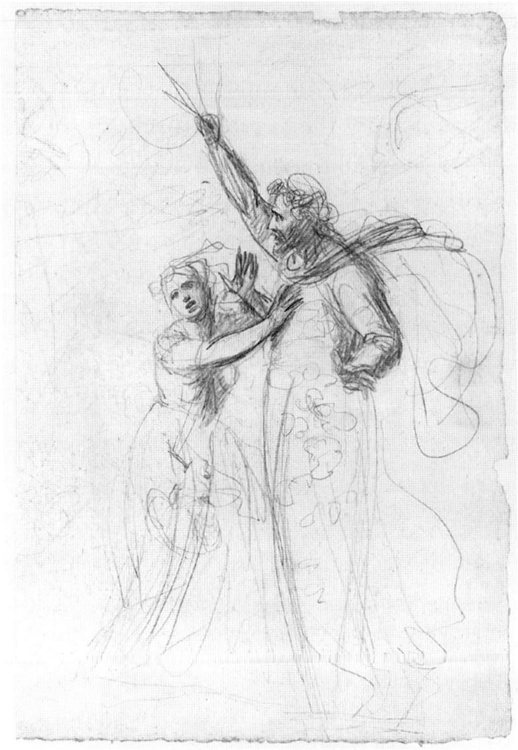

47 George Romney, *Prospero and Miranda*, c. 1786–90.

changing temper, constituting a suite of images revealing the complexities of the play as much through their changing styles as their implied allusions to imagery from Blake or Poussin and the emotional types of Le Brun. They reveal the depth of readings of which Romney is capable in images that disclose through their intimacy a special kind of visual mediation of the play and its movements. To see such work as merely preparatory to unachieved oil paintings is fundamentally to misunderstand the nature of Romney's critical intelligence; at its best, as here, it has a fluency and dynamism as powerful as any other of its day.

IV

While the combination of styles shown in the images of *King Lear* and *The Tempest* is powerfully suggestive as a interpretive medium, many of Romney's wash-drawings function through the use of single, immediate effects. This is the case with the large number of images that address aspects of the supernatural from *Macbeth*, *2 Henry VI* and *A Midsummer Night's Dream* – although here, as will later

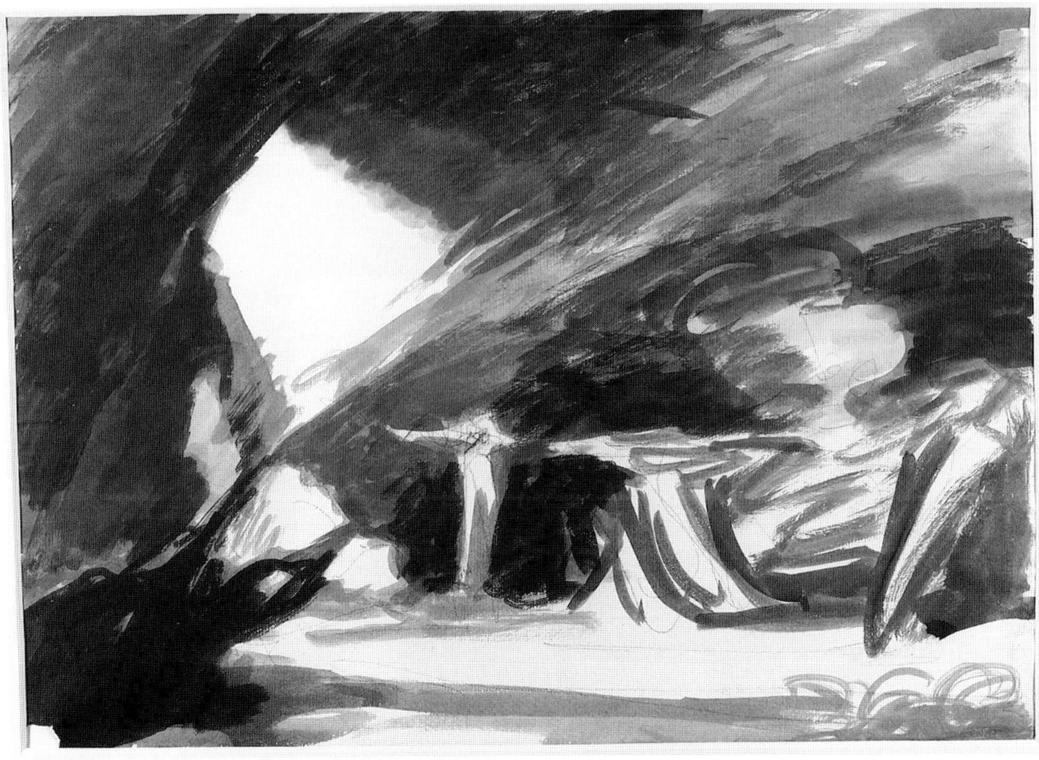

48 George Romney, *A Foregathering of Witches*, c. 1795–1800.

become apparent, echoes of related subjects often inflect the images with a range of other, parallel meanings, sometimes in ways familiar from the combination of portrait and historical painting.

Romney produced more drawings for *Macbeth* than for any other play, concentrating on three episodes: the initial encounter with the witches, the banquet and the cauldron scene. The treatments of the first of these are the most vigorous, and perhaps represent the purest form of a technique first seen in Wootton's painting: the visual embodiment of the play's verbal images of the darkening landscape as a moral emblem of the action. In some, the witches are all but indistinguishable from the heath or its windswept trees; in others, they seem to grow out of the land as an evil emanation, 'fen-sucked fogs' (*King Lear* 2.4.159) made animate. A series of related drawings, probably dating from the second half of the 1790s, shows the witches almost as a single entity in the centre of the composition, standing around the cauldron, with Macbeth before them, arms spread wide so as almost to suggest a serious parody of a crucifixion. All referred to as *A Foregathering of Witches*, perhaps the most forceful is that catalogued as the fourth (Fig. 48).[30] Torrential sweeps

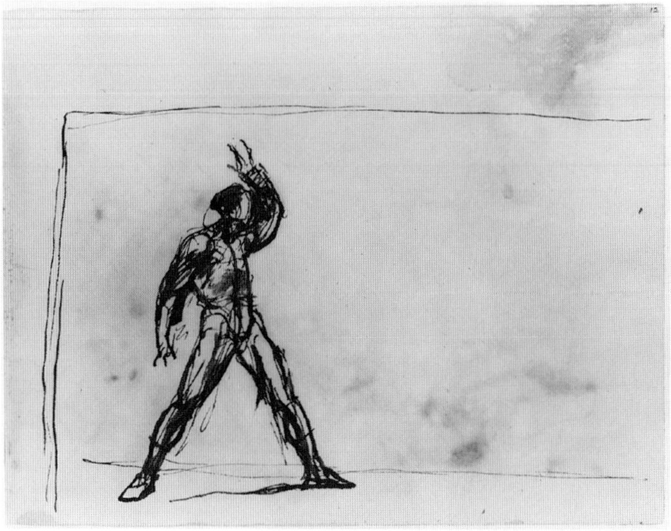

49 George Romney, *Macbeth: Banquet Scene, Figure of Macbeth*, 1790–2.

of wash surround all the figures, revealing the elemental forces unleashed in the confrontation. The power and breadth of execution itself becomes a metaphor of the intense energy of the scene, presenting the viewer in the act of perception with a parallel to Macbeth's condition as 'rapt in the wonder of it' (1.5.5).

The images for the banquet scene repeatedly explore and redefine some or all of three recurrent compositional elements – the figures of Macbeth and Lady Macbeth, a group of diners loosely sketched around a table, and the ghost itself, often occupying the middle ground between the other elements. Striking among them is a wash-drawing of Macbeth from the Folger collection (see Fig. 49)[31] that uses a figure that recurs in many other treatments. Its effect is mainly generated by the near-frenetic energy of the figure's modelling in rapid brush strokes barely contained by the pen outlines, the upraised left arm apparently in motion, the hands suggested by minimal strokes, the head sinister in its small, dark incompleteness. Added to this is its iconographic source. In Paris in 1790, Romney visited Jacques-Louis David. Hayley (p. 149) claims that at this time the painter was at work on *The Oath of the Horatii*,[32] but this cannot be the case since the painting was exhibited in 1784; more likely, Romney saw this painting, and perhaps also the related *Oath of the Tennis Court*,[33] on which David would most likely have been at work, and which develops and extends the figurations of the earlier painting. Romney's image takes its key compositional element, the figure with the upraised arm, as the basis of the figure of Macbeth, and the resemblance produces a particular kind of moral complexity: the heroism of the Horatii, engaged in the protection of the Roman state, and the idealism of the early stages of the revolution in France, are implicitly contrasted with the personal ambition of Macbeth. Together these resonances convey to the figure a moral ambiguity compounded of an ironic statement of loyalty to high political values and the inevitability of a sombre, destructive violence. This not only underscores the moral convolutions of *Macbeth*; it also steps outside the play to add a degree of political immediacy that, in England in the years immediately after the French Revolution, has an insistent threat, bringing a contemporary parallel to Macbeth's actions. The large number of other images of Macbeth in the banquet scene, balanced with the restraining figure of Lady Macbeth and the guests, and executed sometimes in outline and sometimes in dark wash, show a similar energy and disturbance: the existence of so many suggests the impossibility of fixing the scene within a single frame, and this itself reinforces the idea of moral uncertainty as well as stressing again the restless dramatic energies that they all represent.

Of the many treatments of the scene in the Fitzwilliam Museum, one in particular stands out in using a different structure for the figure of Macbeth (Plate 8).[34] Instead of confronting the ghost with raised arms, he recoils with arms outstretched. The comparison is itself significant, suggesting the duality of Macbeth's response between a heroism borrowed from David and a recoil more immediately present in the play's text and perhaps recalling performance in the Garrick tradition. Lady Macbeth stands at the right, opposite Macbeth, with the ghost occupying the intervening space; the isolation of Macbeth further qualifies his moral position, and his recoil perhaps hints at his inability to face the intensity of his guilt and its supernatural manifestations without her aid. What is most striking is the medium. The drawing is executed mainly in thin pen strokes, using the taut lines familiar from the earlier *Lear* images, but the figure of Macbeth itself is splashed with watercolour, applied almost arbitrarily with little relation to the figure's outline. The result is a suggestion of Macbeth's guilt through a visualisation of the imagery of blood that runs throughout the play, from the 'gouts of blood' (2.1.146) on the dagger to Macbeth's admission to Macduff: 'my soul is too much charged/ With blood of thine already' (5.8.5–6). More explicitly, the moral opposition between Macbeth and Banquo is achieved by a visualisation of the corporeal difference between them that includes a reversal of the scene's verbal imagery. When the ghost first appears, Macbeth cries 'Never shake/ Thy gory locks at me!' (3.4.50–51); later, in the cavern scene, he refers to 'the blood-boltered Banquo' (4.1.122). Romney's sketch presents Banquo's ghost in outline, a figure with arms spread wide, its pure whiteness the complete opposite of Macbeth's spattered body. It is Macbeth who is 'blood-boltered'; the extreme difference in

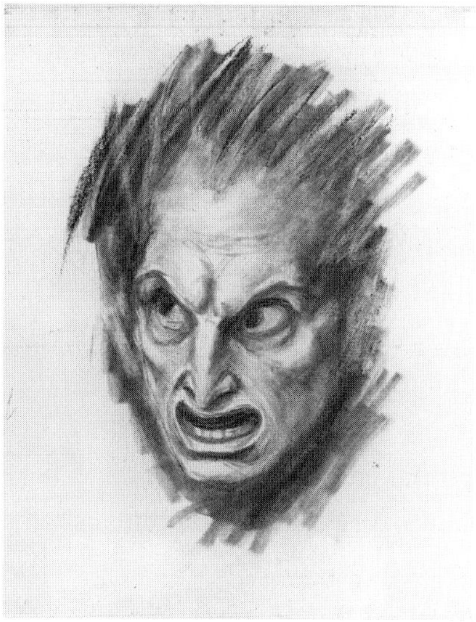

50 George Romney, *Large Head*, c. 1787–90.

tonality between the two figures, coupled with the absence of any similar coloration elsewhere in the image, presents the moral isolation of the figure in wholly visual terms.

The cavern scene is treated in a way that reveals another aspect of Romney's working method: the transferability of scenes and elements from subjects that, while apparently unrelated, are revealed as similar at a very deep level. The links with the series of studies of Lapland witches are perhaps understandable in revealing a fascination with the supernatural, but the other subjects are less obviously related: the studies related to John Howard's prison visits and the fairies from *A Midsummer Night's Dream* are more remote and consequently more suggestive. The motifs of the witches dancing around the cauldron and the fairies dancing before Titania in several instances are visually alike and, while the similarity has more to suggest about the ambivalence of the latter, the pairing is suggestive about both: the supernatural world, it seems, has its own logic, separate from human morality, and the visualisation that Romney gives it conveys this otherness through the free suggestiveness of energetic brush work rather than the detailed explication the scene receives, in different ways, in Reynolds or Fuseli. The likenesses between the cavern scene and the Howard drawings act in a manner similar to the reference to David: by adding an allusion to the contemporary and the actual, they present a direct metaphor of the events of the play that vitalises their horror.

Romney's supernatural images also cover other plays. Some drawings of the conjuration scene in *2 Henry VI* together present a reading of much breadth. One

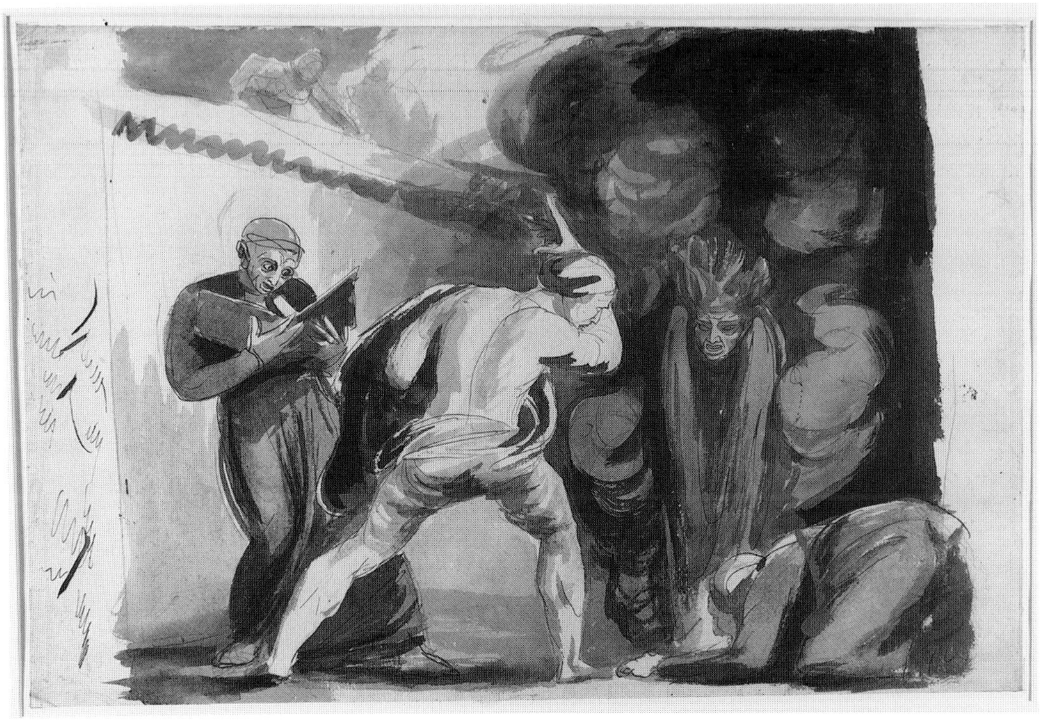

51 George Romney, *Margery Jourdain and Bolingbroke conjuring up the Fiend*, c. 1787–90.

in the Folger collection, inscribed simply *Large Head* and dating from the late 1780s, presents a fiend that combines Le Brun's imagery of horror with powerful, jagged shading to convey a dark, otherworldly sense – almost a hellish halo (Fig. 50).[35] Another presents the whole scene, placing it in Gloucester's garden and including Southwell and Roger Bolingbroke, with the Duchess of Gloucester and Hume looking on from above the wall. In this, the fiend is replaced by swirls of smoke.[36] A third, *Margery Jourdain and Bolingbroke conjuring up the Fiend* (Fig. 51)[37] unites the two and places the earlier image of the fiend within a presentation far more naturalistic, almost in anticipation of the historical authenticity aimed at in many of the Boydell images. The result is a forceful combination of the bravura implication of the wash-drawing and the explicative detail of a formal oil painting, far more effective than the stereotypical Gothic of the image commissioned from John Opie for the Boydell collection[38] (see Chapter 8).

These images represent a small fraction of the pen and ink and watercolour drawings that Romney completed on Shakespearean and related subjects. The loose, rapid execution, poised where necessary against a taut Neo-Classical grace, and the repeated return to similar or closely related scenes, gives them a directness absent from the larger paintings, and confers on them a collective critical insight that allows flexibility and a sense of growth alongside a rare visual statement of ambivalence. Discussing their quality of variation within similarity, Alex Kidson describes them as 'varied almost cinematographically, like successive stills in a film'.[39] This captures their likeness, but distorts their nature: the images should not be seen in series but instead regarded collectively as a meditation on the text they present, with the considered force of a thoughtful, but tentative, reading. Rather than taking on the nature of a sequence of filmic frames, they offer a constellation of possible interpretations, all of equal and simultaneous value.

Romney's achievement in the Boydell images was to show a kind of Shakespearean nationalism that embraced the idea of portraiture and impersonation, but it is the wash-drawings that provide a unique visual understanding of the fluidity of dramatic text. Working from an imaginative response to the page, not to performance, they offer a mirror of the reading experience in visual terms that, through the meditations of a contemporary man of feeling that embrace the sufferings of the contemporary penal system as well as the moral complexities of Macbeth's ambition, are unique in their critical visualisation of the plays' darker aspect.

NOTES

1. William Hayley, *The Life of George Romney, Esq.* (Chichester: W. Mason, 1809), p. 131.
2. *George Romney 1734–1802*; Exh. Cat. (London: National Portrait Gallery and Princeton N.J.: Princeton University Press, 2002), p. 6.
3. Letter from Isaac Reed, 7 November 1796, quoted in John Romney, *Memoirs of the Life and Works of George Romney* (London: Baldwin and Cradock, 1830), p. 240.
4. Evidence of Hayley's library is provided in *A Catalogue of the very valuable and extensive library of the late William Hayley Esq, Removed from his seat at Felpham* (London: Robert H. Evans, 1821). For the reference to Johnson, see 'Ninth Day's Sale', p. 58.
5. Untraced; engraved for the Boydell Shakespeare Gallery by Francis Legat, 1 January 1795, 49.5 × 36.8 (19 ½ × 14 ½).
6. The text here is that presented in the engraving, which follows the Boydell-Steevens edition (see Chapter 9). As no detailed locations are given, the line numbers refer to the edition by Kenneth Muir: The Oxford Shakespeare (Oxford: Clarendon, 1999). Equivalent references to passages from other Boydell engravings are given to the most recent New Cambridge Shakespeare edition.
7. See the engraved version of the head of Cassandra in Hayley's memoir, dated 1786(?).
8. 143.4 × 203 (56 ½ × 80 ⅞), Folger Shakespeare Library, engraved by Benjamin Smith, 29 September 1799, 50.5 × 43.6 (23 ½ × 17 ¼).

9. 191.2 × 121.9 (48 × 66), Petworth House, The National Trust. engraved by Benjamin Smith, 1 December 1803, 31.8 × 30.6 (12 1/2 × 12).
10. Untraced; a version of the image, painted in oil, arguably by Romney himself, over a mezzotint by John Jones, 42.5 × 52 (16 3/4 × 20 1/2) is in the Folger Shakespeare Library.
11. 74.9 × 63 (29 1/2 × 25 15/16), Folger Shakespeare Library. See William L. Pressly, *A Catalogue of Paintings in the Folger Shakespeare Library: 'As Imagination Bodies Forth'* (New Haven: Yale University Press, 1993), pp. 108–10.
12. *Falstaff with the Body of Hotspur*, pen with black ink and grey wash over pencil, 343 × 560 (13 1/2 × 22 1/16), Fitzwilliam Museum Cambridge ('FMC') B.V.129; *Falstaff relinquishing the body of Hotspur*, pen with black ink and grey wash over pencil, 391 × 517 (15 3/8 × 20 3/8), FMC B.V.130. Henderson first played Falstaff at the Haymarket in July 1777 and repeated the role during the following two seasons: the drawings probably date from around this time.
13. See, for example, *Lounger*, 20 May 1786; Anon (Samuel Foote?) *A Genuine Narrative of the Life and Theatrical Transactions of Mr John Henderson* (London: T. Evans, 1777), pp. 32–3 and 44–5.
14. Pen with brown ink over graphite, 25.5 × 39 (10 × 15 1/8), Folger Shakespeare Library ('FSL'). Art Flat b6.41 verso.
15. Pen with brown ink and grey-pink wash over graphite, 30.1 × 40 (11 13/16 × 15 7/8), FSL Art Flat b5.9.
16. 112 × 152.5 (45 × 60), National Gallery of Modern Art, Rome.
17. 59 × 43.8 (23 1/4 × 17 1/4), 29 September 1797. The original measured 301 × 457.2 (118 1/2 × 180); for details of its deterioration see Humphrey Ward and W. Roberts, *Romney* (London: Agnew, 1904), pp. 194–5 and Yvonne Romney Dixon, *'Designs from Fancy': George Romney's Shakespearean Drawings* (Washington D.C.: Folger Shakespeare Library, 1999), p. 178.
18. The image is a copy of the Benjamin Smith engraving coloured by stencil, and is in the Legion of Honor, San Francisco, California.
19. Pen, brown ink and brown wash over pencil on paper, 35.88 × 31.9 (14 1/8 × 12 9/16), *c.* 1786–90, FSL Art Flat b5.8.
20. Pen, brown ink and brown wash over pencil on paper, 36.51 × 30.8 (14 3/8 × 12 1/8), *c.* 1786–90, FSL Art Flat b6.25.
21. Pen and grey ink and grey wash, 55.88 × 63.5 (22 × 25), *c.* 1786–90, FMC L.D.125.
22. Late 1780s; light and dark grey wash over pencil, 38.9 × 53.12 (15 5/16 × 21 1/4), FSL Art Flat b.6.26. Kidson (p. 34) titles it *Prospero and Miranda* and dates it to 1786.
23. Pen and grey ink with grey wash, 35.87 × 27 (14 1/8 × 19 5/16); inscription in pencil on verso, FMC B.V. 0127.
24. 85 × 107.5 (33 1/2 × 42 1/4), Wallace Collection, London.
25. 202 × 232 (79 1/2 × 91 1/4), Abbot Hall Art Gallery, Kendal, Cumbria.
26. Destroyed by fire; coloured mezzotint by Caroline Watson.
27. 70.5 × 92.4 (27 3/4 × 36 3/8), Yale Center for British Art, Paul Mellon Fund New Haven, Conn.
28. *The Tempest: Prospero and Miranda*, *c.* 1786–90, pencil, 54.93 × 37.95 (21 5/16 × 14 15/16), FSL Art Flat b6.37.
29. *The Tempest: Miranda*, 1786–90, pen with grey ink and wash over pencil, FSL Art Flat b6.33 recto.

30. Grey watercolour wash and black ink wash over pencil, 39.7 × 51.8 (15 $^5/_8$ × 21 $^3/_8$), FMC L.D.48.
31. Probably 1790–2, pen and brown ink and brown wash, 15.56 × 19.68 (6 $^1/_8$ × 7 $^3/_4$), FSL Art Vol c59.12.
32. 330 × 425 (129 $^{15}/_{16}$ × 167 $^5/_{16}$), Musée du Louvre, Paris.
33. Pen and bistre wash on paper, 65 × 103 (25 $^5/_8$ × 40 $^1/_2$), Musée du Louvre, Paris.
34. Pen and sepia ink and sepia wash, 38.73 × 56.51 (15 $^1/_4$ × 22 $^1/_4$), FMC LD 0123.
35. Brush with brown wash, 50.6 × 35.9 (19 $^{15}/_{16}$ × 14 $^1/_8$), FSL Art Flat b5.24.
36. *Margery Jourdain and Roger Bolingbroke Conjuring up the Fiend*, c. 1787–90, pale and dark grey watercolour wash over graphite, 37.8 × 48.5 (14 $^7/_8$ × 19 $^1/_{16}$), FSL Art Flat b6.48.
37. *Margery Jourdain and Bolingbroke conjuring up the Fiend*, pen with grey ink and grey wash over pencil, 38.2 × 55.9 (15 $^1/_{16}$ × 22), FMC B.V.135.
38. Untraced; engraved by Charles Gauthier and Robert Thew, 1 December 1796, 50 × 62.5 (19 $^{11}/_{16}$ × 24 $^5/_8$).
39. *George Romney*, p. 217.

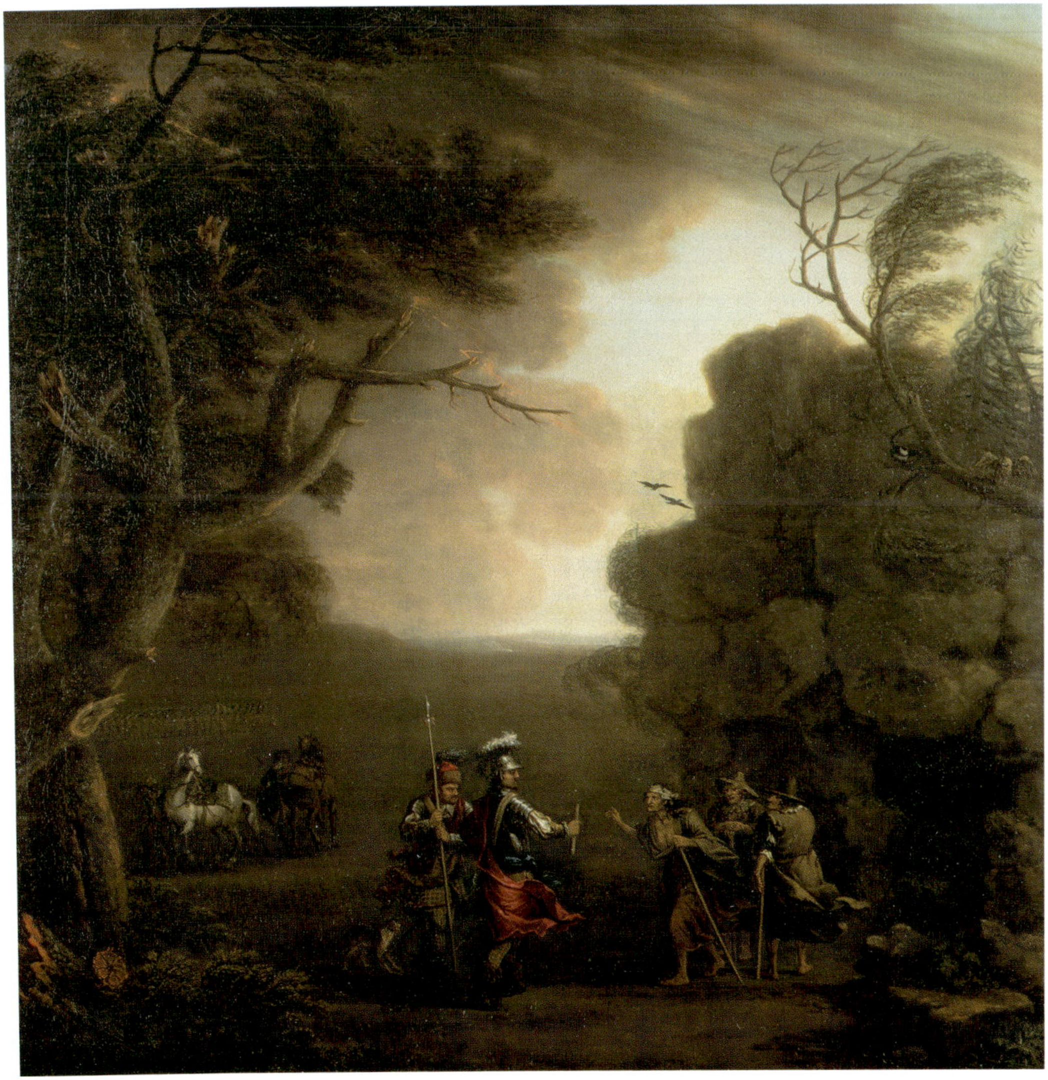

1 John Wootton, *Macbeth and Banquo meeting the Weird Sisters*, 1750.

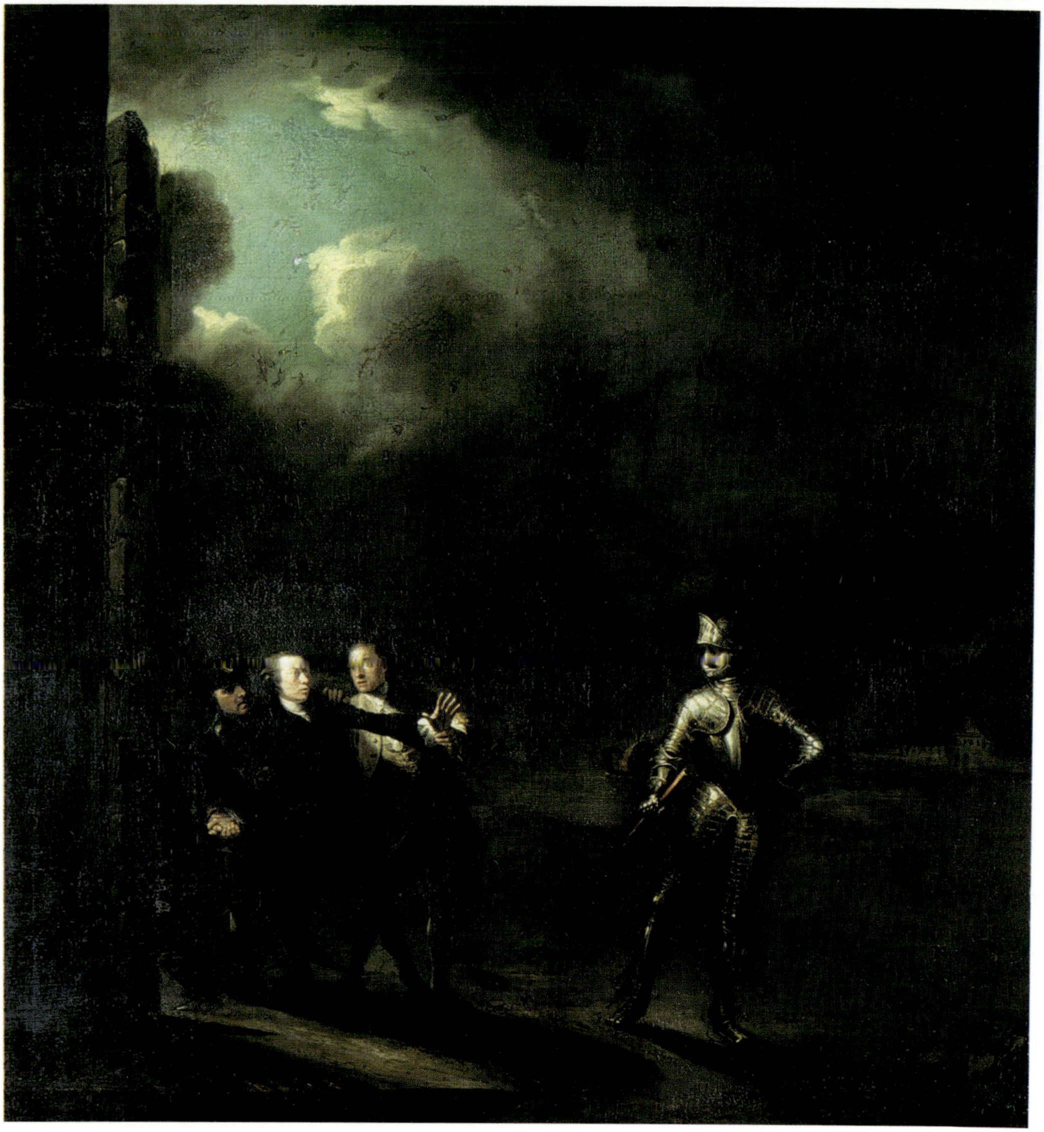

2 Benjamin Wilson, *William Powell as Hamlet encountering the ghost*, 1768–9.

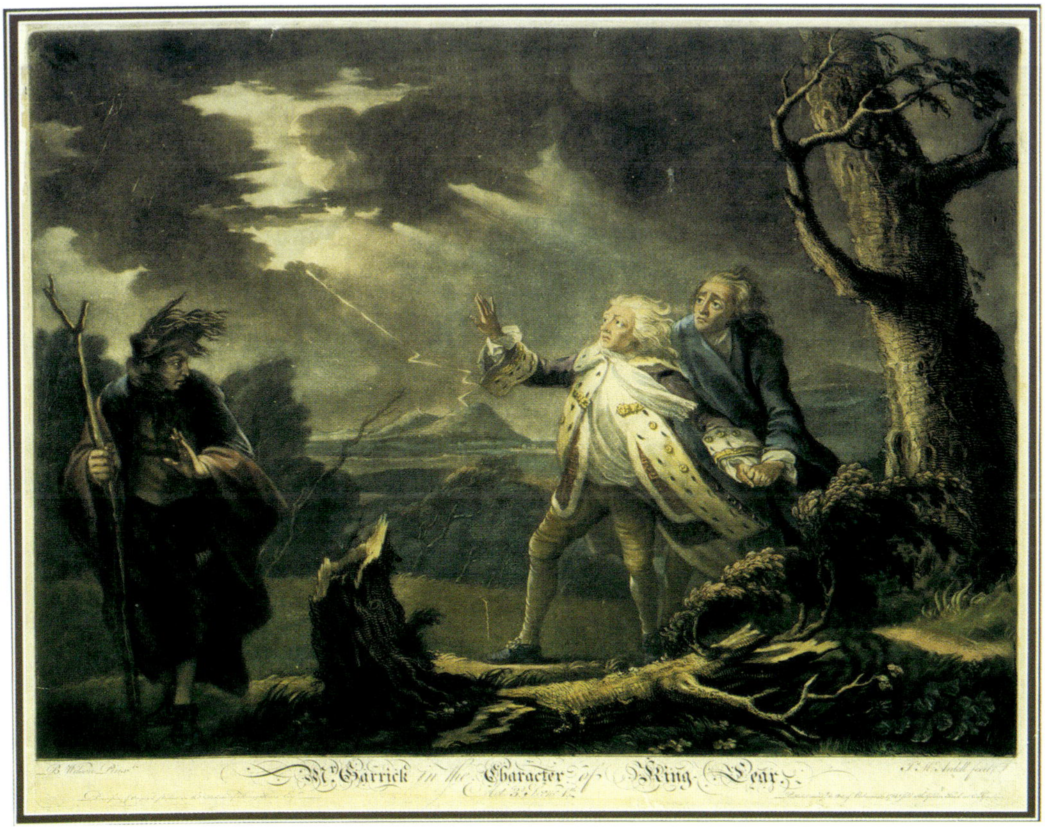

3 Benjamin Wilson, *David Garrick as King Lear*. Mezzotint by James McArdell, 1754.

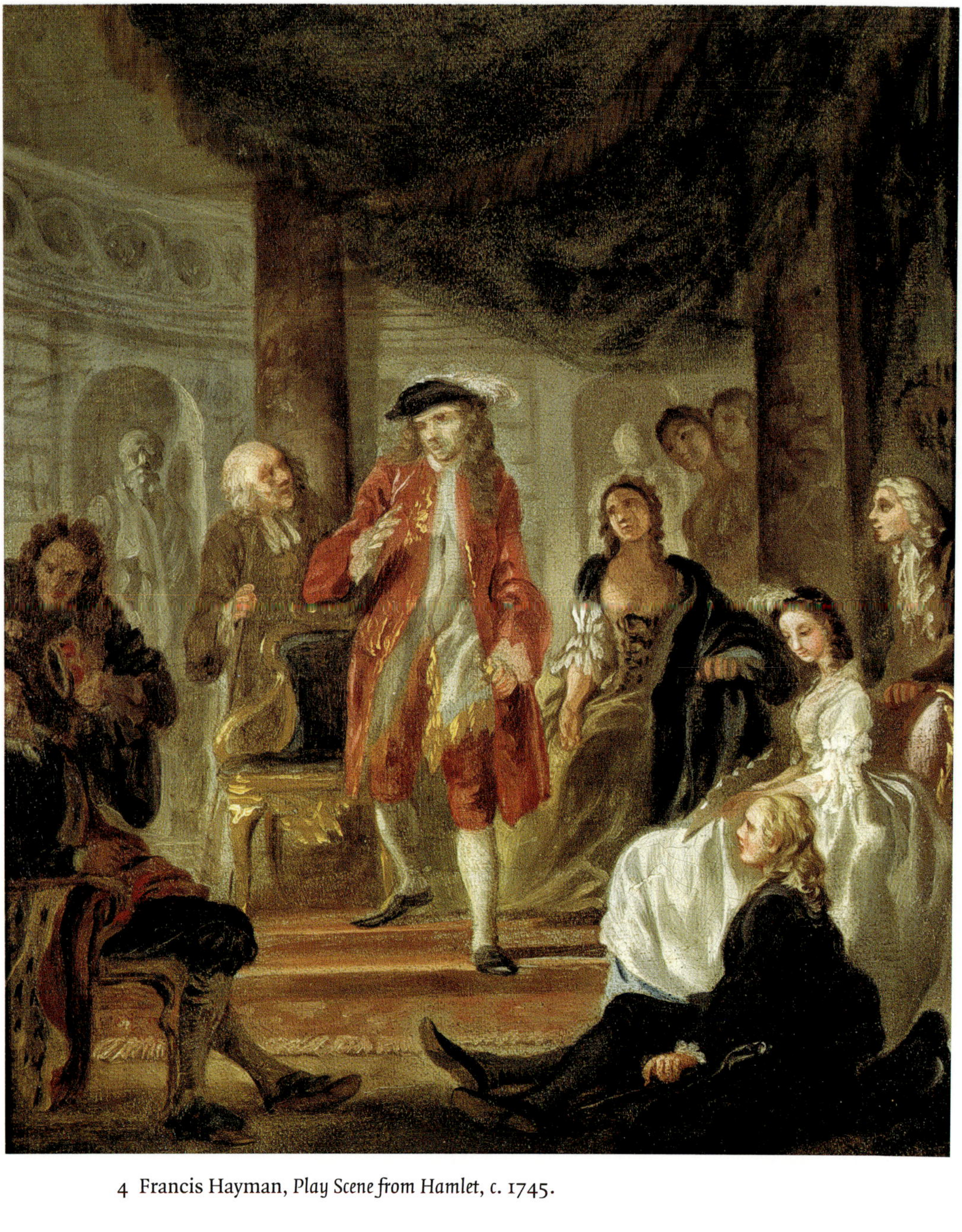

4 Francis Hayman, *Play Scene from Hamlet*, c. 1745.

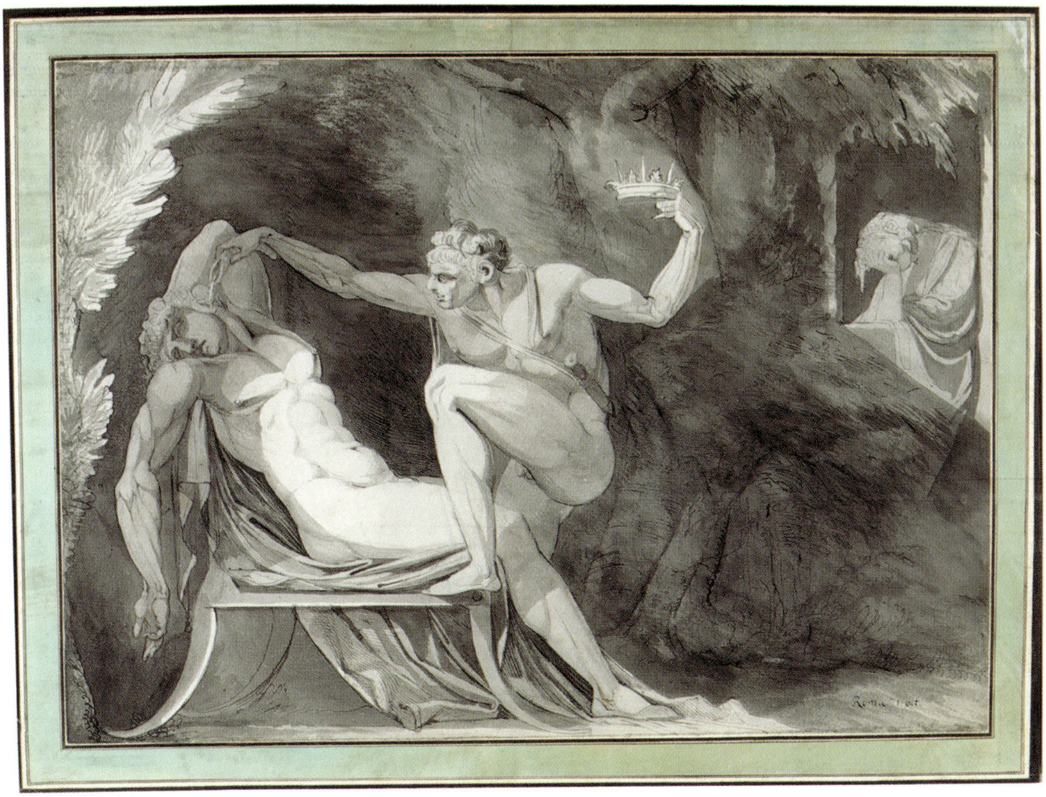

5 Henry Fuseli, *Hamlet, King of Denmark, poisoned by his brother Claudius while sleeping in the garden*, 1771.

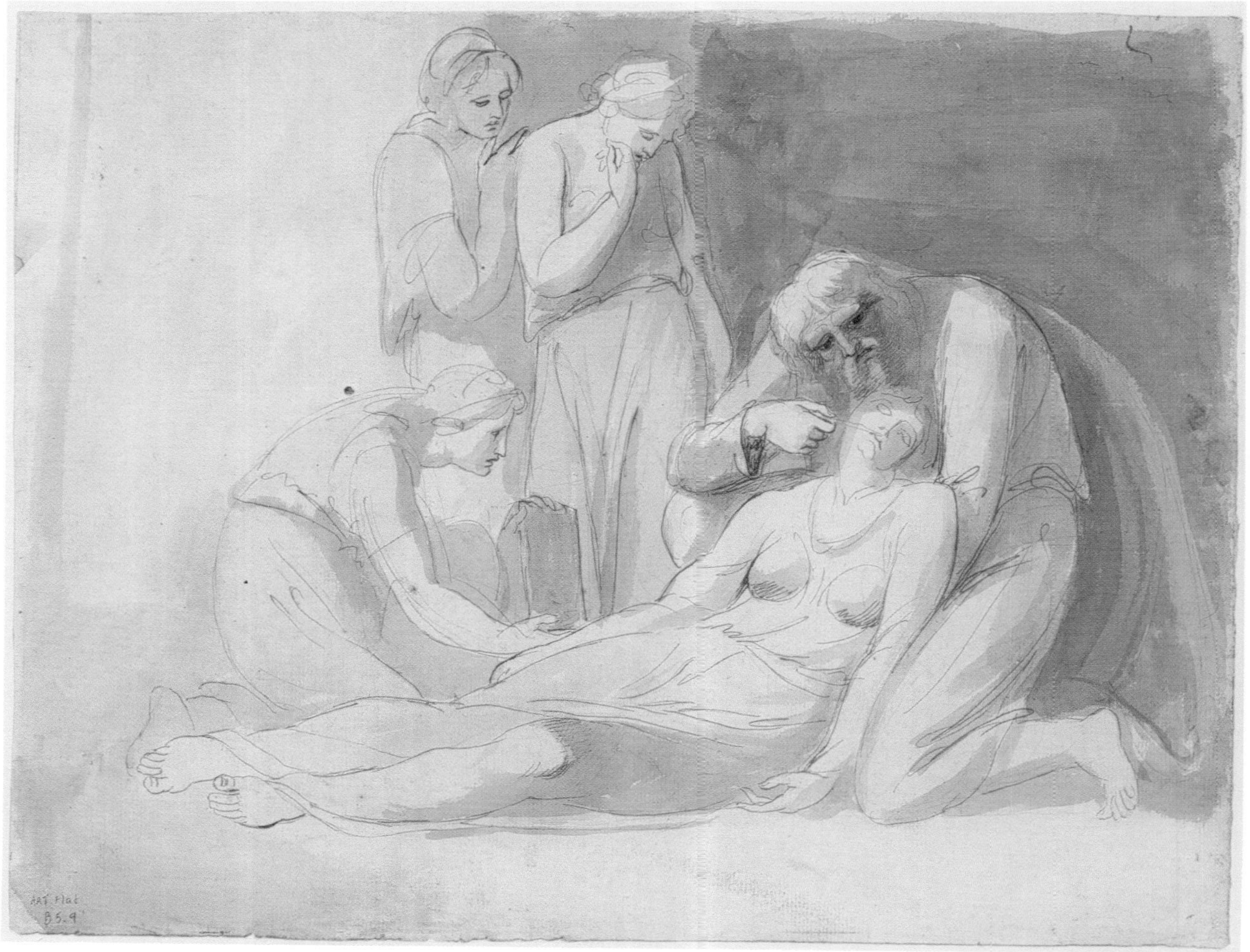

6 George Romney, *The Death of Cordelia*, c. 1775–7.

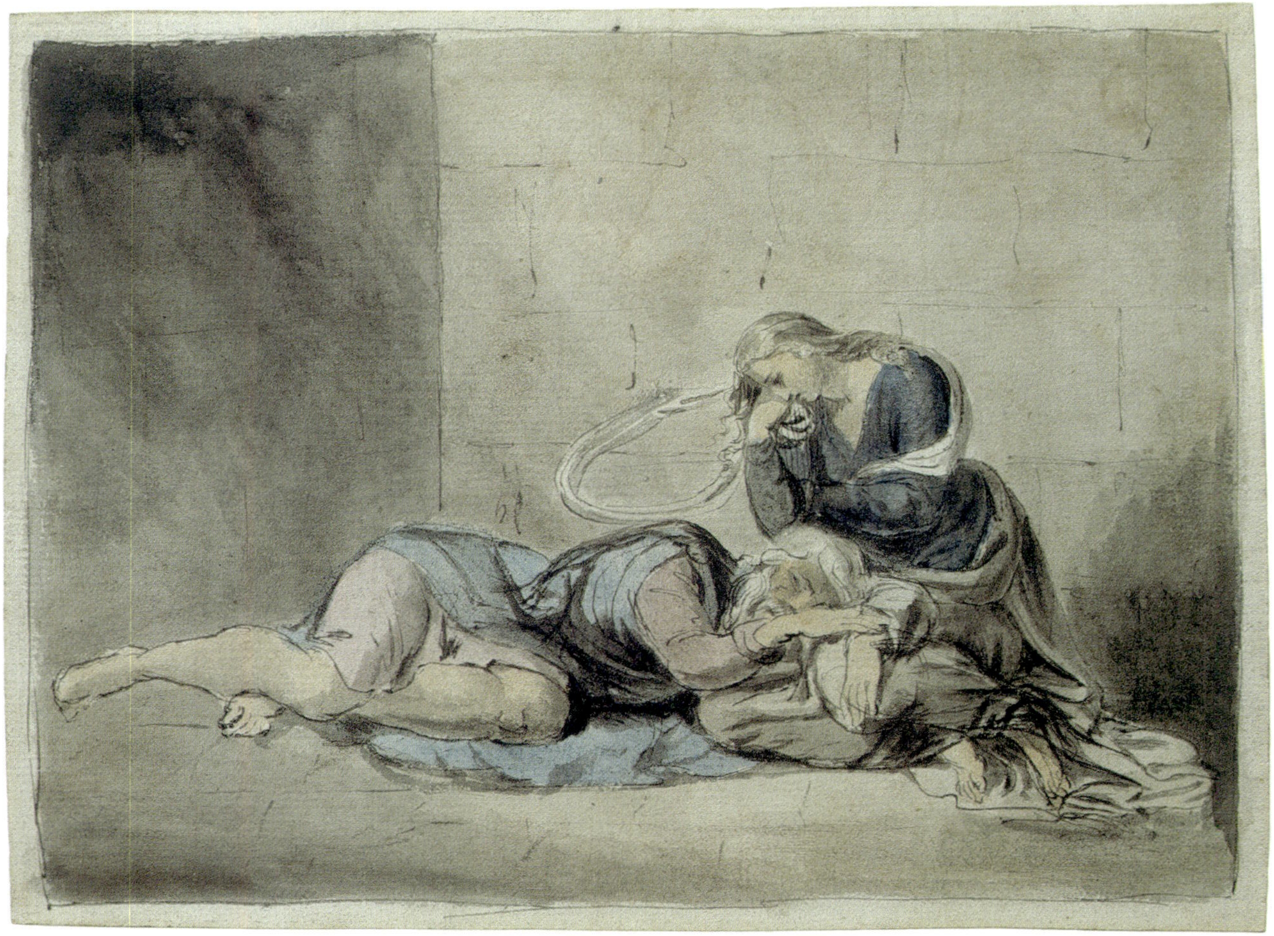

7 William Blake, *Lear and Cordelia in Prison*, c. 1779.

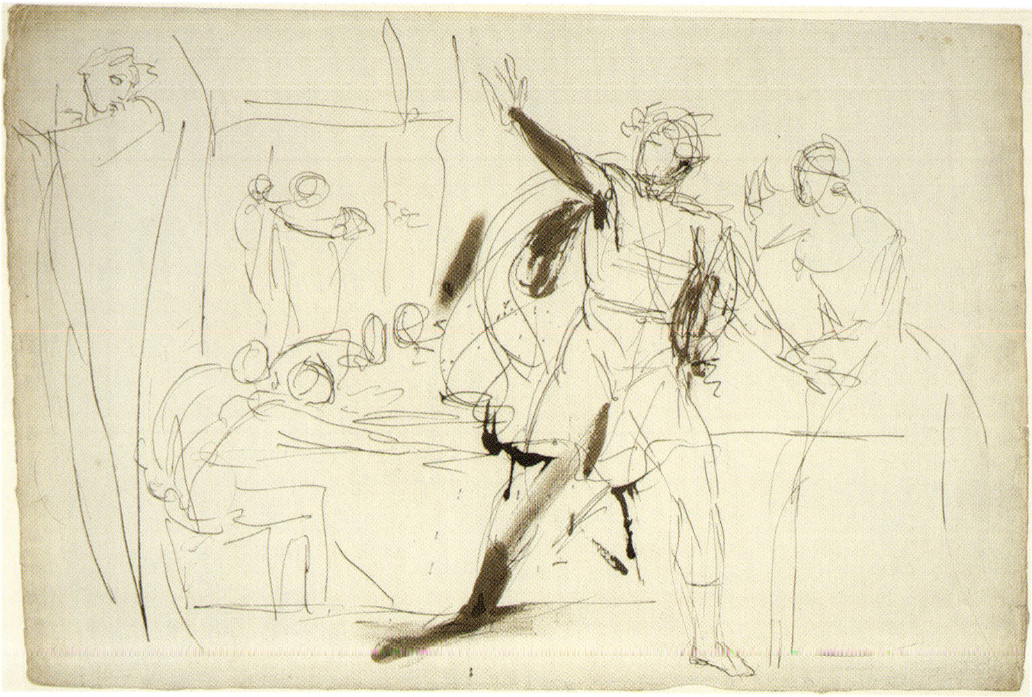

8 George Romney, *Macbeth and Banquo*, c. 1790–2.

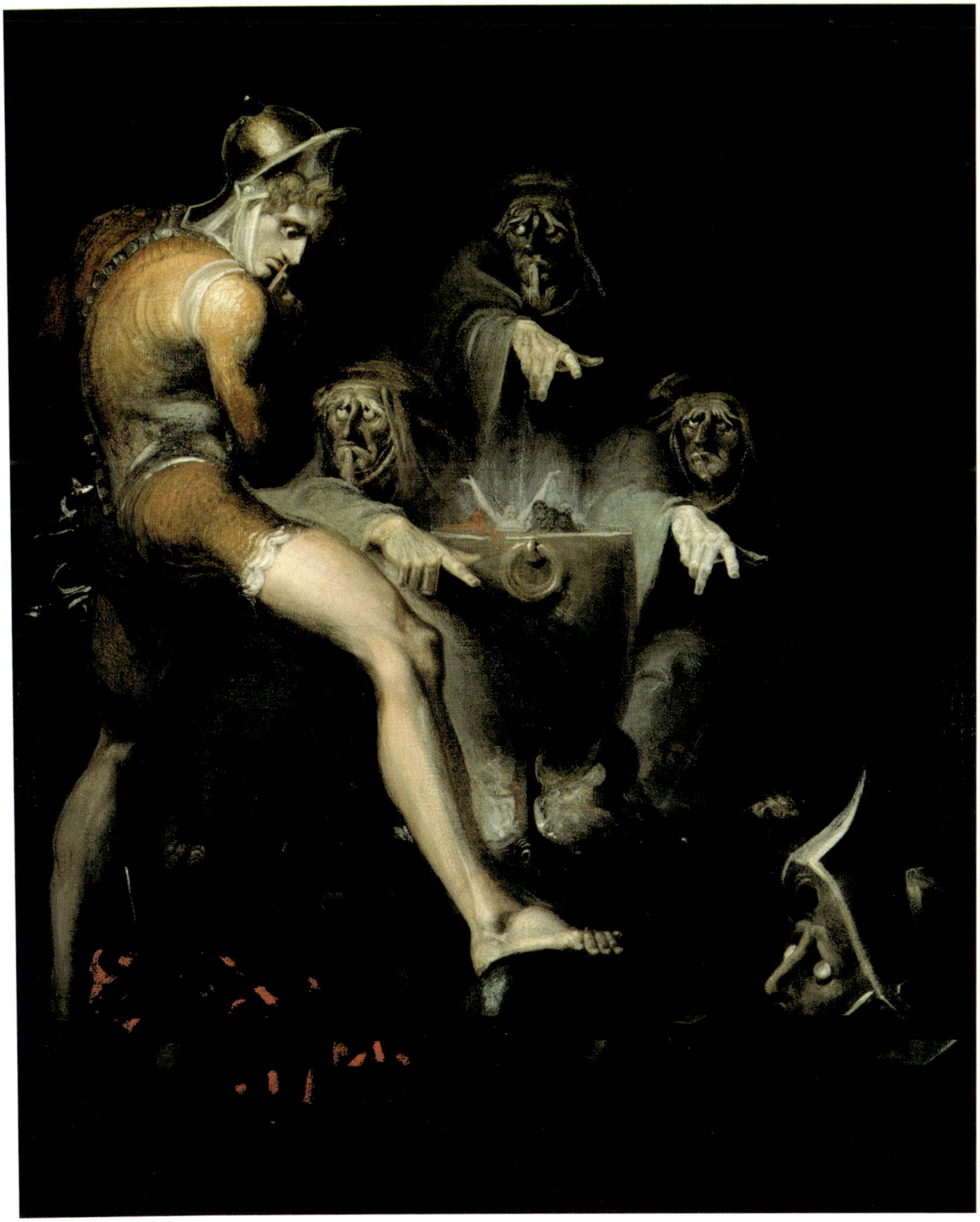

9 Henry Fuseli, *Macbeth consulting the Vision of the Armed Head*, 1793.

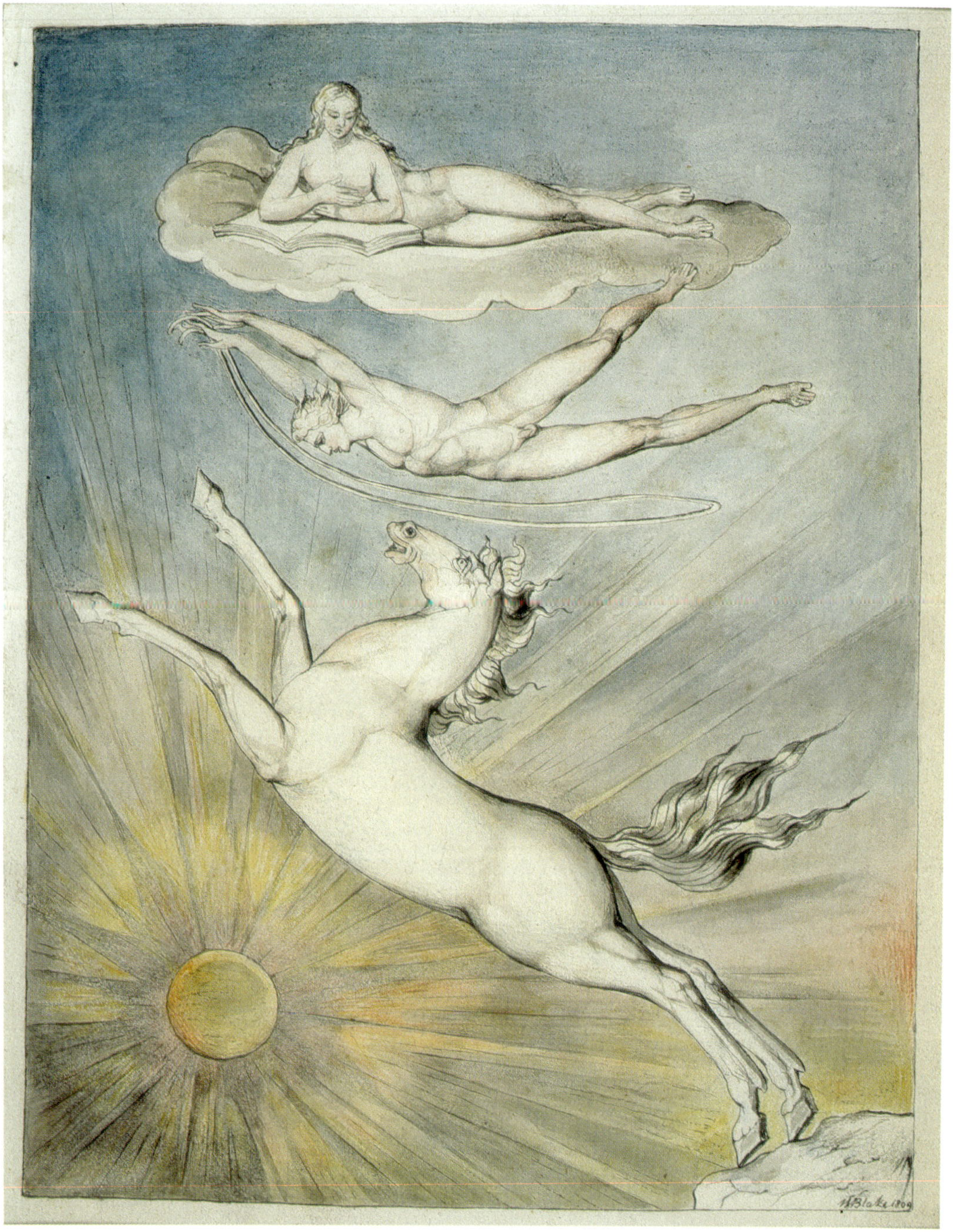

10 William Blake, *Fiery Pegasus*, 1809.

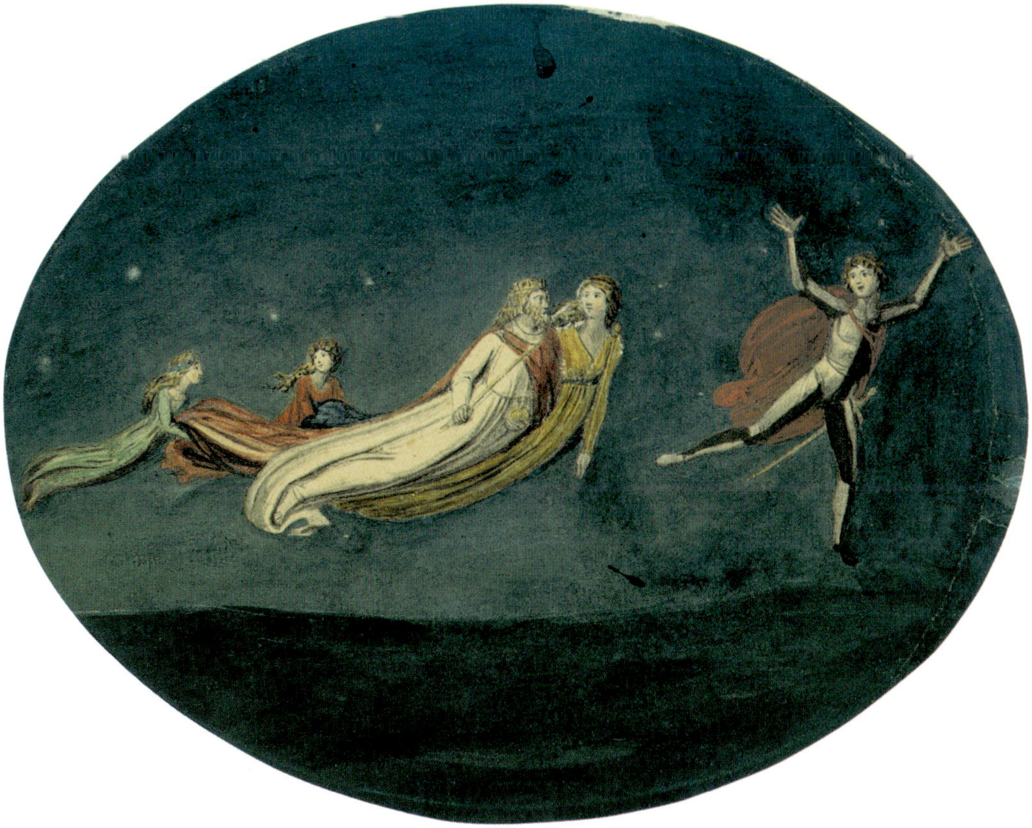

11 William Blake, *Oberon and Titania, preceded by Puck*, c. 1790–3.

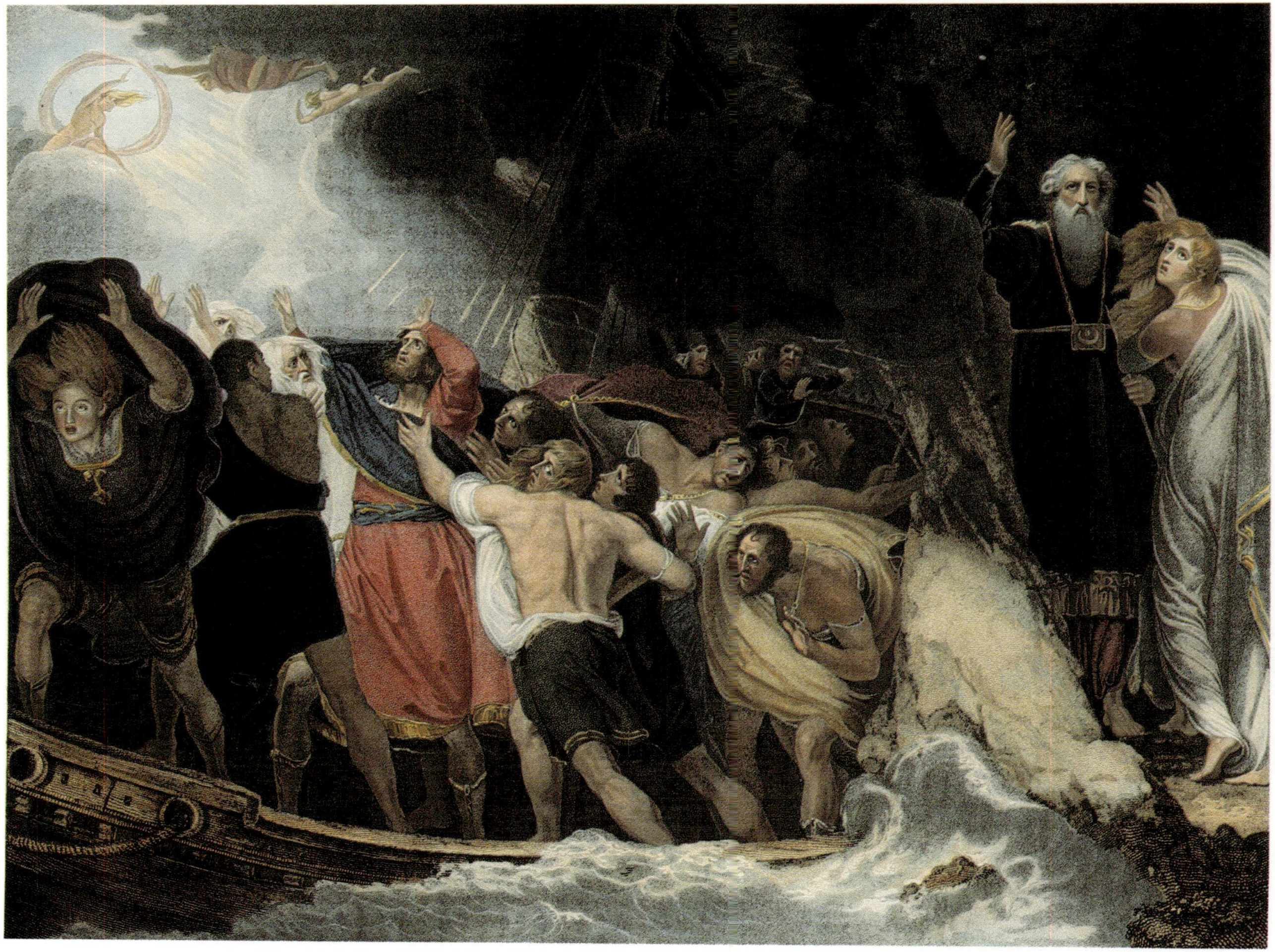

12 George Romney, *The Tempest*. Colour stencil engraving by Benjamin Smith, 1797.

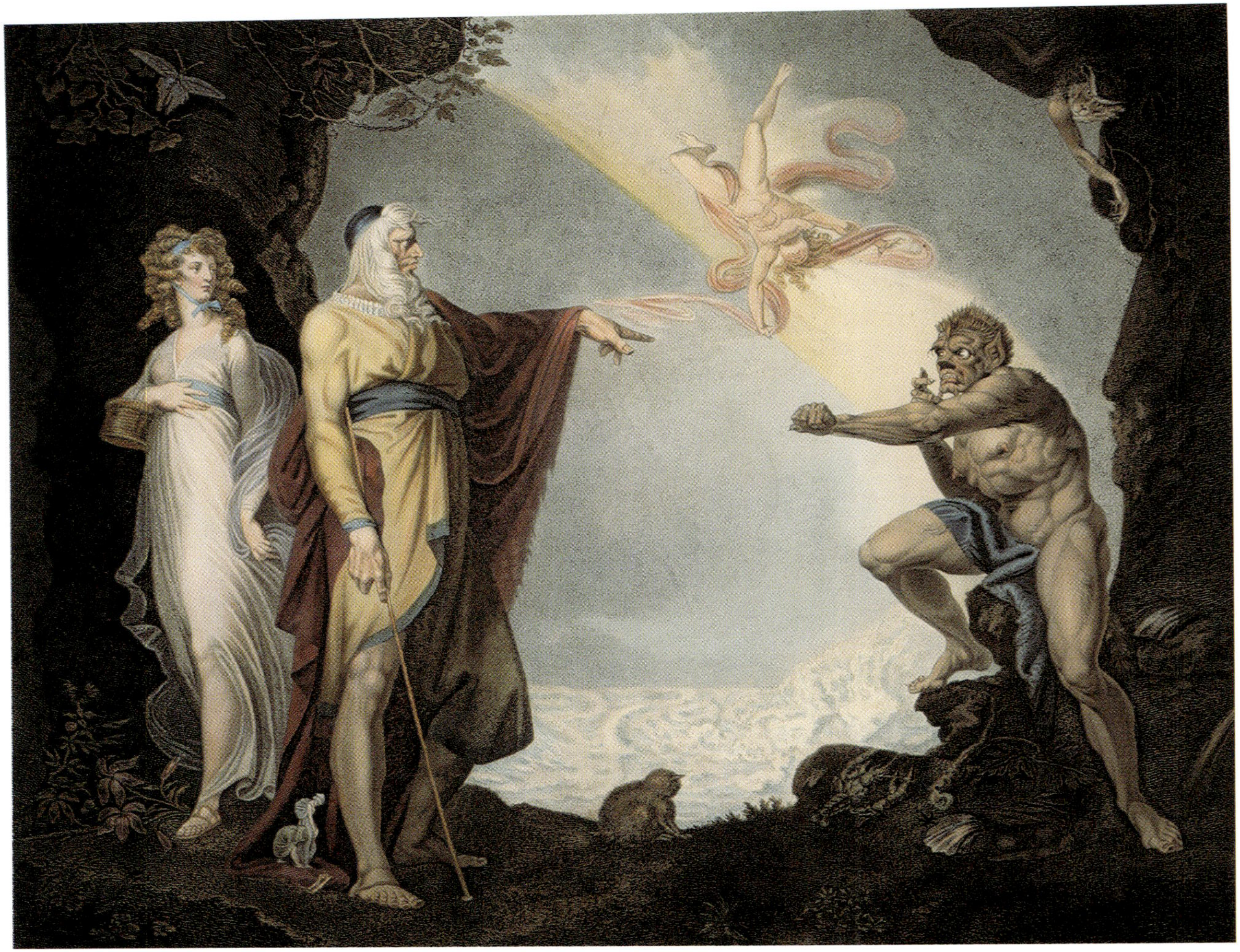

13 Henry Fuseli, *The Tempest*. Line and stipple engraving by Jean Pierre Simon, with hand colouring, 1797.

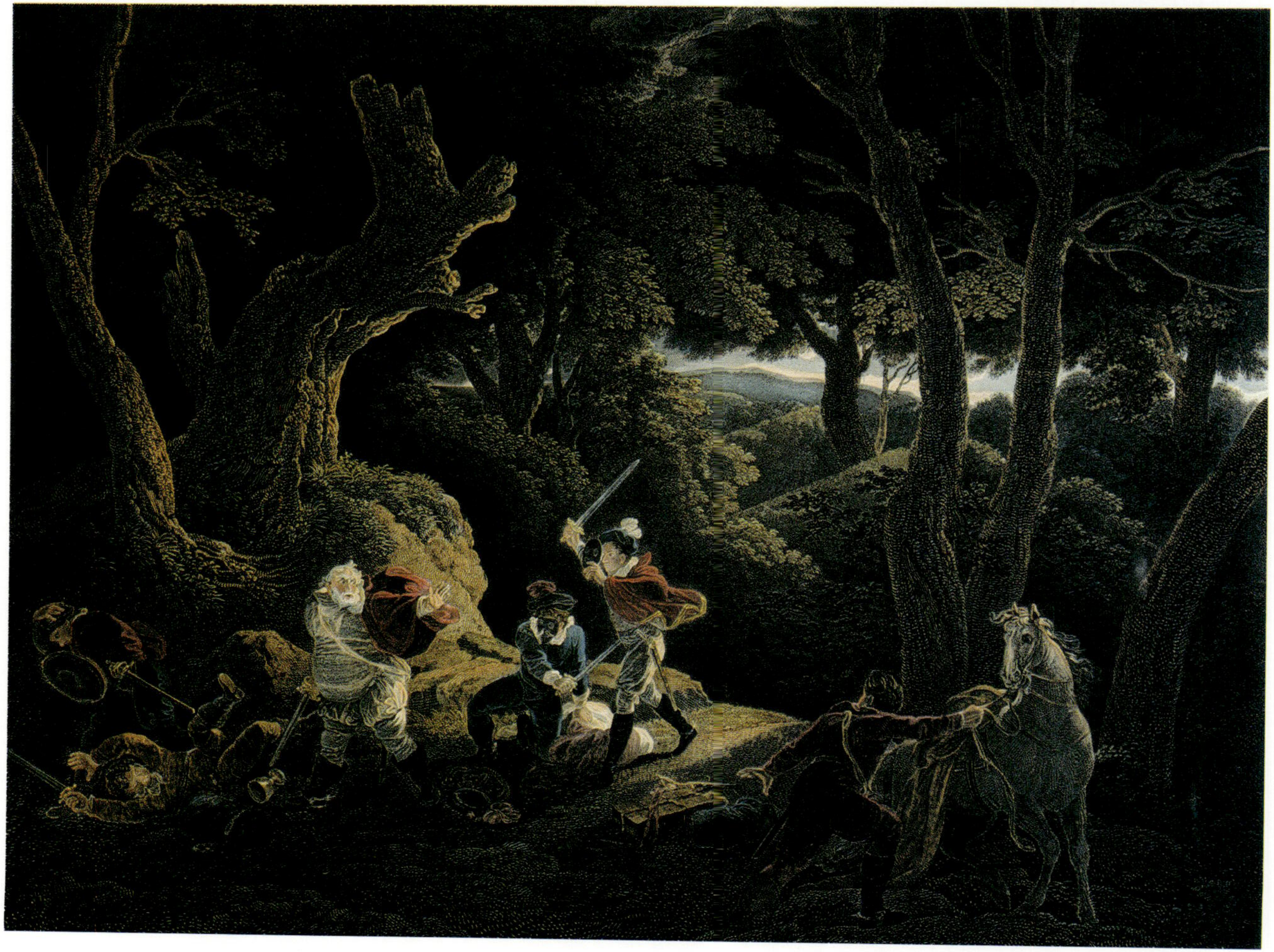

14 Robert Smirke and Joseph Farington, 1 *Henry IV*. Colour stipple engraving by Samuel Middiman, 1797.

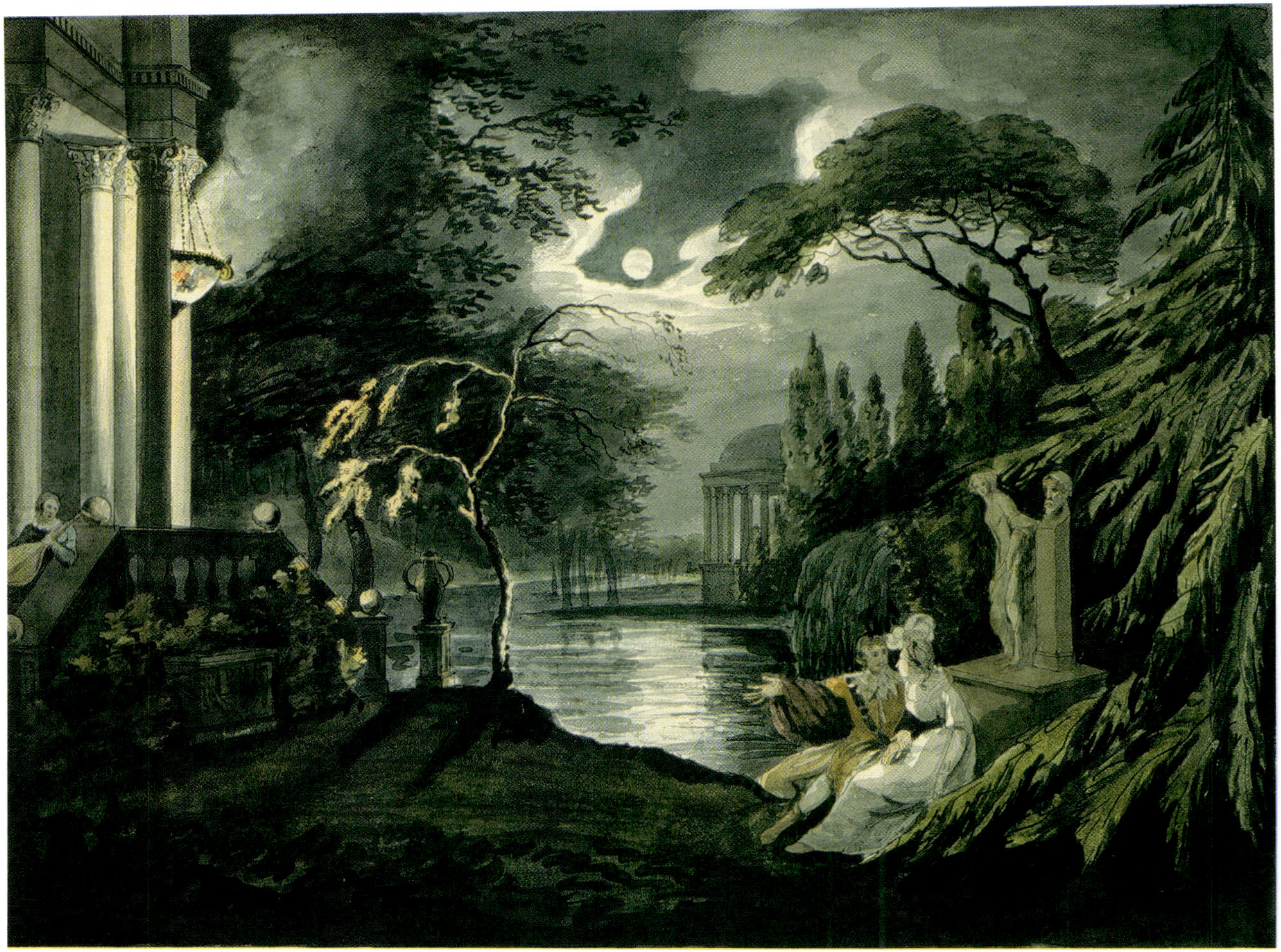

15 W. Jeayes after William Hodges, *The Merchant of Venice*, after 1807. Watercolour in grangerised Heath's Shakespeare.

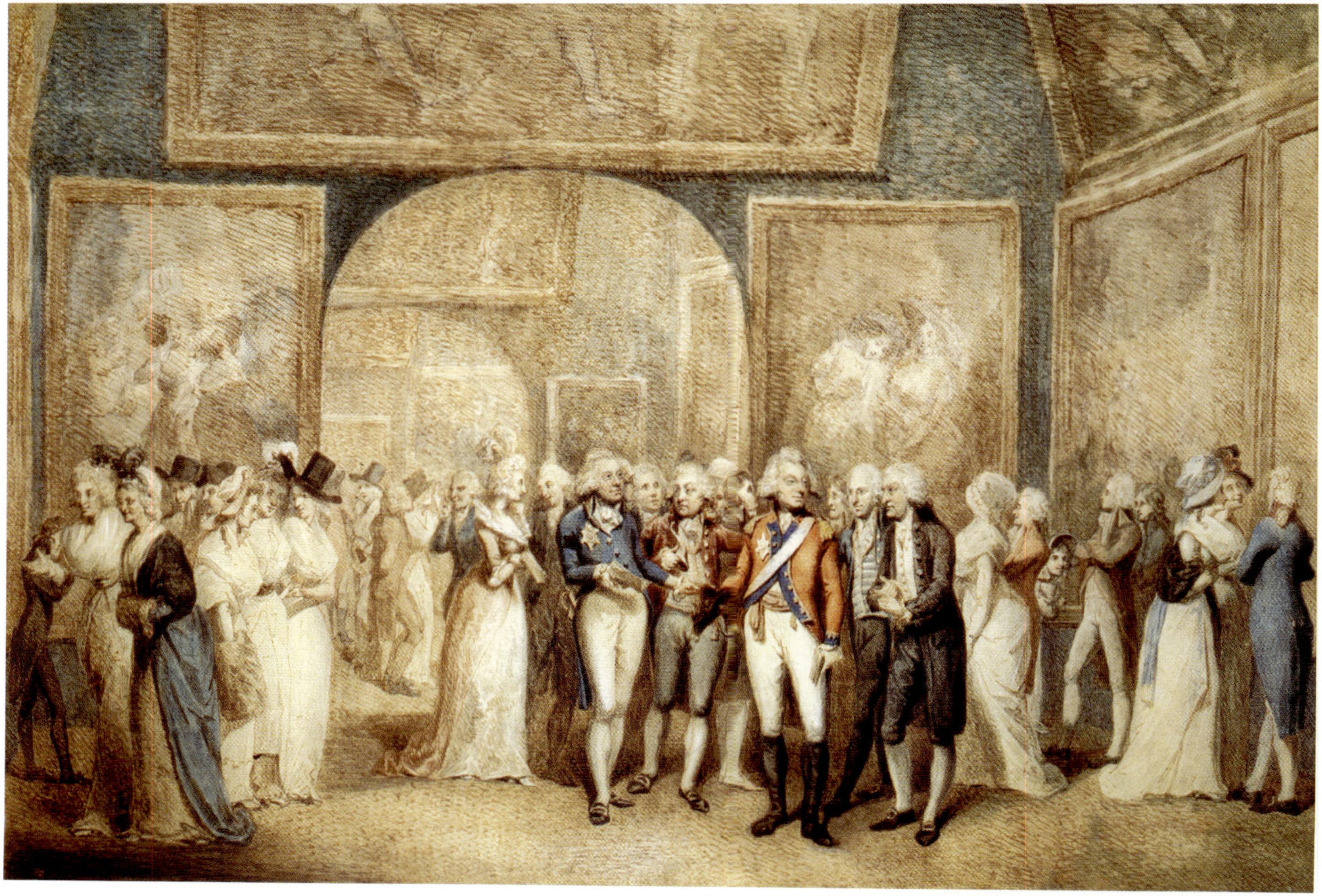

16 Francis Wheatley, *The Opening of the Shakespeare Gallery*, 1790.

CHAPTER 6

'SHAKESPEARE IN RIPER YEARS GAVE ME HIS HAND': WILLIAM BLAKE

I

Romney and Blake at first appear to inhabit quite different intellectual and aesthetic territories. One primarily a portraitist, the other a mythic and prophetic poet and artist, they apparently share very little. Some superficial links are clear: there are images borrowed by Blake from his older colleague and endowed with his own specific mythological meanings; some common friends including John Flaxman and Henry Fuseli; and the shared patronage of William Hayley. Yet from a greater distance the juxtaposition may be more revealing. Both largely self-taught, and reaching maturity when the ideals of Neo-Classicism and the Grand Style were at their height, they found highly personal idioms with which to address these aims. Since the ideas of expression then hovering around the cult of sensibility were moving towards the flood-tide of Romanticism, the incarnations of feeling became an inevitable focus, manifest in different directions in their work with regard to political radicalism, and the supernatural. That Romney spent much of his life as one of the most fashionable London portraitists should not obscure the other aspect of his creative identity; indeed, in its efforts towards unity, fusing Neo-Classicism with epic themes, presenting famous sitters in the guise of heroic figures from history or myth, or in stylistic terms enfolding a Neo-Classical grace with Romantic bravura, his work reveals as many of the complexities of his age as does that of Blake. Blake's initial forays into grand history painting place Shakespeare within an idea of history as nationalistic as that of Hume or Catherine Macaulay, albeit very different, and his figure painting in the illustrations to Dante and Milton shows a fusion of Neo-Classical poise and Romantic thrust that, while different in style, shares the complex unity of Romney. In consequence it is not surprising that, beneath the differences of approach and style, the work of both in connection with Shakespeare should be of originality, critical understanding and no little grace.

The only precise evidence of Blake's knowledge of Shakespeare comes from Benjamin Heath Malkin: 'Shakespeare's Venus and Adonis, Tarquin and Lucrece, and his Sonnets . . . These poems, now little read, were favourite studies of Mr. Blake's early years.'[1] Malkin goes on to say that Blake's father bought him various classical casts, and continues that the 'indulgent parent soon supplied him with money to buy prints, when he immediately began his collection, frequenting the shops of the print-dealers, and the sales of the auctioneers' (p. xix). The period referred to is Blake's study at William Pars' School, which he entered at the age of ten, two years after the first appearance of Johnson's Shakespeare; though there is no evidence, it is certainly possible that the young Blake acquired the *Works* in one edition or another at this time. Quotations from the plays and sonnets appear in the *Notebook*, and the influence of Shakespeare's verse is apparent in the early *Poetical Sketches* of 1769–78, most clearly in Blake's short history play *King Edward the Third*. Blake made extensive annotations to texts that include Reynolds' *Discourses* and the writings of Lavater and Swedenborg, and this practice and his discussion of the Canterbury pilgrims in the *Descriptive Catalogue* suggest that he was a skilful and intense reader. This is also evident in the *Paradise Lost* watercolours, which present the text with an unfailing accuracy and an attention to both narrative progression and verbal moment rivalled only by Fuseli in contemporary visualisations. While producing the series of heads of the poets, including Shakespeare, for William Hayley's library, Blake would, like Romney, have had access to its books, which included Johnson's, Steevens' and Bell's editions of the plays.[2] A more precise suggestion occurs in a letter to Hayley of 28 December 1804 that refers to an engraving of Romeo and the Apothecary that Blake had made, after Fuseli's drawing, for the Rivington Shakespeare of 1805, saying 'I left a good impression of it when I left Felpham last in one of Heaths [sic] Shakespeare.'[3] The volume referred to was an edition, issued in serial parts, which used the text of Johnson and Steevens with plates engraved by Charles Heath,[4] mainly after designs by Thomas Stothard: this, too, was in Hayley's library.[5] The reference may suggest nothing more than Blake's use of the volume as an appropriate place of storage for an engraving, its use as an extra-illustration, or even as a bookmark; but it does confirm that he made some use of an edition of the plays while staying with Hayley, and had access to the most recent editorial decisions and annotations.

Another letter asserts Blake's indebtedness to a range of literary stewards:

Now my lot in the Heavens is this; Milton lovd me in childhood & shewd me his face
Ezra came with Isaiah the prophet, but Shakespeare in riper years gave me his hand[6]

It is this kind of spiritual kinship, linked with the imagined but immediate contact with writers, prophets and thinkers from the past, that defines much of Blake's relationship with Shakespeare; but the images he produced make clear that this is inseparable from detailed and lucid readings of the texts themselves.

Blake shares with Romney an intimacy of utterance quite opposite to the rhetorical distance imposed by the Grand Style of Reynolds, West and Barry. Yet while, with some significant exceptions, Romney's images approach the texts through large movements, aiming at underlying oppositions and groundswells, Blake's start from an address to textual detail, frequently turning a verbal trope into a form that, despite apparently being a direct treatment, adds completely new, and completely visual, denotative and connotative levels, to offer profound insights into the plays' larger identities. Yet his work does not stop there: what makes it unique is its movement beyond these critical readings to the realm of imaginative invention, in the use of Shakespearean texts and concepts as foundational elements within his own mythic universe.

II

In November 1800, William Hayley asked Blake to produce a series of paintings to decorate his recently built library.[7] One of the eighteen heads of poets that he completed was that of Shakespeare (Fig. 52).[8] It uses the head from the Droeshout portrait in the First Folio, surrounded by a wreath woven from English wildflowers, continuing the idea of Shakespeare as the untutored product of the English countryside. On the left, Banquo's ghost points to the show of kings; on the right, Macbeth stands before the three witches. This offers a dense compression of the play, since the postures of the two characters resemble those often found in late eighteenth-century paintings of the first encounter, and here they spread across a much larger temporal span of the play, almost to suggest a dual response to the witches throughout the action, and so reveal their moral ambiguity. The witches themselves, seated before Macbeth, resemble more the spiritual forms found in Blake's allegorical paintings than any stage presentation, and this is confirmed in a comment in the *Descriptive Catalogue* of 1809:

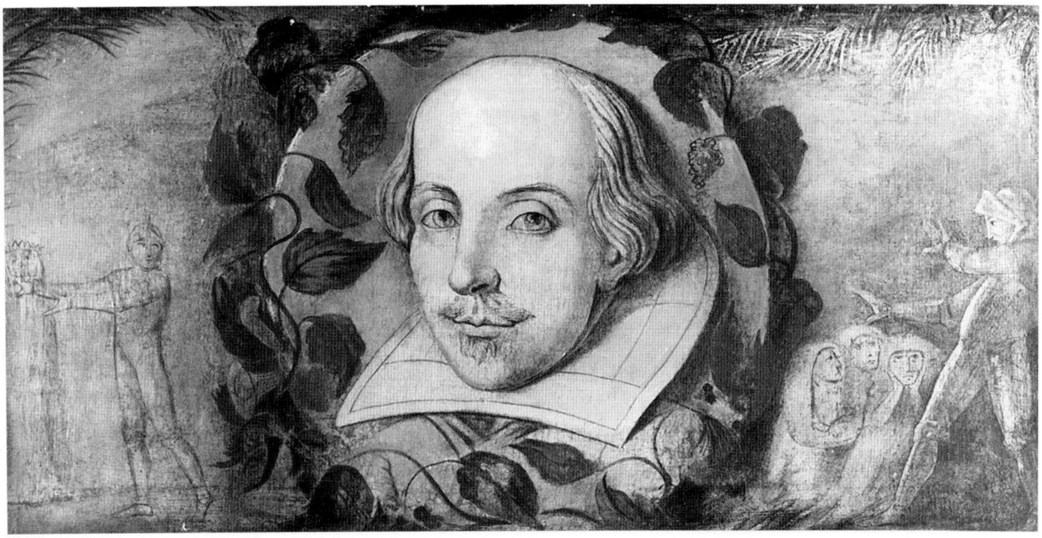

52 William Blake, Head of Shakespeare, *Heads of the Poets*, 1800–1801.

By way of illustration, I instance Shakespeare's Witches in Macbeth. Those who dress them for the stage, consider them as wretched old women, and not as Shakspeare intended, the Goddesses of Destiny[9]

That the allusion is made to support the artist's depiction of Chaucer's Pilgrims as actual and substantial people reveals his approach to the works of both authors: they are texts of human and psychological penetration, not to be addressed with the lightness of Davenant's adaptation.

Perhaps the most striking example of Blake's apparently direct visualisations of verbal metaphor is the colour print *Pity* (*c.* 1795: Fig. 53).[10] Like most of Blake's images it is concerned with both an ostensible subject and a larger implication about human oppositions presented within the artist's own vocabulary of myth and prophecy. The first of two pencil sketches for the print[11] is inscribed 'Shakespeares Pity. And Pity like a naked newborn Babe &c &c F Tatham,' tying the image to the following passage from *Macbeth*:

And pity, like a naked new-born babe,
Striding the blast, or heaven's cherubin horsed
Upon the sightless couriers of the air,
Shall blow the horrid deed in every eye,
That tears shall drown the wind. (1.7.21–5)

Moelwyn Merchant has pointed out[12] that the colour print addresses each aspect of the language, and Martin Butlin describes the approach as 'marvellously literal'.[13]

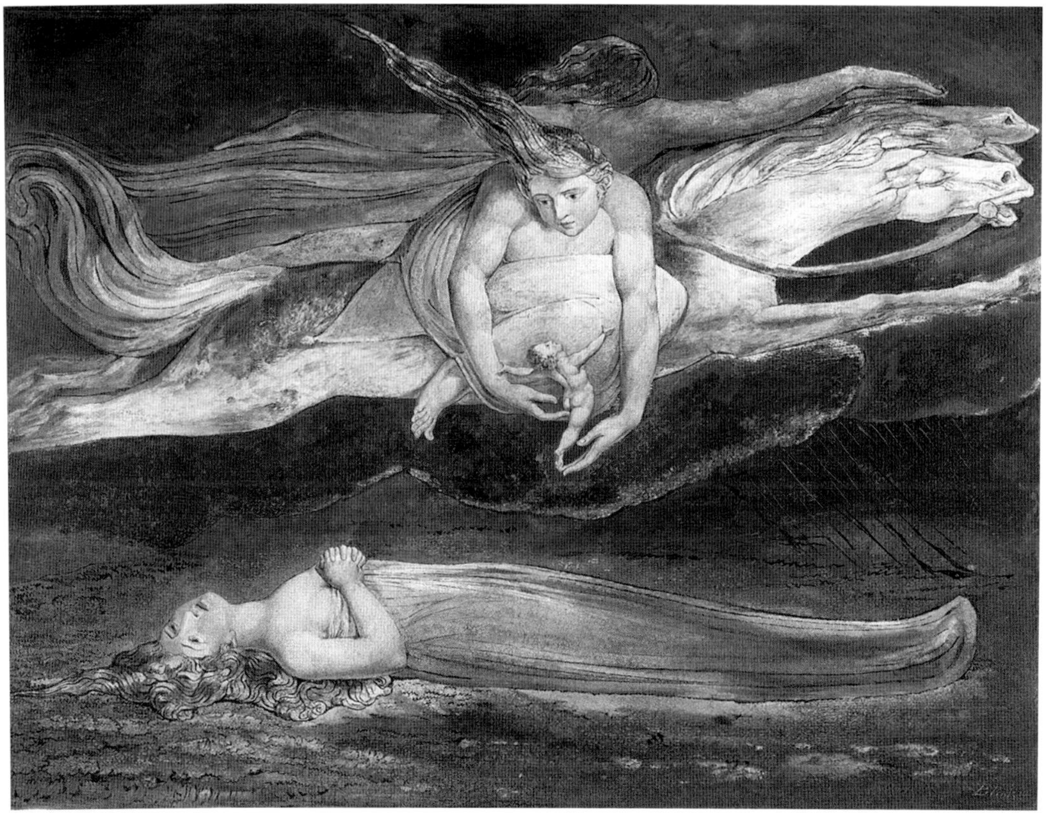

53 William Blake, *Pity*, c. 1795.

Both are in a sense correct; but the manner of visualisation goes further than either suggests, demonstrating the specific quality of Blake's penetration into the verbal processes of Shakespeare's metaphors. The 'sightless couriers of the air' are literally 'horsed', but they are also reinvented at another metaphoric level: the horses add further accretions through their iconography, referring to *Death on a Pale Horse* (1800),[14] painted by Blake in his series of images of the Book of Revelation. This immediately broadens the moral significance of Macbeth's speech, making the judgment universal. Decoding the rest of the image is far harder. The 'naked new-born babe' is not, in literal terms, 'striding the blast', although it certainly confronts the elements, while at the same time being in a relation of dependency or supplication to the female form at the top of the composition. The identity of this figure, in terms of the lines from the play, is far from clear. Perhaps, at the most direct level, it represents the mother of the 'new-born babe;' on successively abstract levels, it may signify the drowned wind, or function emblematically as an embodiment of the object of pity. These levels of signifying show the image moving away from literalism, to function more through presenting a larger affective sense of pity than by offering a precise visual equivalent of the passage. At a more general level still, the process is in turn made universal by the immediate force of the depiction of the storm, visualising in another dimension the last two lines of the passage.

In more ontological terms, the enormity of the image's conjunction of opposites – native, infant vulnerability against apocalyptic force – results in a compound treatment of the passage, completing an effect that simultaneously visualises the verbal trope, reveals its innately literary qualities by the sheer obstinacy of any exact visual equation, and mediates it through further visual associations, in a sense presenting a parable of the reader's reaction through the force of its own idiom. Images by other artists, in other styles, will make forceful use of epic scale and Neo-Classical convention to present visual parallels to the moral scope of the tragedies, or combine details of language to reveal character and incident: Blake's prints and watercolours work quite differently. It is as a treatment not only of the momentary verbal trope, but of the larger function and working of dramatic language on the imagination – both associative and eidetic – when read, that they operate. A major dimension of the effect is to reveal the sheer complexity and variety of the lines and the way that they move from one associative level to another. Remarkable in the later eighteenth century, when examined two hundred years later Blake's images act as a defamiliarising agent of great force in letting readers see afresh lines long familiar, translating them into visual form and in the process paradoxically disclosing their purely literary identity. Martin Butlin's more recent description of the technique as 'visionary literalism'[15] seems the most appropriate way of conveying the print's conjoined lucidity and intangibility.

This quality is again apparent in two watercolours now in the British Museum. In 1809 the Reverend Joseph Thomas commissioned several artists to produce images as extra-illustrations for his second folio of the plays. The commission called for monochrome wash-drawings; Blake produced six watercolours that, because of their breadth of interpretive intelligence and the fact that they are in effect separate images, go far beyond the limits of conventional book illustration and become works in their own right. Of them, perhaps the most striking, and certainly the most revealing of Blake's approach to detailed textual imaging, is the watercolour known both as *Fiery Pegasus* and *As if an Angel Dropped Down from the Clouds* (Plate 10).[16] The image appears next to the speech by Sir Richard Vernon that describes the forces of Prince Hal towards the close of *1 Henry IV*. Fully to grasp the complexity of the image's treatment it is necessary to consider the passage as a whole, as Blake might have read it from the text of the Second Folio:

All furnisht, all in Arms;
All plum'd like Estridges, that with the Winde
Bayted like Eagles, having lately bath'd,
Glittering in Golden Coates, like Images,
As full of spirit as the Moneth of May,
And gorgeous as the Sunne at Mid-summer,
Wanton as youthful Goates, wild as young Bulls.
I saw young *Harry* with his Bever on,
His cushes on his thighes, gallantly arm'd,
Rise from the ground like feathered *Mercury*,
And vaulted with such ease into his Seat
As if an angel dropt downe from the Clouds
To turn and winde a fierie *Pegasus*,
And witch the World with Noble Horsemanship.
(IV.i.97–110)

It is perhaps unsurprising that Blake has selected what is probably the most complex passage in the whole play, containing as it does a textual crux, the discussion of which by editors after Pope takes up over six pages in the *Variorum* of 1936,[17] and to which many subsequent contributions have been made. What is striking is how Blake offers, in visual terms, a reading that reinvents the dynamic thrust of the passage, by focusing on some aspects of the verbal imagery in detail, eliding some together, and largely overlooking others. The depiction of Harry naked removes one of the passage's levels of complexity, the meaning of 'estridges' as either ostriches, with the allusion to the Prince of Wales' feathers with which the force is 'furnisht', or goshawks, which gives associations of hunting as an aristocratic discourse that foreshadows the Prince's skilled horsemanship. As almost a classical nude, the Prince is invested with an elemental identity, a quality of ideal manhood more powerful than any degree of arms or armour would provide. This relates him to the two birds that have been so troublesome to editors, the goshawks that are one meaning of 'estridges' and the eagles to which they are in turn compared. In Blake's reading, the main concern here is with the movement of the figure, who rides upon the air in a direct treatment of the line in the Second Folio's punctuation, 'that with the Winde/ Bayted like Eagles,' and whose lucent clarity suggests the cleanliness implied in 'having lately bath'd'. The loss of the specific reference to the Prince – the absence of the Prince of Wales' ostrich feathers – is compensated for by the visualisation of the power and movement of the birds of prey that are incorporated into the figure. To support this almost metallic cleanliness and vigour, the background of the watercolour draws together the imagery of the midsummer sun, which metonymically represents the image of the line that precedes it and conveys the 'Golden' quality of the line before that: again, Blake's treatment distils the verbal essence into visual terms. The figure's posture, apparently descending from a cloud rather than vaulting from the earth, suggests the stooping angel of the image's alternative title; but the energy of the word 'vaulted' is far from lost, and the motion could be said to combine the two movements as they are embraced in the term 'bating'. The same energy is abundantly present in the horse, the 'fiery Pegasus' that forms the image's other title. The fragment of clifftop on which it stands simultaneously gives a foothold from which the energetic leap takes place and makes material the world that Harry will 'witch . . . with Noble horsemanship'.

The nature of the visualisation is similar to that of *Pity*. Apparently literal, it enfolds a number of other associations and rests on complex acts of selection and reordering to present the larger thrusts of the passage. Anthony Blunt was the first to point out[18] that this passage is the only one mentioned by Burke as an example of the Sublime in literature. Burke finds it Sublime because of 'a richness and profusion of images, in which the mind is so dazzled as to make it impossible to attend to that exact coherence and agreement of the allusions, which we should require on every other occasion'.[19] Blake's vision provides a parallel to the passage's effect in an idiom that also defies precise reading but conveys its energy through another order of metaphor, this time purely visual. In this it is representative of all Blake's treatments of Shakespeare: they provide visual equivalents that seem 'marvellously literal', yet reveal through their own integrity as visual entities the sheer impossibility of any simple transliteration, or statement in other terms, of the plays' language. In consequence they constantly defamiliarise, constantly refresh the language, and impress by reinforcing its distance and unattainability to the reader.

That the image held a major position within Blake's personal imagery is suggested in his own note to a version of the painting, now lost, that he provides in the *Descriptive Catalogue*:

> A Spirit vaulting from a cloud to turn and wind a fiery Pegasus – Shakspeare. The Horse of Intellect is leaping from the cliffs of Memory and Reasoning; it is a barren Rock: it is also called the Barren Waste of Locke and Newton. (*Poetry and Prose*, p. 546)

This act of redefinition and assimilation assumes the power of Hal as an intellectual as well as a physical entity – an embodiment of the Blakean principle 'Energy is Eternal Delight',[20] in short. While this perhaps says more about Blake than about Shakespeare, it reveals another context in which the figure of Hal should be seen: as one of the images in Blake's work that present a very similar figure and, with various degrees of Shakespearean reference, allude to the essence of intellectual or spiritual freedom. The figure of a nude male flying across the upper part of a composition is apparent from early in Blake's work as an embodiment of the spiritual force of imaginative invention. It appears in the frontispiece of the *Songs of Innocence* (1798),[21] and also in the figure of the cloud in *The Book of Thel* (1789–90).[22] In other versions, the male nude, recognisably the same figure yet standing rather than flying, has a more direct relationship with Shakespeare. This is clearest in the engraving *Jocund Day*,[23] where an allusion to Albion is linked with a reference to these lines from *Romeo and Juliet*:

Night's candles are burnt out, and jocund day
Stands tiptoe on the misty mountain tops.
I must be gone and live, or stay and die.
(3.5.9–11)

Here the figure stands before the sun so that light appears to stream directly from it. This inverts the contextual meaning of the quotation, in stressing the vigour of day rather than Romeo's regret that he must now leave Juliet; but the idea of vitality as opposed to death suggested in the last line is transformed into a more personal direction of energy in the lines incised beneath the image, which clarify and extend the reference to Albion:

Albion arose from where he labour'd at the Mill with slaves
Giving himself for the Nations he danced the dance of Eternal Death

The image at one level suggests the freedom of emancipation from industrial slavery through the sacrificial transformation of Albion, the mythic embodiment of the British spirit. That the alternative title is taken from Shakespeare is another embodiment of the particular fabric of patriotic assimilation into which the dramatist has been woven by Blake: Albion's projected triumph is a parallel to the revitalising of the nation metaphorically foreseen in the horsemanship of Prince Hal.

The presentation of the figure of Hal, and the acts of selection, omission and reinvention of linguistic imagery that it involves, are balanced by the addition of two further elements. The most immediately evident is the visualisation of 'fiery Pegasus' in the presentation of the mane and tail of the animal. Although not coloured as flame, their forms and textures clearly recall the monoprint *God Judging Adam* (1795),[24] where the mane of the horse is formed of orange-red flames matching in colour and movement those surrounding God in the chariot of fire that it draws. This is an act of transference of immense imaginative power: together with the deep orange coloration of the sun that suffuses the lower background, it conveys a sense of vigour that forcefully amplifies the dynamic movement of the horse and the Prince.

More puzzling is the female nude who lies reading on a cloud above the composition. Elsewhere in Blake's work, throughout its whole span, a figure reading a large book has connotations of a lifeless, negative stasis – the title page of *Urizen* (1794)[25] and Job and his wife reading in the first plate of *The Book of Job* (1825: Fig. 54),[26] which contains the inscription 'The letter Killeth, the Spirit giveth life', are perhaps the most insistent examples. The figure has been seen as the recording angel, the idea of artistic inspiration, or the embodiment of the reader, but another reading offers itself as closer to the passage from the play. The book is mythic history, the reader a willing participant in the formulation of myth through the act of telling, the element as a whole revealing the way in which Harry's power has already attained the status of legend through the visionary intensity of Vernon's speech. This is imaginative transfer of a high order; it not only captures the tone of this passage, but also conveys the play's emphasis on reporting and chronicling, seen for example in Vernon's later account of Hal to Hotspur (5.2.51–68), and the speech by Hal on the dead Hotspur (5.4.86–100) that is immediately undermined by Falstaff's fictional account (5.2.138–44) of killing Hotspur himself. The concern with chronicle and story also goes beyond this play to suggest the many episodes of self-conscious recording of histories, both personal and dynastic, throughout the Shakespeare canon, from the redefinitions of identity and fortune at the 'gossips' feast' (5.1.405) at the end of *A Comedy of Errors* to the account of the reconciliation of Leontes and Polixenes in *The Winter's Tale*, embracing among other iterations Richard II's darkly ceremonial 'For God's sake, let us sit upon the ground/ And tell sad stories of the death of kings' (3.2.155–6). It is a striking insight into the workings of chronicle in this play and others that again reveals the acuity of Blake's reading. At the same time, it comes inevitably from the play's own reference system: the Hippocrene fountain, from which those who drank were inspired to write poetry, was made to flow when Pegasus stamped his hoofs.[27] This is the final arc in a circle of reference that enfolds the passage in a complex logic of visual association, once more demonstrating the deep relation between word and image in Blake's Shakespearean designs.

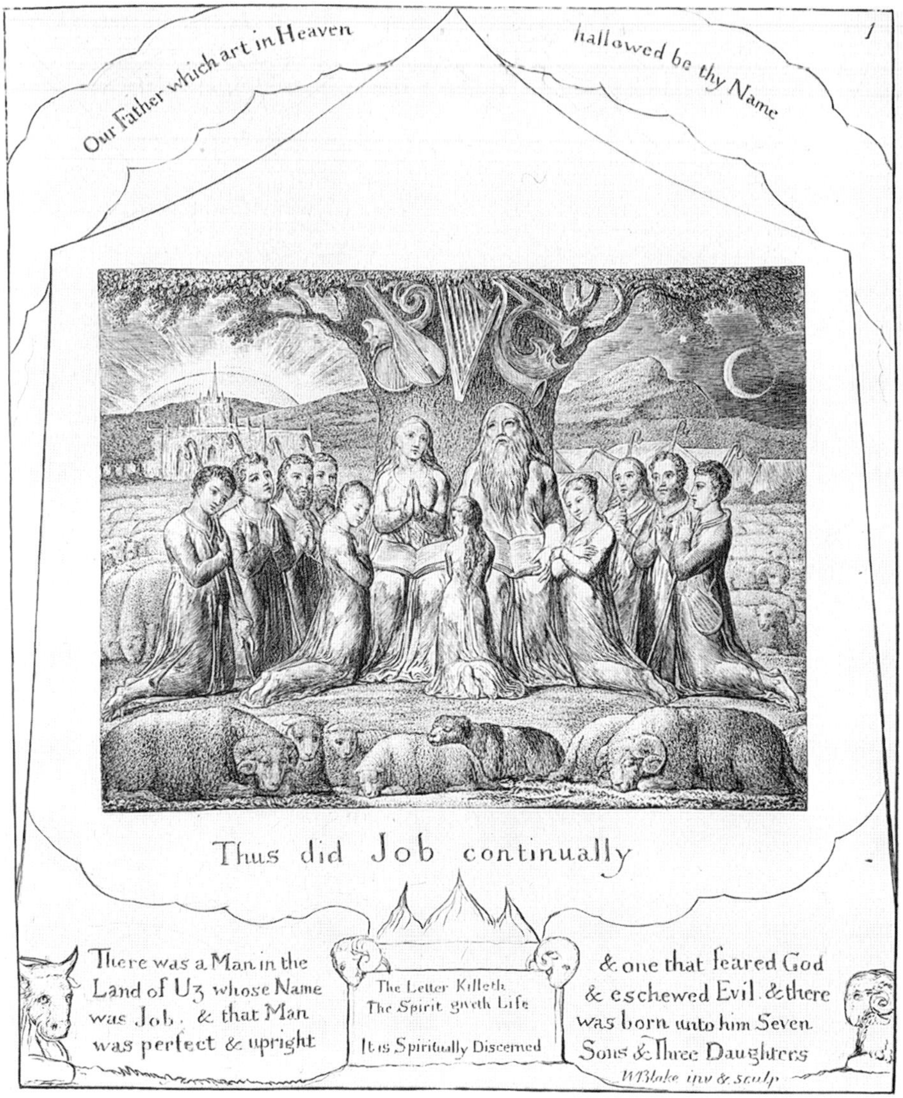

54 William Blake, *The Book of Job*, Plate 1, 1825.

The remaining images in the Thomas folio treat the plays with similar directness, but that depicting Jaques and the wounded stag from *As You Like It* (Fig. 55)[28] is particularly striking for the imaginative insights it discloses through its relationship to Blake's iconographic vocabulary. Jaques is presented directly, outside the perceptual filter of Amiens and the First Lord through which he appears in the text and also, as Chapter 9 will make clear, in the version painted by William Hodges, Sawrey Gilpin and George Romney for the Boydell Shakespeare Gallery. This has the effect of stripping a layer of irony from the speech so that the

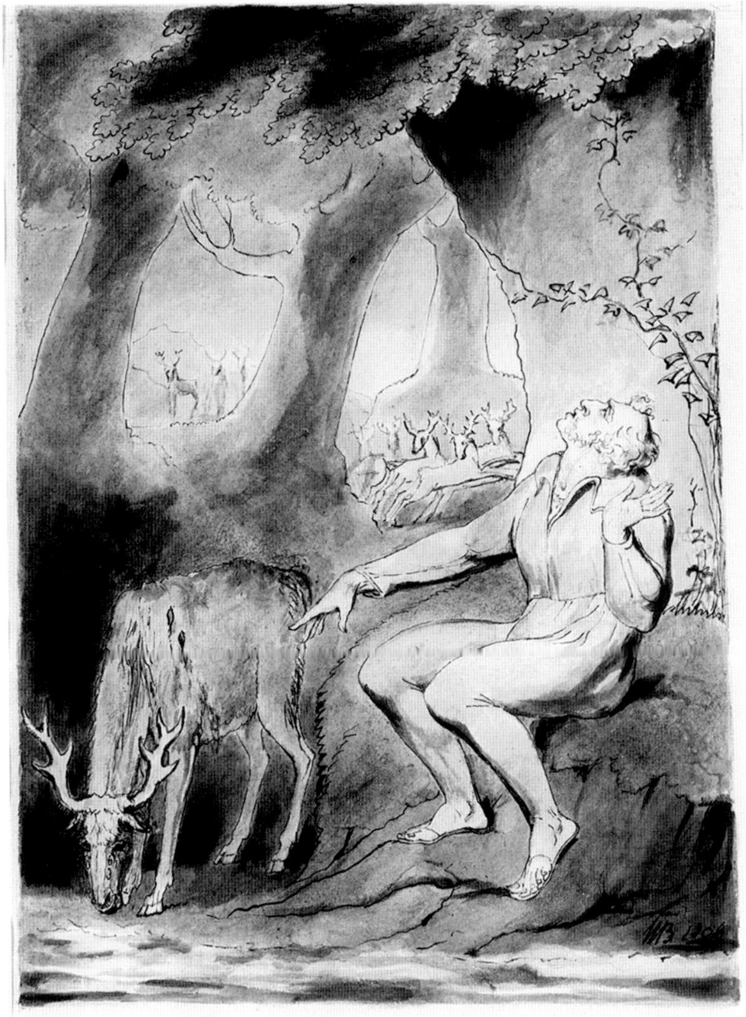

55 William Blake, *Jaques and the Wounded Stag*, 1809.

onlooker is offered, without mediation, the plaint that appears as follows in the Folio:

Sweepe on, you fat and greazy Cittizens,
'Tis just the fashion; wherefore doe you looke
Vpon that poore and broken bankrupt there?
Thus most invectively he pierceth through
The body of the Country, City, Court,
Yea, and this our life, swearing that we
Are meere usurpers, tyrants, and whats worse

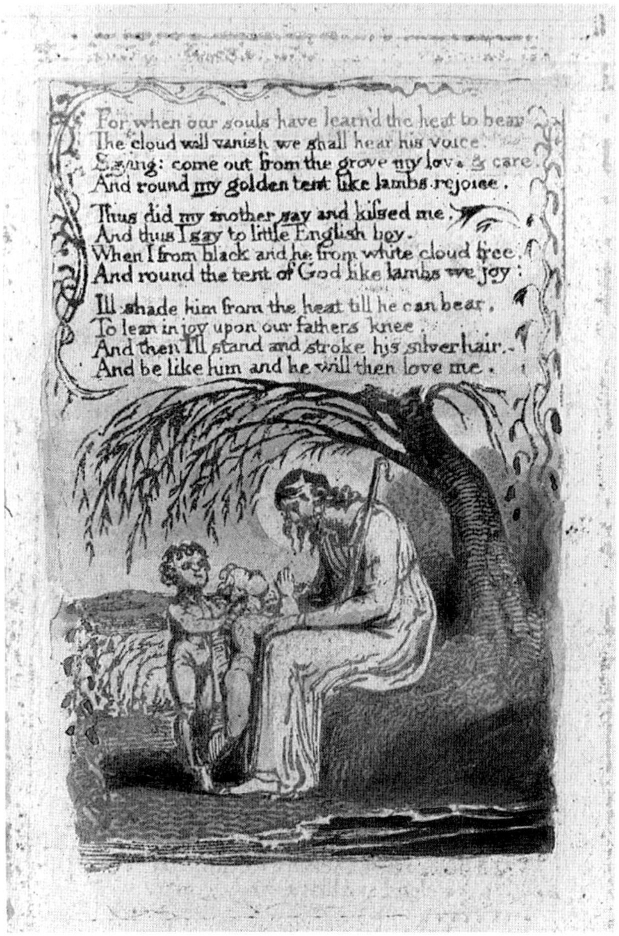

56 William Blake, 'The Little Black Boy', Plate 2, 1789.

To fright the Animals, and to kill them up
In their assign'd and native dwelling place.
(II.i.55–63)

The setting and detail of the image follow the text closely, yet its elements are visualised within Blake's personal iconography, most particularly in the use of the overarching tree that enfolds Jaques and the stag. This is seen often in the earlier illuminated books but is perhaps most fully developed in the second plate of 'The Little Black Boy' from the *Songs of Innocence* (1789: Fig. 56),[29] which presents an idealised vision of a heaven where the white and black children, released from their earthly identities – 'I from black and he from white cloud free' – will play together. In this plate, the figure of God the Father is presented in profile beneath a tree, much like the seated figure of Jaques; the two children stand before Him as does the stag before Jaques. The animal's lowered head has the appearance of the sheep found repeatedly in the early prophetic books, for example, in 'The Shepherd' in the *Songs of Innocence*.[30] These allusions suggest that the image embodies the violation of an ideal unity between the individual and the created world; instead of the satiric reference to Jaques' attempts to 'moralise this spectacle', it shows his anger at heaven for allowing such injustice. What has happened in the act of visual transference is that his response to the stag's lonely suffering has become a serious metonymic statement of the anguish and loss of a fallen world, with the suggestion through its iconography that in heaven things will be otherwise. It is a glimpse into Jaques' own vision that we are offered here, its immediacy a powerful antithesis to the detachment of the First Lord's account: it allows, as it were, the words of Jaques to be heard directly, a shift of emphasis that thoughtfully outweighs the simply comic reading that the passage often receives.

The two images from the Thomas folio reveal insights both into the language of the individual plays and their incorporation into Blake's mythic world view, the former continuing and deepening a tradition of visual criticism, and the latter offering a new dimension of Shakespearean assimilation. At a much deeper level, that explores the structural identity of genre, they work to comment upon larger issues and concerns apparent throughout the canon. *Fiery Pegasus* does this in revealing the process of theatre as mythic history; the Jaques watercolour, by disengaging a level of meaning from the ironic frame in which it appears in the play, makes the onlooker aware of the channelling effect of character when action is reported and not directly presented, and also of the assumptions about identity, in the moralising nature of Jaques' speech, that this impels when characters speak of others. Like many of the plays, *As You Like It* is repeatedly concerned with such fluctuations between recorded action and assumed identity: in reminding us of this Blake once again demonstrates a visual criticism that goes far beyond textual commentary to reveal the armatures on which the plays are built.

III

John Harvey has suggested that Blake's *Tiriel*, significant as the earliest of the prophetic books, rests heavily on a reading of *King Lear*, and that this is given visual statement in the first plate, which might be seen as a reworking of Lear with the dead Cordelia.[31] He develops this by pointing to the resemblance between the tradition of Lear as the bearded prophet examined in Chapter 3 and the figure that exists variously in Blake's work as Urizen, the Old Testament God and other figures in whom anger and reason dominate over compassion. This pairing reveals another dimension of Blake's relationship with Shakespeare, his assimilation of ideas and images into his own private mythology. In the case of Lear, it is hard to discern the exact significance of the borrowing, either as a commentary on Shakespeare or for what it reveals in the work of Blake: certainly, the power of Lear on the heath is a force shared with Blake's dark patriarchs, and probably the most explicit link that may be drawn is in the energy that is both borrowed from Shakespeare's figure and redefined by the allusion to him. The contradiction of moral significance that seemingly results offers itself as further evidence of Blake's assertion, in *The Marriage of Heaven and Hell* (Plate 3: *Poetry and Prose*, p. 34) and elsewhere, that 'Without Contraries is no progression'.

These links show that Shakespeare was a dynamic and immediate force within Blake's creative thought, suggesting a dual relationship with the plays in which the later artist both offers striking visual readings and absorbs and adapts the earlier texts to form part of his own mythological fabric. The fullest understanding of this relationship can be derived from the series of images that, in a number of increasingly personal ways, explore *A Midsummer Night's Dream*. The best known is *Oberon, Titania with Puck and Fairies Dancing* (*c.* 1785: Fig. 57).[32] This has traditionally been related to the final speech of Puck that begins 'If we shadows have offended' (5.1.401), presumably on the basis of the central placing of Puck and the reconciliatory mood that the composition and tone presents, but this is surely incorrect. The setting is the forest and not, as in the final act, the palace; and Puck is addressing Oberon and Titania, not the audience. A far more likely setting is the passage in 4.1 when, after disclosing Bottom to Titania as the object of her love, and removing from him the ass-head, Oberon ritualistically invites:

> Come, my Queen, take hands with me
> And rock the ground whereon these sleepers be.
> (4.1.82–3)

Thus placed, the watercolour adopts a range of new significances within the play's moment and movement. This is the pivot of the play. Before are all the confusions not only of Titania and Bottom but of the earthly lovers; after, the winding of horns to announce the appearance of Theseus and Hippolyta, who will discover and absolve the lovers in their hitherto proscribed pairings, before Bottom attempts to describe his 'most rare vision' (5.1.200). In selecting such a moment Blake not only reveals a strong sense of the play's progress; he shows within it a sense of resolution emblematised by the dancing fairies, a round dance

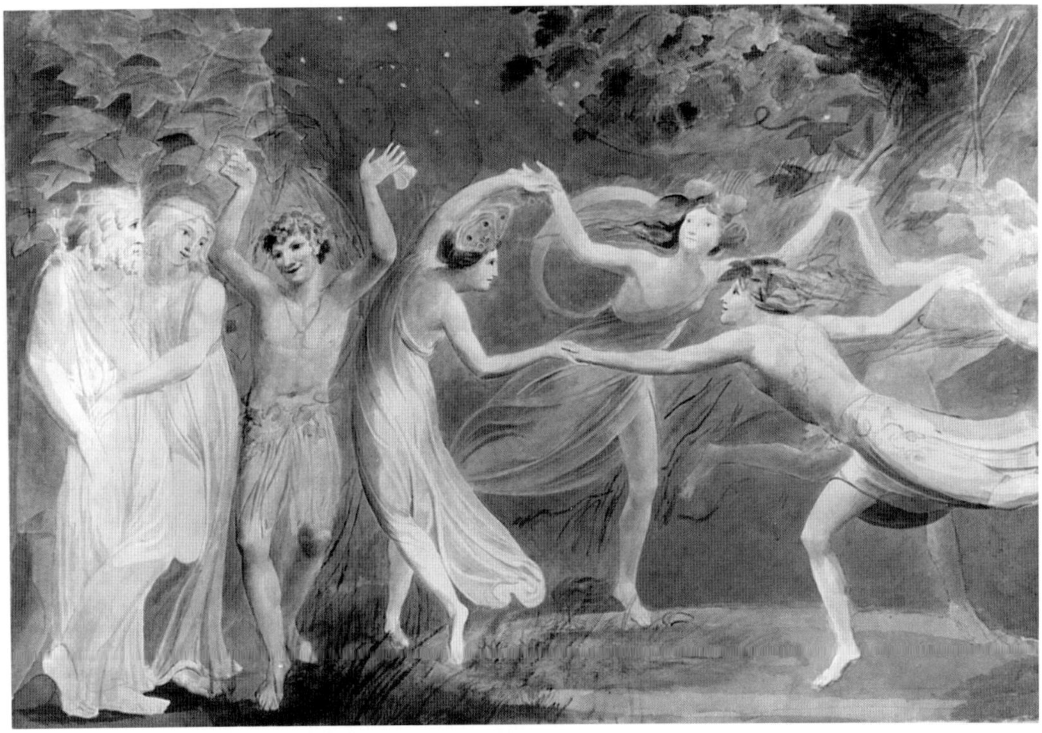

57 William Blake, *Oberon, Titania with Puck and Fairies Dancing*, c. 1785.

that combines supernatural ritual with the Grand Dance to solemnise the end of the court masque. Both use the symbol of the ring to present unity and resolution in the hymeneal contract, but in moving the suggestion out of the court and into the forest Blake sets the marriages within a frame of pantheistic rather than hegemonic sanctity. The compositional resemblance with Romney's *Leveson-Gower Children* of 1777 is strong, suggesting a grace both child-like and Neo-Classical in the fairies' movement, reinforced by the reference to a Roman faun in the delineation of Puck.[33] That, like Romney's painting, Blake's watercolour seems to follow Poussin's *Dance to the Music of Time*, adds another level of suggestion; the fairies, in resembling the dancing seasons, have a power both outside time and over time, and in this an echo of Titania's complaint that 'The seasons alter' (2.1.107) in consequence of the quarrel over the Indian boy becomes faintly audible to salt the resolution.

The location in the forest also places the main weight of the play on the fairy rather than the mortal world, an emphasis extended in the operatic adaptation of the play by Benjamin Britten (1960), which begins with the fairy world and so encloses all the action within its power.[34] Yet Blake's imagery also implies a more equal relation between the two worlds. At one level, all of the characters in the watercolour are recognisable as Neo-Classical figures, much like those from other images Blake produced in the mid-1780s – *Pestilence*,[35] say, or *Joseph making himself known to his brethren*.[36] Oberon and Titania, however, stand apart in their depiction as royalty, recalling the images that Blake had produced when copying the effigies and wall paintings in Westminster Abbey for the Society of Antiquaries in 1774, in particular his drawings of Henry III and Queen Eleanor.[37] At the same time, the figures are clearly of diminutive stature, as their relative size before the leaves makes clear. In a single visual stroke, Blake implies the innate likeness and difference between the human and the fairy worlds of the play within the magical frame of the forest.

The figures of the dancing fairies themselves have more to contribute. One has a moth in her hair: while not developed to the degree it is given in a painting by Fuseli (discussed in Chapter 8), it postulates an intriguing relation between the apparently human figure of the dancer, Bottom's comic attendant, and the natural world. A similar link is shown in the adjacent fairy, who wears 'peaseblossom' in her hair – either the petals of the sweet pea, appropriate for their ethereal texture and pure colour, or a nonce-word using the 'pease' prefix as a diminutive suggesting a blossom of no substance or significance. It is significant that, while the former meaning is immediately apparent in Blake's image, it is the latter that is invariably given as an explanation in editions of the play. The detail again demonstrates the central feature of Blake's imagery: in offering a transliteration as much as a translation into visual terms, it both forces our attention back on to the text to explore the actual diversity of meaning contained in single words or metaphoric tropes and makes us aware of the imaginative imprecision of such utterances. Here, this element of visual processing is enfolded within an awareness of a pivotal moment in the play's action and a sensitivity to the fairies as both unique in their otherness and startlingly human.

Similar figures are used in a much smaller watercolour in the collection of the Folger Shakespeare Library, known as *Oberon and Titania, preceded by Puck* (*c*. 1790–3: Plate 11).[38] The central pair are shown flying through a dark night sprinkled with stars, their trains held by child fairies who fly behind them; their aerial progress suggests the fluent grace of the figures in later images such as *The River of Life* (*c*. 1805).[39] They are preceded by a Puck unique among Blake's figures, dressed in an oddly paradoxical monochrome motley, with arms and legs spread almost as a Vitruvian man. That he carries a sword is most curious of all: this has no source in Shakespeare's text, but instead seems to play further on the equation between human and fairy royalty, implying Puck's role as a courtier or herald. The most likely source of the image is in Oberon's words shortly after the dance celebrated in the earlier Blake watercolour:

Then, my Queen, in silence sad,
Trip we after night's shade;
We the globe can compass soon,
Swifter than the wandering moon.
(4.1.92–5)

There may also be suggestions of Puck's penultimate speech:

And we fairies, that do run
By the triple Hecate's team
From the presence of the sun,
Following darkness like a dream,
Now are frolic (5.1.361–5)

The grace of the characters implies a reading of 'frolic' as *fröhlich* or joyful, and the darkness makes the lines appropriate in both a narrative and a sensual frame. More likely is a combination of attributes of both passages, showing the movement of Oberon and Titania as a royal progress above the world and thus emphasising again their identity as both human and supernatural. Instead of the domestic spite of which Robin Goodfellow is capable, or the fairies' vulnerability, the image concentrates again on their ceremonial enactments, so that within it is contained an implication of the sacramental richness of Oberon's final speech that begins the progress to sanctify the bridal bed:

And each several chamber bless
Through this palace with sweet peace.
(5.1.395–6)

The watercolour's soft darkness is a fitting place for such a resolution.

Related to these watercolours are other images that take as their basis the figures of Oberon and Titania but endow them with with new meanings, making visible the shift from visual criticism of Shakespeare to the assimilation of the play's figures and ideas into Blake's own mythology of creation and growth. The figures have their origin in a page from the notebook of the artist's brother Robert,[40] which shows the two figures lying on a flower, with fairies dancing above them. Another painting, contemporary with the Folger watercolour, is known as *Oberon and Titania on a Lily* (*c.* 1790–3).[41] Something of the implicit meaning of both

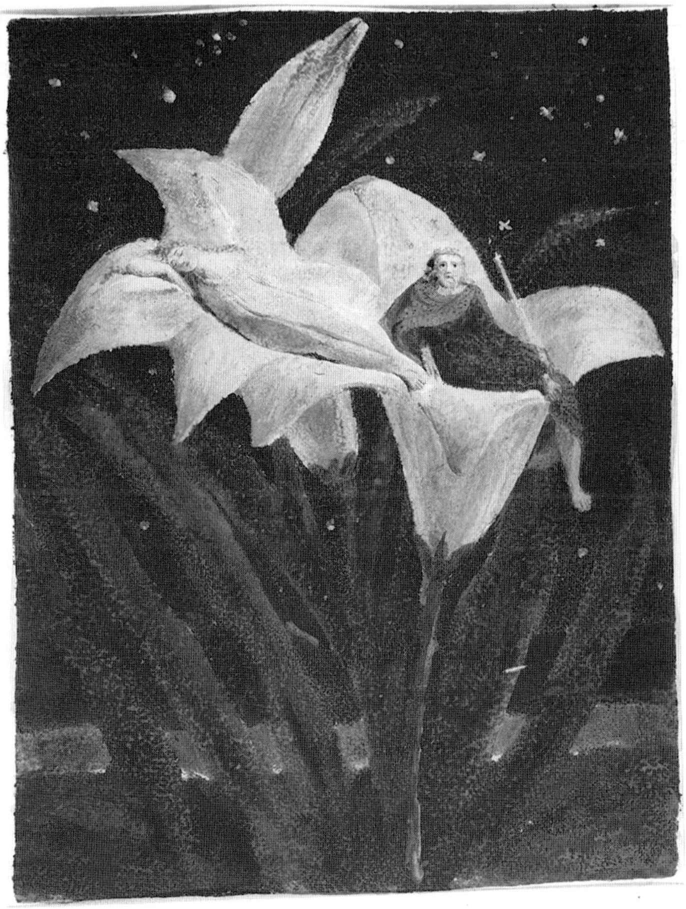

58 William Blake, *The Song of Los*, Plate 5, 1795.

is provided by an image that has no explicit connection to Shakespeare's play, Plate 5 from *The Song of Los* (Fig. 58).[42] This, the central plate in the volume, refers both backwards to 'Africa' and forward to 'Asia', the two parts of the *Song* that, together with *America* and *Europe*, constitute Blake's mythic geography. The king represents the political struggles of America and Europe, the queen the figure of Enitharmon in the latter book, who has slept for 1800 years. Together they represent the hope and joy of the future in a unity of disparate principles within a vegetable – that is, an organic and instinctual – world, as represented by the lily in which they rest, most directly in its forward-leaning bud. What has occurred is a translation of the idea of the unity of opposites within the figures of the *Midsummer Night's Dream* watercolour into Blake's own allegory of political, moral and human oneness, the quality that David Erdman calls 'a paradisal regeneration'[43] that

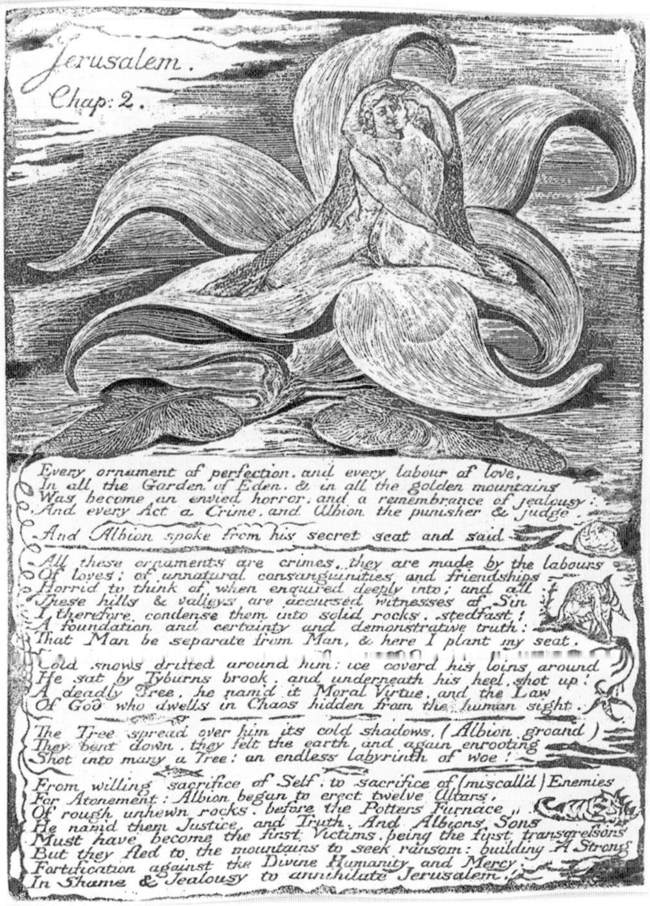

59 William Blake, *Jerusalem*, Plate 28, 1825.

may be seen as a personal annexation of the romance progress of Shakespeare's comedy. This process is again evident in Blake's most ambitious prophetic book, *Jerusalem*, where the same figure is the basis of Plate 28 (Fig. 59). The figures are identified in the text as Albion embracing Vala on the lily of Havilah: again they suggest the generative, redemptive forces of the natural world, here in strong contrast to the horrors of the opening of the book's second chapter. For all these images a sentence in the *Descriptive Catalogue* is revealing, making explicit the link with *A Midsummer Night's Dream*: 'Shakspeare's Fairies also are the rulers of the vegetable world' (*Poetry and Prose*, p. 535).

As well as the drawing by Robert Blake, the images resemble a fragmentary sketch in the *Notebook* (see Fig. 60).[44] This shows a male and female figure

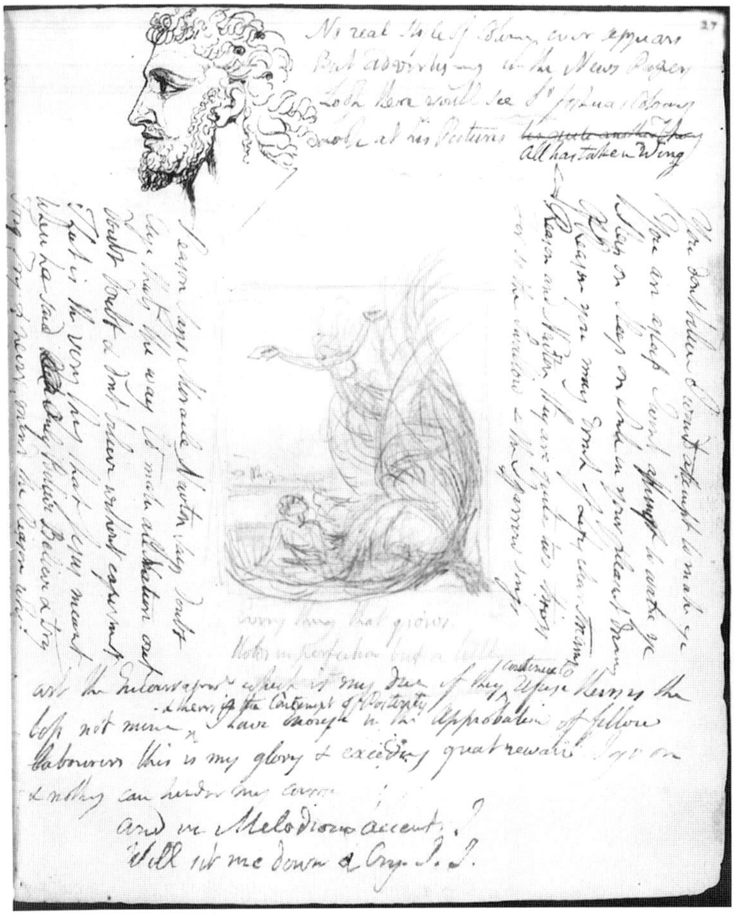

60 William Blake, *Notebook*, p. 21.

embracing within the calyx of a flower. What makes this especially striking are the lines written in Blake's hand beneath it:

every thing that growes
Holds in perfection but a little moment

The lines are from the opening of Sonnet 15, but omit the opening three words – 'When I consider'. The final word is overwritten with another text, and 'but a little' is faded, or may show signs of erasure. Presented with such selectiveness the lines suggest as much a moment of complete fulfilment as a process of transience and loss, with another associated meaning from Blake's 'Auguries of Innocence':

To see a World in a Grain of Sand
And a Heaven in a Wild Flower
Hold Infinity in the palm of your hand
And Eternity in an hour.[45]

This rearrangement redefines the lines of the sonnet into something approaching Blake's belief that 'everything that lives is holy',[46] a prefiguration of the idea of vegetative unity that is the culmination made explicit in the final plate of *Jerusalem*, where 'All Human Forms identified' awake 'into his Bosom in the Life of Immortality'.[47]

Kathleen Raine explores the drawing in relation to a similar figure on the title page of *The Book of Thel*, to show that it shares Shakespeare's concern with time and mutability;[48] but seen in the frame of the Oberon and Titania series, the image has another, equally valuable direction. With the two figures – Oberon and Titania, male and female, reason and compassion – enfolded within the flower, it suggests that the idea of vegetable growth, the basis of so much of Blake's later mythic prophecy, rests in part on a visualised reading of *A Midsummer Night's Dream* and one of the Sonnets. Shakespeare thus visualised is disclosed as central to Blake's prophetic books and the movement they present: visual criticism of Shakespeare has become a very particular kind of insemination in the creative imagination of the artist-reader. As well as enfolding the two Shakespearean characters within Blake's own scheme of creation, this has a more local purpose: as its subtitle makes clear, *Jerusalem* is concerned with *The Emanation of The Giant Albion*, a mythicised history of the past and future of Britain. Despite its intensely personal nature, the imagery has achieved a much more widespread contemporary identity: the involvement of Shakespearean creativity within the notion of an ideal nationhood.

Throughout, the two figures share a visual identity with others that assume greater symbolic valency as Blake's mythology develops, Oberon resembling the form of Urizen, or intellect unmediated by compassion, and Titania recalling the figure of Eve and other female embodiments of pity. This links them to the central figures in another early watercolour, *Lear and Cordelia in Prison* (c. 1779: Plate 7).[49] Writing to Hayley in 1804, Blake refers to Romney's 'picture of *Lear and Cordelia*' as 'an incomparable production . . . about five feet by four, and exquisite for expression; indeed, it is most pathetic; the heads of Lear and Cordelia can never be surpassed'.[50] This must be the large oil included in the Kendal lottery, and now lost; Blake's response shows his respect for the image itself and for the importance of the subject, and it may be that the combination of history, classicism and the personal version of the Grand Style that is apparent in his own work owes something to the same complex of ideas in the work of the earlier artist. The basis of this perhaps lies in the absorption of the image into a mythic recreation of national identity, and it has been suggested that it was prepared as an illustration of Milton's *History of Britain*. A page in the *Notebook* includes 'King Lear' as the fourth of twenty-two 'Subjects for The History of England' (*Poetry and Prose*, p. 672). The immediate setting is nonetheless derived from the stage direction to Act V scene vi of Nahum Tate's *History of King Lear*, the basis of the play's stage presentation in Blake's lifetime:

> Scene, a Prison
> Lear *asleep, with his head on* Cordelia's lap.

The downward glance of Cordelia seems to echo the words with which the scene begins:

> What toils, thou wretched king, hast thou endured
> To make thee draw, in chains, a sleep so sound?
> (Tate, V. vi. 1–2)

This is revealing about Blake's reading, suggesting an acquaintance with the printed text of Tate's play rather than any individual performance, and certainly rather than Shakespeare's play. This should not surprise: if Blake read Tate rather than Shakespeare in preparation for the image he would have encountered a narrative closer to *King Leir*, Geoffrey of Monmouth and the other versions Shakespeare used as his sources, in which the king and his daughters do not die.

Thus far the detail of history; the figures themselves also suggest the painting's more personal, prophetic structure for Blake. Whereas the two figures in the *Midsummer Night's Dream* images may be seen allegorically as presenting various kinds of human opposites, Lear and Cordelia may be far more explicitly defined, as respectively resembling Urizen and Eve, and all their cognates, in Blake's later mythology. In this, they represent two facets of humanity that together compose a lost unity, towards which the figures in the *Los* and *Jerusalem* plates point. The origin of this unity, and the moment of its loss, are suggested most clearly by Blake in his *Descriptive Catalogue*:

> The Strong man represents the human sublime. The Beautiful man represents the human pathetic, which was in the wars of Eden divided into male and female. (*Poetry and Prose*, p. 543)

When the two mythic patterns are related in this image, both gain in associative richness. Blake's myth gains specific resonance by being disclosed within the story of Lear; more significantly, the early dispossession of Cordelia by Lear is revealed in the true enormity of its ramifications, a splintering of the intended unity of selfhood as well as a fracturing of the natural order. The watercolour reveals itself as a supple and resonant dialogue between the idea of British history, the myth of the division of the ideal man as represented in Arthur and the Ancient Britons, the human embodiments of Blake's deeply personal regenerative prophecies, and the human and political ruptures revealed in Shakespeare's *King Lear* as modified by Tate. Again Blake's art stands as an idiosyncratic reading of many of the directions of contemporary British thought, in which the national Shakespeare occupies a fundamental position.

At what stage do Blake's images stop being critical readings of the plays and become part of his own mythology? The question is both insistent and unanswerable, but it implies two central values. One is that, in literal terms, Shakespeare is already a part of the Romantic creative imagination to an extent that is hard to isolate: the most obvious parallel here is with Keats' assimilation of Shakespearean imagery of the natural world. It suggests that Shakespeare painting, and Shakespeare activity in a wider sphere, is already taking on a different identity – a subject returned to in Chapter 10 – and that this particular direction rests almost wholly on the text as it is read rather than performed. The other is that the rich and strange valencies of Blake's imaging remind us of the sheer complexity of the reading process: the translation of compound verbal images into visual forms always moves into fresh areas of metaphoric allusion and suggestion. As well as exerting a powerful aseptic effect in cleansing the text of other accretions of meaning, washing it into a puzzling innocence, it unmasks the reader's share in producing the text: as well as revealing signification, it reminds us that we, like Blake, recreate it at every encounter.

IV

One final irony. Although Blake was excluded from the list of artists commissioned to produce paintings for the Boydell Gallery, he was approached at some time in the 1790s to contribute to it. John Opie had revised his painting of the fourth act of *Romeo and Juliet* by removing some figures from a crowded composition, and Jean Pierre Simon produced an engraving[51] to illustrate the edition of plays published as part of the venture. By this time, the Facius brothers had already produced their engraving of the original version for the volume of large plates.[52] To ensure that both images were the same, Blake was asked to engrave the original version.[53] This he did with complete fidelity, in an engraving technique that makes full use of all the devices available, as comparison with Simon's limited version instantly reveals. It is a masterful piece of execution: every detail of Opie's crowded, awkward composition is presented, with no additions or alterations. In this manner the painter who produced some of the most imaginatively suggestive visual treatments of the plays made his contribution to the largest scheme of Shakespeare illustration of the century.

NOTES

1. *A Father's Memoirs of his Child* (London: Longman, 1806), p. xxxiv.
2. Evidence of this is provided in *A Catalogue of the very valuable and extensive library of the late William Hayley Esq*, 'Ninth Day's Sale', p. 58.
3. *The Complete Poetry and Prose of William Blake*, Revised Edition, ed. David V. Erdman (New York: Doubleday, 1988), Letter No. 54, pp. 759–60; quotation from p. 760.
4. *A new edition of Shakespeare's Plays, from the corrected text of Johnson and Steevens, with prints engraved by Mr. Heath*, 10 Parts (London: Heath and Robinson, 1802–4).
5. *A Catalogue*, 'Twelfth Day's Sale', Lot 2387, p. 76.
6. 'To My Dearest Friend, John Flaxman, these lines'. Letter to John Flaxman, 12 September 1800, *Poetry and Prose*, p. 707.
7. A full account of the heads and their composition is given in William Wells, *William Blake's 'Heads of the Poets' for Turret House, the Residence of William Hayley, Felpham* (Manchester: City Art Gallery, 1969).
8. Pen and tempera on canvas, 41 × 79.5 (16 1/8 × 33). City Art Gallery, Manchester.
9. *A Descriptive Catalogue of Pictures, Poetical and Historical Inventions . . .*, *Poetry and Prose*, pp. 529–51; quotation from p. 535.
10. Colour print finished in pen and watercolour, irregular, 42.5 × 53.9 (16 3/4 × 21 1/4). Tate Britain. Other copies are in the Metropolitan Museum, New York and the Yale Center for British Art (Paul Mellon Collection). For a summary of the processes involved in making the print, see Robin Hamlyn and Michael Phillips, eds. *William Blake*, exh. cat. (London: Tate Publishing, 2000), p. 194.
11. Pencil, 30.5 × 28.3 (12 × 11 1/2), British Museum, London. For an account of the differences between the studies and the prints, see Hamlyn and Phillips, eds. *William Blake*, p. 196.
12. 'Blake's Shakespeare', *Apollo*, LXXIX, 318–25; the reference to *Pity* is on p. 322.
13. *William Blake*, exh. cat (London: Tate Gallery, 1978), p. 63.
14. Pen and watercolour over pencil, 39.5 × 35.1 (15 1/2 × 12 1/4), Fitzwilliam Museum, Cambridge.
15. *Shakespeare in Art*, p. 94.
16. Pen, ink and watercolour, 23.1 × 17.3 (9 1/8 × 7 1/2). British Museum, London.
17. *Henry the Fourth Part I*, ed. Samuel Burdett Hemingway (Philadelphia and London: J. B. Lippincott, 1936), pp. 253–9.

18. *The Art of William Blake* (1959) (London and New York: Harper and Row, 1974), p. 19.
19. *A Philosophical Enquiry into the Origin of our Ideas of the Sublime and the Beautiful*, ed. Adam Phillips (Oxford: World's Classics, 1990), p. 72.
20. *The Marriage of Heaven and Hell*, Plate 4, 'The voice of the Devil'. *Poetry and Prose*, p. 34.
21. Relief etching with watercolour, 10.8 × 6.9 ($4\frac{1}{4}$ × $2\frac{3}{4}$).
22. Although the figure also appears in Plate 3, its main use is in Plate 6, relief etching with watercolour; copy H. 15.3 × 10.8 (6 × $4\frac{1}{4}$), Library of Congress, Rosenwald Collection, Washington D.C.
23. Line engraving, 26.6 × 19 ($10\frac{1}{2}$ × $7\frac{1}{2}$), Rosenwald Collection, National Gallery, Washington D.C.
24. Colour print finished in pen and watercolour, 42.6 × 52.6 ($16\frac{3}{4}$ × $20\frac{11}{16}$), Metropolitan Museum of Art, New York. Two other versions exist, in Tate Britain and Philadelphia Museum of Art, but the New York version is probably the first impression and has the most intense coloration.
25. *The First Book of Urizen*, 1794. Title page, 14.7 × 10.3 ($5\frac{3}{4}$ × $4\frac{11}{16}$), Pierpont Morgan Library, New York.
26. Also known as 'Job and his Family'. Line engraving, 18.4 × 15.0 ($7\frac{1}{4}$ × $5\frac{7}{8}$), Fitzwilliam Museum, Cambridge.
27. Hamlyn, *William Blake*, p. 184.
28. Pen and watercolour, 22 × 15.8 ($8\frac{11}{16}$ × $6\frac{1}{4}$), British Museum, London.
29. Plate 12, relief etching with watercolour, 10.9 × 6.7 ($4\frac{5}{16}$ × $2\frac{5}{8}$).
30. 'Shakespeare and the Ends of Time', pp. 34–5.
31. Plate 4, relief etching with watercolour, 11.0 × 6.9 ($4\frac{5}{16}$ × $2\frac{3}{4}$).
32. Watercolour on paper, 47.5 × 67.5 ($18\frac{11}{16}$ × $25\frac{9}{16}$), Tate Britain.
33. See the account by Robin Hamlyn in *William Blake*, p. 183.
34. For a discussion of the opera's critical and interpretive stance towards the play, see Gary Jay Williams, *Our Moonlight Revels: A Midsummer Night's Dream in the Theatre* (Iowa City: University of Iowa Press, 1997), pp. 199–203.
35. Of the four versions in the Tate collection the most nearly contemporary is that of *c.* 1780–84. Pen and watercolour, 18.5 × 27.5 ($7\frac{1}{4}$ × $10\frac{3}{4}$).
36. Pen and watercolour over pencil, 40.5 × 56 ($15\frac{15}{16}$ × $22\frac{1}{16}$). Tate Britain.
37. *Henry III Head and Shoulders from his Effigy*, pencil, oval, 34 × 29.2 ($13\frac{3}{8}$ × $11\frac{1}{2}$), Bodleian Library Oxford. *Queen Eleanor, Head and Shoulders from her Effigy*, pencil, oval, 33.65 × 29.2 ($13\frac{1}{4}$ × $11\frac{5}{8}$), Bodleian Library, Oxford.
38. Pencil, pen and watercolour, oval, 16.4 × 20.6 ($6\frac{7}{16}$ × $8\frac{1}{2}$).
39. Pen and ink and watercolour on paper, 305 × 336 (12 × $13\frac{1}{4}$), Tate Britain.
40. *Oberon and Titania Reclining on a Poppy*, *c.* 1785–7, watercolour, 20 × 15.5 ($7\frac{7}{8}$ × $6\frac{1}{8}$), British Library.
41. Pen and watercolour, 21.1 × 16.3 ($8\frac{5}{16}$ × $6\frac{7}{16}$), Private collection, USA.
42. In David V. Erdman, ed. *The Illuminated Blake* (London: Oxford University Press, 1975), p. 178.
43. 'The Symmetries of *The Song of Los*', *Studies in Romanticism*, 16 (Spring 1977), pp. 179–88; quotation from p. 180, n.2. See also Erdman's explanatory note to the plate in *The Illuminated Blake*, p. 178.

44. *The Notebook of William Blake: A Photographic and Typographic Facsimile*, ed. David V. Erdman, with the assistance of Donald K. Moore, Revised edition (New York: Readex Books, 1977), p. N21.
45. From the Pickering MS, fair copies made *c.* 1803. *Poetry and Prose*, p. 490.
46. The phrase is first used in the Chorus from 'A Song of Liberty' in *The Marriage of Heaven and Hell*, Plate 27, *Poetry and Prose*, p. 45. It also appears in *A Vision of the Daughters of Albion*, *America: A Prophecy* and *The Four Zoas*.
47. *Jerusalem: The Emanation of The Giant Albion*, Plate 99, *Poetry and Prose*, p. 258.
48. *Blake and Tradition*, The A. W. Mellon Lectures in the Fine Arts, 2 vols. (Princeton: Princeton University Press, 1968), I, pp.106–7.
49. Pen, ink and watercolour, 12.54 × 17.46 ($4\ ^{15}/_{16} \times 6\ ^{7}/_{8}$). Tate Britain.
50. Letter of 4 May, 1804, *Poetry and Prose*, pp. 748–9; quotation from p. 748.
51. Published 1 February 1792, *c.* 16.7 × 27 ($6\ ^{9}/_{16} \times 10\ ^{5}/_{8}$).
52. Published 4 June 1791, 49.5 × 62.5 ($19\ ^{1}/_{2} \times 24\ ^{5}/_{8}$).
53. Published 25 March 1799, 17.0 × 23.9 ($6\ ^{11}/_{16} \times 9\ ^{3}/_{8}$).

CHAPTER 7

'GENERAL IDEAS AND THE FAMILIAR PATHETIC': NEO-CLASSICAL SHAKESPEARE AND JOSHUA REYNOLDS

I

The *Discourses* of Sir Joshua Reynolds, with their stress on revealing the universal within the particular, would seem to offer the clearest model for a Neo-Classical Shakespeare. Yet Reynolds' own paintings of the plays reject such an approach almost completely; and it is also striking that probably the earliest use of the Grand Style for a Shakespeare image, Dance's *Timon of Athens*, is effective largely through the disparity between its style and subject. These circumstances suggest that the Neo-Classical stance was innately at odds with Shakespeare depiction, perhaps reflecting the view, already well established in critical writing, that the plays succeeded through their open rejection of classical methods. Those few images that are avowedly Neo-Classical consequently reveal a way of seeing the plays that runs counter to the main aesthetic current: they are significant in the critical interpretations they offer largely because they manifest a minority reading.

Benjamin West's Shakespeare images probably display the Grand Style at its purest, sharing their idiom with his paintings of episodes from classical history, the Bible and English history. *King Lear and Cordelia* (1784: Fig. 61)[1] employs the devices of classical representation already employed by Dance to generate an epic tone, but does so on an epic scale fitting the dramatist's stature. It is through its resemblance in composition to one of West's classical history paintings, *The Grecian Daughter Defending her Father*,[2] that the canvas discloses its critical meaning: Cordelia is by implication shown as possessing the heroic virtue of loyalty to her father. That the painting was commissioned by the wealthy patron George Bowles suggests that, in both style and production context, the image belongs to a cultural frame best described in Raymond Williams' terms as residual rather

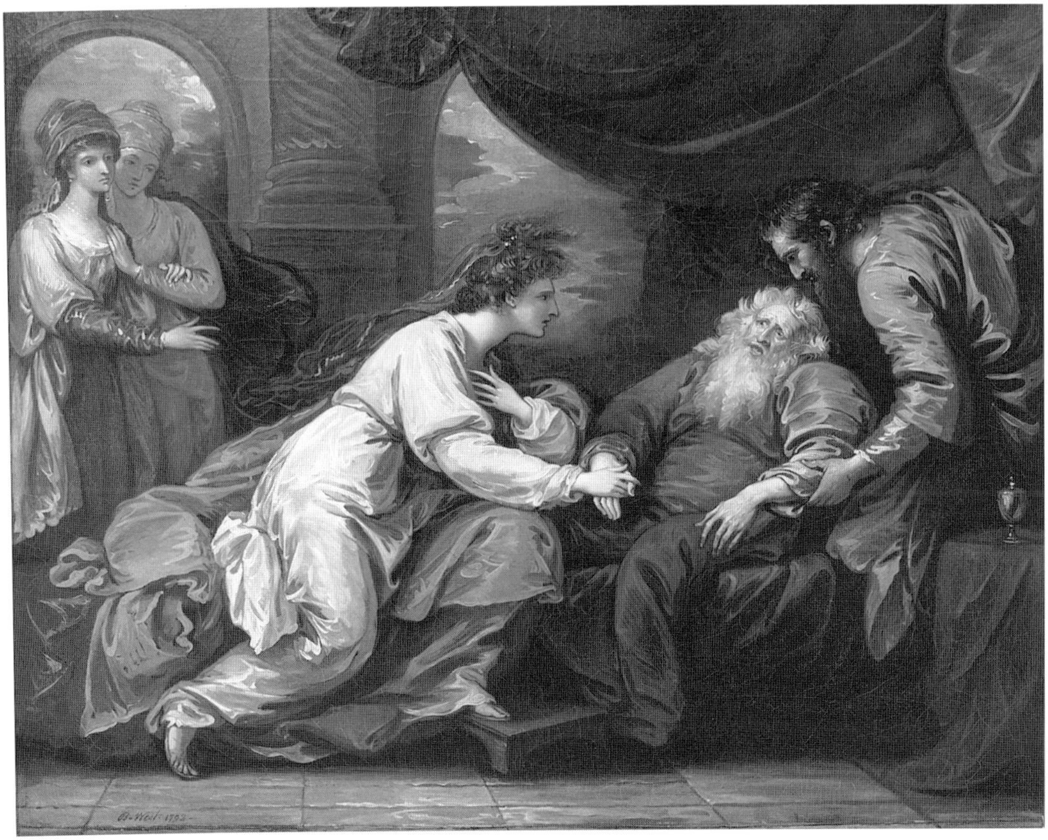

61 Benjamin West, *King Lear and Cordelia*, 1784.

than emergent;[3] and it is this tradition, rather than the indigenous one traced in Chapter 3, that West follows again in *King Lear in the Storm* (1788: Fig. 62),[4] a painting of enormous scale produced for Boydell's Shakespeare Gallery. Although the turbulent composition apparently rejects classical restraint, the figure of Lear himself, modelled on the classical sculpture of the Laocoön[5] that had become fashionable after Winckelmann had praised it in his study of classical art, reveals its fundamental approach. Lear is allied to a classical hero who endures with great dignity the death of one of his children, offering an unusual ennoblement of Lear's suffering on the heath. The allusion also contains an indirect reference to Lessing's *Laocoön*, the theoretical discourse on the relation of the arts of poetry and painting published in 1766. Fuseli had translated Winckelmann in 1765 and, while an English translation of Lessing did not appear until the nineteenth century, it is unlikely that West would not have been aware of the book's ideas, perhaps through Fuseli. The painting in consequence combines a presentation

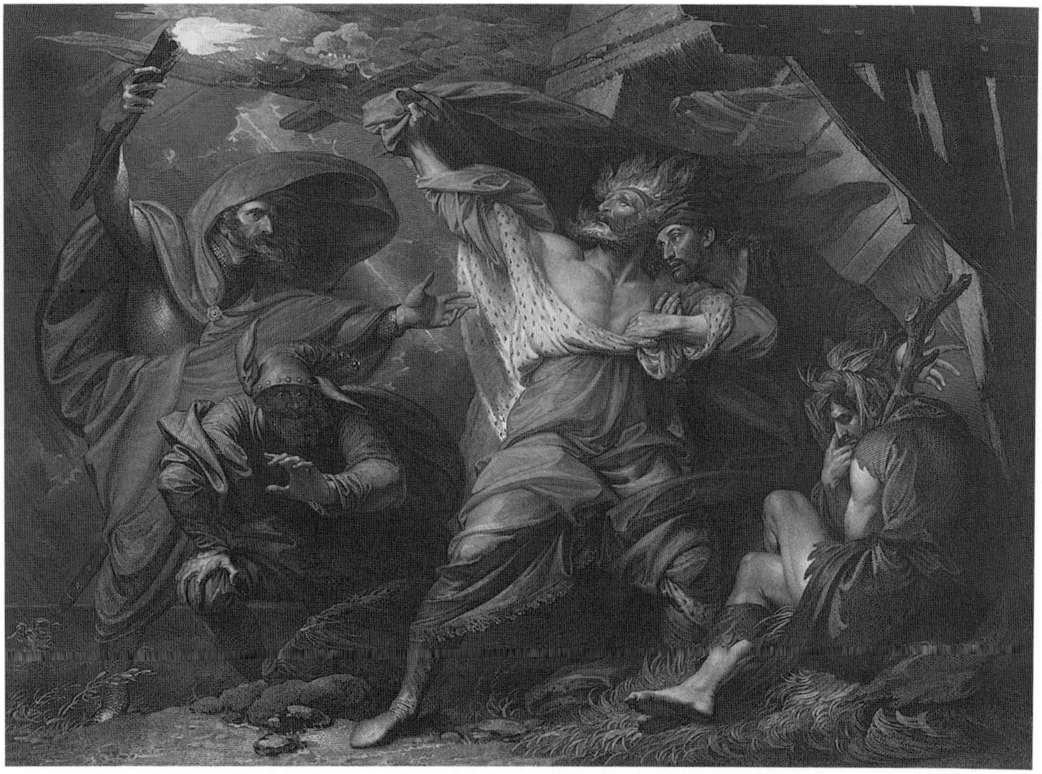

62 Benjamin West, *King Lear in the Storm*. Engraved by William Sharpe, 1793.

of suffering, insistent in its vast scale, with elevating classical allusion and self-reflexive analytical comment, establishing Shakespeare painting within a complex discourse of comparative aesthetics of a sort also found, as later paragraphs will show, in Lawrence and Reynolds.

James Barry's use of Old Master iconography within an epic embodiment of the Grand Style has already been explored in Chapter 3, but another of his images demonstrates a wholly different engagement with its principles. This is *Iachimo emerging from the Chest in Imogen's Chamber* (c. 1788–92: Fig. 63).[6] Like his *King Lear* painting, the image is huge, but whereas in the earlier canvas physical size is a statement of epic feeling, here it enacts a sense of intimate bodily violation. Iachimo and Imogen are separated by a gulf as much moral as physical, emphasised by the material objects that occupy the intervening space that, included in Iachimo's account of the room and its contents, stand metaphorically for the invented bodily possession of Imogen that he reports to Posthumus. It is not only the objects themselves but the lack of structure that they represent that is significant: the disorder in the fragments of classical ornament strewn around

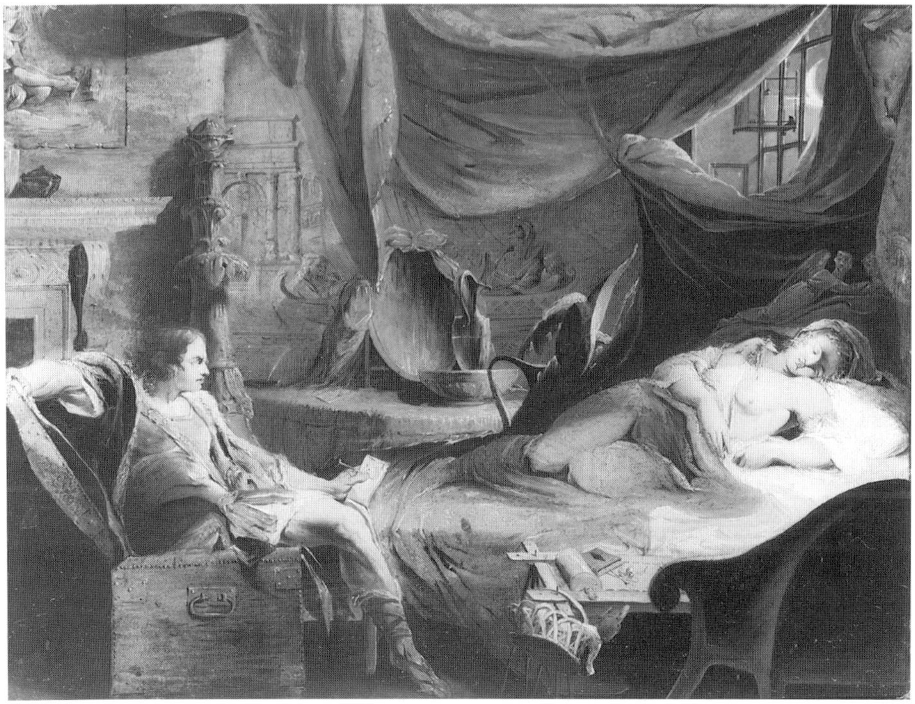

63 James Barry, *Iachimo emerging from the Chest in Imogen's Chamber*, c. 1788–92.

the central passage implies the intended violation, giving the objectification of Imogen inscribed in Iachimo's itinerary a far darker tonality. This is strengthened by the effect of the opening in the elaborate drapery, which acts as a symbol of sexual invasiveness as well as revealing an intrusive moonlight. That in this it balances the picture of 'Chaste Dian bathing' (2.4.82) above Iachimo may also reflect sardonically upon the contrast between these two significations of the moon. But the painting's greatest effect comes from the realisation that, in observing the half-naked woman at the right of the canvas, the onlooker is implicated in the scopophilic act which Iachimo is performing. The painting is a sombre excursion into the darker areas of sexuality and possession presented in the two scenes of the play on which it rests, and as such it succeeds with a power that moves beyond the Neo-Classical principles of Barry's other Shakespeare paintings to convey a modern directoral insight in a disturbing statement of material and sexual incursion.[7]

Another variant of the classical heroic is offered in the paintings of Kemble by Sir Thomas Lawrence, most particularly the first of a series of images of *Coriolanus*. The title reveals its bold simplicity: *John Philip Kemble as Coriolanus before the Hearth of Aufidius* (1788: Fig. 64).[8] The play in which Kemble appeared was

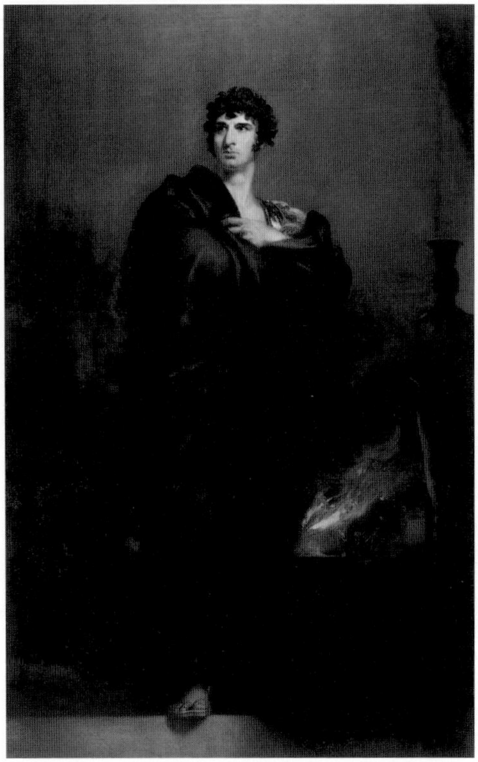

64 Thomas Lawrence, *John Philip Kemble as Coriolanus before the Hearth of Aufidius*, 1788.

Thomas Sheridan's reworking of James Thomson's adaptation, which simplifies the relationship between Coriolanus and Aufidius, but the power of the moment transcends this dilution. In the simple act of showing Kemble awaiting the leader of the Volsces, standing before a domestic architectural feature so redolent of belonging and hospitality, the image crystallises the play's exploration of the psychology of displacement through its central character's shifts of allegiance. That he is depicted as a classical statue, one foot advanced off the hearthstone, much as Maillol's figures take one step off the plinth a little more than a century later, reveals his rejection of the role of hero thrust on him. The painting is made more effective by being one of the few images of actors in character successfully to cross the boundary into astute textual criticism. In a single compositional motif Lawrence makes clear the crisis of identity that Coriolanus suffers, at the same time as the self-referentiality this contains celebrates the classical style of both painting and actor.

The three paintings that Reynolds produced for the Boydell Shakespeare Gallery adopt a markedly different approach. Any formulation of the classical ideal in treatment or technique is carefully modulated through a series of other expressive and conceptual devices, redefining the idea of universality by adapting the painter's earlier techniques to produce images that 'illustrate' Shakespeare in Dr Johnson's sense of the word, interrogating and clarifying aspects of text in both detail and larger movement. Reynolds' reluctance to become involved in Boydell's scheme is often stressed. Northcote recorded his disdain at producing images for reproduction 'as if he thought it degrading himself to paint for a print-seller',[9] and the artist's ill-tempered letters to Boydell,[10] complaining that he could have earned far more by painting portraits, have been taken to reveal a similar contempt. But a letter written soon after the Gallery's inception greets it with enthusiasm, seeing it as a project from which painters and engravers will 'find engagements for eight or ten years',[11] and Reynolds' disparagement of the final use of his paintings does not necessarily connote dismissal of the visual and conceptual challenge they presented. Read closely, the paintings all suggest that Reynolds was developing new applications of his earlier theory and practice that directly engage with the making of visual criticisms of Shakespeare's plays. The result is that, instead of employing an historicised Grand Style and nationalistic stance, they employ a fusion of stylistic elements to enfold a web of allusion and produce sensitive, intellectually rigorous and idiosyncratically witty interpretations.

II

That Reynolds' knowledge of the plays was informed and extensive is apparent from several sources. He copied passages into his commonplace book from Theobald's edition,[12] a habit made fashionable after William Dodd's *Beauties of Shakespear* of 1752. His circle of friends included not only Johnson but Malone, Steevens, and Isaac Reed, and this gave him an awareness at some level of the latest practices in textual editing. His acquaintance with Richard Farmer and Lady Elizabeth Montagu[13] also involved him in critical questions such as the degree to which the plays rested on sources in classical and modern European languages or contemporary works in translation, the exploration of the moral nature of the characters and the plays' use of the supernatural. Most important, he engaged with the texts at a scholarly level by writing a series of notes on separate passages and an unfinished, general essay on the plays.

Five of Reynolds' notes appeared in the final volume of Johnson's edition of 1765 and two in Malone's 1780 supplement, with one remaining unpublished. Of the notes published by Johnson, three concern *Othello*, one *Hamlet* and one *The Merry*

Wives of Windsor. Some offer textual glosses, explaining 'the fellow of this walk' (5.5.20) as Herne the Hunter[14] or reading the Duke's lines to Brabantio (1.3.197–9) as 'let me speak as yourself would speak . . .say what you ought to say' rather than 'speak sententiously' as Johnson suggests (*Life*, I, pp. 146–7). Some attempt to clarify variant readings, suggesting for example that Theobald's correction of 'pierced' to 'pieced' in *Othello* 1.3.217 is incorrect, arguing that 'Shakespeare was continually changing his first expression for another, either stronger or more uncommon' (*Life*, I, p. 149). This is a radical departure from the period's accepted view of Shakespeare as the instinctive writer who never altered his work, and Northcote himself takes issue with this in a footnote – 'I cannot entirely agree with Reynolds' – paraphrasing Ben Jonson to assert that Shakespeare 'never blotted out a line' (*Life*, I, p. 149). The final and most extensive note argues that Lear's 'And my poor fool is hang'd' (5.3.279) refers to the Fool and not Cordelia. Malone disagreed, but printed the note with a tribute to Reynolds' 'ingenious and just'[15] comments, revealing his respect for the artist's opinion.

Other notes are more general. *Macbeth* 1.6 is 'a striking instance of what in painting is termed *repose*' (*Life*, I, pp. 145–6); Ophelia's lines at 4.5.23–6 are unequalled in pathos in the play because they reveal 'the utter insensibility she has to her own misfortune'.[16] Twice Reynolds again takes issue with earlier editors' decisions, rejecting Pope's emendation of Othello's 'desarts idle' to 'desarts wild' (1.3.139) because of Shakespeare's habitual preference for the unusual over the colloquial and familiar,[17] and preferring 'induction' to Warburton's 'instruction' later in the same play (4.1.40), finding the latter 'certainly too forced and far-fetched' (*Life*, I, pp. 150–1).

The individual validity of these notes is less important than the evidence they collectively provide of Reynolds' meticulous attention to the texts. This is translated in the paintings into a concern for detail of setting and action directly counter to the advice in the *Discourses* that heroic paintings should concern themselves only with larger principles. The two approaches come together in another note, unpublished in Reynolds' lifetime, that gives evidence of the visual imagination actively at work. Occurring in a letter to Samuel Parr,[18] it glosses Lady Macbeth's 'screw your courage to the sticking place, / And we'll not fail' (1.7.60–1) by comparison to the ratchet mechanism on a 'wheel engine' or pulley, a visual reading that, while anachronistic, evidences the translation of verbal into visual at a very detailed level. The letter is dated 31 May 1791, when Reynolds' *Macbeth* painting was still unfinished: while the note refers to a much earlier part of the play, it reveals a free commerce between verbal and visual in the artist's imagination at a level of textual moment as well as universal theme.

Reynolds' most extensive writing on Shakespeare is an unfinished essay, reprinted by Hilles from a manuscript and some notes.[19] As this uses quotations from Johnson's edition it is reasonable to suppose both that it was written later than most of the textual notes, and that Johnson's Shakespeare, in one of its forms, was the basis for Reynolds' paintings. Establishing a logical relation between critical writing and artistic practice, always a treacherous task, is particularly difficult with Reynolds, and the essay reflects many commonplace assumptions of contemporary thought: but some of its thrusts are valuable in approaching the paintings. One is a defence of Shakespeare's mingling of tragedy and comedy, another the concluding suggestion that it is 'time for a new code of laws'[20] to replace comparison with the classics when judging such fusions. One passage is particularly suggestive:

> Whether that mixture of grave and gay, the grandeur of general ideas with the familiar pathetic, the artful with the artless – that is, finished passages with the most simple and natural expressions such as every man would use on the same occasion – is it not worth the pains for philosophers and playwrights to examine the cause why we are so delighted with Shakespeare's plays?[21]

This blend of underlying principle with forceful detail is the major practice of the paintings, producing a visual engagement with the plays markedly different from the generalising impulse of Barry and West. The passage also stands metaphorically for the balance of other oppositions that the paintings display: mimetic representation and iconographic reference, and, particularly in the case of *Puck*, conceptual references to tragedy and comedy. This balancing demands the infringement of many of the principles of Neo-Classical universalism, and their combination with aspects of portraiture. Although it cannot quite be seen as anticipating Coleridge's ideas on the organic unity of part and whole, in its empirical use in the Boydell paintings it produces images of critical weight and breadth. At a broader level, it can also be related to the quality of 'double operation', the desire 'to entertain two objects at one time'[22] that Robert E. Moore sees as the basis of Reynolds' understanding of human character, and hence his success as a portraitist.[23] It is tempting, though reductive, to see the Shakespeare paintings in this light: certainly, Reynolds' approach to *A Midsummer Night's Dream* yields its most surprising insights through what may appear to be an egregious series of contradictions.

One of the bases of Reynolds' presentation of scene and character is the mimesis essential to his work as a portraitist. In the Shakespeare paintings this is refined but not dominant: the images do not represent actors playing roles or reflect performance practice but instead visually represent textual detail and larger setting to construct character and idea within a dramatic continuum. To this imaginative immediacy is added the extension of his earlier use of iconographical reference, developing it to a degree seen elsewhere only in the work of Fuseli. Elements from earlier painters, especially Old Masters, are a fundamental part of Reynolds' theory and practice, but they are employed in a variety of ways. His early advice, seen for example in *Discourse III* (p. 49), is merely to study the ancients. By *Discourse VI* (1774) the aim has shifted to imitation, in the assertion that 'no man need be ashamed of copying the antients' (p. 107). Ten years later, *Discourse XIII* defines 'borrowing' as 'that friendly intercourse which ought to exist among Artists' (pp. 216–17) and advocates the construction of '*pasticcio* compositions' (p. 222) with elements from several paintings, particularly for the student developing a vocabulary of forms. Such borrowings, however, should provide only the starting point for the invention of the whole image, and the individual elements, once combined under its overall formal influence, should be completed by following a higher aim. In stating this Reynolds returns to the underlying objective of his earliest pronouncements:

> *The art of seeing Nature*, or in other words, the art of using Models, is in reality the great object, the point to which all our studies are directed. (p. 224)

This ideal is the exact opposite of what it suggests to the unwary present-day reader, denoting the process of seeing through the actual form to the ideal that it merely reflects. When seen against the mimetic presentation of the object or sitter important in Reynolds' work, however, it reveals one level of the duality fundamental to his technique. The duality is shown in another way by the presence of serious or comically conflicting iconographic references within the apparent mimesis. The result of these drives in the Shakespeare paintings is a combination of mimetic presentation of action, buttressed by close textual detail, with both being expanded – sometimes with complex seriousness, sometimes with startling comic richness – by the associations introduced through iconographic allusion.

It is in the use made of iconographic reference that the Shakespeare paintings are most arresting. In his portraits, Reynolds had used earlier images to generate new meanings by the connection forged between the first and subsequent uses. Some paintings flaunt their compositional sources to ennoble the sitter by comparison with an ancient original, as with the depiction of *Captain the Hon. Lord Keppel*[24] in the pose of the Apollo Belvedere. Others create what Horace Walpole was to call 'a special form of wit' in their use of 'borrowed attitudes'.[25] *Master Crewe as Henry VIII* (1776: Fig. 65)[26] has a special quality because of the irrelevance of

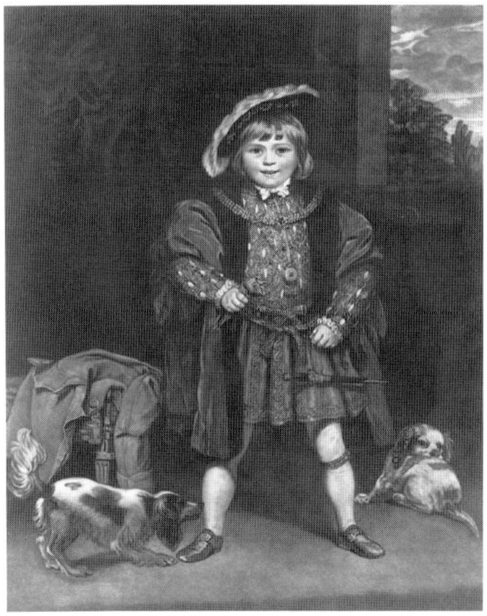

65 Joshua Reynolds, *Master Crewe as Henry VIII*. Engraved by J. R. Smith, 1776.

the reference to the subject, which makes it a fundamentally comic image. Yet the comedy depends on the reader's recognition of both the original and its absurdity in its new setting, an act of interpretive *sprezzatura* that inevitably restricts the circulation of the image to the aristocrat and connoisseur. A special group of paintings are those referred to in Chapter 3 as 'personations', portraits of fashionable men and women adopting the characters of figures from history or literature. Here, the recognition depends on a grasp of the significance of the earlier character, not the earlier image – indeed, many of these paintings, such as those alluded to in *Kitty Fisher as Cleopatra* (1759?),[27] might well have remained unknown to most onlookers. To this group belong two of Reynolds' earlier Shakespeare paintings. Despite including the head of Prospero and a figure of Caliban, *Mrs Tollemache as Miranda* (1773–4: Fig. 66)[28] is more concerned with establishing its central figure as a type of innocence through its comparison with the abstract idea of Shakespeare's character than with exploring the forces driving the play in the manner, say, of Hogarth's painting of *The Tempest*. Allusion is here, certainly; but it works in a very different manner. The same is true of *Mrs Lloyd* (1775–6),[29] which shows a young woman carving on a tree the name of the man then her fiancé, aligning her with the young Orlando in *As You Like It*.

The Shakespeare paintings belong to a larger group of images that use earlier sources in ways that do not immediately yield up their meanings. The complexity they involve, and the problems of interpretation they present, are suggested in a better known, and much discussed, painting: *Garrick between Tragedy and Comedy*

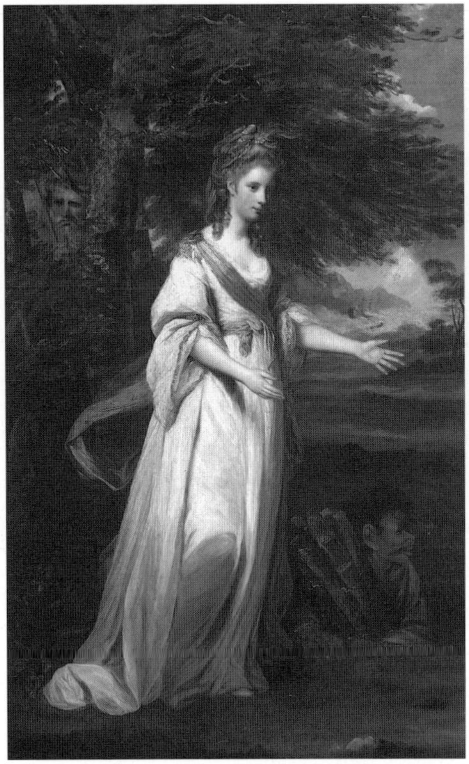

66 Joshua Reynolds, *Mrs Tollemache as Miranda*, 1773–4.

(1762: Fig. 67).[30] The image rests upon the familiar 'Choice of Hercules' trope; but how it is used, and how it should be read, are far from obvious. At the simplest level the image insists on being read as another 'borrowed attitude', in which the onlooker notices the allusion and is amused by its comic incongruity. Presenting an actor's choice of genre as a parallel to a moral dilemma is certainly comic, and it is easy to read the image in this way, with Garrick, who gestures apologetically towards Tragedy as he is hauled off by Comedy, having made a decision resulting not in epic struggle but a successful public career. This enfolds another signification, which has been seen as a satiric thrust at Garrick's self-importance: the relative triviality of the consequence of his choice implies the arrogant self-absorption of an actor quite happy to see himself as Hercules – a quality that many, Reynolds included, had remarked.[31] Richard Wendorf sees this as evidence of Reynolds' insight into his sitters' divided loyalties:[32] moved across to the Shakespeare paintings, the same qualities may be seen to reveal the multiple levels of meaning within the texts, sometimes contradictory, sometimes working across genres.

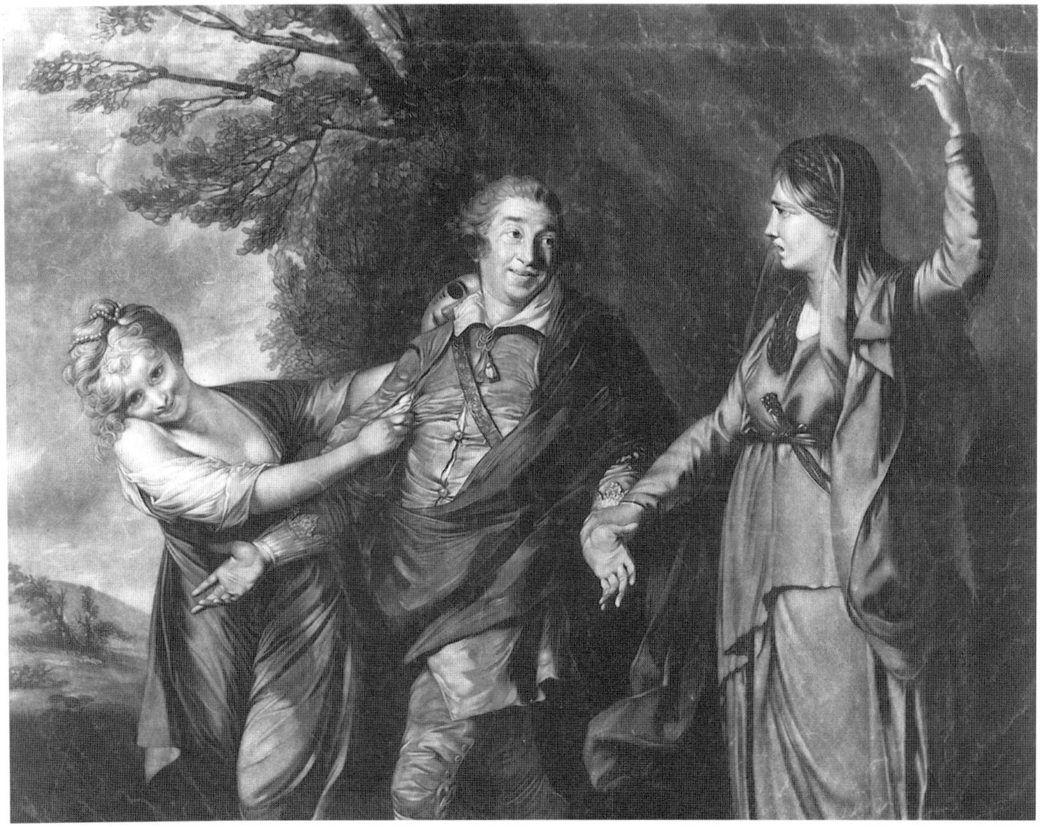

67 Joshua Reynolds, *Garrick between Tragedy and Comedy*, 1762. Mezzotint by Edward Fisher, 1762.

Ronald Paulson suggests another reading.[33] The point of the painting is that the choice is as yet unmade, so that Garrick is revealed as a master of both genres. He is also shown as primarily an actor: able to present both genres, he here acts out the choice between them, in double tribute to his abilities. This reveals the image as in dialogue not only with meaning but with technique, offering a comically new interpretation of the workings of the Choice trope, reinvigorating it by placing it in a context with a wholly new narrative emphasis; and Robert E. Moore[34] develops this further by pointing out that Comedy is depicted in the style of Correggio and Tragedy in that of Guido Reni, a blending of style and idea that gives the image a metacritical dimension. Given the complexity of Reynolds' relations with Garrick, the kind of allusive wit demonstrated in the 'borrowed attitudes' paintings, the extent of his knowledge of Old Master images and his willingness to employ elements from them as compositional sources, such a breadth does not seem in any way unlikely. That many of Reynolds' original commentators did not see this complexity should not surprise us: the most immediate reference was easily decoded, and if another, more private one was there, this would be quite in accord with Reynolds' intellectualism and his delight in the sense of doubleness. Alongside this complexity, of course, the portrait's most immediate meaning remains clear: it is recognisably a depiction of David Garrick.

The range of meanings in the Garrick portrait, their production both by mimesis and by iconographic reference, and the difficulty and incompleteness with which they were approached by many contemporary onlookers together constitute an important reading model for the Shakespeare paintings. Surface identity of character is never in doubt; situation and idea are located and interpreted by visual treatment of textual detail. In addition, these elements function together with multiple levels of iconographic allusion, generating allusive meanings through dialogue with their earlier contexts. Unconventional and at times incongruous, these allusions produce thrusts that make the paintings distinctive and controversial works of Shakespearean criticism.

III

The Death of Cardinal Beaufort (1789: Fig. 68)[35] was the first of Reynolds' three Boydell paintings to be completed, carrying across to Shakespearean painting the issues of allusion and meaning insistent in the subject paintings and in the process creating unique problems in both execution and interpretation. Martin Postle[36] suggests that the composition is influenced by Fuseli's treatment of the same passage, exhibited at the RA in 1774.[37] That Reynolds, then in his sixties and established in due eminence as the first President of the Royal Academy, could be influenced by the 33-year-old Fuseli is revealing about both, suggesting the impact of the younger artist's approach to the scene and an insecurity in the older man that is perhaps hinted at in some of his other subject paintings.[38]

As *Henry VI* was not performed in Reynolds' lifetime, the image could only have originated in Reynolds' reading of the text, almost certainly in Johnson's edition. Johnson found the trilogy as a whole 'more happily conceived, and more accurately finished than those of K. John, Richard II. or the tragick scenes of King Henry IV and V.' and continued, 'Of these plays I think the second the best.'[39] This may explain Reynolds' selection of the scene where King Henry urges repentance on the dying Cardinal – an act that continues the practice of choosing a moment of intense moral election that was earlier analysed by Shaftesbury. The moment is precisely located by the quotation beneath Caroline Watson's engraving:[40]

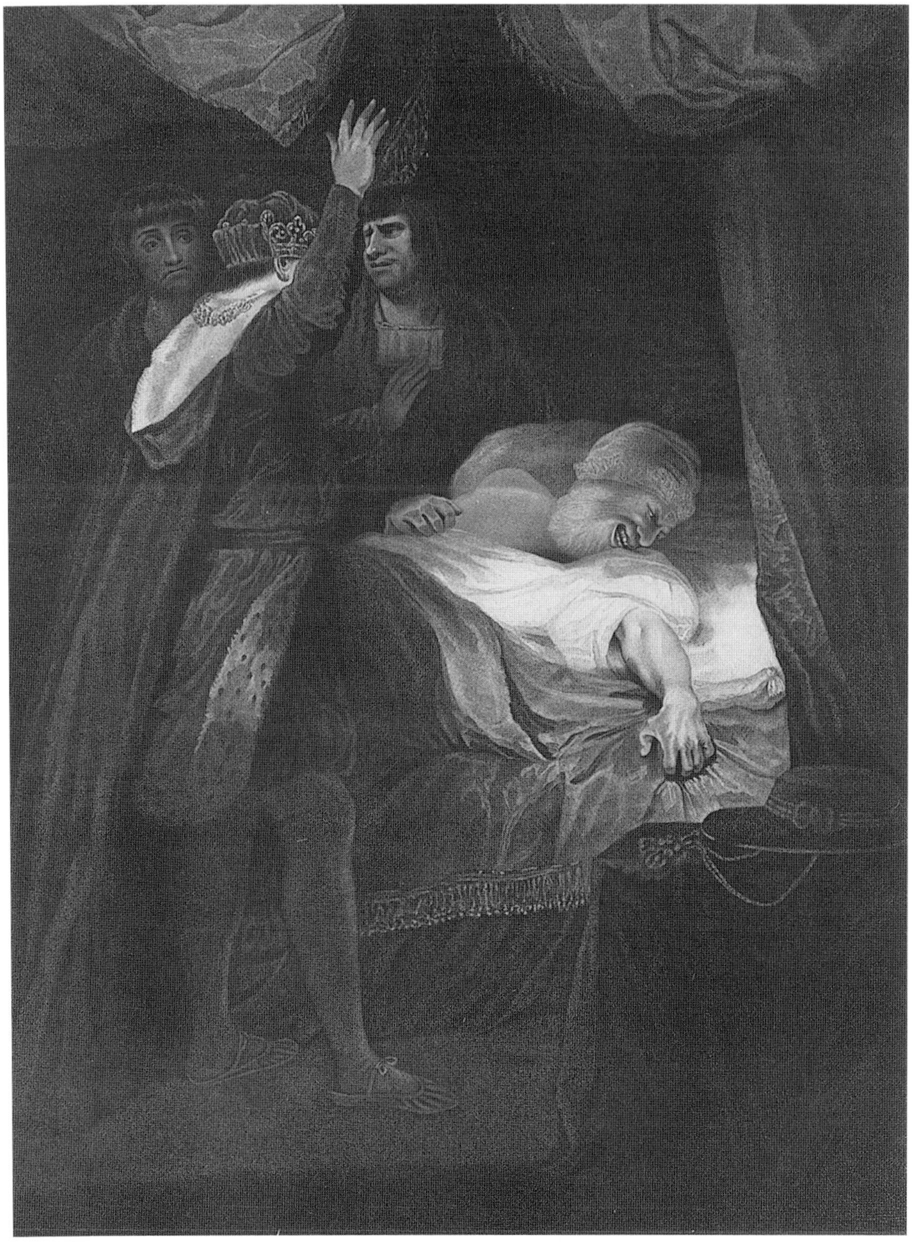

68 Joshua Reynolds, *The Death of Cardinal Beaufort*. Engraved by Caroline Watson, 1792.

Warwick: See how the pangs of death do make him grin!
Salisbury: Disturb him not; let him pass peaceably.
King Henry: Peace to his soul! If God's good pleasure be: –
Lord Cardinal, if that thou think'st on heaven's bliss,
Hold up thy hand, make signal of thy hope. –
He dies, and makes no sign. O God, forgive him!
(3.3.24–9)

Reynolds follows Fuseli's example in using Poussin's *Death of Germanicus* (1626–8)[41] as the compositional basis but, whereas Fuseli includes a large group of figures around the bedside, Reynolds pares down the composition to exclude all unnecessary elements and reducing the setting to a classically draped bed. The two figures that, in the Poussin, look across at each other in the middle ground to provide tension are transformed by Reynolds into Salisbury and Warwick; Poussin's central figure with upraised arm becomes King Henry by the substitution of a crown for a Roman coronet and the shift from an upraised finger to an open hand, more clearly to suggest admonition or appeal. The rearrangement of the dying man's head gives prominence to the death rictus; the absence of other mourning figures similarly emphasises the clenched hand.

Poussin's painting was a very well-known image, one review of Reynolds' painting asserting that 'the print is in the collection of every man of taste',[42] so it may be assumed that Reynolds, with all his earlier experience of the effects of iconographical allusion, did not use it lightly. The greater concentration effected by Reynolds' changes reveals the allusion's main purpose, the presentation of the Cardinal's treachery through an ironic comparison: Germanicus was an imperial general of great heroism and loyalty to the Republic, Cardinal Beaufort a traitor who sought to undermine the monarchy. The omission of the attendant figures also turns the event from an affair of state into an intimate human exchange, and this is given added power by the composition: the King's upraised arm and open hand suggest a forthright, open admonition, while the Cardinal's hand gripped around the sheet denotes a recalcitrance no persuasion may prise open. In this way the moral antitheses of the play are woven into the painting's structure in a striking act of visual mediation. The presentation of the divergence in more personal terms is shown also in the precise rendering of the bed's hangings as silk and velvet instead of the 'drapery . . . nothing more' recommended in *Discourse* IV (p. 62), a treatment that also provides a metaphor of corruption in providing a note of sensual richness, akin to luxury.

The death rictus that is the image's main focus makes visible Warwick's line 'See how the pangs of death do make him grin!' (3.3.24). This Gothic detail, incongruous and over-stated to some viewers, may, as Postle suggests,[43] demonstrate Reynolds' exploration of the strange closeness of tragedy and comedy in moments of complex action in the plays. It also suggests Reynolds' concern to link the precise detail of the text, the 'familiar pathetic', with the larger idea or 'grand design', the close textual reading balanced by the larger awareness of the play's movement seen in the painting's composition and its intense chiaroscuro. Perhaps, too, the allusion to Germanicus offers a more qualified reflection of the play's moral contrasts, inflecting Cardinal Beaufort's final recusancy with its own kind of valour.

In the original painting, a small devil appeared behind the Cardinal's head in embodiment of the 'busy meddling fiend/ That lays strong siege unto this wretch's soul' (3.3.21–2). The figure was painted out, either by Reynolds or some later hand, and removed from the engraving after the proof impressions, in response to criticism from several quarters. Repton found it 'beneath the dignity of the subject and the Artist';[44] *The Times*, Walpole and Burke all agreed.[45] Fuseli made the most cogent objection: 'its ludicrous meanness destroys that terror which is the soul of the scene'.[46] Regardless of its appropriateness or otherwise in terms of taste, the figure appears to violate Reynolds' own principle that 'all smaller things are to be sacrificed to the greater' (*Discourse* IV, p. 58). Why, then, did Reynolds include it? Current taste for the Gothic, manifested in an interest in the supernatural, as shown in many Shakespeare paintings and in writings such as the chapter 'On the Praeternatural Beings' in Elizabeth Montagu's *Writings and Genius of Shakespeare*, may have been an influence. Certainly, a concern for the supernatural runs through all three of Reynolds' Shakespeare paintings; but the fact that Walpole, high priest of the Gothic, criticised the devil, argues against this. Larger considerations are at work, related to the way in which Reynolds reads the plays, going beyond the treatment of a single line to address one of the key forces of *2 Henry VI*.

In embodying the devil, Reynolds is presenting schematically the opposition between Christian grace and diabolic evil enacted repeatedly in the play's text. It is most insistent in Margery Jourdain's conjurations (1.2), but in rejecting these to associate the devil instead with Beaufort Reynolds lays emphasis on the play's recurrent association of diabolism and treachery. Buckingham tells the king that 'naughty persons' have 'practised dangerously against your state,/ Dealing with witches and with conjurers' (2.1.165, 169–70); Suffolk refers to the Duchess' 'devilish practices' (3.1.46); York refers to Jack Cade and his part in the rebellion by saying 'This devil here shall be my substitute' (3.1.371); and as Salisbury and Warwick leave with the king before the arrest of Suffolk the Queen curses them with 'There's two of you, the devil make a third!' (3.2.303). After the death of Beaufort the language of the diabolic continues, now held in stronger opposition against Henry's divinity: Henry speaks of Cade and the rebels in a direct reference to Christ's words from the cross:[47] 'O graceless men! They know not what they do' (4.4.38).

In drawing together all these verbal images the painting offers another solution to the problem of enfolding the temporal traffic of the play within a synchronous visual space, but it is also important at a more immediate critical level. It discloses the presentation of history not as a sequence of events but as a moral struggle existing outside chronology, a way of reading events familiar to Shakespeare's audience as an alternative to the notion of history as a narrative, and apparent not only in *2 Henry VI* but in all the history plays. In making this visible, Reynolds' image provides a major corrective to the reading of the play as a providentialist sequence, and raises provocative questions about the nature of both theatre and painting as instruments of temporal statement in moral, personal, and national frames. This insight may, or may not, compensate for the undoubted faults of the painting, that include as well as the death rictus and the literal devil the concealment of Henry's face by his raised arm, which compromises the character's forthrightness so essential to the workings of the image's moral argument.

Reynolds' first completed exercise in Shakespearean illustration is an experiment in visual criticism, drawing together approaches seen in the portraits, the fancy pictures, the *Discourses*, and the notes and essay on Shakespeare. Its comparative failure suggests not so much Reynolds' lack of interest in the project as his desire to find new ways of addressing the interaction of verbal and visual within a compound moral and historical frame which turns to serious use the playfulness of his earlier iconographic allusion. The insights it offers into the play's imagery, and the different concept of history that this generates, define it is a powerful act of recovery at a time when, as Chapter 8 will make clear, Shakespeare painting was increasingly moving towards a materialist, seamless historiography unaware of the ideological bases on which it rested.

The largest and most ambitious of Reynolds' Boydell paintings is *Macbeth and the Witches*,[48] a treatment of the cavern scene accompanied by the textual passage including the show of kings (4.1). Begun in 1786, it remained unfinished at Reynolds' death six years later, although Robert Thew's engraving was published by Boydell on 1 December 1802 (Fig. 69).[49] Like the *2 Henry VI* image it combines

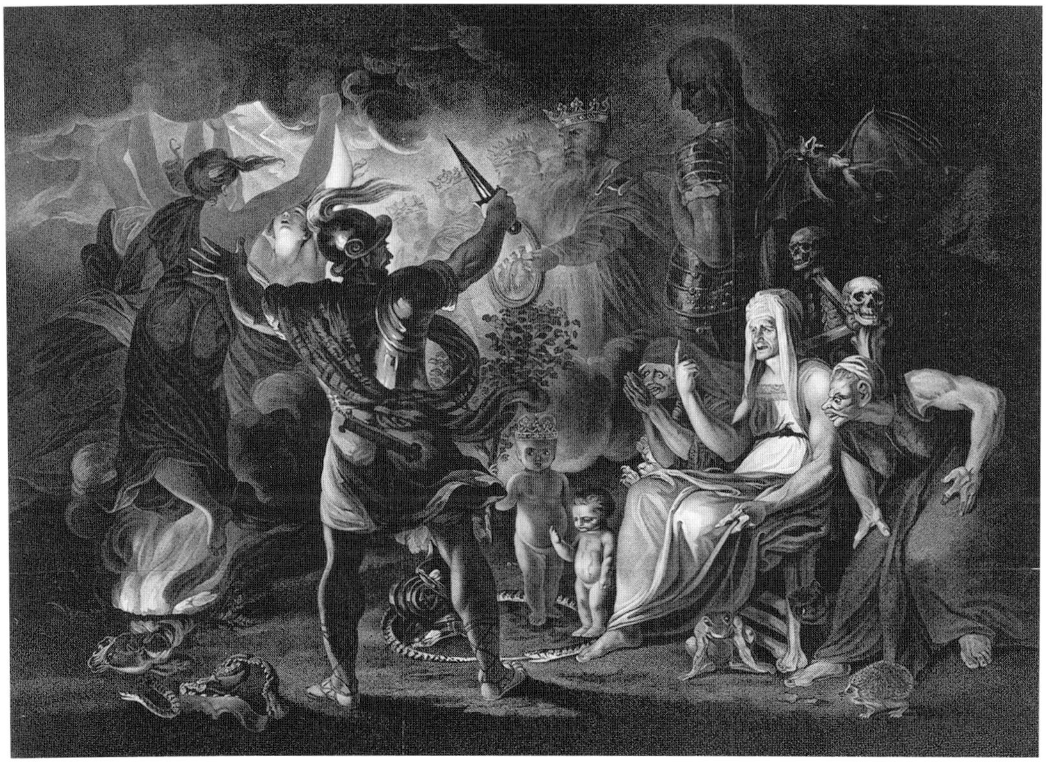

69 Joshua Reynolds, *Macbeth and the Witches*. Engraved by Robert Thew, 1802.

close reading with a conceptual commentary made through iconographic allusion. That the scene is depicted with such precision again reveals Reynolds' use of Johnson's text rather than the theatrical tradition; that the visual presentation of the text encompasses more than a single moment is evident in the range of detail used to present the witches. The cauldron is shown to the left of the dense composition, and the 'ingredience' (4.1.34) named in the witches' chants disposed around the foreground. A snake forms a circle just before Macbeth, its shape suggesting the 'elves and fairies in a ring' (42) that perform the enchantment. Within the coiled snake stand the vision of the crowned child bearing a tree, and the third apparition, the bloody child. Macbeth stares directly at the 'armed head' that appears behind the witches, gesturing to the first of the kings in visual statement of the warning 'Beware the Thane of Fife' (72). This figure is the first in the show of kings that recede through the centre of the composition, and holds a mirror in which the figures are reflected. Reynolds' care in both reading and visualising is apparent here: while only four of the kings are shown, the mirror reflects them all, to present the show of eight kings, neatly preventing the already full composition from becoming cluttered. The three witches retain something of theatrical tradition by looking as much male as female, but this is offset by their origin in the figures of Sibyls and devils from the ceiling and altar wall of the Sistine Chapel, an allusion which adds resonance to their moral ambiguity.[50] The central witch sits on a throne constructed of bones and surrounded by skeletons, perhaps Reynolds' deepest foray into the Gothic.

As well as demonstrating extreme compositional skill, the overall structure reflects Reynolds' detailed textual reading and a sense of the supernatural. The figure of Macbeth itself makes a number of iconographic references that complement and broaden the image's specific visualisations. Turner[51] saw it as a version of Vitruvian man, the Renaissance ideal of humankind as the centre of proportion and judgment both aesthetic and moral inscribed in Macbeth's comment 'I dare do all that may become a man; / Who dares do more is none' (1.7.46–7). In the scene where Macbeth has manifestly gone beyond and beneath human morality through his dealings with the witches the reference conveys forceful mockery. Turner, who exhibited his own work with lines from his own poem titled *Fallacies of Hope*, would perhaps have been especially sensitive to the ironic nuances of such allusions. Another possible reference is to Hogarth's *Mr Garrick in the Character of Richard III*. Macbeth's upper body and outspread arms recall the pose of Garrick seen from behind. The parallel is suggestive. Hogarth's Richard has a premonition of failure in the moment of waking from the dream before battle: Reynolds' Macbeth is presented in a similar moment of realisation. The pairing also implies that, like Richard's, Macbeth's authority is usurped, linking the innate Machiavellian powers of Richard with Macbeth's capitulation to the witches' 'supernatural soliciting' (1.3.129). Perhaps, too, it reflects a concern in contemporary Shakespeare criticism, where different qualities of evil within individual characters were the source of commentary and comparison, and which Reynolds would have known in the work of Elizabeth Montagu and perhaps also William Richardson.[52]

The most striking allusion is to an image that Reynolds would certainly have known closely, since it passed into the ownership of the Royal Academy in 1779: Leonardo's *Virgin and Child with St Anne and St John the Baptist* (c. 1499–1500).[53] The drawing, known also as the Burlington Cartoon, had probably been in England since 1763, and, from 1779 in the collection of Robert Udny, from whom the RA acquired it. Reynolds takes from the cartoon the raised hand and upward pointing finger of St Anne. A common element in images of St John, the device shows the Baptist's role as the forerunner of Christ; Reynolds himself had used it in his own *The Child Baptist in the Wilderness* (1776).[54] The pointing finger in this case indicates the armed head, placed behind the witch in parallel to the figure of the one to come later, but instead of Christian redemption the implication here is of pagan retribution in the line of kings to which it is directed, implying that Macbeth is the moral opposite of John the Baptist in a serious appropriation of Reynolds' earlier technique of comic 'borrowed attitudes'. The reference is most powerful, however, in suggesting that Macbeth saw the witch and her companions as a divine foreshadowing of some ideal future state, not as the 'instruments of darkness' (1.3.123) as which Banquo recognises them,[55] and in this it echoes another element of the image that suggests Macbeth's complete misreading of the witches' moral identity.

This is achieved through an allusion to a convention rather than to an individual painting, although two images are important within it: Tintoretto's *Martyrdom of St Lawrence* (1569–96)[56] and the painting of the same title by Titian (1548–57).[57] The parallel is achieved in general terms by the use of the extreme chiaroscuro of the Tintoretto, offering a single, damning stroke of irony in which Macbeth is compared to a Christian martyr. More specifically, the situation of Macbeth is revealed as an inversion of that of St Lawrence: while the latter is presented before the idol which he refuses to worship, Macbeth stands in the same relation to the power he willingly embraces. The specific setting provides the 'familiar pathetic' to balance the 'general idea' furnished by the chiaroscuro, and again detail and larger movement are united to present a critical reading.

That the painting is unfinished, and currently in a much deteriorated state, inevitably limits critical discussion, yet Thew's engraving can be regarded as complete in practical terms and, like many others in the Boydell collection, makes visible elements and passages of its original now difficult to discern. Within it, a key difference from *The Death of Cardinal Beaufort* is apparent. Whereas that image achieves close textual reading of the play's metaphoric poles of good and evil in a single visual element, *Macbeth* presents a much larger range of Shakespeare's images in precise figurative terms, to be read in conjunction not with a single iconographic reference but with a range of allusions that imaginatively project a reading of the play's moral frame. Vitruvian man, John the Baptist and St Lawrence – both in themselves and in the Old Master convention that presents them – are all enlisted to convey the force of Christian humanism in opposition to the moral darkness of the witches. The antithesis is given further, and more immediate, statement in the visual metaphor of the painting's extreme chiaroscuro. Here, light and dark again do battle, as they do in the atmospheric landscapes of Macbeth's initial encounter with the witches as presented by Wootton and Zuccarelli.

These referential and immediate significances are linked by another element that reveals a further critical statement about the play. In the upper left of the image, billowing clouds suggest the winds and 'yeasty waves' (52) conjured by the witches; beneath them dances another trio of witches, in the seductive female forms that have beguiled Macbeth near the play's opening, countering the muscular hermaphrodites at the right. In showing both versions of the witches – objects of beauty, objects of darkness – the image presents the dualism with which Macbeth sees the apparitions, posing his moral dilemma in direct visual terms that reinforce and are reinforced by the suggestion that he sees the central witch as St Anne.

Once identified, this dualism stands revealed as the major organisational principle of the image, which in turn declares itself as an 'invention' in Fuseli's sense, a structural and conceptual armature in which form and interpretive act are indistinguishable. The duality of the witches, the extremes of chiaroscuro, the dualities of Macbeth himself all stand revealed as a formal visualisation of one of the major linguistic tropes of the play, the sickening antithetical rhythms that encapsulate Macbeth's indecisiveness – 'This supernatural soliciting / Cannot be ill; cannot be good' (1.3.129–30); and his inability to distinguish good and evil appearances, clear from his very first utterance – 'So foul and fair a day I have not seen' (1.3.36). It is this dualism of idea and form that make it, for all the Gothic excesses for which it has been criticised, an astute and compelling visualisation of the play's moral and textual fabric.

IV

Apparently the most straightforward of the three Boydell paintings, Reynolds' *Puck* (1789)[58] is embedded just as firmly as the others within a polyphony of allusion and commentary. Here, though, the references release a free play of meanings that interrogate the serioludic identity of *A Midsummer Night's Dream* and ultimately question the whole nature of the visual statement of literary and philosophical themes. Included in the Boydell edition of the plays rather than the volume of engravings, the painting immediately declares its non-theatrical origins through its naturalistic setting and the disparity of size between the foreground figure of Puck and those of Titania and Bottom to the rear. This dysfunction reflects the image's displacement of time through suspending the play's sequence. The engraving by Luigi Schiavonetti (Fig. 70)[59] includes 'Act 2 Scene 2' in the caption but, as Bottom and Titania are shown asleep at the rear, and they do not appear in this scene, the moment depicted is uncertain. Either the caption defines the image

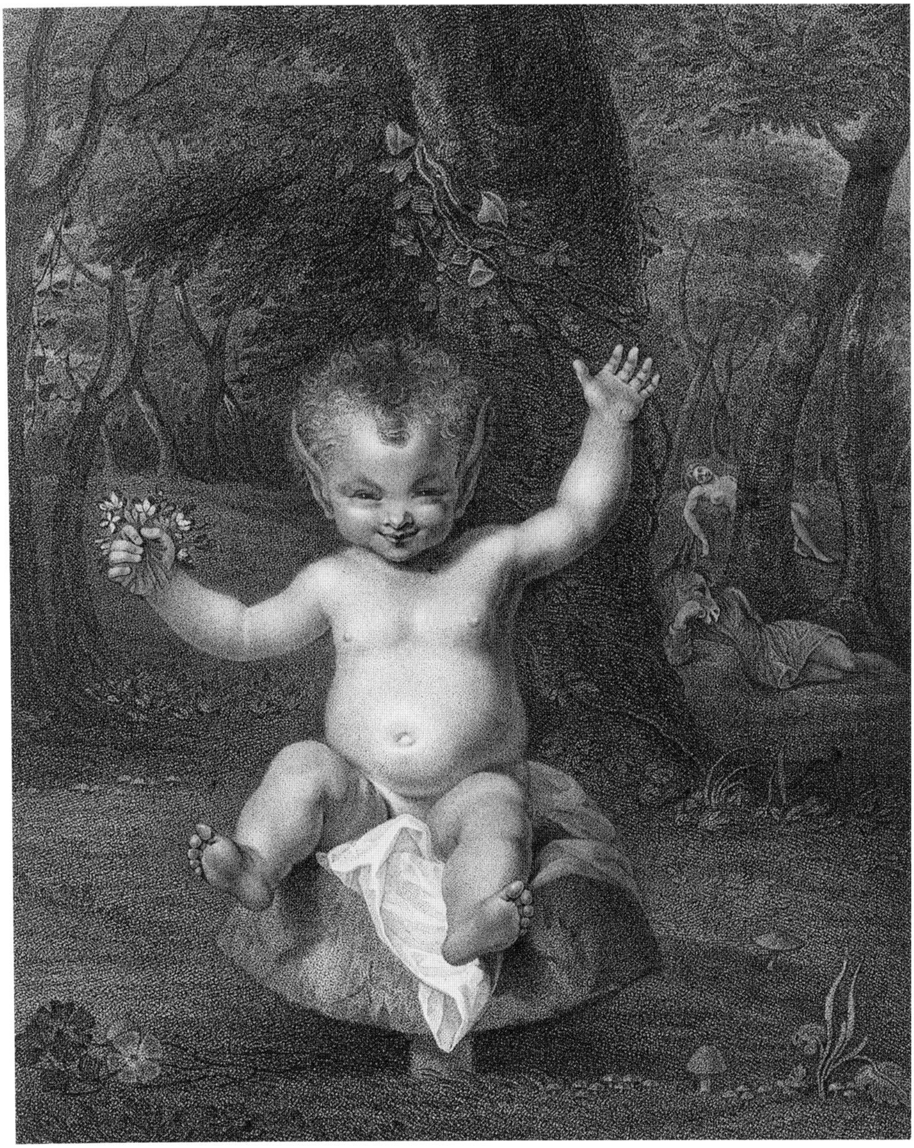

70 Joshua Reynolds, *A Wood – Robin Goodfellow (Puck)*. Engraved by Luigi Schiavonetti, 1799.

as a proleptic representation of the consequences of Puck's actions, or it is a simple error: since the text of the edition gives 'Scene III' as the heading for scene 2 – the divisions throughout follow Capell – and is not corrected even in Steevens' own proof copy,[60] the latter seems more likely. If this is so, the image must come after the courtship scene of Act 4 scene 1 and Puck's entry after line 42, but before the appearance of Oberon, who advances to order Puck to 'undo/ This hateful imperfection of her eyes' (4.1.59–60). Together, the displacement of relationships of space and time visually emblematises the quite different dimensionality of the fairy world. The move away from actuality is continued in the setting, the figures to the rear and the allusions contained in the figure of Puck, all of which reflect the polymorphous quality of the play's events and ideas. The suspension of the action when Titania and Bottom are enmeshed in the plotting of Oberon, of which Puck is the agent, turns the image at one level into a meditation on the nature of their power, and it is in this that the figure of the child-fairy, read in dialogue with the play's action, its mythological resonances, and paintings by Reynolds and others, assumes its multiple significance.

William Cotton relates a visit to Reynolds' studio by Boydell and George Nicol, the writer's grandfather and a guest at the dinner party where Boydell's Shakespeare Gallery was conceived. Seeing a painting of a child, Nicol intervened with a suggestion:

> It can very easily come into the Shakespeare, if Sir Joshua will kindly place him on a mushroom, and give him fawn's ears, and make a Puck of him.[61]

This implies a merging of classical and indigenous mythology, departing from the Robin Goodfellow established in the first exchange between Puck and the Fairy (2.1.32–58). Perhaps because his own treatments show Puck as the spitefully manipulative spirit of the English tradition, Fuseli saw this as a deficiency: 'he surely cannot be mistaken for the Robin of Shakespeare and Milton'.[62] But the dual origin is important in prompting a visual metaphor of the dichotomous Puck, stressing its nature as both homespun and exotic, rustic English sprite and Nordic Pug or Poug. The setting is resolutely English, but this again underscores the play's ambivalence by offering misleading reassurance about the familiarity of the wood.

An unsigned review in the *Morning Post* of 1 May 1789 attacked the child-figure as 'a portrait of a *foetus* taken from some anatomical preparation' and complained that the toadstool on which he sits was 'of such disproportionate magnitude, that it seems to have been brought from *Brobdingnab* [sic] for the occasion, particularly as the trees are very small'. This draws attention to what might today be regarded as compelling features of the character's complexity and otherness, suggesting folk-legends of still-birth, changelings and demonic possessions, aspects seemingly quite fitting to the ambivalent spirit. Present-day viewers may well share a dislike for the figure, but they are unlikely to reject the insight the review finds offered in the painting's contradictory, fugitive identity.

This quality is also implied by the relation between the figure and Reynolds' many other infant-paintings. *The Infant Jupiter*[63] (1774) shares Puck's direct gaze at the onlooker – an address that Hazlitt described as 'doubtful',[64] perhaps missing the point that within the youthful pose is contained an adult forthrightness. Such compression also underlies a better known image, *The Infant Hercules*[65] (1775–8). *Puck* shares both paintings' blurring of child and adult; but, where they achieve the elision by combining events held separate in orthodox chronology, it reveals a power and knowingness in the expression of the figure that is simultaneously childlike and adult in its superiority, rendered mysterious by the suspension of time implied in the forms sleeping behind him.

Reynolds' allusiveness is used to more direct critical purpose in the similarity with his painting *The Infant Dr Johnson*.[66] Painted in 1781–2, this is the image that bears the closest resemblance to the figure of Puck, especially in the enlarged forehead caused by the bowed posture. The comparison draws a comic parallel between the learned editor and the mischievous sprite, a link very much of the kind Reynolds earlier exploits in his 'borrowed attitude' paintings: but it also suggests a comic parallel to the elision between Garrick and Shakespeare seen in many contemporary depictions, most obviously Gainsborough's portrait *Garrick with a Bust of Shakespeare* (1766–9).[67] As Garrick seems to merge with the Bard whom he so revered, so Johnson is wittily combined with one of his most elusive characters. Reference of this sort is quite fitting to Reynolds the painter, who depicted *Mercury as Cut Purse*[68] and *Cupid as Link Boy*,[69] and whose *Garrick between Tragedy and Comedy* has been praised as 'a joke, essentially a parody'.[70]

This would seem to suggest that the main invention of the painting is through a comic depiction of character, making use of many of the techniques of allusiveness from the fancy pictures, especially those that depict children in the attitudes of adults. Detailed textual reference is, however, employed to offset this, in a manner that goes beyond character to suggest the larger moods and movements of the play. In the middle ground, partially concealing Titania, stands a tree which, like the one nearer to the onlooker, is wound round with ivy – a detail now far clearer in Schiavonetti's engraving than in the painting itself. This presents lines spoken by Titania before the moment of the painting:

So doth the woodbine the sweet honeysuckle
Gently entwist; the female ivy so
Enrings the barky fingers of the elm.

(4.1.39–41)

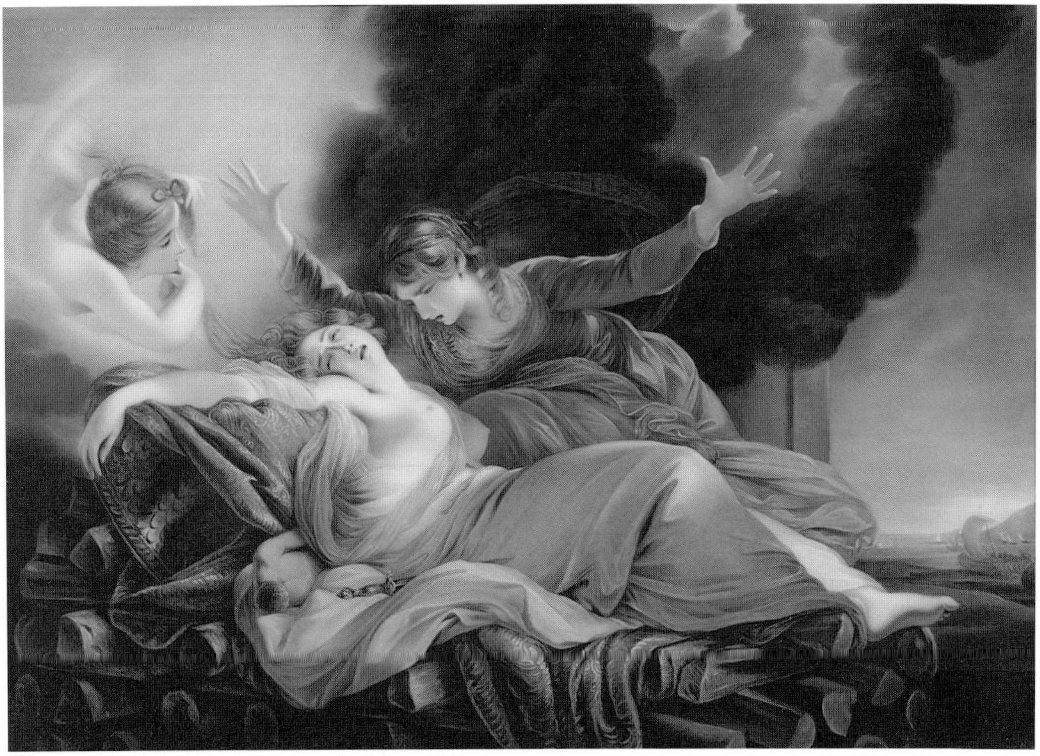

71 Joshua Reynolds, *Death of Dido*, 1781.

That Reynolds catches this echo of Titania's predatory hold over Bottom reveals again his close reading. More significantly, it also works in conjunction with the larger iconographical references apparent in the figure of Titania. Just visible behind the tree and the recumbent figure of Bottom with the ass's head, the naked Titania stretches luxuriantly, right arm flung out to her side, the posture suggesting a drowsy and fulfilled eroticism that adds another note to the relationship with Bottom that is rarely sounded before mid-twentieth century readings. The posture implies that the source of the figure is in Reynolds' own *Death of Dido* (1781: Fig. 71),[71] itself in turn modelled on a fresco after Giulio Romano of *The Sleeping Psyche* (1524–6: Fig. 72).[72]

Critical readings of this allusion will inevitably vary with the onlooker's interpretive stance. It is possible to see it as a simple formal borrowing, of the kind suggested by Reynolds in the earlier *Discourses* cited above. Yet to look at it in this way is to deny all kinds of interpretive statements that, given the rich allusiveness of the other Shakespeare paintings and the complex multiple meanings of the Garrick portrait, appear highly characteristic of Reynolds' sense of doubleness, and also of

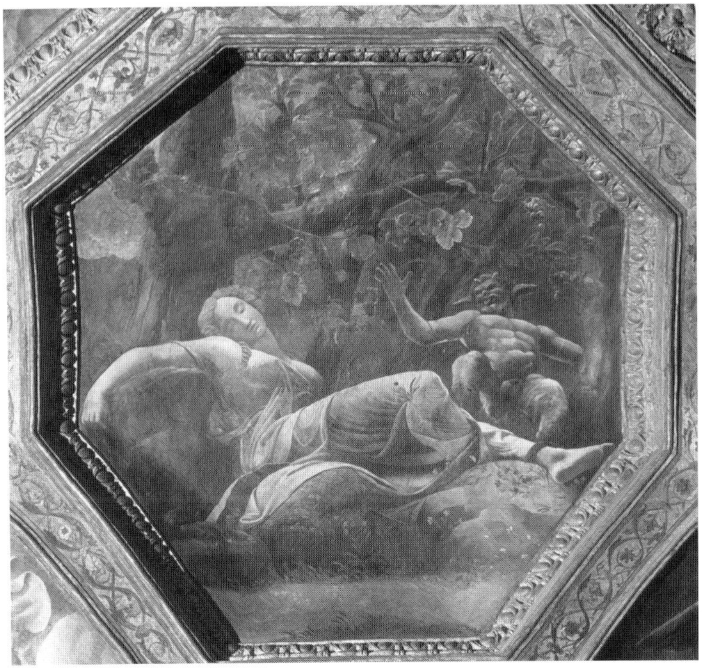

72 After Giulio Romano, *The Sleeping Psyche*, 1524–6.

his powerful sense of humour as demonstrated in the 'borrowed attitudes'. Seen within the larger stream of Reynolds' paintings, it grows quite naturally out of the comic and serious resonances of apparently inapposite pairings that include not only Master Crewe and Henry VIII but the identity of *Three Ladies Adorning a Term of Hymen* (1774)[73] as both an elegantly sweeping neo-classical composition and a comic insinuation of a race past the winning-post of marriage.

In alluding to Dido the image suggests a parity between Titania and Bottom and Dido and Aeneas, the rustic made into a classical hero and the fairy queen turned into the tragic founder of Carthage. In the reference to the fresco, Titania becomes Psyche, the last mortal exalted to a goddess – a form of translation equal and opposite to that undergone by Bottom in the play, and a close parody of the results of the transformation Titania suffers at the hands of Oberon and Puck. The link between Titania as tragic victim offered by the allusion to Dido, and the visualisation of her identity as a predatory parasite in the twining ivy, is achieved by a balance between close textual reading and underlying, universalising reference to a classical hero. It is matched by the other reading that was habitually applied to Dido, the temptress who seduced Aeneas away from his heroic purpose. Bottom becomes Cupid, the lover who visits Psyche only at night when she cannot see him, and against whom she is warned by rumours that he is a fearsome monster – a comic parallel to the actual transformation that Bottom suffers. The presentation of Bottom suggests the Protean identities that he comically wishes to adopt in the rehearsal – 'let me play Thisbe too' (1.2.42); 'Let me play the lion too' (1.2.66); and the gloss he himself offers on his own performance – 'This is Ercles' vein' (1.2.57).

The set of allusions also acts as a commentary on other levels of the play's action. The compound absurdities of the relationship newly constituted between Titania and Bottom – that between a goddess and a soldier hero, and that between the son of the goddess of love and a mortal turned goddess – functions as a parallel to the Pyramus and Thisbe interlude in parodying the amorous vicissitudes of the mortals: both enfold serious, fatal contingencies within comic performance. The total effect is at once sardonic, comic and disturbing – a 'lamentable comedy' (1.2.32–3), in fact, that perfectly mediates the play's own tonality. As well as to the concluding interlude, the painting also recalls, in its dual mythological reference, a passage from Helena's vow to Lysander at the play's outset:

My good Lysander,
I swear to thee by Cupid's strongest bow,
By his best arrow with the golden head,
By the simplicity of Venus' doves,
By that which knitteth souls and prospers loves,
And by that fire which burn'd the Carthage queen
When the false Trojan under sail was seen
I.i.168–74

Titania and Bottom thus constitute a parodic reprise of the confused amorous relations of the mortals, completing the circle that unites the play's levels of action, stressing the female role as that of potential victim and offering further evidence of Reynolds' skill as a close textual reader.

All of these references, and the ambiguities they offer, are held together by their presentation in the shadow of a polymorphous Puck who alludes to the heroic – Hercules, and the familiar – the child portraits. The painting is the fullest visual enactment of what Reynolds valued most in Shakespeare, his linking of tragedy and comedy, through the uniting of the local and the universal. It reveals features of the play's compound tonality unfathomed in critical writing of its own time, and only realised in the theatre more than a century later.

There is one further level of irony in the image. By making allusion to *The Infant Johnson*, so that Puck is presented as a parody of the editor of the very text in which he himself appears, Reynolds contrives to destabilise the whole notion of intellectual commentary on the work of the playwright to which the painting itself contributes. In this, the image offers a visual parallel to the discussion of the nature of theatrical reality that is undergone both in the mechanicals' rehearsal and their performance. Just as this calls into question the whole identity of theatre, so the image problematises the processes of visualisation: an 'illustration' itself both as a critical elucidation and as a visual reworking, it offers a metacritically witty undermining of the whole process of illustration.

V

Reynolds' achievement in his late Shakespeare paintings was to draw together the local and the universal, the moment and the whole, and in one case the comic and the tragic, in a manner that extended his writings on Shakespeare and his theories about iconographic borrowings while revitalising elements from his portraits and subject paintings, appealing to those categories of wit that he had not so much courted but created through his development of the borrowed attitude. But the images raise the insistent question of why they have achieved so little serious critical attention, most particularly with regard to their use of sources. The answer to this lies in both their intrinsic nature and their external circumstances. The Shakespeare paintings' very difference from Reynolds' other images held them apart from his usual audience, and their condition, now seriously deteriorated and not easily accessible, has hindered later discussion. They were painted at a time when Reynolds' admirers, the connoisseurs and patrons who had followed his earlier work, were increasingly being displaced, as Fuseli was also discovering, by a new kind of gallery visitor and print buyer who lacked the experience to decode complex structures of allusion to Old Master paintings and classical texts. It may also be the case that the particular kind of wit, aligned in Chapter 1 with the mock-heroic, may have been something that few would then have recognised when it was not part of a more fully focused comic intent in a portrait. It is edifying to note that a review of *The Death of Cardinal Beaufort* in the *St James's Chronicle* dismissed the painting as 'too like that of Germanicus by Poussin, to claim the distinction of an original composition'.[74] Familiarity with the source obviously does not imply understanding of its effect: recognition of this irony demands a particular grasp of a sense of the double that, at the century's close, was far less pervasive than in the time of Pope and Fielding. As Chapter 9 will show, it is very rarely encountered in the paintings of the Boydell Shakespeare Gallery.

Reynolds' approach to the paintings has a part to play in their comparative neglect, too. Although the images break new ground as a means of textual commentary, they were painted late in the artist's life at a time when his eyesight was failing, allowing little possibility of future development of their new approach. Reynolds was throughout his life primarily a portrait painter, working with the aristocracy and gentry, and as many have stressed he thought it demeaning to produce paintings simply as the basis of reproductive engravings, the only commission that allowed him directly to paint Shakespearean subjects. The paintings that deal with Shakespearean themes before the Boydell commissions, the early head of Lear (*c.* 1762) mentioned in Chapter 3 and the two portraits of society women in Shakespearean character, are far closer to the world of fashionable portraiture than those of the historical or literary painting. It would seem that the painter who had written about Shakespeare, and who was the friend of Shakespearean editors and critics, held himself aloof from Shakespeare painting for reasons that were economic and social as much as aesthetic.

Another, more important, question remains. Why, when so many of his earlier images depended upon the reader's recognition of the armature of allusion on which they are built, did so much of the witty and critical reference of the Shakespeare paintings remain unnoticed? One reason may lie in the paintings' mingling of genres, which made them nearly impossible to read for their original audiences, who had moved away from the subtle rewards of the mock-heroic of the second quarter of the century. Another may be the obscurity of some of the references. Yet, given the range and subtlety of allusion, often comically inapposite, in so many of Reynolds' earlier paintings, and his own ironic wit, such an allusive vocabulary seems quite characteristic of both the painter and the man.

As to why the allusions have not received subsequent comment, the state and availability of the images and their unfashionable place within Reynolds' output are again the most immediate explanation. Another is perhaps simple chance: after all, the origin of *The Death of Dido* in *The Sleeping Psyche* was first noted by Edgar Wind in 1938.[75] Art historical iconography is not alone in coming late to such recognitions: the importance of Apuleius' *The Golden Asse* as a primary source for *A Midsummer Night's Dream* was not established until articles appearing, quite independently of each other, in 1945 and 1948,[76] despite the publication of William Adlington's translation in 1566. Even Fuseli, who produced paintings based on it,[77] did not recognise the connection.

Along with the allusion to the *Laocoön* in West's *Lear*, the Old Master deposition figure in Barry's *Lear and Cordelia*, and Northcote's use of Caravaggio's *Entombment* in his *Richard III*, Reynolds' paintings were rare among the Boydell images in employing a classical frame of reference. Perhaps this is the most reliable explanation of their comparative neglect: for all their individuality, these images make use of a reference system that depends on the classical mock-heroic at a time when other, more direct ways of creating meaning were well established. In part, Romanticism had already laid claim to Shakespeare; but in the more immediate circumstance in which his paintings were seen, the Boydell Gallery, other forces were at work. The most insistent were those generated by the new materialist culture that had already appropriated the texts, and the phenomenon, of Shakespeare, and it is these that are the subject of the next chapter.

NOTES

1. Original version of 1784 now unknown. Version of 1793, 48.1 × 59.9 (19 × 23 9/16), Folger Shakespeare Library, Washington D.C.
2. 1794; oil on panel, 48.3 × 58.4 (19 × 23), Newark Museum, New Jersey.
3. 'Base and Superstructure in Marxist Critical Theory' in *Problems in Materialism and Culture: Selected Essays* (London: Verso, 1980), pp. 40–2.
4. 271.8 × 365.7 (107 × 144), Museum of Fine Arts, Boston. Engraved by William Sharpe, 25 March 1793, 49.5 × 62.5 (19 1/2 × 24 5/8). There is also an oil sketch, 52 × 70 (20 1/2 × 27 1/2), Detroit Institute of Arts.
5. Late 2nd century BC. Marble, height 213.4 (84), Vatican Museum, Rome.
6. 285.75 × 360.7 (112 1/2 × 142), Royal Dublin Society, Dublin.
7. I am indebted to Professor Valerie Wayne, in discussion with whom this reading took shape.
8. 287 × 177.8 (113 × 70), Guildhall Art Gallery, London.
9. James Northcote, *The Life of Sir Joshua Reynolds* 2 vols. (London: Henry Colburn, 1818), II, p. 226.
10. 8 December 1786 and 15 December 1791; nos. 165 and 230 in *The Letters of Sir Joshua Reynolds*, ed. John Ingamells and John Edgcumbe (New Haven and London: Yale University Press, 2000), pp. 176, 229–30.
11. To Charles, 4th Duke of Rutland, 13 February 1787. *Letters*, no. 171, pp. 180–1.
12. See Frederick Whiley Hilles, *The Literary Career of Sir Joshua Reynolds* (Cambridge: Cambridge University Press, 1936), pp. 30–1.
13. Boswell records Johnson's disapprobation of Montagu's work. See *Boswell's Life of Johnson*, ed. George Birkbeck Hill, revised by L. E. Powell, 6 vols. (Oxford: Clarendon, 1936–50), II, p. 88.
14. Hilles, *Literary Career*, p. 27.
15. The note and Malone's comments are reprinted in Hilles, *Literary Career*, pp. 99–100.
16. Ibid., p. 28.
17. Ibid., pp. 28–9.
18. *Letters*, pp. 224–5.
19. Some of the notes are reprinted in *The Literary Career*, and the complete extant text in Frederick Whiley Hilles, *Portraits by Sir Joshua Reynolds* (London: Heinemann, 1952), pp. 107–22.

20. Hilles, *Portraits*, p. 122.
21. Ibid., p. 112.
22. Ibid., p. 119.
23. 'Reynolds and the Art of Characterization', *Studies in Criticism and Aesthetics, 1660–1800: Essays in Honor of Samuel Holt Monk*, ed. Howard Anderson and John S. Shea (Minneapolis: University of Minnesota Press, 1967), pp. 332–57, esp. pp. 340–1.
24. 238.8×147 ($95\frac{1}{2} \times 57\frac{7}{8}$), National Maritime Museum, Greenwich.
25. Horace Walpole, *Anecdotes of Painting in England*, Advertisement to Vol. IV, 1771, ed. Ralph N. Warnum, 3 vols. (London: Swan Sonnenschein, Lowrey, 1881), I, p. xvii, n. 2.
26. 139.7×110.5 ($57\frac{1}{2} \times 43\frac{1}{2}$), Private Collection. Engraved by J. R. Smith, 1776.
27. 76.2×63.5. (30×25), Iveagh Bequest, Kenwood House.
28. 238.8×144.8 (95×58), Iveagh Bequest, Kenwood House.
29. 236×146 ($93 \times 57\frac{1}{2}$), Private collection.
30. 148×183 ($58\frac{1}{4} \times 72$), Private collection. Mezzotint by Edward Fisher, 1762.
31. See 'Reynolds on Garrick' in Hilles, *Portraits*, 86–9.
32. *Sir Joshua Reynolds: The Painter in Society* (Cambridge, Mass. and London: Harvard University Press, 1996), p. 151.
33. *Emblem and Expression: Meaning in English Art of the Eighteenth Century* (London: Thames and Hudson, 1975), pp. 80–2.
34. 'Reynolds and the Art of Characterization', p. 334.
35. 218.5×157.5 ($86\frac{1}{8} \times 62$), National Trust, Petworth House; another version, studio of Reynolds, *c.* 1790, oil on board, 42.5×32.5 ($16\frac{3}{4} \times 12\frac{13}{16}$), Folger Shakespeare Library, Washington D.C. Engraved by Caroline Watson, 56.5×40.5 ($22\frac{1}{4} \times 15\frac{1}{2}$), 1 August 1792.
36. *Sir Joshua Reynolds: The Subject Pictures* (Cambridge: Cambridge University Press, 1995), p. 259.
37. Pen and ink, charcoal and chalk on paper, 65×81.9 ($25\frac{1}{2} \times 32\frac{1}{4}$), Walker Art Gallery, Liverpool.
38. See, for example, Wind's discussion of *The Death of Dido*, '"Borrowed Attitudes" in Reynolds and Hogarth', *Journal of the Warburg and Courtauld Institutes*, II (1938–9) pp. 182–5, esp. p. 183.
39. Johnson's note quoted in *The Plays and Poems of William Shakespeare*, ed. Edward Malone and James Boswell, 21 vols. (London: F.C. and J. Rivington, 1821), XVIII, p. 549.
40. 56.5×40.5 ($22\frac{1}{4} \times 15\frac{1}{2}$), published 1 August 1792.
41. 146×195 ($57\frac{1}{2} \times 76\frac{3}{4}$), Institute of Arts, Minneapolis. This may be the basis of an earlier Reynolds sketch bought by Thomas Holcroft from the artist in 1796, as recorded by Postle (*Subject Pictures*, p. 259) from Reynolds' account books. This work, now lost, may have followed Poussin's composition, of which Reynolds had a copy. The copy might well have been the basis of Fuseli's sketch as well as Reynolds' painting: Fuseli rarely uses the French artist as the basis of his own iconographical references, his taste being far more towards Renaissance Italian models, and the idea of both artists following an Old Master image certainly aligns itself more fully with contemporary ideas of composition.
42. *St James's Chronicle*, 4–12 May 1789.
43. *Reynolds*, pp. 260–1.
44. *The Bee*, p. 41.
45. *The Times*, 7 May 1789; *Anecdotes of English Painting*, XV, p. 206; Hazlitt, 1816, II, pp. 276–7.

46. *Analytical Review*, 1790, VI, p. 330.
47. Luke 23.34.
48. 271.7 × 365.7 (107 × 144), National Trust, Petworth House.
49. 49.5 × 62.5 (19 $^{1}/_{2}$ × 24 $^{1}/_{2}$).
50. See Nicholas Penny, *Reynolds*, Exh. Cat. (London: Royal Academy of Arts and Weidenfeld and Nicholson, 1986), p. 326.
51. British Museum Add. Ms. 46151 fol. 109.
52. *A Philosophical Analysis and Illustration of some of Shakespeare's Remarkable Characters* (London: John Murray, 1774). There is no record of Reynolds' knowledge of this book, but his discussion of Jaques in the unpublished essay resembles Richardson's chapter on the character.
53. Charcoal, black and white chalk on paper, 141.5 × 104.6 (55 $^{11}/_{16}$ × 41 $^{3}/_{16}$), National Gallery, London.
54. 125.73 × 101.28 (50 $^{1}/_{4}$× 39 $^{7}/_{8}$), Minneapolis Institute of Art. This may be a preparatory sketch for the two images, now lost, that he painted in the same year.
55. A similar gesture appears in a mezzotint by John Jones after George Romney's painting, now lost, of *John Henderson as Macbeth*, 19 May 1787, British Museum, London; another version, oil on engraving on canvas, 42.5 × 52 (16 $^{3}/_{4}$ × 20 $^{1}/_{2}$), *c.* 1787, Folger Shakespeare Library, Washington D.C. Here, though, the scene depicted is Macbeth's initial meeting with the witches, and there is no show of kings, so the specific relation of the gesture to Macduff is absent.
56. 93.5 × 118.2 (36 $^{3}/_{4}$ × 46 $^{1}/_{2}$), Private Collection.
57. 500 × 280 (197 × 110), Gesuiti, Venice.
58. Oil on panel, 101.6 × 81.3 (40 × 32), The Earl Fitzwilliam, Milton Park, Peterborough.
59. *A Wood – Robin Good-Fellow*, image 27 × 18.6 (7 $^{3}/_{8}$ × 10 $^{5}/_{8}$), on paper 44.5 × 31 (17 $^{1}/_{2}$ × 12 $^{1}/_{4}$), published September 29, 1799.
60. *The dramatic works of Shakspeare revised by George Steevens*, 9 Vols. (London: Boydell and Nicol, 1802), VIII, p. 24. Proof copy in the Folger Shakespeare Library, PR2752 1791–1802a v8 ShCol.
61. William Cotton, ed. John Burnet, *Sir Joshua Reynolds. Gleanings from his diary, unpublished manuscripts and from other sources* (London: Longman, 1856), pp. 174–5.
62. *Analytical Review*. 1789, IV, p. 106.
63. 49.7 × 35.3 (19 $^{5}/_{8}$ × 13 $^{7}/_{8}$).
64. *Essays on the Fine Arts*, ed. William Carew Hazlitt (London: Reeves and Turner, 1873), p. 33.
65. 303 × 297 (119 × 117), The Hermitage, Leningrad.
66. 61 × 46.3 (24 × 18 $^{1}/_{4}$), Hyde Collection, Houghton Library, Harvard University.
67. 234.95 × 152.4 (92 $^{1}/_{2}$ × 60), Town Hall, Stratford-upon-Avon. Destroyed by fire, 1946. Copy after Gainsborough, after 1769, 114.3 × 75.9 (45 × 30), Folger Shakespeare Library, Washington D.C. Mezzotint by Valentine Green published by John Boydell, 2 April 1769, 59.65 × 38.42 (23 $^{7}/_{8}$ × 15 $^{1}/_{8}$).
68. 1774; 76 × 63.5 (30 × 25), The Faringdon Collection Trust, Buscot.
69. 1774; 76 × 63.5 (30 × 25), Albright-Knox Art Gallery, Buffalo, New York.
70. Penny, *Reynolds*, p. 207.
71. 142.2 × 251 (56 × 98 $^{7}/_{8}$), Royal Collection.

72. Palazzo del Té, Mantua.
73. 233.7 × 290.8 (92 × 114), Tate Britain.
74. 9–12 May 1789.
75. 'Borrowed Attitudes', p. 183.
76. Sister M. Generosa, 'Apuleius and *A Midsummer Night's Dream*: Analogue or Source, Which?' *Studies in Philology*, XLII (1945), pp. 198–204; D. T. Starnes, 'Shakespeare and Apuleius', *Publications of the Modern Language Association*, LX (1945), pp. 1021–50; John Dover Wilson, *Tribute to Walter de la Mare on his Seventy-fifth Birthday*, 25th April 1948, reprinted in *Shakespeare's Happy Comedies* (London: Faber, 1962), pp. 207–19.
77. The paintings both refer to Cupid and Psyche, often treated as a separate episode. In the version by Charles Gildon with illustrations by Hogarth, the transformation is into a lap-dog rather than an ass: this may account for the absence of references in eighteenth-century discussions of the play.

CHAPTER 8

FUSELI, NATURE AND SUPERNATURE

I

From 1780 onwards, almost all of Fuseli's Shakespeare images engage, at one level or another, with the need to reconcile an insistent contradiction: the visual presentation of a complex intellectual debate with the texts in a manner accessible to an increasingly diverse readership. Chapter 4 has suggested how this led to a dilution of style in some of the history paintings, and the adoption of a particular kind of characterisation through posture and expression. Other images show a different response: the development of a complex vocabulary that allowed the artist to satisfy simultaneously his own wish to explore the arcane reaches of the plays' supernatural dimensions and the fashionable tastes for the Gothic, the Sublime and the uncanny. It is in this arena that the dilemma finds the most convincing resolution.

Fuseli's paintings of Shakespearean supernature share the foundation and aim of his earliest literary paintings, in producing a web of iconographic allusion and compositional invention to convey a critical reading of both the moment and the movement of the play. By the end of the century, his work with Lavater had allowed him to develop a taste for the depiction of extreme human states without limiting him to the use of prescribed models, and in the images of the supernatural this combines with his innate grasp of imaginative texts that operated in a metaphoric mode. The focus on supernature also drew on two other aspects of his aesthetic personality, an acquaintance with European folk-mythology and an experimental knowledge of lepidoptera and entomology in general. The two came together, in a manner by no means illogical given the rural foundations of many fairy beliefs, in an emphasis on the forms of the natural world and their mythic exchange with superstition and folklore. Concerned as they often are with states of dream or visionary experience, the supernatural paintings also make frequent use of two stylistic effects, extremes of chiaroscuro and acute perspectival displacements, sometimes within compositions stripped of all but the most essential features, sometimes in images teeming with minute figures compounded of the human and the lepidopteral.

What results is a series of interlocking paradoxes in which the supernatural is made vividly real by strained anatomy and facial expression, the fairy kingdom located precisely within the natural world, and dreams made experientially real through the intensity with which the uncanny is visualised. These qualities give the paintings a compelling appeal to the cult of the Gothic, at the end of the century still enjoying popularity, and also to that of the Sublime, which gained a renewed currency at the same time. Fuseli's visions of the supernatural, the uncanny made knowable, achieved widespread popularity: while the most extreme example of this is the various versions of *The Nightmare*,[1] many of his Shakespeare paintings adopt similarly sensational vocabularies to convey readings of the plays. Perhaps because of the immediate appeal that this generates, the density of their textual reading has been overlooked, their value as serious critical statements obscured by their febrile intensity. In the most successful of these paintings character, situation and relationship are presented with a dynamic ambiguity that functions to explore and magnify the driving forces of the plays with an intellectual energy both innovative and compelling.

Fuseli was of course not alone in focusing on elements of the supernatural within the plays; Macbeth's encounter with the witches had, after all, been among the most popular scenes since 1750. Yet many paintings show the event as a revision of theatre, or use merely conventional forms of the unnatural so that the sense of a confrontation with something genuinely other is at best compromised and at worst annulled. The same is true of many other images that explore supernatural relations. George Romney's sketches of Marjorie Jourdain (see Chapter 5) show him as one of a rare group capable directly of suggesting the uncanny: conversely John Opie, whose version of the same scene was commissioned by Boydell in preference to Romney's,[2] is oddly unsatisfying. The fiend is a conventional Satanic figure emitting a conventional unearthly glow, the figures respond with familiar horror in a fussy composition that diffuses rather than concentrates emotion, and the skull and dead baby at Jourdain's feet are theatrical props. This is stage horror rendered static on the easel: paradoxically, by avoiding any hint of existing also in the realm of nature, the knowable world, it fails to convince in its actuality within the unknowable, and so lacks power to disturb. Most important, it fails to move

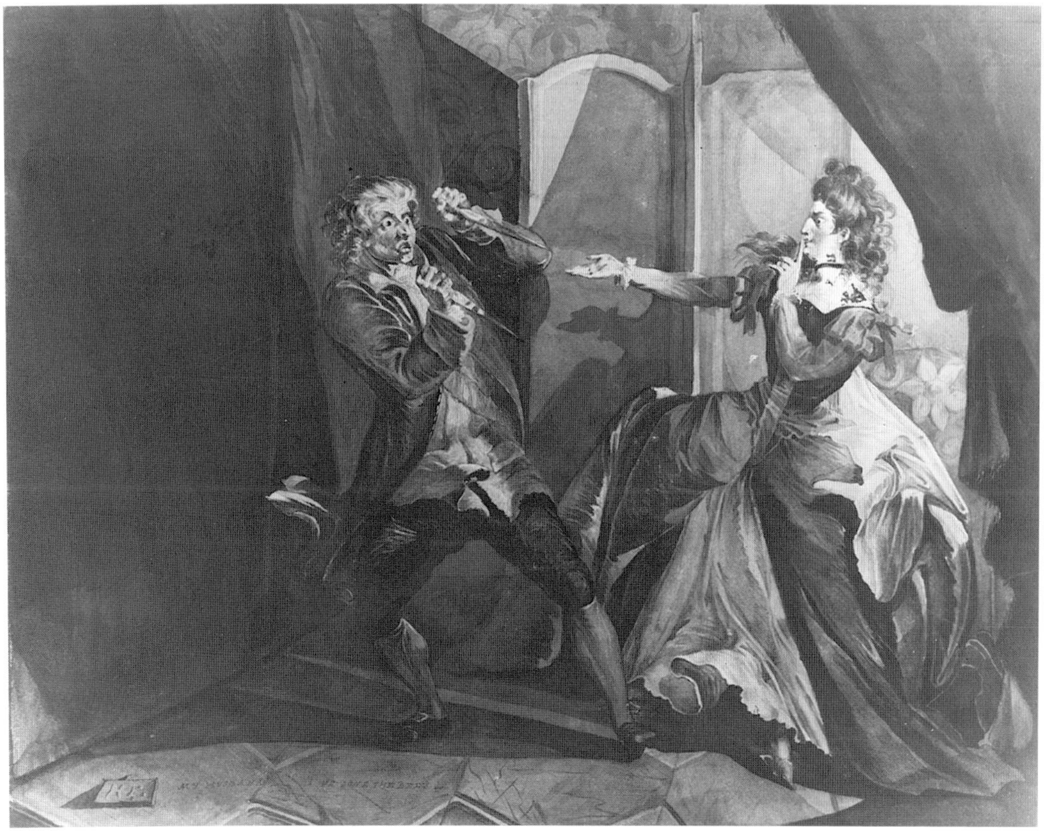

73 Henry Fuseli, *Garrick and Mrs Pritchard as Macbeth and Lady Macbeth after the Murder of Duncan*, 1768.

beyond a superficial reading of the scene and, unlike Romney or Fuseli at their best, offers no critical engagement with the text and its issues.

Fuseli's ventures into the supernatural are of a different order. While the combination of many of his mature effects is seen in images from *A Midsummer Night's Dream*, *The Tempest* and *The Winter's Tale*, the mannerist delineation of the figure and the use of extreme chiaroscuro – the subject of the whole of his sixth Academy lecture[3] – are dominant in images that revisit the most popular Shakespearean scenes, and are apparent from very early in his career. One of the earliest London images is *Garrick and Mrs Pritchard as Macbeth and Lady Macbeth after the Murder of Duncan* (1768: Fig. 73).[4] Apparently owing much to the stage, this already suggests the distortion of body and face more fully exploited later. In 1812 Fuseli revisited the subject in a much larger oil painting, *Lady Macbeth seizing the daggers* (Fig. 74).[5] Distortion is now extreme, in the exaggerated musculature and glaring eyes of

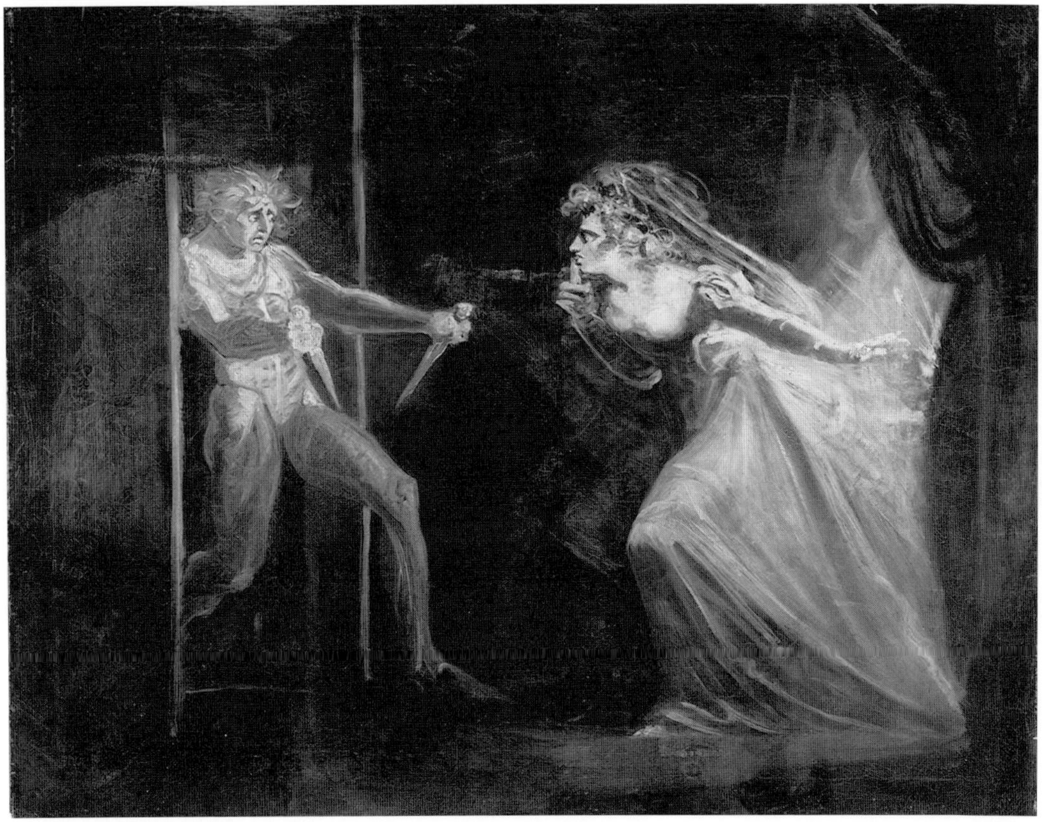

74 Henry Fuseli, *Lady Macbeth seizing the daggers*, 1812.

Macbeth, and the body of Lady Macbeth caught in a single diagonal sweep. In exploring these images as stage history, Stephen Orgel sees the figures as exaggerations of emotional states that reduce the actors to caricature.[6] This is true, but it is only a limitation when the images are seen as performance records: when seen as textual interpretations, they become instead powerful visualisations of the feverish intensity of the moment. This is seen most particularly, and at its most painterly, in the restricted palette of the second treatment of the scene, a single range from dark umber to sickly pale green-ochre relieved only by the red on Macbeth's hands and body. Here, as in Romney's image of the banquet scene, the textual references to blood are powerfully concretised. Desmond Shawe-Taylor suggests that, as well as offering a kind of nostalgic revision of the earlier image and the theatric experience it records, Fuseli is showing the figures in some kind of Dantescan hell,[7] but it is more specifically Shakespearean, prefiguring the grimly comic allusions of the porter scene, and reaching much further forward to Lady Macbeth's sombre, near-final 'Hell is murky' (5.1.31). In this the simple intensity and textual breadth of the mature paintings as visualisations of Shakespeare's supernatural imagery are manifest.

The process of concentration by reduction seen in the change between these treatments of one scene is even more evident in *Macbeth meeting the Witches* (1800–1810).[8] This pares down the encounter to its essential elements, presenting only the heads, shoulders and pointing arms of the witches and the figures of Banquo and Macbeth, their recoil conveyed by extreme chiaroscuro and the angle of their bodies. Earlier depictions of the scene, most of all that prepared for the Boydell Gallery,[9] have been concerned with expressing morality through exaggerated posture or windswept landscape: here there is nothing save two groups of figures within a vast plane of blackness, and the absence of those more explicative elements with which this image is in dialogue – used to the convention, we thus in a sense insert them – contributes to its shock. But the main power rests in the direct impact of the image, realised as it is in minimal terms. That it presents the events through the filter of a sensibility tensed and refined by varieties of the Sublime enhances this, and reveals it as another version of the dialogue between contemporary perception and Shakespeare's text that Fuseli habitually conducts.

The culmination of this intense reduction is seen in *Macbeth Consulting the Vision of the Armed Head* (Plate 9),[10] commissioned for Woodmason's Irish Shakespeare Gallery and completed in 1793. The spectral form of the head is placed right at the foot of the canvas, with Macbeth's body and rapt gaze presenting a compelling diagonal towards it, the witches acting as intensifiers from the middle right. The diagonals stretched right to the limits of the canvas, and the lighting, a gloom almost as concentrated as in the other painting, hold together this unique composition and complete the power of the Sublime that it offers. Extremes of chiaroscuro are matched by an exaggeration of physiognomy that is perhaps the culmination of Fuseli's work with Lavater: the morbid psychology is both inescapable and, in this reading of the play, inevitable.

The canvas also attains a tight integrity through the system of resemblances it establishes, and it is here that its originality as a reading of the play is apparent. Knowles quotes a conversation with Fuseli in which the artist explained the dominant feature of the painting:

> I have endeavoured to show a colossal head rising out of the abyss, and that head Macbeth's likeness – What, I would ask, would be a greater object of terror to you if, some night on going home, you were to find yourself sitting at your own table, either writing, reading or otherwise employed? Would not this make a powerful impression on your mind?[11]

The passage is a very rare instance of the artist commenting directly on the workings of his imagery, but it also reveals the interplay of the domestic and the uncanny that make his supernatural paintings psychologically convincing where so many others fail. The passage does not mention two further elements contributing to the painting's critical effect. The armed head wears a helmet recalling that worn by Banquo in another version of *Macbeth and the Witches*[12] produced at the same time for Woodmason, hinting that Macbeth sees both what he himself might have become, and what he has destroyed. The concentration is extended in one further detail: Macbeth holds his forefinger to his lips, reflecting the gesture of the witches, 'each at once her choppy finger laying/ Upon her skinny lips' (1.3.42–3), in a chilling index of the degree to which they have taken possession of him. All these elements, tightened by Macbeth's posture of recoil and the costume that emphasises his human identity in strong contrast to the spectres around him, are surrounded by bituminous black, again echoing the play's imagery of Satanic darkness. The supernatural and the real are shown in a range of contrasts and elisions, and the result is striking in its psychological reading of the situation of Macbeth, referring to earlier events in the play and again revealing Fuseli's skill in translating temporal into spatial forms.

The same is true of a third treatment of the same play, *Lady Macbeth Sleepwalking* (1783: Fig. 75).[13] While this is concerned with the disturbed state of Lady Macbeth's mind, it shares many features with images that present the supernatural, perhaps as metaphoric enactments of the extreme psychological condition that is its subject. The painting follows convention in showing Lady Macbeth carrying a lighted candle, but breaks significant new ground in its sheer scale, presenting her almost at life size. As with the other *Macbeth* images the setting is minimal, a Tudor arch barely suggested and the doctor and the waiting woman seated rapt against it shown only in the light of the candle. The illumination gives to Lady Macbeth a dynamic power that is echoed in her long stride and outstretched left hand, but this is countered by what is perhaps the most arresting feature of the image. Very rarely does Fuseli present a female character in a form other than that used for the adult fairies in the *Midsummer Night's Dream* paintings, with sharp, angular features and very elaborately styled hair to suggest a combination of spite and sexuality. Lady Macbeth is quite different: her face is the most ordinary, most human face in the artist's output, and instead of being elaborately piled and knotted her hair streams freely behind her. This works in conjunction with the wide, glaring eyes – 'open . . . but their sense are shut' (5.1.21,22) – and the blanched skin, accentuated in contrast to the pale yellow gown and red hair, and emphasised by the darkness by which she is surrounded, to convey a combination of suffering

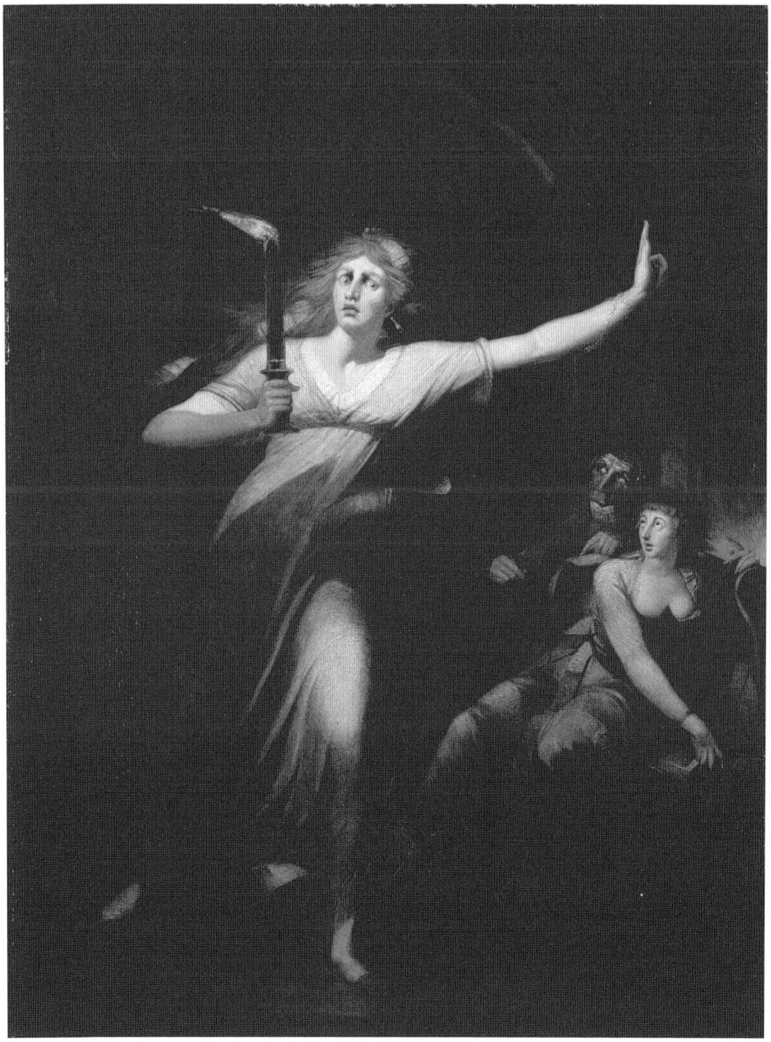

75 Henry Fuseli, *Lady Macbeth Sleepwalking*, 1783.

and physical strength made greater by her otherwise very commonplace appearance. Also important in this is the depiction of the doctor and the serving woman. The former, his face shown considerably foreshortened, is dark and angular; the latter, who wears a fashionably low-cut gown, has about her something of the sexuality familiar from many of Fuseli's female figures but manifestly absent in Lady Macbeth. The resultant contrast further accentuates the apparent ordinariness of the painting's central character.

Once again Fuseli's critical ability to draw together action from temporally separate parts of a play is evident. Denied the sexual determinants obvious in

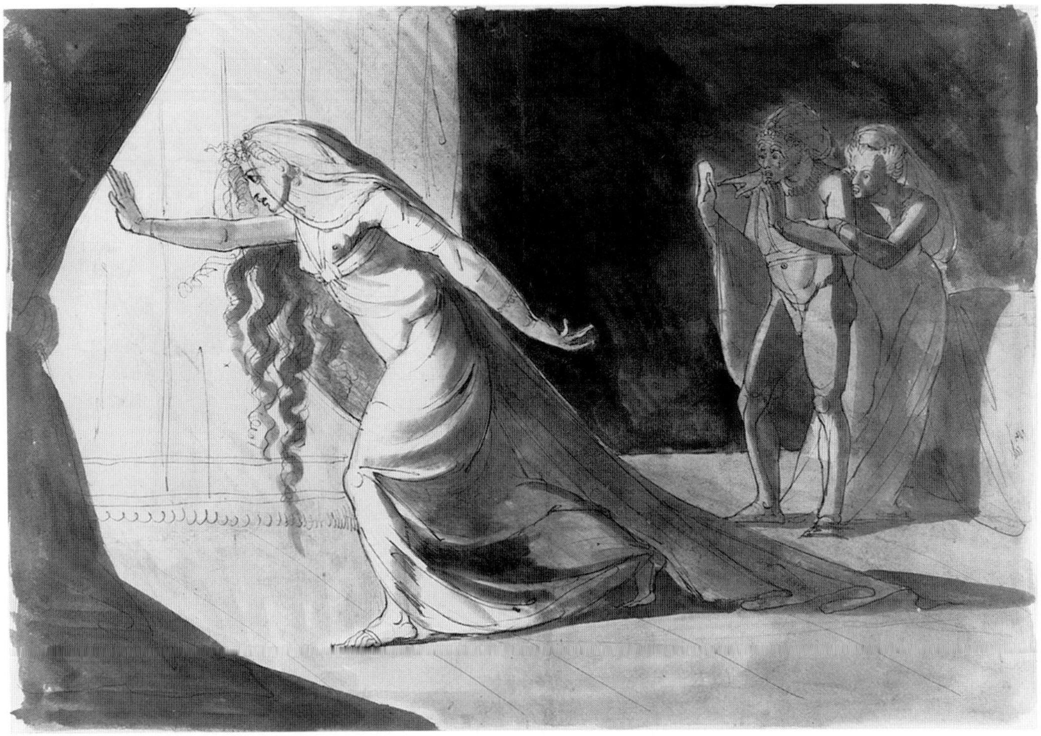

76 Henry Fuseli, *Lady Macbeth Sleepwalking*, 1772.

Fuseli's other female figures, Lady Macbeth appears as if her early invocation 'Come, you spirits/ That tend on mortal thoughts, unsex me here' (1.5.38–9) has been achieved: her power, ambition and sexuality are earlier inseparable, but now her disturbance leaves a sense of displaced and unfocused epic strength. Her invocation continues 'Come, thick night,/ And pall thee in the dunnest smoke of hell' (48–9): this is presented in the near complete blackness by which she is surrounded. Like other images, the painting derives its force from a combination of the everyday and the super-real, intensified by the extremes of light and shade, emphasised by the contrast with the other figures, in a stark simplification of character and action. Here, scale is important: the painting's power cannot be fully experienced when it is seen in reproduction. Comparison with an earlier treatment of the same scene is once more revealing. *Lady Macbeth Sleepwalking* (1772: Fig. 76)[14] uses the Borghese Gladiator as its basis, shown in profile, the outstretched arm of the Gladiator shifted from left to right to reveal the staring gaze and continue the powerful line begun in the diagonals of the legs and body and then turned downwards in the mannerist corkscrew figuration of the hair. That it is Lady Macbeth and not Macbeth who is shown in this allusive stance reattributes power to her, while maintaining the pathos of her sleepwalking, in another version of the combination of energy and pathos Fuseli praised as the embodiment of classical tragedy in the Gladiator. The result is simultaneously to deepen the compassion with which Lady Macbeth is presented in the play and to assign to her the force of the classical hero. The image consequently offers a powerful reading of the play's discussions of the interweavings of power, gender and the nature of the heroic, and this is considerably furthered when the two versions of the same scene are considered together.

That Fuseli can produce something so new and so powerful in visualising these scenes evidences the depth of his imaginative powers, and the degree to which his readings have moved beyond conventions of the Gothic. Implicit within them is the beginning of the imaginative approach to Shakespeare that, following Charles Lamb, will be a strong presence at the start of the new century; but rather than simply denying the possibility of stage performance, they recreate the reading experience with a new form of metaphoric presentation. Most importantly, they present the plays with an immediacy that in no degree lessens their critical integrity; but this has been achieved by the rejection of complex iconographic allusions, while other images produced at about the same time return to this device with all the power and range of the Italian wash-drawings.

II

Fuseli's visual treatments of *A Midsummer Night's Dream* are among the most inventive and profound of his paintings of what might be termed natural supernaturalism. Central are the two large canvases, themselves playing wryly on the 'before and after' tradition of literary painting, *Titania and Bottom* and *Titania's Awakening* that were part of the Boydell Gallery, although both were begun before the scheme had been mooted. These are accompanied by various smaller images of Puck, individual fairies or fairy groups, and followed by two images produced for Woodmason's Irish Shakespeare Gallery, *Titania's Awakening* (1793–4) and *Oberon Squeezing the Love-potion on the Eyes of the Sleeping Titania* (1794). Together they constitute a complex of images that, through the network of reference and allusion they set up within themselves and with further paintings by Fuseli and others, are amongst the most complete explorations of Shakespeare's fairy world. Their inventiveness becomes more apparent when it is recalled that, at the time, the play was regarded as little more than the basis for musical and choreographic elaboration: Garrick's *The Fairies* (1755), although retaining the lovers, treated them with very little seriousness, and any concern in the theatre for the integration

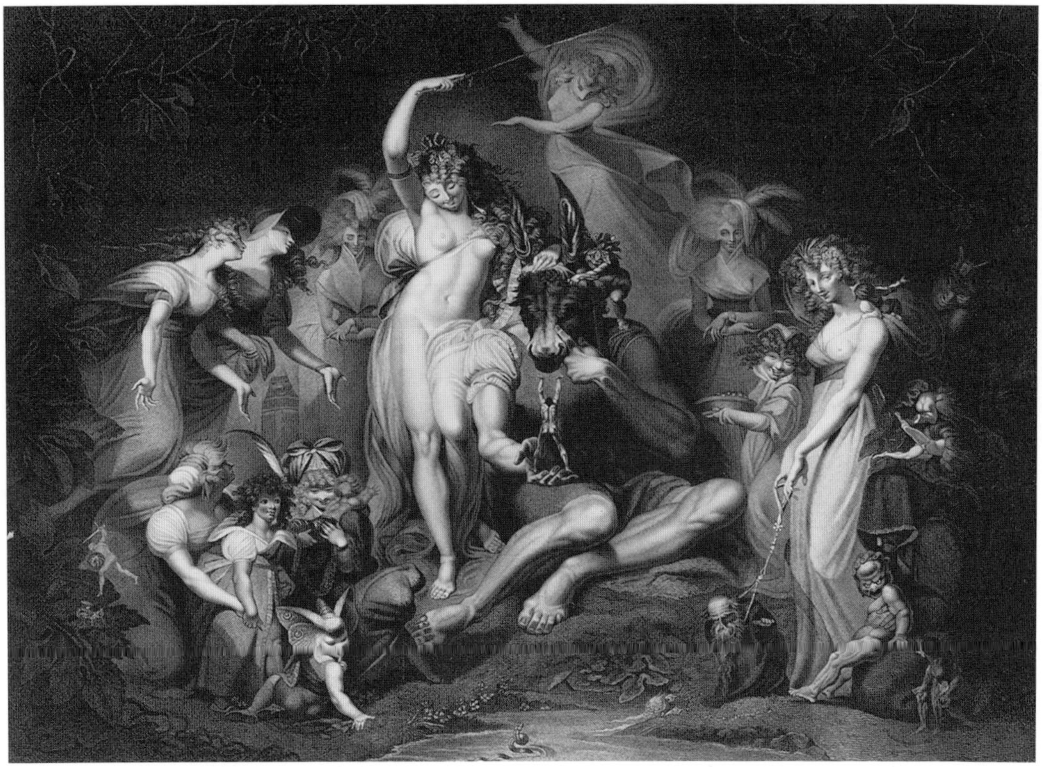

77 Henry Fuseli, *Titania and Bottom*. Engraved by Jean Pierre Simon, 1796.

of the various plot lines and their darker concerns was a very long way off. This gives Fuseli's readings their unique place in the play's history.

In the two large canvases Fuseli's mature ambivalence of representation reaches its peak as a device for critical interpretation. Both immediately declare the absence of the theatrical: the nature of the figures, their relative sizes, and their positioning make any reference to the actual world impossible and reveal that this is the product of an imaginative reading of the text. This does not mean that it is only the supernatural world that is revealed, since the surrounding of the figures by lush foliage both places the figures within Capell's 'wood near Athens' and recalls the origin of the fairy myths in contemporary rural culture. Nor does it suggest a departure from the details of the text, since through close readings it visualises some of the contradictory states of supernature that they embody.

Titania and Bottom (1780–90: Fig. 77)[15] is presented in the engraving above a passage from Bottom's grave debate with Cobweb and Mustardseed (4.1.7–24), and this is one level of its comic activity. But the more serious critical significance of the painting lies in its exploration of the relationship between the fairy and the mechanical through a series of iconographic allusions that, reinforcing elements apparent in the immediate appearance of the figures, reveal it as deeply ambivalent as well as intrinsically comic. Titania's expression of amorous triumph recalls lines significant in implying the power beneath her desire:

Out of this wood do not desire to go:
Thou shalt remain here, whether thou wilt or no.
(3.1.126–7)

Her body's sinuous grace, the left arm encircling Bottom's neck, gives expression to lines that, in a visual metaphor rather than the literal depiction of Reynolds' *Puck*, extend the suggestion of parasitic possession within the apparent tenderness:

Sleep thou, and I will wind thee in my arms . . .
So doth the woodbine the sweet honeysuckle
Gently entwist; the female ivy so
Enrings the barky fingers of the elm.
(4.1.37, 39–41)

The ambivalence of these passages is strengthened by one of the putative sources of the figure, the *Leda and the Swan* attributed to Leonardo.[16] Titania becomes by this association the victim of rape by a God turned animal, revealing the darker nature of Shakespeare's event. Fuseli here develops Puck's comment 'My mistress with a monster is in love' (3.2.6), and Oberon's injunction when squeezing the love juice:

What thou seest when thou dost wake,
Do it for thy true love take;
Love and languish for his sake.
Be it ounce or cat or bear,
Pard, or boar with bristled hair
In thy eye that shall appear
When thou wak'st, it is thy dear.
Wake when some vile thing is near!
(2.2.33–40)

At the same time, the allusion is comic because it compares not only Titania to Leda but Bottom to Zeus. This provides a bathetic parallel to his 'translation', and extends the mystical dimensions of his own account of his dream, full of echoes of

I Corinthians and the first Epistle of St John, by the provision of a pagan equivalent in his elevation to the condition of Zeus.

The classical sculpture known as *The Farnese Bull* from which the raised right arm is taken provides the second iconographic clue to Titania, again presenting her as a mortal victim.[17] It depicts Dirce, second wife of Lycus, king of Thebes, being tied to a bull by Zethus and Amphion, sons of Lycus by his first wife Antiope, as punishment for her cruelty to their mother. Oberon's motives are similar to those of Amphion: both are acts of revenge for a supposed earlier betrayal, showing Titania's vulnerability – also plainly evident in her open posture – and Oberon's spite. By placing the relationship within these classical frames, Fuseli reveals both its comic and serious identities: but it is the ambivalence that defines their use as characteristic of this period of his Shakespeare painting, and which so revealingly matches the tone and movement of this scene and the language of other parts of the play which the image also involves.

Other elements reveal Titania as a supernatural predator, but hint at a similar duality. The two fairies with elegant, imploring gestures at the left of the canvas, and the two that stand still behind her, are familiar from many of Fuseli's images of fairies and fashionable ladies. They wear the classical *empire* style then fashionable from France, suggesting that these are adult figures as aware of sexuality as their human counterparts; that there are two in similar postures perhaps hints at the similar status of Helena and Hermia. Their grace is offset by the fairies that stand on either side of Titania and to her rear. Similarly clothed but with the elaborate head-dresses used in many of Fuseli's courtesan drawings, they suggest the predatory side of Titania, and the balance of the two pairs again hints at the contrary states of being apparent in the mortal lovers.

On the right, another fairy leads on a short string a grey-bearded dwarf dressed as a monk or friar. This image is linked by Gert Schiff[18] to the overcoming of Merlin by the character known variously as Vyvyane, Nimiane and Nimue, who uses her seductive charm (here suggested by her exposed breast) to persuade him to reveal his secret art and leaves him imprisoned in a wood, in a cage invisible to all but himself. Sexual enchantment within a wood suggests itself as an event in which Titania is both seductress and victim, and implicit within the reference is the equation of Bottom with Merlin, the magician, further extending the idea of his mystic translation. There is also a link with another of Fuseli's images of the play, the small *Cobweb* tondo of 1785–6.[19] There, a tiny figure holds on a chain the incubus figure from *The Nightmare*, who may be released to prey on sleeping women: the allusion here is not to *A Midsummer Night's Dream* but to Mercutio's speech about Queen Mab in *Romeo and Juliet*:

This is the hag, when maids lie on their backs,
That presses them and learns them first to bear
(1.4.92–3)

In the convergence of these two references the ambivalence of the relationship between Bottom and Titania is again emblematised.

To the right of the friar crouches a hooded figure holding a strange red-headed dwarf, perhaps a changeling, again suggesting Titania's dark powers. Her role as sexual predator is suggested by the fairy children in the lower left-hand corner of the painting. All have the same angular features that project a spiteful energy; the lowest, with hair distorted to resemble the wings of a moth to suggest the character with that name, takes to an extreme the elaborate hair styles of Fuseli's courtesans and adds to them a macaronic pun that reinforces the play's dark sexuality: in the Swiss-German dialect spoken by Fuseli, the word *toggeli* means both 'butterfly' and 'incubus'.[20] Immediately behind this figure, a tiny fairy-gladiator attacks an insect within a flower, giving visual identity to a line from the beginning of the scene where the fairies disperse, 'Some to kill cankers in the musk-rose buds' (2.2.3). The presentation of this figure in heroic classical pose is a use of allusion for purely comic purposes, mimicking the link between Bottom and Zeus and revealing the integrity of the image down to its tiniest details, all of which are closely related to the play's text. These tiny figures reflect Fuseli's expertise in entomology, which spills over into his writings in a way that confirms the ambivalence of its visual use. In a review of a study of British butterflies he talks of the enthusiasm with which a fashionable woman 'mounts the head with ribbons *en papillon*';[21] in one discussing a volume on the insects of Georgia he compares the Linnaean system of classification to the hierarchy of 'Greek and Trojan demi-gods'.[22] These passages reveal the kind of conceptual link the artist was habitually forging, and suggest another source of the imaginative richness of the paintings as critical documents.

Almost in the very centre of the composition stands a tiny male nude seen from behind who stands with upraised arms on Bottom's hand, a figure that, from its position, is most probably Mustardseed. As well as giving this fairy a disturbingly incongruous human form, adding to the general sense of physical and moral disproportion, the figure is further disruptive through its iconography, coming from *The Execution of St John* by Andrea del Sarto, a figure of which Fuseli made several copies in his Italian years.[23] It is used elsewhere by Fuseli as an image of controlling violence, for example in *Hephaistos Bia and Cratus chain Prometheus to a Rock in the Caucasian Mountains* (c. 1810),[24] a drawing of Hephaistos hammering a stake through the heart of the supine Prometheus. It also appears in

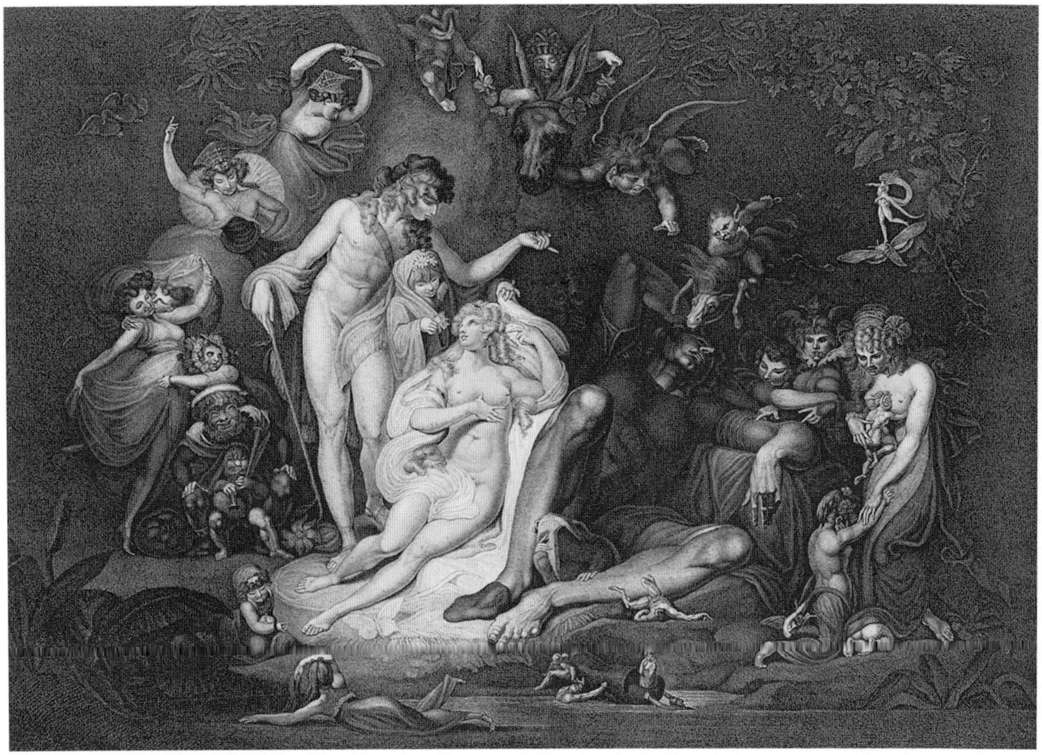

78 Henry Fuseli, *Titania's Awakening*. Engraved by Thomas Ryder and Thomas Ryder Jr., 1803.

Blake's engraving after Fuseli's design to illustrate a passage in Part I, Canto III of Erasmus Darwin's *The Botanic Garden*. Titled 'Fertilisation of Egypt',[25] the engraving represents the dog Anubis before the Nile in flood. Duality is present even here: Anubis in Hellenistic mythology is both celestial and infernal so that, the link implies, even at their apparently most insignificant and innocuous, the fairies are potentially satanic. This nexus of allusion quite reverses the usual readings of the fairies' paying court to Bottom: Fuseli's private iconography betrays his own sense of the grotesquely absurd, but when decoded also reveals the seriousness and threat within Bottom's parodic levée before the fairies in which he becomes a potential victim, just as he is enthralled by Titania.

Titania's Awakening (1785–9: Fig. 78)[26] continues this visual explication, largely by charting the duality of Puck and the fairies through a series of visual tropes, each of which qualifies and undermines the others, while simultaneously implying the same dualism in other areas of the text. What is most immediately striking about the image is that it reveals the central characters, Oberon and Titania, as essentially different from the fairies by presenting them *en grisaille*, arranged in the manner of a Neo-Classical sculpture. To convey their otherness by relating them to one of the most elevated forms of contemporary art is a statement at once comic and richly suggestive, placing them by implication beyond the fairy world and within a human order of moral responsibility, an association that anticipates by at least a century the later theatrical fashion of having the same actors play the fairy king and queen and the rulers of the Athenian court. The inclusion of a figure that is surely the Indian Boy between Oberon and Titania within this serioludic parody of Canova raises questions about the always equivocal status of this character, who is mentioned earlier in the text (2.1.20–27) but neither speaks nor is recorded as being on stage. Rarely if ever discussed by critics or shown in images – the Rowe frontispieces are perhaps the only other eighteenth-century visualisations[27] – the boy has only recently come to be included in productions, especially those that scrutinize issues of ethnicity or colonisation.[28] Fuseli's treatment is provocatively imprecise: is the boy at the centre of a trope of familial harmony, or is his closeness to Oberon proof of male victory in the battle for his allegiance? Fuseli's exploration of the sinister implications of colonisation at all its levels is clear in *The Tempest* design (see Chapter 4), and the composition of *Titania's Awakening* may be read as a parallel to the darker acts of mental colonisation visited upon Titania by Oberon, and the mutual colonisations of Titania and Bottom. At the same time, the boy's expression, richly-coloured costume and imprecise ethnicity adds a balancing suggestion of deep, sensual exoticism of the sort suggested in Donne's 'Indias of Spice and mine'.[29]

The social implications of the difference between the fairy court and the world of the mechanicals are implied by the presentation of Bottom, a figure gross in size and attitude: the stylistic opposition neatly hypostatises the social gradations innate to the play. Here the moral difference appears at first sight quite straightforward, the elegant gestures and light tonalities of the figures surrounding Oberon implying a reconciliatory impulse towards Titania while the dark and graceless forms around Bottom suggest themselves as the inhabitants of a dream. Yet the opposition is more apparent than actual, as the groups contain aspects that undermine or overthrow their surface meanings. The dualism of the fairies is best seen in the two groups of female forms in the upper left and lower right hand quadrants of the ring surrounding the central figures of Oberon, Titania and Bottom. Despite the fluent movements, accentuated by the contrast with the recumbent Bottom, their iconography reveals a strong element of potential evil. They resemble the aerial ring of fairies in Fuseli's later painting *The Shepherd's Dream* (1793),[30] a treatment of the transformation of rebel angels into forms compared by Milton to those who enchant a lonely shepherd in *Paradise Lost*, I, 768–92. As an explanation of the origin of fairies, the passage is supported by folklore and establishes an important principle of their duality: at any time, it is suggested, these fairies may return to forms of diabolic grossness.

Ambivalence of an equivalent kind is implicit within the sexuality of the fairies. The lowest figure of the left-hand group is being held and kissed from behind by a male fairy in an action uneasily hovering between child's game and adult assault: its source in Hogarth's 'Noon', one of *The Four Times of the Day* (1738), emphasises the sinister aspect, the note of predatory sexuality adding a species of human evil to counter the fairies' seeming innocence. A drawing dated 1813, *Two lovers embracing by a keyboard instrument*,[31] repeats the poses; there, it is an event overtly and consensually erotic, and its anticipation by the child fairies projects an uneasy sense of pre-adolescent sexuality that colours the reading of the rest of the image, offering a destabilising alternative to conventional views of fairy innocence. This note continues in the fairy adults who, like those in the earlier painting, are fashionably dressed, a placement within a contemporary human activity that has important results. Sexual intrigue in the fairy court, it implies, is as complex as that in human society, and this recalls the quarrel between Oberon and Titania, which involves a mutual accusation of infidelity and begins with Titania's banishment of the fairies and the remark 'I have forsworn his bed and company' (2.1.62), a sexual combat familiarly human. A complementary duality is seen in the second group in the lower right quadrant of the fairy circle, that combines apparently nurturing gestures with the spiky features and elaborate coiffeur seen repeatedly in Fuseli's erotic drawings. The child fairy is being comforted; but only because she is turning away from the strange scene before her, and the absurdity of the union of Titania and the ass is emphasised in its physical grossness by this fragment of visual narrative.

Fuseli's depiction of Puck makes visible something repeatedly present in the text, his ability rapidly to change form. This is shown in the structure of the language as much as its content: the word 'sometime' or 'sometimes' appears four times in lines 36 to 52 of 2.1, in which Puck identifies himself by describing some of his protean identities. The image actualises this by presenting Puck no less than five times. The figure on the left of the painting, below the group of ostensibly good fairies, is usually regarded as that of Puck[32] and this is confirmed by its iconography. The figure first appears in a drawing illustrating Milton's 'L' Allegro' dating from 1785.[33] There it represents 'Laughter holding both his sides' (line 32); here, it represents directly Puck's line 'then the whole choir hold their hips and loffe' (2.1.55). Puck's other, darker persona is suggested in the smaller figure crouched in his lap, who plays upon a recorder or horn. This implies not only Puck's ability to assume several voices to 'Mislead night-wanderers' (2.1.39), but more particularly his use of this to torment Demetrius and Lysander in 3.2, and, in the presence of the horn, hints at the figure's origin in the legend of Huon of Bordeaux.[34]

Three other forms present Puck. The elf holding the ass-head above Titania appears benevolent, since he is Puck restoring Bottom to his natural state; but again this is countered by the figure's iconography. Tomory (p. 101) identifies the motif in 'Rêve Magique', one of a series of witchcraft etchings by Claude Gillot called *Scènes Humoristiques*, in which the floating head of an ass forms part of a horrific dream. This suggestion is extended by the gnome on horseback galloping over Bottom's head, easily recognisable as the principal figure of Fuseli's celebrated painting *The Nightmare* (1781).[35] In this atmosphere of immanent duality, the dream which translates Bottom to a state of divine vision might just as easily have been of satanic import, and the use of the incubus gnome uncomfortably echoes the relationship between Titania and Bottom. A further layer of significance is provided in a passage from the most complete source of legends about Puck, *Robin Goodfellow; his mad prankes, and merry Jests* that probably dates from the late sixteenth century. While it is unlikely that Fuseli was aware of this text, it supports in a very specific way the larger folk legends that he obviously knew when Robin describes his actions in the adopted form of 'The Fairy Called Gull:'

> Many times I get on men and women, and so lye on their stomackes, that I cause their great paine, for which they call me by the name of Hagge, or Night-mare.[36]

Seen in this way, the incubus becomes Puck himself in one of his more strongly vindictive forms. Since it is he who places the ass-head on Bottom's shoulders, it is he who is responsible for the dream or 'Nightmare' Bottom undergoes, and Puck's presence as the 'Nightmare' incubus is a logical extension in visual form of the text's implications. The fairy between these apparently benevolent and clearly evil forms of Puck, who looks towards the 'Gull' figure with arm outstretched, is revealed as another depiction of Puck by his similarity to the character in the *Cobweb* tondo. Here the ambiguity is immediate: is the figure beckoning on the incubus Gull or restraining it?

The multiple uncertainties of these images continue in the tiny, biomorphic forms that inhabit the peripheries of both, more visibly so in the engravings because the bitumen-based paint that Fuseli used in these passages has greatly darkened with age. As uncertain in origin as in significance, they occupy the images' borders as if moving out of visual and into psychological space, and again disturb because of their half-familiar, half-uncanny identities, reaffirming the paintings' success because of their fusion of these opposed states. The treatments of slightly different textual moments that Fuseli produced for Woodmason are markedly less successful than the earlier ones precisely because they lack this quality: neither *Titania Awakes, surrounded by attendant fairies, clinging rapturously to Bottom, still wearing the ass's head*[37] nor *Oberon Squeezes the Flower on Titania's Eyelids*[38] has the sense of sheer otherness within the apparently everyday that is so compelling in the Boydell visualisations.

It remains extremely unlikely that anyone looking at the images on their first exhibition would have decoded all of the references that have been gradually unravelled by later art historical research into Fuseli's own canon and all the other sources employed, yet this does not undermine the paintings' power as visualisations of the play and its compound states of being. Contemporary responses suggest that, while the complex iconography was inaccessible, the painting impressed overall because of its breadth and imaginative power. The *St James's Chronicle* conveys this well: 'This is the best Picture we have ever seen by this Artist. He discovers a strong poetick fancy in personifying the different fairies.'[39] Private responses are much harder to come by, but a comment in a manuscript guide to the prints, written for Isabel Eustis Francis by her mother or father, refers to both paintings in terms of approval not used for any of the other images: 'both pictures perfect representations of a dream'.[40]

The initial effect is much the same today: viewers are drawn into this strange world by the tangible presentation of the unknowable, as a few moments listening to comments before *Titania and Bottom* in Tate Britain will confirm. That it is possible to decode the images and find within them a reading of the play of such sophistication – in its humour as well as its darkness – does not negate the visceral response. In this regard the two paintings represent perhaps the most satisfactory solution to Fuseli's earlier dilemma: that the images retain their mystery allows many readers to experience them as an immediate statement of fairy otherness, while the web of allusion offers, for those who care to decode it, a reading of the play's dualities unique within critical statements of its own time and for many decades to come.

One detail impresses, both in itself and because of the long chain of relationships it forges between the supernatural paintings. One of the fairies in the lower passage of *Titania Awakes* is a tiny male figure with the wings of a moth. The moth is an element that appears in different forms in many of the supernatural paintings, most notably in the elaborate hair of the fairy in the Boydell *Titania and Bottom*, beneath Titania's feet in the *Awakening*, and also at the extreme right of the same painting, where it is being ridden by a small fairy. Significantly, it appears again in two of the three surviving versions of *The Three Witches* (1783).[41] Though now considerably faded, its original import is revealed in the mezzotint by John Raphael Smith (1785),[42] where it is clearly revealed as a death's head moth. This provides another alternative to the earlier signification, which has about it both the *toggeli* pun and another verbal-visual wordplay common in later paintings, which exploit the dual meaning of the Greek *psyche* for both butterfly and spirit. At this level, Fuseli's paintings of the supernatural develop a close set of internal references: as with Romney's images of *Macbeth* and *A Midsummer Night's Dream*, the fairies and the witches occupy a single, imagined yet psychologically real world alternating between gossamer lightness and dark threat, to which the human characters, all alike, are subject.

III

In the published volume of the Boydell prints, Fuseli's treatment of *The Tempest* (Plate 13) comes after Romney's split-scene version of the play's opening. The juxtaposition is revealing. Whereas Romney concentrates on the physical storm, presenting the generative tensions between Prospero, Alonso and Ferdinand, Fuseli dramatises the conflict between Prospero and Caliban, with the storm shown in limited detail in the background and without the sinking ship. A difference in styles also emphasises a difference in concerns; while Romney visualises the scene as a modified history painting, omitting the figure of Caliban completely and presenting Ariel as a threefold classical spirit, Fuseli presents an opposition of forces within the play that are both supernatural and located firmly within the natural world. The detail of the setting reflects the play's linguistic concern, shown most often through Caliban, with the natural history of the island, and with balancing it against Prospero's magic. This is achieved by placing the onlooker within Prospero's cave looking out on the tempest, the events framed by the two warring characters. The location within the text is as usual denoted by the quotation beneath the engraving:

For this, be sure, to-night thou shalt have cramps,
Side-stitches that shall pen thy breath up; urchins
Shall, for that vast of night that they may work,
All exercise on thee: thou shalt be pinch'd
As thick as honey-combs, each pinch more stinging
Than bees that made them. (1.2.326–31)

Although the original has been lost,[43] a coloured version of the engraving exists in the Legion of Honor in San Francisco (Plate 13). This suggests that the central passage of the painting used what was for Fuseli an exceptionally light, transparent blue. Such colouring emphasises several elements of the composition, most notably by providing an extreme contrast to the darkness and threat of the conflict taking place before it: once more, chiaroscuro becomes an important dimension of Fuseli's critical practice.

The confrontation of Prospero and Caliban initially implies the simple oppositions of good and evil that generations of critics have embedded in the play; but the similarity of their gestures also hints at an underlying likeness between the two characters, reflecting visually the tonal parity of their linguistic sparring in which Caliban's 'A south-west blow on ye,/ And blister you all o'er!' (1.2.324–5) is set against Prospero's equally spiteful response given above. The postures, strikingly alike, present the two not in the precise hierarchy postulated in the play's opening but as equal opponents. All of this defamiliarises and complicates the relationship of power and morality that exists between the two at the play's start, and the ambivalence it generates is furthered by the suggestion in their outstretched arms of the creation from the Sistine Chapel, setting the onlookers to wonder how far this aggressive Caliban is Prospero's creation, as implied in the latter's admission 'this thing of darkness, I / Acknowledge mine' (5.1.274–5). Perhaps, too, it serves as a reminder of the willingness with which Caliban greets the parody-magicians Stephano and Trinculo, an allusion repeated elsewhere in the image.

This re-vision of the conflict, revealing possible similarities beneath the moral extremities assumed in many readings of the play, is matched by the showing of other aspects in deepened perspective. Miranda's expression of disdain, directed past Prospero to Caliban, states visually her words to the 'Abhorred slave' (1.2.351) in the speech at this time habitually reattributed to Prospero, both in performance and on the page. Johnson himself continued this practice, with an explanatory note:

> This speech which the former edition give [sic] to Miranda is very judiciously bestowed by Mr Theobald on Prospero.[44]

Rowe follows the Folio in giving the speech to Miranda, as does Pope. It is unclear whether Fuseli attributes the speech to her or not, but it is certainly apparent from the depiction of Miranda that she shares Prospero's attitude to Caliban. This Miranda is a sensually cognisant woman, whose revulsion rests on a full understanding of sexuality as a dimension of her identity. Her depiction in Fuseli's habitual *empire* costume, and with the aquiline features and elaborate coiffeur of figures from both *Macbeth* and *A Midsummer Night's Dream*, reinforces this: here is no parody maiden, but a mature woman aware of her own power and her own needs. In the centre of the composition, suffused by the uncharacteristically pure blue light, Ariel's headlong plunge suggests grace, but perhaps also the fall of a rebel angel, a link made explicit by Fuseli's later use of a near-identical figure in *Uriel observing Satan's Flight* (1802) to illustrate *Paradise Lost* Book III.[45] As the threatening force of Prospero reveals the redemptive potential of Caliban, so the darker origins of Ariel are hinted at; while, at the same time, the notion of Miranda as the inheritor of a fortunate fall has the merest suggestion.

This ambivalence is enhanced by the landscape setting of the image, which uses a device familiar from many of Fuseli's mature literary paintings in which the central figures are surrounded by an area of darkness populated by animate beings of a different order. Behind Prospero's head is a large butterfly or moth familiar from many of Fuseli's paintings of the supernatural world, perhaps in his own extension of the pun on 'psyche' for both butterfly and spirit, as well as a more general ambivalence between the beauty of the butterfly and the darker associations of the moth. At the magician's feet are two tiny figures, a standing woman apparently with wings and a kneeling, hooded man, familiar from his appearance before Bottom in the earlier *Titania and Bottom*. These two again define the extremes of Prospero's magic, from angelic to sinister, and the polarities are perhaps united in the pair of arms that reach out from the earth towards Prospero: do they belong to a figure called into existence or one buried by his magic power? An answer is perhaps supplied by the use of a similar figure in the frontispiece engraving to Darwin's *Botanic Garden*, 'Flora attired by the Elements'.[46] Here, the figure reaches up to give rings to the goddess, embodying the gift of the element of Earth; the allusion in the *Tempest* image may suggest another statement of Prospero's earth-magic, while its ambiguous nature allows for the threatening elements of the power to remain evident. By contrast, the characterisation of Caliban is subtly achieved through forms from the natural world that together offer a very specific reading. The obvious attributes here would be 'the charms / Of Sycorax – toads, beetles, bats' (1.2.340–1) with which Caliban curses Prospero immediately after the passage quoted beneath the engraving. Instead, the attributes are in part those good things of the island that Caliban offers to Stephano and Trinculo, along with his service, later in the play:

I prithee let me bring thee where crabs grow;
And I with my long nails will dig thee pig-nuts,
Show thee a jay's nest, and instruct thee how

To snare the nimble marmoset. I'll bring thee
To clust'ring filberts, and sometimes I'll get thee
Young scamels from the rock. (2.2.144–9)

Some of these are pictured directly, others suggested by association. The animal above Caliban is identifiable by posture and form as 'the nimble marmoset'; the crab is shown at his feet. The variety of rich vegetation, a lobster and two large shells close by reflect in more general terms the close relation between Caliban and the natural world seen throughout the play, as well as more explicitly suggesting Caliban's references to 'filberts' and 'pig-nuts' here, and to 'berries' and 'fish' a little earlier (2.2.137, 138). These benevolent elements offset the wild and threatening appearance of Caliban: here, as with Prospero, Fuseli employs the device of conveying moral ambivalence through the use of attributes that identify and extend key aspects of the text's imagery. A final ambiguity is added in the cat at the centre of the image. Not mentioned in the text, this is an addition from Fuseli's own imagination, perhaps as a familiar spirit for Prospero, although one far more domesticated than the 'brindled cat' of the witches in *Macbeth* (5.1.1) and thus perhaps a hint at the ultimate benevolence of his magic.

These contradictory details remain unresolved, and properly so, since this is an image of the beginning of the play where the nature of Prospero's magic and his intentions are, despite his reassurances to Miranda, not yet clear. The uncertainty is further accentuated by the image's viewpoint. The normal perspective of the stage is reversed and the onlooker placed within Prospero's cave, looking out on to the storm. In the act of watching, the onlookers are implicated in the play's action and the moral frame of its discussion of colonisation and ownership, becoming either the colonised or the colonist, Caliban or Prospero. Within this setting, Fuseli employs the natural and the supernatural as inseparable partners within the play's dynamic: it is a vision of the play wholly contemporary in its concern with the powers of nature and supernature, a relocation within the territory of Romantic speculation that balances Hogarth's depiction of the play's forces within an earlier frame of religious and moral antitheses. Strikingly, Fuseli here avoids the more obvious allusions to colonisation found in his earlier fresco design (see Chapter 4): the antitheses here are more general, going beyond the actual into the realm of the supernatural, as well as being within a territory that, as the faces and postures of all three characters remind us, remains alarmingly human.

Fuseli produced only one other image from *The Tempest*, known simply as *Ariel* (*c.* 1800–10: Fig. 79).[47] While it may be located at the very end of the play, it shares

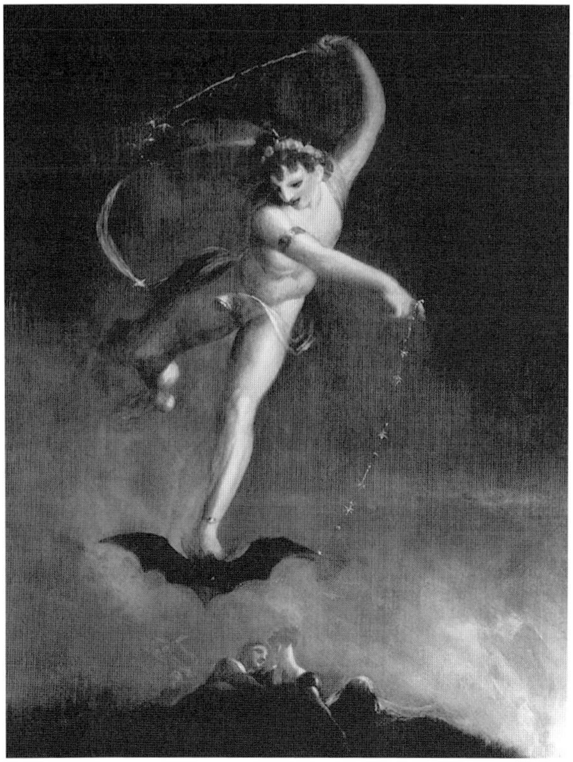

79 Henry Fuseli, *Ariel*, c. 1800–10.

with several of his other images including the *Winter's Tale* tondi the characteristic of not alluding to one specific moment but rather bringing together wider aspects of the play's language and movement. Ariel's movement illustrates a line from his final song, 'On the bat's back I do fly' (5.1.91), and beneath him sit Ferdinand and Miranda embracing, with next to them a barely discernibly fairy figure. The pure energy of Ariel is presented directly in the diagonal slant of his body, and echoed in the jewels on the chain with which he is leading the bat. The absence of contradictory figures in the corners or foreground suggests that this is an image of resolution, but the balancing absence of Prospero makes clear that this has been achieved solely in Ferdinand, Miranda and Ariel. Overall, however, the tone is lucid and dynamic, and this rejection of the more sombre aspects of the play suggests a new lightness in Fuseli's approach, that will be developed in the images produced for the Rivington Shakespeare.

Yet this, too, is an ambiguous image. Ariel has certain resemblances to the central figure in the surviving version of the Boydell *Puck* (c. 1810–20: Fig. 80)[48] sharing the frontal depiction and the string of orbs or jewels which, in that image,

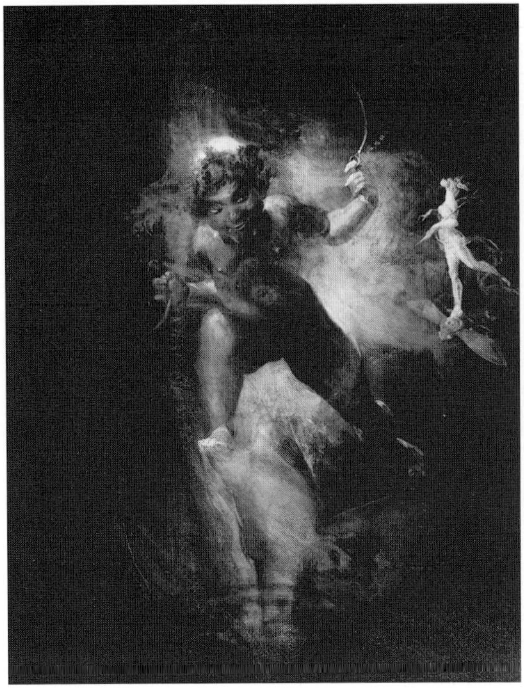

80 Henry Fuseli, *Puck*, c. 1810–20.

brilliantly visualises the claim to 'put a girdle round about the earth/ In forty minutes' (2.1.175–6). Puck wears an expression compounded of scowl and leer: once the link with Ariel is made, it is hard to avoid speculation about the relation of the two, and the moral dualism seen so often appears once again. To the left of Puck appears a fairy riding on a bat's back, the posture adopted, with vigour and grace, by Ariel. Here, the figure is one of the female fairies that populate the larger paintings of *A Midsummer Night's Dream*, and is taken directly from one of the tiny figures in the interstices of *Titania's Awakening*. There it flies not over the reconciled figures of Oberon and Titania but over the two fairies nursing changelings. When Ariel is seen within these references the dark suggestiveness of Fuseli's network of allusions begins to insinuate itself. The primary force of the image of Ariel acts to present the character as a bringer of joy and resolution, reading the end of the play as condign with the ending of the earlier, so-called 'happy comedies': but the allusions suggest a darker possibility within Ariel, whose treatment of Stephano, Trinculo and Caliban comes remarkably close to Puck's misleading night-wanderers. This constitutes a reminder that the resolution of those earlier plays is subtly qualified, and achieved only after struggle and reversal. It is one of Fuseli's most instinctual, most joyous paintings, avoiding the gloomy uncertainties of the earlier fresco design, lightly postulating between the realms it depicts – fairy and human, nature and supernature – a similar confluence in the play. But the delicate tonality and grace of movement is matched by the subtle suggestion in its iconography that all has not been easily achieved, and in this and in the fact that the lovers are physically under the power of Ariel in this image it draws together the sweep of the play's movement in recalling Prospero's earlier directive:

this swift business
I must uneasy make, lest too light winning
Make the prize light. (1.2.449–51)

V

In 1785–6 Fuseli produced a series of four small tondi based on *The Winter's Tale*, which mark a new departure in his approach to the painting of the plays. While they rest on suggestions made in the text, each one draws together aspects widely separate to construct moods or events not dwelt with in detail in the play, exploring both the fairy world and the indigenous rural mythology of the play by employing elements seen in the *Midsummer Night's Dream* paintings and elsewhere.

Three are explicitly concerned with Perdita, and show various aspects of her childhood and early maturity that are touched upon by Time, who refers to her as 'now grown in grace/ Equal with wond'ring' (4.1.24–5)[49] before announcing his concern with 'A shepherd's daughter,/ And what to her adheres' (4.1.27–8). What results in the images is the combination of many elements familiar from Fuseli's earlier explorations into fairy mythology. Writing of one of these images, Gert Schiff[50] draws attention to aspects which are evident in them all in quoting Florizel's description of her as 'no shepherdess, but Flora/ Peering in April's front' (4.4.2–3). This quality of the rural deity is combined in Fuseli's images with a supernatural note first sounded by the Shepherd when, on finding the abandoned child, he says to his son:

take up, take up, boy; open't.
[The Clown unwraps the bundle]
So, let's see; it was told me I should be rich by the fairies.
This is some changeling (3.3.112–4)

A little later, on discovering the gold Antigonus has earlier left with the baby, the Shepherd continues 'This is fairy gold, boy, and 'twill prove so' (3.3.118). These

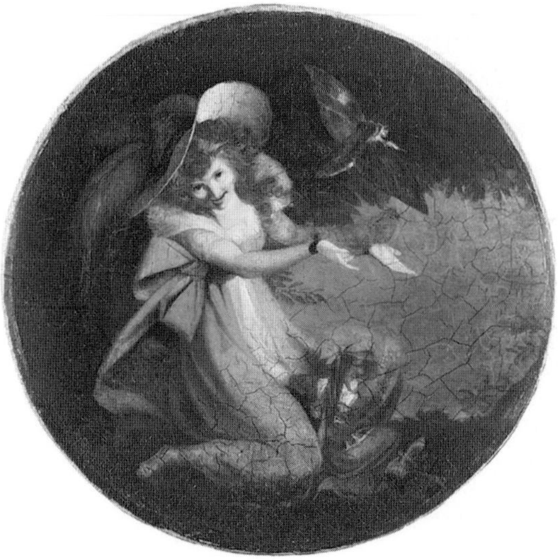

81 Henry Fuseli, *Young Woman with a Butterfly and Small Fairy*, 1785–6.

two strands are joined in Fuseli's paintings in another version of his habitual linking of the worlds of nature and supernature, to offer commentary of a very specific kind on the character and the play.

While these aspects are basic to all four of the images, each one addresses other parts of the text and seems to present a separate stage in the growth of Perdita. Three of them, and perhaps the fourth, can be seen as a chronological sequence; but this approach would limit the breadth of view so that, like Romney's wash-drawings of *The Tempest*, they are better considered as a meditation on aspects of the character of Perdita that are suggested in the second half of the play. The earliest in the play's chronology is *Young Woman with a Butterfly and Small Fairy* (Fig. 81).[51] Here a younger Perdita looks out at the onlooker as she apparently releases a large coloured butterfly. The symbolism is clear enough; as the butterfly emerges from its chrysalis, so she has emerged into womanhood, apparently from the basket or 'bearing-cloth' (3.3.111) which lies at her feet, in which she was left by Antigonus. This is enriched by the presence of another butterfly on the ground, recalling the tiny figures in the foreground of the *Midsummer Night's Dream* paintings. With the tree beneath which she sits, this develops the play's imagery of natural abundance; seen through the Shepherd's references to 'fairy gold', it again combines the natural and the supernatural. That the image recalls the country portraits of Gainsborough is further suggestive of a rural ideal, but with the added edge of Fuseli's awareness of folk belief and the erotic inflection that it is given through the direct, provocative gaze of the subject and the association with

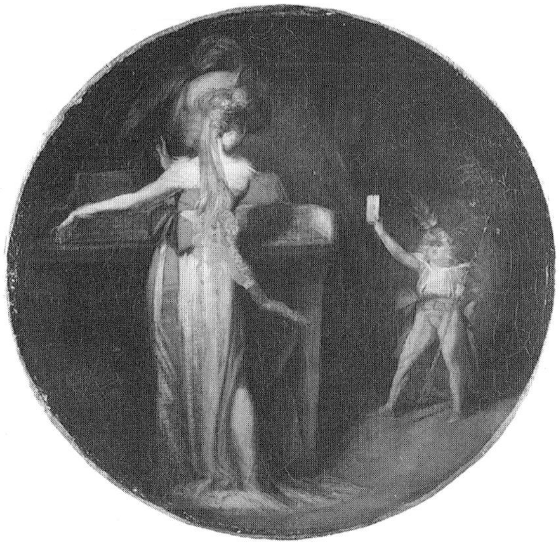

82 Henry Fuseli, *Young Woman at a Spinet and Elfin Messenger*, 1785–6.

Fuseli's other work in which this is more explicit. This reading is supported by the possibility of another instance of the verbal-visual play Fuseli employs elsewhere, here with reference to two colloquial expressions. The idea of Perdita's emergence into adulthood is supported by the idioms *wie ein Schmetterling aus der Puppe kriechen*, to emerge from a chrysalis or blossom into flower, and *wie ein Schmetterling hin und her flattern*, to flit from one girl to the next. With suitable gender modifications, this suggests both the emergence of Perdita into the adult world in the guise of the floral kingdom celebrated at the shepherds' feast, and also the flirtatious quality suggested by the gaze. In the dialogue between the two readings thus generated, Fuseli's image suggests an ambiguity within Perdita to offer a view of the character far more searching than those found in contemporary performance or criticism. It is an index of the simultaneous breadth and concentration of Fuseli's outlook that his deep knowledge of entomology is used here as the source of visual metaphor linked with his strong literary sense, the whole tensely united by the underlying erotic charge.

Young Woman at a Spinet and Elfin Messenger (Fig. 82)[52] continues this multivalence. Showing Perdita standing at the keyboard of a virginal, it seems of little relevance to the play, but becomes pertinent when read alongside a figure touched on in the *Dream* paintings, the use of a young woman playing a spinet in seventeenth-century emblematology 'to represent the transition between virginity and the breaking of the hymeneal chord'.[53] This is another motif that appears elsewhere in Fuseli's painting, for example in *Nude woman listening to a Girl playing upon a Spinet*,[54] developed from a sketch listed by Schiff as *Paraphrase of Titian's Venus and the Organ player* (1800–5).[55] The allusion to Titian's *Venus and Cupid with an Organist* (see Fig. 35) has already been noted in Chapter 4 with reference to *Queen Katherine's Dream* (see Fig. 34); but whereas there it forms the basis of a series of references to the senses, in the other images it becomes overtly erotic. In the *Paraphrase* sketch not only does the organ player, as in Titian's original, look directly at the genitals of the naked Venus: she is raised on one elbow in a far more assertive pose and directly returns his stare. The sketch is prefigured in the Spinet tondo in two ways. Perdita's left hand is raised elegantly above the keyboard, as is that of the organ player; and she looks directly into the eyes of the fairy messenger who is holding a letter in his uplifted hand. The image suggests a visual metaphor of Perdita's sexual maturity in which she takes over the interrogatory role of the organ player, perhaps amplifying the flirtatious gaze in the *Butterfly* tondo and extending her social function in the sheep-shearing scene into something more dominantly intimate. There, on Florizel's repeated exhortation, she forgets her inappropriate elevation as something 'goddess-like prankd up' (4.4. 10) and takes on the role of the hostess; here, it seems that she has celebrated womanhood by asserting control in courtship. This is, of course, totally in accord with Fuseli's own more explicit sexual imagery as demonstrated in the series of *symplegma* drawings[56] and, less openly, in any number of other paintings and sketches. As so often with Fuseli, dialogue with convention takes a highly personal inflection that also runs through his own erotic discourse. In the discussion of Perdita, it offers another reading of her character and role. Not only does it invert the playful eroticism of Florizel's references to the pagan gods' taking on disguises for the purpose of courtship, but it also redefines her role in the giving of flowers to her guests at the feasts: she becomes not Flora, but an amorous Hymen. That the image includes another fairy figure, and is enfolded in leaves and flowers, again combines the two worlds of pastoral and faery.

The third image, known simply as *Perdita* (Fig. 83),[57] comes closest to her presentation in the events of the play. Perdita occupies the centre of the image, dressed for the sheep-shearing feast as the embodiment of Flora. What seems to be provided by the image is a meditation on the combination of the mature Perdita as a nature goddess and the language of fairy possession that surrounds her abandonment and discovery. This allows for the inclusion of the ambiguous fairy-figures in the upper left quadrant of the tondo, familiar from other paintings on related themes: it is as if Perdita has survived them and reached maturity as a goddess in Ferdinand's eyes, and is now waiting to take on her role as rural hostess, imaged in a version of the traditional fairy-tale setting of the sleeping

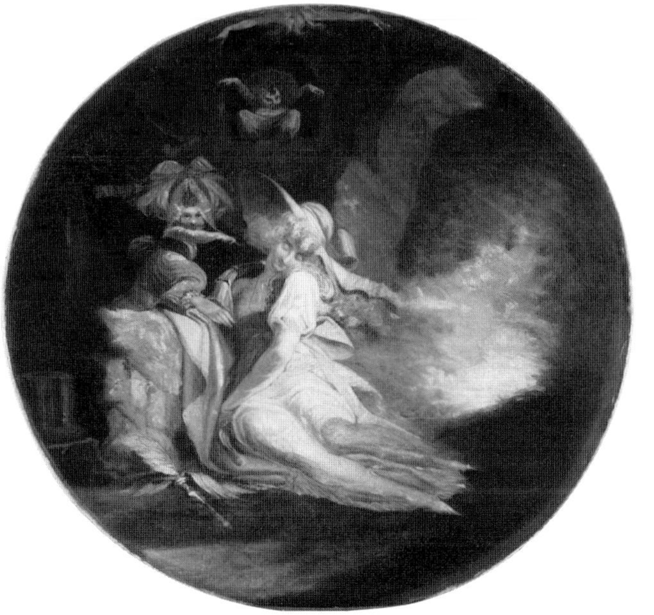

83 Henry Fuseli, *Perdita*, 1785–6.

princess. By including the fairies alongside the rustic feast-dress of Perdita, Fuseli has drawn together the two extremes of her life as presented in the play. The result is that the image encloses the range covered in the two other tondi, as well as presenting a self-contained critical statement that reveals the close links between the worlds of fairy mythology and rural life.

Seen together, the three images offer an extension of the play that, taking its cue from specific details of the text, fills in the sixteen-year interval in the life of Perdita. The imagery of the natural world, in the enclosed, flowering spaces by which the central character is surrounded, continues the rural discourse that is one strand of the sheep-shearing scene, and this is balanced by the elves and fairies that develop the supernatural strain of the play's action and language. The eroticism of the series foreshadows her marriage to Florizel and offers a gloss on the jealousy of Leontes with which the play began. Another reference underlies the images: they exist in dialogue with the tradition of engravings of individual characters that was a popular strand of Shakespeare imaging. *Perdita* and the *Butterfly* tondo also refer, in the costume of the central character, to the tradition of open-air portraiture developed by Gainsborough. The first of these is enriched by the addition of levels of textual analysis and commentary simply absent in most character studies; the second, by a parodic thrust inflected with a flirtatious, challenging eroticism. These qualities of painterly self-reflection if

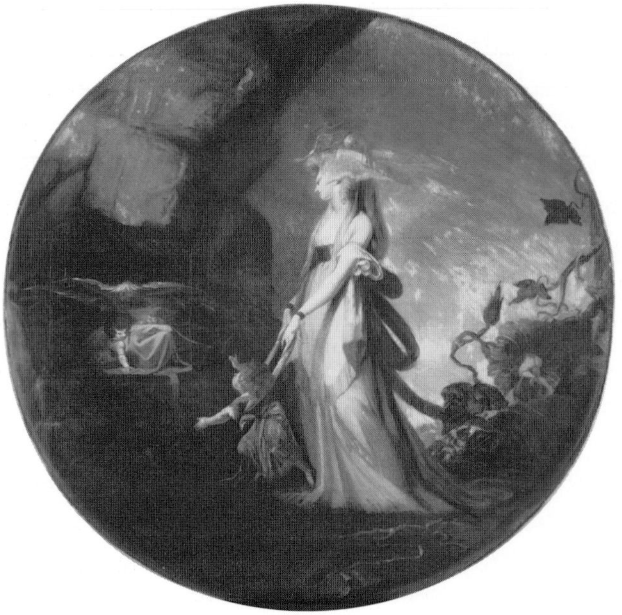

84 Henry Fuseli, *Mamillius in Charge of a Lady of the Court*, 1785–6.

anything make the dialogue between image and text more resonant still because of the awareness of the different media it creates.

Mamillius in Charge of a Lady of the Court (see Fig. 84),[58] the remaining tondo, stands a little apart from the others: its relationship rests on its treatment of the words of Mamillius at the beginning of the second act:

HERMIONE Pray you sit down by us,
And tell 's a tale
MAMILLIUS Merry or sad shall't be?
HERMIONE As merry as you will.
MAMILLIUS A sad tale's best for winter; I have one
Of sprites and goblins.
HERMIONE Let's have that one, good sir.
Come on, sit down, come on, and do your best
To fright me with your sprites; you're powerful at it.
MAMILLIUS There was a man –
HERMIONE Nay, come sit down, then on.
MAMILLIUS Dwelt in a churchyard – I will tell it softly,
Yon crickets shall not hear it.
HERMIONE Come on then, and give't me in mine ear.
Enter Leontes, Antigonus and Lords. (2.1.22–32)

The passage is intriguing because, while it suggests itself as the winter's tale from which the play takes its title, the tale itself is absent, deferred by the interruptions from Hermione about how it should be told and finally prevented by the entry of Leontes. There is no sequence to the tale, but a good deal of atmosphere, and the exchange, with Hermione's instructions and Mamillius' questions, is as much about the business of telling as about a tale itself. All that the audience hears is concerned with the setting: the tale exists in the circle of magic, mythology, and rural legend. In this, it shares qualities visualised in the other three images: a dual relation of fairy and rustic lore within a tale hinted at but never told. This very particular narrative deferral binds together the four images, allowing the onlooker to recognise the quality as part of the play's own peculiar identity.

Fuseli's image unites the two elements by showing a landscape inhabited by strange fairy shapes familiar from the other supernatural paintings of the mid 1780s. At the right, the fairy who disappears into the calyx of a flower is quoted from *Titania's Awakening*; to the left, the two fairies seated on a shelf of rock recall the central figure from the roughly contemporary *Cobweb* tondo, while above them is the bat-like figure from Fuseli's *Tempest* paintings. Together they suggest the imaginings of a folk mythology. The image is linked more closely to the structure of the passage from the play by the way in which the figure of Mamillius is reaching out to them: they come to represent the unattainable other, fascinating but remote, of the terrifying folk-tale, here given another dimension of deferral in the tale's incompleteness. The narrative circumstances of the episode are reinforced by the presence of the female courtier leading the child, representing the heavily gendered location of the start of the scene. Fairy-exoticism, the familiar setting of the countryside, the narrative circumstance of the play, and the unachieved status of the tale are all brought together in the image: Mamillius reaches for the fairy world as we reach for the narrative, and each becomes metaphoric of the other, at the same time as the image becomes a visual metaphor of the play text.

The two dialogues of these four images, with character and with the tradition of character-illustration, reveal simultaneously the limitations of many earlier, conventional character depictions and the extreme narrative subtlety and risk of *The Winter's Tale*. At the same time they invite the onlooker to speculate further about the childhood and youth of this central, yet perplexing, character whose history is lost, as her name suggests. Fuseli's suite of Perdita images becomes almost a Stanislavskian exploration of character, an experiment in visual criticism that builds on the text's lacunae, simultaneously to explode the earlier tradition of visual character studies and to prepare the ground for nineteenth- and twentieth-century appropriation and adaptation of character. This is a response to Shakespeare's play of a new order of originality, that offers as much a personal creative meditation as a critical reading. In Shakespeare painting it is matched only, appropriately enough, in the work of Blake (see Chapter 6); in the critical reading of *The Winter's Tale*, it is a conceptual forebear of Auden's *The Sea and The Mirror*.[59]

VI

To refer to these works as Fuseli's supernatural paintings is to diminish them both in terms of their subjects and because they move towards something far richer in their approach to painting as a critical act. The insistent conundrum of the triangular relation of painting, text, and reader, which for Fuseli is always creatively confused by the use of arcane iconographic sources, is solved in the paintings of *A Midsummer Night's Dream* by a triumphal reversal in which this sheer otherworldly inaccessibility constitutes their mesmeric attraction. That they simultaneously make detailed and suggestive critical comments through an accretion of allusive layers is not necessarily contradictory or ironic. the power derived from this palimpsest is apparent even if its origins remain obscure. It becomes clear through the movement from these images to those of *The Tempest*, and most completely in the *Winter's Tale* tondi, that the level of intellection is that rare kind in which the creative and the critical, those absurd categories, are imaginatively and exultantly collapsed into each other. The allusion to Auden is doubly appropriate, since his composition is as rare in literary tradition as Fuseli's remains in painterly ones. What surrounds Fuseli's work, most of all in the Boydell Gallery, cannot make the leap to this kind of invention, and what comes after it simply has other concerns. In both Auden and Fuseli the temper of imagination has another continuity. The successors of both these forms are most properly those works that return to the medium in which they find their origin. Only in the Shakespearean theatre, in those productions that unite precision of textual reading with the bold stroke of interpretive utterance, is this quality realised – and, it must be said, realised very rarely. It is not that the imaginative circle is completed, but that the spiral of interpretive recreation continues to ascend.

This process is, of course, not the concern of this book, except in that in some ways it foreshadows the varieties of looping back and forth between stage and imagination that are a very particular dimension of Shakespeare visualisation in the nineteenth century. At the close of the eighteenth, the visual imagination worked for most painters and readers in different ways, with images often functioning as much as a critique of social processes as of the plays themselves. The paintings that surrounded those of Fuseli and Reynolds on the walls of the Boydell Shakespeare Gallery demonstrate these functions in many different ways, and the engravings made from them offer in consequence a different kind of reading experience from those produced to satisfy earlier tastes. These images, and the cultural forces that they enact, are the subject of the next chapter.

NOTES

1. The earliest was produced in 1781, 101 × 127 (40 × 50), Detroit Institute of Art, with at least two others following before 1790. It was also engraved, and formed the basis of a number of political cartoons; see D. H. Weinglass, *Prints and Engraved Illustrations By and After Henry Fuseli* (Aldershot: Scolar, 1994), pp. 55–7.
2. Presumably because it was ready earlier, conceivably because Opie would be paid less: here as elsewhere for the Gallery the absence of records is complete. The painting itself is now lost; engraved by Charles Gauthier Playter and Robert Thew, published 1 December 1796, 50 × 62.5 ($19\frac{3}{4}$ × $24\frac{5}{8}$).
3. The whole of Fuseli's sixth Academy lecture is devoted to this topic: see Knowles, *Life and Writings*, II, pp. 273–301.
4. Watercolour with touches of white bodycolour on card, 32.3 × 39.4 ($12\frac{3}{4}$ × $15\frac{1}{2}$), Kunsthaus Zürich.
5. 101 × 127 ($39\frac{3}{4}$ × 50), Tate Britain.
6. *Authentic Shakespeare*, pp. 246–7, 251–2.
7. In Jane Martineau et al., *Shakespeare in Art*, exh. cat. (London: Merrell, 2003), p. 119.
8. 87 × 112 ($34\frac{1}{4}$ × $44\frac{1}{8}$), Richard J. Carrott, Riverside, California.
9. Untraced; engraved by James Caldwell, published 23 April 1798, 50 × 63 ($19\frac{11}{16}$ × $24\frac{13}{16}$).
10. 167.7 × 134.3 (66 × $52\frac{7}{8}$), Folger Shakespeare Library, Washington D.C.
11. Knowles, III, pp. 189–90.
12. 167.7 × 134.6 (66 × 53), National Trust, Petworth House.
13. 221 × 160 (87 × 63), Musée du Louvre, Paris.
14. Pen and grey wash on card, 30.7 × 43.2 ($12\frac{1}{8}$ × 17), British Museum, London.
15. 216 × 274 (85 × $107\frac{7}{8}$), Tate Britain. Engraved by Jean Pierre Simon, published 29 September 1796, 49.5 × 62.5 ($19\frac{1}{2}$ × $24\frac{5}{8}$).
16. Galleria Borghese, Rome.
17. Marble, height 370 ($145\frac{5}{8}$), Museo Archeologico Nazionale, Naples. See Tomory, *The Life and Art of Henry Fuseli*, p. 100.
18. *Henry Fuseli*, p. 62.
19. 45.7 ($18\frac{1}{2}$) diameter, Pierre Jeannerat, London.
20. The pun was first identified by Gert Schiff (*Henry Fuseli*, p. 107) in the discussion of its use in Fuseli's *Belinda's Awakening* (1780–90) that treats *The Rape of the Lock*.
21. Review of *The Papilios or Butterflies of Great Britain* by W. Levin, *Analytical Review*, XXII (December 1795), p. 583.

22. Review of *Rarer Lepidopterous Insects of Georgia* by J. E. Smith, *Analytical Review*, XXVII (January 1798), pp. 1–2.
23. For example, *Henker mit Kopf eines Enthaupteten (Executioner with the head of a decapitated man)*, 1777, pen and sepia ink over pencil on paper, 22.7 × 18.5 ($8\,^{15}/_{16} \times 7\,^{1}/_{4}$), Staatliche Kunstsammlungen, Weimar.
24. Pencil watercolour and ink, 35.9 × 30.2 ($14\,^{3}/_{16} \times 11\,^{7}/_{8}$), Auckland Art Gallery Toi i Tamaka.
25. *The Botanic Garden; A Poem, in Two Parts. Part I. Containing The Economy of Vegetation*. Engraving, 13.0 × 7.8 ($5\,^{1}/_{8} \times 3\,^{1}/_{16}$), facing p. 127.
26. 222 × 280 ($87\,^{3}/_{8} \times 110\,^{1}/_{4}$), Kunstmuseum, Winterthur. Engraved by Thomas Ryder and Thomas Ryder Jr., published 1 December 1803.
27. See Stuart Sillars, 'An Eighteenth-century *Midsummer Night's Dream* Illustration', *British Journal for Eighteenth-Century Studies*, Vol. 4 No. 2 (Summer 1981), pp. 80–8.
28. For a discussion of the issues raised by such productions, see Margo Hendricks, '"Obscured by dreams": Race, Empire and Shakespeare's *A Midsummer Night's Dream*', *Shakespeare Quarterly*, Vol. 47 No. 1 (Spring 1996), pp. 37–60.
29. 'The Sun Rising', *John Donne, The English Poems*, ed. A. J. Smith (Harmondsworth: Penguin, 1971), pp. 80–1.
30. 154 × 215 ($60\,^{5}/_{8} \times 84\,^{5}/_{8}$), Tate Britain.
31. Private collection, untraced; pencil on paper partly washed in orange, 23.5 × 18.3 ($9 \times 7\,^{1}/_{2}$), Christie's sale, 14 April 1992. See *Drawings by Henry Fuseli, R.A. From a Private Collection*, auction cat., (London: Christie's, 1992), pp. 50–51.
32. See for example Peter Tomory, *The Life and Art of Henry Fuseli* (London: Thames and Hudson, 1972), p. 169.
33. Pencil heightened with white, 33 × 41.1 ($13 \times 16\,^{3}/_{16}$), Auckland Art Gallery Toi i Tamaki.
34. In this text, translated from the French in 1570 by Lord Berners, Huon 'had about his neck a rich horn'. The text is reprinted in *Illustrations of the Fairy Mythology of* A Midsummer Night's Dream, ed. James Orchard Halliwell (London: Shakespeare Society, 1845), pp. 91–119; quotation from p. 97.
35. 101 × 127 (40 × 50), Detroit Institute of Art, Chicago.
36. Reprinted as *The Mad Pranks and Merry Jests of Robin Goodfellow*, intro. J. Payne Collier (London: Percy Society, 1841), p. 42. Collier's introduction asserts that, while the text is reprinted from a rare copy dated 1628, there is 'little or no doubt' that it first appeared before 1588 (Introduction, p. vi.).
37. 169 × 135 ($66\,^{1}/_{2} \times 53\,^{1}/_{8}$), Kunthaus Zürich.
38. 169 × 135 ($66\,^{1}/_{2} \times 53\,^{1}/_{8}$), Private collection, Switzerland.
39. 5–7 May 1789.
40. *A descriptive catalogue of the prints from Boydell's Shakspeare gallery done for the benefit of my daughter isabel eustis [francis] in two volumes, one hundred prints* [sic]. c. 1800. The manuscript notebook is in the Folger Shakespeare Library, S.a.37.
41. 65 × 91.5 ($25\,^{5}/_{8} \times 36\,^{1}/_{8}$), Kunsthaus Zürich, 75 × 90.2 ($29\,^{1}/_{2} \times 35\,^{1}/_{2}$) Royal Shakespeare Theatre, Stratford-on-Avon, 35 × 44.5 ($13\,^{3}/_{4} \times 17\,^{1}/_{2}$), North Carolina Museum of Art, Raleigh.

42. 45.8 × 55.5 (18 5/16 × 21 7/8).
43. Except for the small section with the head of Prospero, now in the City of York Art Gallery. Engraved by Jean Pierre Simon, published 29 September 1797, 49.5 × 62.5 (19 1/2 × 24 5/8).
44. *Works*, I, p. 22.
45. 1802, oil on canvas, 91.5 × 71.5 (36 × 28 1/8), Ulrich Collection, Zürich. Engraved by Charles Warren, 11.5 × 8.8 (4 1/16 × 3 1/2), *Paradise Lost* (London: du Roveray, 1802), I, facing p. 93, to illustrate lines 740ff.
46. 24.8 × 17.8 (9 3/4 × 7). The image refers to Volume I Canto I lines 69–80. That the figure of Flora bears some resemblance to that of Miranda in costume, facial features and the position of the right hand may strengthen the allusion.
47. 92.7 × 71.5 (36 1/2 × 28 1/4), Folger Shakespeare Library, Washington D.C.
48. 102 × 82 (40 1/8 × 33 7/16), Folger Shakespeare Library, Washington D.C.
49. *The Winter's Tale*, ed. Stephen Orgel, The Oxford Shakespeare (Oxford: Clarendon, 1996). All subsequent quotations are from this edition.
50. *Henry Fuseli*, p. 60.
51. *Mädchen mit Schmetterlingen, zwischen ihren Knien kleine Fairy*, diameter 46.5 (18 5/16), Erben Leon Bollags, Zürich.
52. *Mädchen am Spinett und Elfenbote*, diameter 46.5 (18 5/16), Erben Leon Bollags, Zürich.
53. Tomory, *Fuseli*, p. 169.
54. *c.* 1800, 71 × 91 (27 9/10 × 36 4/10), Kunstmuseum, Basle. See Frederick Antal, *Fuseli Studies* (London: Routledge, 1956), p. 102.
55. Watercolour and body colour, 40 × 31.5 (15 3/4 × 12 3/8), Kunsthaus Zürich.
56. For example, *Symplegma of a Man and Three Women*, 1809–10, pencil heightened with colour, 18.0 × 24.5 (7 7/8 × 9 5/8), Victoria and Albert Museum, London.
57. Diameter 43 (17 1/4), Hinton Ampner, The Ralph Dutton Collection (The National Trust).
58. Diameter 43 (17 1/4), Hinton Ampner, The Ralph Dutton Collection (The National Trust).
59. *The Sea and The Mirror: A Commentary on Shakespeare's 'The Tempest'*, 1944, ed. Arthur Kirsch (Princeton, N.J. and Oxford: Princeton University Press, 2003).

CHAPTER 9

'A MAGNIFICENT SCHEME, IF IT CAN BUT BE EFFECTED':[1] BOYDELL, CRITICISM AND APPROPRIATION

I

In November 1786 Josiah Boydell entertained to dinner his uncle, the print-publisher Alderman John Boydell. Among the other guests were the artists Benjamin West, Paul Sandby, and George Romney; the King's Bookseller George Nicol; and the poet and patron William Hayley. At some stage in the evening, the idea of what was to become the Boydell Shakespeare Gallery was raised. Exactly who made the suggestion would later be much disputed, but the result was clear: the commissioning of a number of paintings from a diversity of British artists, each one treating a scene from one of the plays, that would together establish a national school of painting to equal those from the rest of Europe.[2] The paintings would be reproduced as large-format engravings that would make the images familiar in England and beyond, and also prove a sound commercial venture. When the Prospectus was issued on 1 December 1786, in addition to the 'Series of Large and Capital Prints,' it offered 'A Most Magnificent and Accurate Edition' of the plays, edited by George Steevens.[3] Both would be issued in serial parts, of which 'one number, at least, shall be published annually', and sold by subscription.

The scheme progressed on an ambitious scale. A new gallery, designed by George Dance, was built at 52 Pall Mall, on the site of the house owned by the dramatist and publisher Robert Dodsley. Located in the newly fashionable area of London, close to Piccadilly and St James's and in the same street as Christie's auction rooms, the Gallery was an immediate success when it opened at noon on 4 May 1789 (see Plate 16), with 34 paintings by 18 artists. An advertisement in *The Times* reminded subscribers to collect their 'Tickets of Perpetual Free Admission' and then announced 'Admittance to the Public, One Shilling'.[4] The next year a further 22 paintings were added, and from 1791 the prints were displayed, as they became available, on the lower floor. A catalogue was issued that contained extensive passages from the plays, in some cases including the complete scene depicted, and rarely of less than three pages.[5] Humphry Repton produced *The Bee*,[6] a 54-page pamphlet review, ostensibly independent, but in fact written at Boydell's instigation; it contained short appraisals of each painting, often in comparison with the text. When the Gallery reopened after an expansion in 1802 another catalogue was issued, listing 167 paintings by 33 artists, again accompanied by lengthy quotations.[7] A final version, published in 1805 – 'being the last time the pictures can ever be seen as an entire collection' – gave short passages for the first 20 images and then simply listed titles, act and scene numbers and the characters shown.[8]

These publications suggest that the images were the subject of serious discussion, not only as paintings but as critical enactments of the scenes they presented: that the first catalogue contained nearly 100 pages and was issued in plain boards makes clear that it was intended to be bound in the purchaser's own more elaborate style, perhaps as a work of reference to the large prints as they became available. Both features show the venture in its social and critical terrain: concerned with the plays and their discussion, it is also part of a commercial exchange, available not only to those who would formerly have commissioned paintings but to those of a lower but still affluent rank, who would have their books bound for them and could afford costly subscriptions. Repton's involvement is similarly important: the choice of a garden designer and theorist suggests a milieu of the country house at once aristocratic and uniquely English. The Gallery's social and aesthetic position is emblematised in the sculpture by Thomas Banks, *Shakespeare between the Dramatic Muse and the Genius of Painting*, that adorned the upper story of the building's façade (see Fig. 2). Based on the tomb of Lorenzo de'Medici by Michelangelo, it revisited the Choice trope discussed by Shaftesbury, with the muse of painting proclaiming the dramatist to the onlooker – who in practical terms was the fashionable citizen walking down Pall Mall – as 'the proper Object of her pencil'.[9] In its self-reflexive idiom it wittily proclaimed Shakespeare's annexation by painting: metaphorically, it stood for the subsumption of the plays into a new level of material culture.

Important though the display of the paintings was, both for Boydell's revenue and as a form of discourse critical as well as social, the main thrust lay in the production of the engravings. The effective supremacy of prints over paintings as cultural objects was now quite clear: paintings were primarily the first stage in the production of reproductive engravings. While income from the Gallery was important for Boydell, the sale of engravings was potentially far more lucrative since it would last longer and exploit a wider market. A major consequence of this has been overlooked by earlier critics who dismiss as negligible many of the Boydell images:[10] the change in status of the individual work has repercussions on the structures and devices used to transmit meaning and the ideological assumptions they enfold. The images of Reynolds, West, Fuseli and a handful of others are important in the wider current of eighteenth-century English art and as works of Shakespearean criticism; but those produced by less renowned artists have as much to reveal in defining a wider response to the plays. Painting in England in the eighteenth century was always a fundamentally commercial as well as an aesthetic endeavour,[11] and this gained an extra dimension with the spread of large-scale engraving. Boydell's scheme is the most complete embodiment of the unity between these impulses within a force-field of social, cultural and intellectual resonances: the result is that the engravings transmit their textual readings within ideological, conceptual and emotional frames made genuinely contemporary by the simple need to sell.

The original scheme was to reproduce the paintings both as large engravings and as quarto plates to illustrate the edition of the plays. In 1794, however, Boydell commissioned another series of paintings, mainly from established book illustrators, that would serve the latter function after display in the Gallery. Almost all of them depict, in vertical format, two or three figures before a setting appropriate to the play, and lack the scale and breadth, both literal and conceptual, of the large paintings. When the large prints finally appeared in volume form in 1805, they numbered 100 rather than the 72 promised in the Prospectus; of these, 16 were also reproduced as small engravings, although there seems no clear reason for their selection. One obvious assumption is that there were insufficient images for each play, suggesting a lack of overall planning apparent in many other dimensions of the scheme.

The first serial part of the edition was available, in its turquoise boards for subsequent binding, in January 1791. The earliest folio prints bear the date 4 June 1790 – two images of *Much Ado* by Peters and Hamilton and the first of Northcote's three treatments of *Richard III*. In March 1791, the final *Much Ado* image appeared, and with it the second *Richard III*, but it was not until June 1795 that the last engraving for this play was issued. This was presumably a combination of production circumstance and marketing strategy: the engravings became available in no particular order, depending on the time it took to produce the plates, so that delaying publication until all images for one play were complete made no commercial sense. Issuing them in a random order was also sound commercial practice, since it would encourage subscribers to maintain their interest in acquiring the whole series instead of stopping when certain plays were completed.

Little detail survives of the subscription procedure, and that which does is far from clear. The remark made by Malone in a letter to Lord Charlemont that 'there were not above twenty names among them that anybody knew'[12] refers to those subscribing before the Gallery opened, and may owe its origin to traditional English aristocratic disdain. The only surviving list is that made available for signature in the Gallery itself, comprising 80 pages of vellum on the first of which is written, in flowing copperplate, *The Signatures of the Subscribers to Shakespeare.*[13] After those of the King, Queen and Prince of Wales, it contains 752 names, far short of the eventual total of 1,384. It is not clear whether all the signatories purchased both prints and edition (from the second proposal of 1790[14] it was possible to choose either, or both), so that at best it can give only a rough idea of what may have been the composition of the subscribers, and even less of their origins or ideologies.

It is, however, abundantly evident that the cost of subscribing to the whole scheme – 54 guineas (£56.70) for the prints and 36 guineas (£37.80) for the edition – and the scale of the volumes, two imperial folios and nine large quartos respectively, would have restricted its availability to those of significant means, not only for its purchase but also for its storage and display. The combined price was the equivalent of an annual income – in many cases a generous one – for a clergyman, schoolmaster or merchant, and was approaching twice the annual fees, including board, for a pupil at Eton. Consequently, if Winifred Friedman's claim that many of the subscribers were 'members of the new middle classes'[15] has any truth, the term must be defined as referring to those who lived in town houses in the newer parts of London – Berkeley Square, Grosvenor Square, Cavendish Square and most recently Bedford Square – and had arrived there through commerce or industry rather than inheritance. The surviving list in large measure supports this, but embraces a range of interests. Of the 752 signatories, roughly a tenth can be located within the aristocracy – earls, peers and baronets – with nearly three hundred giving addresses in London, often in the newer streets and squares. There are subscriptions from the Bodleian; the library of the University of Edinburgh; the libraries of King's and Emmanuel Colleges, Cambridge; Chetham's Library, Manchester; Bristol Library Society; and three booksellers, a small figure that suggests the unlikelihood of further sales. Among the more familiar names are Warren Hastings, returned in 1785 from his role as Governor-General of India; Josiah Wedgwood, Queen's Potter and inventor of the famed 'jasper ware'; Thomas Coutts, the banker; John Julius Angerstein, the instigator of the modern Lloyd's insurance market, whose collection of paintings would later form the nucleus of the National Gallery; Charles James Fox, the politician; and Uvedale Price, the writer and landscape theorist. Those from further afield include Johann Samuel Steinhübel in Eperies in Hungary; Jacob Friedrich von der Nüll (?) in Vienna; Jacques de Bulhakov, Membre de l'Academie Imperiale de St Petersburg; William Burroughs Esq., Advocate General of Bengal; John Barker Church of New York; and Robert Burton of 'Richmond Virginiae'.

Just as important are the names, less known, of those from outside London, of which there are a good 200.[16] They include Valentine Jones, Bailbrook House, Near Bath; Edmund Battersbee, Stratford upon Avon; Francis Wilson, Vauxhall, Surry [sic]; Will'm Green, Stanway Hall, Colchester; B (?) Malkin, Hackney; Rev'd John Lamb DD, Shelswell(?) Oxon; Sam'l Knight, Milton, Cambridgeshire; George C. George of Penryn Cornwall Esq; and George Bowles, Wanstead Grove. There are ten addresses in Scotland, two in Monmouthshire, and one in Guernsey: there are two Members of Parliament and two professors. The names of about forty women appear: they include Mary Hockley, Hants; Ann Fisher, Ealing Park; Henrietta Maria Goddard, Harley Street, Miss Shallon, Chesham, Bucks; Mary Stratton, Chalent House, near Westbury, Wilts; Catherine Hussey of Lamberhurst; Phoebe Webster; Catherine Blackburne, Liverpool; and Anne Damer, who had produced the two terracotta bas-reliefs that were reproduced on the title pages of the volumes of prints. In some ways the absences are as revealing: the list does not contain the names of major literary or theatrical figures, locating the practice of reading the edition and the prints within a different discursive setting, although their signatures may have appeared on the other list or lists now untraced.

In addition to the subscribers, the prints were seen and owned by those who purchased individual numbers, containing four or five prints, or single impressions, available at one guinea; no list remains of either group. Another aspect of the Gallery of which little evidence survives is the transatlantic marketing of the prints. The Philadelphia *General Advertiser* of 4 December 1792 carried an advertisement offering the first number and inviting subscriptions, at the auction house of A. Hubley: no list has come to light. An index of the images' breadth of exposure is, however, suggested by the presence of two of the prints, Fuseli's *Titania and Bottom* and Smirke's treatment of the Induction from *The Taming of the Shrew*, among the collection of Thomas Jefferson at Monticello, where they still hang.[17] Since Jefferson was in the habit of discussing his art collection with his guests, the discourse surrounding these images in this setting must be counted among the earliest American critical explorations of Shakespeare.

Apart from the clues given in the surviving subscription list, there is little to reveal the subscribers' interests, outlooks or familiarity with the plays. That the prints themselves had as accompanying text the central word 'Shakspeare', archaically spelled to give an antiquarian rather than a scholarly authority, flanked by ten or twelve lines (from Steevens' edition, and personally proof-read by him[18]) to fix the image within the play, suggests a desire to make the images more readily understood by those with little textual knowledge. Repton's allusion in *The Bee* to the paintings as showing 'scenes with which we are all acquainted' (p. 5) may well include an element of flattery in welcoming his readers into an educated, fashionable circle. The limitation of audience through wealth may suggest a contraction of ideological breadth, but it is pertinent to remember here that political allegiances in the eighteenth century did not always follow the patterns that a twenty-first century reader would assume. While the ideological bases of the paintings are in many instances consistent, there are areas, most particularly with regard to the landscape, where a far greater range of readings is possible.

Whatever the nature and limits of the readership, it is clear that the range of styles and stances of the painters themselves was broad, since the scale of the venture meant that almost every available painter was asked to contribute. Boydell broke from his practice of employing British artists in only two cases, 'Angelica' (Angelica Kauffman) who was 'looked upon as an English Artist' and 'Mr Ramberg a Foreigner' who had 'resided here many years'.[19] At its conclusion, the Gallery contained paintings by 33 artists, whose work was reproduced by 46 printmakers. Some, most notably the images discussed in preceding chapters, made complex use of iconographical reference and other devices to construct compositional inventions of much critical weight. Other painters, whose earlier experience might have been with Rococo landscapes, sporting paintings or book illustration, brought a different expertise to the task. The result is a collection of wide variation in style and approach, and inevitably also in quality, but within this variety the principle laid down by Jonathan Richardson still holds good: the images select a significant moment of the action as the basis of depiction, rather than presenting the forces of the play schematically as does Hogarth. The moment is made explicit in each engraving by the quotation presented beneath it; its relation to the rest of the play, in terms of character, action, ideas or language, often determines the nature and value of the analytical readings that ensue.

How the scenes were chosen is not known. No record exists of Boydell's having issued instructions to individual artists of the kind Hayman received from Hanmer, and there is certainly no evidence of there having been any overall scheme or systematic approach to the plays. Instead, it seems that individual artists approached Boydell with suggestions for subjects, ideas about treatments, or requests for commissions.[20] In some cases, paintings had been begun before the scheme was mooted. Fuseli's *Midsummer Night's Dream* images come into this category, and Northcote's first image from *Richard III* was completed and exhibited before the 1786 dinner – indeed, Northcote claimed that its existence was one reason for the Gallery's foundation.[21]

If Boydell offered no suggestions, others did. Edward Jerningham's *The Shakspeare Gallery* urges the rejection of 'mawkish portraits' and instead advocates a higher form:

From these we turn to scenes of higher aim
Where Eagle-Genius soars to nobler game;
Where Fancy, Reason, Taste, in one conjoin'd
Unfold the workings of th' impassion'd mind.
Now to the laurell'd, academic band,
To ev'ry artist's emulative hand,
Munificence upholds her sacred prize,
And bids the daring reach it from the skies[22]

The coming together of the three qualities in the third line, and the reference to the 'academic band', suggest an enterprise that is intellectual and aesthetic in its pursuit of the highest principles of the academy, and the implicit rejection of sentiment reinforces the painting of Shakespeare as a high endeavour. The remainder of the poem 'attempts to point out new subjects for future exhibitions' ('Advertisement', unnumbered); of the twenty or so suggestions, four, including Juliet's awakening in the tomb and 'The hair-dishevelled prophetess of Troy' (p. 14), later became subjects of the Gallery. This is not to imply that the poem recorded Boydell's instructions, or had any influence, but rather that the idea of selecting passages for painting was being given serious thought in the years before the Gallery opened.

More detailed suggestion is offered in a much more substantial publication, *Imperfect Hints towards a new edition of Shakespeare*, which appeared in two parts, the first of about 150 pages and the second of over 200, in 1787–8.[23] Beginning with an outline plan of the edition, which would follow precedent and include earlier prefaces and a selection of poems on Shakespeare, it then gives detailed recommendations for images illustrating thirteen of the plays. Some are reprints of images from earlier editions, some copies of Old Master paintings, and some suggestions for new images. Its value is in showing the extent of serious critical concern for the visualisation of character, scene and action, although the suggestions almost without exception have no bearing on the paintings produced for the Gallery. Almost all of the proposed images rest on theatrical precedent, those for *The Merchant of Venice* for example repeatedly stressing the need to reproduce the gestures of Macklin as Shylock.

Quite the opposite approach is taken by a letter in the *Gentleman's Magazine* in 1788. This urges the rejection of 'the meretricious foppery of the modern stage', stressing by implication the superior power of the imagination:

> To prevent such expectations from taking root in the minds of tasteless individuals, it would not have been amiss had Messrs. Boydell advertised us, that their first instruction to their artists was, to forget, if possible, they had ever seen the plays of Shakespeare, as they are absurdly decorated in modern theatres.[24]

This is the approach followed by most of the Boydell images, although a few incorporate aspects of recent performances. William Hamilton's treatment of *Love's Labour's Lost* (1793),[25] for example, and John Downman's *As You Like It* (late 1780s?)[26] both reproduce Sarah Siddons' posture and gestures, but fill the surrounding space with a pastoral landscape and architectural forms, fashionable Gothic in the former and rather confused Neo-Classical in the latter. In general, the stage has been displaced by what has by now become the dominant cultural mode: a realist, personal narrative, apparent in the novel, history, or landscape painting, with all the complex organisations of temporal structures that this entails, and all the social, political and related ideological assumptions it enfolds. The chosen scene is presented as a moment perceived by a single organising consciousness, and at this level, with significant exceptions (including those already considered) the uniformity of approach in the collection seems almost complete.

This apparent realism is often filtered through the *sensibilité* or sentimentality that had recently become fashionable. Often, the moment that seemingly is depicted with transparency has been selected because it demonstrates a crisis of feeling within the play, and the action is suspended to allow due weight to the emotion thus generated. Images that do not depict such tableaux often present events that invite sympathy with character or cause, or imbue a landscape with emotional cues to intensify feeling. Coupled with this is the move away, in all but a few images, from the use of classical iconography to a much more immediate referentialism, another component of the predominant materialist mode. Itself an embedding of ideology within image, the stance in turn enfolds other assumptions shared between image and onlooker: to put it in terms familiar from more recent approaches to the growth of Shakespeare activity, the Boydell images are striking as instances of Shakespeare appropriation as much as of Shakespeare criticism.

The process of appropriation is also related to the different settings in which the images were seen. The public, social activity of visiting the gallery was markedly different from the process of viewing and discussing the two volumes of fifty engravings that finally appeared in 1805. The presence of the quotations from the plays, and the possibility of closer exploration of the ways in which they are visualised in the images, turns this into a separate forum for the expression of critical and ideological stances at any point along an axis from contemporary ideological statement (with one of the plays as its starting point) to close textual commentary. The full title of the two volumes is revealing: A *Collection of Prints / from pictures painted for the purpose of illustrating/ the/ dramatic works/ of / Shakspeare/ by the/ artists of Great-Britain* (see Fig. 85). As noted in Chapter 1, for most of the eighteenth century the word 'illustrating' was used primarily in the sense of providing an annotation or commentary, rather than the modern sense of offering visual treatment of a scene. Volumes such as Boydell's doubtless contributed to the shift in meaning; but the idea of the prints as an explanatory critical tool is certainly one dimension of the word's import in the title. In this context, the subscribers assume greater importance: in the social identities they constitute, both separately and in total, they form the other voice in the interpretive dialogue that the collection of prints invite, and which contemporary reading practices support.

The images, their meanings and their reception demand fuller treatment than is here possible, even when the smaller plates for the edition of the plays are excluded. Some key themes do, however, emerge to suggest the place of the collection within the changing terrain of Shakespeare imaging and Shakespeare activity. They are the interlocking concerns with time and narrative, seen through the related discourses of the novel and popular history; the perception and depiction of the landscape as an ideologically freighted cultural form; and the new kinds of reading experience produced by the sequential presentation of images from single plays within the completed Boydell volumes.

II

Although the Boydell Gallery paintings continue to employ approaches first established by Shaftesbury and Richardson, the majority locate them within a larger conceptual frame. Their master fiction is that of the realist novel, the dominant form of a culture increasingly concerned with material entities seen through apparently transparent narrative sequences. That they do this is significant in

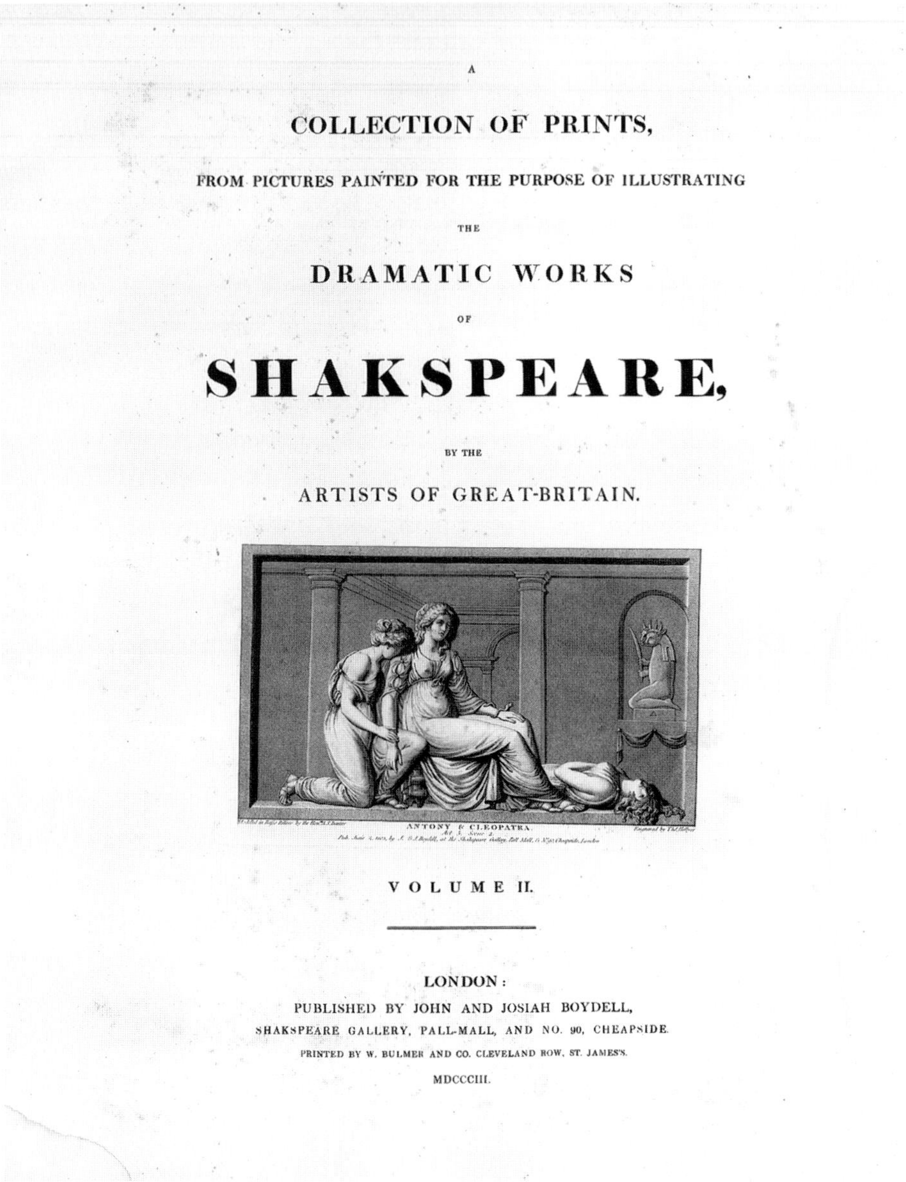

A

COLLECTION OF PRINTS,

FROM PICTURES PAINTED FOR THE PURPOSE OF ILLUSTRATING

THE

DRAMATIC WORKS

OF

SHAKSPEARE,

BY THE

ARTISTS OF GREAT-BRITAIN.

ANTONY & CLEOPATRA.

VOLUME II.

LONDON:

PUBLISHED BY JOHN AND JOSIAH BOYDELL,

SHAKSPEARE GALLERY, PALL-MALL, AND NO. 90, CHEAPSIDE.

PRINTED BY W. BULMER AND CO. CLEVELAND ROW, ST. JAMES'S.

MDCCCIII.

85 Title Page, *A Collection of Prints*, vol. II, 1805. By permission of the Folger Shakespeare Library.

revealing a political ideology that rejects the more functionally subversive, self-reflexive and self-ironising forms of the novel that are an important counter thrust, especially in the work of many women novelists who simultaneously extend and undermine the novel's structures and voices, including Anna Maria Bennett, Charlotte Smith and Jane West – writers whose work found visual equivalents in the satirical prints of Gillray and Rowlandson. Boydell's images are moulded from an innate concern with time, history and narrative so insistent that, even when it is displaced by Fuseli, West and a few others, its presence still remains an essential part of the effect through the shock of its absence. The exchange between the time of the isolated moment and the longer extent of the dramatic text is complicit in a broader relation between the historical period of the play's composition, that of its historical setting, and the larger concept of how history and narrative, in both fact and fiction, are constituted in the aesthetic of the image's production.

This principle rests on the simultaneous growth of the novel and of popular history as narrative forms. The publication in 1753 of Charlotte Mary Lennox's *Shakespeare Illustrated*, with its implicit assumption that narrative realism in the novel was superior to the performative mode of the theatre,[27] reveals that, while the novel and Shakespeare's plays would seem to belong to different cultural frames and reading contexts, the two have converged by the middle of the century through the powerful attraction of the former. David Hume's influential *History of England* (1754–62) engaged in direct competition with the novel for fashionable readers' attention by employing the rival genre's methods. Concerned with the roles of individuals, often sentimental and frequently using invented or reconstructed dialogue, it aimed at presenting a lively and emotionally engaging story with clearly signalled plot lines. It is no chance coincidence that Tobias Smollett was charged with continuing Hume's history to the present after the philosopher's death in 1776; nor is it insignificant that Northcote and Smirke, prolific in their work for Boydell, produced illustrations for the edition published by Bowyer in 1792. The proximity was also physical: Bowyer opened his Historic Gallery in 1793 to display the paintings from which these illustrations were taken, in rooms a few doors away from Boydell's Gallery in Pall Mall. At the same time as the novel was confirming its status as a particular but unquestioned form of reality, history borrowed its structures, enfolding the growing awareness of nationhood within a narrative of individuals and feelings: the temporal concerns of both were given spatial statement in painting.

Within the stances and forms of the Boydell Gallery, the two genres elide. This is most obvious in the presentation of a moment of sentimental intensity within a setting of assumed accuracy of period or location. Treatment of events from a single viewpoint is inevitable within the terms of a visual culture dominated by representationalism, but with Shakespeare imaging it often has the effect of denying the multivalence that is the essence of drama as a dialogic form. Depending on the image, this may result in the flattening out of the generative conflicts by which a play is driven in action, idea, and diction or act instead to concretise them, providing a spatial analogy for the temporal debates of the text. The need for a continuous, involving narrative leads to a desire to present visually events reported, not shown, in the text; and a concern for materiality of presentation itself reflects a larger ideological concern to establish history as an actuality rather than a debate. These factors come together to produce a stance markedly different from those apparent in images of an earlier generation. Zoffany, Hayman or Wilson were content to repeat the mixture of styles and costumes of the contemporary stage without a thought for what would later be called historical accuracy; at a deeper ideological level, Hogarth was able to manipulate historical distances to voice biting criticisms of immediately contemporary political situations. By contrast, the Boydell images of the same plays employ painstakingly accurate architectural forms, complemented by specific elements such as the elaborate canopy and the stance of the king in what, after Holbein, had become the pose from which he was immediately recognised and from which he derived his character, in the Rev. Matthew Peters' treatment of the closing scene of *Henry VIII*.[28] This reveals a very particular ideology: materiality of form is allied to a simple, single view of the historical process which, despite the counter thrusts of Catherine Macaulay, is dominated by a Tudor providentialism in which the history plays move to a glorious and inevitable conclusion in the reign of Elizabeth. The importance of this in defining national identity is particularly strong during the years between the American and French revolutions, when a large proportion of the paintings for the Gallery were completed.

Another dimension of novelistic materialism in the Boydell images is the representation of events narrated rather than enacted in the text, which assimilates them into the continuous narrative constructed by the omniscient narrator of novel or history. This erasure of the distinction between presented and described action not only changes the literary mode from dialogic to diegetic: it also offers new opportunities for comment on language, character and narrative device. Fuseli had, of course, already done this in 1771 in his image of the poisoning of old Hamlet (see Chapter 4), but this image makes reference to thematic and linguistic elements of the whole play and so moves far beyond the constraints of novelistic visualisation. The plays are now rewritten as a seamless progress presented through the eyes of a narrator not only all-knowing but all-seeing.

The transference of the plays into this idiom is revealed most completely in James Northcote's three *Richard III* images. It is instantly evident in their concern with one subject, the murder of the princes in the tower that, seen through the writings of Hume, becomes the major historiographical reinvention of the

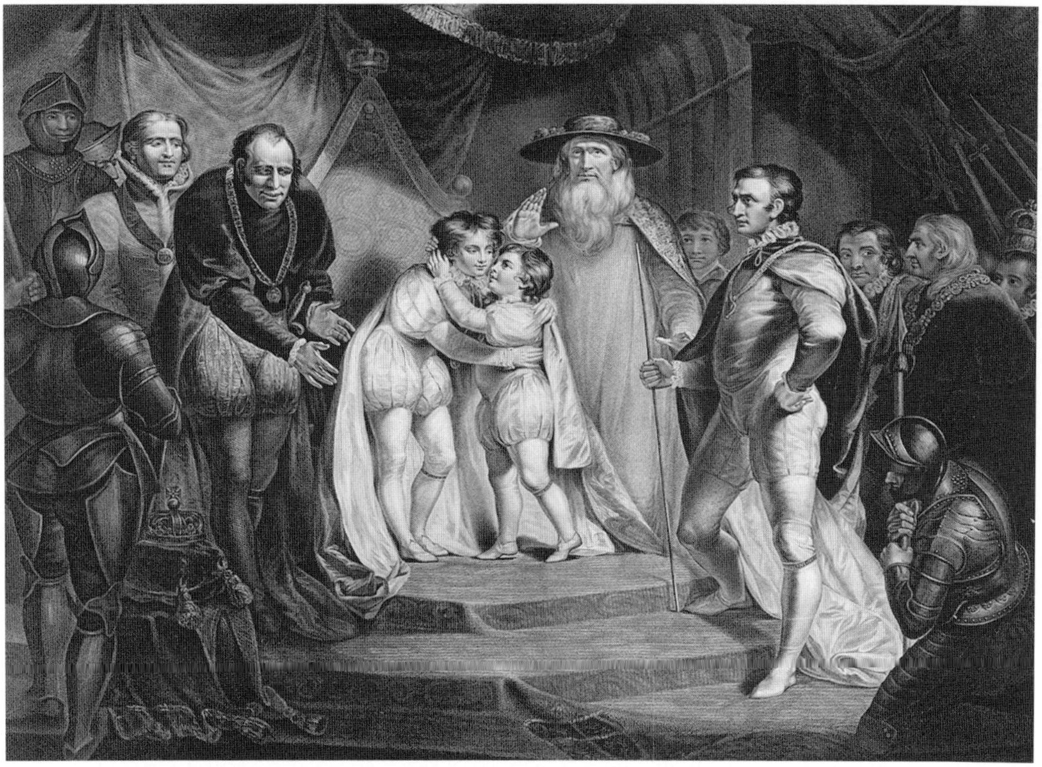

86 James Northcote, *Richard III*, 1. Engraved by Robert Thew, 1791.

play, presenting Richard as the epitome of evil and the murder as his diabolic climacteric. As well as the older sources in More and Edward Hall, Hume drew on more recent writing. John Pointon's *Chronological History of England*, revealingly subtitled *An Impartial Abstract of the most Remarkable Transactions*, gives this account in 1714:

King Richard, to secure the Government to himself, causes his 2 nephews, the Innocent King *Edward* V. and his brother, the Duke of *York*, to be miserably murdered.[29]

This tone is directly rendered in the Boydell images. The first (see Fig. 86)[30] shows the princes in dazzling whiteness before Richard, in terms whose novelistic character-drawing is implicit, as Humphry Repton reveals in the style of his account in *The Bee*, which, like Pointon's account, characterises the main figures through the simple, unqualified terms of the popular romance:

We may observe the innocent salutation of the children, and the contrast between the villainy of *Gloucester* and the manly openness of *Lord Hastings*.[31]

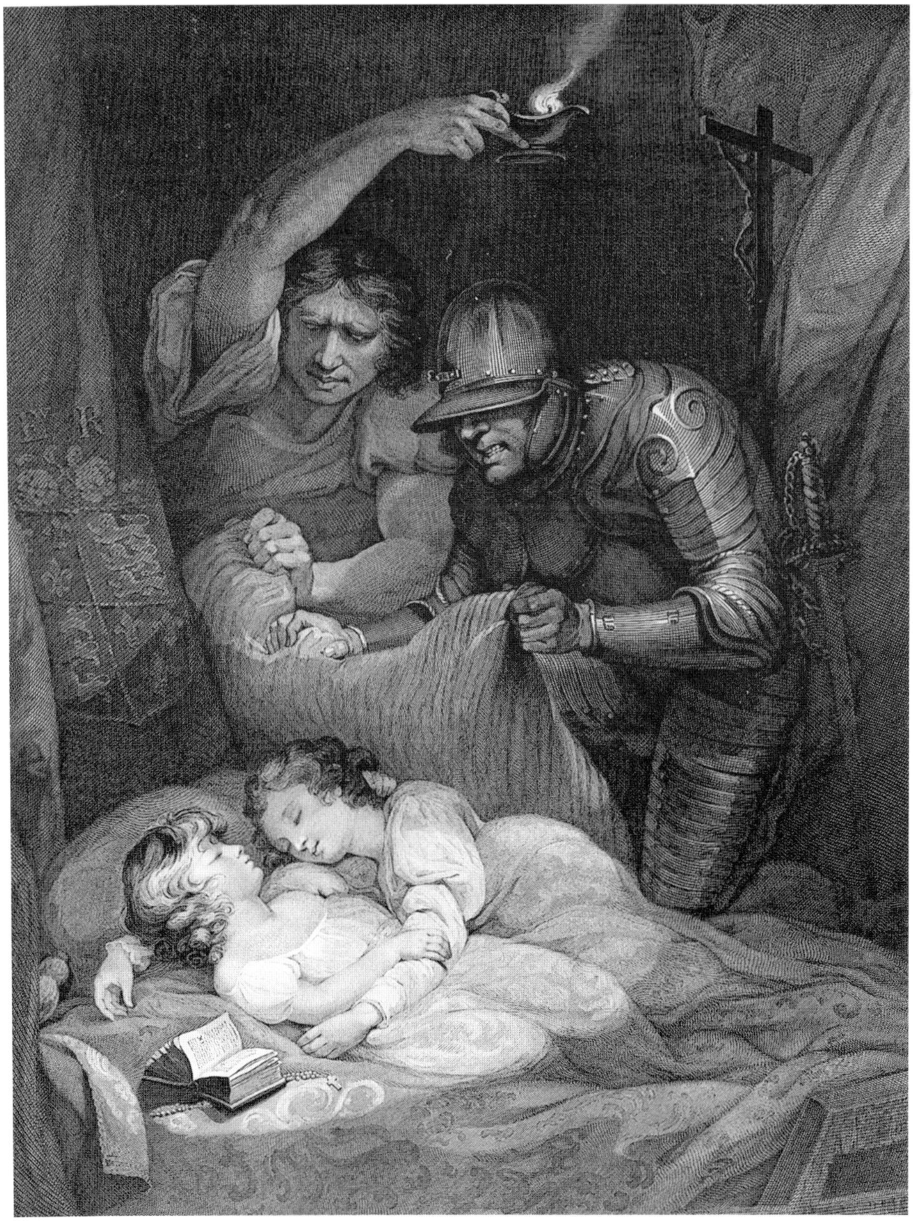

87 James Northcote, *Richard III*, 2. Engraved by Francis Legat, 1790.

To novelistic tradition is added art historical reference: Richard wears the medallion of the order of the garter and the garter itself, continuing the tradition begun by Hogarth. The second image (see Fig. 87) approaches the murder more closely.[32] It visualises the details of Shakespeare's text, the princes' lips 'four red roses on a stalk', their arms 'alabaster innocent', and the 'book of prayers' transformed into an illuminated missal (4.3.12, 11, 14). The episode is reported, not presented, in the play: Tyrell's speech tells of the events whereas Northcote shows them, offering the moment just before the murder in an act of translation that adopts the idiom of the novel in two dimensions, first by presenting action through the eyes of an omniscient narrator and secondly by suspending it at the moment of maximum sentiment just before the killing.

The third image (see Fig. 88)[33] develops further the novelistic history. In the play, Tyrell speaks briefly of the princes' burial:

The chaplain of the tower hath buried them;
But where, to say the truth, I do not know.
(4.3.29–30)

Again, the image dwells on sentiment, showing the bodies being handed down a staircase and ennobling the moment by borrowing the composition of Caravaggio's *Entombment of Christ* (1602–4)[34] which Northcote would have seen in Rome. This is a rare instance in the Boydell collection of the use of Biblical Old Master iconography, but whether or not the original readers established the link the emotional power of the image is still strong, deriving from the situation, and enhanced by the upraised hands at the lower left: a gesture commonly associated with nurture or supplication is turned to darker narrative purpose. The most revealing element of the image is its physical setting. Shakespeare makes no mention of the place of burial, but More places it 'at the stayre foote, metely depe in the grounde under a great heape of stones'[35] and Hume follows this almost exactly:

After suffocating them with the bolster and pillows, they showed their naked bodies to Tyrrell, who ordered them to be buried at the foot of the stairs, deep in the ground under a heap of stones.[36]

Clearly, Northcote's image follows the details recorded by More: Lennox's dicta about Shakespeare's inferiority to his sources have been read in literal terms and applied not to a novel but to a work of history, so close has the relation come between them. Hume's narrative, given added authenticity by a footnote allusion to its source in More, is here silently absorbed into Shakespeare's text: the play, its source and the image elide to form part of the great novel of English history. Once more, comparison with Hogarth is revealing. In his painting of Garrick as Richard, the focus is on character and event through a structure that breaks the limits of theatric record by the overlapping of events and the use of incongruous iconographic reference. In Northcote's paintings, details and situations selected from the play are embedded within a novelised history whose outcome is never

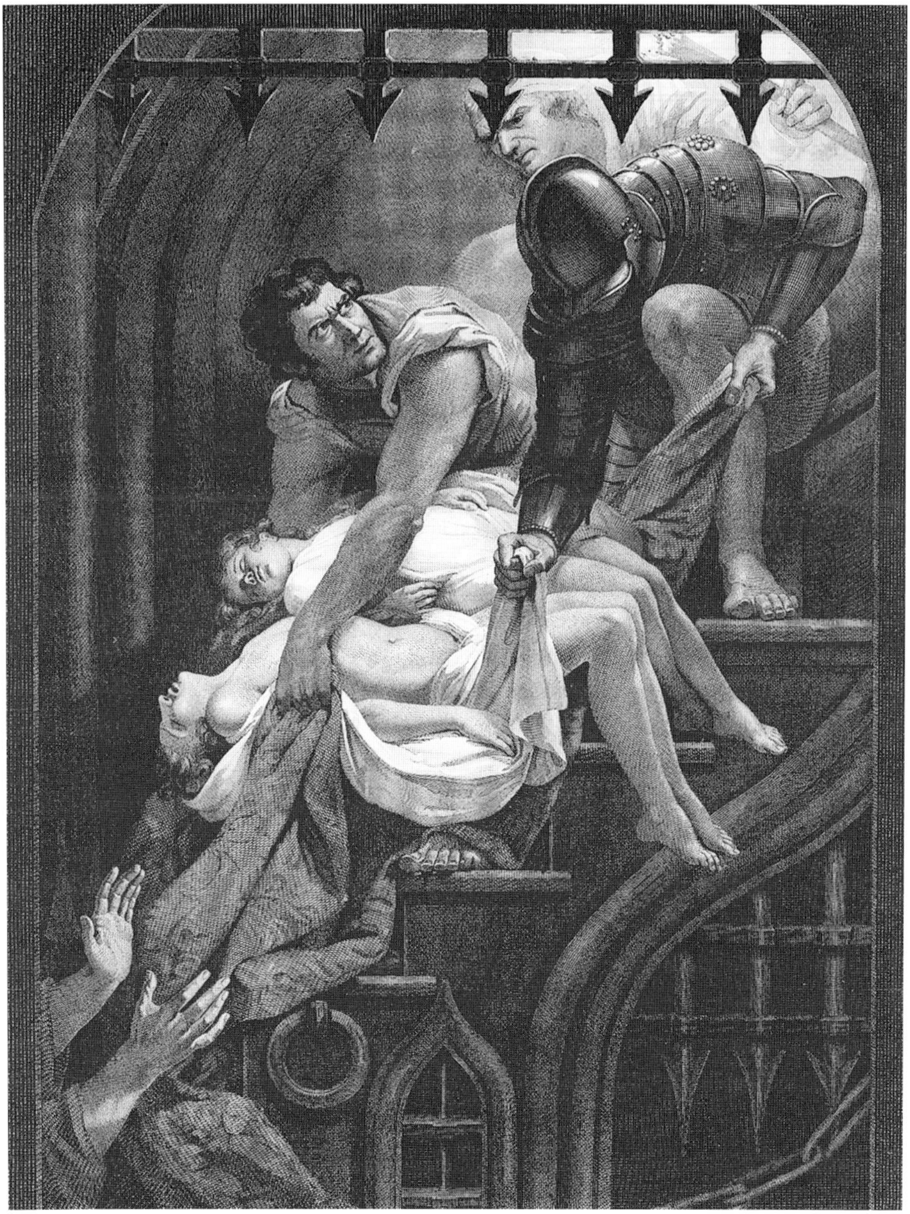

88 James Northcote, *Richard III*, 3. Engraved by William Skelton, 1795.

in doubt and which has achieved almost the stature of a folk-belief. The providentialist narrative is important to the contemporary reader because it reinforces the founding of the Tudor dynasty that will culminate in a key moment of English greatness, the 'England of Elizabeth', of which Shakespeare is of course a central pillar. This historical narrative bears heavy ideological freight: reinforcing

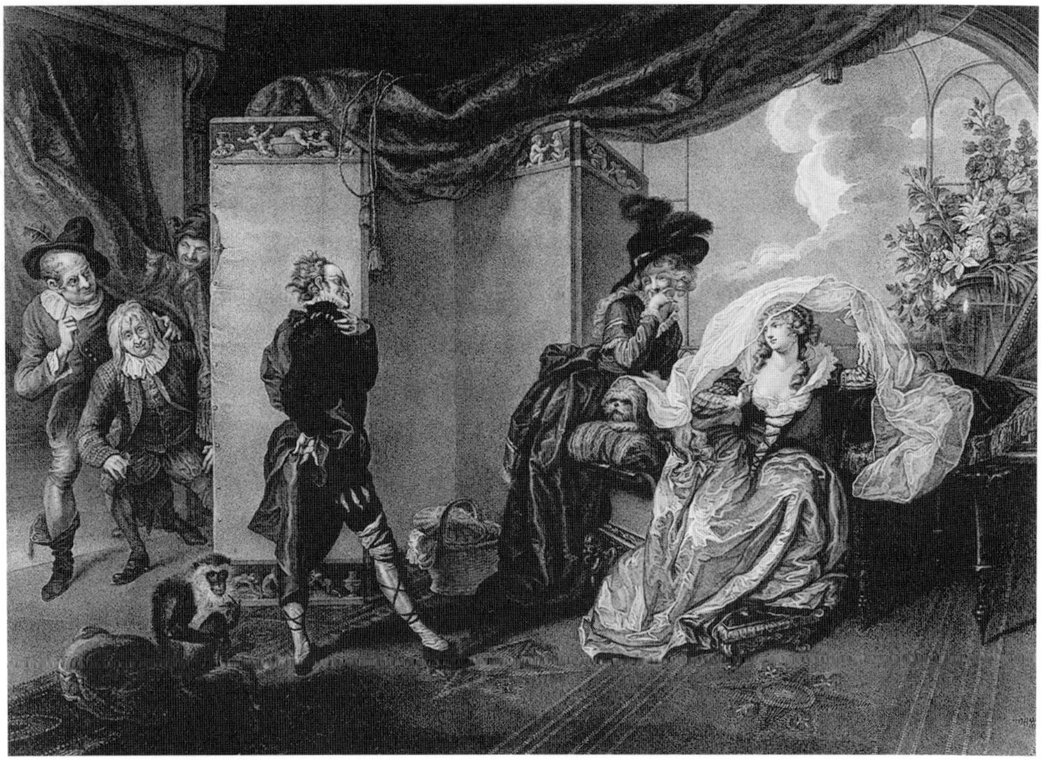

89 Johann Heinrich Ramberg, *Twelfth Night*. Engraved by Thomas Ryder, 1794.

stable rule under king and parliament and an inevitable progress to the good, it invariably offers a Tory interpretation of history that many of Boydell's subscribers would have shared.[37] But along the way, a key element has been lost: the play's ambivalence, which through its action, its tense interplay between characters, and most powerfully the force of Richard's character in scenes such as the courtship of Queen Anne, accounts for its magnetic force whether read or on stage. In focusing on a single aspect of the play's action Northcote's images deny this power, and turn *The Tragedy of Richard III* into a chapter of populist history.

Concern for material actuality does not always run alongside concern for truth to the text's historical period, or contemporary ideological statement. When a play is relocated within a different time, physical details can make valuable comments about action and idea. The most striking instance of this occurs, significantly enough, in one of the few images produced by painters not English by birth, Johann Heinrich Ramberg's painting of *Twelfth Night* (1789: Fig. 89).[38] It depicts Malvolio's performance cross-gartered before Olivia, but places it in the world of Restoration comedy. This immediately suggests a set of relationships quite different, placing the absurdity of Malvolio's appearance within a series of interlocking pretences and stratagems to suggest the dark conquest peculiar to that genre. Malvolio is attended by a small monkey, suggesting both a later court and the animal's traditional association with lust, a link used by Hogarth in the second *Harlot's Progress* plate. Malvolio's smile, and the exaggerated angle of his head, coupled with his receding hairline, reveal his absurdity very clearly within this new frame, while Olivia's appearance and elaborate costume reinforce the new temporal setting and emphasise their difference in age. The classical frieze on the screen, showing cupids playing with animals, suggests both the feral nature of Malvolio's courtship and the sexual self-consciousness of the Restoration stage.

This is extended in two more temporal dimensions. The image enlarges the reference by including Sir Toby and Aguecheek, who do not enter until much later, and Feste, half hidden behind a curtain, who has no part in the scene. Their presence serves mainly to guide the onlooker's response and so point up the absurdity of the event, but it has another purpose. As Sir Toby and Aguecheek observe Malvolio, Feste observes them, and the suggestion of intrigue has about it a hint of the sombre theatre of eavesdropping and espionage familiar in *Hamlet*, approximately contemporary with *Twelfth Night* in the canon. Malvolio's ridiculous behaviour is further darkened by the knights: neither is young, and the absurdity of Malvolio is transferred across to them in a more general statement of a kind familiar from the ageing lovers of the Restoration stage. More important, it offers a reminder of the melancholy at the passage of time that is the play's pedal note: 'Youth's a stuff will not endure' (2.3.46). Time, especially an instant of time, is used more positively in the treatment of Olivia. In exasperation at the display she has thrown back the veil that she has earlier habitually worn before visitors. This marks a significant move forward: the rejection of Malvolio denotes the end of her mourning for her dead brother, and after this the return to the world, and the courtship that will end with the marriage, implausible or miraculous, to Sebastian. All these kinds of time ripple through and across each other in a meditative visual treatment of the text's moment and movement. A temporal dialogue is present here, too; but the voices are those of two different kinds of theatre, and the visual intelligence that draws them together, and the concerns with materialism that it embraces, lead us back to the play's identity, not away from it.

III

The most direct way in which the Boydell Gallery images lift the plays out of theatrical spaces into a setting in accord with contemporary ideas of experiential realism occurs through their use of landscape. The simplest images use the approach established in the 1740s and merely place mimicked stage events before a landscape setting. Others go further and employ the natural world as a means of conveying mood. John Hoppner's treatment of *Cymbeline* 3.4[39] places Pisanio and Imogen in a setting of elaborate shagginess suggesting the cult of the picturesque, the wildness of which echoes the emotional intensity of the encounter, where Imogen is shown baring her breast and inciting Pisanio to kill her. Raphael West's version of the narrated episode in *As You Like It* 4.3[40] where Oliver reports his being saved by Orlando employs a grotesquely exaggerated, gnarled tree as the major feature to convey the tensions and dangers of the scene, while Angelica Kauffman's painting of *Two Gentlemen of Verona* 5.3[41] uses the setting in a similar, though less extreme, way. These are immediate uses of the landscape that continue a tradition in Shakespeare painting reaching back to John Wootton, but alongside them in the Boydell collection are images that use landscape more subtly to engage in a negotiation between Shakespearean themes and those insistent within contemporary ideologies.

During the later decades of the eighteenth century the English landscape became the subject of wide-ranging ideological investment.[42] Changes in agriculture turned it into an industrial base; first enclosure, and then revolutionary ideas from America and France, politicised it; studies such as *The Natural History of Selborne* (1789) made it the site of scientific enquiry; a range of discourses concerning agriculture, reproduction, sexuality and property freighted it heavily with attitudes towards gender; and the various discourses and philosophies of Romantic individualism made it the centre of emotional and psychological symbolism. Visual representations by Gainsborough, Richard Wilson, George Morland and others drew together these strands in various interweavings; the tradition of portraiture, for example, that placed an aristocratic woman, or a land-owning couple, before a cultivated landscape, ensured that images of property were also deeply engendered. The painted landscape provides one of the most revealing sites of ideological reinvention of the plays in the Boydell images, and perhaps one of the most diverse in the kinds of landscapes presented and the ideological freights they carry.

One subset of landscape ideology concerns the forest. Elizabeth Hackendorn Cook has drawn attention to the visit of George III to the New Forest in 1789 as a statement of Englishness in revealing the independence and freedom of the dwellers in the forest, figures no longer under feudal power but enjoying the protection and patronage of a monarch newly restored to health and known – not wholly satirically – as 'Farmer George'.[43] This is one level of the ideological substructure of Samuel Middiman's engraving, after Robert Smirke and Joseph Farington, of the robbery scene (2.2) from *I Henry IV* (Plate 14).[44] While the figures are shown in carefully accentuated lighting, the dominant figuration is the landscape, a lush and diverse afforestation, primarily of ancient native oaks, whose tactile qualities are rendered with great skill by Middiman's stipple. While the original is lost, a coloured engraving[45] gives some clue to its nature in its deep earth tones and soft greens. The reader is led carefully through the events, with the aid of lines from the play beneath the engraving, by the direction of the light and the extended arm of Falstaff. In the very centre stands Prince Henry, mask before his face, with Poins attending him. It is a strong statement of the literal centrality of the monarch to the native forest, but contemporary ideology enriches it further.

From the seventeenth century onwards, forests and in particular royal forests were important largely for the production of naval timber. At the end of the eighteenth century a series of Royal Commissions had reported that timber production was insufficient, and that it should be supplemented or farmed out to private contractors.[46] The forest presented by Middiman is not a careful plantation; none of the trees would be of much value for naval building, that in the centre being a fashionably picturesque blasted oak and the others being sinuously twisted to form attractive compositions. Further, the play of light not only presents Falstaff and Hal in an exaggerated chiaroscuro, but turns the trees into pleasing aesthetic objects. The implication is that Hal is a type of the new monarch taking possession of a forest so ancient and English that there is no need for it to be turned into naval timber; it is not a Garden of Eden that is presented, but a Forest of Albion, and the ideal monarchy that is to come with Prince Hal is balanced against that offered by the restored George III. A new period of prosperity is perhaps hinted at in the fact that the young Prince is masked. In 1723 the 'Black Act' imposed a death penalty on 'any person . . . being armed . . . and having his or their faces blacked, or being otherwise disguised'[47] in a royal or other forest, in a draconian attempt to reduce poaching and other offences. The act also forced the local hundred to pay for any damage caused, making it a societal, rather than specific, punitive measure. By the 1790s its implementation was much relaxed, but it was not repealed until 1823. In Farington's image the presence of the king in a forest, armed and concealed behind a black mask, suggests a new national wellbeing: even the monarch can burlesque an action the judicial consequences of which were resented and feared in the middle years of the century, in a ludic celebration of a new harmony within the forest community and the nation that it metonymically represents. That the trees are all oaks reinforces the national identity, and introduces a theatrical echo;

in 1759 Garrick included the song 'Hearts of oak' in his play *Harlequin's Invasion*, and it became a nationalistic rallying cry throughout the succeeding years of war in Europe and America. It shares with Farington's image the transfer of the epithet from the literal oaks to the quality of forthright strength promoted as the essence of all things English, used in the image as a metaphor of the vigour of Prince Hal and George III.

The image also has another resonance, in recalling a passage from Book II of Richard Payne Knight's *The Landscape*, published by Boydell's printer, Joseph Bulmer, at the Shakespeare Printing Office, in 1794.[48] The sharing of publishers suggests the close link between Shakespeare and the physical identity of the nation; further, considered in the light of the poem's publication just before the painting was begun, and of Farington's friendship with Knight, the following lines become particularly relevant:

While uncorrupted still, on every side,
The ancient forest rose in savage pride;
And in its native dignity display'd
Each hanging wood and ever verdant glade;
Where every shaggy shrub and spreading tree
Proclaim'd the seat of native liberty;
In loose and vary'd groups unheeded thrown,
And never taught the planter's care to own.
(II.35–42)

The wild forms of the trees are an image of innate English freedom, the refusal of the 'levelling' that gave material form to the rejection of revolutionary sentiments from France. Payne Knight's rival, Uvedale Price, made the link explicit in reference to republicanism: 'despotism is the most complete leveller'.[49] This is, of course, only one section through a complex continuum in which formal gardens moved in and out of fashion, in both France and England, where they had earlier been rejected as reflecting the power of the French monarchy. But in this particular cultural moment, the confluence of a designed wilderness with the Shakespearean 'native woodnotes wild' to evidence the untamed English spirit is given visible form in Farington's treatment of *I Henry IV*.

What stands revealed here is the supple interweaving of contemporary ideologies with the perception of Shakespeare's text: while offering little in the way of textual criticism, the image powerfully states the degree to which the plays have become imbricated within the texture of national life and the fashioning of national identity. Just as the production of *Henry VIII* was extended by the addition of a Coronation procession in the year of George III's accession, so the text of *I Henry IV* is being visualised within a very clear contemporary imperative. That it has gonc largely without comment reinforces its innateness: it is, after all, the shared ideology that goes unremarked.

The presence of Hal in the forest as emblem of the restored monarch taking possession of his kingdom should also be seen within a larger contemporary circumstance. In 1789 a 'day of General Thanksgiving'[50] for the king's recovery was marked by a service in St Paul's Cathedral, before which the king processed through streets bordered with specially erected scaffolding to accommodate the crowds. On the way from Westminster to St Paul's the procession passed the newly completed Boydell Gallery in Pall Mall; Boydell himself, as an Alderman, took part in a separate procession to the Cathedral; and the ceremony took place on 23 April, St George's Day and by common fiction the birthday of Shakespeare. In the shadow of this event, and the royal visit to Windsor Forest, the Farington-Smirke image further evidences the inseparable interweaving of Shakespearean and national narratives.

If here it seems that the weight of signification lies more in contemporary event than in Shakespearean criticism, the balance is partially redressed in two images by Peters that mediate contemporary critical readings of *The Merry Wives of Windsor* through images of gender and landscape, using conventions of dress and setting that connote an ideologically saturated past. The first (see Fig. 90)[51] treats the passage in 2.1 where Mistress Ford and Mistress Page compare their letters from Falstaff and find them identical. In the play it is a turning point, since from it stems the plot to avenge Falstaff's treatment of all women alike as objects of sexual fulfilment. This conventional act of selection however involves other imperatives.

Peters' canvas places the event firmly in the tradition of the Anglo-French *galanterie*, a Rococo image of an elaborately dressed woman, often in a garden or a richly furnished interior, in which a trivial event becomes the peg on which to hang a scene of carefully delimited sensuality. Ruthven Todd's reference to 'the "nice" drawing-room pornography of the Rev. Matthew William Peters, R.A., or his like'[52] is just right: Peters is respectable as both clergyman and academician, the pictures harmlessly, publicly, flirtatious. Yet the ideology is more complex and more exploitative, importantly moving that which in the play might be seen as the redressing of gender imbalance into a frame that, for all its apparent inconsequence, imposes a relation of power based on voyeurism and an assumed natural order both recent and constructed. This is achieved largely through a series of references. While in the play the letter is the pivot of Falstaff's unmasking and

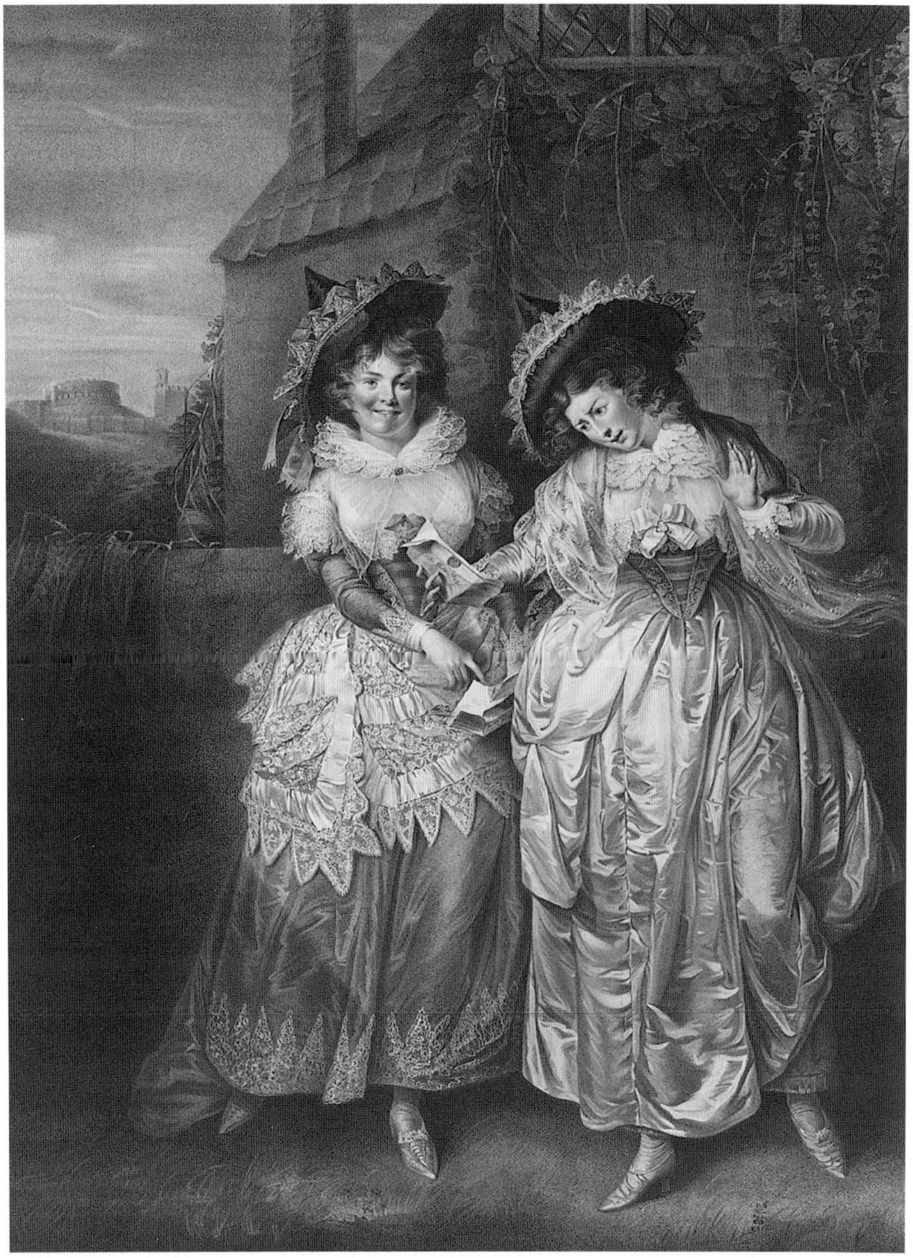

90 The Rev. Matthew William Peters, *The Merry Wives of Windsor*, I. Engraved by Robert Thew, 1793.

the women's revenge, in the tradition of *galanterie* it stands for something different, a liaison willingly entered into: although the meaning is clear from the text of the play, from the associative power of the convention its significance is quite undermined, the evidence of Falstaff's duplicity conveniently erased by its stylistic contextualisation.

Both the women in the image wear very elaborate costumes of lace and satin, modelled on those in portraits by the artist who in the eighteenth century was always referred to as Vandyke, the spelling revealingly conferring a partial, honorary Englishness. Robert Thew's engraving is masterly in depicting the subtle gradations of tone and texture of the fabrics: the open sensuality turns the figures into symbols of sexual willingness, immediately negating any power they derive from their resolve to unmask Falstaff. That the women are objects of sensual pleasure is shown also in their body language, the open arms and splayed feet – important erotic zones for the time – presenting poses of welcome and invitation. That both are blushing introduces an element of ambiguity, teasingly drawing in the male onlooker by suggesting a blend of modesty and arousal. While Page's frown suggests anger, her expression is softened by the pairing with Ford's smile and direct gaze, suggesting demure complicity. Humphry Repton's response to the painting captures the tone:

> How insensible to beauty must that man be, who can think of faults with such a Mrs Ford before his eyes! She is surely the most wicked, seducing object of desire, that ever tempted man, to make a fool of him. (*The Bee*, p. 11)

The immediate sensuality and objectification provided by the 'white satin drapery' (ibid., p. 11) is deepened by the temporal relocation. Anthony van Dyck was painter to Charles I, whose court was renowned for its intellectual seriousness; but the period is also presented in eighteenth-century historical writing as one of royalist order, the prelapsarian state from which England is expelled by the actions of revolutionary republicans, a group especially antithetical after the events of 1776 and 1789. The two perhaps combine in Johan Zoffany's use of van Dyck costumes in his court portraits. In the Peters image, the view of women as sensual objects and the ideal royalist order come together in a hierarchical society that is made to appear ideologically neutral because of the lightness of the tone and the simple immediacy of the realist convention.

This process of historicised justification is enhanced by the setting. Placed before a high wall, the two women become the property of the onlooker, who stands by implication within the same garden, but this is no *hortus conclusus*; instead it becomes the site of politicised sexual possession. Behind the wall stands a poetically rustic cottage, its leaded windows and thatched roof suggesting immemorial Englishness. It is overgrown with creeping plants that form part of the textural range encompassing the lace and satin of the dresses, and the women's complexions and hair. Sexual availability is thus lodged within an irrefragible natural order, but that this order is part of an innately English historical and royal structure, already implied by the reference to Charles I, is stressed by the presence of a key element in the left background: Windsor Castle, a building that to the image's first readers referred to far more than the play's title.

The king's return to live at Windsor in 1789 marked the culmination of the castle's redefinition as an architectural emblem of Englishness that began with its partial rebuilding in the fashionable Gothic style and the commissioning from Benjamin West of a series of huge paintings in the King's Audience Chamber, depicting scenes from the reign of Edward III.[53] Not only was this period the apogee of the chivalric code; it also witnessed the conquest of France and the rapid rise of the merchant classes, culminating in the division of Parliament into two chambers. National identity, valour and government were all established, and West's paintings duly projected them: in the words of a recent analyst, 'the glory and the virtue were strictly English'.[54] The link with Shakespeare as the embodiment of the English genius and the patriotic thrust of the Boydell Gallery is clear: it is significant that *The Merry Wives of Windsor* has five paintings devoted to it, more than any other play except *As You Like It*, which had more only because of the presentation of Smirke's 'Seven Ages' sequence as a self-contained unit. Van Dyck was George III's favourite painter: the link between order of state and order of sexual power is impressed repeatedly in the image and the circumstances surrounding it. The location of images of sexually available women within this doubly historicised setting and the allusions to earlier English monarchs as emblems of propriety makes the ideological stance irrefutable. The difference from Fuseli's erotica is more than visual and sexual: whereas his images show women actively engaged in pleasuring both men and each other, albeit in postures which destabilise relations of power, the direction is usually one of personal psychology rather than a wholesale restructuring of gender politics. Instead, Peters offers an image assertively decorous that enfolds a statement of gender relations within a landscape instinct with the sanctifying power of monarchical tradition.

As well as being engraved by Thew for the large prints, the painting was also engraved by Joseph Saunders for the edition of the plays.[55] This print differs in key details which, though in part the consequence of its size and medium, nonetheless redetermine its meaning. Thew's stipple engraving, which gives a soft, shimmering effect to clothing, hair and foliage, is replaced by line engraving, making the textures far less sensual so that the presentation of the figures as objects of sexual fantasy is at once diminished. This has much to suggest about the relation between the full-size prints and those produced for the edition. The employment of engravers more technically skilled for the large images and the resultant use of subtler techniques to modify meaning and response suggests that the main concern of the venture is not deepening and enriching the reading experience but presenting the author-function 'Shakespeare' reconstituted within contemporary ideology in the large prints, which in consequence act as emblems of their owners' cultural discernment.

Similar forces operate within Peters' second *Merry Wives* image (see Fig. 91),[56] which shows Mistress Page and Mistress Ford putting Falstaff into the buckbasket. Again the costumes are elaborate in their acculturated sensuality; again the presence of foliage places this within an implied natural order. That this is questioned by the women's apparent empowerment is not seriously threatening: it is an action located somewhere along an axis between playful female revenge and a male fantasy of female sexual dominance. Historical sanction is given by the stone tracery and leaded glass of the window; social hierarchy is maintained by the commercial passage of a boat on the river seen through it; and the narrative urgency injected by the page at the right serves more to enhance an element of sexual excitement than to further the plot.

Any power allotted to the two women is firmly contained within this frame: in this it is unlike Fuseli's treatment of the same theme (1792: Fig. 92)[57] which, though nothing like as explicative as his private drawings, contains in the angular sexuality of the two women and their elaborate hair an engagement with the issues of power that – for Fuseli as much as for many present-day readers, though clearly not for Peters – the scene generates. Falstaff appears in an even more foreshortened form, legs splayed as before, while Mistress Page and Mistress Ford, in the form of the elaborately coiffed women from the fairy paintings and the erotica, place linen on top of him. The whole is contained within a very precise structure of intersecting diagonals, resembling the five-point drawings the artist completed as compositional exercises, with the result here of placing Falstaff's head at the level of the women's genitals and in this further recalling the erotic drawings, many of which also include two women and one man. The location within a Rococo interior, with mirrors reflecting the women and the grotesque sculpture at the right, suggests a mood of carnival: the page peering round the door at the right is more a voyeur than a lookout. All this sharpens the erotic tensions within the scene and invests them with a hint of menace at the inversion of power between the genders, revealing darker undertones in a way that Peters'

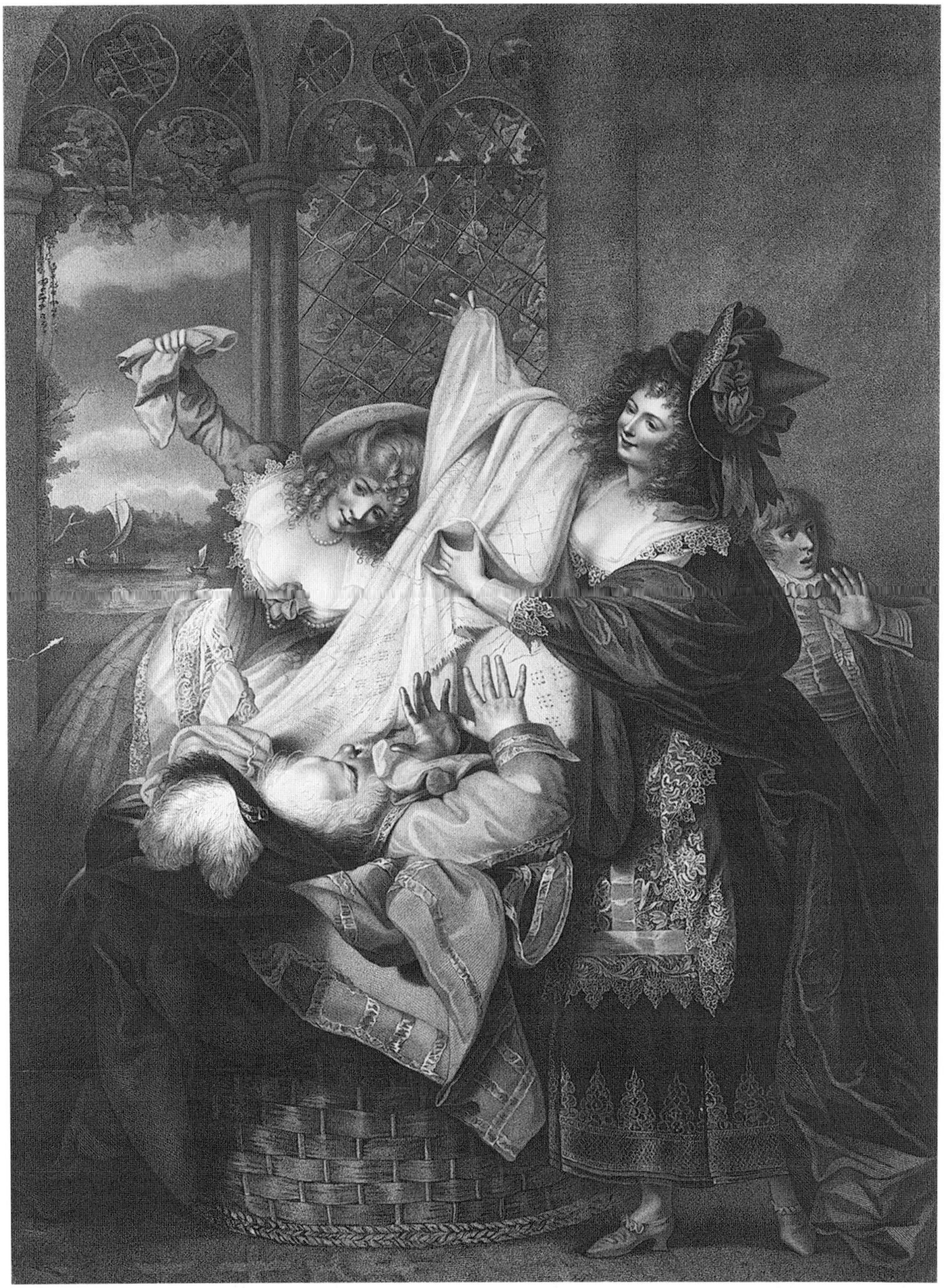

91 The Rev. Matthew William Peters, *The Merry Wives of Windsor*, 2. Engraved by Jean Pierre Simon, 1793.

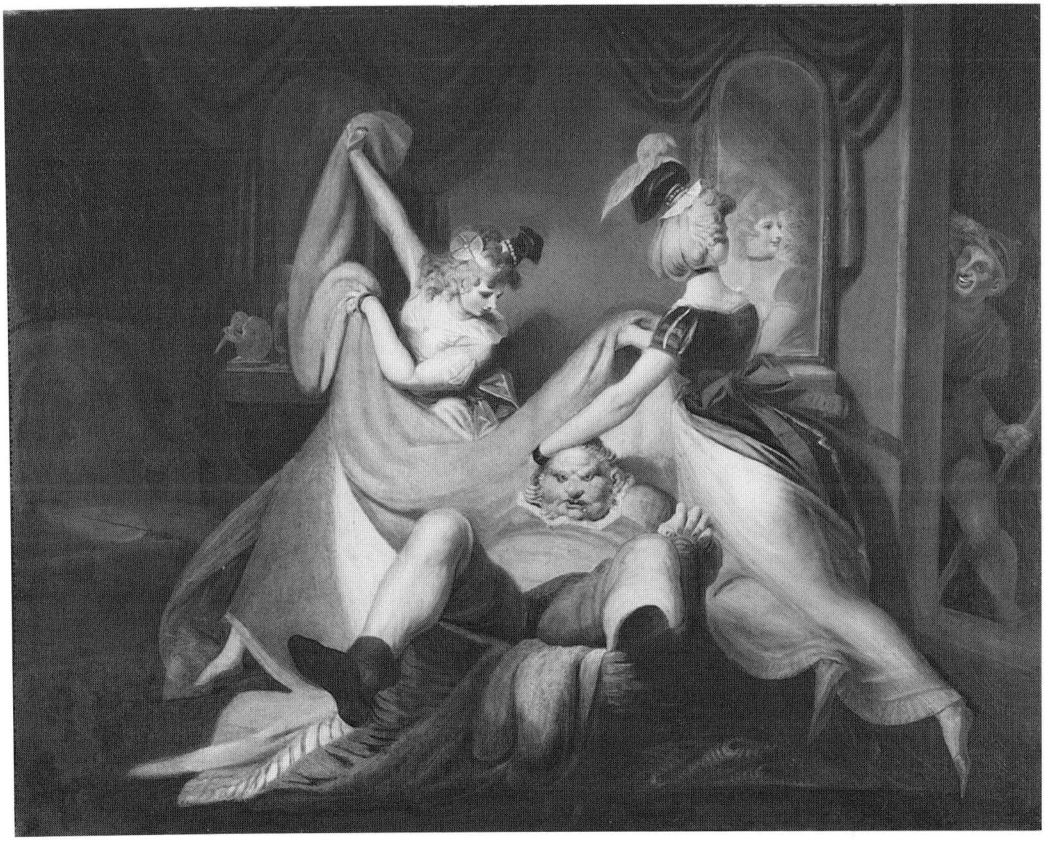

92 Henry Fuseli, *Falstaff in the Buckbasket*, 1792.

version manifestly does not. The difference is illuminating for reasons that go beyond the individual scenes the images present. Fuseli's critical intelligence, here as habitually, seizes on issues of language and idea within the play; Peters takes the action and characters and places them within a physical and ideological location that reflects contemporary ideas of gender and nationhood.

Landscapes of political and gender ideologies are matched in the Boydell collection by those that reflect a new climate of feeling. One that does this very precisely, in a way that has much to suggest about the changing aesthetic of which the gallery was a part, is William Hodges' painting of Jaques and the wounded stag from *As You Like It* 2.1 (c. 1788–9: Fig. 93).[58] This establishes a critical dialogue on the affective relationship between individual and landscape as it is presented in the play and as it appears in contemporary writing and philosophy, along the way revealing the structural influence of the novel at several levels in the visual reconceptualisation of the text. It is one of two Boydell images that treat episodes of the play that

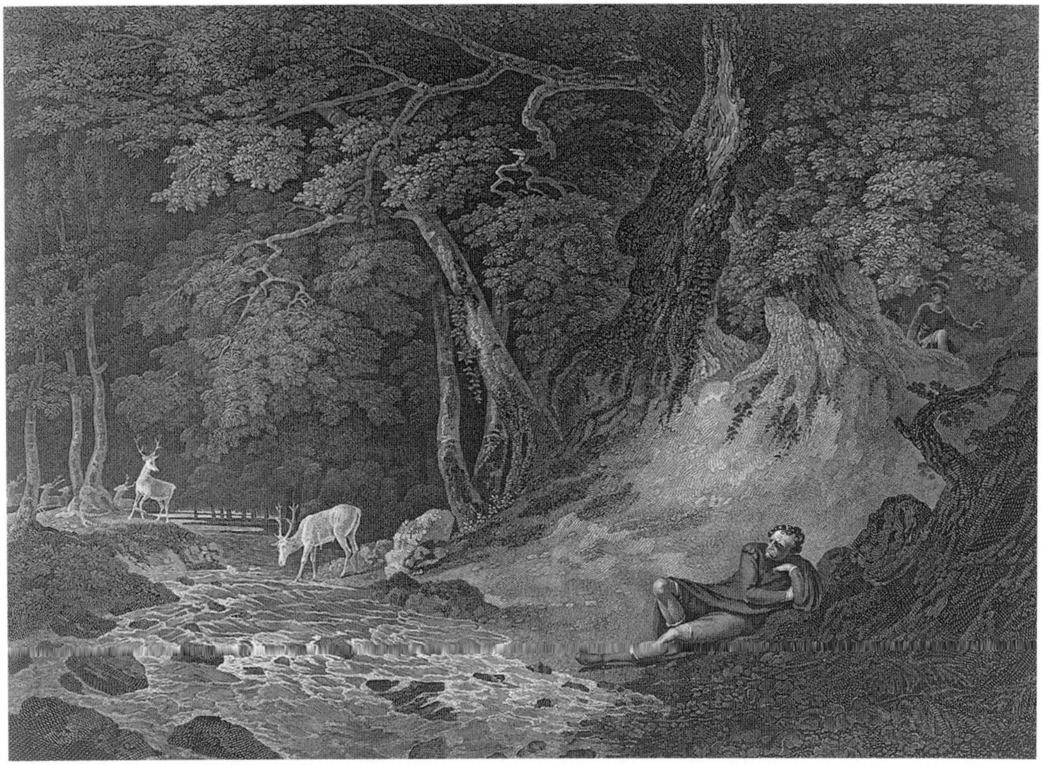

93 William Hodges, *As You Like It*. Engraved by Samuel Middiman, 1791.

are reported, not acted, the other being Raphael West's image discussed earlier. Tieck's impatient objection to the depiction, as in the West, of 'that which is external, or merely narrated',[59] has more than a little value. Although the grotesquely distorted tree, already remarked, uses the setting as an emotional symbol to guide the onlooker's response, and the threatening forms of the snake and the lion are immediate visualisations of the reported danger to Oliver, the image overlooks one central dimension of the passage in the play, its effect on Rosalind; in consequence, it paradoxically confines rather than extends the onlooker's critical grasp of the text. Quite the reverse is true of Hodges' painting, even though it presents an event unfolded in the play through the reports of Amiens and the First Lord.

While to some degree this is a reflection of stage production, Kemble in 1723 having begun the practice of having Jaques speak the words himself, the engraving owes more to the multiple layers of narrative realism of the novel, embracing as it does Jaques, the stags that he is contemplating, and the figures of Amiens and the First Lord concealed behind a tree, the whole enclosed within an extensive naturalistic landscape seen by a single observer-narrator. The image's shift of emphasis, in its use of a number of discourses of landscape, produces a revealing contemporary critical statement: the landscape, the stag, the figure of Jaques and those of the two Lords all contribute to a complex dialogue between contemporary and late sixteenth-century aesthetics of feeling.

The lines printed beneath the engraving are apparently neutral in introducing the events:

To-day my lord of Amiens and myself,
Did steal behind him, as he lay along
Under an oak, whose antique root peeps out
Upon the brook that brawls along this wood
(2.1.29–32)

Their presence prepares the well informed reader for Jaques' own words which 'moralise this spectacle' (2.1.44) and, with the presence of the two observers behind the tree and the exaggerated grief evident in the face of Jaques, the satiric slant seems clear enough. Yet the presence of the wood and the wounded deer in such explicit detail insists that the injury to the natural world be taken seriously. This is amplified by the figuration of Jaques not only in the position historically sanctioned for the melancholic, as demonstrated in Isaac Oliver's portrait of Herbert of Cherbury,[60] but in that adopted by Sir Brooke Boothby in a celebrated portrait by Joseph Wright exhibited at the Royal Academy as recently as 1781.[61] This shows the aristocrat lying before a brook beneath a tree, clutching a slim book with one word on its spine: Rousseau. The reference to Wright's painting reveals a newness of approach in alluding not to an Old Master painting but to a celebrated contemporary image. The allusion validates Jaques's sadness by placing it within a Rousseauiste statement of the unity of the natural world. That Jaques is presented beneath a large, dead oak tree confirms this: all nature mourns the wounding of the stag.

Another level of contemporary reference is provided by the similarity of Jaques' pose to that of Harley, the central character in an immensely popular novel, Henry Mackenzie's *The Man of Feeling* (1771). Jaques' posture and location exactly mirror Harley's:

When he was not peculiarly attracted by the reasonable creation, he would sometimes consort with a species of inferior rank, and lay himself down to sleep by the side of a rock, or on the banks of a rivulet.[62]

Mackenzie seems clearly to be drawing on the tradition of melancholy contemplation that includes Jaques: as with the link to the Wright portrait, the relation is as much that of parallel lines of influence from earlier texts as of direct borrowing from a more recent one. Once the link with the novel is established it discloses another key element of Middiman's image. As well as celebrating and valorising sentimental reflections on nature, the novel satirises them: Harley is a figure of ridicule as well as respect to the novel's narrator, a relationship that parallels that between Jaques and the First Lord. These links reveal in Middiman's engraving a debate about the nature of melancholy and the idea of sympathetic suffering between humankind and the natural world, voiced through references to both current and earlier ideas about the workings of the affections, in which they are both validated and ridiculed. Fundamental to this is the use of two large-scale novelistic practices, the rewriting of the event in terms of a continuous narrative and the presentation of a naturalistic setting, along with more local references to the writing of Mackenzie and Rousseau. These allusions work together to create a dialogue on the natural world that reinvigorates that of *As You Like It*, presenting it in contemporary terms that, more than any allusions to classical or Renaissance art, are part of the discourse of landscape familiar in late eighteenth-century ideological debate. A sense of this immediacy most likely underlies a contemporary review that asserted 'The Composition and Effect of this landscape are truely poetick.'[63]

While the images of landscape so far discussed suggest single ideological readings, a range of possible ideologies is suggested by Hodges' image of the final act of *The Merchant of Venice*.[64] The painting itself is now lost, but a contemporary watercolour copy (Plate 15) suggests that the canvas itself was an image of some richness.[65] The text quoted beneath the image begins with the line 'How sweet the moonlight sleeps upon this bank!' (5.1.54), and the image's initial effect is in conveying this tonal richness. The landscape is heavily Claudean, the setting suggesting an English estate constructed with such a painting as its model. The Palladian front, the temple and the lake all suggest Stourhead, the estate constructed from the 1720s for the banker Henry Hoare by Colen Campbell and Henry Flitwick, but the implications are much more general. As has been pointed out, towards the end of the century the English country estate underwent a change from 'emblematic to expressionistic forms';[66] instead of the specific meanings of one locale, the affective responses produced by such settings in general are played on in this image, successfully employing the rich associations they would have had for Boydell's subscribers, to present the play's conclusion as a statement of sensory and emotional fullness.

The system that the image advances is a version of Shakespeare's order that readers of the image may see either as genuinely organic or as ironically hieratic:

beneath the 'patens of bright gold' (5.1.59) Lorenzo explains the harmonious relationship that is echoed by the herm and nymph behind them. Important in this ambivalence are the image's narrative fulcrum and its iconography. The compositional element of the man and woman seated on a bench within an estate had been used in country-house paintings from the middle of the century, and is perhaps best known in Gainsborough's *Mr and Mrs Robert Andrews* (*c.* 1750).[67] It may be read as encoding a variety of relationships between the individuals and the land that surrounds them. Recent critics such as David Solkin[68] see such paintings as presenting ownership of the woman along with animals, crops and other produce of the estate; others, including Anne Bermingham, see in it a harmonious relation of 'organicism' between the estate's owners and the natural world.[69] What is important in relating this to Hodges' image is not merely that, at a time of political uncertainty within England and Europe, the idea of land and land ownership is being heavily historicised as well as idealised, but that the resultant vision remains open to diverse readings of its presentation of the hierarchical scheme implicit in the passage quoted beneath the engraving and developed in the lines that follow, a latter-day envisioning of what has come to be called the great chain of being. For republican or Whiggish readers, the relation is one that is exploitative at every level; for high and moderate Tories, it is a relation properly hierarchic revealing a stewardship based on the sharing of roles between man and wife, owner and worker, human and vegetative, in which each partner has responsibilities as well as powers. Placing the scene within a generic English country house, Hodges skilfully allows either reading. In consequence, at a time when political allegiances were by no means predictable according to wealth and status group, the image acquires greater flexibility.

It is pertinent here to recall Hodges' career. As the artist engaged to accompany Captain Cook to the South Pacific, and as painter for Warren Hastings in India, few could have had experience of so many different landscapes, or of the political approaches to them as notions of ownership and national identity: his moral landscapes *Effects of Peace* and *Consequences of War*,[70] both contemporary with the *Merchant of Venice* painting, drew an angry response from the Prince of Wales because of their anti-authoritarian tone. This gives a further edge to the placing of this scene within what might be termed an open encryption, and suggests the availability of a Shakespeare for all political aesthetics. Importantly, too, it is an essentially English landscape: as well as the notion of an aesthetic homecoming for its artist, within its appropriation of French landscape painting and Italian architectural principles it offers an ideal English country house, and of this Shakespeare is revealed as the *genius loci*.

While Hodges' experience and outlook may lead us to think of the image as satirical, it is hard to contest that the image suggests a conclusion serene, sensuous and untroubled by dissent. A reading of the text itself suggests otherwise. The fifth act begins with Lorenzo's 'In such a night' speech which becomes a litany of lost loves, moves through the melancholy of Jessica's troubled 'I am never merry when I hear sweet music' (5.1.69) and ends with what, within the warmth of the romance conclusion, is the bawdy disruptiveness of the ring conceit, far removed from a willing acceptance of the placing of man and woman within an organic hierarchy. The detail of Hodges' image goes right against this, displacing it by a view of the scene in which Lorenzo explains the order to a listening Jessica and the presence of the lute in Stephano's hand represents the music of the spheres as well as 'your music, madam, of the house' (5.1.98), both of which rest on a hierarchy natural and mathematical. It is a seductive, but selective, reading with much to suggest about contemporary views of the play's conclusion.

The debates generated within and between all the images discussed in these paragraphs reveal the use of acculturated landscape to present a reading of Shakespeare's text rich in contemporary assumptions about gender, hierarchy, authority and feeling. Landscapes interact with a range of other ideological components, including shifts of feeling and their presentation through a narratorial viewpoint that moves beyond simple realism to allow a range of interpretations, including the self-ironising. The complicity of contemporary ideology within the visual mediation of Shakespeare's text and the landscapes, literal, temporal and perceptual, in which this takes place is the inescapable result of the social processing that the text undergoes in its reinvention for a range of late eighteenth-century readers.

IV

The last few pages have considered Hodges' visualisation of the last act of *The Merchant of Venice* as a single engraving, to be examined and discussed by its owner perhaps in a country house outside Bath, or rooms in Albany or Lincoln's Inn. Other perspectives are opened by considering it in conjunction with the image before it in the Boydell volume, Robert Smirke's treatment of Shylock's house in Act 2 (see Fig. 94).[71] Offering no deep insights, the image nonetheless works skilfully to suggest the future consequences of past actions. While Shylock's speech to Jessica engraved beneath it includes the adjuration to 'Lock up my doors' (2.5.28) and 'stop my house's ears – I mean my casements' (2.5.33), the heavy drapes stand open to reveal an unguarded balcony; while Jessica holds a pair

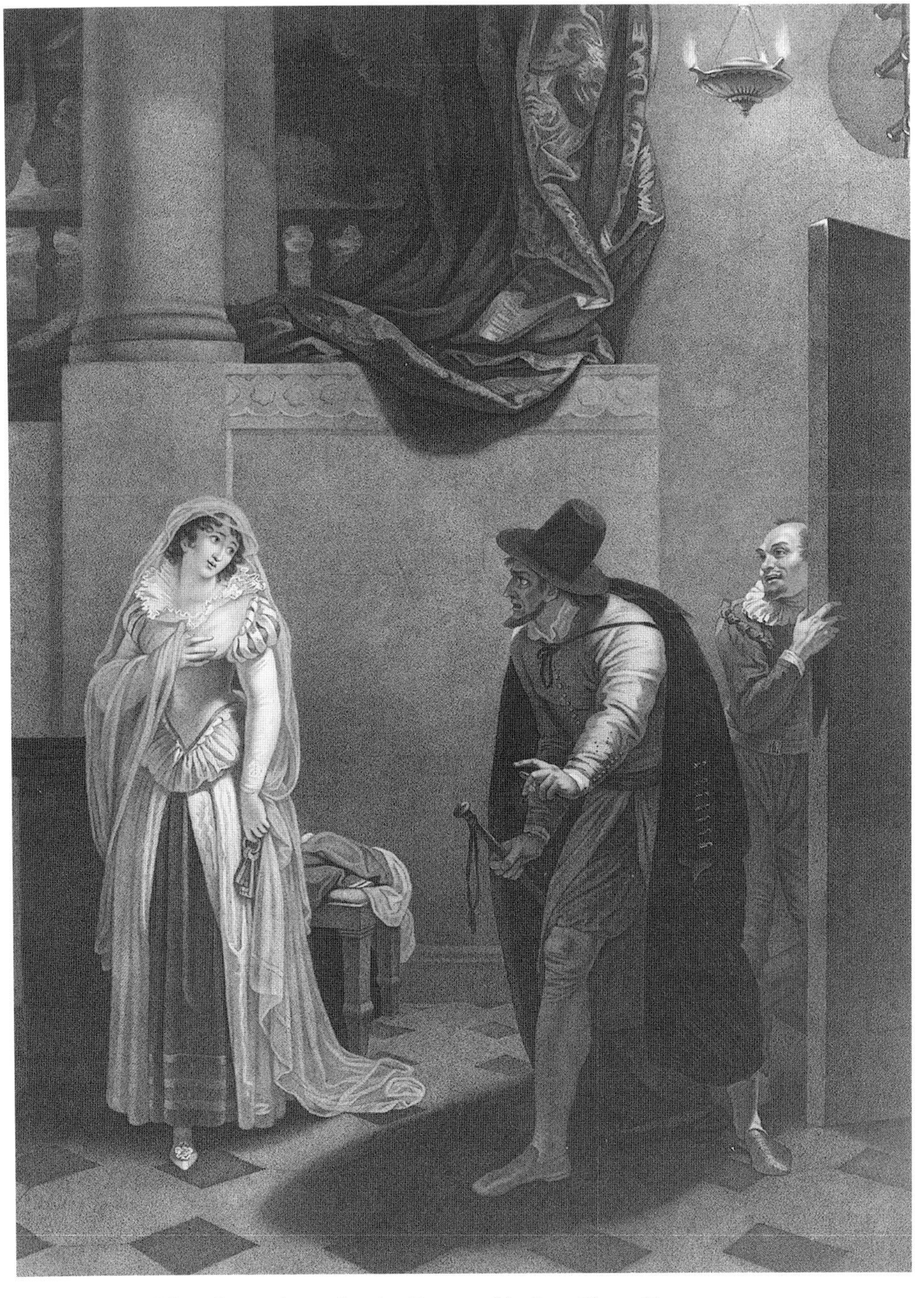

94 Robert Smirke, *The Merchant of Venice*. Engraved by Jean Pierre Simon, 1795.

of heavy keys, Lancelot holds the door open behind Shylock, and the placing of the two in the same plane, slightly behind Shylock, implies the conspiracy for her elopement forged in the preceding scenes. That Jessica and Lancelot are shown in strong light and Shylock in shadow weaves the conspiracy more fully into the engraving's composition.

When the two engravings are seen sequentially, a reading of the play emerges that foregrounds the romance movement of the Jessica–Lorenzo plot. Jessica moves from the constraints of her father's house to the freedom and fulfilment of Belmont and life with Lorenzo, a shift underlined by the movement from a contained, inner space to one that, though also man-made, is defined by the apparent freedom and sensuality of nature in the richness of the foliage and the broad swathes of moonlight that wash over the couple. Within this physical movement is enfolded Jessica's change of state from imprisoned daughter to wife enfranchised through love – a conventional reading of the romance progress of the play and of the trajectory of the so-called 'happy comedies' that would have found few opponents from the late eighteenth century for a hundred years or more, regardless of the hierarchical relation within which Jessica is placed by the verbal and visual rhetorics of the second engraving. What is also intriguing about the sequence is its avoidance of what for many decades had been the main concern of the play in the theatre, the plot concerning Antonio, Shylock and the pound of flesh.[72] It is a reading that, in addition to the openness of the second image, not only ignores the dark strains of the Antonio–Shylock plot and the unresolved dissonances of the final scene; it also positions the play firmly within a convention of romance comedy.

This approach suggests the importance of reading the engravings in sequence. In the Shakespeare Gallery in Pall Mall, individual paintings were hung as they became available, in accord with the pressures of available space as well as from larger aesthetic considerations. When the prints were finally issued in the two imperial folio volumes, a different priority was established, with the images of each play presented in sequence, and the plays arranged not in what was then thought to be the order of composition but in the order of the First Folio. This presentation of each play through a series of between two and five images effectively constitutes a wholly new reading experience, in which the texts are mediated through visual representation to build an overall interpretation of action, language and idea in the moments selected and the features they emphasise.

Examining the images within this serial progression raises important, and often overlooked, implications about the sequential reading experience they generate.

Some fifty years before the popularity of extensively illustrated editions of the plays, at a time when reading texts rarely had more than a single engraving as frontispiece, they constitute a wholly new method of reading in which the texts' moment and movement are presented in almost completely visual terms. Even the Boydell–Steevens edition with which the folio volumes are roughly contemporary does not offer such a process, its images being carefully selected for their composition and presentation of characters so that they fit the size of a folio page; the interpretive freedom of the large plates is absent. The translation of the plays into a set of visual treatments, both unprecedented and overlooked in earlier critical studies, offers a wholly new way of reading the plays on both literal and interpretive levels.

One of the more suggestive sequences is provided by the three Boydell images of *Much Ado about Nothing*. The first, by Peters (see Fig. 95),[73] shows the third act, with Beatrice overhearing Hero and Ursula in the garden speaking of Benedick's love for her. This image plays more directly with the voyeurism implied in the artist's treatments of *The Merry Wives of Windsor*. Cultural resonances are again generated by van Dyck costumes, yet the suggestion is closer to Ramberg's realignment of *Twelfth Night* within the social and aesthetic assumptions of Restoration comedy. This is achieved both in the sumptuous costumes and in the riotous foliage of the setting, almost suggestive of a female empowerment of the sort some have found in the banquet of sense in Wycherley's *The Country-Wife*, where the impotent Horner becomes the focus of unleashed female desire.[74] That the classical urn is covered in ungovernable foliage continues the eruptive rejection of male authority. Yet this is no Irigarayan overthrow: it is a wilfulness carefully kept within bounds by the explicit meaning of the image as defined by the play's events. Beatrice overhears the whisperings of Hero and Ursula, but the whole plan has been laid by Don Pedro after his conversation with Leonato in 2.1: just as he remains in control of the action in the play, so the male onlooker retains power in the image, seeing both the women talking and the woman overhearing. Given the elaborate foliage it almost becomes a scientific enquiry into the communicative habits of another species, and the distance of status that this implies is quite in accord with the mode of presentation. This power relation presents a powerfully immediate metaphor of Don Pedro's manipulation of Beatrice's feelings, which reveals the customary barbed humour of the mature comedies and problem plays. There is one further instance of control: in the large engraving the word PETERS is inscribed on the base of the classical urn. Overgrown it may be, but the power remains with the male artist and the male onlooker, and in this the image reveals itself more openly

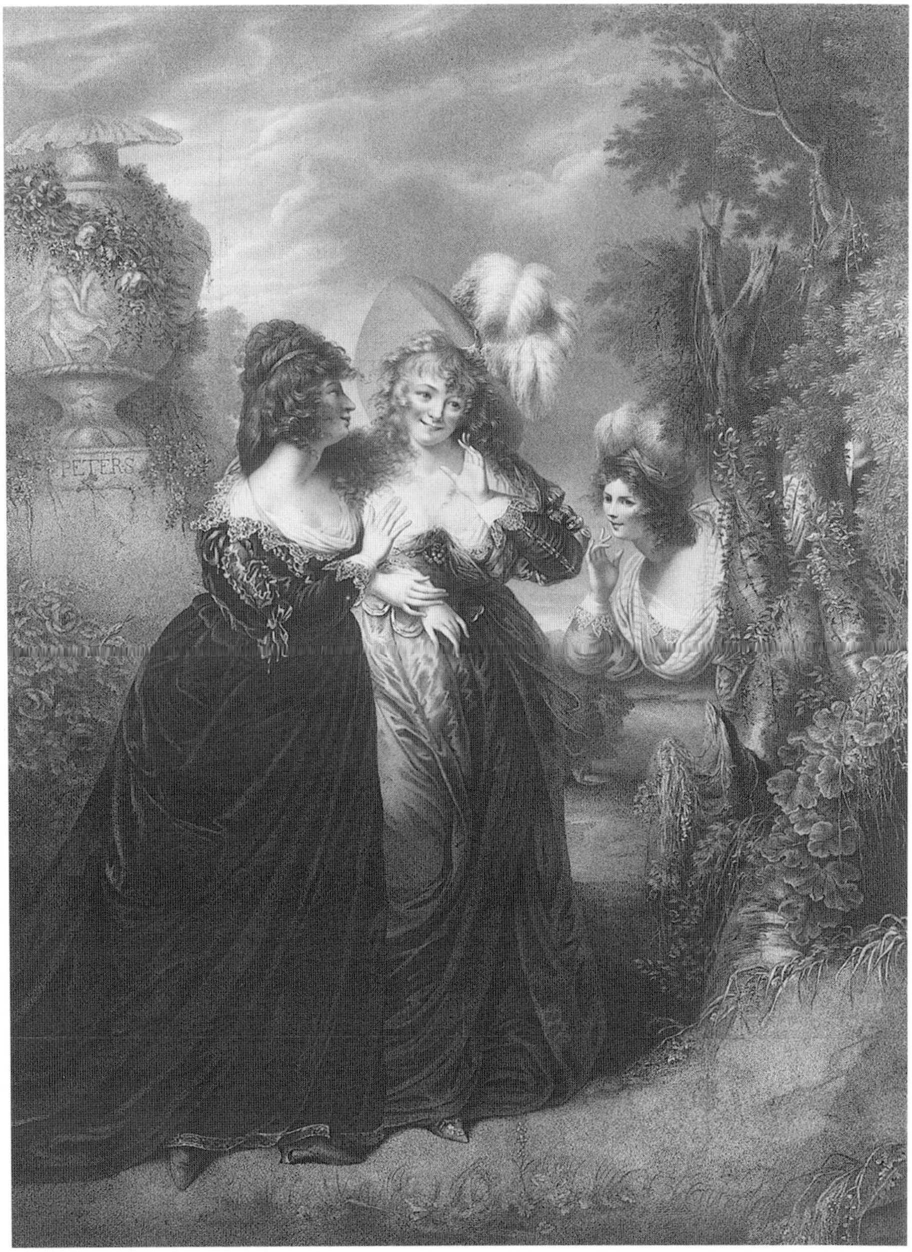

95 The Rev. Matthew William Peters, *Much Ado about Nothing*. Engraved by Jean Pierre Simon, 1790.

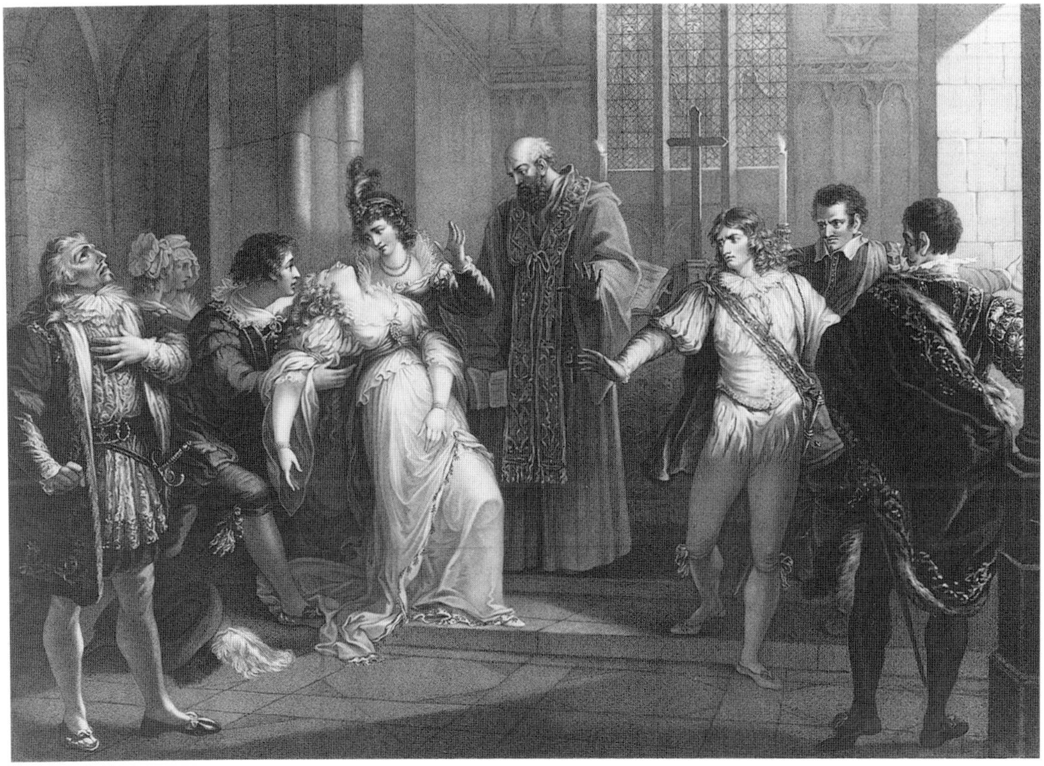

96 William Hamilton, *Much Ado about Nothing*. Engraved by Jean Pierre Simon, 1790.

as evidence of the late eighteenth-century gender politics that underlie the whole image from the mere selection of this phase of Don Pedro's plan, rather than his similar deception of Benedick in 2.3. The two scenes could have made a suggestive pairing in the tradition of dual images: instead, the inference is that only Beatrice may be manipulated in this way and that the event is somehow both uniquely female in its visual discourse and contained within a precise male hegemony. The inscription is significantly missing in the quarto plate,[75] resulting in a diminution of the image's range of meanings, implying in the large print a separation of Shakespeare as cultural and ideological object from the textual actuality of the plays.

Peters' image is followed by William Hamilton's treatment of 4.1 (see Fig. 96).[76] The characters' placement and gestures suggest that the composition may relate to a performance, and the figure of Claudio resembles Kemble, who had played the part for the first time at his wife's Drury Lane benefit on 30 May 1788.[77] But the origin is less important than the image's moment, located precisely by the engraved text:

LEON: Hath no man's dagger here a point for me?
BEAT: Why, how now cousin? wherefore sink you down?
[*Hero swoons*]

JOHN: Come, let us go: these things, come thus to light,
Smother her spirits up.
(4.1.102–5)

Evidence of the detailed reading of the play as a whole is provided in Hero's costume; while it is not possible to judge the accuracy of colouring, the dress resembles in many other features the account given by Margaret:

Cloth o'gold, and cuts, and laced with silver, set with pearls, down sleeves, side sleeves, and skirts, round underborne with a bluish tinsel (3.4.14–16)

A similar care is present in the ways in which the treatment reveals the scene's pivotal nature. The immediate narrative impact is shown in Leonato's despair, Hero's swoon, and the departure of Claudio with Don John and Don Pedro; as the *St James's Chronicle* claimed, the figures are 'described with great force of genius by the Artist, and powerfully engage our compassion'.[78] Later developments are also implied. Leonato's elaborate gesture foreshadows the extremity of his rejection of his daughter later in the scene, and also hints at his elaborate feigning of the anger of bereavement at the beginning of Act 5: the gesture that at first appears exaggeratedly theatrical becomes, when seen in the play's longer perspective, an astute visualisation of the contribution of character to the dynamics of the plot. The conciliatory gestures of the Friar foreshadow a more immediate event: his intervention to suggest a solution in the pretended death of Hero. The origin of the 'biting error' (3.4.170) that the Friar detects at the base of the accusation is suggested in the figure of Margaret between Leonato and Benedick: her complicity is further intimated by her placing at the left of the image in parallel with Don John at the right, with arm flung out motioning Claudio to leave. That his face is shown in shadow further suggests his guilt.

All of this is amplified by the image's place in the continuous reading offered by the sequence. There is little to link it stylistically with Peters' scene, but it is clear that a similar manipulative device underlies it – this time, Don John's earlier luring of Leonato to see Borachio and a waiting-woman at Hero's window – so that the play's recurrent trope of overhearing and overlooking is present by implication. Visually, another link is implied by a comment of Friedman's: 'the drama of the moment has provided Hamilton with the opportunity to show a charming and slender woman in an extreme pose'[79]. More recent critics might view the

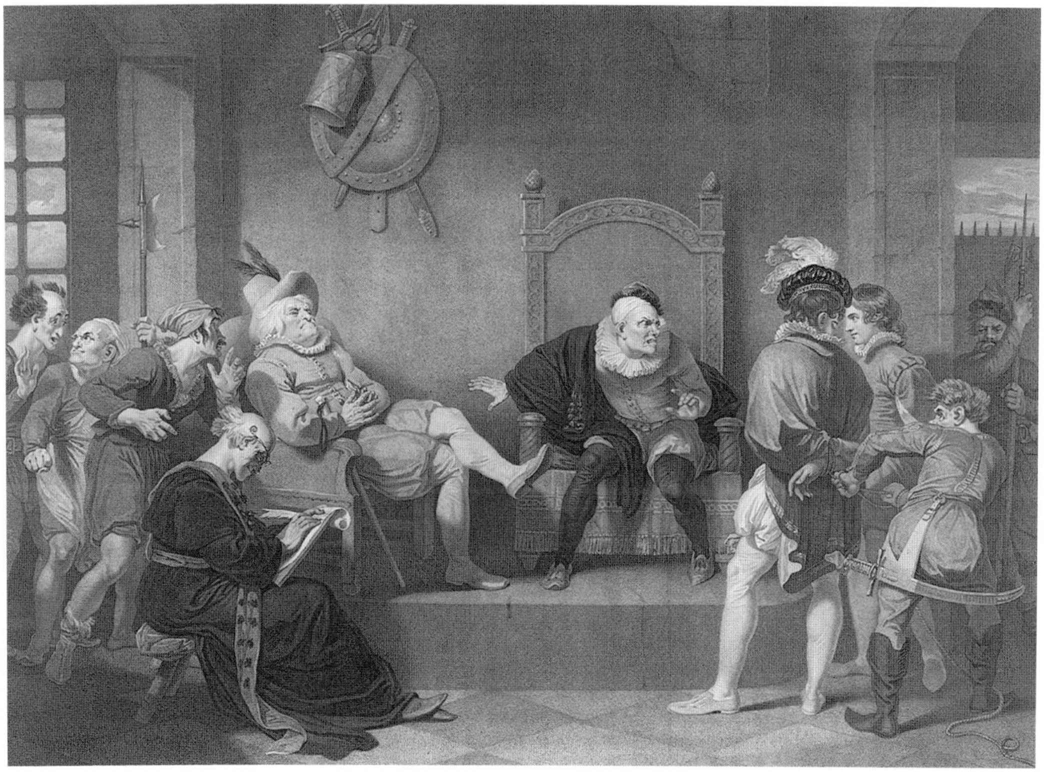

97 Robert Smirke, *The Examination of Conrade and Borachio*. Engraved by John Ogbourne, 1791.

image less moderately: it presents Hero as another female victim of male manipulation, and the posture offers further scopophilic pleasure, drawing another line of continuation both in the critical reading of the play and its contemporary recontextualising to link it to the Peters image and so unify more completely the reading experience.

The play's other level of action is presented in the third and final engraving, Robert Smirke's *The Examination of Conrade and Borachio* (Fig. 97),[80] located by a bare two lines: 'O villain! Thou wilt be condemned into everlasting redemption for this' (4.2.47–8). The image at once presents itself within a minor genre of Shakespeare painting that includes treatments by Hogarth, Hayman and Durno of Falstaff and the recruits, Bunbury's comic rural images, and Smirke's own Boydell painting of Pompey and Froth before Escalus. Here, however, the comic elements, especially the conventional use of exaggerated expressions and bodily forms, are carefully restrained. The faces of the watch follow physiognomic convention in having the distorted features of those not of noble birth, in contrast to the purer forms of their two prisoners, and the Sexton is presented in a mildly satirised form through the traditional guise of the bald, short-sighted schoolmaster. The most extreme expression is adopted by Dogberry. The closest resemblance here is to the figure of the fiend in one of Romney's sketches of Margery Jourdain conjuring, itself based on Le Brun's depiction of anger. The force of his verbal outburst, reproduced beneath the engraving, is much enhanced: overall the image conveys both the comic absurdity in which the scene is richly provided and an element of its seriousness. Dogberry speaks after the First Watchman has revealed the nature of the plot against Claudio; his anger may thus be read as quite serious, in response to the event itself regardless of the complicity of Conrade and Borachio. Instead of attempting a visual translation of the scene's many malapropisms, the image has as its point of focus an expression that fuses comedy with misdirected, and alarming, fury. While the *St James's Chronicle* might have been over-generous in seeing Smirke as 'an Artist who may prove a second HOGARTH', its claim that 'He has fully possessed himself of the spirit of the Autour [sic], yet avoided caricature' is a valid response.[81]

Seen as a sequence, the three images present a reading of the play that follows a trajectory from the deceptively innocuous tonalities of the Peters, in which apparently humorous deception is gathered into later gender politics, through a carefully contextualised treatment of the play's crisis as Hero faints, to a statement of anger within a comedic frame. All contain a suggestion of eventual resolution: the plot of Don Pedro leads to the marriage of Beatrice and Benedick, the figures of the Friar and Leonato suggest the deception that will reveal the falsity of Claudio's accusation, and the anger of Dogberry is the beginning of the process that unmasks Don John, revealing a narrative drive towards resolution that neatly draws together all the levels of plotting. In a visual sense, too, the images reveal a unity within different modes of action. The compositions rest on an opposition that presents a force basic to the play: the 'kind of merry war' (1.1.45–6) of Beatrice and Benedick, the plot of Don Pedro and Don John, Claudio's rejection of Hero, the absurd law-keeping of Dogberry and Verges all exemplify this. The result is to offer a visualisation of the play's modalities that, probably at a subconscious level for most of the engravings' readers, provides insistent and disturbing insights. This opposition contains another complexity: the uncertain tone of each image, poised between the extremes of comedic and tragedic action, presents a visual mediation of the play's verbal mode, with its constant use of violent expressions within an apparently comic setting.

The reading experience the Boydell *Collection of Prints* offers remains unique because of the size of the images, which itself imposes a rhetorical distance and slows the process of reading. In a very few cases, such as Fuseli's paired images of *A Midsummer Night's Dream*, or Northcote's three treatments of the Princes in *Richard III*, the progress is explicit and manipulated with care and deliberation by the artist; but in the groups of images produced by different artists, with different approaches, the result is suggestive in a different and perhaps more valuable way. A sequence of stylistically diverse engravings presents the onlooker with a range of critical engagements with the play that offers an early equivalent of reading three critical analyses of the text produced from different ideological standpoints. The parallel becomes closer when the common eighteenth-century practice of reading is recalled: placed on a reading table, the images would become the subject of social and critical debate. Seen thus, the engravings constitute a distinct form of experiencing the plays that combines the immediacy of the theatre with the depth of detailed textual study, verbalised within a social space of shared discourse.

Read in sequence, the visualisations of each play in the Boydell *Collection* offer a new way of looking at the texts that in its selection of key moments both unfolds a narrative and distances the reader from it, so presenting characters, ideas and linguistic tropes in a complex new form. This would be taken up on a far different scale by Howard's *Spirit of the Plays of Shakespeare* in the 1830s, and by the heavily illustrated editions such as that of Howard Staunton, with images after Sir John Gilbert, in 1864. The link is suggestive; it is one of many ways in which the *Collection of Prints*, for all its roots in a range of eighteenth century aesthetic and cultural assumptions, points forward to a new relation between the verbal and the visual in Shakespeare activity in the century to come.

NOTES

1. *The Manuscripts and Correspondence of James, First Earl of Claremont*, Report of Royal Commission on Historical Manuscripts, 2 vols. (London: H.M.S.O., 1891–4), letter of 9 June 1787, II, p. 51.
2. The event is discussed in Geoffrey Ashton, 'The Boydell Shakespeare Gallery: Before and After' in *The Painted Word*, ed. Peter Cannon-Brookes (London: Heim, 1991), pp. 37–43; Sven H. A. Bruntjen, *John Boydell, 1719–1804: A Study of Art Patronage and Publishing in Georgian London*, PhD thesis, Stanford University, 1974 (New York and London: Garland, 1985); Winifred H. Friedman, *Boydell's Shakespeare Gallery*, PhD thesis, Harvard University, 1974 (London and New York: Garland, 1976); W. M. Merchant, *Shakespeare and the Artist* (London: Oxford University Press, 1959).
3. Victoria and Albert Museum Library, London, *Boydell Publication Proposals*, 103.B. Reprinted in Bruntjen, *John Boydell*, pp. 252–6.
4. *The Times*, 7 May 1789, p 1.

5. *A catalogue of the pictures in the Shakspeare gallery Pall-Mall* (London: Sold at the place of exhibition, 1789).
6. *The Bee; or, a companion to the Shakspeare gallery: containing a catalogue-raisonné of all the pictures; with comments , illustrations and remarks* (London: T. Cadell, 1789).
7. *A catalogue of the pictures, &c. in the Shakspeare gallery, Pall-Mall* (London: W. Bulmer, 1802).
8. *The Exhibition of the Shakspeare gallery, Pall-Mall: being the last time the pictures can ever be seen as an entire collection* (London: W. Bulmer, 1805).
9. From the description, headed 'A Model, by Mr Banks, R. A. of the intended Alto-relievo, to be placed in the front of the Gallery, towards Pallmall', *A Catalogue . . .* (1789), p. 98.
10. 'It is an unhappy irony that the most ambitious attempt to illustrate Shakespeare should give the general impression of a massive irrelevance, an important by-way in this history.' Merchant, *Shakespeare and the Artist*, p. 66. 'Considering the vast outlay, Boydell's enterprise can hardly be called successful from a modern painter's point of view. Only a few good pictures were the result . . .' Sadekichi Hartmann, *Shakespeare in Art* (Boston: L. C. Page, 1901), p. 61.
11. For an extensive account of this, see David Solkin, *Painting for Money: The Visual Arts and the Public Sphere in Eighteenth-Century England* (New Haven and London: Yale University Press, 1992).
12. *The Manuscripts and Correspondence of James, First Earl of Charlemont*, II, p. 51.
13. *Boydell Shakespeare Subscription List*, Boston Public Library, Rare Book Department, RBD 366 Ms.G.164.2.
14. Bound with a subsequent Gallery Catalogue, Folger Shakespeare Library PR 2883 B7 1790 Cage.
15. Friedman, *Boydell's Shakespeare Gallery*, p. 69.
16. Names are transcribed as accurately as possible from the form in which they appear on the subscription list. They are reproduced by kind permission of the Rare Books Collection, Boston Public Library.
17. See Susan R. Stein, *The Worlds of Thomas Jefferson at Monticello* (New York: Abrams, 1999), p. 185. I am indebted to Dr Stein for providing additional information on the images.
18. A letter from Boydell to Steevens of December 24 1789 encloses 'a specimen of the Writing under the first Plate of Shakspeare' with the request that he 'look it over & correct it.' *George Steevens Correspondence*, Folger Shakspeare Library, C.b.10.16.
19. Letter to Sir William Hamilton, 1 January 1793. Folger Shakspeare Library Y.c.255.4.
20. Two letters in the Folger collection, one from a Mrs Cosway (Y.c.626 (1)) and one from James Barry, probably the miniaturist John Barry (Y.c.97 (1)), ask for instructions about the scenes and treatments the Alderman would like, but otherwise no correspondence or other record survives of any instructions being issued, or of any overall plan.
21. Stephen Gwynn, *Memorials of an Eighteenth Century Painter* (London: T. Fisher Unwin, 1896), p. 205.
22. *The Shakspeare Gallery, a poem by Mr Jerningham* (London: J. Robson, 1791), p. 4.
23. London: Logographic Press, J. Walter. The title page gives no author, but the copy in the Folger Shakespeare Library bears the manuscript addition 'By Samuel Felton Esq'.

24. Unsigned letter, 'Cautions in judging of the Paintings from Shakespeare,' *The Gentleman's Magazine*, Vol. LVIII, Part II, No. 3 (September 1788), pp. 778–9.
25. Untraced; engraved by Thomas Ryder, published 4 June 1793, 50 × 63 (19 ¾ × 24 ¾).
26. Untraced; engraved by William Satchwell Leney, published 4 June 1800, 49.5 × 63 (19 ½ × 24 ¾).
27. For a discussion of this process and the debate surrounding it, see Jonathan Brody Kramnick, 'Reading Shakespeare's Novels: Literary History and Cultural Politics in the Lennox-Johnson Debate', *Modern Language Quarterly*, Vol. 55 No. 4 (December 1994), pp. 429–53.
28. Untraced; engraved by John Collyer, published 1 December 1803, 50.5 × 63.5 (20 × 25).
29. *A Chronological History of England: or, an impartial abstract of the most remarkable transactions . . . that have happen'd in the several kings' reigns, since the first attempt by Julius Caesar, upon this southern-part of Great Britain*, 3 vols. (Oxford: Lintott, 1714–21).
30. Untraced; engraved by Robert Thew, published 1 March 1791, 49.5 × 62.5 (19 ½ × 24 ½).
31. *The Bee*, p. 44.
32. 1789? Untraced; engraved by Francis Legat, published 4 June 1790, 56 × 41 (22 × 16 ⅛).
33. 1794? Untraced; engraved by William Skelton, published 4 June 1795, 55.5 × 40.5 (21 ¾ × 16).
34. Oil on canvas, 300 × 203 (118 × 80); Pinacoteca Vaticana, Rome.
35. *The history of Kyng Richard the third*, in *The Workes of Sir Thomas More Knyght, sometyme Lorde Chauncellour of England, wrytten by him in the Englysh tonge*, 1557, Facsimile edition, intro. K. J. Wilson, 2 vols. (London: Scolar Press, 1978), p. 69.
36. David Hume, *The History of England, from the Invasion of Julius Caesar to the Revolution in 1688*, 1762 (New York: Worthington, 1880).
37. Herbert Butterfield's influential *The Whig Interpretation of History* (London: Bell, 1931) offers a critical reading of the assumptions of a later and more self-reflexive historiography, but is a valuable correlative to the assumptions of the much earlier period discussed here.
38. 157.8 × 220.7 (62 × 86 ½), Yale Center for British Art, New Haven. Engraved by Thomas Ryder, 50 × 63.5 (19 $^{11}/_{16}$ × 25), published 4 June 1794.
39. Untraced; engraved by Robert Thew, published 4 June 1801, 50 × 63 (19 $^{11}/_{16}$ × 24 ¾).
40. Untraced; engraved by William Charles Wilson, published 1 December 1798, 49.5 × 63 (19 ½ × 24 ¾).
41. Untraced; engraved by Luigi Schiavonetti, published 1 August 1792, 50.5 × 63.5 (20 × 25).
42. Recent works which have been influential in exploring this include Anne Bermingham, *Landscape and Ideology: The English Rustic Tradition, 1740–1860* (Berkeley and London: University of California Press, 1986); Linda Colley, *Britons: Forging the Nation, 1707–1837* (New Haven and London: Yale University Press, 1992); Carole Fabricant, 'The Literature of Domestic Tourism and the Public Consumption of Private Property', in Felicity Nussbaum and Laura Brown, eds., *The New Eighteenth Century: Theory, Politics, English Literature* (London and New York: Methuen, 1987); and Gerald Maclean, Donna Landry and Joseph P. Ward, eds., *The Country and the City Revisited: England and the Politics of Culture, 1550–1850* (Cambridge, Cambridge University Press, 1999).
43. 'Crown forests and the female georgic: Frances Burney and the Reconstruction of Britishness', in *The Country and the City Revisited*, pp. 196–212.

44. Untraced; engraving published 29 September 1797, 50.5 × 63.5 ($19\frac{3}{4}$ × 25).
45. Size as above; Legion of Honor, San Francisco, California.
46. See *The Country and the City Revisited*, pp. 200–202.
47. 9 George I c. 22, quoted in E. P. Thompson, *Whigs and Hunters: the Origin of the Black Act* (Harmondsworth: Penguin, 1977), Appendix I, pp. 270–7. Quotations taken from p. 271.
48. Richard Payne Knight, *The Landscape: A Didactic Poem. In Three Books. Addressed to Uvedale Price Esq.* (London: Bulmer, Shakespeare Printing Office, 1794).
49. *Essays on the Picturesque, as compared with the Sublime and the Beautiful; and, on the Use of Studying Pictures, for the Purpose of Improving Rural Landscape* (London: J. Mawman, 1810), note to p. 31 line 12, I, pp. 374–5.
50. 'Domestic Occurrences', *Gentleman's Magazine* LIX.4 Part (April 1789), pp. 366–70. Quotation from p. 370.
51. Untraced; engraved by Robert Thew, published Dec. 24 1793, 64 × 46 (25 2/10 × $18\frac{1}{8}$). Also engraved as one of the Quarto plates by James Saunders, published 4 June 1800, 17.3 × 27.2 ($6\frac{13}{16}$ × 10.$\frac{11}{16}$).
52. *Tracks in the Snow: Studies in English Science and Art* (London: Grey Walls Press, 1946), p. 81.
53. For example, *The Institution of the Order of the Garter*, oil on canvas 287 × 448.3 (113 × 176), HM the Queen, Windsor.
54. Allen Staley, *Benjamin West: An American Painter at the English Court* (Baltimore, Md.: Baltimore Museum of Art, 1989), p. 68.
55. Published 4 June 1800, 17.3 × 27.2 ($6\frac{13}{16}$ × $10\frac{11}{16}$).
56. Untraced; engraved by Jean Pierre Simon, published 24 December 1793. 64 × 46.5 ($25\frac{3}{16}$ × $18\frac{1}{4}$).
57. *Falstaff in the Buckbasket*. Oil on canvas, 137 × 170 cm (54 × 67), Kunsthaus, Zurich.
58. Oil on canvas, 92.1 × 123.2 ($36\frac{1}{2}$ × $49\frac{1}{2}$) Yale Center for British Art, Paul Mellon Fund, New Haven, Conn. Engraved by Samuel Middiman, 50 × 63 ($19\frac{11}{16}$ × $24\frac{3}{4}$), published 29 September 1791.
59. 'Die Kupferstiche nach der Shakspeare-Gallerie in London. Briefe an einen Freund'. 1793. *Kritische Schriften*, I, 3–34.
60. *c.* 1610–15, body colour on vellum, 22.86 × 17.78 (9 × 7), the Earl of Powis.
61. Oil on canvas, 148.6 × 207.6 ($58\frac{1}{2}$ × $81\frac{3}{4}$), Tate Britain.
62. *The Man of Feeling*, ed. Brian Vickers (London: Oxford University Press, 1967), p. 84.
63. *St James's Chronicle*, 19–21 May 1789.
64. Untraced; engraved by John Browne, published 1 December 1795, 49.5 × 63 ($19\frac{1}{2}$ × $24\frac{13}{16}$).
65. Copy by W. H. Jeayes in the grangerised copy of *The Plays of William Shakespeare, from the Corrected text of Johnson and Steevens* (London: John Stockdale, 1807). From the collection of George C. George. Vol. VI, *The Merchant of Venice*, facing p 103. Folger Shakspeare Library PR 2752 1802 Copy 2 v3 Sh Col.
66. Peter de Bolla, 'The Charmed Eye', in *Body and Text in the Eighteenth Century*, ed. Veronica Kelly and Dorothea E. von Mucke (Stanford, Calif: Stanford University Press, 1994), pp. 89–111. Quotation from p. 93. See also John Dixon Hunt, *Garden and Grove* (London: Dent, 1986), *passim*.

67. 69.8 × 119.4 (27 1/2 × 47), National Gallery, London.
68. *Richard Wilson: the Landscape of Reaction*, Exh. Cat. (London: Tate Gallery, 1982).
69. *Landscape and Ideology: The English Rustic Tradition, 1740–1860* (London and New York: Thames and Hudson, 1987), p. 29.
70. Both untraced.
71. Untraced; engraved by Jean Pierre Simon, published 1 December 1795, 64 × 46 (25 3/16 × 18 1/8).
72. The workings of this in terms of both theatre and visual representation through the nineteenth century are explored by Stephen Orgel in *Imagining Shakespeare* (London and New York: Palgrave Macmillan, 2003), pp. 144–62.
73. Untraced; engraved by Jean Pierre Simon, published 4 June 1790, 64 × 46.4 (25 3/16 × 18 1/4).
74. See, in particular, Harold Weber, 'Horner and his "Women of Honour": The Dinner Party in *The Country-Wife*'. *Modern Language Quarterly*, Vol. 43 No. 2 (June 1982), pp. 107–120.
75. Engraved by James Heath, published 1 March 1791, 15.6 × 22 (6 1/8 × 8 5/8).
76. Untraced; engraved by Peter Simon, published 4 June 1790, 50 × 63 (19 3/4 × 24 13/16).
77. Charles Beecher Hogan, *The London Stage 1660–1800. Part 5: 1776–1800*, Vol. 2 (Carbondale, Ill: Southern Illinois University Press, 1968), p. 1061.
78. 7–9 May 1789.
79. *Boydell's Shakespeare Gallery*, p. 181.
80. 1789? 154.9 × 215.9 (61 × 85), Royal Shakespeare Theatre Gallery, Stratford-on-Avon. Engraved by John Ogborne, published 1 March 1791, 50 × 63 (19 3/4 × 24 13/16).
81. 14–16 May 1789.

CHAPTER 10

SUMMATIONS AND DEPARTURES

In November 1803 Boydell announced that he could no longer meet the demands of his creditors. Different reasons have been given for the failure. To some, the quality of the prints was too poor, the use of stipple engraving being encouraged to save money. Others ascribed it to the war with France in 1793, which increased the cost of high-quality paper and prevented the vital sales of prints abroad. Perhaps the most likely cause was the sheer cost: the fees of both painters and engravers had to be met, the latter far higher because of the time involved, and Boydell's continued investment in other ventures magnified his difficulties. In 1804, an Act of Parliament licensed the sale of lottery tickets for the disposal of the paintings, and the lottery was held on 28 January 1805, six weeks after Boydell's death. The holder of the winning ticket, the sixty-second to be drawn, was 'Mr. Tassie, of Leicester Square, a gentleman celebrated for his love of the arts'.[1] Josiah Boydell, John's nephew, who himself contributed seven paintings to the Gallery, offered £10,000 for the collection. Tassie preferred to have the paintings auctioned individually by Mr. Christie; the total raised for the sale of 167 paintings was £6,182. One of the ironies of this was that the disposal did far more to further international awareness of the paintings than any other move, since many are now in public and private collections throughout the world.

The failure of the Boydell Shakespeare Gallery does not mark the end of Shakespeare painting as a serious critical endeavour, but it certainly suggests itself as a point at which the nature of such imaging began to change. There were various ventures of the same kind, notably Woodmason's Irish Shakespeare Gallery, but even Fuseli, who vigorously supported the venture and contributed extensively to it, did not produce for it images of the critical intensity and concentration of his earlier work, with the significant exception of the *Macbeth Consulting the Vision of the Armed Head* discussed in Chapter 8. One reason for the move away from galleries of this sort was financial; it became apparent that commissioning and reproducing work of sufficient quality was simply not commercially valid. Shortly, other forces would take over: the great Victorian moral impulse of aesthetic education through public collections, beginning with the building of the Victoria and Albert Museum, and the instigation of the Chantrey Bequest in the 1850s, meant that paintings were made available by public institutions, not private commercial enterprises, other of course than the private galleries which grew to satisfy the rather different demands of collectors.

One aspect of the Shakespeare Gallery did, however, look forward: the publication of the Boydell-Steevens edition of the plays in serial parts combining text and image. Within ten years of its appearance, Rowlandson and Coombe collaborated on *Dr Syntax* and Ackermann issued *The Microcosm of London*. In 1822, Cruikshank produced the phenomenally successful *Life in London*. In the 1830s, Dickens began producing *Sketches by Boz* in the same form, and the illustrated serial novel became the dominant cultural form for the next thirty years. That all these – and, to a limited extent, the ten-part illustrated Shakespeare issued by Charles Heath from 1802 to 1804 – succeeded where the Boydell venture failed may relate to their less ambitious format, and their more overtly populist stance. It certainly has to do with the nature and costs of their production, which was far less elaborate, on a much smaller physical scale, and above all far more rapid, with parts available at regular intervals to obviate the long delay in recovering initial costs. All these forces have a direct impact on Shakespeare imaging, their results perhaps most directly seen in the popular Victorian editions of the plays such as that edited by Howard Staunton, with illustrations by Sir John Gilbert, that first appeared in monthly instalments.[2] New techniques of paper-making and block engraving made it possible to produce this simply and cheaply; the railway network facilitated rapid and extensive distribution; the result was a genuinely popular text of strikingly high quality, both materially and conceptually.

In appearance and structure the edition was very different from Boydell's Shakespeare. Instead of special fonts and expensive paper, it was produced with existing designs on wood-pulp stock: above all, it was a heavily illustrated edition in which the images were cut into the text instead of being separate plates. Word and image were carefully integrated in the volumes, the *mise-en-page* allowing the plays to progress in compound verbal and visual terms. This contributed to a change in the way images were read: the practice of standing round a large volume, pausing to examine an engraving to explore its subtleties through a dialogue both social and intellectual, gave way to an individual experience in which image and word

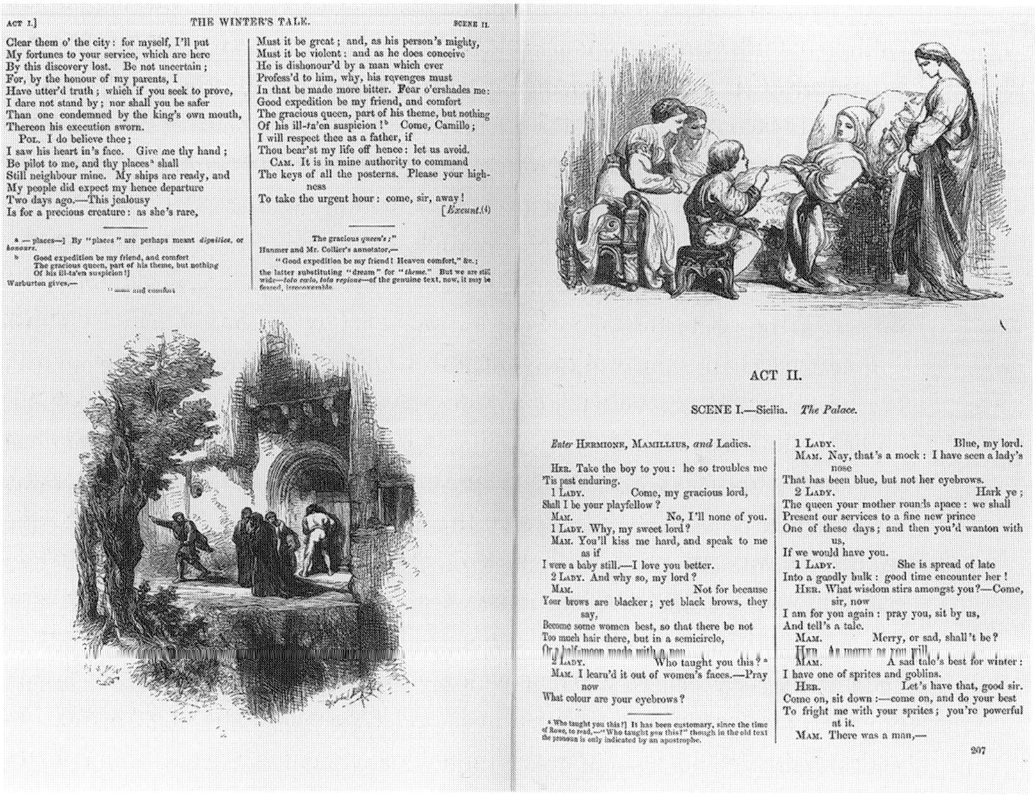

ACT I.] THE WINTER'S TALE. SCENE II.

Clear them o' the city: for myself, I'll put
My fortunes to your service, which are here
By this discovery lost. Be not uncertain;
For, by the honour of my parents, I
Have utter'd truth; which if you seek to prove,
I dare not stand by; nor shall you be safer
Than one condemned by the king's own mouth,
Thereon his execution sworn.
POL. I do believe thee;
I saw his heart in's face. Give me thy hand;
Be pilot to me, and thy places[a] shall
Still neighbour mine. My ships are ready, and
My people did expect my hence departure
Two days ago.—This jealousy
Is for a precious creature: as she's rare,
Must it be great; and, as his person's mighty,
Must it be violent: and as he does conceive
He is dishonour'd by a man which ever
Profess'd to him, why, his revenges must
In that be made more bitter. Fear o'ershades me:
Good expedition be my friend, and comfort
The gracious queen, part of his theme, but nothing
Of his ill-ta'en suspicion![b] Come, Camillo;
I will respect thee as a father, if
Thou bear'st my life off hence: let us avoid.
CAM. It is in mine authority to command
The keys of all the posterns. Please your highness
To take the urgent hour: come, sir, away!
[*Exeunt.*(4)

a —places—] By "places" are perhaps meant *dignities*, or *honours*.

b Good expedition be my friend, and comfort
The gracious queen, part of his theme, but nothing
Of his ill-ta'en suspicion!]
Warburton gives,—
"— and comfort
The gracious *queen's*;"
Hanmer and Mr. Collier's annotator,—
"Good expedition be my friend! Heaven comfort," &c.;
the latter substituting "dream" for "*theme*." But we are still wide—*toto cœlo, toto regione*—of the genuine text, now, it may be feared, irrecoverable.

ACT II.

SCENE I.—Sicilia. *The Palace.*

Enter HERMIONE, MAMILLIUS, *and* Ladies.

HER. Take the boy to you: he so troubles me
'Tis past enduring.
1 LADY. Come, my gracious lord,
Shall I be your playfellow?
MAM. No, I'll none of you.
1 LADY. Why, my sweet lord?
MAM. You'll kiss me hard, and speak to me as if
I were a baby still.—I love you better.
2 LADY. And why so, my lord?
MAM. Not for because
Your brows are blacker; yet black brows, they say,
Become some women best, so that there be not
Too much hair there, but in a semicircle,
Or a half-moon made with a pen.
2 LADY. Who taught you this?[a]
MAM. I learn'd it out of women's faces.—Pray now
What colour are your eyebrows?
1 LADY. Blue, my lord.
MAM. Nay, that's a mock: I have seen a lady's nose
That has been blue, but not her eyebrows.
2 LADY. Hark ye;
The queen your mother rounds apace: we shall
Present our services to a fine new prince
One of these days; and then you'd wanton with us,
If we would have you.
1 LADY. She is spread of late
Into a goodly bulk: good time encounter her!
HER. What wisdom stirs amongst you?—Come, sir, now
I am for you again: pray you, sit by us,
And tell's a tale.
MAM. Merry, or sad, shall't be?
HER. As merry as you will.
MAM. A sad tale's best for winter:
I have one of sprites and goblins.
HER. Let's have that, good sir.
Come on, sit down:—come on, and do your best
To fright me with your sprites; you're powerful at it.
MAM. There was a man,—

a Who taught you this?] It has been customary, since the time of Rowe, to read,—"Who taught *you* this?" though in the old text the pronoun is only indicated by an apostrophe.

207

98 John Gilbert, Page opening from *The Winter's Tale*. Engraved by the brothers Dalziel, 1858.

formed a single progress, the subtle narrative effects of which have been sympathetically explored by Peter Holland.[3] This integration brought with it a move away from the effects achieved in the finest eighteenth-century images, a continuous movement through the text displacing the visual concentration of a concept or verbal strand evident throughout the play that moved temporal statement across into spatial presentation. A page-opening from *The Winter's Tale* (III. 206–7, Fig. 98) demonstrates the different way of conveying the play's movement. At the left hand, Camillo is shown ushering Polixenes away from the Bohemian court; at the right, Hermione is shown with Mamillius and her attendants. This balance reveals the change from exterior and escape to an interior relationship defined by gender and enclosure, in so doing disclosing one of the play's main oppositions; but the visualisation in two frames presents a diachronic sequence quite different from the synchronic statements found in earlier paintings.

A different approach was evident in the work of Frank Howard, *The Spirit of the Plays of Shakespeare*.[4] Published in 1833, this consisted of a set of between twelve and twenty images for each play that presented it in the form of a sequence of 'outline plates', each keyed to a separate page containing about a dozen lines of quotations. This almost presented the plays in the form of a graphic novel, not least because it rearranged the events into a novelistic sequence, placing events merely reported in a simple chronological order. With some exceptions, the quality of the plates is poor, and the separation of text and image offered an inconvenient reading experience with neither the visual power of the Boydell prints nor the integration of the Staunton-Gilbert edition; but the volume significantly expands the range of reading practices through which the texts were assimilated.

Material circumstances of this kind joined with changes in sensibility to form a reflexive, mutually modifying equation that acted upon Shakespeare imaging. Probably the single most important development was the move away from literary painting towards a concern with landscape that, with the single and glorious exception of William Blake, became the dominant form in English Romantic painting. It was this, rather than the heroic literary school that the Alderman had hoped would emerge from his Gallery, that established the national identity of English painting. An aesthetic of seemingly immediate experiential involvement began to displace one of literary mediation – ironically enough, since it owed much of its force to the literary presentation of landscape that can be traced back as far as the 1740s. The change may be seen in very specific terms by comparing William Hodges' image of Jaques and the wounded stag with a treatment of the same scene by John Constable (Fig. 99). Instead of the compound examination of melancholy, or the meditation on theodicy found in Blake's watercolour, Constable's image approaches the scene as a naturalistic, experiential landscape in which morality and melancholy reflection have no place. Like Hodges' painting it was produced for reproduction, but in a strikingly different context, the volume of mezzotints by David Lucas titled *English Landscape Scenery*.[5] Using the very loose style of his mature work to involve the onlooker, Constable's image is part of a different, fundamentally Wordsworthian tradition of landscape in which the equation between inner and outer actualities is the main concern. Except in the unspoken assumptions of this tradition, Constable does not engage, as does Hodges, with the aesthetics of feeling, and does little to address the larger issues of the play, instead placing it within an experienced landscape that, except for the presence of Amiens and the First Lord, almost completely ignores the levels of irony surrounding the presentation of Jaques' reported speech. As Northcote relocates *Richard III* within a novelised history of England, Constable places *As You Like It* within a discourse of national identity defined by landscape: the two together represent something of the range of discourses to which a reinvention of Shakespeare

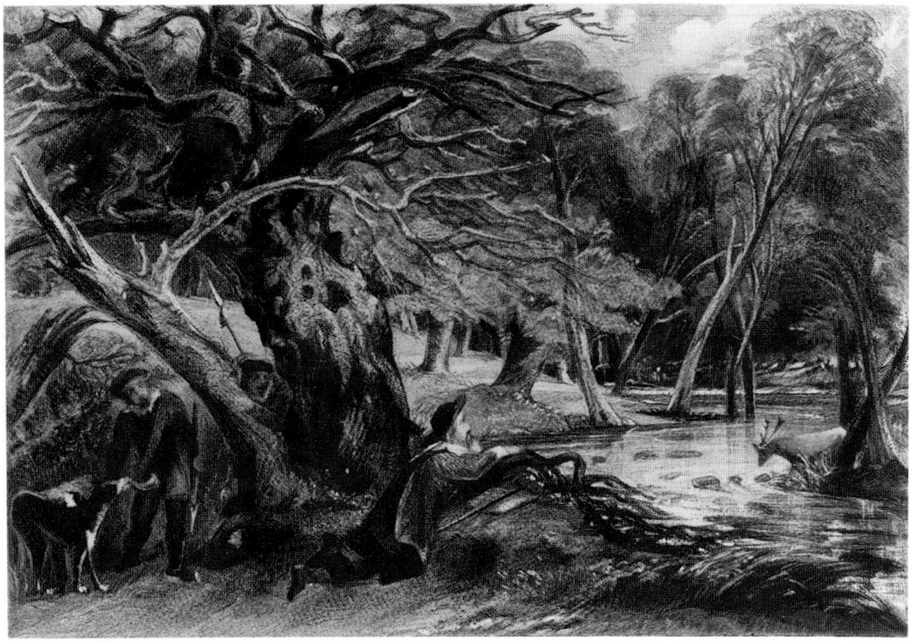

99 John Constable, 'Jaques and the Wounded Stag'. Mezzotint by John Lucas, 1845.

was central, and reveal how much they had changed between the 1780s and the 1840s.

Changes in painterly form are matched by shifts in the way the plays were approached. The growing interest in their verbal structures, from which even stage production was regarded as a trivialising distraction, was explicitly linked to the damaging effect of painting by Charles Lamb, who supplemented his claim that Lear in the theatre 'has nothing in it but what is painful and disgusting'[6] by asking rhetorically 'What injury (short of the theatres) did not Boydell's Shakespeare Gallery do me with Shakespeare?'[7] Certainly, if performance was too egregious a traduction of the literary texts, adaptation into easel-painting would be a reappraisal far too radical: the private reading experience was one of many elements to displace the shared aesthetic assimilation of the Shakespeare painting, although its modification in the illustrated edition, and in adaptation as prose narrative, especially for children, both became acceptable alternatives. Such experience was enhanced by the fashion for portraits of Shakespearean characters, of which Charles Heath's *Shakespeare's Heroines* has already been cited as some kind of culmination.

Despite Lamb's strictures, the relation between text and theatre enjoyed a renewed closeness, perhaps because the gap between performance and textual editing began to narrow sharply, emblematised by the return of Lear's Fool to the stage in 1838. The concern for stage realism that began at about this time, to climax in the work of Beerbohm Tree, is related to a similar concern for realism in painting. Specific examples also reveal the closeness of the links: Daniel Maclise's *Malvolio and Olivia* (1840),[8] perhaps based on a performance featuring Ellen Tree as Viola in 1839, was influential in the design and staging of a production of *Twelfth Night* with Ellen Chapman as Maria, Caroline Heath as Olivia and Walter Lucy as Malvolio in 1858, reversing the earlier tradition of paintings borrowing from stage precedent. That this is evidenced by a contemporary photograph reveals the growth of the new medium as a further aesthetic impulse. Many artists in England saw photography as a rival to their mimetic abilities, and so moved towards a style that concerned itself with minute representation of detail. This aided the newly circular relationship between painting and stage design, with the stage photograph forming a significant intermediate form. In turn, editions such as the mid-century Tallis Shakespeare used retouched photographs of actors in character, with the addition of painted scenery, as the basis of their illustrations. Yet these added little in critical terms to the plays' unfolding, being of interest largely for the performance styles they record.

Aside from the various kinds of illustrated editions, nineteenth-century Shakespeare imaging took a variety of forms. John Martin's *Macbeth* (1820)[9] is rare in presenting within the initial encounter with the witches the force of justice, symbolised in the livid vortex of sea, rock and cloud in which the natural world is shown to avenge the murders. Turner, from whom Martin borrowed this compositional form, produced few Shakespeare images: *Queen Mab's Cave* (*c*. 1846)[10] is a late exercise in light and colour as much as a critical reading, and the inclusion of a figure of Shylock with knife and scales in the foreground of *The Grand Canal: A Street Scene in Venice* (*c*. 1837)[11] is a reference to what had become, by then, the cultural emblem by which most English viewers knew the Italian city. Painting the plays was considerably revitalised by the original members of the Pre-Raphaelite Brotherhood, a term now used with confused and flattening breadth. Hunt and Millais did much to revive interest in Shakespeare painting, but after the initial iconographic impulse their images took on a more direct approach, focusing on the hyper-real depiction, often with implicit moral commentary, of a single moment. The Victorian obsession with time, in what Tennyson called 'the passion of the past',[12] militated strongly against a tradition allowing the corporeal concentration of a sequential narrative within a single image, as a number of paintings that could only present narrative or thematic consequences in three related images confirm – not only Augustus Egg's *Past and Present* but literary topics such as Arthur Hughes' *Eve of St Agnes* (1856)[13] and his *As You Like It* triptych (1871–3).[14] Holman Hunt's *Claudio and Isabella* (1850–3),[15] painstaking in its presentation of an instant of moral dilemma, offers little new as a critical reading of the forces of the play and works as a post-Keatsian medieval pendant to Hunt's *Awakening Conscience* (1853–4):[16] the morality, not the literary-visual text, is the focus in what Martin Meisel sees as a concern to present visually the 'Moment of Truth',[17] but the focus on the fictive concept of a single revelatory instant has deep consequences for the visualisation of longer sequential patterns. William Dyce's *Henry VI at Towton* (1858–60)[18] further denies any possibility of a literary or theatric imagination through its intense presentation of landscape. Neither advances beyond its initial impact to offer a lasting critical insight into the text it visualises. Rossetti's *Death of Lady Macbeth* (*c.* 1875)[19] certainly actualises an essential moment reported, not enacted, in the play; but it is hard not to see it as another page in his collection of 'Stunners'.

There are, of course, exceptions: Millais's *Ophelia* (1850–1),[20] for all its obsessive detail, does release a larger truth: the open arms of the dying woman suggest a mature sexuality that Hamlet failed to understand – as have generations of critics and readers. That the posture also suggests a crucifixion is a resonance unheard by most onlookers, and the shock which greeted a female crucifixion image in the 1990s implies that it will remain unacknowledged – unfortunately so, since it says much about sacrifice and suffering in a character too easily sentimentalised in the large numbers of later images, from Arthur Hughes[21] to J. W. Waterhouse.[22] It is unfortunate that an image so valuably provocative is regarded by so many through anecdotes about its origins, in terms that deny its critical and moral seriousness, both within and without its heavily gendered framing. The same artist's earlier *Ferdinand lured by Ariel* (1849)[23] relocates the multiple identities of the spirit within an English landscape and hints at the power of evil he contains; in depicting the figures in isolation against a meticulous botanical setting it moves away from any possibility of a larger critical handling, but the initial disturbance caused by the spectral coloration of Ariel is suggestively troubling.

Images such as these apart, nineteenth century Shakespeare painting quickly becomes a branch of Victorian genre painting, a prey to fashions of taste in fairies, childhood and noble heroines displaced from a larger sense of the plays' movement and driving ambivalences that characterises the most powerfully effective of the eighteenth-century images. The fairy-paintings of Joseph Noel Paton, full of succulent nude fairies and grotesque elves with phallic probosces, at least move away from the mimetic deliberation that, in the works of Dyce, Leighton and others riding on the flood tide of Arnoldian culture, removes any sense of literary imagination from the images. Richard Dadd is one of the few who presented the ambivalence of the fairy world, or indeed approached it in terms that moved beyond the eroticism often quite literally thinly veiled in the work of most of his contemporaries. The sentiment of the moment, a tyrannical naturalism and a scopophilia made respectable through the association with Shakespeare, came to dominate.

Qualitative comparisons are, however, invalid: nineteenth-century Shakespeare paintings clearly operate in a different way, and act on quite different assumptions, from their eighteenth-century predecessors, the great paintings of Hogarth, Fuseli and even relatively minor figures such as Hodges or Hayman. Perhaps this is the result of two developments that exist in different but related areas of literary production. The growth of the realist novel that had already manifested itself as a major influence on the outlook fundamental to the Boydell images became in the nineteenth century the overwhelming way of seeing, dominating the theatre, annexing large tracts of poetry, and – with the willing collaboration of photography – taking charge of almost every level of painting. Allied to this was the growth of Shakespearean criticism as a branch of the nascent discipline of literary criticism. The lectures of A. C. Bradley that would be published as *Shakespearean Tragedy* in 1904 were given in Liverpool and Glasgow at the same time as Whistler produced his *Ellen Terry as Lady Macbeth*,[24] and the relation seems more than one of chance temporal coincidence. Voluptuously serpentine in clinging green and gold – the overtones of Keats's 'Lamia' are hard to avoid – she holds the crown above her head in an insistent revelation of the ambition that is, in Bradleian terms, her tragic flaw. She is revealed in full sexual power, and the image conveys a true sense of performance; yet ultimately it exists in the genre of character portraits, not visual criticism.

Assessing the eventual achievement of the visual texts explored in these pages is of necessity limited by the imponderable equation it confronts. Making verbal assessments of visualisations of structures themselves arising from extensive verbal syntaxes may be suggestively revealing, but may as easily be simplistic and reductive. That so little has been said and done to assimilate these images into a mainstream of Shakespeare criticism – when, if ever, there was such a thing – does not necessarily imply that their critical mediations of the plays were not grasped by their original and subsequent onlookers. It may instead confirm the difficulty of stating critical readings that, presented visually, are assimilated at a level beneath words. Certainly, a tenacious tradition arose, not only in the endeavour to present the plays in visual form, but also to interpret them through more specific streams of iconographical convention and configuration. That complex acts of criticism were produced is evident from the foregoing pages; and certainly, the images were seen and, in many instances, reproduced, so that an awareness at some level, beyond or beneath the verbal, was manifest in their onlookers. Perhaps this is itself the best evidence of the force of the images: that, at the time of their production, a large number of the images achieved success in a variety of ways and on many levels. That they are not better known or more highly valued perhaps has much to do with the historical growth and compartmentalisation of academic subject areas, which pull against any equation or elision of the verbal and the visual.

It is tempting to see within the century a move towards the wider dissemination of Shakespeare imaging, paralleling the greater availability of Hogarth's engravings in increasingly cheaper editions. But this is manifestly not the case. Those images that were available in engravings remained limited in circulation, as much through their large size as through their cost, which only rarely dropped below £1, at a time when a popular novel could be obtained for a quarter of that sum. The inclusion of so many Shakespeare images in Vauxhall Gardens in the 1740s represented a widespread extension of the visibility of such work, that otherwise would remain the province of the wealthy and those with time and money to invest in gallery going: here, as so often, the concept of an expanding middle class needs to be seen with very considerable caution, referring to the new merchant and administrative ranks. Many of the images circulated within a group restricted by interest and social contact as much as financial resources. Sir William Hamilton's collection of ancient vases furnished the iconographical basis of two of Fuseli's most subtly suggestive images of *Hamlet*: Hamilton was the original owner of Zuccarelli's *Macbeth*, sold at auction to the collector and patron the Duke of Grosvenor, but not before it had been seen and admired by William Lock, who commissioned another version. An amateur artist himself, Lock produced drawings much admired by Fuseli, who praised in particular a sketch of Lady Hamilton, who was the model for Romney's *Cassandra Raving*. This apparently closed circle did produce tangential outgrowths: Lock's version of the Zuccarelli was engraved by Woollett, and Romney's painting by Legat, for Boydell. But the larger geometry remains the model until the changes in production discussed above allowed the celebration of Shakespeare as a national property, and in high Victorian times a national duty, to become more fully dispersed.

Of the images themselves, the most incisive reveal the separate identities of a number of critical, interpretive voices. Hogarth's referential palimpsests disclose the ironic use of allusion within a frame that quite deliberately employs the plays as a critique of contemporary politics and society, revealing their explorations of human corruption as a phenomenon outside time. They also fulfil an essential function of drawing the plays into an arena of contemporary moral and political debate, extended into the compound social and political spaces of Vauxhall Gardens by the images produced by Hayman and his circle. Hogarth's awareness of the performative aspects of Shakespeare's texts finds continuation in Romney's constellations of readings of the same scene, that reveal through their fugitive immediacy a fine and instinctual grasp of the plays and their issues that at the same time metaphorically discloses the constant change of the theatric progression. Fuseli's allusions, rich and strange in their depth and breadth, fuse the intellectual and the emotional into readings suggestive of the plays' darker sexuality and issues of power. Reynolds uses iconography to offer both specific textual insights and – in *Puck* – richly comic sensual games that address serious concerns about genre. Blake reveals a paradoxical grasp both of the identity of the plays' language and of the impossibility of its translation into purely visual terms, at the same time assimilating Shakespeare's texts into his own personal mythography in another manifestation of the dialogue between the texts and contemporary creative practice. The Boydell paintings and prints offer another version of assimilation, while suggesting a wholly new reading experience through the progress of images by different artists. Within the individual stances of these works – and those of less prolific artists including Wootton, the Runciman brothers, and Nathaniel Dance – may be discerned detailed construals of the plays' moments and movements that are unsaid elsewhere in the century's extensive catalogue of responses to the plays, and suggest the wider freedoms of more recent production and criticism.

One reason for this breadth, ironically enough, is the curious happenstance of these images' existence at a time when theatre production and published editions were in a condition of continuous flux, and criticism had not asserted itself into a position of dominance. The painters also had the great advantage that the discipline of English Literature had not established itself in the universities, so that the plays, even allowing for the increasing weight of cultural nationalism they had to bear, were not yet worn down by the crushing weight of syllabuses and approved interpretations. Without these limits, the painters of the eighteenth century were free to present new ways of direct and implied interpretation, making iconographical allusion, translating verbal into visual and temporal into spatial. At their finest, they established the unique place of the analytical Shakespearean image as the fourth limb that, with production, editing and criticism, completes the parallelogram of forces that drives Shakespeare activity in the eighteenth century. In consequence they become a part of the collaborative process through

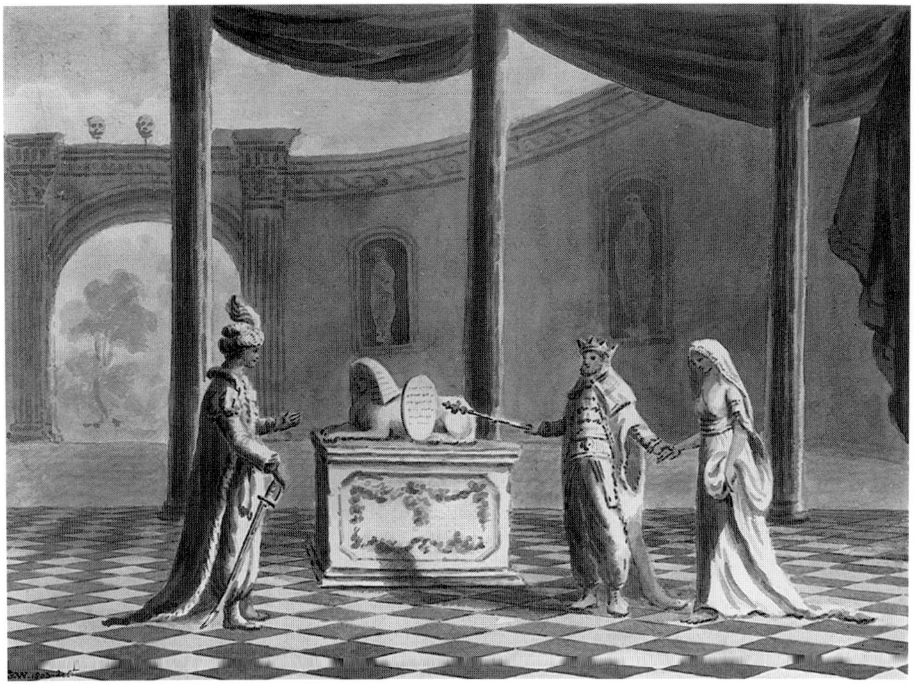

100 George Webbe, *Pericles*, watercolour, after 1807, from a grangerised copy of Heath's *Shakespeare*.

which readers, artists, critics and performers all weave their own changing textual fabric into the entity, sometimes consensual, sometimes controversial, that constitutes the plays and the canon.

At another level, the value of these images resides in their constant stress, through their physical immediacy, on the difference between the visual and theatrical text, reminding the onlooker repeatedly of the otherness of the dramatic entity and revealing in the implicit dialogue between the two media the sheer difficulty of stating either within prose that strives towards critical explication. The act of reading a painting, of relating it to the text, and of distilling its critical spirit is as much aesthetic as intellectual, and inevitably this book has negotiated interpretive obstacles that remove the immediacy of the initial moment, of turning the corner as in some picturesque garden to be confronted with a startling new perspective.

For this reason, it is important at this stage to hand back the act of visual criticism to the image and to the reader, and for this I advance one final image, with no comment but its textual location. It is a watercolour of *Pericles*, dating from some time soon after 1807, included in a grangerised edition of the plays in the

Folger Shakespeare Library (Fig. 100). Beneath it appear these lines from the play, spoken by Antiochus:

> Read the conclusion then;
> Which read and not expounded, 'tis decreed -
> As these before thee, – thou thyself shalt bleed
>
> 1.1.57–9

Inscribed on the verso are the words 'Presented to Geo. C. George of Penryn Cornwall for his Shakespeare Collection By George Webbe Esquire of Falmouth, Cornwall.'[25] An image of a riddle in the play, it enacts itself the puzzle of the visual critical act. Its workings, like those of all the images discussed in these pages, are ultimately concerned with a gaze that goes beyond and beneath words; within it is constituted the new text, critical and creative, that is the image itself.

NOTES

1. Algernon Graves, 'A new light on Alderman Boydell and the Shakespeare Gallery', *The Magazine of Art*, No. 201 (July 1897), pp. 143–8. Quotation from p. 147.
2. *The Plays of Shakespeare. Edited by Howard Staunton. The Illustrations by John Gilbert. Engraved by the Brothers Dalziel* (London: Routledge, monthly instalments, 1856–8), 3 vols., 1858.
3. 'Performing Shakespeare in Print: Narrative in Nineteenth-Century Illustrated Shakespeares', *Victorian Shakespeare, Vol. 1: Theatre, Drama and Performance*, ed. Gail Marshall and Adrian Poole (London and New York: Palgrave Macmillan, 2003), pp. 47–72.
4. *The spirit of the plays of Shakspeare, exhibited in a series of outline plates illustrative of the story of each play drawn and engraved by Frank Howard with quotations and descriptions*, 5 vols. (London: T. Cadell, 1833).
5. It appeared as plate 27 and was issued by Lucas in 1845. See Andrew Wilton, *Constable's 'English Landscape Scenery'* (London: British Museum, 1979).
6. 'Theatralia No 1. On Garrick and Acting; and the Plays of Shakespeare, considered with reference to their fitness for Stage Representation', *The Reflector*, 4 (1811), p. 308.
7. Letter to Samuel Rogers, December 1833. *The Letters of Charles and Mary Lamb*, ed. E. V. Lucas (London: Dent and Methuen, 1935), p. 194.
8. 73.6 × 124.5 (29 × 49), Tate Britain.
9. 50.1 × 71 (19 ¾ × 28), National Gallery of Scotland, Edinburgh.
10. 92 × 122.5 (36 ¼ × 48 ¼), Tate Britain.
11. 150.5 × 112.4 (59 ¼ × 44 ¼), Huntington Library, San Marino, Calif.
12. The phrase occurs in 'The Ancient Sage', *Tiresias and Other Poems* (London: Macmillan, 1885), which presents a sense of immediate involvement with the past in terms suggesting a parallel to Wordsworth's of oneness with the natural world. See *Tennyson: Complete Poems and Plays*, ed. T. Herbert Warren, rev. Frederick Page (Oxford: Oxford University Press), 1967, p. 511.

13. 68.7 × 123.8 (27 1/16 × 48 3/4), Tate Britain.
14. 71 × 99 (28 × 39) centre panel, 71 × 46 (28 × 18) each wing, Walker Art Gallery, Liverpool.
15. Oil on mahogany panel, 75.8 × 42.6 (29 7/8 × 16 3/4), Tate Britain.
16. 76.2 × 55.9 (30 × 22), Tate Britain.
17. *Realizations: Narrative, Pictorial, and Theatrical Arts in Nineteenth-century England* (Princeton N.J.: Princeton University Press, 19), pp. 359–65.
18. 36.8 × 50.8 (14 1/2 × 20), Guildhall Art Gallery, Corporation of London.
19. Pencil, 46 × 62.2 (18 3/8 × 24 1/4), Carlisle Museum and Art Gallery; another version, pen and sepia ink, 30.5 × 35.6 (12 × 14), Ashmolean Museum, Oxford.
20. 76.2 × 55.9 (30 × 22), Tate Britain.
21. *Ophelia*, 1852, 68.7 × 123.8 (27 1/16 × 48 3/4), City Art Gallery, Manchester.
22. *Ophelia*, 1910, 102 × 61 (40 1/8 × 24), Julian Hartnoll.
23. 64.8 × 50.8 (25 1/2 × 20), Makins Collection, Washington D.C.
24. 221 × 114.3 (87 × 50), Tate Britain.
25. *The Plays of William Shakespeare, from the corrected text of Johnson and Steevens*, 11 vols. (London: John Stockdale, 1807), VII, facing p. 7, Folger Shakespeare Library, PR 2752 1807a. c.4 Sh Col.

SELECT BIBLIOGRAPHY

MANUSCRIPT SOURCES

James Barry, Letter to John Boydell, FSL, Y.c.97 (1).

John Boydell, Letters, FSL, Y.c.255(1–5).

Receipts from Henry Fuseli, FSL, Y.d.565 1–3.

Receipt from James Barry, FSL, Y.d.581.

List of paintings commissioned for the 'Shakespeare Gallery', FSL, Y.d.369.

Letter to George Steevens, FSL, C.b.10 (16).

Boydell Shakespeare Subscription List, Boston Public Library, Rare Book Department, RBD 366 Ms.G.164.2.

Marie Cosway, Letter to John Boydell, FSL, Y.c.626(1) and Y.c.97.

James Durno, Letter to John Boydell, *Shakespeareana*, Vol. 1: *Holograph letters*, FSL, W.b.67(42).

Eustis. *a descriptive catalogue of the prints from Boydell's Shakspeare gallery done for the benefit of my daughter isabel eustis [francis] in two volumes, one hundred prints* [sic], C.1800, FSL, S.a.37.

James Gillray, Letter to John Boydell, FSL, ART Flat a5 no.4.

George Steevens Correspondence, FSL, C.b.10.16.

PRINTED SOURCES

Allen, Brian, 'Jonathan Tyers's Other Garden', *Journal of Garden History*, 1.3 (1981), 215–38.

Francis Hayman, Exh. Cat., London and New Haven: Yale University Press, 1987.

Analytical Review.

Anon [Samuel Foote?] *A Genuine Narrative of the Life and Theatrical Transactions of Mr. John Henderson*, London: T. Evans, 1777.

[Samuel Felton] *Imperfect hints towards a new edition of Shakespeare*. 2 vols. London: Logographic Press, J. Walter, 1787–8.

Antal, Frederick, *Fuseli Studies*, London: Routledge, 1956.

Ashton, Geoffrey, *Shakespeare and British Art*, Exh. Cat., New Haven: Yale Center for British Art, 1981.

Balmanno, Mary, 'Reminiscences of Henry Fuseli, Esq, R. A.', *Pen and Pencil*, New York: D. Appleton, 1858.

Balston, Thomas, 'John Boydell, Publisher: "The Commercial Maecenas"', *Signature*, 8, (1948) 3–22.

Barry, James, *An Account of a Series of Pictures, in the Great Room of the Society of Arts . . .* with Addenda, London: Printed for the Author by William Adlard, sold by T. Cadell and J. Walter, 1783.

Bate, Jonathan, 'Shakespearean Allusion in English Caricature in the Age of Gillray', *Journal of the Warburg and Courtauld Institutes*, XLIX, (1986), 196–210.

Shakespeare and the English Romantic Imagination. Oxford: Clarendon, 1986.

Shakespearean Constitutions: Politics, Theatre, Criticism 1730–1830, Oxford: Clarendon, 1989.

'Pictorial Shakespeare: Text, Stage, Illustration'. *Book Illustrated: Text, Image and Culture, 1770–1930*, ed. Catherine J. Golden. New Castle, Delaware: Oak Knoll Press, 2000, pp. 31–59.

Bate, Jonathan, ed., *The Romantics on Shakespeare*, Harmondsworth: Penguin, 1992.

Bate, Jonathan and Russell Jackson, eds., *Shakespeare: An Illustrated Stage History*, Oxford: Oxford University Press, 1996.

Baxandall, Michael, *Patterns of Intention: On the Historical Explanation of Pictures*, New Haven and London: Yale University Press, 1985.

Bennet, M., intro., *Ford Madox Brown 1821–1893*, Liverpool: Walker Art Gallery, 1964.

Bentley, G. E. Jr., *Blake Records*, Oxford: Clarendon, 1969.

Bermingham, Anne, *Landscape and Ideology: The English Rustic Tradition, 1740–1860*, Berkeley and London: University of California Press, 1986.

Betty, William Henry West, *Young Albert, the Roscius, exhibited in a series of characters from Shakespeare and other authors*, London: S. & J. Fuller, 1811.

Bindman, David, ed., *The Thames and Hudson Encyclopaedia of British Art*, London and New York: Thames and Hudson, 1985.

Blake, William, *The Notebook of William Blake: A Photographic and Typographic Facsimile*, ed. David V. Erdman, with the assistance of Donald K. Moore, 1973, revised edn, New York: Readex Books, 1977.

The Complete Poetry and Prose of William Blake, ed. David V. Erdman, New York: Doubleday, 1988.

Blunt, Anthony, *The Art of William Blake*, 1959, London and New York: Harper and Row, 1974.

Boase, T. S. R., 'Illustrations of Shakespeare's Plays in the 17th and 18th centuries', *Journal of the Warburg and Courtauld Institutes*, X, (1947), 83–108.

English Art 1800–1870, Oxford: Oxford University Press, 1959.

Bolla, Peter de, 'The Charmed Eye', Kelly, Veronica and Dorothea E. von Mucke, eds., *Body and Text in the Eighteenth Century*, Stanford, Calif: Stanford University Press, 1994, 89–111.

Boswell, James, *Boswell's Life of Johnson*, ed. George Birkbeck Hill, rev. L. E. Powell, 6 vols., Oxford: Clarendon, 1936–50.

[Boydell, John] *Catalogue raisonné d'un receuil d'estampes d'apres les plus beaux tableaux qui soient en Angleterre. Les planches sont dans la possession de Jean Boydell, et ont été gravées par lui, & les meilleurs artistes de Londres*. A Londres: Chez le Proprietaire, Graveur, & Marchand d'Estampes, Cheapside, 1779.

Boydell Publication Proposals, Victoria and Albert Museum Library, London. 103.B.

A Catalogue of the Pictures, &c. in the Shakespeare Gallery, Pall-Mall, London: Printed by W. Bulmer and Co., Cleveland-Row, for the proprietor, and sold at the place of exhibition, 1802.

The Exhibition of the Shakspeare Gallery, Pall-Mall; Being the Last Time the Pictures can ever be seen as an entire collection, London: Printed by W. Bulmer and Co., Cleveland-Row, for the proprietor, and sold at the place of exhibition, 1805.

Bradley, A. C., *Shakespearean Tragedy: Lectures on 'Hamlet', 'Othello', 'King Lear', 'Macbeth'*, London: Macmillan, 1904.

Le Brun, Charles, *A Method to learn to Design the Passions*, translated by John Williams, London: J. Huggonson, 1734, The Augustan Reprint Society Publication Numbers 200–1, Los Angeles; University of California, 1980.

Bruntjen, Sven H. A., *John Boydell (1719–1804): A Study of Patronage and Publishing in Georgian London*, PhD Dissertation, Stanford University, 1974, New York and London: Garland, 1985.

Bulwer, John, *Chirologia: Or, the Naturall Language of the Hand, Composed of the Speaking Motions and Discoursing Gestures thereof, whereunto is added Chironomia: Or, the Art of Manuall Rhetoricke*, London: Tho. Harper, 1644.

Burke, Edmund, *A Philosophical Enquiry into the Origin of our Ideas of the Sublime and the Beautiful*, ed. Adam Phillips, Oxford: World's Classics, 1990.

Burke, Joseph, *English Art 1714–1800*, Oxford: Oxford University Press, 1976.

Burnim, Kalman A., *David Garrick: Director*, first publ. 1961, Carbondale, Ill.: Southern Illinois University Press, 1973.

Butlin, Martin, *William Blake*, Exh. Cat., London: Tate Gallery, 1978.

The Paintings and Drawings of William Blake, 2 vols., New Haven and London: Yale University Press, 1981.

Butterfield, Herbert, *The Whig Interpretation of History*, London: Bell, 1931.

Cannon-Brookes, P., ed., *The Painted Word: British History Painting: 1750–1830*, London: Heim Gallery, 1991.

Chamberlain, Arthur B., *George Romney*, Freeport NY: Books for Libraries, 1971.

The Manuscripts and Correspondence of James, First Earl of Claremont, Report of Royal Commission on Historical Manuscripts, 2 Vols., London: H. M. S. O., 1891–4.

Christie's, *Drawings by Henry Fuseli, R. A. From a Private Collection*, Auction Catalogue, Tuesday 14 April 1992, London: Christie's, 1992.

Clark, Sandra, ed., *Shakespeare Made Fit: Restoration adaptations of Shakespeare*, London: Dent, 1997.

Clayton, Timothy, *The English Print 1688–1802*, Paul Mellon Centre for Studies in British Art, New Haven and London: Yale University Press, 1997.

A Collection of Prints, from pictures painted for the purpose of illustrating the Dramatic Works of Shakspeare, by the artists of Great-Britain, 2 vols., London: John and Josiah Boydell, 1803.

Colley, Linda, *Britons: Forging the Nation, 1707–1837*, New Haven and London: Yale University Press, 1992.

Collier, J. Payne, ed., *The Mad Pranks and Merry Jests of Robin Goodfellow: Reprinted from the Edition of 1628.*, London: Percy Society, 1841.

Cooper, Anthony Ashley (3rd Earl of Shaftesbury), *A Notion of the Historical Draught or Tablature of the Judgement of Hercules, according to Prodicus, lib II Xen[ophon] de Mem[orabilia] Soc[ratis]*, London: A. Baldwin, 1713.

Cotton, William, ed. John Burnet, *Sir Joshua Reynolds. Gleanings from his diary, unpublished manuscripts and from other sources*, London: Longman, 1856.

Cyclopaedia; or, an universal dictionary of arts and sciences, with the supplement, and modern improvements, London: Strahan (vol. 1) and J. F. C. Rivington (vols. 2–5), 1786.

Darwin, Erasmus, *The Botanic Garden*, London: J. Johnson, 1791.

Davies, Thomas, *Dramatic Miscellanies*, 2 vols., London: T. Davies, 1784.

A Description of Vauxhall Gardens. Being a proper companion and guide for all who visit that place, London: S. Hooper, 1762.

Derrida, Jacques, *Acts in Literature*, ed. Derek Attridge, London and New York: Routledge, 1992.

Dixon, Yvonne Romney, *Catalogue Raisonné of the Drawings of George Romney in the Folger Shakespeare Library*, PhD Dissertation, University of Maryland, 1977.

'Designs from Fancy': George Romney's Shakespearean Drawings, Seattle and London: University of Washington Press, 1998.

Dodsley, R. ed., *The Preceptor: Containing A General Course of* EDUCATION. *Wherein the first principles of polite learning are laid down in a way most suitable for trying the Genius, and advancing the Instruction of* YOUTH, London: R. Dodsley, 1748.

Dryden, John, *Of Dramatick Poesie, An Essay, 1668, The Works of John Dryden. XVII. Prose 1668–1691*, ed. Samuel Holt Monk, Berkeley and Los Angeles Calif. and London: University of California Press, 1971.

Eco, Umberto, *The Limits of Interpretation*, Bloomington, Ind: Indiana University Press, 1990.

Edelstein, T. J., *Vauxhall Gardens*, New Haven: Yale Center for British Art, 1983.

Erdman, David V., 'The Symmetries of *The Song of Los*', *Studies in Romanticism*, 16 (Spring 1977), 179–88.

von Erffa, Helmut and Allen Staley, *The Paintings of Benjamin West*, New Haven and London: Yale University Press, 1986.

Evans, Dorinda, *Mather Brown: Early American Artist in England*, Middletown, Conn: Wesleyan University Press, 1982.

Evans, Robert H., *A Catalogue of the very valuable and extensive library of the late William Hayley Esq, Removed from his seat at Felpham*, London: Robert H. Evans, 1821.

Fabricant, Carole, 'The Literature of Domestic Tourism and the Public Consumption of Private Property' in Nussbaum, Felicity and Laura Brown, eds., *The New Eighteenth Century: Theory, Politics, English Literature*. New York, 1987.

The Farington Diary, 26 May 1804.

Fielding, Henry, *Tom Jones*, ed. R. P. C. Mutter, Harmondsworth: Penguin, 1966 repr. 1985.

Friedman, Winifred H., *Boydell's Shakespeare Gallery*, New York: Garland, 1976.

Fuseli, Henry, *Reflections on the Painting and Sculpture of the Greeks: with Instructions for the Connoisseur, and an Essay on Grace in Works of Art*, London: Printed for the Translator, and sold by A. Millar, 1765.

Remarks on the Writings and Conduct of John James Rousseau, London: Printed for T. Cadell, (successor to Mr. Millar); J. Johnson and B. Davenport; and J. Payne, 1767.

The Mind of Henry Fuseli. Selections from his Writings with an Introductory Study by Eudo C. Mason, London: Routledge and Kegan Paul, 1951.

Remarks on the Writings and Conduct of J. J. Rousseau, 1767, ed. Karl S. Guthrie, The Augustan Reprint Society Los Angeles: Clark Memorial Library, University of California, 1960

The Collected English Letters of Henry Fuseli, ed. David H. Weinglass, Millwood, New York: Kraus, 1982.

Garrick, David, *Romeo and Juliet by Shakespeare with Alterations and an additional scene*, London: J. and R. Tonson and S. Draper, 1750.

Gay, John, ed. Daniel O'Connor, *The Beggar's Opera*, London: Gowans and Gray, 1922.

Generosa, Sister M., 'Apuleius and *A Midsummer Night's Dream*: Analogue or Source, Which?' *Studies in Philology*, XLII (1945), 198–204.

Gentleman's Magazine.

Gilchrist, Alexander, *Life of William Blake*, 1863, 2 vols., London: Macmillan, 1880.

Goffen, Rona, *Titian's Women*, New Haven and London: Yale University Press, 1997.

Goodwin, Gordon, *British Mezzotinters: James McArdell*, London: A. H. Bullen, 1903.

Gowing, Lawrence, 'Hogarth, Hayman and the Vauxhall Decorations', *Burlington Magazine*, XCV, 1953, 4–19.

Graves, Algernon, 'A new light on Alderman Boydell and the Shakespeare Gallery', *The Magazine of Art*, No. 201, July 1897, 143–8.

'Boydell and his Engravers', *The Queen*, CXVI (1904) 178–9, 328–9, 444–5, 524–5, 794–5, 1002–3.

The Poems of Gray and Collins, ed. Austin Lane Poole, London: Oxford University Press, 1919.

Gwynn, S., *Memorials of an Eighteenth Century Painter*, London: T. F. Unwin, 1896.

Habicht, Werner, D. J. Palmer and Roger Pringle, *Images of Shakespeare: Proceedings of the Third Congress of the International Shakespeare Association*, 1986, London and Toronto: Associated University Presses, 1988.

Halliwell, James Orchard, *Illustrations of the Fairy Mythology of 'A Midsummer Night's Dream'*, London: Shakespeare Society, 1845.

Hamilton, William, *Collection of Etruscan, Greek and Roman Antiquities, from the Cabinet of the Honble Wm. Hamilton*, 2 vols., Naples: F. Morelli, 1766–7.

Collection of Engravings from Ancient Vases, mostly of pure Greek workmanship discovered in sepulchres in the kingdom of the Two Sicilies but chiefly in the neighbourhood of Naples during the course of the years 1789 and 1790 now in the possession of Sir Wm. Hamilton, 4 vols., Naples: W. Tischbein, 1791–5.

Hamlin, Robin, 'An Irish Shakespeare Gallery', *Burlington Magazine*, CXX (1978), 515–29.

Hammerschmidt-Hummel, Hildegard. *Die Shakespeare-Illustration (1594–2000)*, Wiesbaden: Harrassowitz Verlag and Mainz: Akademie der Wissenschaften und der Literatur, 2003.

Hartmann, Sadikichi, *Shakespeare in Art*, Boston: L. C. Page, 1901.

Harvey, John, 'Shakespeare and the Ends of Time: the Illustrations'. *The Cambridge Review*, May 1966, 25–48.

Hayley, William, *Poetical Epistle to an Eminent Painter*, London: T. Payne, 1778.

The Life of George Romney, Esq., Chichester: W. Mason, 1809.

Hazlitt, William, *Essays on the Fine Arts*, London:[?], 1873.

Heath, Charles, *The heroines of Shakespeare; comprising the principal female characters in the plays of the great poet. Engraved in the highest style of art, from drawings by eminent artists.* London and New York: London Printing and Publishing Company, n.d. (1883).

Hendricks, Margo, '"Obscured by Dreams": Race, Empire and Shakespeare's *A Midsummer Night's Dream*', Shakespeare Quarterly, Vol. 47 No. 1 (Spring 1996), 37–60.

Hill, John, *The Actor: A Treatise on the Art of Playing*, 2nd ed. revised, London: R. Griffiths, 1755.

Hilles, Frederick Whiley, *The Literary Career of Sir Joshua Reynolds*, Cambridge: Cambridge University Press, 1936.

Portraits by Sir Joshua Reynolds, London: William Heinemann, 1952.

Hogan, Charles Beecher, *The London Stage 1660–1800. Part 5: 1776–1800*, Vol. 2, Carbondale, Ill: Southern Illinois University Press, 1968.

Hogarth, William, *The Genuine Works of William Hogarth illustrated with biographical anecdotes, a chronological catalogue, and commentary*, by John Nichols and George Steevens, 3 vols., London: Longman, Hurst, Rees, and Orme, 1808–17.

The Analysis of Beauty, ed. Ronald Paulson, New Haven and London: Yale University Press, 1997.

Howard, Frank, *The spirit of the plays of Shakspeare, exhibited in a series of outline plates illustrative of the story of each play drawn and engraved by Frank Howard with quotations and descriptions*, 5 vols., London: T. Cadell, 1833.

Hume, David, *The History of England, from the Invasion of Julius Caesar to the Revolution in 1688*, 1762, New York: Worthington, 1880.

Hunt, John Dixon, *Garden and Grove*, London: Dent, 1986.

Indicator, 20 October 1819.

Jaffe, Patricia, *Drawings by George Romney*, Cambridge: Fitzwilliam Museum, 1977.

Jenkins, Ian and Kim Sloan, *Vases and Volcanoes: Sir William Hamilton and his Collection*, London: British Museum, 1996.

Jerningham, Edward, *The Shakspeare Gallery, a poem by Mr Jerningham*, London: J. Robson, 1791.

Johnson, Samuel, *Miscellaneous Observations on Macbeth*, London: E. Cave, 1745.

Johnson, Samuel, ed., *The Plays of William Shakespeare, in eight volumes, with the corrections and illustrations of various commentators, to which are added notes by Sam. Johnson*, London: J. and R. Tonson, 1765.

Dr Johnson on Shakespeare, ed. W. K. Wimsatt. Harmondsworth: Penguin, 1969.

John Keats: The Complete Poems. ed. John Barnard, Harmondsworth: Penguin, 1988.

Kelly, John Alexander, *German Visitors to English Theaters in the Eighteenth Century*, Princeton N.J.: Princeton University Press and London: Oxford University Press, 1936.

Kendall, Paul, *Richard III, the Great Debate*, London: Folio Society, 1965.

Kermode, Frank, 'The Mature Comedies', in *Early Shakespeare (Stratford-upon-Avon Studies III)*, ed. J. R. Brown, and B. Harris).

Kidson, Alex, *George Romney 1734–1802*, Exh. Cat., London: National Portrait Gallery and Princeton N.J.: Princeton University Press, 2002.

Knight, Richard Payne, *The Landscape: A Didactic Poem. In Three Books. Addressed to Uvedale Price Esq*, London: Bulmer, Shakespeare Printing Office, 1794.

Knowles, John, *The Life and Writings of Henry Fuseli*, 3 vols., London: Colburn and Bentley, 1831.

Kramnick, Jonathan Brody, 'Reading Shakespeare's Novels: Literary History and Cultural Politics in the Lennox–Johnson Debate', *Modern Language Quarterly* Vol. 55 No. 4, December 1994, 429–53.

Lamb, Charles, 'On the Genius and Characters of Hogarth', *Reflector*, 2, 1811, 61.

'Theatralia No 1. On Garrick and Acting; and the Plays of Shakespeare, considered with reference to their fitness for Stage Representation,' *Reflector*, 4, 1811.

The Letters of Charles and Mary Lamb, ed. E. V. Lucas, London: Dent and Methuen, 1935.

Langford, Paul, *A Polite and Commercial People: England 1727–1783*, Oxford: Oxford University Press, 1989.

Lavater, John Caspar, *Essays on Physiognomy: designed to promote the knowledge and the love of mankind*, translated from the French by Henry Hunter, 3 vols. (London: printed for John Murray; H. Hunter; and T. Holloway, 1789–98).

Leslie, C. R. and Tom Taylor, *The Life and Times of Sir Joshua Reynolds*, 2 vols., London: John Murray, 1865.

Licht, Fred, Simona Tosini Pizzetti and David H. Weinglass, eds., *Füssli pittore di Shakespeare: Pittura e teatro 1775–1825*, Exh. Cat. Milan: Electa, 1997.

Locke, John, *An Essay Concerning Human Understanding*, ed. John W. Yolton, London: Dent, Everyman's Library, 1961.

[Lockman, John?], *A Sketch of the Spring-Gardens Vauxhall. In a letter to a noble lord*, London: G. Woodfall, n.d. [1751?].

Lounger, 20 May 1786.

Mackenzie, Henry, *The Man of Feeling*, ed. Brian Vickers, London: Oxford University Press, 1967.

Maclean, Gerald, Donna Landry and Joseph P. Ward, eds., *The Country and the City Revisited: England and the Politics of Culture, 1550–1850*, Cambridge, Cambridge University Press, 1999.

Macmillan, Duncan, *Painting in Scotland: The Golden Age*, Oxford: Phaidon, 1986.

Malkin, Benjamin Heath, *A Father's Memoirs of his Child*, London: Longman, 1806.

Manchester City Art Gallery, *'For Friendship's Sake': William Blake and William Hayley*, Exh. Cat., Manchester: City Art Gallery, 1969.

Martineau, Jane, et al., eds., *Shakespeare in Art*, London and New York: Merrell, 2003.

Mawer, John (trans.), *Oppian's Cynergeticks. Translated into English verse*, York: Thomas Gent, 1736.

McKenzie, Alan T, '"The Countenance You Show Me": Reading the Passions in the Eighteenth Century', *The Georgia Review* 32 (1978), 758–83.

intro. *A Method to learn to Design the Passions*, trans. John Williams from the French of Charles LeBrun, 1734, Los Angeles: Augustan Reprint Society Nos 200–201, 1980.

McTighe, Sheila, *Nicholas Poussin's Landscape Allegories*, Cambridge: Cambridge University Press, 1996.

Meisel, Martin, *Realizations: Narrative, Pictorial, and Theoretical Arts in Nineteenth-century England*, Princeton N.J.: Princeton University Press, 1983.

Merchant, W. Moelwyn, *Shakespeare and the Artist*, London: Oxford University Press, 1959.

'Blake's Shakespeare', *Apollo*, LXXIX, (1964), 318–25.

'*A Midsummer Night's Dream*: A Visual Re-creation', *Early Shakespeare: (Stratford-upon-Avon Studies III)*, ed. J. R. Brown and B. Harris, London: Edward Arnold, 1961, rev. 1967.

Comedy, Critical Idiom Series, London: Methuen, 1972.

Milton, John, *Paradise Lost*, London: J. Tonson, 1725.

Moore, Robert E, 'Reynolds and the Art of Characterization', *Studies in Criticism and Aesthetics, 1660–1800: Essays in Honor of Samuel Holt Monk*, ed. Howard Anderson and John S. Shea, Minneapolis: University of Minnesota Press, 1967, 332–57.

More, Thomas, *The history of Kyng Richard the third*, in *The Workes of Sir Thomas More Knyght, sometyme Lorde Chauncellour of England, wrytten by him in the Englysh tonge*, 1557, Facsimile edition, intro. K. J. Wilson, 2 vols., London: Scolar Press, 1978.

Morgann, Maurice, *An Essay on the Dramatic Character of Sir John Falstaff*, London: T. Davies, 1777.

Morning Chronicle, 21 April 1795.

Munro, Jane, *Shakespeare and the Eighteenth Century*, Exh. Cat., Cambridge: Fitzwilliam Museum, 1997.

Myrone, Martin, *Henry Fuseli*, British Artists Series, London and Princeton, N.H.: Tate Gallery and Princeton University Press, 2001.

Nicolson, Benedict, *Joseph Wright of Derby: Painter of Light*, London: Routledge and New Haven: Yale, 2 Vols., 1968.

Northcote, James, *The Life of Sir Joshua Reynolds*, 2 vols., London: Henry Colburn, 1818.

Noyes, Robert Gale, *The Thespian Mirror: Shakespeare and the Eighteenth-century Novel*, Providence, R.I., 1953.

Ogden, James, 'Lear's Blasted Heath', *Durham University Journal*, 49 (1987) 19–26.

Ogden, James, and Arthur Scouten, eds., *Lear from Study to Stage: Essays in Criticism*, London: Associated University Presses and Madison, Wis: Fairleigh Dickinson University Press, 1997.

Orgel, Stephen, *The Authentic Shakespeare and Other Problems of the Early Modern Stage*, London and New York: Routledge, 2002.

Imagining Shakespeare: A History of Texts and Visions, London and New York: Palgrave Macmillan, 2003.

Panofsky, Irwin, *Studies in Iconology: Humanistic Themes in the Art of the Renaissance*, New York: Oxford University Press, 1939.

Pape, Walter and Frederick Burwick, eds., *The Boydell Shakespeare Gallery*, Bottrop, Essen: Pomp, 1996.

Paulson, Ronald, *Hogarth's Graphic Works*, London and New Haven: Yale University Press, 1965.

'Hogarth the Painter', *Burlington Magazine*, CXIV, 1972, 71–9.

Emblem and Expression: Meaning in English Art of the Eighteenth Century, London: Thames and Hudson, 1975.

Book And Painting: Shakespeare, Milton and the Bible: Literary texts and the Emergence of English Painting, Knoxville: University of Tennessee Press, 1982.

Penny, Nicholas, *Reynolds*, Exh. Cat., London: Royal Academy of Arts and Weidenfeld and Nicholson, 1986.

Pointon, John, *A Chronological History of England: or, an impartial abstract of the most remarkable transactions . . . that have happen'd in the several kings' reigns, since the first attempt by Julius Caesar, upon this southern-part of Great Britain*, Oxford: Lintott, 3 vols., 1714–21.

Postle, Martin, *Sir Joshua Reynolds: The Subject Pictures*, Cambridge: Cambridge University Press, 1995.

Powell, Jocelyn, *Restoration Theatre Production*, London: Routledge, 1984.

Pressly, William L., *The Life and Art of James Barry*, New Haven and London: Yale University Press, 1981.

A Catalogue of Paintings in the Folger Shakespeare Library: 'As Imagination Bodies Forth'. New Haven and London: Yale University Press, 1993.

Price, Uvedale, *Essays on the Picturesque, as compared with the Sublime and the Beautiful; and, on the Use of Studying Pictures, for the Purpose of Improving Rural Landscape*, London: J. Mawman, 1810.

Prochno, Renate, *Joshua Reynolds*, Weinheim: VCH, 1990.

Raine, Kathleen, *Blake and Tradition*, The A. W. Mellon Lectures in the Fine Arts, 2 vols., Princeton: Princeton University Press, 1968.

Reflector, II (1811), p. 61.

Repton, Humphry, *The Bee; or, a Companion to the Shakespeare Gallery; containing a catalogue-raisonné of all the pictures; with comments, illustrations and remarks*. London: T. Cadell, 1789.

Reynolds, Joshua, *Discourses on Art*, ed. Robert R. Wark, New Haven and London: Yale University Press. Third edition, revised, 1997.

The Letters of Sir Joshua Reynolds, ed. John Ingamells and John Edgcumbe, New Haven and London: Yale University Press, 2000.

Richardson, George, *Iconology; or, A collection of emblematical figures: containing four hundred and twenty-four remarkable subjects, moral and instructive; in which are displayed the beauty of virtue and the deformity of vice: the figures are engraved by the most capital artists from original designs; with explanations from classical authorities*, London: G. Scott, 1779. Introductory notes by Stephen Orgel, New York and London: Garland Publishing, 1979.

Richardson, Jonathan, *Essay on the Theory of Painting*, London: Bettesworth, 1715. Reprinted Menston, Yorkshire: Scolar Press, 1971.

An Essay on the Whole Art of Criticism as it Relates to Painting. London: Bettesworth, 1719. Reprinted, with *An Argument in Behalf of the Science of the Connoisseur, as Two Discourses*, London: Bettesworth, 1719. Reprinted as *Aesthetics: Sources in the Eighteenth Century*, 4. Bristol: Thoemmes Press, 1998.

Richardson, William, *A Philosophical Analysis and Illustration of some of Shakespeare's Remarkable Characters*, London: John Murray, 1774.

Ripa, Cesare, *Iconologia: or, moral emblems*, ed. Pierce Tempest and Isaac Fuller, London: B. Motte, 1709.

Rococo: Art and Design in Hogarth's London, Exh. Cat., London: Victoria and Albert Museum, 1984.

Romney, John, *Memoirs of the Life and Works of George Romney Esq.*, London: Baldwin and Cradock, 1830.

St James's Chronicle, 4–21 May 1789.

Salamon, M. C., *Shakespeare in Pictorial Art*, Studio special number, London: The Studio, 1916.

Santaniello, A. E., intro. *The Boydell Shakespeare Prints*, New York and London: Blom, 1968.

Schiff, Gert, *Johann Heinrich Füssli, 1741–1825: Text und Oeuvrekataloge*, 2 vols., Zürich: Berechthaus and Munich: Prestel, 1973.

Henry Fuseli 1741–1825, Exh. Cat., London: Tate Gallery, 1975.

Seary, Peter, *Lewis Theobald and the Editing of Shakespeare*, Oxford: Clarendon Press, 1990.

Shakespeare, William, *The Works of Shakespeare*, ed. Nicholas Rowe, 6 vols., London: J. Tonson, 1709.

The Works of Shakespeare, ed. Alexander Pope, 6 vols., London: J. Tonson, 1725.

The Works of Shakespeare, ed. Lewis Theobald, 7 vols., London: Bettesworth, 1733.

The Plays of William Shakespeare, in eight volumes, with the corrections and illustrations of various commentators, to which are added notes by Sam. Johnson, London: J. and R. Tonson, 1765.

A new edition of Shakespeare's Plays, from the corrected text of Johnson and Steevens, with prints engraved by Mr. Heath, 10 Parts, London: Heath and Robinson, 1802–4.

The Dramatic Works of Shakespeare, revised by George Steevens, 9 vols., London: W. Bulmer & Co, Shakespeare Printing Office, 1802.

The Plays of William Shakespeare, ed. A. Chalmers, London: Rivington, 1805.

The Plays of William Shakespeare, from the corrected text of Johnson, London: John Stockdale, 1807.

The Plays of Shakespeare. Edited by Howard Staunton. The Illustrations by John Gilbert. Engraved by the Brothers Dalziel, London: Routledge, monthly instalments, 1856–8; 3 vols., 1858.

Henry The Fourth Part 1, ed. Samuel Burdett Hemingway, The Variorum Shakespeare, Philadelphia and London: J. B. Lippincott, 1936.

Henry IV, Part I, The Oxford Shakespeare, ed. David Bevington. Oxford: Oxford University Press, 1987.

William Shakespeare: the Tragedy of King Richard the Third. Parallel Texts of the First Quarto and the First Folio with Variants of the Early Quartos, ed. Kristian Smidt. Oslo: Universitetsforlaget and New York: Humanities Press, 1969.

The Winter's Tale, ed. Stephen Orgel, Oxford: Oxford University Press, 1966.

Shawe-Taylor, Desmond, 'Eighteenth-Century performances of Shakespeare recorded in the Theatrical Portraits at the Garrick Club', *Shakespeare Survey 51: Shakespeare in the Eighteenth Century*. Cambridge: CUP, 1988.

Siddons, Henry, *Practical Illustrations of Rhetorical Gesture and Action*. London, 1807.

Sillars, Stuart, 'Musical Iconography in *The Beggar's Opera*', *British Journal for Eighteenth-century Studies*, Vol. 1 No. 3 (Autumn 1978), 182–5.

'An Eighteenth-century *Midsummer Night's Dream* Illustration', *British Journal for Eighteenth-century Studies*, Vol. 4 No. 1 (Spring 1981).

Visualisation in Popular Fiction, 1860–1960: Graphic Narratives, Fictional Images, London and New York: Routledge, 1995.

'King Lear: towards a visual history', *Lear from Study to Stage*, ed. A. H. Scouten and James Ogden, London: Fairleigh Dickinson University Press, 1997.

'Jaques and the Wounded Stage', *Dialoging on Genres: Essays Presented to Andrew Kennedy*, ed. Ulf Lie and Anne Holden Rønning, Oslo: Novus, 2001.

Simon, Robin, 'Hogarth's Shakespeare', *Apollo*, CIX, 1979, 213–20.

Smart Alastair, 'Hogarth or Hayman', *Apollo*, CIX, 1979, 208–12.

'Dramatic Gesture and Expression in the Age of Hogarth and Reynolds', *Apollo* 82 (1965), 90–97.

Solkin, David H., *Richard Wilson: the Landscape of Reaction*, Exh. Cat., London: Tate Gallery, 1982.

Painting for Money: The Visual Arts and the Public Sphere in Eighteenth-century England, New Haven and London: Yale University Press, 1992.

Sotheby's, *The Art of Shakespeare: Property of a Mid-Western Private Collector*, Auction catalogue, Tuesday November 10, 1998. New York: Sotheby's, 1998.

Spectator, 1 July 1709.

Staley, Allen, *Benjamin West: An American Painter at the English Court*, Baltimore, Md: Baltimore Museum of Art, 1989.

Starnes, D. T., 'Shakespeare and Apuleius', *Publications of the Modern Language Association*, LX (1945), 1021–50.

Struebe, Isabel C., *The Life and Works of William Hodges*, PhD dissertation, New York University 1978, New York: Garland, 1979.

Studing, Richard, *Shakespeare in American Painting: A Catalogue from the Late Eighteenth Century to the Present*, London and Toronto: Associated Universities Press, 1993.

Summers, Montague, 'The First Illustrated Shakespeare', *The Connoisseur*, CII, (1938), 305–9.

Sunderland, John, 'Mortimer, Pine and some Political Aspects of English History Painting', *Burlington Magazine*, CXVI, 1974.

John Hamilton Mortimer: His Life and Works, London: Walpole Society, LII, 1988.

Tate, Nahum, *The History of King Lear*, ed. James Black, Regents Renaissance Drama Series, London: Edward Arnold, 1976.

Theobald, Lewis, *Shakespeare Restored: or, A Specimen of the Many Errors, as well Committed, as Unamended, by Mr Pope in his Late Edition of this Poet*, London: Franklin, Woodman, Lyon and Davis, 1726.

Thompson, E. P., *Whigs and Hunters: The Origin of the Black Act*, Harmondsworth: Penguin, 1977.

Tieck, Ludwig, 'Die Kupferstiche nach der Shakspeare-Gallerie in London. Briefe an einen Freund'. 1793. *Kritische Schriften*, I, 3–34.

Todd, Ruthven, *Tracks in the Snow: Studies in English Science and Art*, London: Grey Walls Press, 1946.

Tomory, Peter, *The Life and Art of Henry Fuseli*, London: Thames and Hudson, 1972.

Walpole, Horace, *Anecdotes of Painting in England*, ed. Ralph N. Warnum, London: Swan Sonnenschein, Lowrey, 1881.

Horace Walpole's Miscellaneous Correspondence, II, ed. W. S. Lewis and John Riely with the assistance of Edwine M. Martz and Ruth K. McClure, New Haven: Yale University Press and Oxford: Oxford University Press, 1980.

Ward, Humphry and W. Roberts, *Romney: A Biographical and critical essay with a Catalogue Raisonée of his Works*, 2 vols., London: Agnew, 1904.

Warton, Joseph, 'The Enthusiast, or the Lover of Nature', London: R. Dodsley, 1744.

Waterhouse, Ellis, *Reynolds*, London: London. 1973.

Wax, Carol, *The Mezzotint: History and Technique*, London: Thames and Hudson, 1990.

Weber, Harold, 'Horner and his "Women of Honour": The Dinner Party in *The Country-Wife*'. *Modern Language Quarterly*, Vol. 43 No. 2, June 1982, 107–120.

Weinglass, David H., *Prints and Engraved Illustrations by and after Henry Fuseli: A Catalogue Raisonné*, Aldershot, 1994.

Wells, William, *William Blake's 'Heads of the Poets' for Turret House, the Residence of William Hayley, Felpham*, Manchester: City Art Gallery, 1969.

Wendorf, Richard, *Sir Joshua Reynolds: The Painter in Society*, Cambridge, Mass. and London: Harvard University Press, 1996.

West, Shearer, *The Image of the Actor*, London: Pinter, 1991.

Williams, Gary Jay, *Our Moonlight Revels: A Midsummer Night' Dream in the Theatre*, Iowa City: University of Iowa Press, 1997.

Williams, Raymond, 'Base and Superstructure in Marxist Critical Theory', *Problems in Materialism and Culture: Selected Essays*, London: Verso, 1980.

Wilson, John Dover, *Tribute to Walter de la Mare on his Seventy-fifth Birthday*, 25th April 1948, reprinted in *Shakespeare's Happy Comedies*, London: Faber, 1962.

Wilton, Andrew, *Constable's 'English Landscape Scenery'*, London: British Museum, 1979.

Wimsatt, W. K. ed., *Dr Johnson on Shakespeare* (1960), Harmondsworth: Penguin, 1969.

Wind, Edgar, '"Borrowed Attitudes" in Reynolds and Hogarth', *Journal of the Warburg and Courtauld Institutes*, II, 1938–9, 182–5.

Young, David, *Something of Great Constancy*, New Haven and London: Yale University Press, 1966.

INDEX